Labor Economics and Labor Relations

Labor Economics and Labor Relations

Robert J. Flanagan
Stanford University

Robert S. Smith
Cornell University

Ronald G. Ehrenberg
Cornell University

Scott, Foresman and Company

Glenview, Illinois
Dallas, Texas Oakland, New Jersey Palo Alto, California Tucker, Georgia London, England

Cover photo by Eric Futran.

Acknowledgments

p. 209: From "Overinvestment in College Training?" by Richard B. Freeman in *The Journal of Human Resources,* Summer 1975. Copyright © 1975 by the Board of Regents of the University of Wisconsin System. Reprinted by permission of the University of Wisconsin Press.

p. 332: "Union Membership As a Percent of Potential Union Membership by Country, Selected Years, 1900-1975" from *Profiles of Union Growth: A Comparative Statistical Portrait of Eight Countries* by George Sayers Bain and Robert Price, p. 170. Reprinted by permission of Basil Blackwell Publisher.

p. 456: Reprinted, with permission, from S. Herbert Unterberger and Edward C. Koziara, "The Demise of Airline Strike Insurance," *Industrial and Labor Relations Review,* 34 (October 1980): 84. Copyright © 1980 by Cornell University. All rights reserved.

p. 606: From Paul A. Samuelson and Robert M. Solow, "Our Menu of Policy Choices," *The Battle Against Unemployment,* edited by Arthur M. Okun. Copyright © 1965 by W. W. Norton & Company, Inc. Reprinted by permission.

Library of Congress Cataloging in Publication Data

Flanagan, Robert J.
    Labor economics and labor relations.

    Includes bibliographical references and index.
    1. Labor economics. 2. Industrial relations.
I. Ehrenberg, Ronald G. II. Smith, Robert Stewart
III. Title.
HD4901.F46   1984   331   83-27127
ISBN 0-673-15620-6

1 2 3 4 5 6-KPF-89 88 87 86 85 84

Preface

Labor Economics and Labor Relations analyzes modern labor-market behavior and gives the reader an understanding of labor unions and the institutional framework in which collective bargaining takes place. It summarizes empirical evidence that supports or contradicts each major proposition, and illustrates in extensive detail the usefulness of labor-market analysis in understanding public policy and labor relations. We believe that showing students the social implications of concepts enhances the motivation to learn those concepts; that using the ideas of each chapter in an analytic setting allows students to see them in action.

The extensive use of detailed policy and labor-relations applications constitutes a major innovation in this text. Insights from economic analysis clarifying the discussion of many issues in labor relations is a second unique feature.

Labor Economics and Labor Relations is designed for one-semester or one-quarter survey courses in labor economics and labor relations at either the undergraduate or MBA level for students who do not necessarily have extensive backgrounds in economics or labor relations. We have taught such courses over the last decade. The undergraduate courses require only principles of economics as a prerequisite, and the graduate courses often have no prerequisites. It is our experience that it is not necessary to be highly technical in one's presentation in order to convey important concepts, and that students with limited backgrounds in economics and labor relations can comprehend a great deal of material in a single course. Accordingly, while this text provides a comprehensive treatment of modern labor economics and labor relations, it is written in a style that makes the important concepts in the field accessible even to those without backgrounds in intermediate-level microeconomics.

This book draws heavily on Ehrenberg and Smith's *Modern Labor Economics: Theory and Public Policy,* which is also published by Scott, Foresman and Company, and which is designed for courses in labor economics that do not give heavy emphasis to the institutional framework of collective bargaining. The response to that book has been overwhelmingly positive and we have tried to preserve its best features in *Labor Economics and Labor Relations.* We have, however, eliminated much of the more technical material (including the appendices) that was found in *Modern Labor Economics* and, in places, simplified presentations considerably. We have also eliminated several topics, such as household production function and allocation of time models, that quite properly do not belong in an introductory survey course. Finally, we have integrated into the text what we believe to be the most comprehensive and modern treatments of labor law and labor history, the nature of unions, collective bargaining and dispute resolution, the nature of labor agreements, and the effects of unions on compensation, productivity, and working conditions.

The first part of the book examines market forces. Chapter 2 presents an overview of demand and supply in labor markets so that the students will see from the outset the interrelationship of the major forces at work shaping labor-market behavior. This chapter can be skipped or skimmed by students with strong backgrounds in economics or by students in one-quarter courses. Chapters 3 to 5 are concerned primarily with the demand for labor, while Chapters 6 to 9 focus on labor-supply issues. Chapters 10 and 11 integrate an analysis of demand and supply with issues in employee compensation and labor-market discrimination.

Unions and collective bargaining are treated in Chapters 12–17, where the economic analysis developed in earlier chapters is integrated with legal explanations and principles of collective behavior to examine the nature of relationships and contracts between employers and employees in a union environment. Chapters 12 and 13 take a close look at the nature of union organizations (tracing both the forces determining the growth of unions and the factors influencing their internal decision-making), and the legal environment of labor-management relations. Having identified the main components of an industrial-relations system, we then turn to the bargaining process. Collective-bargaining strategy and structure are discussed in Chapter 14, and the consequences of a breakdown in negotiations—labor disputes and methods of dispute resolution—are covered in Chapter 15. The outcome of a completed set of negotiations, a labor agreement, and implications for the employment relationship are examined in Chapter 16. Finally, the effects of unions on compensation, productivity, and working conditions are reviewed in Chapter 17.

The concluding two chapters of the book deal with the macroeconomic issues of unemployment and inflation. We also extend our analysis of the industrial-relations system in Chapter 19 to consider the effect of unions on inflation and on the efficacy of some anti-inflation policies.

As noted above, *Labor Economics and Labor Relations* recognizes that many students have only a limited background in economics and labor relations. All of the necessary analytic tools are carefully developed in the text, and each chapter builds on material that precedes it. We begin the text at a very simple level and explain the derivation of each major concept or tool. We then increase the degree of difficulty in later chapters as the student becomes more familiar with our terminology and methods of analysis.

The text has a number of unique pedagogical features in addition to the use of public-policy and labor-relations examples. First, each chapter contains boxed examples that represent applications of that chapter's theory in managerial, historical, or cross-cultural settings. Several of these examples contrast collective-bargaining arrangements in the United States with the very different institutional frameworks for labor relations found in other countries. Second, each chapter contains discussion or review questions that give students the opportunity to apply what they have learned to specific policy questions. Third, lists of selected readings at the ends of chapters refer students to more advanced sources of study.

Substantively, *Labor Economics and Labor Relations* differs from previous textbooks for survey courses in labor economics and labor relations in a number of ways. First and foremost is its extensive emphasis on public-policy applications and on economic analysis of labor-relations issues. The book also attempts to integrate institutional features, such as the existence of internal labor markets, directly into the theoretical models—explaining the institutions within the context of these models rather than discussing them separately. Also, the discussion and analysis of labor relations in the private and public sectors is contrasted and integrated on a chapter-by-chapter basis rather than treated separately. Finally, the coverage of topics in this book is far more comprehensive than in most texts, and the discussion of a number of the more common topics is much more thorough than that found in other texts. For example, our chapter on discrimination includes a unique section on the conceptual issues involved in affirmative-action planning and a discussion of comparable worth.

Acknowledgments

As the following list of academic acknowledgments indicates, we have had the benefit of substantive and pedagogical comments from numerous friends and colleagues at universities and colleges throughout the country; to these people we are indebted:

George Borjas	*University of California, Santa Barbara*
John F. Burton	*Cornell University*
Glen Cain	*University of Wisconsin, Madison*
James Chelius	*Rutgers University*
Barry Chiswick	*University of Illinois, Chicago Circle*
David Estenson	*University of California, Berkeley*
Donald Frey	*Wake Forest University*
Gilbert Ghez	*Roosevelt University, Chicago*
Daniel Hamermesh	*Michigan State University*
V. Joseph Hotz	*Carnegie-Mellon University*
George Johnson	*University of Michigan*
Lawrence Kahn	*University of Illinois, Urbana*
Harry C. Katz	*Massachusetts Institute of Technology*
Randall King	*University of Akron*
H. Gregg Lewis	*Duke University*
Charles Link	*University of Delaware*
J. Peter Mattila	*Iowa State University*
Jacob Mincer	*Columbia University*
Kevin J. Murphy	*University of Tennessee*
George Neumann	*University of Chicago*
Randall Olsen	*Ohio State University*
Jeffrey Perloff	*University of California, Berkeley*
Cynthia Rence	*Michigan State University*
Jennifer Roback	*Yale University*
Sherwin Rosen	*University of Chicago*
Arthur Schwartz	*University of Michigan*
N. J. Simler	*University of Minnesota*
James P. Smith	*University of California, Los Angeles*
Sharon P. Smith	*American Telephone and Telegraph*
Michael Wachter	*University of Pennsylvania*

We also wish to thank those who have helped us in other ways. Frank Brechling, George Delehanty, Dale Mortensen, John Pencavel, Orme Phelps, Med Reder, and Lloyd Ulman were our teachers, and it was they who gave us a foundation and interest in labor economics and labor relations. Jean Brown, El Vera Fisher, and Patricia Kauppinen typed many drafts of this text in manuscript form, and we wish to thank them for their dedication and patience.

Table of Contents

Labor Economics and Labor Relations

Chapter 1

INTRODUCTION

This book presents a comprehensive—and understandable—application of economic analysis to the behavior of, and relationship between, employers and employees. The aggregate compensation received by employees from their employers was $1,856 billion in 1982, while all *other* forms of personal income that year—from investments, self-employment, pensions, and various government welfare programs—amounted to $714 billion. The *employment* relationship, then, is clearly one of the most fundamental relationships in our lives, and as such it is one that attracts a good deal of legislative attention.

In order to understand the employment relationship and the huge array of social problems and programs, it is essential to develop a mastery of the fundamentals of labor economics, labor union behavior, and the institutional framework in which collective bargaining takes place.

As economists who have been actively involved in the analysis of labor union behavior and the evaluation of labor-related programs adopted or considered by the government, we obviously believe labor economics is useful in understanding the effects of these institutions and policies. What is perhaps more important for the nature of this text is that we also believe that the analysis of public policy can be useful in teaching the fundamentals of labor economics and labor relations. We have therefore incorporated such analyses into each chapter with two pedagogical reasons in mind. First, we believe that showing students the relevance and social implications of concepts to be studied enhances the motivation to learn. Second, using the concepts of each chapter in an analytical setting serves to reinforce understanding by permitting the student to see them "in action."

The Labor Market

There is a rumor that one recent Secretary of Labor attempted to abolish the term "labor market" from departmental publications. He believed it demeaned workers to implicitly think of labor as being bought and sold like so much grain, oil, or bonds. True, labor is somewhat unique. Labor services can only be rented; workers themselves cannot be bought and sold. Further, because labor services cannot be separated from workers, the conditions under which such services are rented are often as important as the price. Put differently, *nonpecuniary factors* —such as work environment, risk of injury, personalities of managers, and flexibility of work hours—loom larger in employment transactions than they do in markets for commodities. Finally, there are a host of institutions and pieces of legislation influencing the employment relationship that do not exist in other markets.

Nevertheless, the circumstances under which employers and employees rent labor services clearly constitute a "market" for several reasons. First, institutions have developed to facilitate contact between the buyers and sellers of labor services. This contact may come through the want ads, the union hiring hall, employment agencies, placement offices, or at the factory gate.

Second, once contact is arranged, information about price and quality is exchanged. Employment applications, interviews, and even "word-of-mouth" information from friends are illustrative of this kind of exchange in the market for labor.

Third, when agreement is reached, some kind of *contract* is executed, covering compensation, conditions of work, job security, and even duration of the job. At times the contract is formal, such as with collective-bargaining (union-management) agreements. At times the agreement is unwritten and informal, with only an implied understanding between the parties based on past practices and experience. Nonetheless, it is often useful to think of the employment relationship as governed by a contract.

It is worth noting that labor "contracts" typically call for employers to compensate employees for their *time* and not for the product they produce. Only 14 percent of American workers receive piece-rate wages or commissions, where compensation is computed directly on the basis of output. The vast majority are paid by the hour, week, or month. They are paid, in short, to show up for work and (within limits) to follow orders. This form of compensation requires that employers give careful attention to worker motivation and dependability in the selection and employment process. It also produces among workers an interest in developing institutions, such as labor unions, that seek to ensure that the orders workers are asked to follow are reasonable and that managerial discretion is not exercised in an arbitrary manner.

The end result of employer-employee transactions in the labor market is, of course, the placement of people in jobs at certain rates of pay. This allocation of labor serves not only the personal needs of individuals but the needs of the larger society as well. Through the labor market our most important national resource—labor—is allocated to firms, industries, occupations, and regions.

Labor Relations: Some Basic Concepts

In any country, the interactions between employers and employees occur in an *industrial relations system*. The labor market is one element of this system. A second factor is public policy—the nature of the government interventions that create the legal environment surrounding market activities. The nature of employee and employer organization constitutes a third important aspect.

In virtually all countries, irrespective of ideological orientation or stage of economic development, the most important organizational feature of economic growth has been the appearance of *labor unions*. Early in the century, Sidney and Beatrice Webb defined a union as "a continuous association of wage earners for the purpose of maintaining or improving the conditions of their working lives." As such, unions present workers with an alternative to public policy for correcting certain market failures and otherwise advancing their interests. The opposite is also true; workers and unions may turn to public policy to obtain goals that they are unable to achieve through *collective bargaining*.

Collective bargaining consists of negotiations between one or more unions and one or more employers to establish a formal *labor agreement* that specifies compensation, hours of work, and other conditions of employment that are to apply to the employers and employees over the term of the agreement. Collective bargaining can be a more effective method of quickly establishing change at the workplace than can the atomistic operation of a competitive market, because negotiations are usually conducted under the threat of collective action (such as a strike or lockout) rather than the threat of individual action (such as a quit). The labor agreement (or collective-bargaining agreement or labor contract) effectively provides a system of industrial governance for workers and their employers for the time that it is in effect. As a result, the rules established in labor agreements can have an important effect on labor-market behavior.

In many respects the modern study of the industrial-relations system reveals the interplay (and often tension) between market forces and institutional rules in determining the employment relationship. The interplay is often quite complicated. Institutional rules established in collective bargaining or through public policy may alter the normal outcomes of the labor market. At times, however, institutional rules may simply codify normal market outcomes. Consider the announcement of a newly negotiated labor agreement providing for a wage increase of five percent over the previous wage level. Are the wages of union members now five percent higher than they would have been in the absence of the union, or did employers simply postpone until negotiations a five percent wage increase that they would have given anyway? Quite possibly, the result is a combination of both forces, but it should be clear that even though a wage increase is associated with the activity of collective bargaining, it may not be the *result* of collective bargaining. Determining the actual impact of the collective-bargaining agreement is a much more complicated task.

This example illustrates that labor-relations outcomes occur in markets that operate under certain principles. To understand the constraints the market imposes on labor relations, we must understand economic behavior. For most of the labor force, moreover, the content of the employment relationship is not established through collective bargaining. It is therefore important to understand the role of economic behavior and legal institutions in shaping the employment arrangements in nonunion organizations.

Labor Economics: Some Basic Concepts

Labor economics is the study of the workings and outcomes of the market for labor. More specifically, labor economics is primarily concerned with the behavior of employers and employees in response to the general incentives of wages, prices, profits, and nonpecuniary aspects of the employment relationship (such as working conditions). These incentives serve both to motivate and limit individual choice. The focus in economics is on inducements for behavior that are impersonal and apply to wide groups of people as opposed to incentives that are more personal in nature.

In this book we will study the relationship between wages and employment opportunities; the interaction between wages, income, and the decision to work; how general market incentives affect occupational choice; the relationship between wages and undesirable job characteristics; the incentives for, and effects of, educational and training investments; the incentives for workers to join unions; how the bargaining tactics and structure adopted by labor and management influence the outcome of collective bargaining; the interplay between dispute-settlement procedures and the likelihood that strikes will occur; and the effects of unions on wages, productivity, and turnover. In the process, we will analyze the effects of such social policies and labor-market institutions as the minimum wage, overtime legislation, pension reform regulations, the Occupational Safety and Health Act, welfare reform, payroll taxes, unemployment insurance, immigration policies, the rise in the mandatory retirement age, antidiscrimination laws, collective-bargaining legislation, and dispute-resolution procedures.

Our study of the employment relationship will be conducted on two levels. Most of the time we will be using economic theory to analyze "what is"; that is, we will be explaining people's behavior, using a mode of analysis called *positive economics.* Less commonly, we will be using *normative* economic analysis to judge "what should be."

Positive Economics

Positive economics is a theory of behavior in which people are typically assumed to respond favorably to "benefits" and negatively to "costs." In this regard, positive economics closely resembles Skinnerian psychology, which views behavior as shaped by rewards and punishments. The rewards in economic theory are pecuniary and nonpecuniary gains (benefits), while the punishments are forgone opportunities (costs). For example, a person motivated to become a surgeon because of the earnings and status surgeons command must give up the opportunity to be a lawyer and be available for emergency work around the clock. Both the benefits and costs must be considered in making this career choice. Likewise, a firm deciding whether to hire an additional worker must weigh the wage and salary costs against the added revenues or cost savings made possible by expanding its work force. And every union must at some point weigh the benefits and costs of striking for an improved offer rather than accepting what is on the table.

Scarcity. The most all-pervasive assumption underlying economic theory is that of resource scarcity. According to this assumption, individuals and society alike do not have the resources to meet all their wants. Hence, any resource devoted to satisfying one set of desires could have been used to satisfy other wants, which means that there is always a cost to any decision or action. The real cost of using labor hired by a government contractor to build a road, for example, is the production lost by not devoting this labor to the building of an airport or some other good. Thus, in popular terms, "there is no such thing as a free lunch," and we must always make choices and live with the rewards and costs these choices bring us. Moreover, we are always constrained in our choices by the resources available to us.

Rationality. The second basic assumption of positive economics is that people are *rational* in the sense that they have an objective and pursue it in a reasonably consistent fashion. When considering *persons,* economists assume that the objective being pursued is *utility maximization;* that is, people are assumed to strive toward the goal of making themselves as happy as they can (given their limited resources). Utility, of course, encompasses both pecuniary and nonpecuniary dimensions. When considering the behavior of *firms,* which are inherently nonpersonal entities, economists assume the goal of behavior to be that of *profit maximization.* Profit maximization is really just a special case of utility maximization—where pecuniary gain is emphasized and nonpecuniary factors are ignored. When considering the behavior of *unions,* economists assume that the goal is the maximization of the welfare of the union membership. This, too, is a type of utility maximization, but it is complicated by the fact that individual workers often have very different ideas about what their union should do for them.

The assumption of rationality implies a *consistency* of response to general economic incentives and an *adaptability* of behavior when those incentives change. These two characteristics of behavior underlie predictions about how workers and firms will respond to various incentives. Rationality cannot be directly "proven," however, and it has been suggested that even totally habit-bound or unthinkingly impulsive people would be forced to alter their behavior in predictable ways if the resources at their command change.[1] Thus, while we will maintain the assumption of rationality throughout the textbook, it is clear that this assumption is not absolutely necessary to the derivation of at least *some* of the behavioral predictions contained herein.

The Models and Predictions of Positive Economics

Behavioral predictions in economics flow more or less directly from the two fundamental assumptions of rationality and scarcity. Workers must continually make choices, such as whether to look for other jobs, accept overtime, seek promotions, move to another area, or acquire more education. Employers must also make choices concerning, for example, the level of output, and the mix of machines and labor to use in production. Unions, as complex political organizations, must choose among alternative combinations of wages, fringe benefits, and nonpecuniary working conditions to maximize membership welfare. Economists usually assume that when making these choices, employees, employers, and unions are guided by their desires to maximize utility, profit, or membership benefits, as the case may be, and that they weigh the costs and benefits of various decisions in a reasonably careful way.

One may object that these assumptions are unrealistic and that people are not nearly as calculating, as well-informed about alternatives, or as well-endowed with a set of choices as economists assume. Economists are likely to reply that if people are not calculating, are totally uninformed, or do not have any choices, then most predictions suggested by economic theory will not be supported by real-world evidence. They thus argue that the theory underlying positive economics should be judged on the basis of its *predictions* and that there may be *enough* information, calculation, and available options to make the theory useful in explaining or predicting a wide range of behavior.

The reason that we need to make assumptions and create a relatively simple theory of behavior is that the actual workings of the labor market are almost impossibly complex. Millions of workers and employers interact daily—all with their own set of motivations, preferences, information, and perceptions of self-interest. Collective bargaining has resulted in the existence of close to 200,000 labor agreements in the United States alone. A detailed description of the individual outcomes and the processes that determine them would clearly be both of limited feasibility and of limited usefulness. What we need to discover are generalizations or general principles that provide useful insights about the employment relationship. These principles could not be expected to predict or explain behavior with the same accuracy as the laws of physics predict the movement of an object through space, because we are dealing with human beings capable of making choices. Nevertheless, we hope to show in this book that a few forces are so basic to labor market behavior that they alone can predict or explain much of the outcomes and behaviors we observe in the labor market.

---

[1]Gary Becker, "Irrational Behavior and Economic Theory," *Journal of Political Economy* 70, 1 (February 1962): 1–13.

Any time we attempt to explain a complex set of behaviors and outcomes using a few fundamental influences we have created a *model* of such behavior. Models are not intended to capture every complexity of behavior; in fact, they are created for the express purpose of stripping away random and idiosyncratic factors so that we can focus on general principles. An analogy from the physical sciences might make the nature of models and their relationship to actual behavior more clear.

Using calculations of velocity and gravitational pull, physicists could predict where a ball would land if it were kicked with a certain force at a given angle to the ground. The actual point of landing might vary from the predicted point due to wind currents and any spin the ball might have—factors that were ignored in the calculations. If 100 balls were kicked, none might ever land exactly on the predicted spot, although they would tend to cluster around it. The accuracy of the model, while not perfect, may be good enough for a football coach to make a decision about whether to attempt a field goal or not. The point is that we usually need to know just the *average tendencies* of outcomes for policy purposes. To estimate these tendencies we need to know the important forces at work but must confine ourselves to few enough influences so that calculating estimates remains feasible.

Normative Economics

Any normative statement—a statement about what *ought* to exist—is based on some underlying value. The value premise upon which normative economics rests is that of *mutual benefit*. A mutually beneficial transaction is one in which there are no losers and, therefore, one that everyone in society could support. A transaction can be unanimously supported when

(a) all parties affected by the transaction gain,
(b) some gain and no one else loses, or
(c) some gain and some lose from the transaction, but the gainers fully compensate the losers.

When the compensation in (c) takes place, case (c) is converted to case (b). In practice, economists often judge a transaction by whether the gains of the beneficiaries exceed the costs borne by the losers, thus making it *possible* for there to be no losers. If the losers sustain losses that the gainers could not possibly compensate, then the transaction could never be mutually beneficial to all, and the wisdom of the transaction must be questioned.

To illustrate a mutually beneficial transaction, suppose that people who formerly owned and operated small subsistence farms in West Virginia—earning the equivalent of $4,000 per year—take jobs in the growing coal mining industry at $15,000 a year. Assuming the switch in jobs is voluntary, these workers are clearly better off. The income gain of $11,000 per year may be offset to some extent by the disagreeableness of working in a mine, but the fact that they voluntarily choose to move into mining tells us that they believe their utility will be enhanced. Mine owners likewise enter into the transaction voluntarily, implying that they obtain at least $15,000 in output from these new workers. The transaction benefits the parties it affects, and as a result it benefits society as a whole. There has been an increase in social output from $4,000 to $15,000 per worker, but, more important, there has been an increase in the overall utility of workers (the miners are better off and no one else is worse off).

To illustrate a transaction that is not mutually beneficial, suppose that society sought to increase the income of these same subsistence farmers by giving them a cash allowance raised by taxing others. This program would simply transfer money from the pockets of some people to the pockets of others, with no increase in output. There is no possibility for the gainers (farmers) to compensate the losers (those taxed), so unanimous consent about the transaction could not be secured. While economists would not say that this transaction is bad or unwarranted, it cannot be justified on the grounds of mutual benefit. Some other ethical principle—not based on unanimous consent—would have to be invoked in order to justify the transaction. (One such principle is that the rich should share their wealth with the poor.)

Normative economics, then, is the analysis of actual and potential transactions to see if they conform to the standard of being mutually beneficial. Transactions may fail to meet this standard—or transactions that meet the standard may not occur—for one of several reasons.

Ignorance. First, people may be ignorant of some important facts and thus led to make decisions that are not in their self-interest. For example, a worker who smokes may take a job in an asbestos-processing plant not knowing that the combination of smoking and inhaling asbestos dust substantially raises the risk of disease. Had the worker known this, he or she would have stopped smoking or changed jobs—but both transactions were "blocked" by ignorance.

Transactions barriers. Second, there may be some barrier to the completion of a transaction that could be mutually beneficial. Often, these barriers are created by government laws. For example, a firm may be willing to offer overtime to production workers at rates no more than 10 percent above their normal wage. Some workers may be willing to accept overtime at the 10 percent premium. However, this transaction—which is desired by both parties—cannot legally be completed in most instances because of a law (the Fair Labor Standards Act) requiring almost all production workers to be paid a 50 percent wage premium for overtime. In this case, overtime will not be worked and both parties will suffer.

Another kind of barrier to mutually beneficial transactions may be the expense of completing the transaction. Unskilled workers facing very limited opportunities in one region may desire to move in order to take better jobs. Alternatively, they may want to enter job training programs. In either case they may lack the funds to finance the desired transaction.

Nonexistence of market. A third reason why transactions that are mutually beneficial may not occur is that it may be impossible or uncustomary for buyers and sellers of certain resources to transact. As an illustration, assume a woman who does not smoke works temporarily next to a man who does. She would be willing to pay as much as 50 cents per hour to keep her working environment smoke-free, and he could be induced to give up smoking for as little as 25 cents per hour. Thus, the potential exists for her to give him, say, 35 cents per hour and for both to benefit. However, custom or the transience of their relationship may prevent her from offering him money in this situation, and the transaction would not occur.

Normative Economics and Government Policy

The solution to problems that impede the completion of mutually beneficial transactions frequently involves government intervention. In cases where a government law is creating the barrier to transaction, the "intervention" might be to repeal the relevant law. Laws prohibiting women from working overtime, for example, have been repealed in recent years as their adverse effects on women have become recognized.

In other cases, however, the government may be able to undertake activities to reduce transactions barriers which the private market would not undertake. We will cite three examples, each of which relates to a barrier discussed above.

Public goods. First let us take the case of information and its dissemination. Suppose that workers in noisy factories are concerned about the effects of noise on their hearing but that to ascertain these effects would require an expensive research program. Suppose further, that a union representing sawmill workers considers undertaking such research and financing the expensive undertaking by selling its findings to the many other unions or workers involved. The workers would then have the information they desire—albeit at some cost—which they could use to make more intelligent decisions concerning their jobs.

The hitch in the above scheme is that the union doing the research may not have any customers *even though* others find the information it produces valuable. The reason for the lack of customers is that as soon as the union's findings are published to its own members or its first customers, the results can easily become public knowledge—and thus available *free* from newspapers or by word-of-mouth. Other unions may be understandably reluctant to pay for information they can get free, and the union doing the research ends up getting very little, if any, reimbursement for its expenses. Anticipating this problem, the union will probably decide not to undertake the research.

The information in the above example is called a *public good*—a good that can be consumed by any number of people at the same time, including those who do not pay for it. Because nonpayers cannot be excluded from consuming the good, no potential customer will have incentives to pay. The result is that the good never gets produced by a private organization. Because the government, however, can *compel* payment through its tax system, it becomes natural to look to the government to produce public goods. If information on occupational health hazards is to be produced on a large scale, it is quite possible that the government will have to be involved.

Capital market imperfections. A second example of a situation in which the government might have to step in to overcome a transaction barrier is the case where loans are not available to finance job training or interregional moves even though such loans could conceivably help workers facing a very poor set of choices to have access to better opportunities. Loans such as these are not typically provided by the private sector, because they are not "backed" (secured) by anything other than the debtor's promise to pay them back. Banks cannot ordinarily afford to take the risks inherent in making such loans, particularly when the loan recipients are poor, because a number of defaults could put them out of business (or at least lower their profitability). This lack of available loans to finance worthwhile transactions represents a "capital market imperfection."

The government, however, might be willing to make loans in the above situation even if it faced the same risk of default, because enabling workers to move to areas of better economic opportunity could improve social welfare and strengthen the economy. In short, because society would reap benefits from encouraging people to enter job training programs or move to areas where their skills could be better utilized, it may be wise for the government to make the loans itself.

Establishing market substitutes. A third type of situation in which government intervention might be necessary to overcome transaction barriers is the case where the market fails to exist for some reason. In the example, a smoker and nonsmoker were temporarily working next to each other, and their transitory relationship prevented a mutually beneficial transaction from taking place. A solution in this case might be for the government to impose the same result that a market transaction would have generated—and require the employer to designate that area to be a nonsmoking area.

In this case, as in the other examples of government intervention mentioned above, it is important to emphasize that when government does intervene, it must make sure that the transactions it undertakes or imposes on society create more gains for the beneficiaries than they impose in costs on others. Since it is costly to produce information, for example, the government should only do it if the gains are more valuable than the resources used in producing it. Likewise, the government would only want to make loans for job training or interregional moves if these activities enhanced social welfare. Finally, imposing nonsmoking areas would be socially desirable only if the gainers gain more than the losers lose. Thus, while normative economics suggests a role for government in helping accomplish mutually beneficial transactions, the role is not an unlimited one.

Plan of the Text

With this brief review of basic concepts and principles in mind, we turn now to the specific subject-matter areas of labor economics and labor relations. The study of the employment relationship is mainly a study of the interplay between employers and employees—or between demand and supply—and between market forces and institutional rules. The first part of the book develops the analysis of market forces. Chapter 2 presents a quick overview of demand and supply in the labor market, allowing the student to see from the outset the interrelationship of the major forces at work shaping labor market behavior. (This chapter contains many concepts that will be familiar to students who have a good background in microeconomics.) Chapters 3–5 are concerned primarily with the demand for labor, while Chapters 6–9 emphasize labor supply issues. Chapters 10 and 11 integrate the analysis of demand and supply in studying issues in employee compensation and labor market discrimination.

Unions and collective bargaining are treated in Chapters 12–17, where the economic analysis developed earlier in the book is integrated with legal analysis and principles of collective behavior to examine the nature of relationships and contracts between employers and employees in a union environment. We noted earlier that an industrial-relations system consists of the interaction of employee and employer organizations, the government (which creates a particular legal or public policy environment), and the market. The nature of labor markets and the market behavior of employers, as indicated above, are analyzed in the earlier chapters of the book. Chapters 12 and 13 respectively examine the nature of union organizations (tracing both the forces determining the growth of unions and factors influencing their internal decision-making) and the legal environment of labor-management relations.

Having established the nature of the main actors in an industrial relations system, we then turn to the bargaining process. Collective-bargaining strategy and structure are discussed in Chapter 14 and the consequences of a breakdown in negotiations—labor disputes and methods of dispute resolution—are covered in Chapter 15. The outcome of a completed set of negotiations is a labor agreement. The nature of labor agreements and their implications for the employment relationship are examined in Chapter 16. The effects of unions on compensation, productivity, and working conditions are reviewed in Chapter 17.

The final two chapters deal with the macroeconomic issues of unemployment and inflation. In Chapter 19 (on inflation) we extend our analysis of the industrial-relations system to consider the effect of unions on inflation and on the efficacy of some anti-inflation policies.

REVIEW QUESTIONS

1. Using the concepts of normative economics, when would the labor market be judged to be at a point of optimality? What imperfections might prevent the market from achieving this point?
2. Are the following statements "positive" or "normative" in nature? Why?
   a. Society should not prohibit women from working more than 40 hours per week.
   b. If women are prevented from working overtime, they will not be as valuable to employers as their male counterparts of similar skill.
   c. If the military draft is prohibited, military salaries will increase.
   d. The military draft *compels* people to engage in a transaction they would not voluntarily enter into; it should therefore be avoided as a way of recruiting military personnel.

SELECTED READINGS

Ryan C. Amacher, Robert D. Tollison, and Thomas D. Willet, eds., *The Economic Approach to Public Policy* (Ithaca, N.Y.: Cornell University Press, 1976).

John Dunlop, *Industrial Relations Systems* (New York: Holt, Rinehart, and Winston, 1958).

Milton Friedman, *Essays in Positive Economics* (Chicago: University of Chicago Press, 1953).

Assar Lindbeck, *The Political Economy of the New Left: An Outsider's View* (New York: Harper & Row, 1971).

Chapter 2

OVERVIEW OF THE LABOR MARKET

Every society—regardless of its wealth, form of government, or the organization of its economy—must make certain basic decisions. It must decide what to produce, how to produce it, the quantities to be produced, and how the output shall be distributed. These decisions require finding out what consumers want, what technologies for production are available, and what the skills and preferences of workers are; deciding where to produce; and coordinating all such decisions so that, for example, the millions of people in New York City and the isolated few in an Alaskan fishing village can each buy the milk, bread, meat, vanilla extract, mosquito repellent, and brown shoe polish they desire at the grocery store. The process of coordination involves creating incentives so that the right amount of labor and capital will be employed at the right place at the required time.

These decisions can, of course, be made by administrators employed by a centralized bureaucracy. The amount of information this bureaucracy must obtain and process to make the, literally, millions of needed decisions wisely and the amount of incentives it must give out to ensure that these decisions are coordinated are truly mind-boggling. It boggles the mind even more to consider the major alternative to centralized decision making—the decentralized marketplace. Millions of producers striving to make a profit observe prices that millions of consumers are willing to pay for products and the wages millions of workers are willing to accept for work. Combining these pieces of information with data on various technologies, they decide where to produce, what to produce, whom to hire, and how much to produce. No one is in charge, and while there are no doubt imperfections that impede progress toward achieving the best allocation of resources, millions of people find jobs that enable them to purchase thousands of items they desire each year. The production, employment, and consumption decisions are all made and coordinated by price signals arising through the marketplace.

The market that has the job of allocating workers to jobs and coordinating employment decisions is the *labor market*. With roughly 100 million workers and 5 million employers in the United States, thousands of decisions about career choice, hiring, quitting, compensation, and technology must be made and coordinated every day. This chapter will present an overview of what the market does and how it works. For those students who may have already mastered microeconomic theory, this chapter can provide a review of basic concepts.

The Labor Market: Definitions, Facts, and Trends

Every market has buyers and sellers, and the labor market is no exception: the "buyers" are employers and the "sellers" are workers. Because there are so many buyers and sellers of labor at any given time, the decisions that are made in any particular case are influenced by the behavior and decisions of others. A firm, for example, may decide to increase compensation in a situation where other employers are doing likewise in order to remain "competitive" in its ability to attract and hold workers. Likewise, an employee may choose to go into personnel work, for example, if he or she discovers that teachers or social workers are having a difficult time finding jobs.

The *labor market* is thus composed of all the buyers and sellers of labor. Some of these participants may not be active at any given moment in the sense that they are not out seeking to find new jobs or new employees. But on any given day, thousands of firms and workers will be "in the market" trying to transact. If, as in the case of doctors or mechanical engineers, buyers and sellers are searching throughout the entire nation for each other, we would describe the market as a *national labor market*. If buyers and sellers only search locally—as in the case of secretaries or automobile mechanics—the labor market is a *local* one.

Some labor markets, particularly those where the sellers of labor are represented by a union, operate under a very formal set of rules that partly govern buyer-seller transactions. In the construction and longshoring trades, for example, employers must hire at the union hiring hall from a list of eligible union members. In other cases, the employer has discretion over who gets hired but is constrained by a union-management agreement in matters like the order in which employees may be laid off, procedures regarding employee complaints, the compensation schedule, the workload or pace of work, and promotions. The markets for government jobs and jobs with large nonunion employers also tend to operate under rules that constrain the authority of management and ensure "fair" treatment of employees. When a formal set of rules and procedures guide and constrain the employment relationship *within* a firm, an *internal labor market* is said to exist.[1]

---

[1]P. Doeringer and M. Piore, *Internal Labor Markets and Manpower Analysis* (Lexington, Mass.: D. C. Heath and Company, 1971).

In many cases, of course, labor market transactions are not made within the context of written rules or procedures, as is clearly the case in most transactions where the employee is changing employers or newly entering the market. Written rules or procedures generally do not govern within-firm transactions—such as promotions and layoffs—among smaller, nonunion employers. While jobs in this sector of the labor market can be stable and well paid, many are not. Low-wage, unstable jobs are sometimes considered to be in the *secondary labor market.*[2] We will discuss the concept of secondary labor markets in greater detail in Chapter 11 on discrimination.

When we speak of a particular labor market—for taxi drivers, say—we are using the term *labor market* rather loosely to refer to the companies trying to hire people to drive their cabs and the people seeking employment as cab drivers. The efforts of these buyers and sellers of labor to transact and establish an employment relationship constitute the "market" for cab drivers. However, neither the employers nor the drivers are confined to this market, and in fact both could simultaneously be in other markets as well. An entrepreneur with $100,000 to invest may be thinking of operating either a taxi company or a car wash, depending on the projected revenues and costs of each. A person seeking a cab-driving job may also be trying to find work as an electronics assembler. Thus, all the various "labor markets" that we can define on the basis of industry, occupation, geography, transaction rules, or job character are really interrelated to some degree. We speak of these narrowly defined labor markets for the sake of convenience, and doing so should not suggest that people are necessarily or permanently locked in to a market that is somehow independent of other markets.

The Labor Force and Unemployment

The term *labor force* refers to all the people who are either employed or who would like to be employed for pay at any given time. Those who are not employed for pay but who would like to be are *the unemployed.*[3] People who are not employed and are neither looking for work nor waiting to be recalled from layoff by their employers are not counted as part of the labor force. The total labor force thus consists of the employed and the unemployed.

In 1980 there were 107 million people in the labor force, representing 64 percent of the entire population over 16 years of age. An overall *labor force participation rate* (labor force divided by population) of 64 percent is substantially higher than the rates around 60 percent that have prevailed throughout the last 30 years, as can be seen by referring to the data in Table 2.1. This table also indicates the single most important fact about labor-force trends in this century;

---

[2]Doeringer and Piore, *Internal Labor Markets and Manpower Analysis.*

[3]The official definition of unemployment for purposes of government statistics includes those who have been laid off by their employers, those who have been fired or have quit and are looking for other work, and those who are just entering or reentering the labor force but have not found a job as yet.

Table 2.1 Labor Force Participation Rates by Sex, 1900–1980 (in percent)

Year	Total		Men		Women	
	Of Those Over 14	*Of Those Over 16*	*Over 14*	*Over 16*	*Over 14*	*Over 16*
1900	54.8 (100)		87.3 (100)		20.4 (100)	
1910	55.7 (102)		86.3 (99)		22.8 (112)	
1920	55.6 (102)		86.5 (99)		23.3 (114)	
1930	54.6 (100)		84.1 (96)		24.3 (119)	
1940	52.2 (95)		79.0 (91)		25.4 (125)	
1950	53.4 (98)	59.9	79.0 (91)	86.8	28.6 (140)	33.9
1960	55.3 (101)	60.2	77.4 (89)	84.0	34.5 (169)	37.8
1970	55.8 (102)	61.3	73.0 (84)	80.6	39.9 (196)	43.4
1980	—	64.3	—	78.0	—	51.7

Note: Index numbers, with 1900 = 100, are shown in parentheses. From 1900–1930, the labor force was defined as those "gainfully employed." Gainful workers were those who, whether they were working at the time or not, reported themselves as having an occupation at which they usually worked. In 1940, the present concept of labor force replaced the concept of gainful worker, with the result that inexperienced people looking for their first job were now counted in the labor force. It is the judgment of Clarence D. Long, *The Labor Force Under Changing Income and Employment,* p. 45, that intercensal comparisons remain meaningful despite this change.

Sources for data on ages 14 and older:
  1900–1950: Clarence D. Long, *The Labor Force Under Changing Income and Employment* (Princeton: Princeton University Press, 1958), Table A-2.
  1960: U.S. Department of Commerce, Bureau of the Census, *Census of Population, 1960: Employment Status,* Subject Reports, PC(2)-6A, Table 1.
  1970: U.S. Department of Commerce, Bureau of the Census, *U.S. Census of Population, 1970: Employment Status and Work Experience,* Subject Reports, PC(2)-6A, Table 1.

Source for data on ages 16 and older:
  U.S. President, *Employment and Training Report of the President* (Washington, D.C.: U.S. Government Printing Office), transmitted to the Congress 1981, Table A-1.

namely, *labor force participation rates for men are falling while those for women are increasing dramatically.* These trends and their causes will be discussed in detail in Chapter 6.

The ratio of those unemployed to those in the labor force is the *unemployment rate.* While this rate is crude and has several imperfections, it is the most widely cited measure of labor market conditions. When the unemployment rate is in the 3–4 percent range in the United States, the labor market is considered *tight*—indicating that jobs in general are plentiful and hard for employers to fill and that most of those who are unemployed will find other work quickly.[4] When the unemployment rate is higher—say, 7 percent or above—the labor market is described as *loose,* in the sense that workers are abundant and jobs are relatively easy for employers to fill. To say that the labor market as a whole is loose, however, does not imply that there are no shortages; to say it is tight, of course, can still mean that in some occupations or places those seeking work exceed the number of jobs available at the prevailing wage.

---

[4]Some people are beginning to argue that labor markets are "tight" when unemployment is around 5 percent or even a bit more. This issue will be discussed in Chapter 18.

Table 2.2 displays the overall unemployment rate for the first 81 years of this century. The data clearly show the extraordinarily loose labor market during the Great Depression of the 1930s and the exceptionally tight labor market during World War II. However, when the average unemployment rate of the earliest long stretch of nonwar years (1900–1914) is compared with that of the latest long stretch of nonwar years (1954–65), we see that unemployment in nonwar, nondepression years is slightly higher now than before (4.4 percent from 1900–1914 vs. 5.3 percent from 1954–65). What is very different is that the *range* within which the unemployment rate fluctuates is much narrower now. In 1900–1914, the unemployment rate varied from 0.8 percent to 8.5 percent, while from 1954–65 the range was 4.2 percent to 6.8 percent. It is evident, then, that the labor market is more stable now than at the turn of the century. Chapter 18 will present a more detailed analysis of the determinants of the unemployment rate.

Industries and Occupations: Adapting to Change

As we pointed out earlier, the labor market is the mechanism through which workers and jobs are matched. Over the years in this century, the number of certain kinds of jobs has expanded and the number of others has contracted. Both workers and employers had to adapt to these changes in response to signals provided by the labor market.

An examination of the industrial distribution of employment from 1900 to 1970 reveals the kinds of changes the labor market has had to facilitate. Table 2.3 discloses a major shift: *agricultural employment has declined drastically while employment in service industries has expanded.* Manufacturing jobs have increased proportionately to the increase in total employment, so their employment share has remained more or less constant. The largest employment increases have been in the service sector. Retail and wholesale trade, which increased from 9.2 percent of employment in 1910 to 20 percent in 1970, showed the largest increases in nongovernment services. However, the largest percentage increase has been in government employment—which quadrupled its share of total employment over the 70-year period. Some describe this shift in employment from agriculture to services as a shift from the *primary* to the *tertiary* sector (manufacturing being labeled the *secondary* sector). Others describe the shift to services as the arrival of the "post-industrial" state. In any case, the shift in employment has been accompanied by large population movements off the farms and to urban areas. These population movements have also been largely coordinated by the labor market, as Chapter 9 will show.

The combination of shifts in the industrial distribution of jobs and shifts in the production technology within each sector has also necessitated that workers acquire new skills and work in new jobs. Table 2.4 shows that a large increase in *white-collar,* or nonmanual, jobs has taken place concurrently with a large decline in agricultural jobs. Manual workers and personal-service workers have shown relatively modest increases since 1900. The largest single gain has come about in clerical jobs, although professional and technical jobs (teach-

Table 2.2 Unemployment Rates for the Civilian Labor Force over 14 Years Old, 1900–1981

Year	Rate	Year	Rate	Year	Rate
1900	5.0	1916	4.8	1932	23.6
1901	2.4	1917	4.8	1933	24.9
1902	2.7	1918	1.4	1934	21.7
1903	2.6	1919	2.3	1935	20.1
1904	4.8	1920	4.0	1936	17.0
1905	3.1	1921	11.9	1937	14.3
1906	0.8	1922	7.6	1938	19.0
1907	1.8	1923	3.2	1939	17.2
1908	8.5	1924	5.5	1940	14.6
1909	5.2	1925	4.0	1941	9.9
1910	5.9	1926	1.9	1942	4.7
1911	6.2	1927	4.1	1943	1.9
1912	5.2	1928	4.4	1944	1.2
1913	4.4	1929	3.2	1945	1.9
1914	8.0	1930	8.9	1946	3.9
1915	9.7	1931	15.9		

Note: After 1966, unemployment rates for only those 16 and over are published. The differences between the rates for those over 14 and over 16 in the years where both were computed are very small. Therefore, a parallel series in this table was not considered necessary. The rates shown from 1967 on relate to those over 16, and the prior data related to those over 14.

   In 1957 the definition of the term *unemployed* was changed to include those who 1. were waiting to be called back to a job from which they had been laid off; 2. were waiting to report to a new wage or salary job scheduled to start within the next 30 days (and were not in school during the survey week); or 3. would have been looking for work except that they were temporarily ill or believed no work was available in their line of work or in the community. Prior to 1957, part of group 1 above—those whose layoffs were for definite periods of less than 30 days—were classified as employed, as were all of the persons in group 2 above. This new definition was also applied to unemployment data for the years 1947–1957.

ers, engineers, lawyers, and so forth) have also increased disproportionately fast.

Labor markets must work very effectively if enormous shifts in the industrial and occupational distribution of employment are to be accomplished without long delays or undue hardship. There is disagreement over how effectively and humanely labor markets operate, but there can be no disagreement that the labor market has an incredibly large and important role to perform in society.

The Earnings of Labor

The actions of buyers and sellers in the labor market serve both to allocate and to set prices for various kinds of labor. From a social perspective, these prices act as signals or incentives in the allocation process—a process that relies primarily on individual and voluntary decisions. From the worker's point of view, the price of labor is important in determining income—and hence purchasing power.

Table 2.2 (continued)

Year	Rate (old series)	Rate (new series)	Year	Rate
1947	3.6	3.9	1958	6.8
1948	3.4	3.9	1959	5.5
1949	5.5	5.9	1960	5.6
1950	5.0	5.3	1961	6.7
1951	3.0	3.3	1962	5.6
1952	2.7	3.1	1963	5.7
1953	2.5	2.9	1964	5.2
1954	5.0	5.6	1965	4.6
1955	4.0	4.4	1966	3.8
1956	3.8	4.2	1967	3.8
1957	4.0	4.3	1968	3.6
			1969	3.5
			1970	4.9
			1971	5.9
			1972	5.6
			1973	4.9
			1974	5.6
			1975	8.5
			1976	7.7
			1977	7.1
			1978	6.1
			1979	5.8
			1980	7.1
			1981	7.6

SOURCES: 1900–1954 (old series): Stanley Lebergott, "Annual Estimates of Unemployment in the United States, 1900–1950," *The Measurement and Behavior of Unemployment,* NBER Special Committee Conference Series no. 8 (Princeton, 1957), pp. 213–239.

1955–1957 (old series): U.S. Bureau of the Census, *Annual Report on the Labor Force,* Current Population Reports, Series P-50 (1955, 1956, 1957).

1947–1966 (new series): U.S. Bureau of Labor Statistics, *Employment and Earnings,* vol. 13, no. 7 (January 1967), Table A-1.

1967–1981: U.S. President, *Economic Report of the President* (Washington, D.C.: U.S. Government Printing Office, February 1982), p. 266.

The *wage rate* is the price of labor per working hour.[5] The *nominal wage* is what workers get paid per hour in current dollars; nominal wages are most

---

[5]In this book, we define the hourly wage in the way most workers would if asked to state their "straight-time" wage. It is the money a worker would lose per hour if he or she has an unauthorized absence. When wages are defined in this way, a paid holiday becomes a "fringe benefit," as we note below, because leisure time is granted while pay continues. Thus, a worker paid $100 for 25 hours —20 of which are working hours and 5 of which are time off—will be said to earn a wage of $4.00 per hour and receive time off worth $20.

An alternative is to define the wage in terms of actual hours worked—or as $5.00 per hour in the above example. We prefer our definition, because if the worker seizes an opportunity to work one less hour in a particular week, his or her earnings would fall by $4.00, not $5.00 (as long as the reduction in hours does not affect the hours of paid holiday or vacation time for which the worker is eligible).

Table 2.3 Employment Distribution by Major Industrial Sector, 1900–1970 (in percent)

Year	Agriculture[a]	Goods-Producing Industries[b]	Nongovernment Services[c]	Government Services[d]
1900	38.1	37.8	20.0	4.1
1910	32.1	40.9	22.3	4.7
1920	27.6	44.8	21.6	6.0
1930	22.7	42.1	28.1	7.1
1940	18.5	41.6	31.1	8.8
1950	12.1	41.3	36.4	10.2
1960	6.6	41.4	38.8	13.2
1970	3.8	39.8	40.5	15.9

Note: From 1900 to 1930, employment refers to "gainful workers." From 1940 on, employment refers to experienced civilian labor force. Where applicable, persons not assigned to an industry were assumed to have the same employment distribution as those who were.
[a]Agriculture includes forestry and fishing.
[b]Included are manufacturing, mining, construction, transportation, communications, and public utilities.
[c]Included are trade; personal, professional, and business services; entertainment; finance; and real estate.
[d]Includes federal, state, and local government workers.

SOURCES: 1900–1940: U.S. Bureau of the Census, *Historical Statistics of the United States, Colonial Times to 1957,* 1960. Table D57-71.
    1950: *U.S. Census of Population 1950,* Subject Reports. Vol. IV, Chapter 1D, 1955. Table 15.
    1960: *U.S. Census of Population 1960,* Subject Reports. PC (2)-7F. 1967, Table 1.
    1970: *U.S. Census of Population 1970,* Subject Reports. PC (2)-7B. 1972, Table 1.

Table 2.4 Occupational Distribution of Experienced Civilian Labor Force, 1900–1980 (in percent)

	1900	1910	1920	1930	1940	1950	1960	1970	1980
White-collar workers	17.6	21.0	25.0	29.4	31.1	36.6	42.2	47.5	52.2
Professional and technical	4.3	4.6	5.4	6.8	7.5	8.6	11.3	14.6	16.1
Managers	5.9	6.5	6.6	7.4	7.3	8.7	8.5	8.1	11.2
Clerical	3.0	5.2	8.0	8.9	9.6	12.3	14.9	17.8	18.6
Sales	4.5	4.6	4.9	6.3	6.7	7.0	7.5	7.0	6.3
Manual workers	35.8	37.5	40.2	39.6	39.8	41.1	39.7	36.6	31.7
Craft workers	10.6	11.4	13.0	12.8	12.0	14.2	14.3	13.9	12.9
Operatives	12.8	14.4	15.6	15.8	18.4	20.4	19.9	17.9	14.2
Laborers (nonfarm)	12.5	11.8	11.6	11.0	9.4	6.6	5.5	4.7	4.6
Personal-service workers	9.1	9.4	7.9	9.8	11.8	10.5	11.7	12.9	13.3
Domestics	5.4	4.9	3.3	4.1	4.7	2.6	2.8	1.5	1.1
Other[a]	3.6	4.5	4.5	5.7	7.1	7.9	8.9	11.3	12.3
Farm workers	37.5	30.4	27.0	21.2	17.4	11.8	6.3	3.1	2.8
Farmers and farm managers	19.9	16.3	15.3	12.4	10.4	7.4	3.9	1.8	1.5
Farm laborers	17.7	14.2	11.7	8.8	7.0	4.4	2.4	1.3	1.3

Note: From 1900–1930, employment data relate to "gainful workers." From 1940 on, data relate to experienced civilian labor force.
[a]Included are attendants, barbers, cooks, guards, janitors, police, practical nurses, ushers, waiters, etc.

SOURCES: 1900–1950: U.S. Bureau of the Census, *Historical Statistics of the United States, Colonial Times to 1957,* (1960), Table D72-122.
    1960: U.S. Bureau of the Census, *Census of Population 1960,* Subject Reports, PC(2)-7A, 1967, Table 1.
    1970: U.S. Bureau of the Census, *Census of Population 1970,* Subject Reports, PC(2)-7A, 1972, Table 1.
    1980: U.S. President, *Employment and Training Report of the President* (Washington, D.C.: U.S. Government Printing Office, 1981), p. 149.

useful in comparing the pay of various workers at a given time. To compare the pay of workers over long periods of time we need to account for changes in the purchasing power of a dollar. Nominal wages divided by some index of prices constitute the definition of *real wages.* Real wages are normally expressed as an *index number*[6]—which provides a rough notion of how the purchasing power of an hour of work compares over time or across cities or countries.

We often apply the term *wages* to the payments received by workers who are paid on a salaried (monthly, for example) basis rather than an hourly basis. The term is used this way merely for convenience and is of no consequence for most purposes. It is important, however, to distinguish among *wages, earnings,* and *income.* The term *wages* refers to the payment for a *unit* of time, while *earnings* refers to wages multiplied by the number of time units (typically hours) worked. Thus, earnings depend on both wages and the length of time the employee works. *Income*—the total spending power of a person or family during some time period (usually a year)—includes both earnings and *unearned income,* which includes dividends or interest received on investments and transfer payments received from the government in the form of food stamps, welfare payments, unemployment compensation, and the like.

Table 2.5 shows the long-run trends in earnings and wages for U.S. manufacturing production workers. While real weekly earnings were about three and one quarter times higher in 1981 than in 1914, the fall in paid weekly hours from 49 to about 40 represented an additional gain in the general standard of living for workers. Probably the best index of living standards is how much workers receive *per hour,* and Table 2.5 shows that real hourly wages were four times as high in 1981 as in 1914, which implies that an hour of work paid for four times more goods and services in 1981 than in 1914.

The actual increase in living standards attainable by the ordinary worker is perhaps even greater than indicated in Table 2.5. Both wages and earnings are normally defined and measured in terms of direct monetary payments to employees (before taxes for which the employee is liable). *Total compensation,* on the other hand, consists of earnings plus *fringe benefits*—benefits that are either payments-in-kind or deferred. Examples of *payments-in-kind* are employer-provided health care or health insurance, where the employee receives a service or an insurance policy rather than money. Paid vacation time is also in this category,

---

[6]An index number is expressed as a fraction of some base, where the base is set equal to 100. To understand how index numbers are constructed, please refer to the last column in Table 2.5, where the index of real hourly wages in 1980 is listed as 403. This means that hourly real wages were four times higher in 1980 than in the base year, which was chosen arbitrarily as 1914.

To arrive at an index of *real* hourly wages requires that we calculate an index of nominal wages *and* an index of prices. An index of nominal wages can be constructed for each year with 1914 as a base by dividing the wage in each year by $0.22—the hourly wage in 1914—and multiplying by 100. This fixes the index at 100 in 1914 and yields an index number of 3305 for 1980 [(7.27 ÷ 0.22) × 100]. The Consumer Price Index, which is based on "pricing out" an unchanging market basket of goods from year to year, is 820 for the year 1980 if 1914 is the base year. Dividing the price index (820) into the index for nominal wages (3305) and multiplying by 100 gives us the figure of 403 noted in the table.

Table 2.5 Average Wages and Earnings of Production Workers in Manufacturing, 1914–1981

Year	Weekly Earnings (current dollars)	Average Weekly Hours Paid For	Average Hourly Wage (current dollars)	Consumer Price Index (1914 = 100)[a]	Index of Real Weekly Earnings (1914 = 100)	Index of Real Hourly Wages (1914 = 100)
1914	10.92	49.4	0.22	100	100	100
1920	26.02	47.4	0.55	199	120	126
1925	24.11	44.5	0.54	174	127	141
1930	23.00	42.1	0.55	166	127	151
1935	19.91	36.6	0.54	137	133	179
1940	24.96	38.1	0.66	140	163	214
1945	44.20	43.5	1.02	179	226	259
1950	58.32	40.5	1.44	240	223	273
1955	75.70	40.7	1.86	266	261	318
1960	89.72	39.7	2.26	295	278	348
1965	107.53	41.2	2.61	314	314	378
1970	133.73	39.8	3.36	386	317	396
1975	189.51	39.4	4.81	536	324	408
1980	288.62	39.7	7.27	820	322	403
1981	317.60	39.8	7.98	905	321	401

[a]The figures in this column should be interpreted with some caution. They are generated by pricing out a fixed "market basket" of consumer goods each year. Over time, however, new goods have become available and old ones improved in quality, so that comparability of the "baskets" used in making the index diminishes over time.

SOURCES: U.S. Bureau of the Census, *Historical Statistics of the United States, Colonial Times to 1970* (Washington, D.C.: U.S. Government Printing Office), 1975.

U.S. Department of Labor, Bureau of Labor Statistics, *Handbook of Labor Statistics 1977,* Bulletin 1966 (Washington, D.C.: U.S. Government Printing Office), 1977.

U.S. President, *Economic Report of the President* (Washington, D.C.: U.S. Government Printing Office, February 1982).

since employees are given days off instead of cash. Deferred payments can take the form of employer-financed retirement benefits, including Social Security taxes, where employers set aside money now that enables their employees to receive pensions later.

In 1976, earnings as conventionally defined constituted only 75 percent of the total compensation of manufacturing production workers. Vacations, pensions, and health care were the largest categories of fringe benefits. Because fringe benefits were virtually nonexistent before 1940, we can assume that total earnings and total compensation were essentially the same in the early 1900s. If earnings in more recent years are adjusted to reflect fringe benefits, we arrive at the conclusion that real compensation per hour around 1980 was more than five times higher than in 1914 for the typical manufacturing worker.

The next section will shift from the foregoing brief description of labor market *outcomes* over time to an analysis of how the market *operates* to generate these outcomes. This analysis of labor market functioning is the central focus of labor economics.

How the Market Works

The study of the labor market begins and ends with an analysis of the demand for and supply of labor. On the demand side of the labor market, we will study employer behavior regarding the hiring of labor. On the supply side, the behavior of both workers and potential workers will be explored. The interaction of demand and supply is basically what determines working conditions, employment and compensation levels, and the allocation of labor to various occupations, industries, and employers. One can thus think of any labor market outcome as always affected, to one degree or another, by the forces of both demand and supply. To paraphrase economist Alfred Marshall, it takes both demand and supply to determine economic outcomes just as it takes two blades of a scissors to cut cloth.

In this chapter we present the basic outlines and broadest implications of the simplest economic model of the labor market. In later chapters we will add some complexities to this basic model and explain assumptions and implications more fully. However, the simple model of demand and supply presented here generates some rather profound insights into labor market behavior which can be very useful in the formation of social policy. Every piece of analysis in this text is either an extension or modification of the basic model presented in this chapter.

The Demand for Labor

Firms are in the business of combining various factors of production—mainly capital and labor—to produce goods or services that are sold in a product market. Their total output and the way in which they combine labor and capital depends on 1. product demand, 2. how much labor and capital they can acquire at given prices, and 3. the choice of technologies available to them. When we study the demand for labor, we are interested in finding out how the number of workers employed by a firm or set of firms is affected by changes in one or more of these three forces. To simplify the discussion, we will study one change at a time and hold all other forces constant.

Wage changes. Of primary interest for most purposes is the question of how the number of employees (or total labor hours) demanded varies when wages change. Suppose, for example, that we could vary the wages facing a certain industry over a long period of time but keep the technology available, the conditions under which capital is supplied, and the relationship between product price and product demand all unchanged. What will happen to the demand for labor when, say, the wage rate is *increased?*

First, higher wages imply higher costs and, usually, higher product prices. Because consumers respond to higher prices by buying less, employers would tend to reduce their level of output. Lower output levels, of course, imply lower employment levels (other things equal). This decline in employment is called a *scale effect*—the effect on desired employment of a smaller scale of production.

Second, as wages increase (assuming the price of capital does not change, at least initially), employers have incentives to cut costs by adopting a technology that relies more on capital and less on labor. Thus, if wages were to rise, desired employment would fall because of a shift toward a more "capital-intensive" mode of production. This second effect might be termed a *substitution effect* because as wages rise, capital is *substituted* for labor in the production process.

The effects of various wages on employment levels might be summarized in a table showing the labor demanded at each wage level. Table 2.6 is an example of such a *demand schedule.* The relationship between wages and employment tabulated in Table 2.6 could be graphed as a *demand curve.* Figure 2.1 shows the demand curve generated by the data in Table 2.6. Note that the curve has a negative slope—indicating that as wages rise, less labor is demanded.

A demand curve for labor tells us how the desired level of employment—measured in either labor hours or number of employees—varies with changes in the price of labor when other forces affecting demand are held constant. These other forces, to repeat, are the product demand schedule, the conditions under which capital can be obtained, and the set of technologies available. If wages change and these other factors do not, one can determine the change in labor demanded by moving up or down along the demand curve.

Table 2.6 Labor Demand Schedule for a Hypothetical Industry

Wage Rate	*Desired Employment Level*
$3.00	250
4.00	190
5.00	160
6.00	130
7.00	100
8.00	70

Note: Employment levels can be measured in number of employees *or* number of labor hours demanded. We have chosen here to use number of employees.

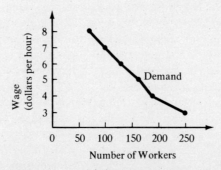

Figure 2.1   Labor Demand Curve

Changes in other forces affecting demand. What happens when one of the other forces affecting labor demand changes?

First, suppose that *demand for the product* of a particular industry were to increase, so that at any output price more of the goods or services in question could be sold. Suppose in this case that technology and the conditions under which capital and labor are made available to the industry do not change. Output levels would clearly rise as firms in the industry sought to maximize profits, and this *scale* (or *output*) *effect* would increase the amount of labor demanded. (As long as the relative prices of capital and labor remain unchanged, there is no *substitution effect.*)

How would this change in the demand for labor be illustrated using a demand curve? Since the technology available and the conditions under which capital and labor are supplied have remained constant, this change in product demand would increase the labor desired at any wage level that might prevail. In other words, the entire labor demand curve *shifts* to the right. This rightward shift, shown as a movement from D to D' in Figure 2.2, indicates that at every possible wage rate the number of workers demanded has increased.

Second, consider what would happen if the product demand schedule, technology, and labor-supply conditions were to remain unchanged, but *the supply of capital* changes so that capital prices fall to 50 percent (say) of their prior level. How would this change affect the demand for labor?

Our analysis of this situation is exactly the same as our analysis of a wage change. First, when capital prices decline, the costs of producing tend to decline. Reduced costs stimulate increases in production and these increases will tend to raise the level of desired employment at any given wage. The scale effect of a fall in capital prices thus tends to increase the demand for labor at each wage level —which can be represented in Figure 2.3 by a shift to the right of the labor demand curve.

The second effect of a fall in capital prices would be a substitution effect, whereby firms adopt more capital-intensive technologies in response to cheaper capital. Such firms would substitute capital for labor and would use less labor to produce a given amount of output than before. With less labor being desired at

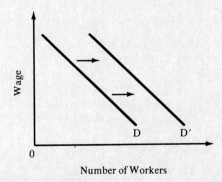

Figure 2.2 Demand for Labor Shifts Due to an Increase in Product Demand

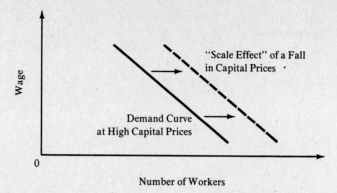

Figure 2.3 Demand for Labor Shifts Due to "Scale Effect" Resulting from Fall in
Capital Prices

each wage rate, the demand-for-labor curve shifts to the left, as shown in Figure
2.4. In some cases this leftward-shifting tendency of the substitution effect would
be stronger than the rightward-shifting tendency of the scale effect; in other cases,
the scale effect would be stronger.

The hypothesized changes in product demand and capital supply just discussed have tended to *shift* the demand curve for labor. It is important to
distinguish between a *shift* in a demand curve and *movement along* a curve. A
labor demand curve graphically shows the *labor desired* as a function of the *wage
rate* (the wage is on one axis and the number employed is on the other axis of
the graph). When the *wage* changes and other forces are held unchanged, one
moves along the curve. However, when one of the *other forces* changes, the labor
demand curve will *shift.* Unlike wages, these forces are not directly shown when
the demand curve for labor is drawn. Thus, when they change, a different relationship between wages and employment will prevail, and this shows up as a shift
of the demand curve. If more labor is desired at any given wage rate, then the

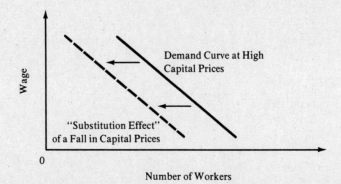

Figure 2.4 Demand for Labor Shifts due to "Substitution Effect" Resulting from
Fall in Capital Prices

curve has shifted to the right. If less labor is demanded at each wage rate that might prevail, then the demand curve has shifted left.

Market, industry, and firm demand. The demand for labor can be analyzed on any one of three different levels.

1. To analyze the demand for labor *by a particular firm,* we would examine how an increase in the wage of machinists (say) would affect their employment by a particular aircraft manufacturer.
2. To analyze the effects of this wage increase on the employment of machinists *in the entire aircraft industry,* we would utilize an industry demand curve.
3. Finally, to see how the wage increase would affect the *entire labor market* for machinists, in all industries in which they are used, we would use a market demand curve.

We will see in Chapters 3 and 4 that firm, industry, and market labor demand curves will vary in *shape* to some extent, because *scale* and *substitution effects* have different strengths at each of the three levels. However, it is important to know at this point that the scale and substitution effects of a wage change work in the same direction at each level, so that firm, industry, and market demand curves *all slope downward.*

Long run vs. short run. One can also distinguish between *long-run* and *short-run* labor demand curves. Over very short periods of time, employers find it difficult to substitute capital for labor (or vice versa), and customers may not change their product demand very much in response to a price increase. It takes *time* to fully adjust consumption and production behavior. Over longer periods of time, of course, responses to changes in wages or the other forces affecting the demand for labor will be larger and more complete.

In Chapters 3 and 4 we will draw some important distinctions between short-run and long-run labor demand curves. At this point, we only need to point out that while these curves will differ, *they both slope downward.* Thus, an increase in the wage rate will reduce the demand for labor—although perhaps by different amounts—in both the short and long run.

The Supply of Labor

Having looked at a simple model of behavior on the buyer (or demand) side of the labor market, we now turn to the seller (or supply) side of the market. For the purposes of this chapter we will assume that workers have already decided to work and that the question facing them is what occupation and what employer to choose.

Market supply. To first consider the supply of labor to the entire market (as opposed to the supply to a particular firm), let us suppose that the market we are considering is the one for stenographers. How will supply respond to changes in the wages stenographers might receive? In other words, what does the supply schedule of stenographers look like?

If the salaries and wages in *other* occupations are *held constant* and the wages of stenographers rise, we would expect to find more people wanting to become stenographers. For example, suppose that each of 100 people in a high-school graduating class has the option of becoming an insurance agent or stenographer. Some of these 100 people will prefer to be insurance agents even if stenographers are better paid, because they like the challenge and sociability of selling. Some would want to be stenographers even if the pay were comparatively poor, because they hate the pressures of selling. Many, however, could see themselves doing either job; for these the compensation in each occupation would be a major factor in their decision. If stenographers were higher paid than insurance agents, more would want to become stenographers. If the pay of insurance agents were higher, the number of people choosing the insurance occupation would increase and the supply of stenographers would decrease. Of course, at some ridiculously low wage for stenographers, *no one* would want to become one.

Thus, the supply of labor to a particular market is positively related to the wage rate prevailing in that market, holding other wages constant. That is, if the wages of insurance agents are held constant and the stenographer wage rises, more people will want to become stenographers because of the relative improvement in compensation (as shown graphically in Figure 2.5).

As with demand curves, each supply curve is drawn holding other prices and wages constant. If one or more of these other prices or wages were to change, it would cause the supply curve to *shift.* As the salaries of insurance agents *rise,* some people will change their minds about becoming stenographers and choose to become insurance agents. Fewer people would want to be stenographers at each level of stenographic wages as salaries of insurance agents rise. In graphical terms (see Figure 2.6), increases in the salaries of insurance agents would cause the supply curve of stenographers to shift to the left.

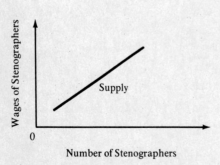

Figure 2.5   Supply Curve for Stenographers

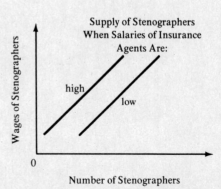

Figure 2.6   Labor Supply Curve for Stenographers Shifts as Salaries of Insurance Agents Rise

Supply to firms. Having decided to become a stenographer, the decision then moves to which offer of employment to accept. If all employers were offering stenographic jobs that were more or less alike, the choice would be based on compensation. Any firm unwise enough to attempt paying a wage below what others pay would find it could not attract any employees (or at least it could not attract any of the caliber it wants). Conversely, no firm would be foolish enough to pay more than the going wage, because it would be paying more than it would have to pay in order to attract a suitable number and quality of employees. The supply curve to a firm, then, would be horizontal, as can be seen in Figure 2.7. The horizontal supply curve to a firm indicates that at the going wage, a firm can get all the stenographers it needs. If it pays less, however, supply shrinks to zero.

The difference in slope between the market supply curve and the supply curve to a firm is directly related to the type of choice facing workers. In deciding whether to enter the stenographic labor market or not, workers must weigh both the compensation *and* the job requirements of alternative options (such as being an insurance agent). If wages of stenographers were to fall, fewer people would want to enter the stenographic market. However, not everyone would withdraw from the market, because the jobs of insurance agent and stenographer are not perfect substitutes. Some people would remain stenographers after a wage decline because they dislike the job requirements of insurance agents.

Once having decided to become a stenographer, the choice of which employer to work for is a choice between alternatives where the job requirements are nearly the *same*. Thus, the choice must be made on the grounds of compensation alone. If a firm were to lower its wage offers below those of other firms, it would lose all its applicants. The horizontal supply curve is, therefore, a reflection of supply decisions made among alternatives that are perfect substitutes for each other.

We have argued that firms wishing to hire stenographers must pay the going wage or lose all applicants. While this may seem unrealistic, it is not. If a firm offers jobs *comparable* to those offered by other firms but at a lower level of total compensation, it might be able to attract a few applicants of the quality it desires because a few people will be unaware of compensation elsewhere. Over time, however, knowledge of the firm's poor relative pay would become more widespread, and the firm would find it had to rely solely on less qualified people to

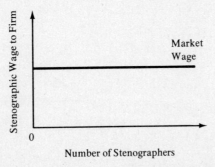

Figure 2.7 Supply of Stenographers to a Firm

fill its jobs. It could secure quality employees at below-average pay only if it offered *noncomparable* jobs (more pleasant working conditions, longer paid-vacations, and so forth). This factor in labor supply will be discussed in Chapter 7. For now, we will assume that individual firms, like individual workers, are usually *wage takers;* that is, the wages they pay to their workers must be pretty close to the going wage if they face competition in the labor market. Neither individual workers nor firms can set a wage much different from the going wage and still hope to transact. (Exceptions to this general proposition will be noted in later chapters.)

The Determination of the Wage

The wage that prevails in a particular labor market is heavily influenced by the forces of demand and supply, whether or not the market involves a labor union. However, because unions are labor-market institutions designed to alter the market outcome, we will first discuss wage determination in the case of nonunionized labor markets.

The equilibrium wage. Recall that the market demand curve indicates how many workers employers would want at each wage rate, holding capital prices and consumer incomes constant. The market supply curve indicates how many workers would enter the market at each wage level, holding the wages in other occupations constant. These curves can be overlaid on the same graph to reveal some interesting information, as shown in Figure 2.8.

For example, suppose the market wage were set at W_1. At this low wage, demand is large but supply is small. More importantly, Figure 2.8 indicates that at W_1 demand *exceeds* supply. At this point, employers will be competing for the few workers in the market and a "shortage" of workers would exist. Firms' desires to attract more employees would lead them to increase their wage offers, thus driving up the overall level of wage offers in the market.

As wages rise, two things happen. First, more workers would choose to enter the market and look for jobs (a movement along the supply curve); second, at the

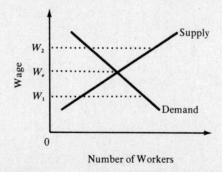

Figure 2.8   Market Demand and Supply

same time increasing wages would induce employers to seek fewer workers (a movement along the demand curve). If wages were to rise to W_2, supply would exceed demand. Employers would desire fewer workers than the number available, and not all those desiring employment would be able to find jobs—resulting in a "surplus" of workers. Employers would have long lines of eager applicants for any opening. These employers would soon reason that they could still fill their openings with qualified applicants even if they offered lower wages. Further, if they could pay lower wages they would want to hire more employees. Some employees would be more than happy to accept the lower wages if they could just find a job. Others would leave the market and look for work elsewhere as wages fell. Thus, demand and supply would become more equal as wages fell from the level of W_2.

The wage rate at which demand equals supply is the *market-clearing* or *equilibrium* wage. At W_e in Figure 2.8, employers can fill the number of openings they have, and all employees who want jobs in this market can find them. At W_e there is no surplus and no shortage. All parties are satisfied, and no forces exist that would alter the wage. The market is in equilibrium in the sense that the wage will remain at W_e.

The equilibrium wage is the wage that eventually prevails in a market. Wages below W_e, for example, will not prevail because the shortage of workers leads employers to drive up wage offers. Wages above W_e likewise cannot prevail because the surplus leads to downward pressure on wage rates. The market-clearing wage, W_e, thus becomes the *going wage* that individual employers and employees must face. In other words, wage rates are determined by the market and "announced" to individual market participants. Figure 2.9 graphically depicts "market" demand and supply in panel (a) along with the demand and supply curves for a typical firm in that market in panel (b). All firms in the market pay a wage of W_e, and total employment of L equals the sum of employment in each firm.

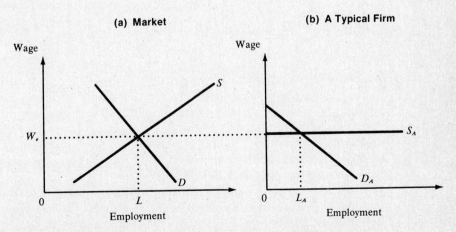

Figure 2.9 Demand and Supply at the "Market" and "Firm" Level

Disturbing the equilibrium. What could happen to change the equilibrium (market) wage once it has been reached? Once equilibrium has been achieved, changes could arise from shifts in either the demand or the supply curve. For example, let us consider what might happen to the wages of stenographers (the majority of whom at present are women) if job opportunities for women in management and other prestigious fields were to improve. The greater availability and improved pay for women in these alternative careers would probably cause some women to leave the stenographer market and seek work in these other fields. Fewer women would want to become stenographers at the going wage. As Figure 2.10 shows, the market supply curve for stenographers would shift to the left.

As can be seen from Figure 2.10, after the supply curve has shifted, W_e is no longer the market-clearing wage. There is now a shortage of stenographers because demand exceeds supply at W_e. As employers scramble to fill stenographic jobs, the wage rate is driven up. The new equilibrium wage is W'_e, which of course is higher than W_e. Better opportunities for women in management would thus lead to a smaller supply of stenographers, and to fill stenographic jobs the wage rate paid to stenographers would have to rise. The end result of the improved opportunities elsewhere would be to increase the wages of stenographers.

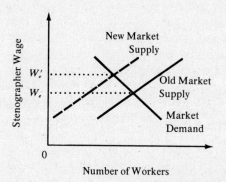

Figure 2.10 New Labor Market Equilibrium after Supply Shifts Left

Shifts of the demand curve to the right would also cause wages to rise. Suppose, for example, that the increase in paperwork accompanying greater government regulation of industry causes firms to demand more stenographic help than before. Graphically, as in Figure 2.11, this greater demand would be represented as a rightward shift of the demand curve. This rightward shift depicts a situation in which, for any given wage rate, the number of stenographers desired has risen. The old equilibrium wage (W_e) no longer equates demand and supply. If W_e were to persist, there would be a labor shortage in the stenographer market (because demand would exceed supply). This shortage would induce employers to improve their wage offers and eventually drive up the stenographic wage to W^*_e.

Both the leftward shift of supply and the rightward shift in demand initially created shortages—shortages that led to increases in the market wage rate. The

EXAMPLE 2.1

The Black Death and the Wages of Labor

A tragic example of what happens to wages when the supply of labor suddenly shifts occurred when plague—the Black Death—struck England (among other European countries) in 1348–51. Estimates vary, but it is generally agreed that plague killed between 17 and 40 percent of the English population in the short period of time. This shocking loss of life had the immediate effect of raising the wages of laborers. As supply shifted to the left, a *shortage* of workers was created at the old wage levels, and competition among employers for the surviving workers drove the wage level dramatically upward.

Reliable figures are hard to come by, but many believe wages rose by 50–100 percent over the three-year period. A thresher, for example, earning two and one-half pence per day in 1348 earned four and one-half pence in 1350, while mowers receiving 5 pence per acre in 1348 were receiving 9 pence in 1350. Whether the overall rise in wages was this large or not, there was clearly a labor shortage and an unprecedented increase in wages. A royal proclamation—commanding landlords to share their scarce workers with neighbors and threatening workers with imprisonment if they refused work at the pre-plague wage—was issued to deal with this shortage, but it was ignored. The shortage was too severe and market forces simply too strong for the rise in wages to be thwarted.

The discerning student might wonder at this point about the *demand* curve for labor. Did it not also shift to the left as the population—and the number of consumers—declined? The answer is that it did, but that this leftward shift was not as pronounced as the leftward shift in supply. What happened was that, while there were fewer customers for labor's output, the customers who remained consumed greater amounts of goods and services per capita than before. The money, gold and silver, and durable goods that had existed prior to 1348 were divided among many fewer people by 1350, and this rise in per capita wealth was associated with a widespread and dramatic increase in the level of consumption—especially of luxury goods. Thus the leftward shift in labor demand was dominated by the leftward shift in supply, and the predictable result was a large increase in wages.

SOURCES: Harry A. Miskimin, *The Economy of Early Renaissance Europe 1300–1460* (Englewood Cliffs, N.J.: Prentice-Hall, Inc., 1969); George M. Modlin and Frank T. deVyver, *Development of Economic Society* (Boston: D.C. Heath, 1946); Douglass C. North and Robert Paul Thomas, *The Rise of the Western World* (Cambridge: Cambridge University Press, 1973); Philip Ziegler, *The Black Death* (New York: Harper & Row, 1969).

supply-caused shift, however, led to a fall in employment (as compared to the old equilibrium level of employment). Conversely, the demand-caused shift induced an increase in the equilibrium level of employment.

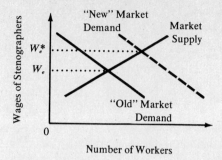

Figure 2.11   New Labor Market Equilibrium after Demand Shifts Right

Equilibrium wages can also fall, of course. Although *money* wages are rarely cut, in a period of rising prices *real* wages can fall quite readily anyway. Between 1976 and 1977, for example, money wages for nonagricultural production workers rose by 8.0 percent (from $203.70 per week to $219.91), but their real wages fell by 3 percent because prices rose by 11 percent.[7] Money wages in an occupation can also fall relative to wages in other occupations. Thus, when we speak of a declining wage rate it can imply a decline *relative to product prices or to other wages* as well as a fall in the money wage rate.

A fall in the equilibrium wage rate will occur if there is increased supply or reduced demand. An increase in supply would be represented by a rightward shift of the supply curve, as more people enter the market at each wage (see Figure 2.12). This rightward shift causes a surplus to exist at the old equilibrium wage *(W_e)* and leads to behavior that reduces the wage to W_e'' in Figure 2.12. Note that the equilibrium employment level has increased. What could cause this rightward shift of the supply curve? For stenographers, the causes of increased supply at each wage could be 1. a greater desire among people to become stenographers, or 2. reductions in the wages of competing occupations (such as insurance agents in our example above).

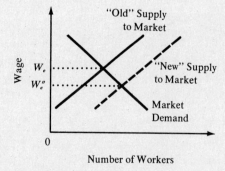

Figure 2.12   New Labor Market Equilibrium after Supply Shifts Right

---

[7]U.S. President, *Economic Report of the President* (Washington, D.C.: U.S. Government Printing Office, January 1980), Tables B-36 and B-49.

A decrease (leftward shift) in demand would also cause a decrease in the equilibrium wage, although such a shift would be accompanied by a fall in employment, as we can see in Figure 2.13. The leftward demand shift causes a surplus at the original equilibrium wage *(W_e)*. When firms find the ratio of applicants to openings is greater than usual and when workers find that jobs are harder to come by, downward pressure on the wage will exist and the market-clearing wage falls to W_e^{**}. Money wages may go up, but any increases will be smaller than those received in other occupations. Sadly for the authors, the decline in demand for college professors brought on by a number of financial and demographic pressures offers an excellent example of a "surplus" market. The result was a 17 percent decline in real, after-tax income for college professors over the 1967–78 period.

It is possible, of course, for equilibrium to be disturbed by shifts in both demand and supply at the same time. These simultaneous shifts might either reinforce each other or work against each other. An example of a reinforcing shift is where a leftward shift in demand is accompanied by a rightward shift in supply, as shown in Figure 2.14. If the demand curve alone shifted, wages would fall from W_{1-1} to W_{2-1}, but when accompanied by a rightward shift in supply wages fall to W_{2-2}.

Shifts may also tend to work against each other. For example, if the invention

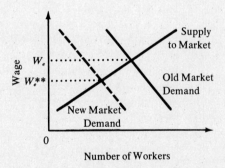

Figure 2.13   New Labor Market Equilibrium after Demand Shifts Left

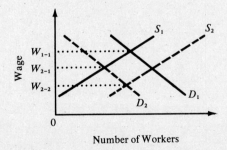

Figure 2.14   New Labor Market Equilibrium after Supply Shifts Right and Demand Shifts Left

and spread of tape-recording devices reduced the demand for people with stenographic skills at the same time that opportunities for women outside the clerical occupations were increasing, it would be difficult to predict the effects on stenographers' wages (see Figure 2.15). The leftward shift of demand exerts downward pressure on wages, while the leftward shift of supply has a tendency to cause wages to rise. The ultimate effect depends on which force is greater. In panel (a) of Figure 2.15, the forces generated by the contraction of demand were dominant, and the equilibrium wage is depicted as falling from W_{1-1} to W_{2-2}. In panel (b) of Figure 2.15, however, the contraction of supply was dominant, and wages are shown as rising from W_{1-1} to W_{2-2}.

Applications of the Theory

The preceding section presented a simple model of how a labor market functions. Although this model will be refined and elaborated upon in the following chapters, the model is adequate to explain many important phenomena, including those that follow.

The Allocation of Labor to Inhospitable Climates

The labor market, as we emphasized earlier, performs the task of matching employers and employees. In accomplishing this task it fulfills the important social role of allocating a scarce resource—labor—among potential users. Moreover, this allocation takes place voluntarily. Our model of the labor market explains how this allocation happens and with what effects.

Any society wanting to allocate its resources by taking into account the wishes of both consumer and worker must invent a mechanism that readily reflects both sets of wishes. The market is just such a mechanism. The wishes of consumers are expressed through the labor demand schedules of employers. The

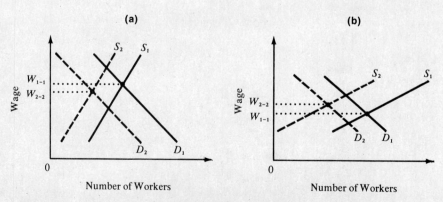

Figure 2.15   New Labor Market Equilibria after Supply and Demand Shift Left

more of a particular output consumers want and the more they are willing to pay for it, the more labor (and capital) will be demanded by producers. For example, Figure 2.16 shows that firm A has a stronger demand for workers than does firm B; therefore, at a wage of W_0, it hires more workers.

The labor market also reflects worker preferences. If all jobs were alike, preferences would not be important. However, jobs vary in difficulty, level of tension, location, working conditions, hours, security, and so forth. Workers will understandably be more reluctant to do some kinds of work than other kinds, and the allocation process must take this reluctance into account. The supply curves to various labor markets are a convenient way to represent worker preferences. When the jobs are pleasant, many people will be willing to offer their services at each wage level. When jobs are distasteful, fewer will be willing to do so.

The effect of worker preferences on the allocation of labor can be understood by comparing two labor markets where the job *duties* are the same but where the conditions of work are radically different. Let us suppose, for example, that one market is offering clerical jobs in the continental United States, while the other market is offering such jobs with companies building a pipeline in a harsh, inhospitable, remote location near the Arctic Circle. If wages were equal in both places, the jobs near the Arctic Circle would not be filled, as workers prefer more hospitable climates. To attract workers to the unappealing location requires that compensation be higher there. The high wages cause employers to economize on the use of labor in these places—most, in fact, would not even locate there. Some, however, have such strong incentives for locating there that they are willing to pay the high wages. The high wages, of course, serve to compensate workers for the inhospitable location of their jobs.

The building of the trans-Alaska pipeline in the mid-1970s provides an example of how disagreeable working conditions affect wages. The work entailed long hours (84 hours a week), cruel winter weather (frequently 55 degrees below zero), and anything but a normal personal life (dormitory living). Under these conditions, it took hourly wages 50 percent higher than those received by similarly skilled workers in the continental United States, with time and one-half for overtime and double time on Sundays, to recruit and hold the required labor

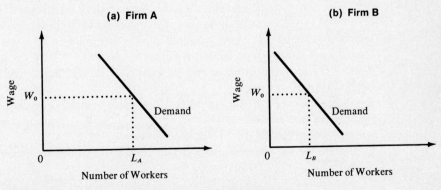

Figure 2.16   The Demand for Labor in Two Firms

force. However, workers who chose to work there could make $60,000 per year —almost four times what they could make in roughly the same job located in the continental United States.

EXAMPLE 2.2

Restricted Labor Supply in the Soviet Union

Examples of the effects of a restricted labor supply to areas where the weather is extraordinarily harsh can be found in socialist, as well as capitalist, countries. In the Soviet Union, where production is centrally planned but labor is recruited voluntarily through the use of incentives, workers in the Far North are paid wages and supplements that are 60–180 percent higher than in the populated areas in central, southern, and western Russia. Only part of the differential is to compensate workers for the higher costs of living in Northern Siberia. Even a society that philosophically prefers wage equality must pay its workers in the Far North a *real wage* much higher than elsewhere if it hopes to voluntarily assemble a work force large enough to produce in that region.

SOURCE: Paul R. Gregory and Robert C. Stuart, *Soviet Economic Structure and Performance*, 2nd ed. (New York: Harper & Row, 1981), pp. 190–92.

The Accommodation of "Baby Boom" Workers

During the late 1970s, the overall labor market was forced to accommodate a huge influx of new workers searching for jobs. These new entrants were people born in the late 1950s—a period of the so-called "baby boom." The number of 20-year-olds in the population in 1977 was 44 percent larger than the number in 1962 and equally large compared to the numbers projected for 1992.[8] Thus, there was a "bulge" in the number of inexperienced workers seeking jobs. What can we predict would happen as this bulge in supply hit the labor market?

First, new entrants are, by definition, inexperienced workers, and such workers are not very good substitutes for experienced workers. Inexperienced workers tend to be offered *entry-level jobs,* while more complicated or responsible jobs higher up on the career ladder are reserved to some extent for experienced workers. Thus, the experienced and the inexperienced are, to a degree, in different labor markets.

What happens when a big bulge of population enters a labor market? The sheer increase in population will shift the supply curve to the right, because there will be more people offering themselves for work at every wage level. Figure 2.17 illustrates this shift from S_1 to S_2. This shift in supply, if not accompanied by

---

[8]Data for this section were obtained from Finis Welch, "Effects of Cohort Size on Earnings: The Baby Boom Babies' Financial Bust," *Journal of Political Economy 87,* 5 (October 1979): S65–98.

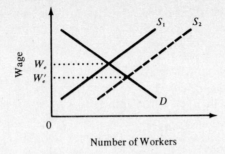

Figure 2.17   Labor Market Equilibrium for Teenagers after Population Increase

a correspondingly large shift in demand, will have the effect of reducing wages. (Figure 2.17 shows that the equilibrium wage fell from W_e to W'_e.)

Did the "baby boom" bulge in the late 1970s cause wages of inexperienced workers to fall? To answer this question we must pick a standard against which to measure the fall. Money wages rarely fall, especially during periods when prices are rising. We could, therefore, measure whether *real wages* fell over some time period. However, real wages have tended to rise due to improvements in technology—a force we would like to filter out if possible so that we can focus only on changes produced by the shift in supply.

The best way to measure the fall in the wages of inexperienced workers is to compare their wages to those of adults in their peak earnings years. These adults will be the beneficiaries, along with inexperienced workers, of technological advances, but they are far enough removed from the "baby boomers" in experience that the bulge of new labor force entrants will not affect their wages directly. Measured against this group, earnings of new entrants fell dramatically in the late 1970s.

Table 2.7 tells the story. In every educational category, the proportion of inexperienced workers in the labor force increased during the period from 1967 to 1975—a clear indication that the number of young workers was increasing faster than the number of older workers. This abnormally large rise in employment was accompanied by a 12–15 percent decline in the earnings of new workers relative to adults. Thus, as our model of labor-market behavior suggests, the large increase in employment necessary to accommodate the "baby boom" entrants was facilitated by a decline in their wage. The influx of inexperienced workers created a "surplus" at the former wage level, and as new workers competed for jobs the wage level was driven down.

Effects of Unions

Although we will discuss the role and effects of unions on the labor market later in this text, it is important here to briefly establish that the model outlined in this chapter can also apply to unions. This analysis will look only generally at the effects of unions on wages. Later chapters will analyze union effects on wages in

Table 2.7 Economic Position of New Entrants in Labor Force, by Level of Schooling

Years of School Completed	Percent of Work Force with Less than 5 Years of Experience in Each Schooling Category		Weekly Wages of New Entrants Relative to Peak Earners	
	1967–69	1973–75	1967–69	1973–75
8–11 years	8.9	15.4	0.53	0.46
12 years	15.0	20.8	0.63	0.55
1–3 years of college	19.0	25.2	0.59	0.52
4 or more years of college	18.7	22.9	0.63	0.54

SOURCE: Finis Welch, "Effects of Cohort Size on Earnings: The Baby Boom Babies' Financial Bust," *Journal of Political Economy* 87, 5 (October 1979): S65–S98.

more detail and will also examine their effects on productivity, turnover, and wage differentials across race and sex groups.

Unions represent workers and, as such, primarily affect the *supply* curves to labor markets. They can affect these supply curves in two ways. First, most unions operate under labor-management agreements—called *contracts* or *collective-bargaining agreements*—that permit employer discretion in the selection of workers. These contracts cover wages, other forms of compensation, working conditions, procedures for employee complaints, and rules governing promotions and layoffs. The provisions of the contracts are the result of a bargain struck between management and all workers collectively. In effect, workers band together, agree to a bargaining position, and negotiate as a group. All are bound by the final provisions of the contract—which means that all must receive the agreed-upon wage.

Many of the most prominent collective-bargaining agreements, in effect, are industrywide. These agreements, which include those in the auto, steel, rubber, coal, and trucking industries, affect the supply curves in the relevant labor markets by making them horizontal. No one can get paid more or less than the wage agreed upon in the contract (see Figure 2.18).

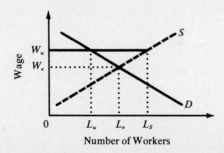

Figure 2.18   Effects on Labor-Market Equilibrium of Industrywide Unions

In Figure 2.18, the supply curve without a union is S, and the market-clearing wage is W_e. However, the union raises the wage above W_e to W_u, the wage specified in the contract, by preventing firms and workers from offering or accepting wages below W_u. The result is a wage above equilibrium, employment levels below those that would prevail if the wage were lower, and a "surplus" of labor (at W_u, L_s workers want work in these jobs but only L_u can find work). Because the wage cannot fall, the surplus remains and will manifest itself in long lines of workers applying for job openings with union employers.

The graphical analysis was based on the assumption that unions raised the wage above market-clearing levels. This is probably a useful assumption, given that unions certainly intend to do this. Not all unions have the power to affect wages much, for reasons we will discuss in Chapter 4. If these unions agree to wages equal to W_e, the market equilibrium wage, then clearly they do not affect wage or employment outcomes in the labor market.

The second way in which some unions affect the supply to markets is by *directly* limiting supply. Some unions operate under agreements in which employers hire all labor from the union and in which the union controls who and how many members it lets in. The dual power of being able to restrict its membership and to require employers to hire only union members permits the union to set the level of labor supply to the market (see Figure 2.19).

In Figure 2.19, S_u represents the level of supply determined by union policy and W_u the resulting wage. S_u is drawn as a vertical line because wage increases or decreases do not affect supply. Supply is set at L_u by union policy.

The wage and employment levels under the union—W_u and L_u—can be compared to the lower wages *(W_e)* and higher employment levels *(L_e)* that would prevail in the absence of a union. The major difference between this case, where unions control supply, and the more common situation, in which employers choose workers but make contracts with all workers collectively, is that there is no surplus of workers standing at the employer's hiring gate. The long line of disappointed people is at the union's office. Examples of labor unions that control

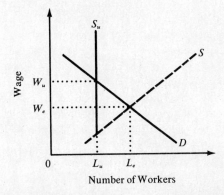

Figure 2.19   How Unions that Control Supply of Labor to a Market Affect Labor Market Equilibrium

supply are those representing skilled construction workers, longshoring workers, and theater lighting technicians.[9]

The model of labor market behavior presented in this chapter has here been used to explain how unions affect wages. If unions are successful in driving such wages above equilibrium, the model can also be used to analyze the consequences of this wage increase. First, as wages rise above the market-clearing level, employment will be reduced. Second, as union wages rise the number of people wanting union jobs will increase. However, the limited job opportunities will make it difficult for many of these people to find work, and a "surplus" of labor will come to exist in the unionized markets. (See Chapters 3 and 17 for an analysis of union effects on wages and employment in nonunion labor markets.)

Who Is Underpaid and Who Is Overpaid?

In casual conversation one often hears a worker say that he or she is "underpaid." Just as often one hears employers claiming workers are "overpaid." Clearly, each is using a different standard for judging wages. People tend to judge the wages paid or received against some notion of what they "need," but there is no universally accepted standard of need. A worker may "need" more income to buy a larger home or finance a recreational vehicle. An employer may "need" greater profits to pay for sending a child to college. In general, almost all of us feel we "need" more income!

Despite the difficulties of assessing needs, there are still important reasons for defining "overpaid" and "underpaid." For example, the public utilities commissions in every state must consider and approve rate increases requested by the telephone, gas, and electric companies. These companies desire increases partly to keep up with production costs, which the companies obviously want to pass on to consumers. Suppose, however, that a public utilities commission observes that the *level* of wages paid by these companies or the *increases* in such wages are "excessive." In the interests of holding down consumer prices, it may want to consider adopting a policy whereby excessive labor costs cannot be passed on to consumers in the form of rate increases. Instead, it may decide that such costs should be borne by the company or its shareholders. Obviously, such a policy would require a definition of what constitutes "overpayment."

We pointed out in Chapter 1 that a fundamental value of normative economics is that, as a society, we should strive to complete all those transactions that are mutually beneficial. Another way of stating this value is to say that we must strive to use our scarce resources as effectively as possible—which implies that output should be produced in the least costly manner so that the most can be obtained from such resources. This goal, combined with the labor market model

---

[9]This is not to say that all unions that *can* control supply are equally prone to do it. Some may fear the presence of a large number of qualified workers outside the union, and figure that it is better to take them in, collect their dues, and ration jobs among all members than to face stiff nonunion competition. Restricting entry into the union is *most likely* where employers *must* hire only union workers.

outlined in this chapter, suggests a useful definition of what it means to be overpaid.

We will define workers as *overpaid* if their wages are higher than the market equilibrium wage for their job. Because a labor "surplus" exists for jobs that are overpaid, a wage above equilibrium has two implications (see Figure 2.20). First, employers are paying more than they have to in order to produce (they pay W_H instead of W_e). They could cut wages and still find enough qualified workers for their job openings. In fact, if they did cut wages they could expand output and make their product cheaper and more accessible to consumers. Second, more workers want jobs than can find them (Y workers want jobs, and only V openings are available). If wages were reduced a bit, more of these disappointed workers could find work. A wage above equilibrium thus causes consumer prices to be higher and output to be smaller than is possible, and it creates a situation where not all workers who want the jobs in question can get them.

With this definition of overpayment, the public utilities commission in question would want to look for evidence that wages were above equilibrium. The commission might be able to compare wages paid by utilities to those of comparable workers in the general labor market. Doing so would require measures of worker quality, of course—data that are hard to quantify in some cases. Alternatively, the commission could look to employee behavior for signs of above-market wages. If wages are above those for comparable jobs, current employees will be *very* reluctant to quit, because they know their chances of doing better are small. Likewise, the number of applicants will be unusually large.

An interesting—although perhaps extreme—example of above-equilibrium wage rates could be seen in New York City in 1974–75. New York City fire fighters and police officers during this period were receiving salaries roughly 40 percent greater than skilled mechanics and machinists working in the city and some 50 percent greater than area truck drivers. Perhaps the most convincing evidence of "overpayment" and the attendant surplus is that there were enormous numbers of qualified applicants who had passed job-related tests and were waiting for openings. For fire fighters, there were about 12,000 qualified applicants—compared to a total employment of only 10,000—at a time when the city was not even hiring fire fighters. For police officers, there were more than 42,000

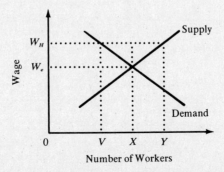

Figure 2.20 Effects of an Above-Equilibrium Wage

qualified applicants on the waiting list, 23,000 current employees, and no hiring to speak of.[10]

An even larger surplus existed for sanitation workers, whose $14,770 yearly salary (in 1974 dollars) was 60 percent higher than the area average for laborers/materials handlers. In that department, there were 36,849 on the waiting list of people who had passed a job-related examination—or 3.4 qualified applicants for each current employee! Again, hiring was almost nil during this period. These numbers clearly point to a labor "surplus"—and thus to "overpayment."

To better understand the social losses attendant to overpayment, let us return to the principles of normative economics. Can it be shown that reducing overpayment will create a situation where the gainers gain more than the losers lose? Suppose in the case of sanitation workers that *only* the wages of *newly hired* sanitation workers were lowered—to $10,000, say. Current workers thus do not lose, but many laborers working at $9200 per year (the prevailing wage for them in 1974) will jump at the chance to take a $10,000-a-year job. Taxpayers, knowing that garbage-collection services can now be expanded at lower cost than before will increase their demand for such services, thus creating jobs for these new workers.[11] Thus, some workers gain while no one loses—and social well-being is clearly enhanced.[12]

Employees can be defined as *underpaid* if their wage is below equilibrium. At below-equilibrium wages employers have difficulty in finding workers to meet the demands by consumers, and a labor "shortage" thus exists (firms want more workers than they can find at the prevailing wage). They also have trouble keeping the workers they do find. If wages were increased, output would rise, and more workers would be attracted to the market. Thus, an increase would benefit the people in society in *both* their consumer and worker roles. Figure 2.21 shows how a wage increase from W_L to W_e would increase employment to V from X (at the same time wages were rising).

A classic example of below-equilibrium wages were those in the U.S. Army. In 1962, for example, when the military draft was in effect, the military paid enlisted personnel salaries and allowances that came to around 80 percent of the earnings of comparably aged civilian workers. Total compensation was so low for the job that an enormous gap between demand and supply existed. As a result,

---

[10]Sharon P. Smith, *Equal Pay in the Public Sector: Fact or Fantasy* (Princeton, N.J.: Industrial Relations Section, Princeton University, Research Report Series No. 122, 1977), p. 20.

[11]These new workers, of course, have wanted sanitation jobs with New York City all along, but the high wage prevented job opportunities in that field from expanding.

It should be noted that if the wages of *current* sanitation workers were lowered, city taxpayers could obtain their current level of service for less money. Their gains (in tax savings) equal the income losses of sanitation workers, and if we are to arrange the transaction so that no one loses, the gainers would have to compensate the losers by restoring their lost income. For this reason we have assumed that salaries for current sanitation workers are not cut.

[12]If the workers who switch jobs are getting paid approximately what they are worth to their former employers, these employers lose $9200 in output but save $9200 in costs—and their welfare is thus not affected. The presumption that employees are paid what they are worth to the employer is discussed at length in Chapter 3.

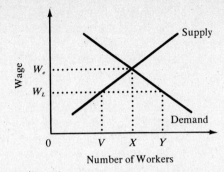

Figure 2.21   Effects of a Below-Equilibrium Wage

a large percentage of all new recruits had to be *drafted* in order to deal with the shortage. A decade later, when shortages could no longer be met through conscription, salaries and allowances for enlisted personnel had risen to 95 percent of the civilian wage.

How do these definitions of underpayment and overpayment accord with notions of fairness or equity? They square very well with the concept of *horizontal equity*—treating equals equally. If the equilibrium wage were paid to each worker in a particular labor market, no one would be underpaid or overpaid. Equal workers would receive equal pay for essentially the same work.

These definitions, however, are ambiguous in relation to the concept of *vertical equity*—treating different groups differently. How can we justify paying a professor more or less than a sanitation worker? The answer suggested by our definitions is that it is less a matter of justice than it is of getting the job done. We have to pay professors and sanitation workers whatever it takes to get them to provide the level of services we desire. If so few people want to collect garbage that it requires a relatively high wage to attract them, so be it. If we are to have this valuable service performed without resorting to involuntary servitude, there is no choice but to pay the wages necessary to attract the required number and quality of workers.

Labor "Shortages": A Policy Application

The government is frequently urged to undertake programs designed to cope with perceived labor shortages. Underlying these proposals is usually an assumption that market forces are not working effectively to generate an adequate supply of workers to the occupations in question, but this assumption is often based on concepts or reasoning that are faulty. We can use the insights developed in this chapter to point out two common errors in this assumption and the dangers of not recognizing them.

Wrong definition of shortage. Perhaps the most common error is to define a "shortage" in terms that are independent of demand. For example, a recent book on occupational safety and health argued that there was a shortage (in 1973) of

19,700 industrial nurses even though the same book estimated that the number of jobs available for such nurses exceeded their supply by only 700.[13] In what sense does the author perceive a "shortage"?

It is clear that the author's definition of a shortage is inconsistent with the concept as we have defined it. According to our definition a shortage exists if, at the prevailing wage rate for a given occupation, demand exceeds supply. If the figures quoted above for industrial nurses are correct, a minor shortage of 700 may be said to exist. The author, however, ignores what demand *actually* is and bases his definition of a shortage on what he feels demand *should be!* He argues that to do an "adequate" job of protecting workers from the dangers of health hazards on the job, we "need" to have 19,700 more nurses than we currently have. His definition is thus based on a perception of *"need"* as compared to supply— rather than on *demand* as compared to supply.

The distinction between a needs-based definition of a shortage and a demand-based definition is not a trivial matter of semantics. The central problem addressed by economics is that resources are scarce, so that our individual or social *needs* for newer cars, larger houses, cleaner air, better schools, and more mass transit will not necessarily get translated into *demand*. That workers would be healthier if we employed 19,700 more industrial nurses no more indicates that these nurses would be hired than the fact that all families would be happier with five-bedroom houses suggests more such homes could be sold! Given limited resources, firms and homeowners alike may not choose to pay the added costs of meeting the "need."

Acceptance of a needs-based definition of labor shortage by the government poses two related dangers. Declaring that the "shortage" of industrial nurses amounts to 19,700 may imply to new workers that many more jobs are available than in fact actually exist. Many might mistakenly enter the field believing the opportunities are better than they really are. The other danger is that the government might uncritically adopt expensive programs to increase supply in an environment where the added workers would not find jobs available in the field.

In the 1960s, for example, the government initiated a $300 million program to increase the supply of professional nursing graduates by 29 percent in five years. The program was adopted after a report by the Surgeon General calculated a huge shortage of nurses based on a needs approach. The report contended that 50 percent of direct patient care should be provided by registered nurses (as opposed to nursing aides), because below this level patient satisfaction is significantly reduced. The problem with trying to increase the supply of nurses to meet this "shortage" was that at the time supply did not seem to be falling short of effective demand!

The hallmark of a shortage (as we have defined it) is a wage rate that rises faster than average. If demand exceeds supply at the prevailing wage, firms with unfilled vacancies will attempt to attract workers by offering higher wages, and thus wages in the shortage occupation rise relative to those in occupations not

---

[13]Nicholas Ashford, *Crisis in the Workplace* (Cambridge, Mass.: MIT Press, 1976), p. 455.

experiencing a shortage. (Put differently, shortages exist because the wage rate is below market-clearing levels; the market response is for these wages to rise.) There is no evidence that, as of the mid-1960s, nursing salaries were rising faster than average.[14] The relationship of these salaries to all workers, all female workers, and all female professional workers remained essentially constant from 1950 to 1963, showing no tendency to rise. This fact suggests that the effective demand for nurses did not exceed supply at the prevailing wage,[15] and the essential balance between demand and supply probably explains why the supply of nurses rose by 3 percent, and not by 29 percent, as a result of the government program.[16] Future employment and salary prospects simply did not seem attractive enough to lure more students to the field.

What the Surgeon General and the government failed to recognize was that the problem they perceived in providing adequate patient care was one of *demand,* not supply. Nurses were in abundant enough supply to fill available jobs; it was the number of *jobs* that was the "problem." Ironically, a program shifting the *demand* for nurses was initiated later in the 1960s when Medicare and Medicaid were adopted, and the labor market responses to this program indicate a properly functioning market. Nursing salaries rose relative to those in other occupations, and the number of nurses employed rose quickly (mainly because the higher wages attracted many who were *already* trained as nurses back into the field). These responses suggest that the government's efforts to cure a "supply" problem in the nursing market using subsidies were unnecessary as well as unproductive.

Wrong conclusion of market failure. For a prolonged period in the 1950s, firms complained of unfilled vacancies for engineers despite the fact that wages in this market were rising faster than average. The market signals (of a rising wage) seemed to be working, but the shortage did not appear to abate. This situation led some to conclude that the market was not functioning effectively and that government "help" was required (in the form of engineering educational subsidies).[17]

The above conclusion was based on the partially *correct* analysis that a rising wage should cure a shortage in two ways. First, as wages rise more workers will be attracted to the occupation in question. Second, the increased wage dampens demand by firms. What the conclusion *missed,* however, is that a shortage can

---

[14]Donald Yett, *An Economic Analysis of the Nursing Shortage* (Lexington, Mass.: Lexington Books, 1975), p. 160.

[15]Many economists believe the nursing labor market is dominated by just a few buyers of labor in each city, as we will discuss in Chapter 3. While a lack of competition on the employer side of the market does have a bearing on the perception of shortages (as we will see), it will nevertheless be true that if hospitals were trying to hire beyond current levels, they would behave in a way that would drive nursing salaries up.

[16]Yett, *An Economic Analysis of the Nursing Shortage.*

[17]*See* Kenneth Arrow and William Capron, "Dynamic Shortages and Price Rises: The Engineer-Scientist Case," *Quarterly Journal of Economics* 73, 2 (May 1959): 292–308.

continue despite rising wages if the demand curve *continues to shift* to the right (or the supply curve continues to shift to the left).

To illustrate this point, suppose that the market for engineers begins in equilibrium, but that a shortage occurs when the demand for engineers shifts to the right for some reason. (As Figure 2.22 shows, the demand curve would shift from D_0 to D_1.) Suppose further that it takes a year or two for firms and workers to adjust to the shortage. (A longer adjustment period can cause other problems, which will be discussed in the Chapter 8 section on "cobweb models.") Workers need time to perceive the salary increases and shift occupational plans. Firms need time to discover that their problem of unfilled vacancies is not a random event and to initiate wage increases as a response. However, if no further changes in demand or supply occur, wages would rise to W_1 in a year or two, and the shortage would be over.

Suppose, though, that in the year or two after the *initial* shift in demand, the demand curve shifts *again* (to D_2, say). Figure 2.22 shows how the rise in wages to the level of W_1 would not alleviate the shortage, because after this second shift W_2 is the market-clearing wage. A shortage would continue to exist, and it would persist as long as the demand curve continued to move out and as long as the adjustment to it by firms and workers was not instantaneous!

Something like this pattern appears to have caused the prolonged shortage of engineers in the 1950s. The shortage was felt most acutely among research and development (R & D) engineers and was the apparent result of an increase in R & D expenditures by the federal government. As these expenditures continued to increase, the market never had time to fully adjust before the next increase was felt.[18] The market was not failing; indeed, engineering salaries and employment levels were rising just as theory predicts! The market was simply being asked to facilitate a *series* of changes in demand, and the adjustment to one change was not completed before the next one was felt.

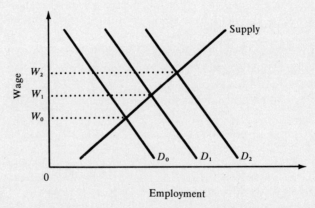

Figure 2.22   A Shortage Persists when the Demand Curve Continues to Shift

---

[18]Arrow and Capron, "Dynamic Shortages and Price Rises."

REVIEW QUESTIONS

1. The Central Intelligence Agency (CIA) finds out that compensation for coal miners in the Soviet Union is rising much faster than compensation in general in that country. It knows that the Soviet labor market is free in the sense that it relies on incentives (not compulsion) in the allocation process.

What can the CIA infer from this sharp rise in mining wages? Can it infer that coal output is increasing? Explain your answers.

2. Analyze the impact of the following changes on wages and employment in a given occupation:

a. a fall in the danger of the occupation.

b. an increase in product demand.

c. increased wages in other occupations.

3. What would happen to the wages and employment levels of engineers if government expenditures on research and development programs were to fall? Show the effect graphically.

4. Suppose a particular labor market is in equilibrium. What could happen to cause the equilibrium wage to fall? If all money wages rise each year, how will this market adjust?

SELECTED READINGS

John T. Dunlop and Walter Galenson, eds., *Labor in the Twentieth Century* (New York: Academic Press, 1978).

Simon Rottenberg, "On Choice in Labor Markets," *Industrial and Labor Relations Review* 9, 2 (January 1956): 183–99; Robert J. Lampman, "On Choice in Labor Markets: Comment," *Industrial and Labor Relations Review* 9, 4 (July 1956): 629–36; and "On Choice in Labor Markets: Reply," *Industrial and Labor Relations Review* 9, 4 (July 1956): 636–41.

Donald Yett, *An Economic Analysis of the Nursing Shortage* (Lexington, Mass.: Lexington Books, 1975).

Chapter 3

THE DEMAND FOR LABOR

The demand for labor is a derived demand. In most cases, employers hire labor not for the direct satisfaction that such an action brings them, but rather for the contribution they believe labor can make towards producing some product for sale. Not surprisingly, then, employers' demand for labor is a function of the characteristics of demand in the product market. Employers' demand is also a function of the characteristics of the production process—more specifically the ease with which labor can be substituted for capital and other factors of production. Finally, the demand for labor is a function not only of the price of labor, but also of the prices of other factors of production. This chapter and the next will illustrate how knowledge of the characteristics of the demand for labor can be used in various policy applications.

For purposes of making or evaluating social policy, the demand for labor has two important features. The first is that it can be shown theoretically—and demonstrated empirically—that labor demand curves slope downward. The second important feature of the demand for labor is the *degree of responsiveness* of this demand to changes in the wage. While it is always true that the quantity of labor demanded declines as the wage increases, in some cases this decline is larger than in other cases. For most policy issues, the degree of responsiveness is of critical importance. Thus, Chapter 4 will discuss the forces that determine this responsiveness and suggest ways in which policy makers can make some guesses about the degree of responsiveness in situations where explicit empirical estimates are not available.

When analyzing the demand for labor, two sets of distinctions are typically made. First, one must specify whether one is concentrating on demand by *firms* or on the demand curves for an entire *market*. As noted in Chapter 2, firm and market labor demand curves will have different properties, although they will both slope downward. Second, one must specify the *time* period for which the demand curve is drawn: the short run or the long run. The *short run* is defined as a period over which a firm's capital stock is fixed; the only input that is free to be varied is labor. The *long run* is defined as a period over which a firm is free to vary all factors of production, in this case both labor and capital. This distinction between short run and long run is a conceptual one, and the two concepts do not necessarily correspond closely to any actual period of calendar time. For example, an owner of a steel mill may find that it takes several years to construct a new steel plant, in which case anything less than two years might be considered the short run. In contrast, the owner of a small firm that hires people to shovel driveways may find that he can vary his capital stock instantaneously (by buying new shovels). In this case, the firm may never face the short run; it will always be involved in making decisions about both labor and capital! However, in spite of the fact that the short run and long run do not correspond neatly to specified calendar periods of time, the distinction does allow us to be more specific about the different forces that influence the demand for labor.

A Simple Model of Labor Demand

Our analysis of the demand for labor will begin with a simple model that yields very basic, but fundamental, behavioral predictions. To simplify the discussion, this model is derived using the four assumptions noted below. Later on in the chapter, two of the assumptions are dropped to see what difference they make. A third assumption is dropped in Chapter 5.

The Assumptions

In analyzing employers' demand for labor, we will make four assumptions. First, we will assume that employers seek to maximize *profit* (the difference between the revenue they take in from the sales of their product and their costs of production). This is a standard assumption of positive economics, but it is not absolutely necessary to derive the fundamental conclusion of the chapter—namely, that the demand for labor is a downward sloping function of the wage rate.[1]

Second, we will initially assume that firms employ two homogenous factors of production—labor and capital—in their production of goods and services. That is, we assume that there is a two-factor *production function* that indicates how various amounts of labor *(L)* and capital *(K)* can be combined to produce output *(Q):*

---

[1] Totally impulsive or random demand patterns are consistent with downward-sloping demand curves if people or firms have limited resources—a point made by Gary Becker, "Irrational Behavior and Economic Theory," *Journal of Political Economy* 70, 1 (February 1962).

$$Q = f(L,K). \qquad (3.1)$$

In equation (3.1) f stands for "a function of" and is used to represent a *general* mathematical relationship between Q and the factors of production. The *specific* relationship between Q and the two factors of production depends on the technology utilized. Later in this chapter we relax this two-factor assumption, noting that there are many different categories of labor. Firms also use other inputs besides *capital* (defined as machinery, equipment, and structures) in their production process, including materials and energy. Chapter 4 will discuss issues relating to energy usage.

Third, we will assume that the hourly wage cost is the only cost of labor. We will initially ignore the existence of hiring and training costs as well as those fringe benefit costs (like holiday pay, vacation pay, and sick leave as well as many forms of social insurance) that do not vary with weekly hours of work. By ignoring these costs here and by assuming that the length of the work week is fixed, we gloss over the distinction between the number of employees that a firm hires and the total number of person-hours[2] of labor that it employs. In Chapter 5 we will drop our simplifying assumption and consider the question of how the firm determines its optimal length of work week—as well as how hiring, training, and nonvariable fringe benefit costs affect the demand for labor.

Finally, we will initially assume that both a firm's labor market and its product market are competitive. If the firm's labor market is competitive, we can treat the wage rate that it must pay its workers as given; if its product market is competitive, we can treat the product price it faces as given. (Both of these assumptions are relaxed later in the chapter.) The following analyses of labor demand by the firm, in both the long and the short run, are primarily verbal.

Short-Run Demand for Labor by Firms

In the short run, when a firm's capital stock *(K)* and production function are not free to vary, the number of units of output that a firm produces can change only if it changes the number of units of labor that it employs—see equation (3.1). The additional output that can be produced by a firm when it employs one additional unit of labor, with capital held constant, is called the *marginal product of labor* (MP_L). For example, if a car dealership can sell 10 cars a month with one salesperson and 21 cars a month with two, the marginal product of hiring one salesperson is 10, and the marginal product of hiring the second is 11 cars per month. If a third equally persuasive salesperson were hired and sales rose to 26 per month, the marginal product of hiring the third salesperson is 5 cars per month. These hypothetical data are summarized in Table 3.1.

Table 3.1 shows that adding an extra salesperson increased output (cars sold) in each case. As long as output *increases* as labor is added, labor's marginal product (the change in output brought about by adding another unit of labor) is

---

[2]Person-hours, also called labor-hours, are calculated by multiplying the number of employees times the average length of work week per employee.

**Table 3.1 The Marginal Product of Labor in a
Hypothetical Car Dealership
(capital held constant)**

Number of Salespersons	Total Cars Sold	Marginal Product of Labor
0	0	
1	10	10
2	21	11
3	26	5

positive. In our example, however, the marginal product of labor increased at first (from 10 to 11), but then fell (to 5). Why?

The initial rise in marginal product is *not* because the second salesperson is better than the first; we ruled out this possibility by our assumption (stated above) that labor is homogeneous. Rather, the rise could be the result of the two generating promotional ideas or helping each other out in some way. Eventually, however, as more salespeople are hired, the marginal product of labor must fall. A fixed building (remember capital is held constant) can contain only so many customers, and thus each additional increment of labor produces progressively smaller increments of output. This law of *diminishing marginal returns* is an empirical proposition that derives from the fact that as employment expands, each additional worker has a progressively smaller share of the capital stock to work with.

For expository convenience, we will assume that the marginal product of labor is always decreasing.[3] Figure 3.1 shows a marginal-product-of-labor schedule *(MP_L)* for a representative firm. In this figure, the marginal product of labor is tabulated on the vertical axis and the number of units of labor employed on the horizontal axis. The negative slope of the schedule indicates that each addi-

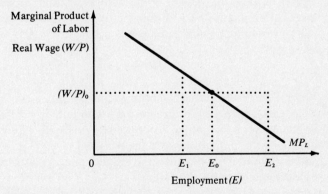

Figure 3.1 Demand for Labor in the Short Run

---

[3]We lose nothing by this assumption, because we show later in this section that a firm will never be operated at a point where its marginal product of labor schedule is increasing.

tional unit of labor employed produces a progressively smaller (but still positive) increment in output.

The marginal product of labor is measured as units of added output per unit increase of labor. Suppose we denote the money (nominal) wage rate that the firm pays per unit of labor by W and its product price per unit of output by P. These variables have dimensions of dollars per unit of labor and dollars per unit of output, respectively. Thus, the *real wage rate* that the firm pays—its money wage divided by its price level *(W/P)*—also has the dimension *units of output per unit of labor.* For example, if a woman is paid \$10 per hour and the product she makes sells for \$2, she gets paid—from the firm's point of view—five units of output per hour (10 ÷ 2). These five units represent her real wage, and because the real wage and the marginal product of labor are both measured in the same dimension, we can plot both on the vertical axis of Figure 3.1.

In the short run, a firm's demand-for-labor curve coincides with the downward-sloping portion of its marginal-product-of-labor schedule. This result arises from the assumption that firms seek to maximize profit. In order to accomplish this objective, a firm should employ labor up until the point that the marginal revenue (or additional revenue) it receives from hiring the last employee is just equal to its marginal (or additional) cost of employing that worker. Since a firm's profit is simply equal to revenues minus costs, if its marginal revenue exceeds its marginal cost, overall profits can be increased by expanding employment. Analogously, if its marginal revenue is less than its marginal cost, a firm is losing money on the last unit of labor hired, and it could increase its profit by reducing employment. As a result, the only employment level that is consistent with profit maximization is that level at which the marginal revenue of hiring the last unit of labor is just equal to its marginal cost.

Given the assumptions that we have made, the marginal cost of an additional unit of labor is simply the money wage rate *(W)* that must be paid. The marginal revenue of hiring an additional unit of labor, or labor's *marginal revenue product (MRP),* is equal to the value of the additional output produced. *MRP* equals the marginal product of labor multiplied by the additional revenue that is received per unit of output *(MR):*

$$MRP = (MP_L) \cdot (MR). \qquad (3.2)$$

Because we assumed that the firm sells its output in a competitive market—and hence that product price does not vary with output—the additional revenue per unit of output is simply the firm's product price *(P)*. Thus, for firms that operate in competitive output markets, the marginal revenue product obtained from an additional unit of labor equals the product price for the firm's output multiplied by its marginal product of labor:

$$MRP = (MP_L) \cdot P. \qquad (3.3)$$

The marginal revenue of labor is just equal to its marginal cost—and profits are maximized by the competitive firm—at the point where the marginal revenue product equals the money wage:

$$P \cdot (MP_L) = W. \tag{3.4}$$

Dividing both sides of equation (3.4) by the firm's product price yields an alternative way of stating the profit-maximizing condition, which is that labor should be hired until its marginal product equals the real wage:

$$MP_L = \frac{W}{P}. \tag{3.5}$$

Given any real wage (by the market), the firm should thus employ labor to the point at which the marginal product of labor just equals the real wage. In other words, *the firm's demand for labor in the short run is equivalent to the downward-sloping segment of its marginal-product-of-labor schedule.*[4] To see that this is true, pick any real wage—for example, the real wage denoted by $(W/P)_0$ in Figure 3.1. We have asserted that the firm's demand for labor will be equal to its marginal-product-of-labor schedule and consequently that the firm would employ E_0 employees. Now suppose that a firm initially employed E_2 workers as indicated in Figure 3.1, where E_2 is any employment level greater than E_0. At the employment level E_2, the marginal product of labor is less than the real wage rate; the marginal cost of the last unit of labor hired is therefore greater than its marginal revenue product. As a result, profit could be increased by reducing the level of employment. Similarly, suppose instead that a firm initially employed E_1 employees, where E_1 is *any* employment level less than E_0. Given the specified real wage $(W/P)_0$, the marginal product of labor is greater than the real wage rate at E_1 —and consequently the marginal revenue that an additional unit of labor produces is greater than its marginal cost. As a result, a firm could increase its profit level by expanding its level of employment.

Hence, to maximize profit, given any real wage rate, a firm should stop employing labor at the point where any additional labor would cost more than it would produce. This profit-maximization rule implies two things. First, the firm should employ labor up to the point where its real wage equals the marginal product of labor—but not beyond that point. Second, its profit-maximizing level of employment will lie in the range where its marginal product of labor is *declining.* (If $W/P = MP_L$, but MP_L is *increasing,* then adding another unit of labor will create a situation where marginal product *exceeds* W/P. As long as adding labor causes MP_L to exceed W/P, the profit-maximizing firm will continue to hire labor. It will only stop hiring when an extra unit of labor would reduce MP_L below W/P, which will only happen when MP_L is declining. Thus, the only employment levels that could possibly be consistent with profit maximization are those in the range where MP_L is decreasing.)

The demand curve for labor can therefore be thought of in two equivalent ways. It may be thought of as the *downward-sloping section of the firm's marginal-*

---

[4]One should add here, "provided that the firm's revenue exceeds its labor costs." Above some real wage level this may fail to occur, and the firm will go out of business (employment will drop to zero).

product-of-labor schedule—in which case it indicates how many units of labor will be hired at each *real wage.* Alternatively, it can be thought of as the *downward-sloping portion of the firm's marginal revenue product of labor schedule*—which is simply the *marginal product* schedule multiplied by *marginal revenue* (or product price, for a competitive firm). In this second case, the labor demand curve indicates the profit-maximizing level of employment for any given *money* wage. Which version of the demand curve one employs depends solely on analytical convenience, because they are equivalent alternatives. In Example 3.1, which reviews some of the important aspects of the demand for labor in a concrete way, it is more convenient to express the demand curve in terms of marginal revenue product of labor.

EXAMPLE 3.1

Store Detectives and the Optimal Rate of Shoplifting

At a business conference one day, a department store executive was boasting that his store had reduced theft to 1 percent of total sales. His colleague shook her head slowly and said, "I think that's too low. I figure it should be about 2 percent of sales."

How can more shoplifting be better than less? The answer is based on the fact that reducing theft is costly in itself! A profit-maximizing firm will not want to take steps to reduce shoplifting if the added costs it must bear in so doing exceed the value of the savings it generates.

The table below shows a hypothetical marginal revenue product *(MRP)* schedule for department-store detectives. Hiring one detective would, in this example, save $50 worth of thefts per hour. Two detectives could save $90 worth of thefts each hour, or $40 more than hiring just one. The *MRP* of hiring a second detective is thus $40. A third detective would add $20 worth more to thefts prevented, and thus adds $20 more to revenues.

Number of Detectives on Duty During Each Hour Store is Open	Total Value of Thefts Prevented per Hour	Marginal Value of Thefts Prevented per Hour (MRP)
0	$ 0	$—
1	50	50
2	90	40
3	110	20
4	115	5
5	117	2

The *MRP* does *not* decline from $40 to $20 because the added detectives are incompetent; in fact, we shall assume that all are equally alert and well trained. *MRP* declines, in part, because surveillance equipment (capital) is fixed; with each added detective, there is less equipment per person. However, the *MRP* also declines because it becomes progressively harder to generate savings. With just a few detectives, the only thieves caught will be the more obvious, less-experienced shoplifters. As more detectives are hired it becomes possible to prevent theft by the more expert shoplifters, but they are harder to detect and fewer in number. Thus, *MRP* falls because theft prevention becomes more difficult once all those who are easy to catch are apprehended.

To draw the demand curve for labor we need to determine how many detectives the store will want to employ at any given wage. For example, at a wage of $50 per hour, how many detectives will the store want? Using the *MRP* = *W* criterion it is easy to see that the answer is ''one.'' At $40 per hour, the store would want to hire two, and at $20 per hour the number demanded would be three. The demand for labor curve that summarizes the store's profit-maximizing employment of detectives is given in the accompanying graph.

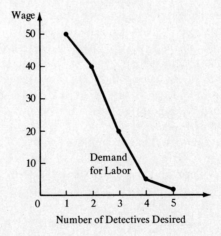

The graph illustrates a fundamental point: the demand for labor curve in the short run slopes downward because it *is* the *MRP* curve—and the *MRP* curve slopes downward because of diminishing marginal productivity. The demand curve and the *MRP* curve coincide, as demonstrated by the fact that if one were to graph the *MRP* schedule in the table, one would arrive at exactly the same curve as in our graph. When one is hired, *MRP* is $50; when two are hired, *MRP* is $40; and so forth. Since *MRP* always equals *W* for a profit maximizer, the *MRP* and labor demand curves expressed as functions of the money wage must be the same.

> Another point to be made in this example is that there is some level of shoplifting that the store finds more profitable to tolerate than to eliminate. At high wages for store detectives, the store will find it profitable to eliminate less theft than it will at lower wages. To say the theft rate is "too low" thus implies that the marginal costs of crime reduction exceed the marginal savings generated, and the firm is therefore failing to maximize profits.

It is important to emphasize that the marginal product of any given individual is *not* a function solely of his or her personal characteristics. It should be clear from Figure 3.1 and from Example 3.1 that the marginal product of a worker depends upon the number of employees that the firm has already hired. Similarly, an individual's marginal product depends upon the size of the firm's capital stock; increases in the firm's capital stock shift the entire marginal-product-of-labor schedule up. It is therefore incorrect to speak of an individual's productivity as being an immutable factor that is associated only with his or her characteristics, independent of the characteristics of the other inputs that he or she has to work with.

Marginal productivity and the allocation of baseball players. The fact that one's marginal productivity is not independent of other inputs being used helps explain the allocation of certain professional baseball players across the various teams. Before 1975, professional baseball players were bound to the team for which they played. They could choose not to play baseball, of course, but they could not choose the baseball team for which they would play. Being bound to a team naturally limited their options and held down their salaries. Other teams could not bid them away from the team to which they were bound; the only way a player could change teams was if both owners involved agreed between themselves on a price at which the player would be sold to the new team.

In 1975, a labor-relations ruling was issued (and later followed by a collective-bargaining agreement) that allowed certain players the right to become *free agents,* which meant that these players could sell their services to any team. Owners initially objected to the free-agent system. One argument they advanced was that it would harm competitive balance among the teams by enabling the best and richest teams to grab up all the star players. Our observations about marginal productivity and profit maximization can be used to evaluate—and refute—the owners' contention about competitive imbalances.

If team owners are profit maximizers, they will hire a star only if the extra revenue he will generate is greater than his salary. That is, the star's *MRP* must not be lower than his wage. If a team is *already* loaded with stars, an additional good player will not bring in very much in terms of added revenues. However, if a team has no star—or very few—the addition of the *same* good player will quite possibly generate a lot in added revenues. Thus, because the *MRP* of a star will probably be lower, *other things equal,* on the best teams, these teams will tend to be the least willing to put up money for the star free agents. Capital stock is one of the "other things" that must be held equal for this prediction to hold, however. For example, if team quality is held constant, one's *MRP* will be higher on teams that have larger stadiums and larger television markets.

The above considerations suggest that the teams that will bid most aggressively for the free agents will be those that tend to have poorer records or are located in areas with large potential markets. Although there are instances to the contrary, it is interesting to note that 27 of the first 38 "star-quality" free agents signed with teams that had poorer records than the team they were on—and of the remaining 11, 7 signed with teams located in larger markets.[5] Thus, free agency has neither had, nor could be expected to have, harmful effects on the competitive balance of professional baseball teams. If anything, it has helped to equalize the distribution of talent across teams.

Objections to the marginal productivity theory of demand. Two kinds of objections are sometimes raised to the theory of labor demand introduced in this section. The first objection is that firms do not know what labor's MP_L is, that almost no employer can ever be heard uttering the words "marginal revenue product of labor," and that the theory assumes a degree of sophistication on the part of employers that just is not there. This objection can be answered as follows: whether employers can verbalize the profit-maximization conditions or not, they must instinctively *know* them in order to survive in a competitive environment. Competition will "weed out" employers who are not good at generating profits, just as competition will weed out pool players who do not understand the intricacies of how speed, angles, and spin affect the motion of bodies through space. Yet one could canvas the pool halls of America and probably not find one player who could verbalize Newton's laws of motion! The point is that firms can *know* rules without being able to verbalize them. Those who are not good at maximizing profits will not last very long in competitive markets. Conversely, the ones who survive are those who, whether they can verbalize the general rules or not, *do* know how to maximize profits.

The second objection to the marginal productivity theory of demand is that in many cases it seems that adding labor while holding capital constant would not add to output at all. For example, one secretary and one typewriter can produce output, but it might seem that adding a second secretary (holding the number of typewriters constant) could produce nothing extra, since that secretary would have no machine on which to work. The answer to this objection is that the second secretary could address envelopes by hand—a slower process, but one that would free the secretary at the typewriter to type more letters per day. The two secretaries could trade off using the typewriter, so that neither becomes fatigued to the extent that mistakes increase and typing speeds slow down. The second secretary could also answer the telephone and in other ways expedite

---

[5]The authors are indebted to Theo Smith and his enormous collection of baseball cards for these data.

work. Thus, even with technologies that seem to require one machine per person, labor will generally have an *MRP* greater than zero (capital held constant).

Long-Run Demand for Labor by Firms

In the long run, employers are free to vary their capital stock as well as the number of workers that they employ. An increase in the wage rate will affect their desired employment levels for two reasons. First, wages affect employment through a *scale* or *output effect.* A profit-maximizing firm will produce up to the point where the marginal revenue from the last unit of output produced is just equal to its marginal cost of production. Now an increase in the wage rate tends to increase the marginal cost of production without affecting the marginal revenue. As a result, at the firm's previous equilibrium level of output, marginal cost *exceeds* marginal revenue. The firm is losing money on the last units of output that it produces, and it can increase its profits after the wage increase by cutting back on its production level. Reducing output will generally cause the firm to reduce its usage both of capital and of labor.

The second reason why an increase in the wage rate affects a firm's desired employment level in the long run is that it induces *factor substitution.* In order to maximize profit, a firm must be minimizing the cost of producing whatever level of output it produces. This cost minimization is achieved when the last dollar the firm spends on employing capital yields the same increment to output as the last dollar that the firm spends employing labor. To illustrate this point, let us assume that a firm has a given level of output, *Q,* and is considering changing its mix of capital and labor to see if it can reduce cost. Suppose it finds that a dollar's worth of labor adds one unit of output to production, but a dollar's worth of capital adds two units to output. If it decreased its employment of labor by the equivalent of a dollar, and increased its employment of capital by the equivalent of 50 cents, it could produce output level *Q* at a lower cost! The *current* mix of capital and labor in this example is clearly not profit-maximizing, and extending this reasoning leads to the conclusion that the firm will reach its optimal mix of inputs only when an added dollar spent on (or taken away from) labor and an added dollar spent on (or taken away from) capital lead to equal changes in output.

To better understand factor substitution, let *C* represent the rental cost per period of a unit of capital equipment. This rental cost depends upon a number of things, including the purchase price of new capital equipment, the interest rate that a firm must pay on borrowed funds, and various provisions that affect the income-tax treatment of firms' investment expenditures (the specific formula for *C* need not concern us here). Now, if a firm is to minimize the cost of producing any given level of output, it must employ labor and capital up until the point that the marginal cost of producing the last unit of output is the same regardless of whether capital or labor is employed in generating that last unit. A formal way of stating this requirement is that the wage divided by the marginal product of labor (which is the cost of producing an added unit of output using just labor) must equal the cost of capital *(C)* divided by the marginal product of capital *(MP$_K$)*:

$$(W/MP_L) = (C/MP_K). \tag{3.6}$$

We can rewrite equation (3.6) as

$$(W/C) = (MP_L/MP_K). \tag{3.7}$$

Equation (3.7) indicates that in order to be minimizing its cost of production, a firm must employ capital and labor up until the point that their relative marginal costs are just equal to their relative marginal productivities.

Consider what happens when wages increase and capital costs do not. The increase in *W/C* distorts the equality in equation (3.7), and the left-hand side is now greater than the right-hand side. Since the marginal cost of producing a unit of output is now greater when a firm adds new labor than when it adds new capital, the firm has an incentive to substitute capital for labor—to increase its usage of capital and decrease its usage of labor. The increase in usage of capital leads to a decline in the marginal product of capital, while the decrease in usage of labor leads to an increase in the marginal product of labor. Eventually the equality in equation (3.7) is restored, with fewer workers employed.

Market Demand Curves

The demand curve (or schedule) for an individual firm indicates how much labor that firm will want to employ at each real wage level. A *market demand curve* (or schedule) is just the *summation* of the labor demanded by all firms in a particular labor market at each level of the real wage.[6] If there are three firms in a certain labor market, and if at *(W/P)$_0$* Firm A wants 12 workers, Firm B wants 6, and Firm C wants 20, then the market demand at *(W/P)$_0$* is 38 employees. More importantly, because market demand curves are so closely derived from firm demand curves, they too will *slope downward* as a function of the real wage. When the real wage falls, the number of workers that existing firms want to employ increases. In addition, the lower real wage may make it profitable for new firms to enter the market. Conversely, when the real wage increases, the number of workers that existing firms want to employ decreases, and some firms may be forced to cease operations completely.

---

[6]If firm demand curves are drawn as a function of the money wage, they represent (as we noted) the downward-sloping portion of the firms' marginal revenue product curves. In a competitive industry, the price of the product is "given" to the firm, and thus at the firm level the marginal revenue product of labor has imbedded in it a given product price. When aggregating labor demand to the *market* level, product price can no longer be taken as given, and the aggregation is no longer a simple summation. However, the market demand curves drawn against money wages, like those drawn as a function of real wages, slope downward—which, at this point, is all that is important.

EXAMPLE 3.2

Coal Mining: The Interaction Between Technology and Wages

That wage increases have both a *scale effect* and a *factor substitution effect,* both of which tend to reduce employment, is widely known—even by many of those pushing for higher wages. John L. Lewis was president of the United Mine Workers during the 1920s, 1930s, and 1940s, when wages for miners were increased considerably with full knowledge that this would induce the substitution of capital for labor. According to Lewis:

Primarily the United Mine Workers of America insists upon the maintenance of the wage standards guaranteed by the existing contractual relations in the industry, in the interests of its own membership. . . . But in insisting on the maintenance of an American wage standard in the coal fields the United Mine Workers is also doing its part, probably more than its part, to force a reorganization of the basic industry of the country upon scientific and efficient lines. The maintenance of these rates will accelerate the operation of natural economic laws, which will in time eliminate uneconomic mines, obsolete equipment, and incompetent management. . . .

The policy of the United Mine Workers of America will inevitably bring about the utmost employment of machinery of which coal mining is physically capable. . . . Fair wages and American standards of living are inextricably bound up with the progressive substitution of mechanical for human power. It is no accident that fair wages and machinery will walk hand-in-hand.

SOURCE: John L. Lewis, *The Miners' Fight for American Standards* (Indianapolis: The Bell Publishing Company, 1925), pp. 40, 41, 108.

Figure 3.2 shows a hypothetical market demand-for-labor curve *(D₀)* and a labor supply curve *(S₀)*. (Disregard the curve labeled D_1 for the moment.) The supply curve has been drawn as an upward-sloping function of the real wage, since higher real wages induce more individuals to enter this labor market. In this competitive labor market, the equilibrium real wage *(W₀)* and employment *(E₀)* levels are determined by the intersection of the labor demand and supply curves. If the real wage were lower than W_0, the number of workers that employers would want to hire would exceed the number of individuals who want to work. Employers, facing unfilled positions, would be forced to raise their real wage offers to eliminate the job vacancies. In contrast, if the real wage were above W_0, employers would face an excess supply of applicants. The number of individuals willing to work would exceed the number of employees firms want to hire, and employers would eventually realize that they could reduce their real wage offers and still attract the necessary workers.[7]

---

[7]The reduction in real wages need not occur through a reduction in money wages. Rather, all that is required during a period when prices are rising is that money wages remain constant or rise less rapidly than product prices.

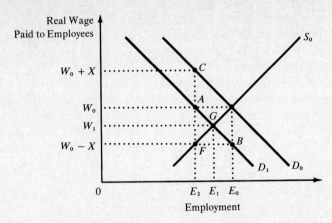

Figure 3.2 Who Bears the Burden of an Employer-Financed Payroll Tax?

Policy Application: Who Bears the Burden of the Payroll Tax?

In the United States, several social insurance programs are financed by payroll taxes. Employers, and in some cases employees, make mandatory contributions of a fraction of the employees' salaries, up to a maximum level (or taxable wage base), to the social insurance trust funds. For example, the Social Security retirement, disability, and Medicare programs (OASDHI) are financed by a payroll tax paid by both employers and employees, while in most states the unemployment insurance and workers' compensation insurance programs are financed solely by payroll-tax payments made by employers. It is not clear just why payroll taxes on *employers* are so heavily used in the social insurance area. There seems to be a prevailing notion that such taxes result in employers "footing the bill" for the relevant programs—but this is not necessarily the case.

With our simple labor market model we can show that the party making the social insurance payment is not necessarily the one that bears the burden of the tax. Suppose for expository convenience that only the employer is required to make payments and that the tax is a fixed dollar amount *($X)* per employee rather than a percentage of payroll. Now consider the demand curve D_0 in Figure 3.2 —which is drawn in such a way that desired employment is plotted against the real wage *employees receive*. Prior to the imposition of the tax, the wage employees receive is the same as the wage employers pay. Thus, if D_0 were the demand curve before the tax was imposed, it would have the conventional interpretation of indicating how much labor a firm is willing to hire at any given wage. However, *after* imposition of the tax, employer wage costs are $X above what employees receive. Thus, if employees receive W_0, employers will face costs of $W_0 + X$. They will no longer demand E_0 workers; rather, because their costs are $W_0 + X$, they will demand E_2 workers. Point *A* becomes a point on a *new* demand curve, formed when demand shifts down because of the tax (remember, the wage on the vertical axis of Figure 3.2 is the wage *employees receive* and not the wage employers pay). Only if employee wages fell to $W_0 - X$ would the firm want to continue hiring E_0 workers—for then *employer* costs would be the same as before the tax. Thus, point B is also on the new, shifted demand curve. Note that with a tax of $\$X$, the new demand curve (D_1) is parallel to the old one and that the vertical distance between the two is X.

Now the tax-related shift in the demand curve to D_1 implies that there is an excess supply of labor at the previous equilibrium real wage of W_0. This surplus of labor creates downward pressure on the real wage, and this downward pressure continues to be exerted until the wage falls to W_1, the point at which the quantity of labor supplied just equals the quantity demanded. At this point, employment has also fallen to E_1. Thus, *employees* bear part of the burden of the payroll tax in the form of *lower wage rates and lower employment levels.* The lesson is clear: the party legally liable to make the contribution (the employer) is not necessarily the one that bears the full burden of the actual cost.

Figure 3.2, however, does suggest that employers will bear at least *some* of the burden of the tax, because the wages received by employees do not fall by the full amount of the tax ($W_0 - W_1$ is smaller than X, which is the vertical distance between the two demand curves). The reason for this is that, with an upward-sloping supply curve, employees withdraw labor as their wages fall, and it becomes more difficult for firms to find workers. If wages fell to $W_0 - X$, the withdrawal of workers would create a labor shortage that would serve to drive wages to some point (W_1 in our example) between W_0 and $W_0 - X$. Only if the labor supply curve were *vertical*—meaning that lower wages have no effect on labor supply—would the *entire amount of the tax* be shifted to workers in the form of a decrease in their wages by the amount of X, as shown in panel (a) of Figure 3.3.

In general, the extent to which the labor *supply curve* is *vertical* determines the proportion of the employer payroll tax that gets shifted to employees' wages. The more vertical the supply curve—that is, the less responsive labor supply is to changes in wages—the higher the proportion of the tax that gets shifted to workers in the form of a wage decrease. Panel (a) of Figure 3.3 shows that a payroll tax on the employer will depress employee wages more with supply curve S_0' than with supply curve S_0'' (the wage corresponding to point L is lower than that corresponding to point M). It must also be pointed out, however, that to the degree employee wages do *not* fall, employment levels *will:* employment losses with supply curve S_0'' are larger than with curve S_0'. When employee wages do not fall much in the face of an employer payroll tax increase, employer labor costs are increased—and this increase reduces the quantity of labor they demand.

The other major influence on the extent to which payroll taxes are shifted to employees is the shape of the demand curve. If the demand curve is relatively horizontal—meaning that employer demand is very sensitive to changes in labor costs—there will be relatively large employment losses and strong downward pressures on employee wages. On the other hand, if employer demand is not very responsive to labor costs—and the demand curve is more vertical—both employment losses and employee wage changes will be small. These two conclusions are illustrated by the two sets of demand curves in panel (b) of Figure 3.3. The wage

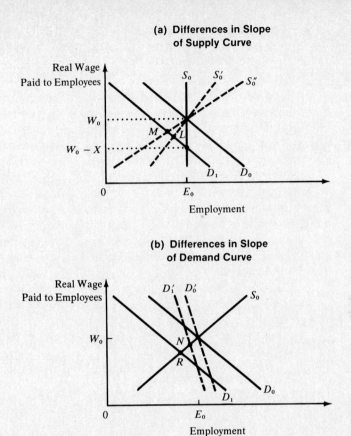

(a) Differences in Slope of Supply Curve

(b) Differences in Slope of Demand Curve

Figure 3.3 Conditions that Affect the Shifting of an Employer Payroll Tax

and employment levels for each initial demand curve $(D_0$ and $D_0')$ are assumed to be the same $(W_0$ and $E_0)$. When an employer payroll tax of X is imposed, it shifts *both demand curves down by the vertical distance of* X, so that the new curves are D_1 and D_1'. Point N, which lies on the relatively vertical demand curve D_1', is a lot closer to W_0 and E_0 than is point R—the intersection between the supply curve and the relatively horizontal demand curve D_1.

A number of empirical studies have sought to ascertain what fraction of employers' payroll tax costs are actually passed on to employees in the form of lower wages or lower wage increases. Although the evidence is by no means unambiguous, two recent studies concluded that less than half of employers' payroll tax contributions are actually shifted onto labor in the form of real wage decreases.[8]

---

[8]Ronald G. Ehrenberg, Robert Hutchens, and Robert S. Smith, *The Distribution of Unemployment Insurance Benefits and Costs,* Technical Analysis Paper No. 58, ASPER, U.S. Department of Labor, October 1978; Daniel Hamermesh, "New Estimates of the Incidence of the Payroll Tax," *Southern Economic Journal* 45 (February 1979): 1208–19.

Modified Models of Labor Demand

Monopoly in the Product Market

We have assumed so far that firms take product prices as given. If a firm faces a downward-sloping demand curve for its output—so that as it expands employment and output, its product price falls—then the marginal revenue it receives from the last unit of output it produces is not the product price. Rather, the marginal revenue is less than the product price, because the lower price applies to all units it sells, not just the marginal unit. As a result equation (3.4) must be modified in the presence of product market monopoly. In the short run, labor should be employed up until the point at which the wage rate just equals the marginal revenue product of labor _(MRP)_—which, for a firm facing a downward-sloping demand curve in the output market, equals the marginal product of labor multiplied by the marginal revenue _(MR)_:

$$(MR)\ (MP_L)\ =\ W. \tag{3.8}$$

Now one can express the demand for labor in the short run in terms of the real wage by dividing both sides of equation (3.8) by the firm's product price, _P_, to obtain

$$\frac{MR}{P} \cdot MP_L\ =\ \frac{W}{P}. \tag{3.9}$$

Since marginal revenue is always less than a monopoly's product price, the ratio _(MR/P)_ in equation (3.9) is less than one. As such, the demand-for-labor curve for a firm that has monopoly power in the output market will lie below and to the left of the demand-for-labor curve for an _otherwise identical_ firm that takes product price as given. Put another way, just as output is lower under monopoly than it is under competition, other things equal, so is the level of employment.

The _wage_ rates that monopolies pay, however, are not necessarily different from competitive levels even though _employment_ levels are. An employer with a product market monopoly may still be a very small part of the market for a particular kind of employee—and thus be a _price taker_ in the labor market even though a _price maker_ in the product market.[9] For example, a local utility company may have a product market monopoly, but it will have to compete with all other firms to hire secretaries and thus must pay the going wage.

There are circumstances, however, where economists suspect that product market monopolies might pay wages that are _higher_ than competitive firms would

---

[9] A _price taker_ is someone who is such a small part of a particular market that he or she cannot influence market price. Thus, to such a person, the market price is a given. A _price maker_ is someone with enough monopoly power that he or she can influence prices.

pay.[10] The monopolies that are legally permitted to exist in the United States are regulated by governmental bodies in an effort to prevent them from exploiting their favored status and earning monopoly profits. This regulation of profits, it can be argued, gives monopolies incentives to pay higher wages than they would otherwise pay for one of two reasons. First, regulatory bodies allow monopolies to pass on the costs of doing business to consumers. Thus, while unable to maximize profits, the managers of a monopoly can enhance their *utility* by paying high wages and passing the cost along to consumers in the form of higher prices. The ability to pay high wages makes a manager's life more pleasant by making it possible to hire people who might be more attractive or more personable or who have other characteristics managers find desirable.

Second, monopolies that are as yet unregulated may not want to attract attention to themselves by earning the very high profits usually associated with monopoly. They, too, may therefore be induced to pay high wages in a partial effort to "hide" their profits. The excess profits of monopolies, in other words, may be partly taken in the form of highly preferred workers—paid a relatively high wage rate—rather than in the usual monetary form.

The evidence on monopoly wages, however, is not very clear as yet. Two studies suggest that monopolies *do* pay higher wages than competitive firms for workers with the same education and experience, while a third finds no such evidence.[11]

Monopsony in the Labor Market

When only one firm is the buyer of labor in a particular labor market, such a firm is called a *monopsonist.* Because the firm is the only demander of labor in this market, it can influence the wage rate. Rather than being a *price (wage) taker,* and facing the horizontal labor supply curve that competitive firms are confronted with, monopsonists face an upward-sloping supply curve. The supply curve confronting them, in other words, is the *market* supply curve. To expand its work force, a monopsonist must increase its wage rate. (In contrast, a competitive firm can expand its work force while paying the prevailing market wage as long as that wage is not below market-clearing levels.)

The unusual aspect of a *firm's* being confronted with an upward-sloping labor supply curve is that the *marginal cost of hiring labor exceeds the wage.* If a competitive firm wants to hire 10 workers instead of 9, the hourly cost of the additional worker is equal to the wage rate. If a monopsonist hires 10 instead of

---

[10]For a full statement of this argument, see Armen Alchian and Reuben Kessel, "Competition, Monopoly, and the Pursuit of Money," H. G. Lewis, ed. *Aspects of Labor Economics* (Princeton, N.J.: Princeton University Press, 1962).

[11]James Dalton and E. J. Ford, "Concentration and Labor Earnings in Manufacturing and Utilities," *Industrial and Labor Relations Review* (October 1977): 45–60; Ronald Ehrenberg, *The Regulatory Process and Labor Earnings* (New York: Academic Press, 1979); Leonard W. Weiss, "Concentration and Labor Earnings," *American Economic Review* 56, 1 (March 1966): 96–117.

9, it must pay a higher wage to all workers *in addition to* paying the bill for the added worker. For example, suppose that a monopsonist could get 9 workers if it paid $7 per hour but that if it wishes to hire 10 workers it would have to pay a wage of $7.50. The labor cost associated with 9 workers is $63 per hour (9 times $7), but the labor cost associated with 10 workers is $75 per hour (10 times $7.50). Hiring the additional worker costs $12 per hour—which is far higher than the $7.50 wage rate![12]

The fact that the marginal cost of hiring labor is above the wage rate affects the labor market behavior of monopsonists. In maximizing profits, any firm should hire labor until the point where marginal revenue product equals marginal cost. Since the marginal cost of hiring labor for a monopsonist is *above* the wage rate, it will stop hiring labor at some point where marginal revenue product is above the wage rate. In terms of Figure 3.4, the monopsonist hires E_M workers because at that point marginal revenue product equals marginal labor costs (point *X*). However, the wage rate necessary to attract E_M workers to the firm—which can be read off the supply curve—is W_M (see point *Y*). Thus, wages are below marginal revenue product for a monopsonist.

If the market depicted in Figure 3.4 were competitive, each firm in the market would hire labor until marginal revenue product equalled the wage. Thus, if the demand curve in that market were the same as the marginal revenue product curve shown, the wage rate would be W_C and the employment level would be E_C—and the conventional result would be obtained. Note that in a market that is monopsonized, wages and employment levels are *below* W_C and E_C.

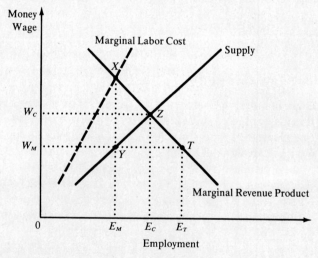

Figure 3.4   The Effects of Monopsony

---

[12]We assume here that the monopsonist does not know which workers it can hire for $7 per hour and which workers could only be hired at $7.50. All it knows is that if it wants to hire 10 workers it must pay $7.50, while if it wants to hire 9 it can pay only $7.00. Therefore, all workers get paid the same wage.

Examples of pure monopsony in the labor market are difficult to cite: an isolated coal-mining town or a sugar plantation, where the mine or sugar company is literally the only employer, are examples that are increasingly rare. However, some employers may be large relative to the market and may, therefore, find themselves confronted with an upward-sloping supply curve.

Some economists argue that the market for registered nurses—particularly in a small town—is partially monopsonized. Hospitals employ the majority of registered nurses, and in many small towns there is only one hospital. These hospitals, it is argued, behave like monopsonists and pay lower wages than they otherwise would.[13]

If the market for registered nurses is characterized by monopsony, this situation could help explain why the nursing shortage discussed in Chapter 2 was perceived to exist even though nursing salaries were not being bid up. At wage W_M in Figure 3.4, the monopsonized employer (the hospital in this case) will hire only E_M workers because that is where marginal revenue and marginal cost are equal. However, *if* it could do all its additional hiring at W_M, it would *like* to hire E_T. Since at W_M supply falls short of E_T, there might appear to be a shortage! In this case, then, hospitals find themselves in the position of wanting to hire more nurses at E_M—and being unable to do so—while at the same time being unwilling to raise wage offers necessary to increase employment beyond E_M! The "shortage" is thus more apparent than real.

Another market that may be monopsonized is the market for public-school teachers outside of metropolitan areas.[14] However, there is not much evidence that private firms in metropolitan areas have monopsony power. Wages that these firms pay appear to be essentially unaffected by the concentration of employment in the hands of a very few employers.[15]

More Than Two Inputs

Thus far we have assumed that there are only two inputs in the production process: capital and labor. In fact, labor can be subdivided into many categories (for example, labor can be categorized by age, race, sex, by educational level, and by occupation). Other inputs besides capital that are used in the production process include materials and energy. If a firm is seeking to maximize profits, in the long run it should employ all inputs up until the point that the additions to output received from spending the last dollar on each input are equal. This generalization of equation (3.6) leads to the somewhat obvious result that the

[13]Richard Hurd, "Equilibrium Vacancies in a Labor Market Dominated by Non-Profit Firms: The 'Shortage' of Nurses," *Review of Economics and Statistics* 55, 2 (May 1973): 234–240; C. R. Link and J. H. Landon, "Monopsony and Union Power in the Market for Nurses," *Southern Economic Journal* 41 (April 1975): 649–59.

[14]Ronald Ehrenberg and Gerald Goldstein, "A Model of Public Sector Wage Determination," *Journal of Urban Economics* 2 (April 1975): 223–45.

[15]*See* Robert L. Bunting, *Employer Concentration in Local Labor Markets* (Chapel Hill: University of North Carolina Press, 1962).

demand for *any* category of labor will be a function not only of its own wage rate, but also of the wage rates of all other categories of labor and of the prices of capital and other inputs.

The demand curve for each category of labor will be a downward-sloping function of the wage rate paid to workers in the category, for the reasons discussed earlier. Changes in the prices of the other categories of labor or in the prices of other inputs may shift the entire demand curve for a given category of labor either to the right or to the left. If an increase in the price of one input shifts the demand for another input to the left, as in panel (a) of Figure 3.5, the two inputs are *gross complements;* if a price increase shifts the demand for labor to the right, as in panel (b) of Figure 3.5, the two inputs are *gross substitutes.* Whether two inputs are complements or substitutes is a function both of the production process and product demand conditions.

Consider our earlier example of a snow-removal firm. Suppose that snow can be removed using either unskilled workers (with shovels) or skilled workers who drive snowplows, and let us focus on the demand for the skilled workers. Other things equal, an increase in the wage of skilled workers will cause the employer to employ fewer of them; their demand curve is a downward-sloping function of their wage. If the wage rate of unskilled workers increases, the employer would want to employ fewer unskilled workers than before—and more of the now relatively cheaper skilled workers—to remove any given amount of snow. To the extent that this substitution effect dominates over the scale effect (the higher unskilled wage leading to reduced output and employment of all inputs), the demand for skilled workers would shift to the right. In this case, skilled and unskilled workers are gross substitutes. In contrast, if the price of snowplows went up, the employer would want to cut back on their usage, which would result in a reduced demand, at each wage, for skilled workers who drive the snowplows. Skilled workers and snowplows are gross complements in this example.

To answer many policy questions requires knowledge of the characteristics of demand curves for particular categories of labor. For example, would a subsidy

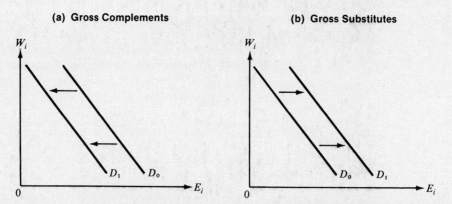

Figure 3.5   Effect of an Increase in the Price of One Input *(j)* on the Demand for Another Input *(i)*

paid to employers who hire teenagers significantly increase teenage employment? The answer depends upon how responsive the demand for teenage labor is to their wage. How would an *investment tax credit,* an implicit subsidy paid to employers for increasing their capital stock, affect the employment of skilled and unskilled workers? The answer here depends upon the extent to which the cost of capital affects the demand curves for skilled and unskilled workers. To take a final example, how does government legislation that prohibits sex discrimination by requiring equal pay for equal work affect the employment levels of males and females? To answer this, one needs to know how the legislation affects male and female wages and then how responsive the demand curve for *each* type of labor is to *both* wage rates.

In each of the above examples, the effect of a policy depends upon the responsiveness of one variable to another. Economists refer to this responsiveness as an *elasticity,* or the percentage change in one variable induced by a given percentage change in another variable. For example, the *own-wage elasticity of demand* for a category of labor is defined as the percentage change in the demand for the category induced by a one percent increase in its wage rate. *Cross-wage elasticity of demand,* or the elasticity of demand for factor i with respect to the price of factor j, is defined as the percentage change in the demand for category i induced by a one percent change in the price of factor j. Since the magnitude of various elasticities of labor demand are so important for policy discussions, the next chapter will be devoted to a discussion of the determinants of elasticities of demand and will apply this concept to various policy issues. The following discussion of minimum-wage legislation should illustrate the use of the analytical tools developed so far.

Policy Application: Minimum-Wage Legislation

History and Description

The *Fair Labor Standards Act of 1938* was the first major piece of protective labor legislation adopted at the national level in the United States. Among its provisions were a minimum-wage rate, or floor, below which hourly wages could not be reduced, an overtime-pay premium for workers who worked long workweeks, and restrictions on the use of child labor. The minimum-wage provisions were designed to guarantee each worker a reasonable wage for his or her work effort and thus to reduce the incidence of poverty.

When initially adopted, the minimum wage was set at $0.25 an hour and covered roughly 43 percent of all nonsupervisory wage and salary workers— primarily those workers employed in larger firms involved in interstate commerce (manufacturing, mining, and construction). As Table 3.2 indicates, both the basic minimum wage and coverage under the minimum wage have expanded over time. Indeed as of January 1, 1981, the minimum wage was set at $3.35 an hour, and about 80 percent of all nonsupervisory workers were covered by its provisions.

It is important to emphasize that the minimum-wage rate is currently spe-

Table 3.2 Minimum Wage Legislation in the United States, 1938–1981[b]

Effective Date of Minimum Wage Change	Nominal Minimum Wage	Percent of Nonsupervisory Employees Covered[a]	Minimum Wage Relative to Average Hourly Wage in Manufacturing	
			Before	After
10/24/38	$0.25	43.4	—	0.403
10/24/39	0.30	47.1	0.398	0.478
10/24/45	0.40	55.4	0.295	0.394
1/25/50	0.75	53.4	0.278	0.521
3/1/56	1.00	53.1	0.385	0.512
9/3/61	1.15	62.1	0.431	0.495
9/3/63	1.25	62.1	0.467	0.508
9/3/64	1.25	62.6		
2/1/67	1.40	75.3	0.441	0.494
2/1/68	1.60	72.6	0.465	0.531
2/1/69	1.60	78.2		
2/1/70	1.60	78.5		
2/1/71	1.60	78.4		
5/1/74	2.00	83.7	0.363	0.454
1/1/75	2.10	83.3	0.423	0.445
1/1/76	2.30		0.410	0.449
1/1/78	2.65		0.430	0.480
1/1/79	2.90		0.402	0.440
1/1/80	3.10		0.417	0.445
1/1/81	3.35		0.403	0.435

[a]Excludes executive, administrative, and professional personnel (including teachers in elementary and secondary schools) from the base. Coverage peaked at 87.3 percent of the nonsupervisory work force in September 1977. As of 1978, however, a court decision eliminated most state and local government workers from coverage. As a result, worker coverage fell from 56,100,000 in 1976 to 51,900,000 in 1978.

[b]As of 1/1/84 the nominal minimum wage was still pegged at $3.35/hour.

cified in *nominal* terms and not in terms *relative* to some other wage or price index. Historically, this definition of minimum wage has led to a pattern of minimum-wage changes that can be represented by Figure 3.6, where time is plotted on the horizontal axis, and the value of the minimum wage relative to average hourly earnings in manufacturing is plotted on the vertical axis. Congress initially specifies the nominal level of the minimum wage (MW_0)—which, given the level of average hourly earnings that prevail in the economy (AHE_0), leads to an initial value of the minimum wage relative to average hourly earnings (MW_0/AHE_0). Now, over time, this relative value declines as average hourly earnings increase due to inflation or productivity growth. The reduced relative value of the minimum wage creates pressure on Congress to legislate an increase in the nominal minimum wage, and after the passage of time (point t_1 in Figure 3.6) Congress returns the relative value of the minimum wage approximately to its initial level. Over time, the process is repeated and the saw-toothed time profile of relative minimum-wage values portrayed in Figure 3.6 emerges. Although it

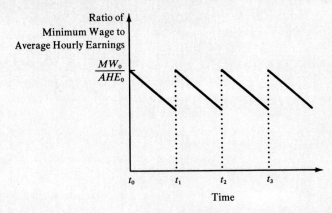

Figure 3.6   Time Profile of the Minimum Wage Relative to Average Hourly Earnings

varies from peak to peak, the value of the minimum wage relative to average hourly earnings in manufacturing after each legislated change has typically been in the range of 0.45 to 0.50 in recent years (see Table 3.2).

A Model with Uniform Coverage

Unfortunately, as with many social programs, minimum-wage legislation may have unintended side effects that work against the program's goals of reducing poverty. Consider the labor market for unskilled workers and assume, initially, that all are covered by minimum-wage legislation. As Table 3.2 indicates, such uniform coverage certainly would not be a reasonable assumption if we wanted to analyze minimum-wage effects during the early years of the legislation. However, a model of full coverage may be more appropriate today than it once was.

Figure 3.7 represents the labor market for unskilled labor, which is in equilib-

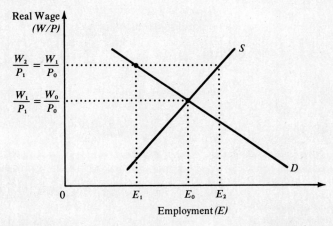

Figure 3.7   Minimum Wage Effects: Uniform Coverage

rium prior to the imposition of the minimum wage with an employment level of E_0 and a *real* wage of W_0/P_0. Now suppose Congress legislates a nominal minimum wage of W_1, which is higher than W_0; this legislation will raise the real wage to W_1/P_0 and reduce the number of employees firms want to hire to E_1. Although a larger number of workers (E_2) are willing to offer their services at that wage rate, no downward pressure is exerted on the money wage because by law the wage cannot be reduced below the nominal minimum. As a result, the immediate impact of the increase in the minimum wage is a decrease in employment and an increase in unemployment (which equals $E_2 - E_1$).[16]

Over time, the government may take actions to stimulate the economy in the hope of reducing unemployment. Such actions invariably include pursuing expansionary monetary and fiscal policy (increasing the money supply and government spending, decreasing taxes) and lead to increases in the price level. However, as the price level goes up, the real minimum wage falls, because the nominal minimum wage is being held constant. As the real wage falls, the number of workers employed increases. If Congress takes no other action but continues to pursue expansionary policies, eventually the price level will rise to P_1, where $(W_1/P_1) = (W_0/P_0)$. That is, the real value of the minimum wage will fall back to the market-clearing level, and employment will return to its initial level. While the immediate impact of the minimum-wage increase was to reduce employment, over a longer period of time this employment reduction is eliminated, at the expense of a higher price level.

The story, however, does not end here. As noted above, Congress periodically increases the nominal minimum to restore its value relative to average hourly earnings. An increase, say, to W_2, where $(W_2/P_1) = (W_1/P_0)$, would again reduce employment to E_1 and create further pressure for the government to take action to reduce unemployment. What results then is a cycle of minimum-wage increases inducing short-run employment losses, inflation reducing the real value of the minimum wage and restoring employment, and then Congress increasing the nominal minimum and starting the process all over.

Periodically, proposals have been introduced into Congress to tie the minimum wage to either the consumer price level or average hourly earnings; the minimum wage would automatically increase each year to maintain a constant value relative to one of these variables. If tied to the former, the net effect of the legislation would be to fix the real wage of low-skilled labor at a level such as

---

[16]The analysis here is somewhat oversimplified. The supply curve in Figure 3.7 indicates the number of workers who want to work at each real wage, under the assumption that any one who wants to work can find employment. However the imposition of a minimum wage that leads to a real wage (W_1/P_0) above the market-clearing level means that not all workers who want to work at that real wage can actually find employment. This reduced probability of finding employment should reduce the actual number of workers seeking employment below the level indicated by the supply curve (E_2). As a result, the actual increase in unemployment will be less than the depicted excess supply of labor $(E_2 - E_1$ in Figure 3.7). Since this complication does not fundamentally alter any of the conclusions in this chapter, we ignore it in the analysis that follows. Jacob Mincer, in "Unemployment Effects of Minimum Wage Changes," *Journal of Political Economy* 84 (August 1976): S87–S104, has presented evidence that higher minimum-wage rates do lead to reduced labor-force participation rates.

(W_1/P_0) in Figure 3.7. Whether such a policy is desirable for low-skilled workers as a group depends upon whether the higher real wage is sufficiently high to compensate low-skilled workers for their employment losses $(E_0 - E_1)$ and upon the income-support programs, such as unemployment insurance, available to unemployed workers.

What's Wrong with the Model?

Early studies of the employment effects of minimum-wage legislation, conducted in the 1940s and 1950s, often found that employment *increased* after minimum-wage increases. They concluded that there are no adverse effects of minimum-wage legislation and that the neoclassical model presented above is all wrong.

These studies, however, do not succeed in disproving the neoclassical model for at least three reasons. First, they ignore the fact that the uniform coverage model is not applicable to the earlier period when coverage was less than complete. Second, they ignore the possibility that employers may not fully comply with increases in the minimum wage; noncompliance would reduce the employment effects of the legislated increase (the noncompliance problem will be discussed later in the chapter). Third, and most important, they ignore the fact that all of the predictions from our models are made holding other factors constant. If other factors are not actually constant, changes in one or more of them may obscure the negative relationship between wages and the demand for labor.

To see the effects of such other factors, consider Figure 3.8—where for simplicity we have omitted the labor supply curve and have focused on only the demand side of the market. Suppose that D_0 is the demand curve for low-skilled labor in year 0, in which year the real wage is W_0/P_0 and the employment level is E_0. Further assume that in the absence of any change in the minimum wage the money wage and the price level would both increase by the same percent over the next year, so that the real wage in year 1 *(*W_1/P_1*)* would be the same as that in year 0.

Now suppose that in year 1, two things happen. First, the minimum wage rate is raised to W_2, which is greater than W_1, so that the real wage increases to W_2/P_1. Second, because the economy is expanding, the demand for low-

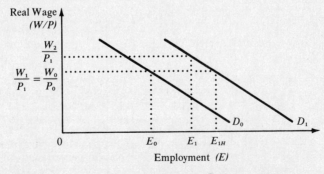

Figure 3.8   Minimum Wage Effects: Growing Demand

skilled labor shifts out to D_1. The result of these two changes is that employment increases from E_0 to E_1 in Figure 3.8.

Comparisons of observed employment levels, such as E_1 and E_0 above, caused the early investigators to conclude that minimum-wage increases had no adverse employment effects. However, this simple before/after comparison is *not* the correct one. Rather, one should ask, "How did the actual employment level in period 1 compare to the level that *would have prevailed in the absence* of the increase in the minimum wage?" Since demand grew between the two periods, this hypothetical employment level would have been E_{1H}. E_{1H} is greater than E_1, the actual level of employment in period 1, so $E_{1H} - E_1$ is the jobs-loss caused by the minimum wage.

In sum, in a growing economy with complete coverage the net effect of a one-time increase in the minimum wage is to reduce the rate of growth of employment. By focusing on only the actual employment growth, the early studies both misunderstood the implications of the neoclassical model and failed to adequately estimate the adverse employment effects of the program.[17]

A Model with Incomplete Coverage

Although minimum-wage coverage has grown over time, with somewhere in the range of 87 percent of all nonsupervisory workers in the private sector being covered by the minimum wage, as late as 1965 more than one-third of these private-sector workers were not covered by minimum-wage legislation. The major uncovered sectors then included retail trade, the service industries, and agriculture; today they include primarily employees in these industries who work for small firms. Since coverage is less than complete, it is useful to present a model of minimum-wage effects under incomplete coverage. (A similar model will reappear in Chapter 17 when we discuss the effects of unions on wages.)

To simplify the discussion, we will assume:

a. that prices are constant (so that we can talk interchangeably about real and money wages),

b. that the labor market for unskilled labor is characterized by a vertical supply curve such that total employment of the unskilled is E_T,

c. that this labor market has a covered and an uncovered sector, and

d. that unskilled workers move back and forth between sectors seeking jobs where the wages are highest.

These assumptions suggest that without a minimum wage, the wage in each sector will be the same. Referring to Figure 3.9, let us assume that this "pre-minimum"

---

[17]It is important to distinguish between a one-time increase in the minimum wage and recurrent increases that, because of inflation, have tended to keep the ratio of the minimum wage to the price level roughly constant after each increase in the minimum (Figure 3.6). In the case of recurrent increases, the main effect of the minimum-wage legislation is to decrease the average *level* of employment rather than to decrease the average (over time) rate of growth of employment.

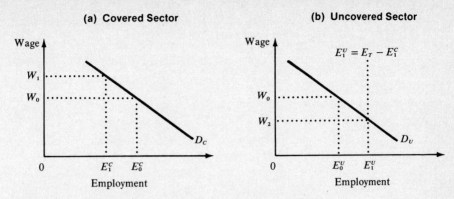

Figure 3.9 Minimum Wage Effects: Incomplete Coverage

wage is W_0 and that total employment of E_T is broken down into E_0^C in the "covered" sector plus E_0^U in the other sector.

If a minimum wage of W_1 is imposed on the covered sector, all unskilled workers will prefer to work there. However, the increase in wages there, from W_0 to W_1, reduces demand—and covered-sector employment will fall from E_0^C to E_1^C. Some workers who previously had, or would have found, jobs in the covered sector must now seek work in the uncovered sector. Thus, to the E_0^U workers formerly working in the uncovered sector are added $E_0^C - E_1^C$ other workers seeking jobs there. Thus, all unskilled workers in the market who are not lucky enough to find "covered jobs" at W_1 now look for work in the uncovered sector,[18] and the supply curve to that sector becomes E_1^U [$= E_0^U + (E_0^C - E_1^C) = E_T - E_1^C$]. The increased supply of workers to that sector drives down the wage there from W_0 to W_2.

As with most government laws, a partial-coverage minimum wage produces both winners and losers. The winners are those covered-sector workers who keep their jobs after the imposition of the minimum and receive the higher minimum wage. The losers are those low-skilled workers who lose their jobs in the covered sector and now are paid lower wages in the uncovered sector. The losers also include those low-skilled workers in the uncovered sector who kept their jobs but now find their real wages depressed, due to the increased supply of labor to that sector. Hence, even in the context of this model, where there are no overall employment effects, it is not obvious that the legislation is desirable on balance. The gains won by some groups must be weighed against the losses suffered by other groups before an unambiguous conclusion can be reached.

---

[18]Under some circumstances it may be rational for these unemployed workers to remain unemployed for a while and to search for jobs in the covered sector. We will discuss this possibility—which is discussed by Jacob Mincer in "Unemployment Effects of Minimum Wage Changes," *Journal of Political Economy* 84 (August 1976): S87–S104—in Chapter 17. At this point we simply note that if it occurs, unemployment will result.

Social Losses

Besides predicting that minimum-wage laws produce both gainers and losers among the poor, this chapter also predicts that such laws will create losses for society as a whole. In the case of full coverage, where government-mandated increases in the real wage create unemployment, the losses of potential output from those who are unemployed is obvious. However, there are also social losses in cases where—as in our Figure 3.9 example of partial coverage above—total employment remains constant. To understand this point requires a quick review of profit-maximization principles.

A firm will hire labor until labor's marginal revenue product equals the money wage rate. In the partial coverage example above (Figure 3.9), unskilled labor—prior to imposition of the minimum wage—would be hired in both sectors to the point where marginal revenue product equalled W_0. Thus, if a worker were transferred from one sector to the other, the value of total output would go down by W_0 in the "sending" sector and up by W_0 in the "receiving" sector. Overall output would remain unchanged by such a transfer.

After the minimum wage has been imposed on the covered sector, however, employment will be reduced there until labor's marginal revenue product equals W_1. Wages in the uncovered sector, in contrast, fall to W_2; employment in that sector will thus increase until labor's marginal revenue product equals W_2. The marginal revenue product in the uncovered sector is now *below* that in the covered sector (W_2 is less than W_1), so that if a worker were transferred from the uncovered to the covered sector output could be increased! (The value of output lost in the uncovered sector by this transfer would be W_2, while the value of output gained in the covered sector would be W_1.)

Since W_1 exceeds W_2, *the value of output can be increased* by transferring labor from the uncovered to the covered sector. This transfer would occur naturally if there were no minimum wage, because workers seeking the higher-paying jobs in the covered sector would bid down wages there, and employment in that sector would expand. Transfers of labor would stop when the wages in each sector were equalized—and as we have shown above, when wages are equal in both sectors of the unskilled labor market there are no further gains to be made by transfers of labor between the two sectors of that market.

With a minimum wage, however, labor *cannot* transfer out of the sector with the lower wage (and lower marginal revenue product) to the higher-wage sector. Wages in the latter sector cannot legally fall, and therefore employment cannot expand there. A beneficial transfer of resources is blocked, and social losses occur. Put differently, total output could be increased with no change in our total resources merely by transferring labor from one sector to another, and the effective prevention of this transfer by the minimum-wage law implies social losses.

The Effects of Monopsony

The preceding analysis of the minimum-wage law has assumed that firms are sufficiently small that their hiring decisions do not affect the market wage for low-skilled workers. That is, we have assumed there is no monopsony in the low-skilled labor market. While this assumption is probably appropriate for most employers of low-skilled labor, it is theoretically possible that monopsony exists in some communities. To understand the effects of a minimum wage on monopsonized markets, consider a "full coverage" model (with only one employer and no uncovered sector).

You will recall from our earlier discussion of the demand for labor by monopsonists that their marginal labor costs are above the wage rate. In maximizing profits, they choose an employment level (E_0 in Figure 3.10) where marginal labor costs equal marginal revenue product (point *A* in Figure 3.10). The wage corresponding to employment level E_0 in Figure 3.10 is W_0.

Suppose, now, that a minimum wage of W_m is set in Figure 3.10. This minimum wage prevents the firm from paying a wage less than W$_m$ and effectively creates a horizontal portion in the supply curve facing the firm (which is now *DACS*). The firm's marginal cost of labor curve is now *DACEM,* because up to employment level E_1 the marginal costs of labor are equal to W_m. The firm, which maximizes profits by equating marginal revenues with marginal costs (which equation now occurs at point *A*), will still hire E_0 workers—but it will pay them W_m instead of W_0. Moreover, if the minimum were set at a wage rate *between* W_0 and W_m, wages *and* employment would increase.

The apparent conclusion that a minimum wage can increase wages without reducing employment in a monopsonized market is subject to two qualifications. First, in the context of Figure 3.10, the minimum wage cannot be set above W_m if employment is to remain at least as large as E_0. Above W_m there would be employment losses. The second qualification is that the firm must remain in business in order for employment not to fall. While an employer may be the only buyer of labor in a particular market, the employing firm may also have many competitors in its product market. If its product market is competitive, its level of profits will be "normal"—which means that if profits were to fall, the firm

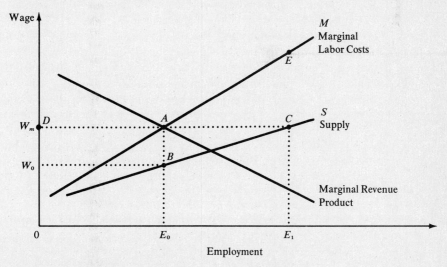

Figure 3.10   Minimum Wage Effects Under Monopsony

would find it could earn more profits in another line of business. If, in our initial example (Figure 3.10), wages rose from W_0 to W_m and employment remained at E_0, firm profits would clearly fall. If the fall were large enough, the firm might go out of business and all E_0 workers would lose their jobs.

Empirical Evidence

Labor economists have devoted much effort to empirically estimating the magnitudes of the effects of minimum-wage legislation on the employment levels of various age/race/sex groups.[19] Although the precise magnitudes of the relationships have yet to be pinned down, it is now widely agreed that increases in minimum wages do reduce employment opportunities, especially among teenagers. The studies use different data and often ask slightly different questions. Virtually all agree, however, that employment opportunities for teenagers have been reduced by the minimum wage—although the *size* of the reduction is in doubt. One recent study, for example, estimates that the 1970 minimum wage raised the cost of hiring 18- and 19-year-olds by 11 percent and reduced their employment by 15 percent.[20] Another recent study, using different data, estimated that the minimum wage reduced *full-time* job opportunities for teenagers but increased the availability of *part-time* work. This latter study found that overall teenage *employment* was not much affected by the minimum wage but that *hours of work* among teenagers fell as a result of the law.[21] These discrepancies in estimated effects of the minimum wage are not unusual, given the complexity of the world and the need for researchers to effectively control for *other* factors that influence teenage employment opportunities. There is no consensus on the effects of minimum-wage legislation on adults—perhaps because far fewer adults are directly affected by the minimum wage (most have wages in excess of the minimum).

Somewhat surprisingly, most research on the minimum wage has focused on its unintended adverse outcome: reductions in employment. Very little research, however, has addressed the question of whether minimum-wage legislation is achieving its intended goal of reducing the incidence of poverty. The few studies that have considered this issue have found that minimum-wage legislation actually has only a minor effect on the distribution of income.[22] This finding is not surprising because not all low-wage workers are members of low-income families;

---

[19]For a very readable, albeit critical, nontechnical survey of economic research on the minimum wage *see* Sar Levitan and Richard Belous, *More than Subsistence: Minimum Wages for the Working Poor* (Baltimore: Johns Hopkins University Press, 1979). For a more sympathetic view, *see* Finis Welch, *Minimum Wages: Issues and Evidence* (Washington, D.C.: American Enterprise Institute, 1978).

[20]Welch, *Minimum Wages.*

[21]Edward Gramlich, "Impact of Minimum Wages on Other Wages, Employment, and Family Incomes," *Brookings Papers on Economic Activity* (1976–2): 409–62.

[22]*See* Edward Gramlich, "Impact of Minimum Wages on Other Wages, Employment, and Family Incomes," and Terry Kelly, "Two Policy Questions Regarding the Minimum Wage" (mimeograph, Washington, D.C.: Urban Institute, 1976).

EXAMPLE 3.3

Minimum Wages in Developing Countries

Does minimum wage legislation reduce employment? The answer depends at least partially on the *level* at which the minimum is set relative to prevailing wages. While in the United States the minimum has stayed at roughly 35 to 50 percent of average hourly earnings, in developing countries the minimum is sometimes set much higher. Not surprisingly the predictions of economic theory are often borne out in situations like the one in Zimbabwe in July 1980. As the *New York Times* reported, a Zimbabwe government decision to set a minimum wage resulted in the dismissal of thousands of workers.

SALISBURY, Zimbabwe, July 6 (Reuters)—A Government decision to set a minimum wage for workers has backfired for thousands with dismissals reported throughout the country.

Officials of the ruling party of Prime Minister Robert Mugabe said today that in the Salisbury area alone more than 5,000 workers were dismissed before the minimum wage bill went into effect last Tuesday.

Worst hit, according to the officials, were domestic servants and farm workers for whom the minimum had been set at $45 a month. Employees in the commercial and industrial sectors, where the minimum had been fixed at $105 a month, have also been dismissed. The officials said that every party office in the country was dealing with hundreds of workers each day complaining of unfair dismissal.

SOURCE: *New York Times,* July 7, 1980.

many low-wage workers, especially among teenagers, are second earners in middle- or upper-income families. Put another way, minimum-wage legislation directly affects low-wage workers, not necessarily low-income families.

The Fair Labor Standards Act has a certain political sanctity because it was the first piece of protective labor legislation adopted at the federal level; very few people would seriously argue for the repeal of the minimum-wage law today. Instead, given the estimates of the adverse effects of the legislation on youth employment opportunities, many people have recently argued that a youth differential or youth subminimum wage should be instituted. Lower wages for teens, they claim, would help alleviate the teenage unemployment problem. While there appears to be empirical support for this proposition, opponents, including organized labor, point out that reducing the wages of teenagers relative to adults would encourage employers to increase their employment of teenagers at the expense of reduced adult employment. Estimates of the likely magnitude of this substitution are required before intelligent policy decisions can be made with respect to a youth differential (see Chapter 4); in the language of some opponents, one should not substitute parents' unemployment for that of their children.

Two additional reasons may help explain why increases in the minimum wage have not had as dramatic effects on employment or the distribution of income as one might expect. First, there is no reason to suspect that all employers comply with the legislation; only limited resources are expended on enforcement of the legislation, and the penalties for employers found to be not complying (paying covered workers less than the minimum) are quite small. Indeed, certain evidence suggests that only 50 to 70 percent of covered workers who would have earned less than the minimum in the absence of the law are actually paid the minimum. The remainder are paid a wage that is illegally low.[23]

Second, our discussion has ignored the possibility that employers may respond to increases in the minimum wage by lowering other forms of nonwage compensation that are *not* covered by the minimum wage law. As Chapter 10 will discuss, nonwage forms of compensation (including holiday, vacation, and sick-leave pay; health insurance; and retirement benefits) now comprise a large, and still growing, share of total compensation. To the extent that employers can respond to increases in the minimum wage by lowering the levels (or more likely the rates of growth) of these benefits, increases in the minimum will have smaller effects on total labor costs—and hence smaller employment effects—than one might have otherwise anticipated.

REVIEW QUESTIONS

1. "It is generally agreed that the volunteer army is a dismal failure—the quality of volunteers is down and the number is not sufficient to meet desired force levels. The only alternatives are to raise the pay of volunteers or to reinstitute a draft system. Since the cost to society is clearly higher in the former than in the latter case, from an economist's perspective a draft system would be preferable." Evaluate this position.

2. Suppose the government were to subsidize the wages of all women in the population by paying their *employers* 50 cents (say) for every hour they work. What will be the effect on the wage rate women receive? What will be the effect on the unsubsidized wage employers pay? (The unsubsidized wage would be the wage women receive less 50 cents.)

3. The Occupational Safety and Health Administration promulgates safety and health standards. These standards typically apply to machinery—which is required to be equipped with guards, shields, etc. An alternative to these standards is to require the employer to furnish personal protective devices to employees—such as ear plugs, hard hats, safety shoes, etc. *Disregarding* the issue of which alternative approach offers greater protection from injury, what aspects of each alternative must be taken into account when analyzing the possible *employment* effects of the two general approaches to the stimulation of safety?

4. In a certain small city with a large university there appears to be a considerable difference in the hourly wage received by people working part time and those of the same skill working full time.

---

[23]Orley Ashenfelter and Robert S. Smith, "Compliance with the Minimum Wage Law," *Journal of Political Economy* 87 (April 1979): 335–50.

a. Using demand and supply curves, and assuming perfect competition, explain the differential in wages.
b. Suppose university enrollments were to fall. What effect would declining enrollments have on the wage differential?
c. Suppose full-time and part-time hours were perfect substitutes in production. How would this affect the wage differential?

SELECTED READINGS

Orley Ashenfelter and Robert Smith, "Compliance with the Minimum Wage Law," *Journal of Political Economy* (April 1979): 335–50.

Charles Brown, Curtis Gilroy, and Andrew Cohen, "The Effect of the Minimum Wage on Employment and Unemployment," *Journal of Economic Literature* (June 1982): 487–528.

Edward Gramlich, "Impact of Minimum Wages on Other Wages, Employment, and Family Incomes," *Brookings Papers on Economic Activity* (1976–2): 409–62.

Sar Levitan and Richard Belous, *More Than Subsistence: Minimum Wages for the Working Poor* (Baltimore: Johns Hopkins University Press, 1979).

Jacob Mincer, "Unemployment Effects of Minimum Wage Changes," *Journal of Political Economy* (August 1976): S87–S104.

Finis Welch, *Minimum Wages: Issues and Evidence* (Washington, D.C.: American Enterprise Institute, 1978).

Chapter 4

ELASTICITIES OF DEMAND FOR LABOR

The previous chapter stressed that the effects of various government policies on employment and wage levels depend crucially on the magnitudes of labor demand elasticities. Given the importance of these elasticities, this chapter will present an extended discussion of the determinants of the elasticities of demand for labor, will summarize the available empirical evidence on the magnitudes of these elasticities, and will then illustrate the importance of this knowledge in a number of policy applications.

Elasticity and Cross Elasticity Defined

The Own-Wage Elasticity of Demand

Recall that the *own-wage elasticity of demand* for a category of labor is defined as the percentage change in its employment *(E)* induced by a one percent increase in its wage rate *(W)*:

$$\eta_{ii} = \frac{\%\Delta E_i}{\%\Delta W_i}. \tag{4.1}$$

In equation (4.1), we have used the subscript i to denote the category of labor i, η to represent elasticity, and the notation $\%\Delta$ to represent "percentage change in." Since the last chapter showed that labor demand curves slope downward, an increase (decrease) in the wage rate will lead employment to decrease (increase); the own-wage elasticity of demand thus is a negative number. What is at issue is its magnitude. The larger its *absolute* value, the larger will be the percentage decline in employment associated with any given percentage increase in wages.

Labor economists often focus on whether the absolute value of the elasticity of demand for labor is greater than or less than one. If it is greater than one, a one percent increase in wages will lead to an employment decline of greater than one percent; this situation is referred to as an *elastic* demand curve. In contrast, if the absolute value is less than one, the demand curve is said to be *inelastic;* a one percent increase in wages will lead to a proportionately smaller decline in employment.[1] If the demand curve is elastic, aggregate earnings (defined here as the wage rate times the employment level) of individuals in the category will decline when the wage rate increases, because employment falls at a faster rate than wages rise. Similarly, if the demand curve is inelastic, aggregate earnings will increase when the wage rate is increased.

To see the importance of the magnitude of elasticity, let us return to our analysis of the minimum wage in a world with *complete coverage.* We saw in Chapter 3 that an increase in the minimum wage would lead to a decrease in employment, if other factors affecting employment were held constant. Does this result imply, from the perspective of low-wage workers as a group, that minimum-wage increases are undesirable? The answer is ambiguous; it depends upon the extent to which the higher minimum wage for those workers who keep their jobs offsets the loss in employment that occurs. There are obvious equity issues involved here that make such comparisons difficult. However, *if* the own-wage elasticity of demand for low-skilled workers is inelastic, an increase in the minimum wage will lead to an increase in aggregate earnings for this group. This increase in aggregate earnings among the low-skilled implies that those who keep their jobs could compensate those who lose them and still be better off.[2] (The fact that *low-skilled* workers, as a *group, might* be made better off by a minimum-wage law does not imply that the gains to *society* as a whole would exceed the losses. Chapter 3 addressed the social losses.)

Figure 4.1 shows that the flatter of the two demand curves graphed (D_1) has greater elasticity than the steeper (D_2). Beginning with any wage ($W,$ for example), given wage changes (to W', say) will yield greater responses in employment with demand curve D_1 than with D_2 (compare $E_1 - E_1'$ with $E_2 - E_2'$).

To speak of a demand curve as having "an" elasticity, however, is technically incorrect. Given demand curves will generally have elastic and inelastic ranges —and while we are usually just interested in the elasticity of demand in the range around the current wage rate in any market, one cannot fully understand elasticity without understanding that it can vary along a given demand curve.

---

[1] If the elasticity just equals -1, the demand curve is said to be *unitary elastic.*

[2] Once we include transfer payments, such as unemployment insurance, in the analysis, it becomes possible for the total income of low-skilled workers (including transfer payments) to increase even if the elasticity is greater than one. See Edward Gramlich, "Impact of Minimum Wages on Other Wages, Employment, and Family Incomes," *Brookings Papers on Economic Activity,* 2 (1976): 409–62.

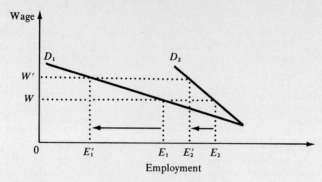

Figure 4.1   Relative Demand Elasticities

To illustrate, suppose we examine the typical straight-line demand curve that we have used so often in Chapters 2 and 3 (see Figure 4.2). One feature of a straight-line demand curve is that at *each* point along the curve a unit change in wages induces the *same* response in terms of units of employment. For example, at any point along the demand curve shown in Figure 4.2, a $2 decrease in wages will increase employment by 10 workers.

However, the same responses in terms of *unit* changes along the demand curve do *not* imply equal *percentage* changes. To see this point, look first at the upper end of the demand curve in Figure 4.2 (the end where wages are high and employment is low). A $2 decrease in wages when the base is $12 represents a 17 percent reduction in wages—while an addition of 10 workers when the starting point is also 10 represents a 100 percent increase in demand. Demand at this point is clearly *elastic.* However, if one looks at the same unit changes in the lower region of the demand curve (low wages, high employment), demand is inelastic. A $2 reduction in wages from a $4 base is a 50 percent reduction, while an

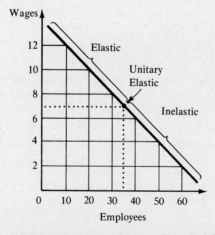

Figure 4.2   Different Elasticities Along a Demand Curve

increase of 10 workers from a base of 50 is only a 20 percent increase. Since the percentage increase in employment is smaller than the percentage increase in wages, demand is seen to be inelastic at this end of the curve.

Thus, the upper end of a straight-line demand curve will exhibit greater elasticity than the lower end. Moreover, a straight-line demand curve will actually be elastic in some ranges and inelastic in others (as shown in Figure 4.2).

The Cross-Wage Elasticity of Demand

Because firms may employ several categories of labor and capital, the demand for any one category can be affected by price changes in the other categories. For example, if the wages of carpenters rose, more people might build brick homes and the demand for *masons* might increase. On the other hand, an increase in carpenters' wages might decrease the overall level of home building in the economy, which would decrease the demand for *plumbers*. Finally, changes in the price of *capital* could increase or decrease the demand for workers in all three trades.

The magnitude of the above effects can be summarized by examining the elasticities of demand for inputs with respect to the prices of other inputs. Recall that in the previous chapter we defined the *elasticity of demand for input i with respect to the price of input j* as the percentage change in the demand for input *i* induced by a one percent change in the price of input *j*. If the two inputs are both categories of labor, these *cross-wage elasticities of demand* are given by

$$\eta_{ij} = \frac{\%\Delta E_i}{\%\Delta W_j},\tag{4.2}$$

and

$$\eta_{ji} = \frac{\%\Delta E_j}{\%\Delta W_i}.$$

If the cross-elasticities are positive (with an increase in the price of one increasing the demand for the other), the two are said to be *gross substitutes*. If these cross-elasticities are negative (and an increase in the price of one reduces the demand for the other), the two are said to be *gross complements*.

Both the sign and magnitude of cross elasticities are important for policy analysis. To return to our minimum-wage example again, would the introduction of a youth subminimum, or youth differential in the minimum wage, be an effective way to increase teenage employment levels? *If* the own-wage elasticity of demand for youth is elastic, a youth differential of, say, 15 percent would lead to a greater than 15 percent increase in teenage employment.[3] However,

---

[3] This actually is an overestimate since it assumes all teens earn the minimum wage. In fact, many earn significantly more; their wages would not be directly affected by a youth differential. Hence, the actual reduction in the average teenage wage would be substantially less than 15 percent.

the story does not end here; one also needs to consider whether *other* groups would face adverse employment effects. If, for example, teens and adult workers are *gross substitutes,* employment of low-skilled *adult* workers would fall if a youth differential were enacted. Estimates of the cross-wage elasticity of demand of adult labor with respect to the teenage wage are thus also required to make intelligent policy decisions. (As later sections will discuss, there *is* evidence that the own-wage elasticity of demand for teenagers is elastic; however, evidence on the size and sign of relevant adult-teenager cross-wage elasticities is generally lacking.[4])

The Hicks-Marshall Laws of Derived Demand

Knowledge of own-wage elasticities of demand is very important for making policy decisions. The factors that influence own-wage elasticity can be summarized by the four "Hicks-Marshall Laws of Derived Demand"—"laws" named after two distinguished British economists, Alfred Marshall and John Hicks, who are closely associated with their development.[5] These laws assert that, other things equal, the own-wage elasticity of demand for a category of labor is high

1. when the price elasticity of demand for the product being produced is high,
2. when other factors of production can be easily substituted for the category of labor,
3. when the supply curves of other factors of production are highly elastic (that is, usage of other factors of production can be increased without substantially increasing their prices), and
4. when the cost of employing the category of labor is a large share of the total costs of production.

Not only are these laws generally valid as an empirical proposition, but the first three can be shown to always hold. There are conditions, however, under which the final law does not hold.

In seeking to explain why these laws hold, it is useful to pretend that we can divide the process by which an increase in the wage rate affects the demand for labor into two steps. First, an increase in the wage rate increases the relative cost of the category of labor in question and induces employers to use less of it and more of other inputs (the *substitution effect*). Second, when the wage increase causes the marginal costs of production to rise, there are pressures to increase product prices and reduce output—causing a fall in employment (the *scale effect*). The four laws of derived demand each deal with substitution or scale effects.

---

[4]*See* Daniel Hamermesh and James Grant, "Econometric Studies of Labor—Labor Substitution and Their Implications for Policy," *Journal of Human Resources* 14 (Fall 1979): 518–42.

[5]John R. Hicks, *The Theory of Wages,* 2nd ed. (New York: St. Martins Press, 1966), pp. 241–47; Alfred Marshall, *Principles of Economics,* 8th ed. (London: Macmillan, 1923), pp. 518–38.

Demand for the Final Product

The greater the price elasticity of demand for the final product, the larger will be the decline in output associated with a given increase in price—and the greater the decrease in output, the greater the loss in employment (other things equal). Thus, *the greater the elasticity of demand for the product, the greater the elasticity of demand for labor will be.* One implication of this result is that, other things equal, the demand for labor at the *firm* level will be more elastic than the demand for labor at the *industry,* or market, level. For example, the product demand curves facing *individual* carpet manufacturing companies are highly elastic, because the carpet of Company X is a very close substitute for the carpet of Company Y. Compared to price increases at the *firm* level, however, price increases at the *industry* level will not have as large an effect on demand because the closest substitutes for carpeting are hardwood, ceramic, or some kind of vinyl floor covering—none of which is a very close substitute for carpeting. The demand for labor is thus much more elastic for an individual carpet manufacturing firm than for the carpet manufacturing industry as a whole. (For the same reasons, the labor demand curve for a monopolist is less elastic than for an individual *firm* in a competitive industry. Monopolists, after all, face *market* demand curves for their product, because they are the only sellers in the particular market.)

Another implication of this first law is that *wage elasticities will be higher in the long run than in the short run.* The reason for this fact is that price elasticities of demand in product markets are higher in the long run. In the short run there may be no good substitutes for a product, or consumers may be locked into their current stock of consumer durables. However, after a period of time, new products that are substitutes may be introduced, and consumers will begin to replace durables that have worn out.

Substitutability of Other Factors

As the wage rate of a category of labor increases, firms have an incentive to try to substitute other, now relatively cheaper, inputs for the category. Suppose, however, that there were no substitution possibilities; a given number of units of the type of labor *must* be used to produce one unit of output. In this case, the first step in the process described above is not present; there is no reduction in employment due to the substitution effect. In contrast, when substitution possibilities do present themselves, a reduction in employment will occur at this stage. Hence, other things equal, *the easier it is to substitute other factors of production, the higher the wage elasticity of demand will be.*

It is important to note that limitations on substitution possibilities need not be solely technical ones. For example, as we shall see in Chapter 14, unions often try to limit substitution possibilities by including specific work rules in their contracts (e.g., minimum crew size for crews in a railroad locomotive). Alternatively, the government may legislate limitations by specifying minimum employment levels for "safety reasons" (for example, each public swimming pool in New

York State must always have a lifeguard present). Such collectively bargained or legislated restrictions make the demand for labor less elastic. Note, however, that substitution possibilities that are not feasible in the short run may well become feasible over longer periods of time, when employers are free to vary their capital stock. For example, if the wages of railroad workers go up, companies could buy more powerful locomotives and operate with larger trains and fewer locomotives. Likewise, if the wages of lifeguards rose, cities might build larger, but fewer, swimming pools. Both adjustments would occur only in the long run, which is another reason why the demand for labor is more elastic in the long run than in the short run.

The Supply of Other Factors

Suppose that as the wage rate increased and employers attempted to substitute other factors of production for labor, the prices of these inputs were bid up substantially. This situation might occur, for example, if one were trying to substitute capital equipment for labor. If producers of capital equipment were already operating their plants near capacity—so that taking on new orders would cause them substantial increases in costs because they would have to work their employees overtime and pay them a wage premium—they would only accept new orders if they could charge a higher price for their equipment. Such a price increase would dampen firms' "appetites" for capital and thus limit the substitution of capital for labor.

For another example, suppose an increase in the wages of unskilled workers caused employers to attempt to substitute skilled employees for unskilled employees. If there were only a fixed number of skilled workers in an area, their wages would be bid up by employers. As in the prior example, the incentive to substitute alternative factors would be reduced, and the reduction in employment due to the substitution effect would be smaller. In contrast, if the prices of other inputs did not increase when employers attempted to increase their usage, other things equal, the substitution effect—and thus the wage elasticity of demand—would be larger.

Note again that prices of other inputs are less likely to be bid up in the long run than in the short run. In the long run existing producers of capital equipment can expand their capacity and new producers can enter the market. Similarly, in the long run more skilled workers can be trained. This observation is an additional reason why the demand for labor will be more elastic in the long run.

The Share of Labor in Total Costs

Finally, the share of the category of labor in total costs is crucial to the size of the elasticity of demand. If the category's initial share were 20 percent, a 10 percent increase in the wage rate, other things equal, would raise total costs by 2 percent. In contrast, if its initial share were 80 percent, a 10 percent increase in the wage rate would increase total costs by 8 percent. Since employers would have to increase their product prices by more in the latter case, output—and hence employment—would fall more in that case. *Thus, the greater the category's share in total costs, the higher the wage elasticity of demand will tend to be.*[6]

Empirical Evidence on Wage Elasticities of Demand

Literally hundreds of studies have been published in recent years that present empirical estimates on the magnitudes of wage elasticities of demand. Some of these studies focus on the aggregate demand for labor in the economy as a whole; others focus on the demand by different industries. Some focus on the demand for different skill classes; still others focus on the demand for different age/race/sex groups. Although our knowledge in a number of these areas is not very precise, it is useful to summarize what we do know.

To be able to draw a particular demand curve with precision requires knowledge of the factors that affect derived demand: the technological possibilities given by the production function (substitutability of capital and labor, labor share in total cost), the supply curve of capital, and the elasticity of product demand. In estimating the elasticity of demand for labor, we do not want to hold these factors constant because they are all crucial in determining the *size* of the elasticity of demand. As a practical matter, however, researchers usually have to estimate demand elasticities holding the *price of capital* constant.[7] This is tantamount to assuming that capital usage can be increased or decreased as wages change with no effect on the price at which capital is supplied; that is, capital supply curves are assumed to be horizontal. All elasticity estimates cited below make this assumption.[8]

The *overall*, own-wage elasticity of demand for labor in the economy as a whole is inelastic and probably in the range of −0.3.[9] This inelasticity is to be expected, because at the level of the economy *as a whole*, scale effects are likely to be small. Workers losing jobs due to wage increases will become self-employed in some cases. There are federal policies and programs designed to maintain national output and create full employment. Foreign goods and services are often very hard to substitute for domestic goods and services. For all these reasons, the *overall* wage elasticity of demand is small.

The own-wage elasticities of demand at the *industry* level tend to vary widely across industries and in the main are also inelastic. Table 4.1 presents a repre-

---

[6]As we noted earlier, this law does not always hold. More specifically, when it is easy for employers to substitute other factors of production for the category of labor but difficult for consumers to substitute other products for the product being produced (low price elasticity of demand), this law is reversed. For a more formal treatment, *see* Hicks, *The Theory of Wages.*

[7]*Capital*, even in a given industry, encompasses so many machines, tools, supplies, and buildings that estimating a supply function is really beyond the capability of the data usually available.

[8]Studies in which the level of *output* or the level of *capital usage* is held constant are ignored here since they assume away either scale or substitution effects.

[9]Daniel Hamermesh, "Econometric Studies of Labor Demand and Their Application to Policy Analysis," *Journal of Human Resources* (Fall 1976): 507–25.

Table 4.1 Representative Estimates of Long-Run Wage Elasticities of Demand, by Industry

Industry	Long-Run Wage Elasticity
Coal mining[a]	
Underground	0.98
Surface	0.86
Manufacturing[b]	0.09 to 0.62
Retail trade[c]	0.34 to 1.20
State and local government[d]	
Employees in education sector	1.06
Noneducation employees	0.38

[a]Derived from estimates presented in Morris Goldstein and Robert S. Smith, "The Predicted Impact of the Black Lung Benefits Program on the Coal Industry" in Orley Ashenfelter and James Blum, eds., *Evaluating the Labor-Market Effects of Social Programs* (Princeton, N.J.: Princeton University Press, 1976).

[b]Daniel Hamermesh, "Econometric Studies of Labor Demand and Their Applications to Policy Analysis," *Journal of Human Resources* (Fall 1976): 507–25.

[c]Philip Cotterill, "The Elasticity of Demand for Low-Wage Labor," *Southern Economic Journal* 41 (January 1975): 520–25.

[d]Orley Ashenfelter and Ronald G. Ehrenberg, "The Demand for Labor in the Public Sector," in Daniel Hamermesh, ed., *Labor in the Public and Nonprofit Sectors* (Princeton, N.J.: Princeton University Press, 1975).

sentative set of estimates for coal mining, manufacturing, retail trade, and the state and local government sector. That the demand for employees in underground mining (located primarily in the East) is more elastic than the demand for employees in surface or strip mining (located primarily in the West) is not unexpected. Surface mining is much more capital intensive, and labor costs are a smaller share of the total costs of production in that sector. That the estimated elasticities at the industry level tend to be in the inelastic range is also not surprising because scale effects at that level are likely to be relatively small in many cases. The elasticity of product demand *for a firm* is very high, as mentioned earlier, but *at the industry level* it is not likely to be very large.

A third set of empirical findings suggests that the own-wage elasticity of demand is higher for production workers than for nonproduction workers. This difference appears to be the result of the greater substitutability between capital and *production* labor than between capital and nonproduction workers.[10]

In general, the more a group of workers is substitutable with capital, the greater will be its elasticity of demand, other things equal. Research to date suggests that capital and unskilled labor are more easily substituted than capital and skilled labor,[11] but whether this translates into a greater own-wage elasticity of demand depends upon the "other things" affecting elasticity: product demand elasticities, share of labor in total cost, and the supply curve for capital. *If* these

---

[10]Hamermesh and Grant, "Econometric Studies of Labor-Labor Substitution."

[11]Hamermesh and Grant, "Econometric Studies of Labor-Labor Substitution."

other factors are more or less the same for skilled and unskilled workers, on average, then the own-wage elasticity of demand will tend to be greater for the unskilled. It appears, for example, that the elasticity of demand for teenage labor may be in the range of -7 to -9 and that it is much higher than the elasticity of demand for adults (who tend to be in more skilled jobs).[12]

All of the evidence cited above has concerned *own-wage* elasticities of demand. As indicated earlier, evidence on *cross-wage* elasticities of demand is generally lacking. We *do* have evidence that teenagers and adults, for example, are substitutes in production,[13] but whether they are *gross substitutes* depends on the *scale effect* as well as on the substitution effect. In other words, we know with some certainty that if teenage wages were reduced by a youth differential in the minimum wage, teenagers would be substituted for adults (at least to some degree) in the production process. However, whether adult employment would go up or down depends also on the scale effect a youth subminimum would create. If scale effects are large, teenagers and adults *could* be gross complements (that is, as teenage wages fell, adult employment would rise despite the substitution against them in the production process). Unfortunately, it is not clear at this point whether teenagers and adults are gross complements or gross substitutes.

Applying the Laws of Derived Demand

Because empirical estimates of demand elasticities that may be required for making decisions are lacking in some cases, it is sometimes necessary to try to guess what these elasticities are likely to be. In making these guesses, we can apply the laws of derived demand to predict these magnitudes for various types of labor. Consider first the demand for unionized New York City garment workers. As we shall discuss in Chapter 12, because unions are complex organizations it is not always possible to specify what their goals are. Nevertheless, it is clear that in most cases unions value both their members' wage *and* employment opportunities. This observation leads to the simple prediction that, other things equal, the more elastic the demand for labor, the smaller the wage gain that a union will succeed in winning for its members. The reason for this prediction is that the more elastic the demand curve, the greater the percentage employment decline associated with any given percentage increase in wages. We can expect that

a. unions would win larger wage gains for their members in markets with inelastic demand curves;

b. unions would strive to take actions that reduce the wage elasticity of demand for their members' services; and

c. unions might first seek to organize workers in markets in which demand curves are inelastic (because the potential gains to unionization are higher in these markets).

---

[12]Hamermesh and Grant, "Econometric Studies of Labor-Labor Substitution."

[13]Hamermesh and Grant, "Econometric Studies of Labor-Labor Substitution."

As we shall see, many of these predictions are borne out by empirical evidence (see Chapters 12 and 17).

Due to foreign competition, the price elasticity of demand for the clothing produced by New York City garment workers is extremely high. Furthermore, employers can easily find other inputs to substitute for these workers; namely, nonunion garment workers in the South (this substitution would require moving the plant to the South, a strategy that many manufacturers have followed). These facts lead one to predict that the wage elasticity of demand for New York City unionized garment workers should be very elastic—a prediction that seems to be borne out by union policies in the industry. That is, because the garment workers' union faces a highly elastic demand curve, its wage demands historically have been moderate. However, the union has also aggressively sought to reduce the elasticity of product demand by supporting policies that reduce foreign competition—and it has, in addition, pushed for higher federal minimum wages in order to reduce employers' incentives to move their plants to the South.

Next, consider the wage elasticity of demand for unionized airplane pilots on commercial scheduled airlines in the United States. The salaries of pilots are only a small share of the costs of operating large airplanes; they are dwarfed by the fuel and capital costs of airlines. Furthermore, substitution possibilities are limited; there is little room to substitute unskilled labor for skilled labor (although airlines can contemplate substituting capital for labor by reducing the number of flights they offer while increasing the size of airplanes). Prior to the deregulation of the airline industry that took place in the late 1970s, many airlines also faced competition on many of their routes and/or were prohibited from reducing their prices to compete with other airlines who flew the same routes. These factors all suggest that the wage elasticity of demand for airline pilots was quite inelastic. As one might expect, their wages were also quite high because their union could push for large wage increases without fear that such an increase would substantially reduce pilots' employment levels. However, after airline deregulation, competition among airline carriers increased substantially, leading to a more elastic labor demand curve for pilots. As a result, many airlines "requested," and won, reduced wages from their pilots.

Finally, consider the wage elasticity of demand for *domestic* farm workers. This elasticity will depend heavily on the supply of immigrants, either legal or illegal, who are potentially willing to work as farm workers at wages less than the wages paid to domestic workers. The successful unionization of farm workers, coupled with union or government rules that prevent illegal immigrants from accepting such employment, obviously will make the demand curve for domestic farm workers less elastic. Similarly, government regulations that either limit the quantity of foreign farm products that can be imported into the United States (quotas), place tariffs on such products, or limit foreign producers from *dumping* (selling their farm products in the United States at prices less than they charge in their own countries) will all reduce the price elasticity of demand for U.S. farm products (and hence the wage elasticity of demand for domestic farm workers). This example indicates how government policies can heavily influence wage elasticities in particular labor markets.

Policy Applications

Knowledge of the magnitudes and signs of wage elasticities of demand are important in many policy applications, as the following examples illustrate.

Market Effects of a Government Training Program

Suppose the labor market for a particular type of clerical worker, say typists, is competitive and is initially in equilibrium. This situation is depicted in Figure 4.3; the initial demand curve is D_0, the supply curve is S_0, and E_0 typists are employed and paid the real wage rate W_0. Suppose also that there is unemployment of unskilled workers in the area and that to remedy this situation the government funds a training program to train these unemployed unskilled workers to become typists.[14] If $E_2 - E_0$ unskilled workers are trained, the supply curve of typists in the market will shift to S_1. At the old equilibrium wage (W_0), the number of typists who want to work will exceed the number that firms want to hire (by $E_2 - E_0$). Downward pressure will be placed on the wage rate and eventually equilibrium will be reestablished at the lower real wage rate of W_1 and the higher employment level of E_1.[15]

Note that even if all trainees were placed in jobs, the net impact of the program is not to increase employment of typists by the number of trainees. Employment has increased by less than the number of trainees, because the

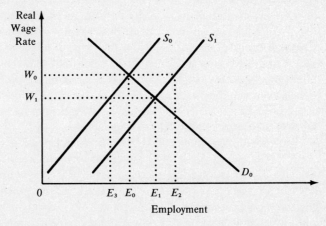

Figure 4.3 Market Effects of a Government Training Program

---

[14]During the late 1970s and early 1980s, the major government training programs for adults were funded under the Comprehensive Employment and Training Act (CETA). See the most recent issue of the *Employment and Training Report of the President* for background data on, and a description of, current training programs (including those funded under the 1982 *Job Training Partnership Act*).

[15]In a period of rising prices real wages can fall without a cut in money wages. All that is required here is that prices rise more rapidly than money wages.

reduction in the real wage rate has induced some previously employed workers to quit their jobs and drop out of the typist labor market. Also, those typists who have kept their jobs are now worse off because their wages are lower than before. Both of these market effects must be taken into account in any evaluation of a training program's effects.

Under what circumstances will both the decline in wages and the loss of jobs by previously employed typists be small? Clearly the answer is, when the wage elasticity of demand for labor is highly elastic. For in this situation, a small decline in wages will lead to a large expansion in the number of employees firms want to hire. Other things equal, trainees should be trained for occupations in which the demand curves are highly elastic.

Of course, this analysis assumes that real wages are flexible in the market for typists, so that initially there is not a shortage of labor in that market. If instead, the real wage could not initially rise above W_1 in Figure 4.3 (which might occur during a period in which wages were directly controlled by federal legislation), then the initial employment level would be E_3. In this situation, employment could increase by the number of trainees and the real wage might not fall. However, if the government attempted to train more than $E_1 - E_3$ new typists, the lesson learned above would apply and employment of typists would not increase by the number trained.

Investment Tax Credit to Reduce Unemployment

An *investment tax credit* allows businesses to subtract a certain percentage of the investments they make in new capital equipment from their tax bills. As such, the credit is an implicit subsidy given to employers for increasing their capital stocks. It has the effect of reducing the price of new capital equipment, which should stimulate such investments. To the extent that this increases the growth rate in the economy, such a tax credit may stimulate employment growth and reduce the unemployment rate. However, working against this scale effect is a substitution effect: the cost of capital is lower because of the tax credit, and this induces the substitution of capital for labor.

Investment tax credits have been part of federal tax legislation since the early 1960s. Indeed, as of 1983 the credit was 10 percent of the purchase price for most capital investments. A policy issue of major interest is whether increasing the level of the tax credit substantially reduces unemployment. Since the cost of the credit to the U.S. Treasury in the form of lost revenue is rather substantial, and because this lost revenue could be used to reduce unemployment in other ways, the effects of the tax credit on employment opportunities is a critical question.

Although the overall effects of an investment tax credit on employment have not been precisely pinned down, we have a fairly good idea which groups would gain or lose from an increase in the credit. As noted above, the data seem to indicate that capital and skilled labor are less substitutable than capital and unskilled labor. Hence, as increases in the investment tax credit reduce the cost of capital, one would expect greater substitution effects—which adversely affect employment levels—among the unskilled. Whether the *actual* level of employment among the unskilled would fall or not depends, as we have emphasized, on the size of the *scale* effect. However, we would expect a tax credit to cause more displacement of unskilled workers than skilled workers.

Employment Tax Credits or Wage Subsidies

As an alternative to an investment tax credit, one might institute a system of payments to employers for increasing their employment levels. When the payment is made directly to employers (for example, when employers are rebated 50 percent of their new employees' wages) the payment is called a *wage subsidy.* If the payment is implicit, in the form of a tax credit, it is called an *employment tax credit.* The analyses, and effects, of both types of payment programs are identical, however. By reducing the price the employer pays for labor, both tend to stimulate employment.

Employment tax credits, or wage-subsidy schemes, can take many forms.[16] They can apply to all new hires or only to increases in firms' employment levels (in which case they are called *marginal* employment tax credits). Since firms typically hire new employees to replace those employees who have quit, retired, or been involuntarily terminated, they would receive subsidies in the former case even if they maintained a constant employment level.

Employment subsidies can also be either *general* or *selective.* A general subsidy is not conditional on the characteristics of the people hired, while a selective, or *targeted,* plan makes payments conditional on hiring people from certain target groups (such as the disadvantaged).

Although European nations have had more experience with employment tax-credit programs than the United States, both general and selective tax-credit programs have been tried in the United States in recent years. For example, a New Jobs Tax Credit was part of the 1977 economic stimulus package passed by Congress. This general, marginal employment tax-credit program was in effect only for 1977 and 1978. Due to limitations on the size of the credit that an employer could receive for each employee (essentially 50 percent of the worker's annual earnings up to a maximum earnings ceiling of $4200), the plan effectively gave employers a proportionately greater subsidy for hiring unskilled and part-time labor than it did for hiring skilled or full-time labor.[17] Because of this, *if* the own-wage elasticities of demand are the same or larger for unskilled or part-time labor *and* if the various skill groups are gross substitutes, one would expect the employment levels of unskilled and part-time workers to be stimulated most by the program.

---

[16]*See* Daniel Hamermesh, "Subsidies for Jobs in the Private Sector," in John Palmer, ed., *Creating Jobs: Public Employment Programs and Wage Subsidies* (Washington, D.C.: Brookings Institution, 1978) for an extended discussion.

[17]For more details of the plan, *see* Orley Ashenfelter, "Evaluating the Effects of the Employment Tax Credit" in U.S. Department of Labor, *Conference Report on Evaluating the 1977 Economic Stimulus Package* (Washington, D.C.: U.S. Government Printing Office, 1979).

EXAMPLE 4.1

The Slowdown in U.S. Productivity Growth

One measure of productivity that is customarily used is *labor productivity,* or output per hour of labor employed. Between 1948 and 1965 this labor productivity grew at a rate of about 3 percent per year in the manufacturing sector. Between 1973 and 1978, however, it grew at a rate of only about 1.5 percent per year. This slowdown in the rate of growth of productivity is particularly disturbing because, as we shall see in Chapter 19, the rate of growth of labor productivity is directly related to both the rate of growth of real wages and the rate of price inflation that occur in the economy.

Not surprisingly, then, economists have expended considerable effort to try to understand the causes of the slowdown in productivity growth. Although the slowdown is not fully understood, a number of factors are known to contribute to it. These factors include, but are not limited to, changes in the age-sex composition of the labor force, government man-dated investments in pollution-abatement equipment (which do not lead to increases in *measured* output since the quality of the environment is not measured in gross national product), and a decline in the capital-labor ratio that has accompanied a slowdown in normal business investment. With less capital to work with, each unit of labor is less productive.

Why has this reduction in capital investment occurred? The answer may hinge on the explosion of energy prices that occurred during the period following the 1974 OPEC oil embargo. Several studies indicate that capital and energy are gross complements and that labor and energy are gross substitutes. Hence, rapid increases in the price of energy should induce employers to reduce their capital stocks and increase employment. Once we realize that energy is an input into the production process and that increases in the price of energy raise the cost of operating capital, it becomes clear why capital/labor ratios have fallen and contributed to the slowdown in measured labor productivity. Government policies to reduce the cost of capital, such as increasing the size of the investment tax credit, could offset energy price increases and stimulate investment, thus increas-ing labor productivity; however, as already noted, the net effect on *employ-ment,* especially of unskilled workers, will not necessarily be favorable.

SOURCES: J. R. Norsworthy, Michael Harper, and Kent Kunze, "The Slowdown in Productivity Growth: Analysis of Some Contributing Factors," *Brookings Papers on Economic Activ-ity,* 2 (1979): 387–423; Edward F. Denison, *Accounting for Slower Economic Growth: The United States in the 1970s* (Washington, D.C.: Brookings Institution, 1979).
Ernst Berndt and David Wood, "Technology, Prices and the Derived Demand for Energy," *Review of Economics and Statistics* 57 (August 1975): 259–68; Edward A. Hudson and Dale Jorgenson, "Energy Prices and the U.S. Economy, 1972–76," *Data Resources Review* 7 (September 1978): 1.24–1.37. The findings, however, are not unambiguous. James Griffin and Paul Gregory, in "An Intercountry Translog Model of Energy and Substitution Responses," *American Economic Review* 66 (December 1976): 845–57, find that capital and energy are gross substitutes.

Preliminary evaluations of the program indicate that it may have had some small positive effect on the overall level of employment; firms that knew of the program's existence seemed to grow more rapidly than firms that did not know.[18] However, one year into the program, less than one-half of all surveyed firms actually knew that the program existed, and one might conjecture that the direction of causation ran from "plans to grow rapidly" to "knowledge of the program," rather than vice versa.[19] That is, firms that were planning to expand their employment, even in the absence of the program, had an incentive to learn about the program so that they could receive the subsidy.

This example again highlights the difficulties social scientists face when they attempt to evaluate the effect of social programs. It also suggests the importance of rapidly disseminating information about the existence of programs; the passage of a law, *per se,* does not guarantee that employers will know about it.

The New Jobs Tax Credit was replaced in 1979 by a Targeted Employment Tax Credit, which was a selective tax credit that subsidized the hiring of unemployed youth (18–24), handicapped individuals, and welfare recipients. To the extent that the demand for teenagers is highly elastic, as the empirical estimates indicate, this program does have the potential to substantially increase youth employment. However, it will be important to examine its impact on the employment levels of the nontargeted groups—especially unskilled adults for whom teenagers may be quite close substitutes. Given the lack of data on demand elasticities for the handicapped and welfare recipients, less can be said about the program's potential effects on these target groups; we will thus have to rely on *ex post facto* (after the fact) evaluations of the program to judge its overall effects.

REVIEW QUESTIONS

1. Suppose Congress has just passed a permanent tax credit applicable to the purchase of machinery. What impact would this tax reduction have on the demand for labor? Under what conditions will the demand for labor be affected *most?*

2. Suppose the government wants to cut expenditures to balance its budget in a way that minimizes the adverse employment effects of such a cutback. Suppose further that it wishes to do this by cutting back expenditures in selected industries (those where employment effects are minimal). Please Identify the criteria the government should use in selecting these industries.

3. Union A faces a demand curve where a wage of $4 per hour leads to demand for 20,000 person hours and a wage of $5 per hour leads to demand for 10,000 person hours. What is the elasticity of demand for this union's labor?

---

[18]*See* Jeffrey Perloff and Michael Wachter, "The New Jobs Tax Credit—An Evaluation of the 1977–78 Wage Subsidy Program," *American Economic Review* 69 (May 1979): 173–79; John Bishop and Robert Haveman, "Selective Employment Subsidies: Can Okun's Law Be Repealed?" *American Economic Review* 69 (May 1979): 124–30.

[19]Perloff and Wachter, "The New Jobs Tax Credit"; Bishop and Haveman, "Selective Employment Subsidies."

Union B faces a demand curve where a wage of $6 per hour leads to demand for 30,000 person hours while a wage of $5 per hour leads to demand for 33,000 person hours.

a. Which union faces the *more* elastic demand curve?

b. Which union will be more successful in increasing the total income (wages times person hours) of its membership?

SELECTED READINGS

Edward F. Denison, *Accounting for Slower Economic Growth: The United States in the 1970s* (Washington, D.C.: Brookings Institution, 1979).

Daniel Hamermesh, "Econometric Studies of Labor Demand and Their Application to Policy Analysis," *Journal of Human Resources* (fall 1976): 507–42.

Daniel Hamermesh, "Subsidies for Jobs in the Private Sector" in John Palmer, ed., *Creating Jobs: Public Employment Programs and Wage Subsidies* (Washington, D.C.: Brookings Institution, 1978).

Daniel Hamermesh and James Grant, "Econometric Studies of Labor-Labor Substitution and Their Implications for Policy," *Journal of Human Resources* (Fall 1979): 518–42.

Jeffrey Perloff and Michael Wachter, "The New Jobs Tax Credit—An Evaluation of the 1977–78 Wage Subsidy Program," *American Economic Review* (May 1979): 173–79.

Chapter 5

EXTENSIONS OF THE THEORY OF DEMAND

Our analyses of the demand for labor in Chapters 3 and 4, for the most part, ignored the substantial *nonwage* labor costs that exist and the *dynamic* nature of firms' employment decisions. These abstractions allowed us to discuss a number of policy issues in the context of a rather simple model. However, a number of other policy issues can be analyzed only in the context of less restrictive models.

This chapter will begin by discussing the magnitudes and growth of various forms of *nonwage* labor costs, including the costs to firms of hiring and training new employees, the costs of legally required social-insurance programs (such as Social Security and unemployment compensation), and the costs of privately negotiated fringe benefits (such as health insurance, vacation and sick-leave pay, and private pensions). These costs typically exceed 20 to 30 percent of employers' payroll costs.

This chapter generalizes our model of employers' demand for labor to incorporate decisions about both the numbers of employees to be hired *and* the average length of the work week for these employees. The fact that many of the nonwage labor costs do *not* vary, at the margin, with weekly hours of work explains why employers may decide to regularly work their employees overtime at legally required premium wage rates rather than increase the level of employment—a phenomenon that has led periodically to the proposal that the legally mandated overtime premium be increased in an effort to discourage employers from authorizing overtime and to encourage them to "spread the work."

Our model of labor demand will also be generalized to explicitly acknowledge the dynamic nature of firms' employment decisions. Employment decisions are often multiperiod in nature. While firms do not always bear the initial costs of employee training, those firms that do must recoup these costs later on. The chapter examines models that incorporate employer-borne hiring and training costs and explores the effects of minimum-wage legislation on teenagers' wage growth, why productivity declines during recessions, and the determinants of voluntary and involuntary labor turnover. The rationales for using hiring standards, such as minimum educational requirements, and for creating internal labor markets are discussed in the context of hiring and training costs.

Nonwage Labor Costs

Although simple textbook models of the labor market often refer to the hourly wage rate paid to workers as the cost of labor, there are in fact substantial *nonwage* labor costs that have important implications for labor market behavior. In general, they fall into two categories: hiring or training costs and fringe benefits.

Hiring and Training Costs

Firms incur substantial costs in hiring and training new employees. *Hiring costs* include all costs involved in advertising positions, screening applicants to evaluate their qualifications, and processing successful applicants who have been offered jobs. One might also include the overhead costs of maintaining employees on the payroll once they have been employed in this category of costs; these costs would include record-keeping costs, the costs of computing and issuing paychecks, and the costs of providing forms to the government (such as W-2 forms to the Internal Revenue Service) about employees' earnings.

New employees typically undergo either formal or informal training and orientation programs. These programs may teach new skills—such as how to use a machine—that directly increase the employees' productive abilities. Alternatively, orientation programs may simply provide newcomers with background information on how the firm is structured—such as who to call if a machine breaks down or where the rest room is. Such information, while not changing skill levels, does increase productivity by enabling workers to make more efficient use of time.

Firms incur at least three types of *training costs:*

1. the *explicit* monetary costs of employing individuals to serve as trainers and the costs of materials used up during the training process;
2. the *implicit* or opportunity costs of the trainee's time (while individuals are undergoing training they are not producing as much output as they could if all of their time were devoted to production activities); and
3. the opportunity costs of using capital equipment and experienced employees to do the training in less formal training situations (for example, if training consists solely of an experienced employee demonstrating how

he or she does a job to a new recruit, the demonstrator may work at a slower pace than normal).

Because a large share of employers' hiring and training costs are implicit in nature, it is not surprising that detailed estimates of the magnitudes of hiring and training costs in the U.S. economy do not exist. Some estimates for individual firms have been made, however, that suggest that the magnitudes are large. For example, a study conducted by the American Management Association in 1960 concluded that the *hiring* and *orientation* costs of new employees varied from around $200 per unskilled laborer to more than $4500 per engineer.[1] This study did not include estimates of training costs, and the costs that were included are not expressed in terms of today's prices. A 1951 International Harvester Company study did include training costs and estimated that its average *hiring* and *training cost* per employee was about $380;[2] in terms of current prices, this figure would be well over $1000. Each of these estimates must be considered only suggestive, however, because the studies are old, the samples are small, and measuring some of these costs is difficult.

Fringe Benefits

We have much better data, however, on the other types of *nonwage* labor costs that firms incur. *Fringe benefits* include *legally required* social-insurance contributions and *privately provided* benefits. Examples of legally required benefits are payroll-based payments employers must make to fund programs that compensate workers for unemployment (unemployment insurance), injury (workers' compensation), and retirement (old-age, survivors', disability, and health insurance—or "Social Security"). Examples of privately provided benefits are holiday pay, vacation and sick leave, private pensions, and private health and life insurance.

Tables 5.1 and 5.2 give some idea of the magnitude and growth of these benefits. Department of Commerce data for the nation as a whole, tabulated in Table 5.1, indicate that forms of compensation other than wages and salaries rose from 6.2 percent of total compensation in 1956 to 15.9 percent in 1982. These data understate the importance of nonwage items in total compensation because they include holiday, vacation, and sick pay as wages. A more comprehensive measure, although for a more limited sample, comes from the biennial U.S. Chamber of Commerce survey of large manufacturing establishments. These data, tabulated in Table 5.2, indicate that total fringe benefits as a percentage of *payroll* (which does not include pension and insurance costs) rose from 20.3 percent to 37.2 percent during the 1957–79 period.

---

[1]*See* Frederick J. Gaudet, *Labor Turnover: Calculation and Costs* (New York: American Management Association, 1960).

[2]This study is cited in Walter Oi, "Labor as a Quasi-Fixed Factor," *Journal of Political Economy* 70 (December 1962): 538–55.

EXAMPLE 5.1

Recruiting Strategies

The fact that recruiting and evaluating job applicants is a costly procedure induces employers to carefully select an overall hiring strategy. An employer wanting to hire *X* employees of a given quality has basically three choices. One is an *intensive-search* strategy, whereby the employer incurs substantial costs in advertising the openings and then interviewing applicants. A second choice is what can be called a *high-wage* strategy. By becoming known as a high-wage employer, an employer can generate large applicant pools very easily—and with so many applicants it can often fill its vacancies with those workers who are *obviously* of high quality (thus saving screening costs). Finally, employers might choose a *training* strategy—where instead of undertaking expensive efforts to ensure a large pool of highly qualified applicants, they accept inexperienced applicants and train them. (The two broad kinds of training offered and who pays for each are discussed later in this chapter.)

Whether a given firm decides on intensive search, higher wages, or greater training as its means of recruiting personnel depends on the relative costs of each strategy to that firm. While firms will differ in the strategy, or mix of strategies, they choose, a study of recruiting in Chicago's clerical labor market did find evidence that intensive search, higher wages, and greater training are indeed substitutes. High-wage firms tended to hire only experienced workers and recruited their applicants through very low-cost sources (word-of-mouth, mainly, but there was some use of newspaper ads). Low-wage firms that hired at the lowest level and trained workers for successively more skilled positions—a feasible strategy in large firms where work can be highly specialized—tended to recruit inexperienced applicants very cheaply from local high schools. Low-wage, smaller firms that needed workers who could perform "up-to-speed" from the very beginning spent the most on search; they tended to use employment agencies (whose fees can be very high) to generate and screen a pool of applicants.

SOURCE: Joseph C. Ullman, "Interfirm Differences in the Cost of Search for Clerical Workers," *Journal of Business* 41, 2 (April 1968): 153–65.

Both data sets indicate, then, an approximate doubling of the share of fringes in total compensation over the last 25 years or so. This increase has occurred in both legally required employer payments and in privately negotiated benefits. (Chapter 10 will discuss *why* fringe benefits have increased as a fraction of total compensation.)

Table 5.1 Compensation of Employees, 1956–1982 (in billions of dollars)

Year	Total	Wages and Salaries (including vacation and holiday pay)	Supplements	Ratio of Supplements to Total (percent)
1956	$ 243.5	$ 228.3	$ 15.2	6.2
1958	258.2	240.5	17.7	6.9
1960	294.9	271.9	23.0	7.8
1962	325.1	298.0	27.1	8.3
1964	368.0	336.1	31.8	8.6
1966	438.3	398.4	40.9	9.3
1968	519.8	469.5	50.3	9.7
1970	609.2	546.5	62.7	10.8
1972	715.1	633.8	81.4	11.4
1974	873.0	763.1	110.0	12.6
1976	1036.8	890.1	146.7	14.1
1978	1299.7	1105.4	194.3	14.9
1980	1596.5	1343.6	252.9	15.8
1982	1855.9	1560.1	295.8	15.9

Notes: "Compensation of Employees" is the income accruing to employees for remuneration for their work.

"Wages and Salaries" consists of the monetary remuneration of employees, including the compensation of corporate officers, commissions, tips, and bonuses, and of payments in kind, which represent income to the recipients.

"Supplements" to wages and salaries consists of employer contributions for social insurance and other labor income. Employer contributions for social insurance comprise employer payments under old-age, survivor's, disability, and hospital insurance, state unemployment insurance, railroad retirement and unemployment insurance, government retirement, and a few other minor social insurance programs. Other labor income includes employer contributions to private pension, health and welfare, unemployment, and workers' compensation funds.

SOURCES: U.S. Department of Commerce, Bureau of Economic Analysis, *Business Statistics, 1975,* p. 6; and U.S. President, *Economic Report of the President* (Washington, D.C.: U.S. Government Printing Office, February 1983), Table B-21.

The Quasi-Fixed Nature of Many Nonwage Costs

The distinction between wage and nonwage costs of employment is important because many nonwage costs are *costs per worker* rather than *costs per hour worked.* That is, many nonwage costs do not vary at the margin with the number of hours an employee works. Economists thus refer to them as *quasi-fixed*—in the sense that once an employee is hired the firm is committed to a cost that does not vary with his or her hours of work.[3]

It should be obvious that hiring and training costs are quasi-fixed; they are associated with each new employee, not with the hours he or she works after the training period. Many fringe costs, however, are also quasi-fixed. For example, in most firms holiday and vacation pay are specified as a fixed number of days per year (which may vary with seniority), and overtime hours do not affect these

---

[3]*See* Oi, "Labor as a Quasi-Fixed Factor."

Table 5.2 Fringe Benefits as a Percent of Payroll in Manufacturing, 1957–1979

Year	Legally Required Payments (employer's share)	Pensions, Insurance	Paid Rest	Pay for Time Not Worked	Other Items	Total Fringe Benefits
1957	4.1	5.8	2.4	6.5	1.5	20.3
1959	4.5	6.1	2.7	6.7	1.6	21.6
1961	5.5	6.8	2.8	7.2	1.3	23.6
1963	5.9	6.7	2.9	7.3	1.4	24.2
1965	5.3	6.7	2.7	7.2	1.7	23.6
1967	6.4	7.0	3.0	7.3	1.9	25.6
1969	6.8	7.6	3.1	7.8	1.7	27.0
1971	6.9	9.9	3.5	8.6	1.7	30.6
1973	8.3	10.2	3.5	8.5	1.5	32.0
1975	8.8	11.6	3.7	10.1	1.9	36.1
1977	9.3	12.9	3.6	9.2	2.3	37.3
1979	10.1	12.1	3.6	8.8	2.6	37.2

Note: "Payroll" (used as the denominator in calculating the above percentages) includes pay for time not worked, such as vacations and holidays, but does not include pension and insurance costs or payroll taxes. "Other items" includes profit sharing, contributions to thrift plans, bonuses, and employee educational benefits.

SOURCE: U.S. Chamber of Commerce, *Fringe Benefits and Employee Benefits* (various issues).

costs. Or to take another example, an employer's unemployment-insurance payroll-tax liability is specified to be a percentage (the tax rate) of each employee's earnings up to a maximum earnings level (the taxable wage base) which in over half of all states was $7000 in 1983. Since most employees earn more than $7000 per year, having an employee work an additional hour per week will *not* cause any increase in the employer's payroll-tax liability.[4]

The quasi-fixed nature of many nonwage labor costs has important effects on employer hiring and overtime decisions. These effects are discussed below.

The Employment/Hours Trade-Off

The simple model of the demand for labor presented in the preceding chapters spoke of the quantity of labor demanded and made no distinction between the number of individuals employed by a firm and the average length of its employees' work week. Holding all other inputs constant, however, a firm can produce a given level of output with various combinations of the number of employees hired and the number of hours worked per week. Presumably, increases in the number

---

[4]This is not true for all fringe benefits. For example, the Social Security (OASDHI) payroll-tax liability of employers is also specified as a percentage of earnings up until a maximum taxable wage base; however, this wage base is considerably higher—$35,700 in 1983. Since this level exceeds the annual earnings of most full-time employees, the employer's payroll-tax liability *is* increased when an employer employs a typical employee an additional hour per week.

of employees hired will allow for shorter work weeks, while longer work weeks will allow for fewer employees, other things equal.

In the short run, with capital and all other inputs fixed, the output *(Q)* a firm can produce is related to both its employment level *(M)* and its average work week per employee *(H)* by the following production function:

$$Q = f(M,H). \tag{5.1}$$

It is reasonable to assume that both inputs in equation (5.1) have positive marginal products ($MP_M > 0$; $MP_H > 0$). That is, increasing the number of employees, holding hours constant—or increasing the average work week, holding employment constant—will lead to increases in output. While remaining positive, each of these marginal products must surely decline at some point. In the case where the number of employees is increased this decline may be due to the reduced quantity of capital that each employee will have to work with or the fact that the firm may be forced to employ lower-quality workers. In the case where the hours each employee works per week are increased, the decline in marginal product may occur because after some point fatigue sets in.

Given this production function,[5] how does a firm determine its optimal employment/hours combination? Is it ever rational for an employer to work his or her existing employees overtime on a regularly scheduled basis, rather than hiring additional employees?

Determining the Mix of Workers and Hours

The fact that certain labor costs are *not* hours-related and others are makes it important to examine the marginal cost an employer faces when employing an additional *worker* for whatever length work week other employees are working *(MC_M)*. This marginal cost will equal the weekly value of the quasi-fixed labor costs plus the weekly wage and variable (with hours) fringe-benefit costs for the specified length of work week. Similarly, it is important to examine the marginal cost a firm faces when it seeks to increase the *average work week* of its existing work force by one hour *(MC_H)*. This marginal cost will equal the hourly wage and variable fringe-benefit costs multiplied by the number of employees in the work force. Of course, if the employer is in a situation in which an overtime premium (such as time-and-a-half or double time) must be paid for additional hours, that higher rate is the relevant wage rate to use in the latter calculation.

Viewed in this way, a firm's decision about its optimal employment/hours combination is no different than its decision about the usage of any two factors of production, which was discussed in Chapter 3. Specifically, to minimize the cost of producing any given level of output, a firm should increase its employment

---

[5]For estimates of such a function, *see* Martin Feldstein, "Specification of the Labor Input in the Aggregate Production Function," *Review of Economic Studies* 34 (October 1967): 375–86. *See also* Sherwin Rosen, "Short-Run Employment Variation in Class-I Railroads in the U.S., 1947–1967," *Econometrica* 36 (July–October 1968): 511–29.

level and its average work week up until the point where spending the last dollar on each yields the same increment to output:

$$\frac{MP_M}{MC_M} = \frac{MP_H}{MC_H}. \tag{5.2}$$

Put another way, the marginal cost of hiring an additional employee (MC_M) relative to the marginal cost of working the existing work force an additional hour (MC_H) should be equal to the marginal productivity of an additional employee relative to that of extending the work week by an hour:

$$\frac{MP_M}{MP_H} = \frac{MC_M}{MC_H}. \tag{5.3}$$

The Fair Labor Standards Act (FLSA) requires that all employees covered by the legislation receive an overtime pay premium of at least 50 percent of their regular hourly wage (time-and-a-half).[6] Now while a large proportion of overtime hours are worked because of disequilibrium phenomena—such as rush orders, seasonal demand, mechanical failures, and absenteeism—a substantial amount of overtime appears to be regularly scheduled. Equation (5.3) indicates why this scheduling of overtime may occur. Although overtime hours require premium pay, they also enable an employer to avoid the quasi-fixed employment costs associated with employing an additional worker. This point can be illustrated by considering what would happen if the overtime-wage premium were to be increased.

Policy Analysis: The Overtime-Pay Premium

Periodically, proposals have been introduced in Congress to raise the overtime premium to double time.[7] The argument made to support such an increase is that even though unemployment remains a pressing national problem, the use of overtime hours has not diminished. Moreover, the argument continues, the deterrent effect of the overtime premium on the use of overtime has been weakened

---

[6]In 1977, approximately 58 percent of all workers were covered by the overtime pay provisions of the FLSA. *See* U.S. Department of Labor, *Minimum Wage and Maximum Hours Standards under the Fair Labor Standards Act* (Washington, D.C.: U.S. Government Printing Office, October 1978). The major categories of noncovered employees include executive, administrative, and professional personnel, outside salespersons, most state and local government employees, and agricultural workers.

[7]One recent attempt was made by Congressman John Conyers of Michigan in HR 1784, introduced into Congress in February of 1979. To quote a supporter of the proposal, "The AFL-CIO endorses the double-time provision as a means of generating additional jobs. The evidence is persuasive that the overtime-pay requirements of the Fair Labor Standards Act have lost their effectiveness as a deterrent to regularly scheduled overtime work." (*See* the statement by Rudolph Oswald, Director of Research, AFL-CIO, in the minutes of the Hearings before the Subcommittee on Labor Standards on HR 1784, October 23, 1979.)

since the FLSA was enacted because of the growing share of hiring and training costs, fringe benefits, and government-mandated insurance premiums in total compensation (see Tables 5.1 and 5.2). As already noted, many of these costs are *quasi-fixed*—or employee-related rather than hours-related—and thus do not vary with overtime hours of work. An increase in them increases employers' marginal costs of hiring new employees relative to the costs of working their existing work forces overtime.

In terms of equation (5.3), the increase in quasi-fixed costs that has occurred causes an inequality between the ratio of marginal productivities and marginal costs at the old equilibrium employment/hours combination:

$$\frac{MP_M}{MP_H} < \frac{MC_M}{MC_H}. \tag{5.4}$$

To restore the equality (and to thus minimize costs) requires increasing the left-hand side of equation (5.4). Given our assumptions of diminishing marginal productivities, if output were to remain constant, employment would have to be reduced and hours worked per employee would have to increase. It is claimed, therefore, that the growth of these quasi-fixed costs has been at least partially responsible for increased usage of overtime hours and that an increase in the overtime premium is required to better "spread the work."[8] Such an increase, by raising the marginal cost of overtime hours relative to the marginal cost of hiring new workers, should induce employers to substitute new employees for the overtime hours employers might otherwise schedule.

Would an increase in the overtime premium prove to be an effective way of increasing employment and reducing unemployment? A number of economists have sought to answer this question. Although the overtime premium is, for the most part, legislatively fixed at a point in time, the ratio MC_M/MC_H varies across establishments because the weekly quasi-fixed costs and the straight-time wage rate vary across establishments. Economists have attempted to estimate the extent to which the usage of overtime hours varies across establishments with the ratio MC_M/MC_H, when all other factors are held constant.[9]

Once this relationship is known, it is possible to simulate what the effect of an increase in the overtime premium would be on overtime hours per employee. For example, suppose that the statistical analyses indicated that the relationship between overtime hours and MC_M/MC_H was given by the line *AB* in Figure 5.1. Consider a representative firm that faced relative marginal costs $(MC_M/MC_H)_0$ and whose employees worked an average of H_0 overtime hours per week. It is a simple matter to compute the effect on the relative marginal cost of an increase

[8]Average weekly overtime hours of work in manufacturing averaged 2.56 hours per employee between 1956 and 1963. However, over the 1964–77 period, the average rose to 3.34 hours per employee, an increase of more than 30 percent.

[9]Since hiring- and training-cost data are not available, these studies utilize data on the other fringe benefits only.

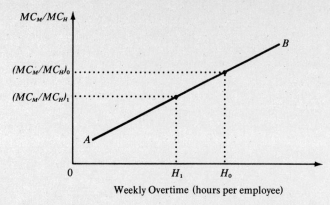

Figure 5.1   Simulating the Effect of an Increase in the Overtime Premium to Double Time

in the overtime premium to double time. If an increased premium caused a decrease to $(MC_M/MC_H)_1$, overtime hours would correspondingly fall to H_1.

Now if one *assumes* that *all* of the reduction in overtime would be converted to new full-time positions, it is possible to estimate what the effect on the employment level would be. The implied results from these studies appear in Table 5.3; these results suggest that employment increases in the range of 0.3 to 4.0 percent would result. At first glance, then, increasing the overtime premium to double

Table 5.3 Estimated Changes in Full-Time Employment Resulting from Increasing the Overtime Premium from Time-and-a-Half to Double Time

Study	Group	Absolute Change	Percentage Change
Ehrenberg (1971)	1966 manufacturing production workers	218,500	1.6
Nussbaum and Wise (1977)	1968 manufacturing production workers	491,400	3.7
	1970 manufacturing production workers	487,700	3.7
	1972 manufacturing production workers	361,900	2.8
	1974 manufacturing production workers	549,700	4.0
	1968–1974 pooled manufacturing interindustry data	320,000	2.0
Solnick and Swimmer (1978)	1972 private nonfarm nonsupervisory workers (low estimate)	159,264	0.3
	1972 private nonfarm nonsupervisory workers (high estimate)	1,521,664	3.1
Ehrenberg and Schumann (1982)	1976 manufacturing workers	—	0.5 to 1.5
	1976 nonmanufacturing nonsupervisory workers	—	1.0 to 2.3

SOURCES: Ronald G. Ehrenberg, "The Impact of the Overtime Premium on Employment and Hours in U.S. Industry," *Western Economic Journal* 19 (June 1971): 199–207; Joyce Nussbaum and Donald Wise, "The Employment Impact of the Overtime Provisions of the FLSA" (Final Report submitted to the U.S. Department of Labor, 1977); Loren Solnick and Gene Swimmer, "Overtime and Fringe Benefits—A Simultaneous Equations Approach" (mimeograph, 1978); Ronald G. Ehrenberg and Paul Schumann, *Longer Hours or More Jobs? An Investigation of Amending Hours Legislation to Create Employment* (Ithaca, N.Y.: New York State School of Industrial Relations, Cornell University, 1982).

time does seem like an effective way of increasing employment and reducing unemployment.

A complete economic analysis, however, suggests that such a conclusion would be an overly optimistic assessment of the effects of a double-time premium.[10] First, these estimates *assume* that the demand for *total* labor hours is completely inelastic with respect to its cost. That is, they ignore the fact that an increase in the overtime premium raises the average cost of hiring labor (even if overtime is eliminated), and that this may induce a shift to more capital-intensive methods of production. Further, to the extent that the cost increase is passed on to consumers in the form of higher prices, a reduction in the quantity of output will occur. Both these *scale* and *substitution effects* should lead to a decline in the number of labor hours purchased by employers; this decline will limit the employment gain associated with any given decline in overtime hours.

Second, these estimates ignore the responses of currently employed workers who would be simultaneously faced with an increase in the overtime premium and a reduction in their hours of work. Although we have yet to discuss the supply side of the labor market in detail, it should be obvious that one possible response to a reduction in overtime hours is for them to *moonlight*—to seek part-time second jobs. Moonlighting would be more likely to occur if the increase in the premium resulted in a decrease in their labor earnings.[11] If increased moonlighting occurred, the creation of new jobs for the unemployed would be further reduced.

Third, these estimates assume that the skill distributions of the unemployed and of those who work overtime are sufficiently similar to permit all of the reduction in overtime to be converted into new full-time employment. However, *if* those working overtime were primarily skilled workers and the unemployed were primarily unskilled, potential employment gains from raising the overtime premium might be considerably smaller than these estimates.

Finally, these estimates assume that the overtime-pay provisions of the FLSA are fully complied with and that they would continue to be fully complied with after an increase in the premium to double time. However, since an increase in the overtime premium would increase the amount employers save by *not* complying with the legislation, such an increase may well lead to a reduced compliance rate, which would further reduce the positive employment effects of the legislation. A number of studies indicate that noncompliance with the overtime-pay provisions is currently at least in the 10 percent range.[12] That is, at least 10 percent of the individuals working overtime who are covered by the FLSA *fail* to receive a premium of at least time-and-a-half. Hence, the possibility of increased noncompliance cannot be dismissed.

---

[10]*See* Ronald G. Ehrenberg and Paul L. Schumann, *Longer Hours or More Jobs? An Investigation of Amending Hours Legislation to Create Employment* (Ithaca, N.Y.: New York State School of Industrial and Labor Relations, Cornell University, 1982).

[11]Formally, this would occur if employers' demand curves for overtime hours were elastic with respect to the overtime wage.

[12]*See* Ehrenberg and Schumann, *Longer Hours or More Jobs?*

Our analysis of the wisdom of increasing the overtime premium to double time, as a means of stimulating employment growth, unfortunately reminds us that policy analysis is never as easy as one might initially hope it would be. The world is complex, and any complete analysis of a policy issue must consider a number of factors. It is in identifying what factors to consider that economic theory is so useful. Indeed, in the present case, even though the *initial* simulations suggested that a double-time premium would lead to an increase in employment, consideration of the *other* factors noted above led to a recommendation against increasing the overtime premium.[13]

Hiring and Training Costs and the Demand for Labor

The models of the demand for labor given in Chapters 3 and 4 were *static,* in the sense that they considered only *current* marginal productivities and *current* labor costs. If all of a firm's labor costs are variable each year, then clearly it will employ labor in *each period* to the point where labor's marginal product equals the real wage.

However, once we begin to consider hiring and training costs, the analysis changes somewhat.[14] Hiring and training costs are usually heavily concentrated in the initial periods of employment and then do not recur. Later on, however, these early "investments" in hiring and training raise the productivity of employees. Once having made the investment, it is cheaper for the firm to *continue* hiring its previous workers than to hire, at the same wage rate, new ones (who would have to be trained). Likewise, with an investment required for all *new* workers, employers will have to consider not only *current* marginal productivity and labor costs but also *future* marginal productivity and labor costs in deciding whether (and how many) to hire. In short, the presence of investment costs—hiring and training expenses—means that hiring decisions must take into account past, present, and future factors.

To illustrate the hiring decision in the face of labor-investment costs, let us consider a firm that is seeking to determine its employment level over a two-period horizon. Suppose the firm incurs hiring and training costs only in the first period (period 0) and that these *direct outlays* amount to $\$H$ per worker. Suppose also that during the initial period, when workers are undergoing training, their actual marginal product schedule is lowered from MP^* to MP_0 (as shown in Figure 5.2) —in other words, MP^*-MP_0 represents the *implicit* costs of training. In the period after training (period 1), the marginal productivity of trained employees is higher (MP_1). Finally, suppose that the wage a firm must pay each employee is W_0 and W_1 in periods 0 and 1, respectively; for now, we take these wages as given by the market, although we will shortly examine how they are determined.

---

[13]Ronald G. Ehrenberg, "The Impact of the Overtime Premium on Employment and Hours in U.S. Industry," *Western Economic Journal* 19 (June 1971): 199–207.

[14]This section draws heavily on Gary Becker's pioneering work, *Human Capital,* 2nd ed. (New York: National Bureau of Economic Research, 1975); and on Oi, "Labor as a Quasi-Fixed Factor." In what follows, all of the wage and hiring and training cost variables are measured in *real* terms.

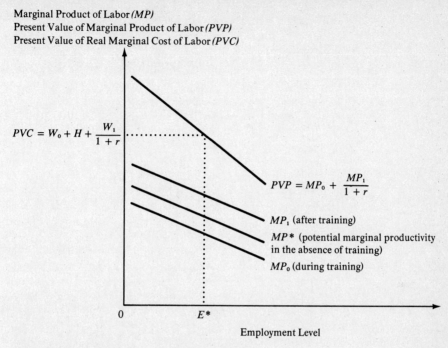

Marginal Product of Labor *(MP)*
Present Value of Marginal Product of Labor *(PVP)*
Present Value of Real Marginal Cost of Labor *(PVC)*

$PVC = W_0 + H + \dfrac{W_1}{1 + r}$

$PVP = MP_0 + \dfrac{MP_1}{1 + r}$

MP_1 (after training)

$MP*$ (potential marginal productivity
in the absence of training)

MP_0 (during training)

0          $E*$

Employment Level

Figure 5.2   Multiperiod Demand for Labor

The Concept of Present Value

In determining its optimal employment level over the two periods, the firm clearly must consider the costs of employing workers in both periods and their marginal products in both periods. A *naive* approach would be to simply add up the costs $(W_0 + W_1 + H)$, add up the marginal products $(MP_0 + MP_1)$, and then stop hiring when the sum of the marginal products that the last worker produces over the two periods is just equal to the sum of his or her wages and hiring and training costs. This approach is naive because it ignores the fact that benefits accruing in the future are worth less to the firm than an equal level of benefits that accrue now. Similarly, costs that occur in the future are less burdensome to the firm than equal dollar costs that occur in the present.

Why should this be the case? The answer hinges on the role of interest rates. A dollar of revenue earned by a firm today can be invested at some market rate of interest so that by the second period it will be worth more than a dollar. Hence, faced with a choice of employing a worker whose marginal product is 5 in period 0 and 2 in period 1, or a worker whose marginal product is 2 in period 0 and 5 in period 1, the firm would prefer the former (if wages for the two workers were equal in each period). The sooner the product is produced and sold, the quicker the firm can gain access to the funds, invest them, and earn interest.[15] Similarly,

---

[15]We are assuming here, of course, that the real price the firm receives for its product is constant and that the real rate of interest is positive.

faced with the option of paying a $100 wage bill today or $100 next period, the firm should prefer the second option. It could earn interest on the $100 in the first period, make the payment in the next period, and have the interest left over. If the firm had made the payment in the initial period, it would not have had the opportunity to earn interest income.

These examples illustrate that firms prefer benefit streams in which the benefits occur as early as possible and prefer cost streams in which the costs occur as late as possible. But how do we compare different benefit and cost streams when benefits and costs occur in more than one period? Economists rely on the concept of *present value,* which we define to be the value *now* of an entire stream of benefits or costs.

Suppose a firm receives the sum of $$B_0$ in the current period and will receive nothing in the next period. How much money could it have in the second period if it invested $$B_0$ at a rate of interest that equals r? It would have its original sum, B_0, plus the interest it earned, rB_0:

$$B_1 = B_0 \,(1 + r). \tag{5.5}$$

Since assets of B_1 can be automatically acquired by investing B_0 at the market rate of interest, B_0 *now and* B_1 *next period are equivalent values.* That is, a person who is offered B_0 now or B_1 in one year would regard the offers as exactly the same as long as $B_1 = B_0 \,(1 + r)$.

Following this line of reasoning, suppose that the firm knows it will receive B_1 in the second period. What is the value of that sum to the firm in the first period? The firm would need to have sum X in the first period in order to invest this sum and wind up with principal plus interest equal to B_1 in period 2:

$$X \,(1 + r) = B_1. \tag{5.6}$$

Dividing both sides by $(1 + r)$,

$$X = \frac{B_1}{1 + r}. \tag{5.7}$$

The quantity X in equation (5.7) is called the *discounted value* of B_1 earned one period in the future.

The *present value* of the firm's earnings over two periods is equal to its earnings in the first period plus the discounted value of its earnings in the second period.[16] Returning to our two-period hiring decision example given at the start of this section, the *present value* of marginal productivity *(PVP)* can now be seen as

$$PVP = MP_0 + \frac{MP_1}{1 + r}. \tag{5.8}$$

---

[16]Earnings in the first period are not discounted because they are received *now,* not in the future.

That is, the value of a worker's marginal productivity *now* to the firm is the marginal productivity in the current period (MP_0) plus the marginal productivity in the second period *discounted* by $(1 + r)$. Likewise, the present value of the real marginal *cost* of labor *(PVC)* is equal to

$$PVC = W_0 + H + \frac{W_1}{1 + r},$$ (5.9)

where r is the market rate of interest. W_0 and H are not discounted because they are incurred in the current period. However, W_1 is discounted by $(1 + r)$ because it is incurred one year into the future.

The present value calculation reduces a stream of benefits or costs to a single number that summarizes a firm's entire stream of revenues or liabilities over different time periods. For example, the *PVC* can be thought of as the answer to the question, "Given that a firm incurs costs of $(W_0 + H)$ this period and W_1 next period per worker, how much does it have to set aside today to be able to cover both periods' costs?" The *PVC* is *less* than $W_0 + H + W_1$, because W_1 is not owed until the second period, and any funds set aside to cover W_1 can be invested now. If it sets aside $W_1/(1 + r)$ to cover its labor cost in the next period, and invests this amount earning a rate of return r, the interest, $r[W_1/(1 + r)]$, plus principal, $W_1/(1 + r)$, available in the next period will just equal W_1. Similarly, the *PVP* can be thought of as the answer to the question, "Given that a worker's marginal product will be MP_0 in this period and MP_1 next period, what is the value of that output stream to the employer today?" The *PVP* is less than $MP_0 + MP_1$ because if the firm were to attempt to borrow against the employee's future marginal product, it could borrow at most $MP_1/(1 + r)$ today and still afford to repay the principal plus interest, $r[MP_1/(1 + r)]$, out of earnings in the second period.[17]

The Demand for Labor

The concept of present value can help clarify what determines the demand-for-labor function in our two-period model. Rather than focusing on the marginal product of labor in each period, an employee's productivity must be summarized

---

[17]More generally, if the firm expects to receive benefits of $B_0, B_1, B_2, \ldots, B_n$ dollars over the current and next n periods, and if it faces the same interest rate, r, in each period, its present value of benefits *(PVB)* is given by

$$PVB = B_0 + \frac{B_1}{1 + r} + \frac{B_2}{(1 + r)^2} + \frac{B_3}{(1 + r)^3} + \ldots + \frac{B_n}{(1 + r)^n}.$$

An analogous expression exists for the present value of costs. The reader should make sure that he or she understands why the denominator of B_2 is $(1 + r)^2$, the denominator of B_3 is $(1 + r)^3$, etc. If one thinks in terms of a series of one-period loans or investments, it should become obvious. For example, X_0 invested for one period yields $X_0 (1 + r)$ at the end of the period. Let us call $X_0 (1 + r) = X_1$. X_0 invested for two periods is equal to its value after one period (X_1) times $(1 + r)$—or $X_2 = X_1 (1 + r)$. But $X_1 = X_0 (1 + r)$, so $X_2 = X_0 (1 + r)^2$. To find the present value of X_2 we divide by $(1 + r)^2$, so that $X_0 = X_2/(1 + r)^2$.

by the *present value* of the marginal-product schedule, which is drawn as the curve *PVP* in Figure 5.2. Similarly, rather than focusing on the hiring and training costs and the wage rates in each period separately, an employer must consider the *present value* of the marginal cost of labor *(PVC)*. To maximize its present value of profits, a firm should employ labor up until the point that adding an *additional* employee yields as much as it costs (when both yields and costs are stated as present values):

$$PVP = PVC, \text{ or } MP_0 + \frac{MP_1}{1 + r} = W_0 + H + \frac{W_1}{1 + r}. \quad (5.10)$$

Given the particular values of W_0, W_1, H, and r that are specified in Figure 5.2, this proves to be the employment level E^*. More generally, the employer's demand-for-labor schedule coincides with the present value of the marginal-product-of-labor schedule.

Now equation (5.10) merely states the familiar profit-maximizing condition —that marginal returns should equal marginal costs—in a multiperiod context. If H were zero, for example, equation (5.10) implies that profits could be maximized when labor is hired so that $MP_0 = W_0$ and $MP_1/(1 + r) = W_1/(1 + r)$—or, since $1 + r$ is the denominator on both sides of the equation, $MP_1 = W_1$. Thus, when H is zero and there are no hiring or training costs, the conditions demonstrated in Chapter 3 are sufficient to guarantee profit maximization in the multiperiod context. However, when H is positive—which means that firms make initial investments in their workers—the conditions for maximizing profits change.

To understand the change in profit-maximizing conditions suggested by equation (5.10), suppose that in the first period the wage the worker receives (W_0) plus the firm's direct outlays (H) exceed the extra worker's output (MP_0). We can call this difference the *net cost* to the firm of hiring an additional worker in the first period (NC_0):

$$NC_0 = W_0 + H - MP_0 > 0. \quad (5.11)$$

In order for the firm to maximize the present value of its profit stream, it must thus get a net *surplus* in the second period—see equation (5.10). If it does not, the firm will not have any incentives to hire the additional worker.

The discounted value of the second period's surplus (G) is defined as:

$$G = \frac{MP_1}{1 + r} - \frac{W_1}{1 + r} = \frac{MP_1 - W_1}{1 + r}. \quad (5.12)$$

From equations (5.10), (5.11), and (5.12), we see that the discounted value of the second-period surplus must equal the net cost (NC_0) in the first period if the firm is to maximize profits:

$$W_0 + H - MP_0 = \frac{MP_1 - W_1}{1 + r}. \tag{5.13}$$

A second-period surplus can *only* exist if wages in that period (W_1) lie *below* marginal product (MP_1). This surplus makes up for the fact that the employer's labor costs in the first period $(W_0 + H)$ were above the worker's marginal product (MP_0).

To this point we have established two things. First, equation (5.10) has shown that in a multiperiod model of labor demand, the firm's demand curve is the same thing as the curve representing the *present value* of labor's marginal product over the periods of hire. Thus, the firm maximizes profits when the present value of its marginal labor costs equals the present value of labor's marginal product. Second, we demonstrated in equation (5.13), that maximizing profits when the firm's labor costs in the first period exceed the worker's first-period marginal product requires wages in the second period to be below marginal productivity in the second period (so that a surplus is generated). The only situations in which a second-period surplus is not necessary to induce the hiring of an additional employee are a. where investment costs (H) are zero in the first period, or b. where investment costs of H exist, but the first-period wage is decreased to such an extent that it equals $MP_0 - H$. In this latter case, employees pay for their own training by accepting a wage in the first period that is decreased by the direct costs of training. Understanding how W_0 and W_1 are determined, then, is central to the task of analyzing the demand for labor in the presence of investment costs. To understand the level and time profile of wages, however, we must first examine the nature of job training.

General and Specific Training

Following Gary Becker, it is useful to conceptually distinguish between two types of training: 1. *general training* that increases an individual's productivity *to many employers* equally and 2. *specific training* that increases an individual's productivity *only at the firm* in which he or she is currently employed.[18] Pure general training might include teaching an applicant basic reading skills or teaching a would-be secretary how to type. Pure specific training might include teaching a worker how to use a machine that is unique to a single employer—or showing him or her the organization of the production process in the plant. The distinction is primarily a conceptual one, because most training contains aspects of both types; however, the distinction does yield some interesting insights.

Suppose (continuing our two-period model) that a firm offers *general* training to its employees and incurs a first-period net cost equal to NC_0 of equation (5.11). This training increases employee marginal productivity to MP_1 in the second period, and the firm scales its wages (W_1) in the second period so that there is a surplus in that period whose present value (G) equals NC_0. What will happen?

---

[18]Becker, *Human Capital.*

The trained employee is worth MP_1 to several other firms, but is getting paid less than MP_1 by the firm doing the training (so that it can obtain the required surplus). The employee can thus get *more* from some other employer—who did not incur training costs and thus will not demand a surplus—than he or she can from the employer offering the training. This situation will induce the employee to quit after training and seek work elsewhere. Assuming all other conditions of employment are the same, the firm would have to pay its employees MP_1 after training to keep them from quitting.

If firms must pay a wage equal to MP_1 after training, they will not be willing to pay for general training of their employees. They either will not offer training or will force the trainees to bear the full cost of their own training by paying wages that are less than marginal product in the period of training by an amount equal to the direct training costs (that is, NC_0 must equal zero). Exceptions to this conclusion can be found in cases where the employee is bound to the firm in some way. For example, the federal government requires employees it has sent to college (in Master of Business Administration programs, for example) to remain in the federal service for a specified number of years or to repay the costs of the training. Similarly, firms may offer to pay for the general training of long-term employees bound to the firm by pension rights or unique promotion opportunities (see Chapter 10 for further discussion).

In contrast, consider an individual who receives *specific training* that increases marginal productivity with the *current* employer to MP_1 in the second period. Since the training is firm-specific, the trainee's marginal product in *other* firms remains at its pretraining level of MP^*. Now the firm that trains the worker *will* have an incentive to offer (and at least partially pay for) the job training, because it can pay a wage above MP^* but below MP_1 in the second period.

Why will it pay above MP^* in the second period? It will do so because if it makes a first-period investment in the worker it does not want the worker to quit. If it pays MP^*, the worker will not have much of an incentive to stay with the firm, since he or she can get MP^* elsewhere too. The higher W_1 is compared to MP^*, the less likely the worker is to quit. Why will the firm pay less than MP_1? As noted earlier, the firm must obtain a surplus in the second period to recoup its first-period investment costs. Thus, the firm prefers *a second-period* wage that is above MP^* and below MP_1:

$$MP^* < W_1 < MP_1. \tag{5.14}$$

This second-period wage is also preferred by employees. If, for example, they were promised a wage equal to MP_1 in the second period, the lack of employer surplus would mean two things. First, employees would be required to pay the *full* cost of training in the first period, and, second, they would live in fear of being laid-off. Since their second-period wage would be equal to their marginal productivity, a firm would not lose much if it laid them off—and *the workers* would lose all of the investment costs incurred in the first period. However, if the workers generate a surplus for the employer, layoff is less likely in the post-training period.

The wage scheme in equation (5.14) thus suggests that both employer and employee should be willing to share in the costs of specific training. If employees bear *all* of the costs of training, then there will be no second-period surplus to protect them from layoff. If employers bear *all* of the costs, they may not be able to pay their employees enough in the second period to guard against their quitting. It is in their *mutual* interest to foster a long-term employment relationship, which can best be done by sharing the investment costs of the first period.

EXAMPLE 5.2

Paternalism in Japan—Is It Rooted in Feudalism or Economics?

In Japan there are many large firms in which employer and employee are mutually committed to a virtual lifetime relationship. These firms almost never lay off workers, and all of their new hires have recently left school. Employees, on the other hand, are given incentives to remain with the firm for their entire career. Wages are strongly linked to seniority, pensions and paid vacations are formulated to encourage a long job tenure, and company loyalty is encouraged through the provision of "paternalistic services," such as company housing, health care, and recreational facilities. James Abegglen describes the consequences of these employment policies:

At whatever level of organization in the Japanese factory, the worker commits himself on entrance to the company for the remainder of his working career. The company will not discharge him even temporarily except in the most extreme circumstances. He will not quit the company for industrial employment elsewhere. He is a member of the company in a way resembling that in which persons are members of families. . . .

While the paternalistic employment relationship described above really pertains to less than half of all Japanese workers—full-time, year-round, predominantly male workers in large firms—the mere existence of such a seemingly permanent employer-employee attachment for so many workers in Japan has drawn much comment. Abegglen views this lifelong relationship as a natural outgrowth of Japan's feudal system prior to industrial development, with its emphasis on the reciprocal loyalty of lord and vassal:

The loyalty of the worker to the industrial organization, the paternal methods of motivating and rewarding the worker, the close involvement of the company in all manner of what seem to Western eyes to be personal and private affairs of the worker—all have parallels with Japan's preindustrial social organization.

Adherents of this explanation seem to conclude that the Japanese system of industrial relations represents a continuation of an ancient, elitist paternalism rather than a system that was consciously chosen for economic reasons by rational industrialists.

An alternative view is that the Japanese system described above finds its roots in profit-maximization calculus. Those who espouse this view argue that Japan's rapid industrialization beginning around 1900 was accompanied by severe shortages of skilled factory workers. Firms competed against each other for skilled labor, and by the end of World War I this fierce competition for workers had led to annual turnover rates of 100 percent for many factories. By 1917 firms were using bribes, cash bonuses, and even physical threats to secure and retain a work force. A government report in 1919 lamented, "The virtue of long and diligent service has been supplanted by a propensity to change jobs."

Faced with such a high degree of employee turnover, firms did not find it profitable to train their own workers; these workers would be gone before they could recoup their investment costs. To reduce the need for constant recruiting, and to induce employees to have long enough job attachments to make training feasible, firms began to offer cash bonuses, company-paid pleasure trips, and shares of company profits to long-term workers. Company housing was provided, and firms took an active interest in improving the quality of worker life both on and off the job. While the "loose" labor markets of the early 1930s provided a setback, industrial growth and attendant labor shortages both during and after World War II fostered the growth of the Japanese system of paternalism throughout the economy. Advocates of this alternative view of Japan's paternalism, such as Koji Taira, argue that the paternalistic system is based more in the need of employers to protect training investments than in feudal tradition.

SOURCES: James C. Abegglen, *The Japanese Factory: Aspects of Its Social Organization* (Glencoe, Ill.: The Free Press, 1958); Clark Kerr, *Industrialization and Industrial Man* (Cambridge, Mass.: Harvard University Press, 1960); Koji Taira, *Economic Development and the Labor Market in Japan* (New York: Columbia University Press, 1970).

Implications of the Theory

Layoffs. One major implication of the presence of specific training is the above-mentioned reluctance of firms to lay off workers in whom they have invested. We have seen that in the post-training period, wages must be less than marginal productivity if the firm is to have any incentives at all to bear some of the initial training costs. This gap between MP_1 and W_1 provides protection against employee layoffs—even in a recession.

Suppose a recession were to occur and cause product demand to fall. The marginal productivity associated with each employment level would fall (from

MP' to *MP''* in Figure 5.3). For workers whose wage was equal to marginal productivity before the recession, this fall would reduce their marginal productivity to *below* their wage—and profit-maximizing employers would reduce employment, as shown in panel (a) of Figure 5.3, in order to maximize profits under the changed market conditions. In terms of Figure 5.3(a), employment would fall from *E'* to *E''*.

For a worker whose wage was *less* than marginal productivity—owing to past specific training—the decline in marginal productivity might *still* leave such

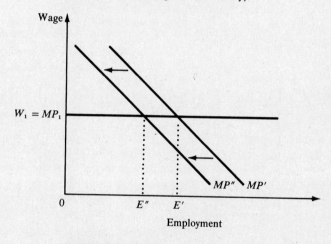

(a) General Training
(a decline in *MP* will reduce employment
for those whose wage = *MP₁* initially)

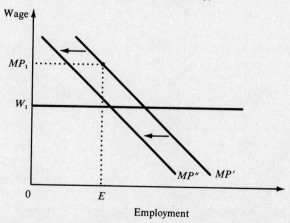

(b) Specific Training
(a decline in *MP* will not necessarily reduce employment
for those whose wage < *MP₁* initially)

Figure 5.3   The Effect of a Decline in Demand on Employment with General and Specific Training

productivity *above* the wage. Firms would not be making enough surplus in the second period to earn back their net labor costs incurred during the training period. However, these costs have already been spent and they cannot get them back. They will not hire and train *new* workers, but neither will they fire the ones they have trained. After all, these trained workers are still generating more than the company is paying them, and to lay them off would only reduce profits further! Thus, as panel (b) of Figure 5.3 shows, workers in whom their employers have invested are shielded to some extent from being laid off in business downturns. Of course, if marginal productivity fell to the point where it was below the wage, even trained workers might be laid off.[19]

Thus, this model suggests that during an economic downswing firms will have an incentive to lay off workers with either no training or with general training but to retain workers who have specific training. Although it is difficult to estimate the extent to which workers have specific training "imbedded" in them, there is some evidence that layoffs are lower for workers with higher skill levels, holding all other things including their *wage rates* constant.[20] Since the divergence between skill (productivity) and wages during the post-training period can be taken as a measure of the extent of specific training, this finding provides some support for the theory.

Labor productivity. A second phenomenon our revised theory of demand can help explain is the fall in average productivity—output per labor hour—that occurs in the early stages of a recession.[21] As demand and output start to fall, firms that have invested in specific training respond by maintaining their specifically trained workers on their payrolls. Such *labor hoarding* causes measured productivity to fall. Of course, the converse of this result is that when demand picks up, firms can increase their output levels without proportionately increasing their employment levels because they, in effect, maintained an *inventory* of skilled labor. Labor hoarding due to specific investments in human capital thus causes average productivity to increase in the early stages of a cyclical expansion and decrease in the early stages of a recession.

Minimum wage effects again. A third implication of our theory has to do with "training" effects of the minimum wage. We have seen that firms will offer *general* training only if the employee fully pays for it. For this to be the case, the employee

---

[19] If the downturn is expected to be short, and if marginal productivity is not too much below the wage, firms might not lay off workers and chance losing them. Why any adjustment would come in the form of layoffs rather than by workers temporarily reducing their wages is discussed in Chapter 18.

[20] For a summary of the evidence, *see* Donald O. Parsons, "Models of Labor Market Turnover: A Theoretical and Empirical Survey" in Ronald G. Ehrenberg, ed., *Research in Labor Economics,* vol. 1 (Greenwich, Conn.: JAI Press, 1977). Parsons also provides evidence on the existence of a negative relationship between quit rates and specific training; as noted earlier, this is another implication of the theory.

[21] *See* the 1977 *Employment and Training Report of the President* (Washington, D.C.: U.S. Government Printing Office, 1977), pp. 23–25.

must receive a first-period wage that is below actual marginal productivity by an amount equal to the direct costs of training. If the minimum wage is set so that receiving such a low wage is precluded, then employers will not offer them training. They may be willing to *hire* workers—if the minimum wage is not above their marginal productivity—but any training would have to take place off the job.

This same analysis would also hold for *specific* training. If the minimum wage prevented the *first* period wage from going low enough, firms offering specific training might *not* be able to offer *second* period wages that are higher than workers' alternative offers. If this is the case, trained workers will always be on the verge of quitting in the second period—which places the firm's first period investment at risk. Under these conditions, firms will have little incentive to offer specific training. Minimum-wage legislation may thus reduce the number of jobs offering training options that are available to low-skilled youths and lower their rates of wage growth. In fact, there is some preliminary evidence that this has occurred.[22]

Credentials or Screening Devices and the Internal Labor Market

The addition of hiring and training costs and other quasi-fixed costs of labor into models of labor demand has been shown in this chapter to lead to numerous insights about firms' employment/hours decisions and about the demand for labor in a multiperiod setting. This final section will sketch several additional extensions of these multiperiod models, including the use of credentials or other screening devices and the internal labor market.

Credentials or Screening Devices

Since firms often bear the costs of hiring and training workers, it is in their interests to make these costs as low as possible. Other things equal, firms should prefer to obtain a given quality work force at the least possible cost. Similarly, they should prefer to hire workers who are fast at learning because such workers could be trained at less cost. Unfortunately, it may prove expensive for firms to extensively investigate the backgrounds of every possible individual who applies for a job to ascertain his or her skill level and ability to undertake training.

One way to reduce these costs is to rely on *credentials,* or *signals,* in the hiring process rather than intensively investigating the qualities of individual applicants.[23] For example, if *on average* college graduates are more productive than high-school graduates, an employer might specify that a college degree is a

[22]Linda Leighton and Jacob Mincer, "Effects of Minimum Wages on Human Capital Formation," in Simon Rottenberg ed. *The Economics of Legal Minimum Wages* (Washington, D. C.: American Enterprise Institute, 1981).

[23]*See* Michael Spence, "Job Market Signaling," *Quarterly Journal of Economics* 87 (August 1973): 355–74.

EXAMPLE 5.3

Coping with Fluctuations in Product Demand: The Use of Product Inventories, Temporary-Help Services, and Reserve Workers

The demand for a firm's product is never constant over a given period. It fluctuates from day to day, week to week, and month to month. If a firm finds it feasible to hold inventories of its finished goods, these fluctuations in demand can be absorbed by *product inventories*—thus permitting the firm to keep its employment and production levels constant during the period. That is, in periods when product demand does not absorb what is produced, the firm stores its unsold output; in periods when demand exceeds output, these stores are drawn down.

Many firms, however, find that the costs of maintaining inventories are very high. Some products are perishable, and they either spoil or become obsolete very quickly. Other products are expensive to make or bulky to store, and keeping inventories of them ties up funds and building space, requires large insurance coverage, and imposes added property taxes on the firm. Still other firms produce services which by their very nature are impossible to produce ahead of demand. How can firms with high inventory costs cope with fluctuating demand?

One way to cope is to hire workers on a temporary basis when product demand is unusually high. As indicated in the text, however, the one-time costs of advertising an opening, screening candidates, and processing the paperwork necessary to put workers on the payroll can be quite high. If the tenure of the job is relatively short, the firm may have insufficient time to recoup these costs. In this case, the firm might consider "renting" workers from a temporary-help service.

Temporary-help services specialize in screening and hiring workers who are then put to work in client plants that need temporary workers. These temporary workers are technically employees of, and receive their paychecks from, the temporary-help service; however, they work under the direction and supervision of the client.

The temporary-help service bills its clients for the time its workers spend under their direction. The hourly charges to its clients are generally *above* the wage the client would pay if it hired directly—a premium the client is willing to pay because it is spared the investment costs associated with hiring. Because obtaining temporary jobs through the temporary-help service also saves employees repeated investment costs associated with searching and applying for the available temporary openings, the employees are willing to take a wage *less* than what they otherwise would receive. The difference between what its clients are charged and what its employees are paid, of course, permits the successful temporary-help service to cover the investment costs necessary in obtaining a match of employer and employee, and to earn a profit.

Hiring of temporary workers is clearly not feasible if a significant amount of specific training must be undertaken before the job can be adequately performed. When job tenure is expected to be short, neither employer nor employee has a long enough time to recoup training costs. (For this reason, temporary help services deal mainly with jobs requiring general training: typing, drafting, simple clerical skills, and so forth.) Where specific training is important, the firm might use *overtime* as a means of meeting fluctuations in product demand. This option, discussed at length in the text, involves paying a substantial wage premium, in some cases leads to problems associated with fatigue, and could cause problems of coordinating production in some industries.

The final option for meeting fluctuations in demand is to hire *reserve workers*—workers who are hired on a full-time basis but who are idle or partially idle some of the time. Some very large plants with easily predicted absentee rates hire and train workers for the specific purpose of filling in for absentees. What may be more common, however, is to keep everyone partially idle during "normal" periods by running production lines at less than maximum speed. During periods of increased demand, production rates can be increased without having to hire more labor or resort to overtime. The cost of reserve workers, of course, is associated with the fact that they are paid even when essentially idle.

Which strategy a firm will choose to cope with product-demand fluctuations depends on the relative costs of each. One study, for example, found greater evidence of the use of reserve workers in industries where product inventory costs are relatively high. If the firm finds that all strategies to meet product-demand fluctuations are too costly, it can exercise its final option and let orders go unfilled—which runs the risk of losing both current and future customers.

SOURCES: Roger LeRoy Miller, "The Reserve Labour Hypothesis: Some Tests of Its Implications," *Economic Journal* 81 (March 1971): 17–35; and Robert S. Smith, "Analysis of Labor Market Adjustments in the Clerical Temporary Help Market: 1953–1960" (unpublished doctoral dissertation, Stanford University), 1971.

requirement for the job. Rather than interviewing and testing all applicants to try to ascertain the productivity of each, the firm may simply select its new employees from the pool of applicants who meet this educational standard. Similarly, if employers believe that married men are less likely to quit their jobs than single men, or that 25-year-olds are less likely to quit than teenagers, they may give preferential treatment to married men and 25-year-olds over single men and teenagers in their hiring decisions.

Such forms of *statistical discrimination*—judging individuals by *group* characteristics—have obvious costs. On the one hand, for example, there may be some high-school graduates who are fully qualified to work for a firm that insists on college graduates. The exclusion of them from the pool of potential applicants imposes costs on them (they do not get the job); however, it also imposes costs on the employer *if* other qualified applicants cannot be readily found. On the other hand, there may be some "lemons" among the group of college graduates, and if the employer hires them he or she may well suffer losses while they are employed. However, if the reduction in hiring costs that arises when *signals* (such as educational credentials, marital status, or age) are used is large, it may prove profitable for an employer to use them even if an occasional lemon sneaks through. Put another way, the total costs of hiring, training, and employing workers may well be lower for some firms when hiring standards are used than when such firms rely upon more intensive investigations of applicant characteristics. (Chapter 11 will return to the issue of statistical discrimination.)

Internal Labor Markets

A major problem with the use of credentials, or screening devices, to predict which applicants will become good employees is that these credentials may only be loosely related to actual productivity on the job. Such personal attributes as dependability, motivation, honesty, and flexibility are difficult to observe using credentials, yet for many jobs such attributes may be crucial. This difficulty with screening is one fact that has induced some firms to adopt a policy of hiring workers at low-level jobs, observing their behavior, and filling all upper-level jobs from within the firm—that is, filling all upper-level vacancies with people whose characteristics have been carefully observed in other jobs the firm has given them to do.

This second approach to the problem of minimizing hiring costs while maximizing the productivity of employees creates an *internal labor market,* because most jobs in the firm are filled from within the ranks of current employees.[24] The hiring done from outside the firm tends to be heavily concentrated at certain low-level "ports of entry." These jobs—such as "general laborer," "machine cleaner," and "packer" for blue-collar applicants or "management trainee" for white-collar applicants—are of sufficiently low responsibility levels that a bad employee cannot do too much damage to the firm or its equipment. However, these jobs do give the firm a chance to observe *actual* productive characteristics of the employees hired, and this information is then used to determine who stays with the firm and how fast and how high employees are promoted.

---

[24]For a detailed discussion of internal labor markets, *see* Peter Doeringer and Michael Piore, *Internal Labor Markets and Manpower Analysis* (Lexington, Mass.: D. C. Heath and Company, 1971). The same general concept has been identified by others as "industrial feudalism," "Balkanization of labor markets," and "property rights" in a job. *See* Arthur Ross, "Do We Have a New Industrial Feudalism?" *American Economic Review* 48, 5 (December 1958): 914; Clark Kerr, "The Balkanization of Labor Markets," in E. Wight Bakke, et al., *Labor Mobility and Economic Opportunity* (Cambridge, Mass.: MIT Press, 1954); and Frederick Meyers, *Ownership of Jobs: A Comparative Study,* Institute of Industrial Relations Monograph Series (Los Angeles: University of California Press, 1964). Other reasons for the existence of internal labor markets are found more recently in Oliver Williamson, et al., "Understanding the Employment Relation: The Analysis of Idiosyncratic Exchange," *Bell Journal of Economics* 16 (Spring 1975): 250–80.

The *benefits* of using an internal labor market to fill vacancies is that the firm knows a lot about the people working for it. Hiring decisions for upper-level jobs in either the blue-collar or white-collar work forces will thus offer few surprises to the firm. The *costs* of using the internal labor market are associated with the restriction of competition for the upper-level jobs to those in the firm. Those in the firm may not be the best employees available, but they are the only ones the firm considers for these jobs. Firms most likely to decide that the benefits of using an internal labor market outweigh the costs are those whose upper-level workers must have a lot of firm-specific knowledge and training that can best be attained by on-the-job learning over the years. For those firms, the number of qualified *outside* applicants for upper-level jobs is relatively small. Firms in the steel, petroleum, and chemical industries tend to rely on internal labor markets to fill vacancies, while those in the garment and shoe industries do not.[25] The former group of industries has highly automated, complicated, and interdependent production technologies that can only be mastered through years on the job. The garment- and shoe-manufacturing industries employ workers who perform certain discrete crafts—skills that are not specific to one firm.

As noted earlier, firms engaged in *specific training* will want to ensure that they obtain a stable, long-term work force—which can learn quickly and perform well later on. For these firms, the internal labor market offers two attractions. First, it allows the firm to observe workers on the job, where it can see firsthand who learns quickly, who is easily motivated, who is dependable, and so forth, and thus make better decisions about which workers will be the recipients of later, perhaps very expensive, training. Second, the internal labor market tends to foster an attachment to the firm by its employees. They know that outsiders will not be considered for upper-level vacancies and that they, therefore, have an inside track on job vacancies. If they quit the firm, they would lose this privileged position. They are thus motivated to become long-term employees of the firm. The full implications of internal labor markets for wage policies within the firm will be discussed in the chapter on compensation (Chapter 10).

Policy Application: Why Do Employers Discriminate in Hiring?

It is commonly asserted that older workers and women are not given the same preference as *prime-aged* men (men between 25 and 55) in filling many jobs—especially the better-paying ones. While this preference may be rooted in prejudice, there may also be an underlying, nondiscriminatory rationale for it. Chapter 11 will discuss discrimination, but this example will point out that what *appears* to be prejudice may be employer behavior designed to avoid losses on hiring and training investments.

To illustrate how the presence of hiring and training costs bears on the issue

---

[25]Doeringer and Piore, *Internal Labor Markets and Manpower Analysis,* p. 43.

of apparent age or sex discrimination, let us assume two people apply for a job where the employer is intending to make a first-period investment of H in hiring and training costs. It is expected that one applicant will be with the firm for two periods, while the other will remain for three periods. Which will the firm prefer to hire?

If it were possible to find workers and train them without cost, firms would not care about the length of their tenure. If one worker quit, a replacement could easily and costlessly be found. Where hiring a worker involves an initial investment by the firm, however, employers will prefer to hire workers with relatively long expected tenures. The longer an employee is expected to be with the firm, the more likely it is the firm will recoup its initial investment costs. Thus, if the two applicants in our example were alike in every respect except their expected length of tenure with the firm, the one expected to remain with the firm for three periods would be preferred.

This preference can be demonstrated by referring back to equation (5.12). Equation (5.12) calculates the present value of a worker's post-training surplus *(G)* for a case where he or she will be employed for just one period after training. To repeat, the present value of the surplus in cases where there is *one* post-training period—which we will call G_1—is calculated as:

$$G_1 = \frac{MP_1 - W_1}{1 + r}. \tag{5.15}$$

If there are *two* post-training periods of employment, the present value of a firm's surplus is found by adding to G_1 the discounted value of the surplus in the second post-training period. The *undiscounted* surplus in this period is the difference between marginal productivity and wages *(MP_2 − W_2)*. However, because this surplus occurs farther into the future than the first period's surplus, it must be more heavily discounted when calculating present value. This is done by dividing *(MP_2 − W_2)* by $(1 + r)^2$—the rationale for which is given in footnote 17. Thus, the present value of a surplus derived over two periods (G_2) is:

$$G_2 = \frac{MP_1 - W_1}{1 + r} + \frac{MP_2 - W_2}{(1 + r)^2}. \tag{5.16}$$

It is obvious, by comparing G_2 and G_1, that the post-training surplus a firm can expect to gain from a worker increases as the expected length of the worker's tenure with the firm goes up, if other things are equal. That is, if the differences between marginal productivity and wages are the same for two workers, the one with the longer tenure will generate more post-training "surplus" for the firm.

Applicants who are very close to retirement will not be seriously considered for jobs that require large employer hiring or training investments (*unless* they accept a low post-training wage). That is, if post-training wages are equal, firms will tend to prefer prime-aged applicants to equally productive older ones whenever there are substantial employer hiring or training investments involved, because the older applicants may retire before the firm can recoup its investment costs. Older workers could redress this imbalance in hiring preferences only by agreeing to work for a lower wage than younger applicants or by paying at least some of the hiring and training costs themselves—conditions that themselves might raise charges of discrimination!

This same reasoning can help explain why women may not have had ready access to jobs requiring sizable initial employer investments. Women—or at least *married* women—have tended to enter and leave the labor force more often than men. Chapter 8 will show, for example, that many married women enter the labor force in their early 20s, drop out to care for children, and then re-enter later on. Chapter 18 will also note that the average white woman worker, aged 25–59, is 15 times more likely to go from having a job to being out of the labor force than a comparable male worker during a one-month period. (For blacks, the probability of going from employment to out of the labor force is 3 times higher for females.) The result of this movement in and out of the labor force among women is that the average length of job tenure for males is about twice what it is for women. That is, the average male worker in 1978 had been on his current job for 4.5 years, while the average woman had been on her job for just 2.6 years.[26]

The shorter average job tenure among women could legitimately induce employers contemplating hiring and training investments to be wary of investing in female workers. This concern has an understandable economic rationale to it, but it also offers a good example of what we earlier called *statistical discrimination* (judging individuals by the characteristics of the group to which they belong). In this case, statistical discrimination could have unfortunate consequences for women who *do* plan continuous careers outside the home. For example, single (never-married) women, aged 25–34, have about the same average job tenure (2.6 years) as men of that age (2.7 years). For single women aged 35–44 the typical length of time on one's current job is 5.7 years, while for men it is only slightly higher (6.9 years). In contrast, the typical married woman worker, aged 35–44, has only been on her job for 3.5 years. Thus, women who never marry are much more likely to have job tenures equivalent to the typical male worker, but a firm using rather general hiring standards (such as age and sex) might not make such distinctions.

In summary, two policy-related points can be drawn from this discussion of hiring and training investments. First, employers may have legitimate economic reasons for preferring to hire employees who are expected to have relatively long job tenures *when* there are significant employer hiring or training investments involved. Thus, it would not necessarily be maliciousness or prejudice that causes older workers and women to have reduced access to jobs that typically require such investments.

---

[26]U.S. Bureau of Labor Statistics, *Job Tenure Declines As Work Force Changes,* Special Labor Force Report No. 235 (Washington, D.C.: U.S. Government Printing Office, 1979). As families become smaller, as household duties become more evenly divided among men and women, and as more women seek *careers,* it is very likely that the labor force behavior of women and men will become more similar.

The second point, however, is that individuals within groups vary, and using group averages to estimate an individual's expected tenure may do a disservice to atypical members of the group. We have seen, for example, that women who never marry have much longer job tenures than married women. Taking this fact into account when screening applicants would make hiring decisions more "fair" to single women but would probably entail added costs to employers. Firms would have to collect data on their applicants to attempt accurate guesses as to which of their female applicants would remain in the labor force continuously or would never marry.

REVIEW QUESTIONS

1. Both low-skilled workers and high-paid professors have high rates of voluntary quits. What do they have in common that leads to a high quit rate?
2. Wages in the U.S. Postal Service have been attacked for being higher than wages elsewhere for people of the same age and education. The Postal Service answers that they *must* pay higher wages than workers could get elsewhere in order to keep their quit rate below the quit rate in other jobs. Are there circumstances under which this argument has any merit?
3. Suppose the government wants to reduce recidivism of ex-convicts by improving their employment prospects and job stability. Suppose further that the government is considering subsidizing half of employer costs incurred in training ex-cons for jobs in their plants. How will this subsidy affect the job prospects and stability of ex-cons, assuming ex-cons are the only group subsidized?
4. Unemployment insurance is financed through a payroll tax levied on the employer. Assume that taxes paid = tax rate $\times$ firm's payroll. Generally speaking, the tax rate increases when a firm lays off workers. Assuming the firm is unable to shift the tax, what effect will abolition of this tax have on the firm's decision to:
   a. lay off workers?
   b. hire workers?
   c. schedule overtime work?
5. In its presentation to the Democratic and Republican national platform committees, the AFL-CIO proposed the following changes to the Fair Labor Standards Act in 1976:
   1. Raise the federal minimum wage to $3.00 per hour (the minimum was then less than $3.00);
   2. Increase overtime pay to double the standard wage (it was then 1½ times the standard);
   3. Reduce the standard work week to 35 hours (down from 40), so that overtime pay would be owed to a worker after 35 hours per week.
   Analyze the employment effects of these proposals.

SELECTED READINGS

Gary Becker, *Human Capital,* 2nd. ed. (New York: National Bureau of Economic Research, 1975).

Peter Doeringer and Michael Piore, *Internal Labor Markets and Manpower Analysis* (Lexington, Mass.: D. C. Heath, 1971).

Ronald G. Ehrenberg and Paul L. Schumann, *Longer Hours or More Jobs? An Investigation of Amending Hours Legislation to Create Employment* (Ithaca N.Y.: New York State School of Industrial and Labor Relations, Cornell University, 1982).

Walter Oi, "Labor as a Quasi-Fixed Factor," *Journal of Political Economy* 70 (December 1962): 538–55.

Michael Spence, "Job Market Signaling," *Quarterly Journal of Economics* 87 (August 1973): 355–74.

Oliver Williamson et al. "Understanding the Employment Relation: The Analysis of Idiosyncratic Exchange," *Bell Journal of Economics* 16 (Spring 1975): 250–80.

Chapter 6

SUPPLY OF LABOR TO THE ECONOMY: THE DECISION TO WORK

This and the next three chapters will focus on issues of *worker* behavior. That is, Chapters 6–9 will discuss and analyze various aspects of *labor-supply* behavior. Labor-supply decisions can be roughly divided into two categories. The first category, which is addressed in this chapter, includes decisions about whether to work at all, and if so, how long to work. Questions that must be answered include whether to participate in the labor force, whether to seek part-time or full-time work, and the length of one's working life. The second category of decisions, which is addressed in Chapters 7–9, deals with the questions that must be faced by a person who has decided to seek work: the occupation or general class of occupations in which to seek offers (Chapters 7–8), and the geographical area in which the offers will be sought (Chapter 9).

This chapter begins with some basic facts concerning labor-force participation rates and hours of work and then moves on to an analysis of the decision to work for pay. This analytical framework is useful in the context of formulating income-maintenance programs.

Trends in Labor-Force Participation and Hours of Work

When a person actively seeks work, he or she is, by definition, in the *labor force*. As pointed out in Chapter 2, the *labor-force participation rate* is the percentage of a given population that either has a job or is looking for one. Thus, one clearcut statistic important in measuring people's willingness to work outside the home is the labor-force participation rate.

Perhaps the most revolutionary change taking place in the labor market today is the tremendous increase in the proportion of women—particularly married women—working outside the home. Table 6.1 shows the extraordinary dimensions of this change. As late as 1950, only 21.6 percent of married women were in the labor force. By 1960 this percentage had risen to 30.6 percent, and by 1980 it had increased to 50.2 percent—almost two and a half times what it had been in 1950.

We need not dwell here on the social changes that have been associated with this increasing tendency for women to seek work outside the home. Changes in family income, child-rearing practices, and the family relationship itself are obvious. Less obvious are the effects on the demand for education by females and on the unemployment rate which will be discussed in Chapters 8, 18, and 19. The longer life span of females is another factor that will affect labor supply and will become an important issue, for example, in funding pension plans (see Chapter 10). Of paramount concern in this chapter are the factors that have influenced this fundamental change in the propensity of women to seek work outside the home.

A second major trend in labor-force participation is the decrease in the length of careers for males—as can be seen in Table 6.2. The overall labor-force participation rate of men has been falling, as was noted in Chapter 2, but the really substantial decreases have been among the very young and the very old. The labor-force participation rate of teenagers fell from 61.1 percent in 1900 to 35.8 percent in 1970—a 41 percent decline—although the growth of the student labor force since World War II has slowed the decrease somewhat. The decrease for

Table 6.1 Labor Force Participation Rates of Females over 16 Years of Age, by Marital Status, 1900–1980 (percent)

Year	All Females	Single	Widowed, Divorced	Married
1900	20.6 (100)	45.9 (100)	32.5 (100)	5.6 (100)
1910	25.5 (124)	54.0 (118)	34.1 (105)	10.7 (191)
1920	24.0 (117)			9.0 (161)
1930	25.3 (123)	55.2 (120)	34.4 (106)	11.7 (209)
1940	26.7 (130)	53.1 (116)	33.7 (104)	13.8 (246)
1950	29.7 (144)	53.6 (117)	35.5 (109)	21.6 (386)
1960	35.7 (173)	42.9 (94)	38.7 (119)	30.6 (546)
1970	41.6 (202)	50.9 (111)	39.5 (122)	39.5 (705)
1980	51.7 (250)	61.2 (133)	44.1 (136)	50.2 (896)

Note: Index numbers, with 1900 = 100, are shown in parentheses.

SOURCES: 1900–1950: Clarence D. Long, *The Labor Force Under Changing Income and Employment* (Princeton: Princeton University Press), 1958, Table A-6.

1960: U.S. Department of Commerce, Bureau of the Census, *Census of Population, 1960: Employment Status* (Subject Reports PC(2)-6A), Table 4.

1970: U.S. Department of Commerce, Bureau of the Census, *Census of Population, 1970: Employment Status and Work Experience* (Subject Reports PC(2)-6A), Table 3.

1980: U.S. President, *Employment and Training Report of the President, 1980* (Washington, D.C.: U.S. Government Printing Office, 1981), Tables A2, B1. (The data for 1980 are not strictly comparable because they are derived from a monthly survey, not the decennial census).

Table 6.2 Labor Force Participation Rates For Males, by Age, 1900–1980 (percent)

	Age Groups				
Year	14–19	20–24	25–44	45–64	Over 65
1900	61.1 (100)	91.7 (100)	96.3 (100)	93.3 (100)	68.3 (100)
1910	56.2 (92)	91.1 (99)	96.6 (100)	93.6 (100)	58.1 (85)
1920	52.6 (86)	90.9 (99)	97.1 (101)	93.8 (101)	60.1 (88)
1930	41.1 (67)	89.9 (98)	97.5 (101)	94.1 (101)	58.3 (85)
1940	34.4 (56)	88.0 (96)	95.0 (99)	88.7 (95)	41.5 (61)
1950	39.9 (65)	82.8 (90)	92.8 (96)	87.9 (94)	41.6 (61)
1960	38.1 (62)	86.1 (94)	95.2 (99)	89.0 (95)	30.6 (45)
1970	35.8 (59)	80.9 (88)	94.4 (98)	87.3 (94)	25.0 (37)
1980			95.4 (99)	82.2 (88)	19.1 (28)

Note: Index numbers, with 1900 = 100, are shown in parentheses.

SOURCES: 1900–1950: Clarence D. Long, *The Labor Force Under Changing Income and Employment* (Princeton: Princeton University Press), 1958, Table A-2.

1960: U.S. Department of Commerce, Bureau of the Census, *Census of Population, 1960: Employment Status,* Subject Reports PC(2)-6A, Table 1.

1970: U.S. Department of Commerce, Bureau of the Census, *Census of Population, 1970:* Employment Status and Work Experience, Subject Reports PC(2)-6A Table 1.

1980: U.S. President, *Employment and Training Report of the President, 1981* (Washington, D.C.: U.S. Government Printing Office, 1980), Table A2. (The data for 1980 are not strictly comparable because they are derived from a monthly survey, not the decennial census. Reliable data for males under 25 are unavailable.)

men over 65 has been even more dramatic—from 68.3 percent in 1900 to 25 percent in 1970 and down to 19 percent by 1980. Participation rates for men of "prime age" have declined only slightly. Clearly, men are starting their careers later and ending them earlier than they were at the beginning of this century.

Other measures reflecting the decisions people make about work are the weekly hours of work, the fraction of people who work *part-time,* and the proportion of people who hold more than one job ("moonlighting"). It is not common for people to think of the *hours* of work as being a *supply* variable that is subject to *employee* choice. After all, don't employers—in responding to the factors discussed in Chapter 5—establish the hours of work? They do, of course, but this does not mean that employees have no choice of, or influence on, their working hours. The *weekly* hours of work offered by employers vary to some extent, so that in choosing employers the worker can also choose hours of work. The range of choice may be limited—70 percent of all full-time plant workers normally worked a 40-hour week in 1973, for example, and most of the rest were within 5 hours of that—but choice does exist. Among full-time, nonsupervisory office workers in 1973, only 59 percent worked 40 hours a week, while 17 percent worked 37½ hours, and 13 percent worked 35-hour weeks.[1] Moreover, firms with

---

[1] U.S. Department of Labor Employment Standards Administration, *1973 Survey of Establishment Characteristics and Practices* (Washington, D.C.: U.S. Government Printing Office, 1979), Table 15.

the same 40-hour standard work week will offer different *yearly* hours of work because of different vacation and holiday policies. Finally, *occupational* choice has a working-hours dimension. The weekly or yearly hours of work are different if one chooses to become a teacher rather than an accountant, a retail clerk rather than a traveling sales representative, or a Wall Street lawyer rather than a small-town one.

Thus employees can, in effect, exercise some choice over their hours of work in the short run by choosing their employment. In the long run, a similar mechanism gives employees some influence on working hours. If employees receiving an hourly wage of $X for 40 hours per week really wanted to work only 30 hours at $X per hour, some enterprising employer would seize on their dissatisfaction and offer jobs with 30-hour weeks—ending up with a more satisfied work force in the process. As noted below, large declines in the average hours worked per week took place in this century well before the advent of unions and of federal legislation concerning hours of work.

Table 6.3 displays the historical change in *actual* weekly hours of work in this century after correcting for the fact that these hours tend to rise in prosperity and fall in recessions.[2] What the table shows is that weekly hours fell steadily until the 1940s but since then have more or less stabilized. Overall, the typical manufacturing worker has 16 more hours of leisure each week than he or she had in

Table 6.3 Average Weekly Hours Actually Worked by Manufacturing Production Workers during the Peak Employment Years in Each Business Cycle, 1900–1973 (excluding 1940–45)

	Average Hours Worked	*Average per Decade Decline in Hours Worked*
1901	54.3	
1906	55.0	
1913	50.9	
1919	46.1	2.2
1923	48.9	
1926	47.8	
1929	48.0	4.6
1948	38.8	
1953	38.6	
1956	38.2	0.3
1969	38.3	
1973	38.0	

SOURCE: The data for 1900–1957 were taken from Ethel Jones, "New Estimates of Hours of Work Per Week and Hourly Earnings, 1900–1957," *Review of Economics and Statistics,* November 1963: 374–85. Data for 1969 and 1973 were calculated from the *Annual Survey of Manufactures,* which contain worker hours worked (exclusive of vacations, sick leave, and holidays).

---

[2] Chapter 2 noted, when defining wages and fringe benefits, that hours of *actual* work and the hours for which an employee is *paid* are two different things. Since World War II, the *paid* hours of work are greater than the *actual* hours of work because of the growing prevalence of paid holidays and paid vacations.

1901—virtually an entire waking day! Yet perhaps equally worth emphasizing is that almost all of this change came in the first 45 years of this century—much of it in the first 30 years when unions and federal legislation could not have exerted much influence. An explanation for this must include an analysis of factors influencing both the demand for, and supply of, weekly hours per worker. The supply factors are considered in this chapter, while the demand-side influences were treated in Chapter 5.

Table 6.4 contains data indicating that the fraction of employed workers who voluntarily work part-time (less than 35 hours per week) has risen from 10.7 percent in 1963 to 14.4 percent in 1977. Partly this rise has occurred because the fastest growing groups in the labor force are teenagers and women—groups for which part-time employment is relatively common. However, it is obvious from Table 6.4 that all major labor-force groups have experienced an increase in the proportion of their members who work part-time.

In contrast to trends in part-time employment, there appears to be no trend in the percentage of workers holding two or more jobs. Since 1956, the proportion of employed workers holding two or more jobs has fluctuated around 5 percent —achieving lows of 4.5 percent in 1959 and 1974 and a high of 5.7 percent in 1963. In 1977 exactly 5 percent of employed workers were "moonlighters."

Because labor is the most abundant factor of production, it is fair to say that this country's well-being is heavily dependent on the willingness of its people to work. As we will demonstrate, leisure and other ways of spending time that do not involve work for pay are also important in generating well-being; however, our economy relies heavily on goods and services produced for market transactions. Therefore, it is important to understand the *work-incentive* effects of higher wages and incomes, different kinds of taxes, and various forms of income maintenance programs.

The question of work incentives, for example, will become of critical importance as our population—through longer life spans and a declining birth rate— gradually becomes older. When this happens, there will be a period when relatively few people of working age will have to support a large number of retirees. Their ability to do this and still maintain current standards of living obviously depends on the age at which older people retire and the fraction of the working-age population in the labor force.

Table 6.4 Percentage of Employed Persons Working Part-Time Voluntarily, 1963 and 1977 (in percent)

Group	1963	1977
All workers	10.7	14.4
Males, 20 years and over	3.5	5.0
Females, 20 years and over	19.5	21.3
Both sexes, 16–19	37.8	45.5

Note: A part-time worker is one who works between 1 and 34 hours a week.

SOURCE: U.S. Department of Labor, Bureau of Labor Statistics, *Handbook of Labor Statistics 1978* (Washington D.C.: U.S. Government Printing Office), Table 21.

A Theory of the Decision to Work

The decision to work is ultimately a decision about how to spend time. One way to use one's available time is to spend it in pleasurable leisure activities. The other major way in which people use time is to work.[3] One can work around the home, performing such *household production* as raising children, sewing, building, or even growing food. Alternatively, one can work for pay and use one's earnings to purchase food, shelter, clothing, and child care.

Because working for pay and engaging in household production are two ways of getting the same jobs done, we will ignore the distinction between them and treat work activities as working for pay. We will therefore be characterizing the decision to work as a choice between leisure and working for pay. Most of the crucial factors affecting work incentives can be understood in this context.

If we regard the time spent eating, sleeping, and otherwise maintaining ourselves as more or less fixed by natural laws, then the discretionary time we have (16 hours a day, say) can be allocated to either work or leisure. Since the amount of discretionary time spent on leisure is time not spent on working, and vice versa, the *demand for leisure* can be considered the reverse side of the coin labeled *supply of labor.* It is actually more convenient to analyze work incentives in the context of the demand for leisure—because one can apply the standard analysis of the demand for any good to the demand for leisure—and then simply subtract leisure hours from total discretionary hours available to obtain the *labor-supply* effects.

A Verbal Analysis of the Labor/Leisure Choice

Since we have chosen to analyze work incentives in the context of the demand for leisure, it is instructive to briefly consider the factors that affect the demand for any good. Basically, the demand for a good is a function of three factors:

1. the *opportunity cost* of the good (which is often but not always equal to *market price*),
2. one's level of *wealth,* and
3. one's set of *preferences.*

For example, heating oil consumption will vary with the *cost* of such oil; as that cost rises, consumption will tend to fall unless one of the other two factors intervene. As *wealth* rises people generally want larger and warmer houses that obviously require more oil to heat.[4] Even if the price of energy and the level of personal wealth were to remain constant, the demand for energy could rise if a

---

[3]Another category of activity is to spend time acquiring skills or doing other things that enhance one's future earnings capacity. These activities will be discussed in Chapters 8–9.

[4]When the demand for a good rises with wealth, economists say the good is a *normal good.* If demand falls as wealth rises, the good is said to be an *inferior good* (traveling or commuting by bus is sometimes cited as an example of an inferior good).

falling birth rate and lengthened life span resulted in a higher proportion of the population being aged and therefore wanting warmer houses. This change in the composition of the population amounts to a shift in the overall *preferences* for warmer houses and thus leads to a change in the demand for heating oil.

To summarize, the demand (*D*) for any good can be characterized as a function of opportunity costs (*C*) and wealth (*V*):

$$D = f(\overset{-}{C}, \overset{+}{V}), \tag{6.1}$$

where *f*—the particular relationship between demand and the variables *C* and *V* for an individual—depends on preferences. The notation above *C* and *V* indicates the direction in which the demand for a good is expected to go when the variable in question *increases*—*holding the other one constant.* The demand would move in the opposite direction if *C* or *V* were to decrease.

Note: Economists usually assume that preferences are given and not subject to immediate change. For policy purposes, the changes in *C* and *V*—not changes in the function *f*—are of paramount interest to us in explaining changes in demand, because *C* and *V* are most susceptible to change by government policy. For the most part, we will assume preferences are *given* and *fixed* at any point in time.[5]

To apply this general analysis of demand to the demand for leisure, we must first ask, "What is the opportunity cost of leisure?" The cost of spending an hour watching television is basically what one could earn if one had spent that hour working. Thus, the opportunity cost of an hour of leisure is very closely related to one's *wage rate*—so closely related, in fact, that to simplify the analysis we will say that leisure's opportunity cost *is* the wage rate.[6]

Next, we must understand and be able to measure wealth. Naturally, wealth includes a family's holdings of bank accounts, financial investments, and physical property. Workers' skills can also be considered assets, since these skills can be, in effect, rented out to employers for a price. The more one can get in wages, the larger is the value of one's human assets. Unfortunately, it is not usually possible to directly measure people's wealth. It is much easier to measure the *returns* from that wealth, because data on total *income* are readily available from government surveys. Economists thus often use total income as an indicator of total wealth, since the two are conceptually so closely related.[7]

---

[5]On occasion the government attempts to influence consumption patterns of people by changing preferences rather than prices. For example, rather than raising cigarette taxes to discourage cigarette consumption, the federal government in the 1970s prohibited cigarette manufacturers from advertising on television, and it even sponsored radio and television campaigns against smoking. The effectiveness of these attempts to change preferences is difficult to assess.

[6]This assumes that individuals can work as many hours as they want at a fixed wage rate. While this assumption may seem overly simplistic, it will not lead to wrong conclusions with respect to the issues analyzed in this chapter. More rigorously, it should be said that leisure's *marginal* opportunity cost is the *marginal* wage rate (the wage one could receive for an extra hour of work).

[7]The best indicator of wealth is one's *permanent,* or long-run potential, *income.* One's current income may differ from one's permanent income for a variety of reasons (unemployment, illness, or being a student, etc.). For our purposes here, however, the distinction between current and permanent income is not too important.

If we replace the general demand function in equation (6.1) with the *demand for leisure function,* it would become equation (6.2):

$$D_L = f(\overset{-}{W}, \overset{+}{Y}), \tag{6.2}$$

where D_L is the demand for leisure hours, W is the wage rate, Y is total income, and f (as before) depends on preferences people have for leisure independent of W and Y. The signs over W and Y indicate what happens to the demand for leisure if the variable in question increases, holding the other variable constant.

If income increases, holding wages (and f) constant, equation (6.2) asserts that the demand for leisure goes up. Put differently, *if income increases (decreases), holding wages constant, hours of work will go down (up).* Economists call this predicted response the *income effect.* The income effect is based on the simple notion that as incomes rise, holding leisure's opportunity cost constant, people will want to consume more leisure (which means working less).

Using algebraic notation, the income effect is defined as the change in the hours of work (ΔH) produced by a change in income (ΔY), holding wages constant (W):

$$\text{Income Effect} = \frac{\Delta H}{\Delta Y}\Big|_{\overset{-}{W}} < 0. \tag{6.3}$$

We say the income effect is *negative* because the *sign* of the *fraction* in equation (6.3) is *negative.* If income goes up (wages held constant), hours of work fall. If income goes down, hours of work increase. The numerator (ΔH) and denominator (ΔY) in equation (6.3) move in opposite directions, giving a negative sign to the income effect.

Equation (6.2) also suggests that *if income is held constant, an increase (decrease) in the wage rate will reduce (increase) the demand for leisure—thereby increasing (decreasing) work incentives.* This *substitution effect* occurs because as the opportunity costs of leisure rise (income held constant), working hours are substituted for leisure hours.

In contrast to the income effect, the substitution effect is *positive.* Because this effect is the change in hours of work (ΔH) induced by a change in the wage (ΔW), holding income constant (Y), the substitution effect can be written as:

$$\text{Substitution Effect} = \frac{\Delta H}{\Delta W}\Big|_{\overset{-}{Y}} > 0. \tag{6.4}$$

Because numerator (ΔH) and denominator (ΔW) always move in the same direction—at least in theory—the substitution effect has a positive sign.

At times, it is possible to observe situations or programs that create "pure" income or substitution effects. Usually, however, both effects are simultaneously present—often working against each other.

A "pure" income effect. Winning a state lottery is an example of the income effect by itself. The winnings enhance one's wealth (income) *independent* of the hours of work. Thus, income is increased *without* a change in the compensation received from an hour of work. In this case, the income effect induces the person to consume more leisure, thereby reducing the willingness to work. (If the change in nonlabor income were *negative,* on the other hand, the income effect suggests that people would work *more.*)

A "pure" substitution effect. In the 1980 Presidential campaign, one of the candidates—John Anderson—proposed a program aimed at conserving gasoline. His plan consisted of raising the gasoline tax but offsetting this increase by a reduced Social Security tax payable by individuals on their earnings. The idea was to raise the price of gasoline without reducing people's overall spendable income.

For our purposes, this plan is interesting because it creates a pure substitution effect on labor supply. Social Security revenues are collected by a tax on earnings, so reductions in the tax are, in effect, an increase in the wage rate.[8] However, for the average person, the increased wealth associated with this wage increase is exactly offset by increases in the gasoline tax.[9] Hence, wages are increased while income is held more or less constant. This program would thus create a substitution effect that induces people to work more hours.

EXAMPLE 6.1

Incentives and Absenteeism

The problem of employee absenteeism is significant and tending to grow over time. A 1947 study of absences in manufacturing industries suggested a daily absentee rate of about 4.3 percent, while recent manufacturing data indicate absentee rates are currently around 7 percent. Are workers becoming more sickly? Are they less motivated? Is the workplace more alienating? Is management more inept? These are some of the many questions that arise concerning this problem. The concepts introduced in this chapter suggest yet another question: is absenteeism caused to some extent by the structure of compensation?

As documented in Chapter 5 (and again discussed in Chapter 10),

---

[8]Social Security taxes are levied on yearly earnings up to some maximum—$35,700 in 1983. Once that maximum level is reached within a year, no more Social Security taxes are paid. People whose yearly earnings exceed the base experience no change in the marginal opportunity cost of leisure, because an additional hour of work per year is not subject to Social Security taxes anyway. However, the marginal opportunity cost of leisure would be increased for many—if not most—workers.

[9]An increase in the price of gasoline will reduce the income people have left for expenditures on nongasoline consumption only if the demand for gasoline is inelastic. In this case, the percentage reduction in gasoline consumption is smaller than the percentage increase in price; total expenditures on gasoline would thus rise. Our analysis assumes this to be the case.

fringe benefits form a large and increasing proportion of total compensation. What has happened over time is that employees have received an ever larger proportion of their pay increases in the form of fringe benefits rather than wages. In some cases, these fringe-benefit packages have included paid sick leave provisions, which serve as an obvious inducement for a certain amount of absenteeism. Because workers can call in sick for a specified number of days per year without losing any pay, it is not surprising that a study of absenteeism among public school teachers found that it was greater in districts with more generous paid sick leave provisions.

However, the growth of fringe benefits frequently offers incentives for greater absenteeism independent of paid sick leave. It is often the case that an absence causes a worker to lose his or her daily wage, but the value of many fringe benefits is invariant with respect to an absence. (For example, the value of a worker's medical insurance policy or future pension benefits is not affected by absence from work in most cases.) Thus, when compensation is increased in the form of fringe benefits rather than wages, an *income effect* on the demand for leisure is created *without a corresponding substitution effect!*

The increased use of fringe benefits as a form of compensation has had a possibly profound effect on the incentives to come to work on days when one is feeling slightly ill, in need of a "break," or has a personal problem. The increased compensation that has accompanied economic growth tends to induce greater consumption of all normal goods, including leisure; however, to the extent *wages* are not increased, the price of leisure is not raised. Thus, the changing structure of compensation suggests that relatively stronger income effects, and correspondingly weaker substitution effects, on the demand for leisure have been accompanying economic growth in recent years.

Because absenteeism is one way that leisure is consumed, it may well be that rising absenteeism is at least partially caused by the increased use of fringe benefits in pay packages. Indeed, absenteeism appears to be higher where fringe benefits are more extensively used; for example, rates are higher in manufacturing than retail trade, and higher in large manufacturing plants than small ones. Moreover, a careful intra-industry statistical study has uncovered evidence suggesting that a compensation package weighted toward fringe benefits rather than wages will be accompanied by greater absenteeism.

Sources: Max Kossoris, "Illness Absenteeism in Manufacturing Plants in 1947," *Monthly Labor Review* 66 (March 1948): 265–67. Janice N. Hedges, "Absence from Work—Measuring the Hours Lost," *Monthly Labor Review* 100 (October 1977): 16–23. Donald Winkler, "The Effects of Sick-Leave Policy on Teacher Absenteeism," *Industrial and Labor Relations Review* 33 (January 1980): 232–40. Steven G. Allen, "Compensation, Safety and Absenteeism: Evidence from the Paper Industry," *Industrial and Labor Relations Review* 34 (January 1981): 207–18.

Both effects occur when wages rise. While the above examples illustrate situations in which the income or substitution effects are present by themselves, normally both effects are present—often working in opposite directions. The presence of both effects creates ambiguity in predicting the overall labor supply response in many cases. Consider the case of a person who receives a wage increase.

The labor-supply response to a simple wage change will involve *both* an income and a substitution effect. The *income effect* is the result of the worker's enhanced wealth (or potential income) after the increase. For a given level of work effort, he or she now has a greater command over resources than before (because more income is received for any given number of hours of work). The *substitution effect* results from the fact that the wage increase raises the opportunity costs of leisure. Because the actual labor supply response is the *sum* of the income and substitution effects, we cannot predict the response in advance; theory simply does not tell us which effect is stronger.

If the *income* effect is dominant, the person will respond to a wage increase by decreasing his or her labor supply. This decrease will be *smaller* than if the same change in wealth were due to an increase in *nonlabor* wealth, because the substitution effect is present and acts as a moderating influence. However, in the case where the *income* effect dominates, the substitution effect is not large enough to prevent labor supply from *declining*. It is entirely plausible, of course, that the *substitution* effect will dominate. If so, the actual response to wage increases will be to *increase* labor supply.

Should the substitution effect dominate, the person's labor-supply curve—relating, say, desired hours of work to wages—will be *positively sloped*. That is, labor supply will increase with the wage rate. If on the other hand, the income effect dominates, the labor-supply curve will be *negatively sloped*. Economic theory cannot say which effect will dominate, and in fact individual labor supply curves could be positively sloped in some ranges of the wage and negatively sloped in others. In Figure 6.1, for example, the person's desired hours of work increase (substitution effect dominates) as wages go up as long as wages are low (below W^*). However, at higher wages, further increases result in reduced hours of work (the income effect dominates); economists refer to such a curve as "backward-bending."

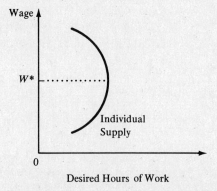

Figure 6.1   An Individual Supply-of-Labor Curve Can Bend Backwards

While economic theory is unable to predict whether the income or substitution effect will dominate in an individual's labor-supply curve, it can bring some useful insights to bear on important policy issues. The work-incentive effect of the personal income tax is an important case in point.

Tax-rate cuts and "supply-side" economics. The election of Ronald Reagan as President in 1980 brought to power an administration persuaded that high rates of inflation (that is, rising prices) and lagging labor productivity could be at least partially overcome by cutting taxes in such a way that investment and work effort would be stimulated.[10] The notion that tax-rate cuts and tax-related investment incentives could be used to stimulate output is central to what came to be called "supply-side" economics. An important element of the supply-side strategy proposed by President Reagan was the Kemp-Roth plan to cut personal income-tax rates across the board by 30 percent over a three-year period.[11] It was believed that cuts in personal income-tax rates would, among other things, increase the incentives of people to work:

> According to supply-siders, large tax-rate cuts would cause an increase in investment and work effort that would reduce fundamental inflationary pressures."[12]

Is the belief by supply-siders that income-tax rate cuts will increase work effort theoretically sound? Suppose, first, that Congress were to lower the income-tax rates of (say) lower income workers but not cut the level of government services provided for this group. A decrease in their income-tax rates is equivalent to an increase in wages, because the workers would take home more income for each hour of work. This wage increase would generate an income and substitution effect, and theoretical reasoning alone cannot predict which effect will dominate. If the substitution effect dominated, labor supply would increase; if the income effect were dominant, the tax cuts would be accompanied by a *fall* in labor supply! The issue is ultimately an empirical question.[13]

The supply-siders who claim that reducing income-tax rates would increase work incentives have a valid point, however, when one considers *general* income-tax-rate reductions. While at any point in time *individuals* or *small* groups of people can experience income effects if their wages change, workers as a *whole* cannot. The potential wealth of a society is more or less fixed at any point in time by the resources and technology it has available to it, and changing the wage rates of workers does not change this potential wealth. (If it did, we could make ourselves, as a society, arbitrarily wealthy by granting ourselves large wage

---

[10]We are indebted to Sharon Smith of AT&T for suggesting this policy application to us.

[11]The plan is named for its Congressional sponsors, Representative Jack Kemp and Senator William Roth. In the summer of 1981, Congress voted to cut taxes 25 percent over 3 years and to adjust tax brackets for inflation thereafter.

[12]"Reagan's Top Problem: Braking Inflationary Expectations," *Business Week,* December 1, 1980: 110.

[13]Later, this chapter will show that the income effect may dominate for men but not for married women.

increases!) Thus, income-tax-rate reductions for everyone would be accompanied by a *substitution* effect but *not* by an *income* effect. The cut in income-tax rates would increase workers' real wage rates—if the government at the same time reduced expenditures so that inflationary pressures did not occur—but it would not immediately affect society's real wealth. There would be a substitution effect with no overall income effect, and labor supply would increase. The *aggregate* supply-of-labor curve, then, must be upward-sloping, as shown in Figure 6.2. *How much* labor supply will increase when tax rates are cut by 25 percent is another question—and the answer is largely unknown at the moment. However, the estimates summarized later in the chapter suggest that the increase would probably be larger for women than men.

To better understand the upward-sloping nature of the aggregate supply-of-labor curve, let us examine in more concrete terms how a general 10 percent reduction in income-tax rates might be handled. While a cut in tax rates would, of course, increase workers' wage rates, it would have the *initial* effect of reducing by 10 percent the revenues available to government. The government might respond to reduced revenues by cutting back on various services it formerly provided: mail delivery on Saturday, educational subsidies, and road-construction funds, for example. Thus, while *wages* would be increased, real income would be held more or less constant by the cut in government services.[14] Workers would have more take-home income but fewer government-provided services.[15] There would be a substitution effect but no overall income effect.

The increase in labor supply caused by the tax cut would serve to increase people's money incomes and reduce their consumption of leisure. Some of the increased earnings would be spent on goods or services, and some would go to

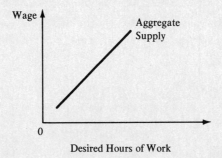

Figure 6.2 The Aggregate Supply-of-Labor Curve Must Be Upward-Sloping at Any Point in Time

---

[14]Some people would be more affected by the governmental spending cuts than others, but the *overall* change in real wealth would be zero.

[15]The alternative to cutting services, at least initially, is to borrow money. However, borrowing increases the money supply if it is done, as is most often the case, from banks—and this would tend to be inflationary. A rise in *prices* would lower the real wage and mitigate any substitution effects (if before-tax money wages remained constant).

the government in the form of taxes.[16] However, whether the increased goods or services are provided privately or by the government, the happiness they generate is offset by the reduced consumption of leisure time. In the short run, to repeat, increased goods and services are offset by reduced consumption of leisure, leaving society equally well off.

In the *long run,* however, real national wealth could be increased *if* the increase in goods and services is channeled into *investment* activities and not immediately consumed. Wage increases that accompany the growth of national wealth *do* generate income effects. However, real national welfare could *only* be increased in the long run and only if current investments were to increase.

The following section introduces indifference curves and budget constraints —material that may already be familiar to students with a background in these fundamentals.

A Graphical Analysis of the Labor/Leisure Choice: The Fundamentals

Graphical analysis requires a level of rigor that is more convincing than verbal analysis and incorporates visual aids that make the analysis easier to understand. The graphical analysis, however, is simply a more rigorous, visible repetition of our verbal analysis; hence, none of the conclusions or definitions reached above will be changed in any way.

Preferences. Let us assume that there are two major categories of goods that make people happy—leisure and money income (which can, of course, be used to buy other goods). Collapsing all goods into two allows our graphs to be drawn in two-dimensional space.

Since both leisure and money can be used to generate satisfaction (or *utility*), these two goods are to some extent substitutes for each other. If one were forced to give up some money income—by cutting back one's hours of work, for example —there would be some increase in leisure time that could be substituted for this lost income to keep the person as happy as before. A very thoughtful consumer/ worker, in fact, could reveal a whole *variety* of combinations of money and leisure hours that would yield him or her this same level of satisfaction.

To understand how preferences can be graphed, suppose a thoughtful consumer/worker is asked to decide how happy he or she would be with a daily income of $64 combined with 8 hours of leisure (point *a* in Figure 6.3). This level of happiness could be called "utility level *A*." Our consumer/worker could name *other combinations* of money income and leisure hours that would *also* yield utility level *A*. Assume that our respondent names five other such combinations. All six combinations of money and leisure that yield utility level *A* are represented by heavy dots in Figure 6.3. The curve connecting these dots is called an *indifference curve*—a curve connecting the various combinations of money and leisure

---

[16]Because earnings are taxed and leisure is not, a 10 percent tax cut that called forth increased labor supply would mean that government revenues would *not* fall by 10 percent in the long run.

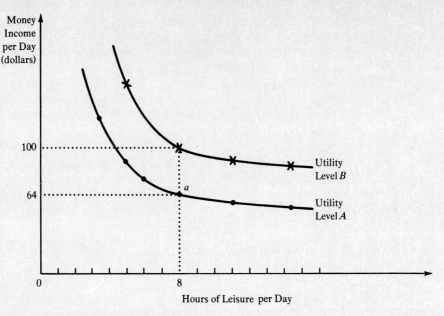

Figure 6.3 Two Indifference Curves for the Same Person

that yield equal utility. (The term *indifference curve* got its name from the fact that, since each point on the curve yields equal utility, a person is truly indifferent about where on the curve he or she will be.)

Our worker/consumer could no doubt achieve a higher level of happiness if he or she could combine the 8 hours of leisure with an income of $100 per day instead of just $64 a day. This higher satisfaction level could be called "utility level *B*." The consumer could name other combinations of money income and leisure that would also yield *this* higher level of utility. These combinations are denoted by the *X*s in Figure 6.3 that are connected by a new indifference curve.

Indifference curves have certain specific characteristics that are reflected by the way they are drawn:

1. Utility level *B* represents more happiness than level *A*. Every level of leisure consumption is combined with a higher income on *B* than on curve *A*. Hence our respondent prefers all points on indifference curve *B* to any point on curve *A*. A whole *set* of indifference curves could be drawn for this one person, each representing a different utility level. Any such curve that lies to the northeast of another one is preferred to any curve to the southwest, because the northeastern curve represents a higher level of utility.
2. Indifference curves *do not intersect.* If they did, the point of intersection would represent *one* combination of money and leisure that yields *two* different levels of satisfaction. We assume our worker/consumer is *not* so inconsistent in stating his or her preferences that this could happen.

3. Indifference curves are *negatively sloped,* because if either money or leisure hours is increased, the other is reduced in order to preserve the same level of utility. If the slope is steep—as at segment *LK* in Figure 6.4—a given loss of income need not be accompanied by a large increase in leisure hours in order to keep utility constant.[17] When the curve is relatively flat—as at segment *MN* in Figure 6.4—a given decrease in income must be accompanied by a large increase in the consumption of leisure to hold utility constant. Thus, where indifference curves are relatively steep, people do not value money income as highly as when such curves are relatively flat —for when they are flat, a loss of income can only be compensated by a large increase in leisure if utility is to be kept constant.

4. Indifference curves are *convex*—steeper at the left than at the right. This shape reflects the assumption that when money income is relatively high and leisure hours are relatively few, leisure is more highly valued than when leisure is abundant and money relatively scarce. At segment *LK* in Figure 6.4, a great loss of income (from Y_4 to Y_3, for example) can be compensated for by just a little increase in leisure, whereas a little loss of leisure time (from H_3 to H_4, for example) would require a relatively large

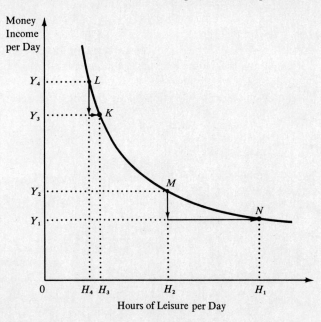

Figure 6.4   An Indifference Curve

---

[17]Economists call the change in money income needed to hold utility constant when leisure hours are changed by one unit the *marginal rate of substitution* between leisure and money income. This marginal rate of substitution can be graphically understood as the slope of the indifference curve at any point. At point *L*, for example, the slope is relatively steep so economists would say that the marginal rate of substitution at point *L* is relatively high.

increase in income to maintain equal utility. What is relatively scarce is highly valued.

Conversely, when income is low and leisure is abundant (segment *MN* in Figure 6.4), income is more highly valued. Losing income (by moving from Y_2 to Y_1, for example) requires a huge increase in leisure in order for utility to remain constant. To repeat, what is scarce is assumed to be highly valued.

5. Finally, different people will have different sets of indifference curves. The curves drawn in Figures 6.3 and 6.4 were for *one person only*. Another person would have a completely different set of curves. People who value leisure more highly, for example, would have had indifference curves that were generally steeper (see Figure 6.5). People who do not value leisure highly will have relatively flat curves.[18] Thus, individual preferences can be portrayed graphically.

Income and wage constraints. Now everyone would like to maximize his or her utility, which could be best done by consuming every available hour of leisure combined with the highest conceivable income. Unfortunately, the resources anyone can command are limited. Thus, all that is possible is to do the best one can, given limited resources. To see these resource limitations graphically requires superimposing constraints over one's set of indifference curves to see which combinations of income and leisure are available and which are not.

Suppose the person whose indifference curves are graphed in Figure 6.3 has no source of income other than labor earnings. Suppose, further, that he or she

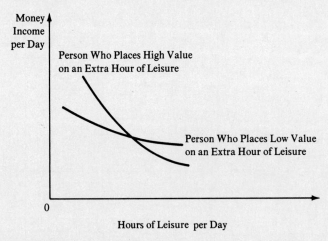

Figure 6.5   Indifference Curves for Two Different People

---

[18]The two curves shown in Figure 6.5 should be compared in *slope* only. Levels of utility for two different people cannot be compared because happiness is not objectively measurable. Figure 6.5 simply shows that people with different preferences will have indifference curves with different *shapes*. The fact that the two curves in Figure 6.5 intersect is thus not important, since the curves are for different people.

can earn $8 per hour. Figure 6.6 contains the two indifference curves drawn in Figure 6.3 but also contains a straight line (*DE*) connecting combinations of leisure and income that are possible for a person with an $8 wage and no outside income. If 16 hours per day are available for work and leisure, and if this person consumes all 16 in leisure, then money income will be zero (point *D* in Figure 6.6). If 8 hours a day are devoted to work, income will be $64 per day (point *M*), and if 16 hours a day are worked income would be $128 per day (point *E*). Other points on this line—the point of 15 hours of leisure (1 hour of work) and $8 of income—are also possible. This line, which reflects the combinations of leisure and income that are possible for the individual, is called the *budget constraint.* Any combination to the right of the budget constraint is not achievable; the person's command over resources simply is not sufficient to attain these combinations of leisure and money income.

The *slope* of the budget constraint is a graphical representation of the wage rate. One's wage rate is properly defined as the increment in income (ΔY) derived from an increment in the hours of work (ΔH):

$$\text{Wage Rate} = \frac{\Delta Y}{\Delta H}. \tag{6.5}$$

Now $\Delta Y/\Delta H$ is exactly the slope of the budget constraint (in absolute value).[19] Figure 6.6 shows how the constraint rises $8 for every one-hour increase

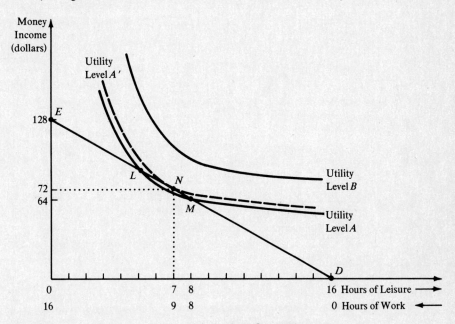

Figure 6.6   Indifference Curves and Budget Constraint

---

[19]The vertical change for a one-unit change in horizontal distance is the definition for *slope. Absolute value* refers to the size of the slope, disregarding whether it is positive or negative.

in work: if the person works zero hours, income per day is zero; if the person works one hour, $8 in income is possible; if he or she works 8 hours, $64 in income can be achieved. The reason the constraint rises $8 for every unit increase in hours of work is because the wage rate the person commands is $8 per hour. If the person could earn $16 per hour, the constraint would rise twice as fast and be twice as steep.

It is clear from Figure 6.6 that our consumer/worker cannot achieve utility level *B*. He or she can achieve *some* points on the indifference curve representing utility level *A*; specifically, those points between *L* and *M* in Figure 6.6. However, if our consumer/worker is a utility maximizer, he or she will realize that a utility level *above A* is possible. Remembering that there are an infinite number of indifference curves that can be drawn between curves *A* and *B* in Figure 6.6—one representing each possible level of satisfaction between *A* and *B*—we can draw a curve (*A'*) that is northeast of curve *A* and is just *tangent* to the budget constraint. Any movement along the budget constraint *away* from the tangency point places the person on an indifference curve lying *below A'*.

An indifference curve that is just tangent to the constraint represents the highest level of utility that the person can obtain given his or her constraint. It is the most northeast curve with an achievable point on it, and no curve superior to it can be reached. If this highest possible curve is denoted as utility level *A'* in Figure 6.6, then point *N* represents the utility-maximizing combination of leisure and income. Thus, our consumer/worker is best off—given his or her preferences and constraints—working 9 hours a day, consuming 7 hours of leisure, and having a daily income of $72. All other possible combinations, such as 8 hours of work and $64 of income, yield lower utility.

The decision not to work. In the example discussed above—and illustrated in Figure 6.6—a point of tangency (*N*) existed between the individual's indifference curve and the budget constraint. That point of tangency indicated the utility-maximizing labor/leisure combination. What happens if there is no point of tangency? What happens, for example, if the person's indifference curves are at every point more steeply sloped than the budget constraint (see Figure 6.7)?

If indifference curves that represent an individual's preferences are very steeply sloped it indicates that the person places a very high value on extra hours of leisure (see Figure 6.5). A very high hourly wage would be required to compensate the person for an hour of lost leisure (that is, an hour of work). If the increase in money income required to compensate the worker for an hour of work (to keep utility constant) is greater than the wage rate at every feasible number of leisure hours, then the person simply will choose not to work. Figure 6.7 indicates that utility is maximized at point *D*—a point of zero hours of work. Point *D* is *not* a tangency point; there can be no tangency if the indifference curve has no points at which the slope equals the slope of the budget constraint. Thus, utility in Figure 6.7 is maximized at a *corner*—a point at the extreme end of the budget constraint—and at this point (*D*) the person does not choose to be in the labor force.

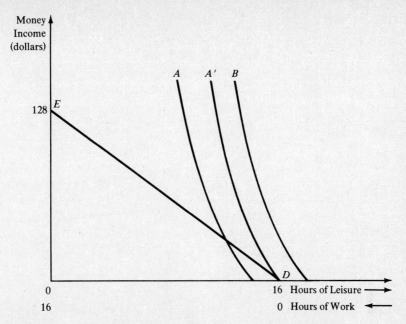

Figure 6.7   The Decision Not to Work Is a "Corner Solution"

The income effect. Suppose now that the person depicted in Figure 6.6 is lucky and falls into a source of income independent of work. Suppose, further, that this *nonlabor* income amounts to about $36 per day. Thus, even if this person worked zero hours per day, his or her daily income would be $36. Naturally, if the person worked more than zero hours, his or her daily income would be equal to $36 plus earnings (the wage multiplied by the hours of work).

The source of nonlabor income has clearly increased our person's command over resources, as can be shown by drawing a new budget constraint to reflect the nonlabor income. As shown by the broken line in Figure 6.8, the end points of the new constraint are:

1. point *d*—zero hours of work and $36 of money income, and
2. point *e*—16 hours of work and $164 of income ($36 in nonlabor income plus $128 in earnings).

Note that the new constraint is *parallel* to the old one. Parallel lines have the same slope; since the slope of each constraint reflects the wage rate, we can infer that the increase in nonlabor income has not changed the person's wage rate.

We have just described a situation in which a pure *income effect* should be observed. Income (wealth) has been increased, but the wage rate has remained unchanged. The previous section noted that if wealth increased and the opportunity cost of leisure remained constant, the person would consume more leisure and work less. We thus concluded that the income effect was *negative;* as income

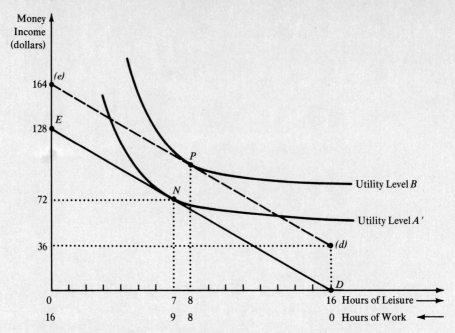

Figure 6.8 Indifference Curves and Budget Constraint (with an increase in nonlabor income)

goes up (down), holding wages constant, hours of work go down (up). This negative relationship is illustrated graphically in Figure 6.8.

When the old (solid) budget constraint was in effect, the person's highest level of utility was reached at point *N*, where he or she worked 9 hours a day. With the new (dashed) constraint, the optimum hours of work are 8 per day. The new source of income, by not altering the wage, has caused an income effect that results in one less hour of work per day.

Income and substitution effects with a wage increase. Suppose that, instead of increasing one's command over resources by receiving a source of nonlabor income, the wage rate for another person were to be increased from $8.00 to $12.00 per hour. This increase, as noted earlier, will cause *both* an income and a substitution effect; the person is both wealthier *and* faces a higher opportunity cost of leisure. Both effects can be illustrated graphically (see Figures 6.9 and 6.10).

Figures 6.9 and 6.10 illustrate the *observed effects* of the wage change as well as the two (hidden) *components* of the observed change: the income and substitution effects. Figure 6.9 illustrates the case where the observed response is to increase the hours of work; in this case, the substitution effect is stronger than the income effect. Figure 6.10 illustrates the case where the income effect is stronger, and the response to a wage increase is to reduce the hours of work. Both cases are plausible. Theory tells us in what direction the income and substitution

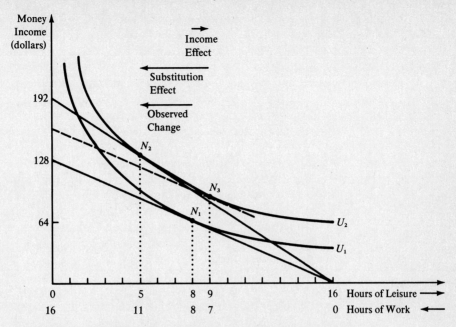

Figure 6.9   Wage Change with Substitution Effect Dominating

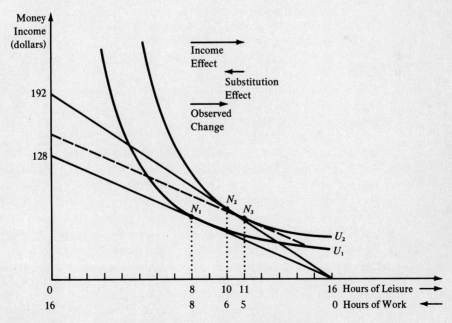

Figure 6.10   Wage Change with Income Effect Dominating

effects should go, but theory does not tell us which effect will be stronger. The difference between the two cases lies *solely* in the shape of the indifference curves (preferences); the budget constraints, which reflect wealth and the wage rate, are exactly the same.

Figures 6.9 and 6.10 show a new budget constraint. We are assuming that no source of nonlabor income exists for the person depicted, so that both the old and new constraints in each diagram are anchored at the same place—zero income for zero hours worked. However, the new constraint rises 50 percent faster than the old constraint, reflecting the 50 percent increase in the wage rate (from $8 to $12 per hour). The left endpoint of the new constraint is now at $192 (16 hours of work times $12 per hour) rather than at $128 (16 hours times $8).

In Figure 6.9, the new constraint implies that utility level U_2 is the highest that can be reached, and the tangency at point N_2 suggests that 11 hours of work per day is the optimum. When the old constraint was in effect, the utility-maximizing hours of work were 8 per day. Thus, the wage increase has caused the person's hours of work to increase by three per day.

This observed effect, however, masks the underlying forces at work. These underlying forces are, of course, the income and substitution effects. These forces are not directly observable, but they are there (and working against each other) nonetheless. A physical analogy can be used to explain how these forces work.

Suppose a riderless boat is set adrift in the Mississippi River on a day in which the wind is blowing *across* the river. The river's current carries the boat downstream, but the crosswind also exerts a force that blows the boat east (say). We observe where the boat is when it passes under a certain bridge. While we *observe* where the boat crosses under the bridge, we cannot directly see the two independent forces that together dictate where the boat ends up. There is the influence of the current and of the wind, and for some purposes it may be useful to measure these effects separately. How would we do it?

We would measure the influence of the current by asking ourselves, "Where would the boat have passed under the same bridge if there had been no wind?" This hypothetical question holds two elements constant: the wind (zero velocity) and the bridge under which the boat passes. The answer to the question is thus designed to identify the "pure" effect of the current. The influence of the wind could be measured by comparing where the boat actually crossed under the bridge with where it *would have crossed* had there been no wind.

Turning now to Figure 6.9, we will identify the income effect (as we did the "current effect") by asking, "What would have been the change in the hours worked if the person had reached indifference curve U_2 (the bridge) by a change in *nonlabor* income with *no* change in the wage rate (no wind)?"

We answer this question by moving the old constraint to the northeast, maintaining its original slope (reflecting the old wage of $8.00), which holds the wage constant. By definition, we must hold the wage constant when dealing with the income effect. However, moving the old constraint hypothetically "allows" nonlabor income to increase so that the person arrives at the new level of utility. The dashed constraint in Figure 6.9 depicts this hypothetical constraint, which is tangent to indifference curve U_2 at N_3. This tangency suggests that had the person received nonlabor income, with no change in the wage, sufficient to reach the new level of utility, he or she would have *reduced* work hours from 8 (N_1), to 7 (N_3) per day. This shift is a graphical "proof" that the income effect is negative, assuming that leisure is a normal good.

The substitution effect can be measured once the pure effect of the wage change is known. We measure the substitution effect as the difference between where the person ends up and where he or she *would* have ended up without a wage change. *With* the wage change, the person represented in Figure 6.9 ended up at point N_2, working 11 hours a day. *Without* the wage change, the person would have arrived at point N_3, working 7 hours a day. The wage change *by itself* (holding utility, or real wealth, constant) caused work hours to increase by 4 per day. This increase demonstrates that the substitution effect is positive.

To summarize, the observed effect of raising wages from $8 to $12 per hour increased the hours of work in Figure 6.9 from 8 to 11 per day. This observed effect, however, is the *sum* of two component effects. The income effect—which operates because an increased wage increases one's real wealth—tended to *reduce* the hours of work from 8 to 7 per day. The substitution effect—which captures the pure effect of the change in leisure's opportunity cost—tended to push the person toward 4 more hours of work per day. The end result was an increase of 3 in the hours worked each day.

Figure 6.10 can be analyzed in the same way. Here, the *observed* effect of the increased wage is a *reduction* in hours of work from 8 to 6 per day (points N_1 to N_2). This change is the result of an income effect, which by itself tended to *decrease* by 3 hours the hours of work per day, and a substitution effect, which tended to *increase* working hours by one per day. The net result of these forces is, of course, a reduction in hours of work by 2 per day.

The differences in the observed effects of a wage increase between Figures 6.9 and 6.10 are due to differences in the shape of the indifference curves—or, in other words, to different preferences. The substitution and income effects worked in their predicted direction in both cases, but their relative strengths are a function of preferences (which are reflected in the shape and placement of indifference curves).

Although theory cannot predict whether the income or substitution effect will dominate, it can be readily understood that the income effect of any given wage change is *larger* for individuals who are *working many hours* for pay than for those who are working few hours. Changes in income represent changes in one's command over resources, and it is clear that a wage increase (say) fosters greater increases in wealth the more hours one works. (In terms of our graphical analysis, it can be seen from Figures 6.9 and 6.10 that the budget constraint representing a wage of $12 per hour lies further to the northeast of the one representing an $8 wage in its upper portion—where more hours are worked.)

Empirical Findings on the Labor/Leisure Choice

This chapter has argued, both verbally and graphically, that the income effect on labor supply is negative and that the substitution effect is positive. While these predictions are often useful for policy purposes—as we saw in the discussions of the work-incentive effect of the income tax—it is also important to know *how large* the two effects are. It is the *relative size* of each effect that determines the ultimate *observed* effect.

Evidence on the absolute and relative sizes of income and substitution effects can be obtained in two different ways:

1. the *time-series study* can be used to look at *trends* in labor-force participation rates and hours of work over time.
2. the *cross-section study* can be used to analyze the patterns of labor supply across individuals at a given point in time.

Time-series studies. Chapter 2 pointed out that real hourly wages rose fourfold from 1914 to 1980. Associated with that rise was a rather sharp decline in the labor-force participation rate of older males, clearly reflecting a trend toward earlier retirement. One can also observe substantial declines in the hours of work. One is therefore tempted to conclude from these trends that the income effect dominates the substitution effect—meaning that when wages rise, the propensity to work will fall.

There are three potential objections to, or problems with, the conclusion that the income effect is larger than the substitution effect. First, the earlier retirement of males can be seen as a function of greater availability of pensions. Pensions pay older people for not working, thereby creating incentives not to work at an elderly age. Interestingly, however, a large part of the decline in labor-force participation rates for elderly males came *before* 1940, during an era when pensions were virtually nonexistent.

A second disturbing fact that raises questions about the relative strength of the income and substitution effects is the much smaller decline in hours of work after World War II. Has the income effect grown weaker relative to the substitution effect? Not necessarily. Hours of work are *jointly* determined by employers and employees, and while rising real wages may be inducing employees to want to work less, a number of developments have led employers to offer incentives for workers to work longer hours (these forces were discussed in Chapter 5). It is important to remember that countervailing forces may well be coming from the *demand* side of the market in determining hours of work.

Third, while we cannot rule out the possibility that the income effect dominates the substitution effect for males, how do we interpret the dramatic rise in participation rates among females? One possible explanation is that preferences among women have changed—particularly since their heavy involvement in the labor market during World War II. For example, the stigma against working wives or mothers has weakened. This change in preferences may explain some of the rising propensity of women to work, but it does not explain the *cause* of the changing preferences. Since women's attitudes may be most strongly influenced by the sheer increase in the number of working women, understanding what started the increase originally is fundamental.

Another theory for the growing proportion of working women is based on the observation that women really have a tripartite choice of how to spend time: leisure, market work, and nonmarket (household) work. The inventions of automatic washers and dryers, frost-free refrigerators, and prepared foods—to name a few—have reduced the time required to perform given household tasks. Being able to perform these tasks faster reduces the savings from staying home instead of working for pay. Thus, yet another force is at work affecting the incentives of women to work for pay.

Finally, it may well be that, because wives have tended to work in the home more—and for pay less—than men and unmarried women, the income effect for them will be smaller and the substitution effect will be larger. The plausibility of a smaller income effect rests on the observation that at any point in time, many married women are out of the labor force and many others are working less than full time. Thus, as noted before, a given wage increase will generate a smaller income effect than it would if virtually all were working (for pay) full time. A larger substitution effect is plausible for married women because household and market work are such close substitutes, whereas market work and leisure are not as close substitutes.

Suppose that women and men have roughly the same preferences regarding leisure and work. These two alternative ways to spend time are substitutes, but they are not close substitutes. Thus, a change in the opportunity cost of leisure may not elicit a large change in the supply of working hours for either sex; leisure and work are simply too different for a large responsiveness to changes in opportunity costs to be observed. However, there are two different types of *work* activity—market work (for pay) and household work—and there is a high degree of substitutability between *these* alternatives. If market work is performed, household chores are hired out to specialists (baby-sitters, cleaning services) or done by machines (frost-free refrigerators). If household work is substituted for market work, these costs of hiring out tasks are saved. Thus, doing household work oneself or working for pay and hiring out these chores represent two ways of getting the same job done. They are very close substitutes, so that when the incentives to pursue one alternative change, a large response in time spent doing the other can be expected. Because married women have traditionally performed household work to a greater extent than have men and unmarried women, we would expect this second influence on the overall substitution effect (the substitution between work activities) to be more important for married women. The substitution effect observed in the above studies is thus plausibly larger for married women.

It is easy to see that looking at *trends* in the propensity of people to work for evidence on the relative strength of income or substitution effects is not completely satisfactory. So many other factors are involved over time that affect these propensities that isolating income and substitution effects is impossible. Indeed, the growth of pensions, changes in employer desires concerning hours of work, time-saving household inventions, and changed attitudes toward working women all cloud our analysis of trends.

Cross-section studies. Numerous studies of labor-supply behavior have relied on cross-sectional data.[20] These studies basically analyze labor-force participation or annual hours of work as they are affected by wage rates (the slope of the budget constraint) and unearned income (how far out the constraint lies). The most reliable and informative studies are those done on large samples of males, primarily because the labor supply behavior of women is complicated by child-rearing and household-work arrangements for which data are sketchy at best. The findings discussed here are of *nonexperimental studies*—studies in which variations in wages and incomes are *observed,* rather than *generated by,* the researchers (findings from experimental studies are summarized later in this chapter in the discussion of income-maintenance programs).

Just about all studies of male labor-supply behavior indicate that the income effect dominates the substitution effect—and thus that males have (individual) negatively sloped supply curves. There is as yet no universal consensus about the *size* of the labor-supply response. However, one careful review study[21] claims that once various statistical and definitional problems are accounted for, the effect of raising a man's wage by 10 percent would be a 1–2 percent reduction in his labor supply. This observed effect is the result of something like a 2.5 percent reduction resulting from the income effect and roughly a 1 percent increase associated with the substitution effect.

The estimates for women are less well defined, perhaps for the reasons cited above. Nevertheless, the results of cross-sectional studies usually indicate that the *substitution* effect dominates, yielding a positively sloped labor supply curve for females.[22] Studies comparable to those for males (noted above) have generally found similar income effects among females, but the substitution effects for women are much larger than those for men, the likely reasons for which were mentioned earlier.[23]

It is interesting—and somewhat heartening—that the results of nonexperimental, statistically sophisticated cross-section studies generally support the observations based on trends over time. Namely, the income effect appears to dominate for males, and the substitution effect appears dominant for females. As noted earlier, the relatively larger substitution effect among women probably reflects the traditional household role of married women rather than sex-related differences in work/leisure preferences.

---

[20]The studies and conclusions reported here are for *individual* wage changes and *individual* supply-of-labor curves. They do *not* pertain to *aggregate* labor supply responses in response to a general wage change (where, as noted earlier, there can be no overall income effect).

[21]George Borjas and James Heckman, "Labor Supply Estimates for Public Policy Evaluation," *Proceedings of the Industrial Relations Research Association* (1978), pp. 320–31.

[22]*See* Jacob Mincer, "Labor Force Participation of Married Women," in *Aspects of Labor Economics* (Princeton, N.J.: Princeton University Press, 1962); Glen G. Cain, *Married Women in the Labor Force* (Chicago: University of Chicago Press, 1966); William G. Bowen and T. Aldrich Finegan, *The Economics of Labor Force Participation* (Princeton, N.J.: Princeton University Press, 1969).

[23]*See* Glen G. Cain and Harold W. Watts, "Toward a Summary and Synthesis of the Evidence," *Income Maintenance and Labor Supply: Econometric Studies* (Chicago: Markham, 1973).

EXAMPLE 6.2

The "Discouraged" vs. the "Additional" Worker

Changes in one spouse's productivity, either at home or in market work, can alter the family's basic labor-supply decision. Consider, for example, a family in which market work is performed by the husband and in which the wife is employed full-time in the home. What will happen if a recession causes the husband to become unemployed?

The husband's market productivity declines, at least temporarily. He may be a highly specialized worker and unable to find similar work at the moment. The drop in his market productivity relative to his household productivity (which is unaffected by the recession) makes it more likely that the family will find it beneficial for him to engage in household production. If the wage his wife can earn in paid work is not affected, the family *may* decide that, to try to maintain the family's prior level of utility (which might be affected by both consumption and *savings* levels), *she* should seek market work and *he* should stay home for as long as the recession lasts. He may remain a member of the labor force as an unemployed worker awaiting recall, and as she begins to look for work she becomes an "added" member of the labor force. Thus, in the face of falling family income, the number of family members seeking market work may increase—a phenomenon akin to the *income effect*.

At the same time, however, we must look at the *wage rate* someone without a job can *expect* to receive if he or she looks for work. This expected wage, denoted by $E(W)$, can actually be written as a precise statistical concept:

$$E(W) = \pi W,$$

where W is the wage rate of people who have the job and π is the probability of obtaining the job. For someone without a job, the price of an hour at home—the opportunity cost of staying home—is $E(W)$. The reduced availability of jobs that occurs when the unemployment rate rises causes the expected wage of those without jobs to fall sharply, for two reasons. First, an excess of labor supply over demand tends to push down real wages (for those with jobs) during recessionary periods. Second, the chances of getting a job fall in a recession. Thus, both W and π fall in a recession, causing $E(W)$ to decline. Noting the *substitution effect* that accompanies a falling expected wage, some have argued that people who would otherwise have entered the labor force become "discouraged" in a recession and tend to remain out of the labor market. Looking for work has such a low expected payoff for them that such people decide that spending time at home is more productive than spending time in job search. The reduction of the labor force associated with discouraged workers in a recession is a force working opposite to the "added-worker" effect—just as the substitution effect works against the income effect.

It is possible, of course, for both the "added-worker" and "discouraged-worker" effects to coexist, because "added" and "discouraged" workers will be different groups of people. Which group predominates, however, is the important question. If the labor force is swelled by "added workers" during a recession, the published unemployment rate will likewise become swollen (the added workers will increase the number of people looking for work). If workers become "discouraged" and drop out of the labor market when they are unemployed, the decline in people seeking jobs will depress the unemployment rate. Knowledge of which effect predominates is needed in order to make accurate inferences about the actual state of the labor market from the published unemployment rate.

We do know that the added-worker effect does exist. Jacob Mincer, in a clever landmark study, found that the labor-market behavior of wives was very sensitive to temporary changes in their husbands' income. In fact, he found that the labor supply of married women was more responsive to temporary than permanent changes in their husbands' income! However, this added-worker effect is confined to the relatively few families whose normal breadwinner loses a job (the overall unemployment rate rarely goes above 10 percent). The fall in expected real wages occurs in nearly *every* household, and remembering that the substitution effect is strong for married women, it is not surprising to find that the discouraged-worker effect is large and predominant. Other things equal, *the labor force tends to shrink during recessions and grow during periods of economic recovery.* As more and more women become regularly employed for pay, the "added worker" effect will probably become smaller relative to the "discouraged worker" effect, because it will be increasingly confined to teenagers.

The dominance of the discouraged-worker effect creates what some call the "hidden unemployed"—people who would like to work but who believe that jobs are so scarce that looking for work is of no use. Because they are not looking for work, they are not counted as "unemployed" in government statistics. Focusing on the period 1973–78, when the overall official unemployment rate went from 4.9 percent to 6.0 percent, can give some indication of the size of hidden unemployment.

In 1973, an average of 4.3 million people were counted as unemployed at any given time—representing 4.9 percent of the labor force. In addition, there were 679,000 people who indicated that they wanted work but were not seeking it because they felt jobs were unavailable to them. This group constituted 1.2 percent of those adults not in the labor force. In 1978, the number of people officially counted as unemployed was 6 million, but there were 850,000 people among the "hidden" unemployed. These 850,000 people represented 1.5 percent of those adults not in the labor force. The rise in the percentage of those out of the labor market for job-related reasons is evidence of the discouraged-worker effect. Incidentally, if "discouraged workers" were counted as unemployed members of the labor force, the unemployment rate would have been 5.6 percent in 1973 and 6.8 percent in 1978.*To count these workers, however, would overlook the possibility that many of them desire only an intermittent labor-force attachment and time their periods out of the labor force to coincide with periods when expected wages are low.

Source: Jacob Mincer, "Labor Force Participation of Married Women," in *Aspects of Labor Economics:* A Conference of the Universities—National Bureau Committee on Economic Research (Princeton, N.J.: Princeton University Press, 1962).

*To say that including "discouraged workers" in unemployment statistics would change the published unemployment rate does not imply that it *should* be done. For a summary of the arguments for and against counting discouraged workers as unemployed, see the final report of the National Commission on Employment and Unemployment Statistics, *Counting the Labor Force* (Washington, D.C., 1979), pp. 44–49.

Policy Applications

Virtually all government income-maintenance programs—from welfare payments to unemployment compensation—have work-incentive effects, and the direction and size of these effects are often critical issues in constructing and enacting such programs. As a society, we have decided to help those among us who are economically disadvantaged for one reason or another. However, it is important to understand how income-maintenance programs can affect the willingness to work. This final section will discuss the labor-supply implications of the unemployment-insurance, workers'-compensation, and welfare programs and their alternatives.

Income-Replacement Programs

Unemployment insurance and workers' compensation are what might be called *income-replacement programs.* Unemployment insurance benefits are paid to workers who have been laid off, permanently or temporarily, by their employers. Workers' compensation is paid to employees who have been injured on the job. Both programs are intended to compensate workers for earnings lost while out of work.[24]

Complete replacement? Given that both the unemployment-insurance and workers'-compensation programs are intended to replace lost earnings, it may seem a bit odd—if not callous—that both programs typically replace roughly just *half*

---

[24]For a complete description of these programs, *see* George E. Rejda, *Social Insurance and Economic Security* (Englewood Cliffs, N.J.: Prentice-Hall, 1976). We will return to the unemployment insurance and workers' compensation programs in the chapters on unemployment (Chapter 18) and compensating differentials (Chapter 7).

of before-tax lost earnings.[25] It is true that most benefits paid out under these programs are not taxed, so that the fraction of *after-tax* earnings replaced is usually somewhat higher than 50 percent. However, it is also true that lost fringe benefits are not replaced, so that lost compensation is far from completely replaced. Why?

The reason for incomplete earnings replacement has to do with work incentives. Both injured and unemployed workers have some discretion over how long they will remain out of work. A man with a lacerated arm might be able to carry out his normal duties with some discomfort after a few days of recuperation, or he might choose to wait until his wound is completely healed before returning to work. An unemployed woman might accept the first offer of work she obtains, or she may prefer to wait a while and see if she can generate a better offer. In both cases the worker has the legal latitude to decide (within some limits) when to return to work. These decisions will obviously be affected by work incentives inherent in the income-replacement programs affecting them.

Replacing *all* of lost income could result in *overcompensation*—by generating a higher level of utility than before the loss of income[26]—and would motivate the recipients of benefits to remain out of work as long as possible. Figure 6.11 shows

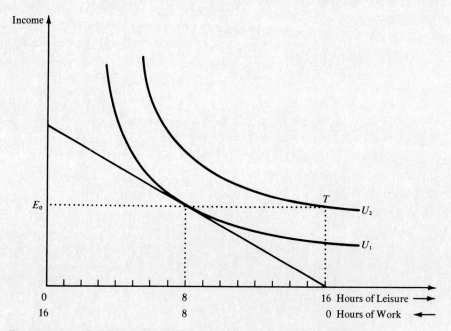

Figure 6.11   Full-Earnings Replacement Overcompensates Workers

---

[25] Both programs are run at the state level and thus vary in their characteristics across states. Benefits in both programs are bounded by minimums and maximums.

[26] We are assuming here that the psychic costs of injury or layoff are small. It could be argued that complete income replacement is justified on the grounds that it compensates for large psychic losses, but our analysis of work-incentive effects would be unchanged.

that before employment ceased, the person earned E_0 and had a level of utility equal to U_1. If, when employment ceases, the worker receives benefits equal to E_0, he or she will be at point T on a higher indifference curve. Before work ceased, the worker earned E_0 and had 8 hours of leisure, whereas at T he or she has E_0 in income and 16 hours of leisure per day. In this case, the recipient would be better off not working than working! Thus, full earnings replacement could clearly inhibit program beneficiaries from returning to work at the earliest possible time (see Example 6.3 for a case where full earnings replacement would *not* completely destroy work incentives).

EXAMPLE 6.3

The Economics of the "Workaholic"

The text discussion of work incentives inherent in income-replacement programs has assumed that more leisure time always increases one's utility. This assumption leads to the conclusion that government income subsidies that are reduced one dollar for every dollar earned will induce people not to work. It was argued that such subsidies essentially reduce wages to zero, and that people will not work if they cannot increase their income by working.

Although the above assumption that an hour of leisure yields more in utility than an uncompensated hour at work may be true for most people, we can all think of people we know who love their work and become bored and restless when away from work. For them, work may be a "hobby," a "calling", or a means of socializing. It seems inconceivable that these people would choose *not* to work even if their money income would be the same whether they did or did not work. Can economic theory deal with these "workaholics" who derive more pleasure from work than from leisure, holding money income constant? The answer is yes.

Let us suppose that a "workaholic" places a positive value on leisure when her working hours are high, but after L' hours of daily leisure are consumed any further increases in leisure cause her to be bored and restless. She places *negative* value on leisure at that point and would prefer to be at work even if she were not paid for it! A graphical representation of this woman's indifference curve is given by the curve *ABCD* in the accompanying figure. Along the arc *ABC,* the indifference curve is negatively sloped, which means that she would be willing to give up some income to obtain more leisure (that is, she places a positive value on leisure). Increases in leisure hours beyond L', however, place her in a range where her indifference curve is positively sloped (segment *CD*). In this range she places a negative value on leisure and would *give up* income if it meant she could avoid the boredom or social isolation of not working.

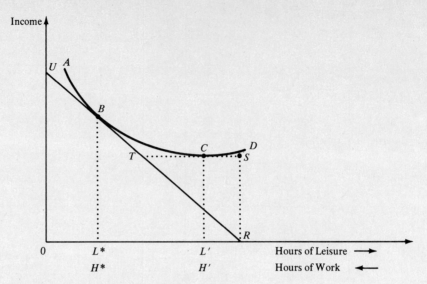

The Work/Leisure Choice of a Workaholic

If our workaholic faced a budget constraint like *RU* in this figure, she would maximize utility at point *B* and work *H** hours per day. However, even if her budget constraint had a horizontal (zero-wage) segment in it (see, for example, the constraint *RSTU* in the figure) she would work! In this latter case, she would maximize utility at point *C* and work *H'* hours. *H'* represents fewer hours than did *H** but is clearly not equal to zero. Economic theory, then, *can* represent and successfully analyze the behavior of "workaholics."

Actual income loss vs. "scheduled" benefits. A second issue in income replacement programs is how to structure workers' compensation for permanent disabilities. Should workers who are either totally or partially disabled receive benefits that replace their *actual* lost earnings, or should they receive benefits according to some impersonal schedule appropriate for people with their disability? One might initially think that replacing actual losses is more fair, but such a program would create an enormous disincentive to work.

Suppose a worker has become partially disabled because of an injury on the job. Suppose this worker lost three fingers on one hand and, being a manual worker, must now seek work in jobs that pay less than he earned before. His new "market" budget constraint might be the line AD in Figure 6.12. If our injured worker earned E_0 before injury, and workers' compensation replaces all earnings loss up to E_0, the workers'-compensation budget constraint facing this worker is like the solid-line constraint $(ABCD)$ drawn in Figure 6.12. This income-replacement constraint has a vertical segment (AB), which indicates that if the person does not work at all he receives a benefit equal to E_0. If he does earn money by taking a job, the difference between E_0 and his actual earnings becomes his

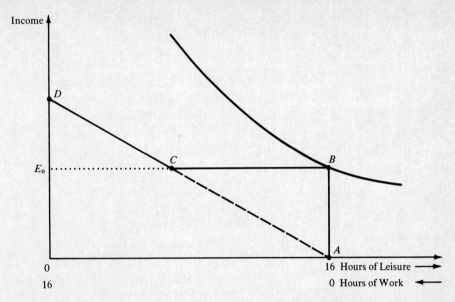

Figure 6.12   Budget Constraint with Actual Income Replacement

disability benefit. Thus, as long as his actual earnings are below E_0, his benefit is such that his total income remains at E_0, which is why the segment BC is horizontal at E_0. The segment CD corresponds to his "market" (unsubsidized) constraint when earnings are above E_0.

Now the interesting thing about Figure 6.12 is that for many people, B—a point of no work at all—is the point of maximum utility. Throughout the horizontal segment, BC, the individual's net wage is zero, as reflected by the horizontal line. If our worker were to earn an extra \$10, the government would reduce his benefits by \$10. In a very real sense, any earnings would be "taxed" away completely in the form of a dollar-for-dollar reduction in benefits. When people cannot increase their income by working, there is usually no incentive to work. There are exceptions, however, where a zero wage *would* be associated with a positive level of work hours—as illustrated in Example 6.3.

One way to avoid the disincentives inherent in replacing *actual* lost earnings for disabled workers is to grant benefits according to some schedule drawn up with reference to the disability but without regard to the individual's actual earnings loss. For example, in the state of New York, a worker losing the first three fingers of one hand receives two thirds of his before-injury weekly wage for a period of 101 weeks irrespective of his actual earnings during or after this 101-week period.[27] After that, he receives no further workers' compensation for that injury. Other states compensate permanent, partial disabilities in a similar manner.

[27]New York State, *Workmen's Compensation Law* (Hempstead, N.Y.: Workmen's Compensation Board, 1970), p. 65.

Using an impersonal schedule of disability benefits preserves at least some incentive to work, because benefits are not reduced if earnings increase. The benefits received become a grant of nonwage income, and they do not alter the recipient's wage rate (price of leisure).

Figure 6.13 contains the "market" constraint (*AD*) and the "actual earnings loss" constraint (*ABCD*) previously depicted in Figure 6.12. Now assume that instead of actual earnings loss, disability benefits for our disabled worker equal E_s no matter how much or how little he earns after the injury. His new constraint is thus *ABE*. This new constraint is parallel to *AD*, his "market" constraint (*ABE* is everywhere E_s higher than constraint *AD*)—reflecting the fact that this form of compensation for injury does not alter his wage rate.

Figure 6.13 provides a graphical demonstration that with "scheduled" benefits there are greater incentives to work than when benefits are based on earnings loss. Our injured worker maximizes utility at point *G* rather than at point *B*, even though both disability benefit programs depicted pay equal benefits for those who cannot or do not choose to work.

The conclusion that scheduled payments offer stronger work incentives than benefits based on actual losses clearly becomes even stronger if the scheduled benefits are reduced below E_s. As benefits are reduced, the constraint *ABE* moves closer to *AD*, and the point of utility maximization moves farther from *G* and closer to *F* (the utility-maximizing point in a world without disability benefits). Maximum work incentives are retained when there is no income-transfer program

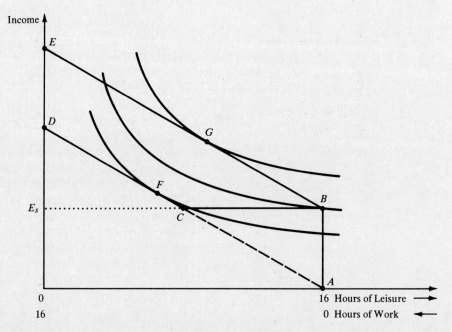

Figure 6.13   Comparing Budget Constraints of Two Disability Programs

—a situation in obvious conflict with the overall *goal* of helping workers who find themselves economically disadvantaged.[28]

While the basic aim is to restore income to disadvantaged workers, it is important to preserve work incentives as much as possible. If we take *AD* as the budget constraint when no benefit program exists and point *F* as the corresponding optimum work effort, it is easy to see from Figure 6.13 that "scheduled" benefits cause only an income effect. The constraint moves out to *ABE*, but it does not change slope. Work effort declines, since point *G* is to the right of point *F*, but it does not cease.[29]

On the contrary, when actual earnings loss becomes the basis for benefits calculation, there is an income *and* a substitution effect—and *both* work in the *same* direction. The benefits simultaneously increase income while *reducing* the wage rate to zero (in the segment *BC* of constraint *ABCD*). The presence of a zero wage rate reduces the price of leisure to zero and is a powerful disincentive to work. It is not surprising that payments for partial disabilities are generally "scheduled" in nature.[30]

Income-Maintenance Programs

Income-maintenance programs—more popularly known as "welfare" or relief" programs—have the goal of *raising* the income of the poor to some minimum acceptable level. They thus differ from income-replacement programs, which were aimed at *restoring* lost income. Because poverty is generally an income-related concept, the benefits paid out under income-maintenance programs generally are affected by the level of the beneficiary's actual income. As we shall see, income-conditioned benefits inevitably reduce work incentives below what such incentives would be with no income-support system for the poor. They simultaneously increase income while reducing the price of leisure (the wage rate)—both of which should cause the demand for leisure to increase and the supply of labor to fall. This fact is the root of much of the controversy welfare programs have generated over the years. Welfare payments have taken two forms in this country, as described below.

The old welfare system. Prior to 1967, welfare took the form of a guaranteed annual income. A welfare worker would determine the "needed" income of the eligible person or family, based on family size, area living costs, and local welfare regulations. Actual earnings would be subtracted from this needed level, and a

---

[28]Chapter 7 will show that workers who are injured may be compensated *in advance* of injury by having higher wages (due to the risk inherent in their job) than they would otherwise have. The *compensating wage differentials* must also be taken into account when establishing programs on post-injury compensation.

[29]An exception to this statement would be a situation in which a person's indifference curves are such that a "corner solution"—as in Figure 6.7—is obtained.

[30]For more details on the Workers' Compensation program, *see* Rejda, *Social Insurance and Economic Security.*

check would be received each month for the difference. If earnings went up, welfare benefits would go down, dollar-for-dollar. This creates a budget constraint like *ABCD* shown in Figure 6.14, where total income is Y_n (the "needed" income) as long as the person is subsidized. There is no incentive to work for many people, because there is a zero wage (segment *BC*) over most normal hours of work.

Thus, the old welfare system served to increase income by moving the budget constraint out from *AC* to *ABC*; this shift created an *income effect* tending to reduce labor supply from points *E* to *F* in Figure 6.14. However, it *also* caused the wage to effectively drop to zero: every dollar earned was matched by a dollar reduction of welfare benefits. This dollar-for-dollar reduction in benefits induced a huge *substitution effect*—causing many to reduce their hours of work to zero (point *B*). The old system clearly had strong disincentives for welfare recipients to find work.

The revised welfare system. Recognizing the nonexistent work incentives for welfare recipients in the old system, the government restructured welfare benefits in 1967 to eliminate the zero wage rate. Welfare recipients were allowed to keep the first $30 of any earnings per month and one third of the rest. Thus, ignoring the first $30, a welfare recipient who earned an extra $100 by working would have his or her benefits reduced by $67. The take-home wage rate thus became, in effect, one third of the market wage. While a take-home wage of one third the market wage clearly reduced the wage rate compared to what it would have been without welfare, it represented a significant improvement in work incentives over the zero wage rate implicit in the old system (see Figure 6.15).

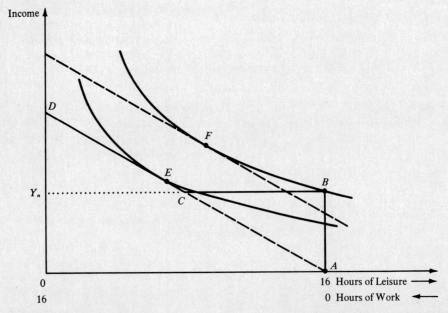

Figure 6.14   Income and Substitution Effects for Old Welfare System

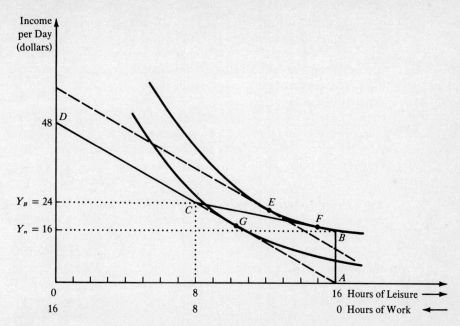

Figure 6.15   Income and Substitution Effects of the Revised Welfare Program

Let us assume that the government had determined that the minimum needed income, Y_n, for the recipient family was $16 per day. It thus guaranteed that the family would have a welfare benefit of $16 if no one worked. Suppose, however, that the family head could earn $3 per hour if she worked, or a total of $48 per day if she worked 16 hours a day. If we ignore the first $30 of monthly earnings that could be kept completely[31] and remember that for every $3 she earned the government reduced her welfare benefit by $2, we can easily see that if she worked 8 hours a day—and thus earned $24—she would be taken off welfare and receive no benefit (two thirds of $24 is $16). An income of $24 thus becomes the *break-even level* of income (Y_B)—the point at which the family is no longer subsidized.

For incomes higher than $24 per day, the family's budget constraint is *CD*, the subsidized or market constraint of which the slope's absolute value is 3 (reflecting the $3 wage). If the family earnings are zero, the welfare benefit is $16 (point *B* in Figure 6.15). If earnings are between $0–$24, the family is subsidized and has a total income (earnings plus subsidy) that falls along segment *BC* in Figure 6.15. Segment *BC* rises from $16 (point *B*) to $24 (point *C*) for 8 hours of work—which suggests this segment has a slope of which the absolute value is one. This slope is one third the slope of *AD*, which reflects the market wage of $3. Therefore, as long as the family is subsidized, the take-home wage rate is one third of the market wage under the revised welfare system.

If one compares constraint *AD* in Figure 6.15 with constraint *ABCD*—the revised welfare system constraint—one can see that the program increases income

[31]To take into account this small sum would complicate our diagram without changing the analysis or its conclusions in any essential way.

and reduces the take-home wage rate (because it "taxes away," in the form of reducing welfare benefits, two thirds of earnings). The increased income alone—with no change in wage—would create an *income effect* that decreases labor supply from points G to E. However, the fact that the take-home wage is reduced below the market wage creates a *substitution effect* that further reduces labor supply to point F.[32] Again, *both* the income and the substitution effect work in the direction of less work *compared to a world with no income subsidies.* However, comparing Figures 6.15 and 6.14, one can see that the revised welfare system had stronger work incentives for welfare recipients, because welfare benefits were not reduced dollar-for-dollar with earnings.

The current welfare system. In 1981 the welfare system was changed so that the budget constraints facing recipients are now a hybrid of the old and the revised systems. If a person receiving welfare finds a job, he or she faces the revised constraint ($ABCD$) analyzed in Fig. 6.15 for four months. That is, for the first four months of work, the recipient's earnings (above $30) are "taxed" at the rate of 67 percent. After that, earnings are "taxed" at 100 percent and the person's constraint becomes $ABCD$ in Figure 6.14. An analysis of this change in the welfare system is useful in making a further point about work incentives.

Our analysis of the welfare system so far has emphasized the work incentive effects on welfare *recipients.* It is true that for those who *continue to receive welfare,* the 1981 return to a 100 percent tax on earnings represents a reduced work incentive as compared to the "revised" system discussed above. However, the 1981 changes may induce some recipients who were previously employed to work longer hours and to leave the welfare rolls.

Consider Figure 6.16. For the individual whose preferences are represented there by indifference curves Z and Z', utility was maximized at point X under the "revised" welfare system when the constraint facing that individual was $ABCD$. However, after the 1981 changes, this individual faces the constraint $ABC'D$ after four months of working, and utility is now maximized at point X'. It is important to note three things about point X': (1) it is a point offering greater utility than point B for this individual (whose indifference curves are relatively flat, which means he or she values income relatively highly), so the person does not cease working; (2) it lies to the left of point X, which suggests that this individual will work longer and consume less leisure than he or she did under the "revised" system; and (3) the individual is now off welfare (utility is maximized along $C'D$ not ABC') but his or her level of utility is reduced as compared to what it was under the "revised" system (utility level Z is no longer possible).

The major point to be made is that whether a given change in the welfare system increases or reduces work incentives depends on one's preferences. You

---

[32]Note that because of the decrease in the take-home wage, the *income effect* of the income-maintenance program described becomes smaller the *more* one works (as long as income is sufficiently low to qualify for the subsidy). Graphically, segment ABC of the constraint in Figure 6.15 is further to the northeast of the market constraint AD in the region where working hours are fewest—and closest near 8 hours of work (the point where the subsidy ends).

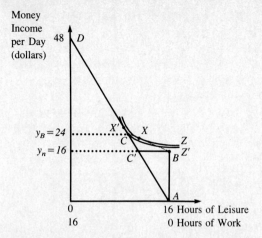

Figure 6.16   The New Welfare System May Increase Work Incentives for the Working Poor

should be able to demonstrate to yourself that for people whose indifference curves are so steep (that is, their preferences for "leisure" are quite strong), they were working very little under the "revised" system, the 1981 changes will reduce work incentives, and they will remain on welfare and cease working entirely. On the contrary, for those whose indifference curves are relatively flat, as was just illustrated in Figure 6.16, work incentives are increased under the 1981 changes. Economic theory is thus very useful in highlighting this frustrating policy problem!

EXAMPLE 6.4

Worker Adjustment to Incentives

The discussion of work incentives inherent in income-replacement and income-maintenance programs assumed that workers are well informed about program characteristics—that is, that they have some intuitive understanding of the budget constraint facing them. It also assumed that workers face a sufficiently large array of choices that they are able to find a set of working hours close to their utility-maximizing set. Students often have a healthy skepticism about the degree to which these assumptions approximate reality. The following example suggests that workers *do* have sufficient knowledge and choice to accomodate their behavior to a given set of work incentives.

The State of Wisconsin, like other states, has an unemployment compensation program that pays unemployed workers a weekly benefit. These benefits are different for different recipients, depending primarily on their pre-unemployment earnings. There is a minimum and a maximum weekly benefit, but for most workers the unemployment benefit is about one half of prior earnings. Also like most other states, Wisconsin has a method of allowing for partial benefits to be paid to unemployed workers who obtain part-time or low-wage work during their period of eligibility for unemployment benefits. Unlike most other states, however, Wisconsin's partial benefit scheme is such that recipients can only receive one of three unemployment benefits: their full weekly benefit, a benefit equal to half their full weekly benefit, or zero. This partial benefit program contains some rather interesting work incentives.

The typical recipient of unemployment compensation in Wisconsin can earn up to one fourth of his or her pre-unemployment earnings with *no loss of benefits.* Being able, in effect, to keep all their earnings up to that point, the wage rate of recipients equals their market wage. This element of the program is graphed in the first figure as segment *CD,* which is parallel to the market constraint (*AB*).

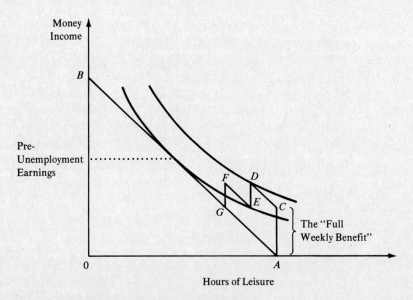

Partial Unemployment Benefits in Wisconsin

However, once current earnings rise above the critical level of one fourth of prior earnings, benefits are reduced to one half the weekly benefit. This abrupt drop in benefits causes an equally abrupt drop in total income. Since working an extra hour past point *D* causes income to drop, the wage, in effect, becomes *negative,* as segment *DE* in the first figure illustrates.

Benefits equalling one half the full entitlement are paid, then, to recipients who earn between one fourth and one half of their prior earnings. When earnings rise just beyond the one-half point, all unemployment benefits cease, and the constraint becomes the "market constraint"—as segments

EF, FG, and *GB* illustrate. The first figure shows a saw-toothed constraint where the market wage alternates with extremely negative wage rates.

A quick look at the first figure indicates that, for many people, point *D* is the utility-maximizing combination of leisure hours and income. People who are not fortunate enough to obtain a job offer where they can earn exactly one fourth of their earnings will try to choose the next best position—which is likely to be at points along the upper portions of *CD* or near point *F*. Points along most of *EF* and the lower portions of *CD* are clearly inferior—in terms of utility—to other points along the constraint running from *C* to *G*.

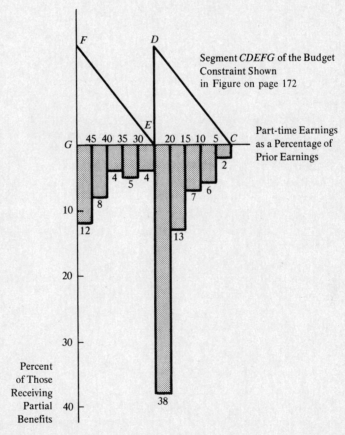

Distribution of Partial Benefits in Wisconsin (1967), by Earnings Level

While it is true that most of those receiving unemployment benefits are completely unemployed, it is interesting to observe whether those who *are* able to find part-time work adjust their behavior as indicated above. In other words, *do* people tend to cluster most at point *D*—where earnings are just equal to one fourth of their prior wages? Are there more people at point *F* and the upper portions of *CD* than along the rest of the constraint running from *C* to *G*?

The answer to both these questions—at least for the year 1967 when a study of the questions was undertaken—is yes. In the second figure, segment *CDEFG* of the first figures budget constraint is superimposed on the distribution of those actually receiving partial unemployment benefits, demonstrating that by far the biggest cluster of people is at point *D,* earning 20–25 percent of their prior earnings. Further, the concentrations of people increase as one moves to the upper ends of each segment (*CD* and *EF*)—with two-thirds of all partial-benefits recipients either at *F* or the upper half of *CD*. Thus, it appears that workers who do find partial employment while receiving unemployment benefits do have the knowledge and inclination to adjust their behavior to the constraints (and the related incentives) facing them.

SOURCE: Raymond Munts, "Partial Benefit Schedules in Unemployment Insurance: Their Effect on Work Incentive," *Journal of Human Resources* 5 (Spring 1970): 160–76.

Welfare dilemmas. Lest the student receive the impression that the obvious solution to this work-incentive problem is to reduce the implicit tax from two thirds to some lower fraction, let us explore what happens if this implicit tax were reduced to one fourth. Under this plan, the welfare recipient would be allowed to keep three of every four dollars earned. If $16 is still the daily benefit when there are no earnings, the break-even level of income becomes $64 (instead of $24). In other words, no matter what their wage rate, people who earn less than $64 per day would receive welfare benefits. Clearly, a low implicit tax rate and a reasonably generous guarantee level are inconsistent with confining welfare benefits to only the needy! This dilemma pervades just about all disputes over welfare policy. That is, reducing implicit tax rates to increase the work incentive leads to an increase in the number of people eligible for benefits.

It is also worth noting here that, because the welfare subsidy is conditioned on income, and because income is to some extent under the control of an individual, it is possible that some people previously above the break-even level of income will reduce their labor supply enough to qualify for the subsidy. This possibility is illustrated in Figure 6.17. Prior to the subsidy, the person depicted maximized utility at point *L*, working 9 hours per day. After the subsidy is instituted and the constraint moves to *ABCD*, this person finds that utility is maximized at point *M*, where hours of work are much fewer. Point *M* is a point of lower money income than point *L*, but the increased leisure time more than makes up for the lost income.

Empirical studies of welfare and work incentives. Although making welfare benefits available to people who were not previously eligible for them will clearly decrease their work incentives, the relevant policy question is: by how much will their work incentives be decreased? Some studies used estimates of income and substitution effects obtained from nonexperimental data in the late 1960s to answer this question. These studies imply that, for males, a guaranteed (zero-

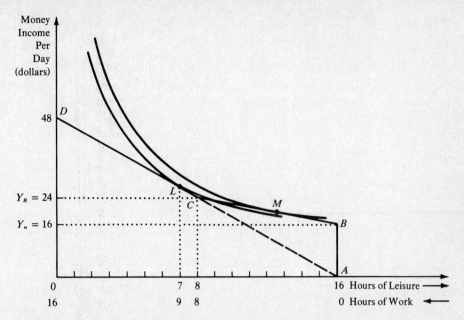

Figure 6.17 Some May Reduce Hours of Work and Money Income Under an Income-Maintenance Program

earnings) benefit of about 75 percent of the poverty level (which was $3300 per year in 1967) and a 50 percent implicit tax rate would cause male labor supply to decrease by 8–15 percent.[33]

Experimental data, however, can also be used to estimate the size of income and substitution effects. Four large social experiments were conducted in New Jersey, Seattle-Denver, Gary (Indiana), and rural North Carolina in the late 1960s and early 1970s for the purpose of measuring labor-supply responses to various alternative income-maintenance policies. They were conceived and funded because researchers and policy makers did not want to rely solely on estimates derived from the nonexperimental studies cited above.

While the details in each experiment varied, the welfare programs offered to the people in the experiments had benefit-guarantee levels (benefits with zero earnings) ranging from 50–125 percent of the poverty level.[34] The implicit tax

---

[33]Borjas and Heckman, "Labor Supply Estimates for Public Policy Evaluation," p. 331.

[34]Poverty level incomes are those below which the federal government considers a family to be living in poverty. These income thresholds are defined for farm and nonfarm families separately and are also calculated by family size and the age/sex of the household head. The threshold in each case is based on the 1963 cost of an inexpensive, but nutritionally sound, food plan designed by the Department of Agriculture. This cost was multiplied by 3, reflecting an assumption that families of three or more persons spend one-third of their income on food, and has been adjusted upward each year since 1963 by changes in the Consumer Price Index. For a nonfarm family of four, the 1976 poverty threshold was $5815, up from $3128 in 1963; by 1982 changes in the Consumer Price Index implied a poverty level of around $9750 per year. (*See* U.S. Bureau of the Census, Current Population Reports, *Consumer Income,* Series P-60, No. 115, issued July 1978 for a more detailed explanation of poverty thresholds.)

rates in each experiment ranged from 30–80 percent. The typical response for males in these experiments was to reduce labor supply by 3–8 percent.[35] The somewhat smaller response than the cross-sectional prediction above is perhaps due to the known and limited duration of each experiment; responses might have been larger if recipients knew the program would be available to them indefinitely.

In examining the labor-supply response of females in these experiments, it is useful to recall two facts from the nonexperimental studies. First, the estimates of income and substitution effects for women are much less precise than for men; second, the substitution effect for market work appears to be larger. Remembering that the substitution effect of income-maintenance programs induces a withdrawal of labor supply, it is not surprising to find that the labor-supply responses of women in the experiments tended to be larger than for men and were also more varied. For wives, the responses ranged from zero decline in Gary to a 55 percent decline among Spanish-speaking wives in New Jersey, with most other estimates in the 15–30 percent range.[36] For female heads of families, the declines ranged from 11 percent in Seattle-Denver to 30 percent in Gary.

Thus the labor supply effects of expanded welfare coverage are not likely to be innocuous. At some point, society will have to decide whether the improvements in social equity that result from more generous welfare programs are counterbalanced by the social losses attendant to reduced labor supply.[37] In making this decision, of course, society may feel quite different about reductions in market work by some groups (say, mothers of small children) than it feels about the labor-supply reductions of other groups.

REVIEW QUESTIONS

1. Is the following statement true, false, or uncertain:
   "Leisure must be an inferior good for an individual's labor supply curve to be backward-bending." Explain your answer.
2. The way the Workers' Compensation system works now is that employees permanently injured on the job receive a payment of $X each year whether they work or not. Suppose the government were to implement a new program where those who do not work at all get $0.5X but where those who do work get $0.5X plus Workers' Compensation of 50 cents *for every hour worked.* What would be the change in work incentives associated with this change in the way Workers' Compensation payments are calculated?

[35]Minorities in the New Jersey experiment were an exception to this finding. They did not decrease their labor supply at all.

[36]For a summary of all the experiments, *see* Robert Moffitt and Kenneth Kehrer, "The Effect of Tax and Transfer Programs on Labor Supply: The Evidence from the Income-Maintenance Experiments" *Research in Labor Economics,* ed. R. Ehrenberg (Greenwich, Conn.: JAI Press, 1981). *Also see* Michael C. Keeley *et al.,* "The Estimation of Labor Supply Models Using Experimental Data," *American Economic Review* (December 1978): 873–87; Robert A. Moffitt, "The Labor Supply Response in the Gary Experiment," *The Journal of Human Resources* 14 (Fall 1979): 477–87; Albert Rees, "An Overview of the Labor-Supply Results," *The Journal of Human Resources* 9 (Spring 1974): 158–80.

[37]The general issue of equity vs. output considerations is treated in a readable manner by Arthur Okun, *Equality and Efficiency: The Big Trade-Off* (Washington, D.C.: The Brookings Institution, 1975).

3. Suppose our welfare system were structured *initially* as follows: all people earning below income \$X would be given a cash grant to bring their income up to \$X. *Draw a graph showing the budget constraint for this program.*

Next, suppose we change the welfare system to incorporate a *work test.* This means that persons who work *fewer* than Y hours get no welfare payment at all. Above Y hours of work, the people receive a welfare payment sufficient to bring up their income to \$X. *Draw in the relevant budget constraint on your graph.*

Now answer the question: *Which system has stronger work incentives? Why?*

4. A secret memo from the President has been found in the trash basket in front of an aide's house. It says, in part, "Although I am in favor of eliminating the capital-gains advantages in the income tax system, I am concerned that we maintain the labor supply of the expert managers who run the industry of this country. By forcing them to pay higher taxes on investment income, we may be affecting their labor market behavior. Please have a labor economist figure out the labor supply effects of this proposed tax reform on the wealthy and report back to me as soon as possible. The analysis should be clear as to what might happen and why. Please have your economist write so that an ordinary human can understand."

Write an analysis for the President. (Note: The capital-gains "loophole" applies to the sale of stocks, bonds, and other assets. If the asset has been held for more than six months, only 40 percent of the gain on the sale—the difference between selling price and cost—is taxable. The President would make the whole gain taxable.)

5. The Secretary of Labor has received the following memo from a member of the President's staff:

"The growth of interest in worker-owned enterprises raises some important questions relating to profit sharing. If workers with no previous investment income begin to receive a portion of profits, the effects on labor supply could be large. Would you please have your staff prepare an analysis of the labor-supply implications of widespread worker participation in profits? The paper should cover the direction of the labor-supply effects as indicated by theory and the likely ways in which these labor-supply effects could be manifested. In particular, however, I am interested in a comparison of the labor-supply effects of alternative bases upon which profits can be shared among workers. Which basis or bases have the smallest labor-supply effects?"

Write the paper avoiding the use of undefined jargon words. In other words, explain the concepts and hypotheses fully.

SELECTED READINGS

William G. Bowen and T. Aldrich Finegan, *The Economics of Labor Force Participation* (Princeton, N.J.: Princeton University Press, 1969).

Glen G. Cain, *Married Women in the Labor Force* (Chicago: University of Chicago Press, 1966).

Glen G. Cain and Harold W. Watts, eds., *Income Maintenance and Labor Supply* (Chicago: Markham, 1973).

H. G. Lewis, "Hours of Work and Hours of Leisure," *Proceedings of the Industrial Relations Research Association* (1957):196–206.

Robert Moffitt and Ken Kehrer, "The Effect of Tax and Transfer Programs on Labor Supply: The Evidence from the Income Maintenance Experiments," in Ronald G. Ehrenberg, ed., *Research in Labor Economics,* 4 (Greenwich, Conn., JAI Press, 1981) 103–50.

J. A. Pechman and P. M. Timpane, eds. *Work Incentives and Income Guarantees: The New Jersey Income Tax Experiment* (Washington, D.C.: The Brookings Institution, 1975).

Chapter 7

COMPENSATING WAGE DIFFERENTIALS AND LABOR MARKETS

Chapter 6 analyzed workers' decisions about *whether to seek employment* and *how long to work*. Chapters 7 and 8 will analyze workers' decisions about the industry, occupation, or firm in which they will work. This chapter will emphasize the influence on job choice of such daily, *recurring* job characteristics as working environment, length of commute from home to work, and risk of injury. The following chapter will analyze the effects of required educational *investments* on occupational choice.

This chapter will present an analysis of occupational choice that emphasizes the importance of both wages and nonpecuniary job characteristics in the allocation of labor to meet social needs. The empirical research on wage patterns will also be examined to see if job choices and the allocation of labor really are made along the lines suggested by these analyses. The final section applies the concepts of this chapter to two very important and controversial government programs: occupational safety and health regulation and affirmative-action plans for hiring women and minorities.

An Analysis of Occupational Choice

If all jobs were exactly alike and located in the same place, an individual's decision about where to seek work would be relatively simple. He or she would attempt to obtain a job where the expected compensation was highest. Any differences in compensation would cause workers to seek work with the highest-paying employers and avoid applying for work with the low-paying ones. The high-paying employers, having an abundance of applicants, might decide they are paying more than they have to in order to staff their vacancies. The low-paying employers would have to raise wage offers in order to compete for workers. Ultimately, if the market works without hindrance, wages of all employers would equalize.

All jobs are not the same, however. Some jobs require much more education or training than others. Some jobs are in clean, modern offices, and others are in noisy, dusty, or dangerous factories. Some permit the employee some discretion over the pace of work at various points throughout the day, while some involve highly rigid assembly-line work. Some are challenging and call for decision making by the employee; others are monotonous. While the influence of educational and training requirements will be discussed at length in the next chapter, we will discuss here how the variations in job characteristics influence individual choice and the observable market outcomes of that choice.

Individual Choice and Its Outcomes

Suppose several unskilled workers have received offers from two employers. Employer X pays $5.00 per hour and offers clean, safe working conditions. Employer Y also pays $5.00 per hour, but offers employment in a dirty, noisy factory. Which employer would the workers choose? Most would undoubtedly choose Employer X, because the pay is the same while the job is performed under less disagreeable conditions.

Clearly, however, $5.00 is not an equilibrium wage in both firms.[1] Because Firm X finds it very easy to attract applicants at $5.00, it will "hold the line" on any future wage increases. Firm Y, however, must either clean up the plant, pay higher wages, or do both if it wants to fill its vacancies. Assuming it decides not to alter working conditions, it must clearly pay a wage *above* $5.00 to be competitive in the labor market. The extra wage it must pay to attract workers is called a *compensating wage differential,* because the higher wage is paid to compensate workers for the undesirable working conditions. If such a differential did not exist, Firm Y could not attract the unskilled workers that Firm X can obtain.

Suppose that Firm Y raises its wage offer to $5.50 while the offer from X remains at $5.00. Will this 50-cent-per-hour differential—an extra $1,000 per year —serve to attract *all* the workers in our group to Firm Y? If it did attract them all, Firm X would have an incentive to raise its wage and Firm Y might want to lower its offers a bit; the 50-cent differential in this case would *not* be an equilibrium differential.

More than likely, however, the 10 percent higher wage in Firm Y would attract only *some* of the group to Firm Y. Some people are not bothered by dirt and noise as much as others are, and these people may decide to take the extra

---

[1]There may be a few people who really do not care about noise and dirt in the workplace. We assume here that these people are so rare—or Firm Y's demand for workers so large—that Y cannot fill all its vacancies with just those who are totally insensitive to dirt and noise.

pay and put up with the poorer working conditions.[2] Others, however, may be very sensitive to noise or allergic to dust, and they will decide that they would rather get paid less than expose themselves to working conditions that are very unpleasant. If both firms can obtain the quantity and quality of workers they want, the 50-cent differential *would* be an equilibrium differential—in the sense that there would be no forces causing the differential to change.

The desire of workers to avoid unpleasantness or risk, then, should force employers offering unpleasant or risky jobs to pay higher wages than they would otherwise have to pay. Put another way, in order to attract a work force, these employers will have to pay higher wages to their workers than firms that offer pleasant, safe jobs to comparable workers. This wage differential serves two related, socially desirable ends. First, it serves a *social* need by giving people an incentive to do—voluntarily—dirty, dangerous, or unpleasant work. Likewise the existence of a compensating wage differential also imposes a financial penalty on employers who have unfavorable working conditions. Second, at an *individual* level, it serves as a reward to workers who accept unpleasant jobs by paying them more than comparable workers in more pleasant jobs.

The allocation of labor. Society has a number of jobs that are either unavoidably nasty or would be very costly to make safe and pleasant (coal mining, deep-sea diving, and coke-oven cleaning are examples). There are essentially two ways to recruit the necessary labor for such jobs. One is to compel people to do these jobs—the military draft being the most obvious American example of forced labor. The second way is to induce people to do the jobs voluntarily.

Most modern societies rely mainly on incentives—compensating wage differentials—to recruit labor to unpleasant jobs voluntarily. Workers will mine coal, collect garbage, and bolt steel beams together 50 stories off the ground, because, compared to alternative jobs for which they could qualify, these jobs pay well. The 1500 commercial deep-sea divers in the United States, for example, who are exposed to the dangers of drowning, the rigors of construction work with cumbersome gear, a lonely and hostile work environment, and several physiological disorders as a result of compression and decompression, made $20,000 to $45,000 per year in the mid-1970s, or about 20 percent to 130 percent more than the average high-school graduate.

As another example, the *failure* to pay sufficiently high wages to U.S. military personnel has occasionally created difficulties in recruiting and retaining such people. While the pay for military recruits with less than two years of service was 14 percent above the pay for civilian youth right after the draft was eliminated in 1973, the relative pay advantage had fallen to 2 percent by 1979. This fall in relative pay for recruits was accompanied by a rather severe short-

[2]The assertion that people are affected differently by noise is documented in *Community Reaction to Airport Noise,* vol. I (report to the National Aeronautics and Space Administration prepared by Tracor, Inc. of Austin, Texas), July 1971. This study showed, for example, that around 10 percent of people are "highly susceptible" to noise annoyance, while around half are "highly adaptable" to airport noises.

EXAMPLE 7.1

Coal Mining in the Soviet Union

Coal mining is a dangerous, but socially necessary, task the world over. Because it is difficult to recruit people to do voluntarily this unpleasant work, compensating wage differentials exist even in economies where "market" incentives are not *philosophically* recognized. In the Soviet Union, for example, the difficulties of recruiting personnel to work in the coal-mining industry have caused the average earnings of miners to be *double* that of the average factory worker. Further, miners in the most unhealthy and arduous jobs work 30 hours a week, compared to 36 hours in the other mining jobs; in addition, they receive a one-time bonus equivalent to over 25 percent of the yearly pay for manufacturing workers.

SOURCE: Radio Liberty Research, June 11, 1979 (RL 179/79).

age in the quantity and ability levels of enlistees, despite the decline in civilian job opportunities that accompanied a large rise in the unemployment rate over that six-year period. By 1982, both the quality and quantity aspects of the military shortage had ended, due partly to a very high civilian unemployment rate, but probably mostly to pay raises that increased the pay for recruits to 18 percent above that of civilian youth. If the government wants to maintain armed services without resorting to the draft, it is clear that military pay must rise to a level sufficient to overcome the hazards and inconveniences of military life.[3]

Compensation for workers. Compensating wage differentials also serve as *individual* rewards by paying those who accept bad or arduous working conditions more than they would otherwise receive. In a parallel fashion, those who opt for more pleasant conditions have to "buy" them by accepting lower pay. For example, if a person takes the $5.00 per hour job with Firm X, he or she is giving up the $5.50 per hour job with less pleasant conditions in Firm Y. The better conditions are being bought, in a very real sense, for 50 cents per hour.

Thus, compensating wage differentials become the price at which good working conditions can be purchased by—or bad ones sold to—workers. Contrary to what is commonly asserted, a monetary value *can* often be attached to events or conditions in which the effects are primarily psychological in nature. Compensating wage differentials provide the key to the valuation of these nonpecuniary aspects of employment.

---

[3]"The Retention Problem," *The Wall Street Journal* (March 19, 1980), p. 24, and an unpublished table provided to us by Robert Lockman, Center for Naval Analyses. What is pleasant or unpleasant is determined in the market at the *margin*. For example, even if most people dislike night work, there might be enough who do not to fill night-shift jobs without a compensating wage differential. *See* Example 7.3 for a fuller discussion of this issue.

In the area of occupational-health-and-safety policy, there is continuous debate about whether to make machines safer or whether to protect the worker from machine hazards with personal protective devices.[4] For example, high noise levels can eventually damage the hearing of workers. The Department of Labor has favored reducing noise levels through engineering changes, such as putting mufflers on—or baffles around—noisy machines. Employer representatives have consistently claimed that such engineering changes are inordinately expensive and that compelling workers to wear earplugs would preserve workers' hearing at much less cost. Because resources are scarce, our society would like to achieve hearing protection at minimum cost, but we must be sure to count *all* the costs. One of the costs of wearing earplugs is the *psychic* cost: they are very uncomfortable for most people to wear. The cost of this discomfort *must* be counted along with the purchase price of earplugs in arriving at the total cost of wearing earplugs.

How could we put a dollar value on earplug discomfort? A straightforward way to determine this dollar value would be to find a set of employers who *require* the use of earplugs as a condition of employment and to compare the wages they pay to those of *comparable* firms that allow, but *do not require,* the wearing of earplugs. If workers do in fact find earplugs more uncomfortable than the noise, wages in the firm that requires their use should be higher—and this wage differential is the estimate of what value workers place on this discomfort.

Suppose, for example, that the research showed that companies requiring earplugs pay 10 cents an hour—or $200 per year—more than *otherwise similar* firms pay for *comparable* labor.[5] Workers accepting work there are indicating by their behavior that they are willing to take $200 per year as compensation for the discomfort they must bear; that is, the cost of the discomfort to them is equal to, or less than, $200 per year. Those refusing to work at the plant place a value higher than that on their discomfort costs, because $200 is insufficient to compensate them. Thus, the cost of discomfort at the margin is $200 per year (that is, to induce one more worker to wear earplugs would require added compensation of about $200 per year).

Before concluding that the psychic costs of wearing earplugs are $200 per year, we must remember that our hypothetical findings above are for the marginal worker. People differ in the amount of discomfort they feel and in the value they place on what they feel. Those most likely to take the extra pay in return for having to wear earplugs are those who are least sensitive to discomfort or most willing to trade discomfort for money. If we were to compel *all* workers in noisy factories to wear earplugs, we would be forcing earplugs on some for whom the costs of discomfort are in excess of $200.

As this example illustrates, compensating wage differentials are the price at which various *qualitative* job characteristics are bought and sold. As such, they

---

[4]The debate about whether or not the government should be involved at all in the occupational safety and health area is discussed later in this chapter.

[5]Firms may be willing to do this if they believe requiring earplugs will reduce workers' compensation claims for hearing loss in the future.

offer a way of placing a value on things that most people think of as "noneconomic." This illustration, of course, does not prove that compensating wage differentials exist or that such differentials are equilibrium prices—issues that will be discussed later in the chapter.

Assumptions and Predictions

We have seen how a simple theory of job choice by individuals leads to the *prediction* that compensating wage differentials will be associated with various job characteristics. Positive differentials (higher wages) will accompany "bad" characteristics, while negative differentials (lower wages) will be associated with "good" ones. However, it is very important to understand that this prediction can *only* be made *holding other things equal.*

Our prediction about the existence of compensating wage differentials grows out of the reasonable assumption that if a worker has a choice between a job with "good" working conditions and a job of equal pay with a "bad" set of working conditions, he or she will choose the "good" job. If the employee is an unskilled laborer he or she may be choosing between an unpleasant job spreading hot asphalt or a more comfortable job in an air-conditioned warehouse. In either case, he or she is going to receive something close to the wage rate unskilled workers typically receive. However, our theory would predict that this worker would receive *more* from the asphalt-spreading job than from the warehouse job.

Thus the predicted outcome of our theory of job choice is *not* that employees working under "bad" conditions receive more than those working in "good" conditions. The prediction is that, *holding worker characteristics constant,* employees in bad jobs receive higher wages than those working under more pleasant conditions. The characteristics that must be held constant include all the other things that influence wages: skill level, age, race, sex, union status, region of the country, and so forth. Because there are many influences on wages *other* than working conditions, our theory leads us to expect employers offering "bad" jobs to pay higher wages than employers offering "good" jobs to *comparable* workers. This theory is based on three assumptions about workers and one concerning employers:

Assumption 1: utility maximization. Our first assumption is that workers seek to maximize their *utility,* not their income. If workers sought to maximize income, they would always choose the highest-paying job available to them. This behavior would eventually cause wages to be equalized across the jobs open to any set of workers, as stated earlier.

In contrast, compensating wage differentials will only arise if some people do *not* choose the highest-paying job offered—preferring instead a lower-paying, but more pleasant, job. This behavior allows the employers offering the lower-paying, pleasant jobs to be competitive for labor. Wages do not equalize in this case. Rather, the *net advantages*—the overall utility from the pay and the psychic aspects of the job—tend to equalize for the marginal worker.

Assumption 2: worker information. The second assumption implicit in our analysis is that workers are aware of the job characteristics of potential importance to them. Whether they know about them before they take the job or find out soon after taking it is not too important. In either case, a company offering a "bad" job with no compensating wage differentials would have trouble recruiting or retaining workers—trouble that would eventually force it to raise its wage.

It is quite likely, of course, that workers will quickly learn of dust, dirt, noise, rigid work discipline, and other obvious bad working conditions. It is equally likely that they will *not* know the *precise* probability of being laid off, say, or injured on the job. However, even with respect to these probabilities, their own direct observation or word-of-mouth reports from other employees can give them enough information to evaluate the situation with some accuracy. For example, the proportion of employees considering their work "dangerous" has been shown to be rather closely related to the actual injury rates published by the government for the industry in which they work.[6] This finding illustrates that, while workers are probably not able to state the precise probability of being injured, they do form accurate subjective judgments about the relative risk among several jobs.

Where our predictions may disappoint us, however, is with respect to *very* obscure characteristics. For example, while we now know that asbestos dust is highly damaging to worker health, this fact was not widely known 40 years ago. One reason information on asbestos dangers in plants was so long in being generated is that it takes more than 20 years for asbestos-related disease to develop. Cause and effect were thus obscured from workers and researchers alike—creating a situation where worker job choices were made in ignorance of this risk. Compensating wage differentials for this danger thus could not possibly arise at that time. Our predictions about compensating wage differentials, then, hold only for job characteristics that workers know about.

Assumption 3: worker mobility. The third assumption implicit in our theory is that workers have a range of job offers from which to choose. Without a range of offers, workers would not be able to select the combination of job characteristics they desire or avoid the ones to which they do not wish exposure. A compensating wage differential for risk of injury, for example, simply could not arise if workers were able to obtain only dangerous jobs. It is the act of choosing safe jobs over dangerous ones that forces employers offering dangerous work to raise wages.

One manner in which this choice can occur is for each job applicant to receive several job offers from which to choose. However, another way in which choice could be exercised is for workers to be (at least potentially) highly mobile. In other words, workers with few concurrent offers could take a job and continue their search for work if they thought an improvement could be made. Thus, even with few offers at any *one* time, workers could conceivably have relatively wide choice over a *period* of time—which would eventually allow them to select the job that maximizes their utility.

---

[6]W. Kip Viscusi, "Labor Market Valuations of Life and Limb: Empirical Evidence and Policy Implications," *Public Policy* 26 (Summer 1978): 359–86.

While there are no general data on the number of concurrent offers a typical job applicant receives, it does seem to be true that job mobility among American workers is relatively high. The reported quit rate in manufacturing is normally between 1–2 percent per month—or about 12–24 percent per year. With job openings from quits and from general business expansion, manufacturing businesses newly hire 3 percent of their employees each month. Turnover is so great, in fact, that the median length of job tenure is 3.6 years—meaning that half of all workers have been on their current job less than three and one-half years.[7]

Another way to understand the amount of choice workers have in the job market is to look at job mobility over time. Consider male, blue-collar operatives (semiskilled workers)—a group of males many believe face severe restrictions on job choice. Among those operatives who were over age 25 in 1965, 18 percent were working in *completely different* occupations by 1970 (almost 9 percent had moved to skilled jobs, 3.5 percent had entered managerial or professional/technical occupations, and 3 percent were in unskilled jobs). The main point is that almost one worker in five had had a major occupational change in that five-year period.[8] Many more, of course, changed their jobs or their place of employment while still retaining semiskilled work. It is thus difficult to conclude that workers are typically lacking in job choice.

Assumption 4: employer profit maximization. As emphasized throughout this text, wages are determined by the interaction of supply and demand. Workers may want higher wages, but employers must be willing to pay them. Why would an employer offering a dangerous job be willing to pay a higher wage than some other firm that offers safer employment?

The assumption here is that the disagreeable aspects of jobs are costly for the employer to eliminate. An employer with a dangerous workplace, for example, can make it safer only by incurring the costs of installing safety devices, training employees, or issuing protective equipment to its workers. In attempting to maximize profits, the firm will attempt to attract its desired work force in the least costly manner. Thus, the firm compares the higher wage costs associated with offering dangerous jobs to the net costs required to make these jobs safer. ("Net" costs are the expenditures on safety less such nonwage savings as reduced machine damage and less worker time lost.) If the wage savings from offering safer jobs exceed the net costs of reducing risk, the firm will decide to offer safer, lower-paying jobs. However, if the net costs of providing more safety are greater than the extra wage costs required to recruit employees for dangerous work, the profit-maximizing employer will choose not to offer safer jobs; instead, higher wages will be offered to attract the desired employees.

In the above case, then, the firms that are willing to pay higher wages do so because they are able to attract workers without having to undertake an expensive

---

[7]Robert E. Hall, "The Importance of Lifetime Jobs in the U.S. Economy," *American Economic Review* 72 (September, 1982): 716-24.

[8]U.S. Bureau of the Census, *Characteristics of the Population, 1970: U.S. Summary,* Vol. I, Sec. 2 (Washington, D.C.: U.S. Government Printing Office, 1973), Table 230. These data do not indicate what fraction of those who changed occupation also changed employers.

EXAMPLE 7.2

Compensating Wage Differentials in 19th Century Britain

English mill towns in the mid-1800s were often places beset by violence and unhealthy living conditions. Infant mortality, a common indicator of health conditions, averaged over 200 per 1000 live births in English towns —a rate well above those that typically prevail today in the poorest African countries! Violence was also a common part of life: crime rates were high, husbands beat wives, parents beat children, and corporal punishment was often used by factory supervisors against child labor.

It is interesting, however, that the conditions varied from town to town and factory to factory. Infant mortality rates ranged from 110 to 344 among English towns in 1834, for example. As a further example, not all factories used corporal punishment as a means of industrial discipline. These differences in conditions have led economic historians to wonder whether workers' *information* and *choice* back then were sufficient to generate compensating wage differentials for the more unpleasant or unhealthy sectors of employment.

More specifically, workers were leaving rural areas to work in towns during this era in English history. Towns where conditions were very unhealthy would be less attractive to potential migrants than towns with a healthier environment if the wages one could receive in each place were equal. If workers had reasonably good information on health conditions and could obtain work in several places, they would tend to gravitate toward the more pleasant places and away from the unhealthy towns. Differences in the relative supplies of migrants should have caused a wage differential to be created; that is, factories in the more squalid towns would have to offer higher wages to compete for migrants. Likewise, factories that used corporal punishment would have had to offer higher wages than firms that did not, if employees had information on working conditions and could exercise choice about where they worked.

While wage and other data from the 1800s are such that research results are probably more suggestive than definitive, two intriguing findings have emerged from studies of compensating wage differentials in nineteenth century England. First, it appears that once the cost of living and regional wage differences are accounted for, wages were higher for unskilled laborers in towns where infant mortality rates were greater. Results using 1834 data, replicated again using 1905 data, suggest that where infant mortality rates were 10 percent greater than average, the unskilled wage was 2–3 percent higher than average. Second, it also appears that male children who worked in factories where corporal punishment was used received wages some 16–18 percent higher than boys of the same age, experience, and literacy who worked in plants where violence was not used. (Because workers receive compensating wage differentials only if employers are willing to pay them, one must entertain the notion that the threat of corporal punishment raised productivity by 16–18 percent.)

Source: Jeffrey G. Williamson, "Was the Industrial Revolution Worth It? Disamenities and Death in 19th Century British Towns," *Explorations in Economic History* 19 (1982): 221–45; Clark Nardinelli, "Corporal Punishment and Children's Wages in Nineteenth Century Britain," *Explorations in Economic History* 19 (1982): 283–95. We are indebted to Professor Ronald Warren, University of Virginia, for calling our attention to this article and for suggesting this general topic as an example.

safety program. The higher wages, in other words, allow them to cut costs elsewhere. The firms that pay lower wages to comparable workers are those that find the provision of safety a cheaper option for attracting labor. In a real sense, these latter firms *must* pay lower wages to remain competitive in the product market, because they have incurred greater safety-related expenses than the firms offering dangerous, higher-paying jobs.

Empirical Tests of the Theory of Compensating Wage Differentials

The prediction that there will be compensating wage differentials for undesirable job characteristics is at least 200 years old. Adam Smith, in his *Wealth of Nations* published in 1776, proposed five "principal circumstances which . . . make up for a small pecuniary gain in some employments, and counterbalance a great one in others."[9] Three of these will be discussed in other chapters: the difficulty of learning the job (Chapter 8), the probability of success (Chapter 10), and the constancy of employment (Chapter 18). However, most relevant to our discussion in this chapter is his assertion that "the wages of labour vary with the ease or hardship, the cleanliness or dirtiness, the honourableness or dishonourableness of the employment."

One would think that 200 years is a sufficient period of time over which to have accumulated substantial evidence concerning an important prediction! Unfortunately, the prediction has only been seriously tested in the last ten years— and even then in only a limited way. The reasons for this lack of evidence are two-fold. First, the prediction is that, *other things equal,* wages will be higher in unpleasant or dangerous jobs. The prediction can be tested validly only if the researcher is able to control for the effects of age, education, sex, region, race, union status, and all the other factors that typically influence wages. Only when the effects of these factors on wages are known can the researcher filter out the

[9]*See* Adam Smith, *Wealth of Nations* (New York: Modern Library, 1937), Book I, Chapter 10.

separate influence on wages of (say) injury risk.[10] Statistical procedures can control for these other factors, but these procedures require large data samples and the use of computers—and only in the last ten years or so have the necessary data and computers been widely available to researchers.

The second problem that has hindered the empirical testing for compensating wage differentials is the problem of specifying, in advance of these tests, job characteristics that are generally regarded as "disagreeable." For example, while some people dislike outdoor work and would have to be paid a premium in order to accept it, others prefer such work and dislike desk jobs. Similar observations can be made about such job characteristics as repetitiveness, chances to make decisions, level of responsibility, and amount of physical exertion. Tests of the theory require selecting job characteristics where there is widespread agreement about what is "good" or "bad" at the margin. For this reason, the most credible and convincing tests of the theory have dealt with the level of *danger* on the job. While people may respond with different intensities to danger, it is difficult to believe that anyone prefers injury to safety; danger is an unambiguous "bad." The risk of injury is also objectively measured from injury rates published by occupation or, more commonly, by industry.

The most striking evidence of compensating wage differentials to date relates to the risk of *fatal* injury on the job. Nine separate studies, all using different data sets—seven from the United States and two from Great Britain—have found that wages are positively associated with the risk of being killed on the job, other things equal.[11] The results suggest that workers receive between $20 and $300 more per year for every one-in-ten-thousand increase in the risk of being killed on the job. (One death for every 10,000 workers is roughly the yearly average for steel mills, while a rate of 10 deaths per 10,000 workers is the average for logging camps.) While these estimates seem small, they do imply that a plant with 1,000 employees could save between $20,000 and $300,000 in wage costs *per year* if it undertook a safety program that would save one life every ten years.

The results for nonfatal injuries are not as supportive of the theory of compensating differentials. Most of these injuries are relatively minor and at least partially compensated for by workers' compensation insurance—which means that the losses incurred by workers are relatively small. Small losses probably do not generate much incentive to obtain large compensating wage differentials, so that any differentials that do exist may simply be too small to distinguish from

---

[10]It is especially important to control for these other influences because safety is probably a normal good (meaning that higher income workers desire more of it). A *simple* correlation of risk levels and earnings is thus negative—not positive as predicted by theory. However, the simple correlation fails to account for all the *other* factors that influence earnings. Only if the influence of these factors can be accounted for would we expect to obtain the predicted positive relationship between earnings and risk.

[11]Eight studies are reviewed in Robert S. Smith, "Compensating Wage Differentials and Public Policy: A Review," *Industrial and Labor Relations Review* 32 (April 1979): 339–52. The ninth is by Alan Marin and George Psacharopoulos, "The Reward for Risk in the Labor Market: Evidence from the U.K. and a Reconciliation with Other Studies," *Journal of Political Economy* 90 (August 1982): 827–53.

other forces that influence wages.[12] It is not too surprising, then, that it has been easier to observe compensating wage differentials for fatal than nonfatal work accidents. The victims of a fatal accident cannot possibly be fully compensated after the fact, so that the sheer magnitude of the losses caused by these accidents motivates those at risk to seek compensating differentials that are large enough to observe.

Policy Applications

The insights provided by the theory of compensating differentials can be applied to some very critical social issues: the federal occupational safety and health program and affirmative-action plans for hiring minorities and women.

Occupational Safety and Health

Are workers benefited by the reduction of risk? In 1970, Congress passed the Occupational Safety and Health Act, which directed the U.S. Department of Labor to issue and enforce safety and health standards for all private employers. The stated goal of the act was to ensure the "highest degree of health and safety protection for the employee."[13] Despite the *ideal* that employees should face the minimum possible risk in the workplace, the discussion below suggests that implementing this ideal as social *policy* may not necessarily be in the best interests of workers.

Suppose a labor market is functioning like our textbook model, in that workers are well informed about dangers inherent in any job and are mobile enough to avoid risks they do not wish to take. In these circumstances, wages will be positively related to risk (other things equal), and workers will sort themselves into jobs according to their preferences. A worker (Person B) who does not worry much about being injured, may decide to accept a more dangerous job because of the higher wage (W_B) being offered. Another (Person A) may find that the higher wage is not enough to compensate him for the higher risk; this kind of worker will take a safer job at lower pay (W_A).

Now suppose the Occupational Safety and Health Administration (OSHA) —the Department of Labor agency that is responsible for implementing the federal safety and health program—promulgates a standard that, in effect, says that any risk level above that faced by Person A (R_A) is illegal. The effects, although unintended and perhaps not immediately obvious, would be detrimental to employees like B. Reducing risk is costly, and the best wage offer a worker can

---

[12]The statistical problem is one of distinguishing the influence of injuries from all the other influences, including random ones, on wages. It is a little bit like trying to locate the position of Pluto in the sky from one's backyard. When Pluto is close to earth, the moon is merely a crescent, there is no haze, and the city is dark, it can be done. If a full moon, great distance from the earth, haze, and ground light are present, Pluto's weak light signal cannot be seen or "filtered" out from all the other stars or planets.

[13]Section 6(b)(5) of the Occupational Safety and Health Act.

EXAMPLE 7.3

What Job Characteristics Produce Dissatisfaction?

Textbooks in personnel management frequently assert that workers become dissatisfied if they are insecure about layoff, perform repetitive tasks, are subject to stress, or do not have some autonomy over how to organize their efforts. Managers are urged to analyze the jobs they offer to see where fatigue, boredom, stress, or lack of freedom can be eliminated.

From casual observation of people each of us knows, however, we are aware that personalities and energy levels differ. Some workers (Air Force pilots, performing artists) seem to thrive on stress; others go to great lengths to avoid it. Some people, like actors, seek jobs where layoff is a common and expected occurrence—and still others seem to prefer controlled, repetitive jobs where decisions and responsibility need not be undertaken. Can these casual observations be reconciled with the "conventional wisdom" of management texts?

The analysis in this chapter has emphasized that workers will tend to avoid jobs with disagreeable attributes. If a very repetitive job, for example, does not pay a wage any greater than a more interesting and available job of comparable skill, only those workers who like repetitive tasks (or at least do not mind them) will apply. If there are not enough workers who like repetitive tasks to fill the openings, a firm will have to raise wage offers so it can attract the workers who find task-repetition a disagreeable job characteristic.

Thus, compensating wage differentials for a job characteristic that many find unpleasant will not arise if the positions can be adequately staffed by workers who are not bothered by this characteristic. Only when the number of people bothered is large relative to demand will firms need to pay compensating differentials, for only then will they need to attract workers who find the job characteristic in question unpleasant. (Economists call these latter workers "marginal," because even with the higher wage rate, they are often close to being dissatisfied enough to quit; their attachment to the firm is therefore "marginal.") If a job characteristic is universally regarded as disagreeable—or is regarded as such by firms' marginal workers—compensating wage differentials should arise. However, if the number of people who do not find the characteristic unpleasant is relatively large, differentials will not be created.

By analyzing the wage differentials associated with various job characteristics, then, one can begin to assess which are regarded as unpleasant by the marginal worker and which are not. Interestingly enough, none of the "disagreeable" characteristics mentioned in the first paragraph are consistently or strongly associated with higher wages, other things being equal. Studies of the effects on wages of repetitive tasks, lack of autonomy, stressful conditions, and job insecurity have *not* provided clear evidence of positive wage differentials. Hence, while many people would find these four job characteristics disagreeable, one must question whether the workers who actually hold jobs with these characteristics find them so.

Because the studies mentioned above are few in number (there are 8) and may have methodological weaknesses, and because labor markets may not work perfectly, one cannot come to strong conclusions at this point about which job characteristics are regarded as unpleasant by workers actually facing them. However, these studies do illustrate a method for analyzing this important issue, and their results raise legitimate questions about aspects of the "conventional wisdom" of personnel management theories regarding job satisfaction.

Sources: Charles Brown, "Equalizing Differences in the Labor Market," *Quarterly Journal of Economics* 94 (February 1980): 113–34; Greg Duncan, "Earnings Functions and Non-pecuniary Benefits," *Journal of Human Resources* 11 (Fall 1976): 462–83; and W. Kip Viscusi, "Wealth Effects and Earnings Premiums for Job Hazards," *Review of Economics and Statistics* 60 (August 1978): 408–16. Other studies are reviewed in Robert Smith, "Compensating Wage Differentials and Public Policy: A Review," *Industrial and Labor Relations Review* 32 (April 1979): 339–52.

obtain at risk R_A is W_A. For Person B, however, wage W_A and risk R_A generate *less utility* than did his higher-wage and higher-risk job! This conclusion can be inferred from B's behavior *if,* as we assumed above, the labor market is characterized by both information and choice. After all, B *could* have worked at the lower risk and wage level before OSHA's standard was promulgated; the fact that he rejected that option and chose instead a higher-wage, higher-risk job suggests that the latter job yielded greater utility, all things considered.

When the government mandates the reduction of risk in a market where workers are compensated for the risks they take, it penalizes workers like B, who are not terribly sensitive to risk and appreciate the higher wages associated with higher risk. The critical issue, of course, is whether workers have the knowledge and choice necessary to generate compensating wage differentials. Many people believe that because workers are ignorant, unable to comprehend different risk levels, or immobile, most do not choose risky jobs voluntarily. If this belief were true, government regulation *could* make workers better off—and, indeed, such conditions almost undoubtedly prevail in some markets. However, the arguments already presented concerning information and mobility, and the evidence of the positive relationship between wages and risk of death, should challenge the assumption that, in general, the labor market fails to generate compensating differentials.

To say that worker utility *can* be reduced by such programs does not, of course, imply that it *will* be reduced. The outcome depends on how well the unregulated market functions and how careful the government is in setting its standards for risk reduction. The following section will analyze a governmental program implemented in a market that has *not* generated enough information about risk for employees to make informed job choices.

How strict should OSHA standards be? Consider a labor market, like that mentioned previously for asbestos workers, where ignorance or worker immobility hinders labor-market operation. Let us suppose also that the government becomes aware of the health hazard involved and wishes to set a standard regulating worker exposure to this hazard. How stringent should this standard be?

The crux of the problem in standard setting is that reducing hazards is costly; the greater the reduction, the more it costs. While businesses bear these costs initially, they will ultimately respond to them by a. cutting costs elsewhere and b. raising prices (to the extent that cutting costs is not possible). Since labor costs constitute the largest cost category for most businesses, it is natural for firms facing large government-mandated hazard-reduction costs to hold the line on wage increases or to adopt policies that are the equivalent of reducing wages: speeding up production, being less lenient with absenteeism, reducing fringe benefits, and so forth. It is also likely—particularly in view of any price increases (which, of course, tend to reduce product demand)—that employment will be cut back. Some of the job loss will be in the form of permanent layoffs that force workers to find other jobs—jobs they presumably could have had before the layoff but chose not to accept. Some of the loss will be in the form of cutting down on hiring new employees who would have regarded the jobs as their best employment option.

Thus, whether it is in the form of smaller wage increases, more difficult working conditions, or being unable to obtain or retain one's first choice in a job, the costs of compliance with health standards will fall on employees. Employees will bear these costs in ways that reduce their earnings below what they *would have been in the absence of OSHA.* These losses may not be immediate or very obvious, since it is hard to know what wages would have been without the OSHA standard. However, the obscurity of this outcome of government regulation does not justify ignoring it.

Suppose a worker believes she has taken a low-risk job, when in fact she is being exposed to a hazard that has a relatively large probability of damaging her health in 20 years. She receives a wage equal to W_A, and believes herself to be at risk level R_A; instead, she faces the higher risk of R_B. If the government discovers that the true risk level faced by this worker and others in similar jobs is R_B, not R_A, what should it do?

One option is to simply inform the affected workers and let them decide for themselves what to do. This option presumes that workers can understand information about relative risks and have enough choices available to avoid jobs they regard as unsatisfactory. However, if the government has little confidence in the ability of workers to understand the information or to find other work, the government could pass a standard that limits employee exposure to this hazard. But what level of protection should this standard offer? Because any employer ordered by the government to reduce risk levels faced by employees must incur added costs, its wage and employment offers to workers cannot be as generous as before. As argued above, it is likely that employees will bear the costs of mandated risk reduction; therefore, it is very important that OSHA set its safety and health standards carefully.

Workers clearly benefit from the risk reduction itself, but because they will probably bear the costs of this reduction, one must ask whether they are willing to pay the price. If the value they place on reduced risk is greater than the wage loss involved, they will be made better off by OSHA's new health standard. If, however, the wage loss they face is large compared to their evaluation of the benefits associated with reduced risk, OSHA's program will make them worse off.

How can one estimate, in a practical way, how much wage loss workers are willing to bear in exchange for a reduction in risk and still feel at least as well off as they are currently? The answer lies in estimating compensating wage differentials in markets that appear to work. Suppose that in a properly functioning market, workers accept wage cuts of $300 per year for reductions in the yearly death rate of 1 in 10,000 (this represents the upper-bound estimates reported on p. 188). These workers appear to feel that, other things equal, $300 is a price they are willing to pay for this reduction in risk. Thus, as noted earlier in the case of earplug use, compensating wage differentials can be used to estimate the value workers place on seemingly intangible aspects of their jobs. The use of such differentials should not be oversold, because the difficulties of establishing which markets are properly functioning are considerable. However, estimating compensating wage differentials is probably the best way of finding out what value workers attach to various job characteristics.[14]

Since one cannot rule out the possibility—indeed, the likelihood—that one way or another workers will ultimately pay for the costs of their reduced workplace risks, economists argue strongly that the government should conduct studies to estimate whether the value workers place on risk reduction is commensurate with the costs of the program. These studies are called *benefit-cost* studies, and they weigh the costs of a program against the value workers (or other beneficiaries) attach to the benefits of (say) reduced risk. Estimates of compensating wage differentials can be very useful in estimating these benefits.

Consider the OSHA standard that reduced the exposure of 90,000 asbestos workers to two fibers of asbestos per cubic centimeter of air. Inhaling airborne asbestos fibers is strongly and persuasively associated with several types of cancer; it is expected that the two-fiber standard will reduce yearly asbestos-related deaths by 4 per 1000 workers. Extrapolating from the *lower-bound* estimates of compensating differentials associated with the risk of death, mentioned on page 188, asbestos workers would probably be willing to pay *at least* $800 per year for this four-in-one-thousand reduction in risk.[15] Because the yearly cost of the asbestos standard comes to roughly $800 per worker, it seems reasonably certain that the workers benefited by the standard would be willing to bear any of the program's costs that are shifted to them.[16] Thus, the asbestos standard almost certainly improves the welfare (utility) of asbestos workers.

---

[14]*See* E. J. Mishan, "Evaluation of Life and Limb: A Theoretical Approach." *Journal of Political Economy* 79, 4 (July/August 1971): 687–705.

[15]The figure of $800 arises from multiplying the lower estimate of $20 for a one-in-ten-thousand reduction in death risk by a factor of 40 (to bring it up to a four-in-one-thousand reduction).

[16]Russell Settle, "Benefits and Costs of the Federal Asbestos Standard," paper delivered at a Department of Labor Conference on Evaluating the Effects of the Occupational Safety and Health Program, March 18–19, 1975.

As another example of benefit-cost analysis, consider two alternative standards limiting the exposure of chemical workers to *acrylonitrile*—a substance used in making acrylic fibers and a certain type of resin. Exposure to acrylonitrile is believed to increase one's chances of contracting cancer; reducing worker exposure from 20 parts-per-million (ppm) of air to 2 ppm would reduce the yearly risk of cancer-related deaths by 8.4 per 10,000 exposed workers. We know from our estimates of compensating differentials that the *most* we can assume workers would be willing to give up to obtain this reduction in risk is about $2500 per year.[17] Since obtaining this new level of risk would cost $2800 per worker (per year), it is conceivable that the standard would improve worker utility if workers bore the costs, but the costs would come very close to outweighing the benefits.

On the other hand, reducing acrylonitrile exposure to 1 ppm would reduce the death rate by 9 per 10,000 exposed workers at a yearly cost of $25,000 per worker. Given that the most workers seem to be willing to pay for a 9 in 10,000 reduction in risk is $2700 per year, there is no chance that a 1 ppm standard could improve their utility if they bore the costs. Thus, while a 2 ppm standard may be worth promulgating, a 1 ppm standard would not be.[18] Perhaps because of the high costs and small benefits, OSHA chose to set the acrylonitrile standard at 2 ppm.

EXAMPLE 7.4

Mandatory Risk Reduction in Coal Mining

The caution with which government should proceed with *mandatory* risk-reduction programs is underscored by events in coal mining. The Federal Coal Mine Health and Safety Act of 1969 directs that miners be offered chest X-rays in order to detect black lung disease. (This disease is technically known as *coal workers' pneumoconiosis*—a condition in which the inhalation of coal dust eventually reduces the functional capacity of the lungs. It is progressive, disabling, and sometimes fatal.) When it appears miners have the disease, their employers must, under the law, offer them jobs in less dusty areas of the mine. These jobs are lower-paid and less prestigious than the dusty jobs at the "face" of the mine. Consequently, only 10 percent of the miners offered such jobs in the 1970s accepted them. The behavior of most miners thus tells us that they were willing to undertake a known risk because the compensation (monetary and psychic) of the dangerous jobs was great enough to offset this risk. A law *compelling* them to leave the dusty jobs would clearly reduce their welfare, at least as they see it.

---

[17]This figure is obtained by multiplying the upper estimate of $300 for a one-in-ten-thousand reduction by 8.4.

[18]This analysis is based on data reported in James Miller, "Occupational Exposure to Acrylonitrile," statement before the Occupational Safety and Health Administration on behalf of Vistron Corporation, Washington, D.C., 1978.

Judging OSHA under alternative norms. In our analysis of OSHA above, we argued that a safety or health standard is socially desirable only if the value workers place on risk reduction is commensurate with the costs of the standard. The implicit assumptions of this analysis were that a. the only beneficiaries of the standard are the workers whose risk is reduced, and b. the benefits can best be measured by the current willingness of employees to pay for risk reduction. Neither assumption is universally accepted.

It is frequently argued that members of society who are not directly affected by the risk-reduction program might be willing to pay *something* for the benefits that accrue to those workers who *are* directly affected. Presumably, this "willingness to pay" is strongest for family members, relatives and close friends, and weakest for strangers. However, even strangers would have some interest in reducing injury and disease if they were taxed to subsidize the medical treatment of those who are injured or become ill. Thus, it is argued, the benefits of OSHA standards extend beyond the direct beneficiaries to other "external" parties whose "willingness to pay" should also be counted.

The major issue for policy making is not whether these external benefits exist but how large they are and whether they are already included in the "willingness to pay" of those directly benefited by an OSHA standard. For example, one could plausibly argue that a worker's *family* might be heavily involved in his or her choice of jobs, so that compensating wage differentials *already* reflect family preferences. Put differently, the opinions and preferences of family members and close relatives *could* affect the preferences of workers directly at risk and thus play a role in determining what jobs such workers choose at what wages. To date, no research has addressed this issue.

Also unclear at present is the degree to which medical care for job-related injuries and illnesses is subsidized by parties who are not direct beneficiaries of an OSHA standard. Workers' compensation insurance premiums, for example, are established at the *industry* level and are subject to some modification based on the experience of the individual firm in that industry; it seems unlikely that one industry's workers subsidize the medical treatment of injured workers in other industries. Since OSHA standards apply to *entire industries,* it does not appear too probable that subsidies by "external" parties through workers' compensation are very large. However, because most occupational *illnesses* are not effectively covered by workers' compensation, treatment of those who contract a disease from their work is paid for by them, their insurance, or public subsidies (Medicare, Medicaid).[19] The likelihood that "external" parties subsidize the treatment of those directly at risk of occupational disease is thus very high; what is unknown at present is the magnitude of the subsidy.[20]

---

[19]When a worker contracts lung cancer, it is usually very difficult to tell whether the cause was job-related, due to personal habits, related to residential location, or a combination of all three. Because it cannot usually be proven to be job-related, workers' compensation does not apply.

[20]This ignorance need not prevent us from making benefit estimates, however. We could, for example, calculate benefits in two different ways. We could first assume no subsidy and use compensating wage differentials as discussed in the text. Alternatively, we could assume a 100 percent subsidy of medical costs and add to the willingness to pay implied by the compensating differentials the medical-cost savings associated with the OSHA standard.

Another argument against using only the apparent willingness of workers to pay for risk reduction as a measure of its benefit is that workers really do not know what is best for themselves in the long run. Society frequently prohibits (or at least tries to prohibit) people from indulging in activities that are dangerous to their welfare; laws against the use of narcotics and gambling are two such examples. Some argue that OSHA standards limiting exposure to dangerous substances or situations fall into the category of preventing workers from doing harm to themselves by being lured into dangerous work; therefore, it is argued that to ask how much they value risk reduction is irrelevant. The conflict between those who claim that workers know what is best for themselves and those who claim they do not can only be resolved on philosophical grounds.

However, one offshoot of the argument that workers do not know best for themselves deserves special mention. Some argue that worker preferences are molded by the environment in which they were raised and that there is no reason to take that environment as "given" or unchangeable. Once all workers at risk are required to wear protective clothing and equipment, and once they are prevented from taking certain risks on the job (in return for higher pay perhaps), their attitudes and preferences will accommodate. A few years ago, for example, wearing hard hats was considered "sissified"; today it is not. Thus, OSHA standards are regarded as an engine for changing worker—as well as employer—attitudes and behavior.

How far one wants to go in imposing present costs on workers to induce a change of attitude is a philosophical issue. We should add, however, that the value judgment underlying normative economics—that of mutual benefit, or making some better off and no one else worse off—is usually interpreted as applying to *current* (observed) preferences. Thus, the policy analyses of this text, by taking preferences and the current set of prices (compensating wage differentials, for example) as given, have implicitly assumed that workers know what is best for themselves. This section has pointed out that *alternative* assumptions *do* exist.

Affirmative-Action Planning

In an effort to end discriminatory hiring practices, all large firms doing business with the federal government are required to prepare an *affirmative-action plan* listing their goals for the hiring of women and minorities for the coming years. If these goals are set too low or if approved goals are not met, the firm could conceivably lose its government contracts. Thus, setting realistic goals is important.

In order to construct and evaluate a realistic affirmative-action plan for hiring new employees, firms must know the *availability* of women and minorities. The concept of availability used by the government has been defined in basically two ways as:[21]

---

[21]U.S. Department of Labor, Office of Federal Contract Compliance Programs, *Compliance Manual* (October 18, 1978).

1. the percentage of minorities or women among those who have the skills required by a specific job group or who are capable of acquiring them;
2. the percentage of minorities and women who can be expected to become available during the period [in which] the ultimate goal is to be achieved.

A construction contractor seeking to hire 20 carpenters for a big job may be required to establish a goal of having six blacks among them if 30 percent of *all* carpenters in the city are black. Alternatively, an automobile manufacturer that will be hiring 20 beginning mechanical engineers may be required to set a goal of having five women among them if 25 percent of *new graduates* in mechanical engineering are female. The particular definition of availability to be used is the one that makes the most sense in the particular situation.

While this flexibility in defining availability undoubtedly helps achieve the goal of setting realistic targets for firms, the government has usually ignored another aspect of availability: the *interest of workers* in a particular employer. In the case of locally recruited minority workers, for example, the government has typically used the percentage of qualified minorities in the entire city or metropolitan area as the measure of availability, regardless of how far away they may live from the place of employment. This measure of availability disregards the fact that people prefer to work near home, other things equal, and that their interest in applying for jobs diminishes as the commuting distance rises. Commuting costs, in terms of both time and money, are seen by workers as negative aspects of employment—aspects to be avoided unless adequate compensation for them is received. Failure to take them into account when trying to measure availability works against the intention of setting realistic hiring goals.

The Timken Company. An illustration of the severity of the commuting issue arose in 1976, when the government declared The Timken Company ineligible to receive government contracts.[22] The reason for debarment was that Timken's plant in Bucyrus, Ohio, set its minority hiring goals based on a 16-mile recruiting radius—an area with a 0.6 percent minority population—and refused to include the town of Mansfield, which is 25 miles from its plant and contains 15 percent minorities. The government concluded that 25 miles—35–45 minutes by car—was a reasonable commuting distance and that Mansfield should thus be included for goal-setting purposes. Characteristically, the government's hiring goal for Timken assumed that workers in Mansfield were equally likely to be interested in a job at Timken as those in Bucyrus. The government thus calculated its measure of availability by drawing a 25-mile radius around the plant and calculating the percentage (3.5 percent) of minorities living in that entire area.

Timken took the case to court and won a reversal. The court, looking at the jobs available in Mansfield and the commuting pattern of its residents, decided that workers living in Mansfield were unlikely to want to commute to Bucyrus. In this decision, the court relied on a survey of 12 major employers in Bucyrus, none of whom restricted the geographical range of their hiring, which showed

---

[22]*Timken Company* v. *Vaughn* 413 F. Supp. 1183 (N.D., Ohio 1976).

only four Mansfield residents out of 2300 workers were working in the Bucyrus firms.

While it is clear that the government was wrong in weighting Mansfield and Bucyrus residents equally in computing Timken's availability, it is not clear that the court was correct in rejecting Mansfield as part of Timken's natural recruiting area.

A model of commuting. We asserted earlier that the cost of commuting to work is viewed by workers as a disadvantage; the higher the cost, the greater the disadvantages of the job. In this respect, commuting costs are like the risk of injury—to be avoided unless compensation is received. Thus, we would expect that workers in general would require higher wages to commute longer distances to otherwise identical jobs. Those who do not mind commuting very much will not require large differentials, but those who are averse to spending time commuting will take jobs far away from home only if the wage differential is large.

On the employer side of the market, there is also a positive relationship between wages and the commuting distances of their workers. Consider a firm that is dissatisfied with its pool of job applicants and wants to enlarge this pool so it can be more selective in hiring. One solution is to raise its wage offers in order to attract more applicants. This higher wage offer will, among other things, attract applicants who live farther away from the plant. The higher wage offer serves to overcome the commuting costs for these workers.

How high the firm is willing to raise its wage offer depends on how much more productive its work force will be. A large, sophisticated, assembly-line plant may be willing to raise its wages a lot to increase the size of its labor market, because it can select the most skilled *and* the most dependable workers. Unsteady workers, or those prone to absenteeism, can impose high costs on an assembly-line producer. A smaller firm looking for workers of the same general skill, but not having a highly interdependent production process, may not obtain a very big increase in productivity if it hires only the most dependable workers. Thus, it may not find that increasing the size of its labor market is as beneficial.

This brief discussion suggests two conclusions of interest in the context of antidiscrimination programs. First, there is a *positive* relationship between wages and commuting distances, other things equal. High-wage firms will have geographically larger recruiting areas than low-wage employers. What this means for affirmative-action planning is that the firm's wage policy—whether its pay rate is high, average, or low for the skills it hires—should play a role in determining the size of its labor market and the availability of minorities or women.

In the Timken case, for example, Mansfield may well have been in Timken's legitimate recruiting area (even if it was not for the other twelve employers) *if* Timken's wage rates were higher than average for the jobs involved. Mansfield workers would not, under any circumstances, be considered as equally "available" as Bucyrus workers, but an important consideration—the wage rate—was ignored by the court in defining the availability of minorities to Timken. This consideration, however, was taken into account in a 1979 court decision, wherein it was held that residents of the District of Columbia were not effectively in the labor pool of a suburban employer because, in part, the employer's wages were lower than those paid in the District.[23]

The second major conclusion suggested by our analysis is that workers select wage offers and commuting distances based on their preferences. People who place a high value on working close to home will accept lower wage offers. These lower offers serve as a compensating wage differential for the desirable characteristic of being able to commute to work quickly and cheaply.

This second conclusion is significant for antidiscrimination policy because women typically work closer to home than do men. Usually having the primary family responsibilities for meal preparation and child rearing, women appear to place a premium on being able to work close to home and their wages will be somewhat lower as a result. Thus, *some* of the gross wage differentials between men and women may well be explained by the generally shorter commutes among women. (Incidently, our analysis here also suggests that firms' recruiting areas for women may be smaller than they are for men—an implication that could be of some importance for affirmative action planning.)

Chapter 11 will return to a closer examination of male-female wage differences. The point here is that the role women traditionally have had as primary homemaker affects their earnings adversely. While assigning women this role may in itself be considered "discriminatory" by some, this form of discrimination is not the direct object of antidiscrimination programs conducted by the government. These programs by themselves cannot completely eradicate male-female earnings differences.

REVIEW QUESTIONS

1. Is the following true, false, or uncertain: "Certain occupations, such as coal mining, are inherently dangerous to workers' health and safety. Therefore, unambiguously, the most appropriate government policy is the establishment and enforcement of rigid safety and health standards." Explain your answer.

2. Statement 1: "Business executives are greedy profit maximizers, caring only for themselves." Statement 2: "It has been established that workers doing filthy, dangerous work receive higher wages, other things equal." Can both of these statements be generally true? Why?

3. It has often been claimed that an all-volunteer army would be entirely made up of soldiers from minority groups or disadvantaged backgrounds. Using what you have learned in this chapter, analyze the reasoning and assumptions underlying this claim.

4. "The concept of compensating wage premiums for dangerous work does not apply to industries like the coal industry, where the union has forced all wages and other compensation items to be the same. Since all mines must pay the same wage, owners of dangerous mines will have to pay the same wage as owners of safe mines. Therefore, compensating differentials cannot exist." Is this statement correct? (Assume wages and other forms of pay must be equal for dangerous and nondangerous work and consider the implications for individual labor-supply behavior.)

---

[23]*U.S.* v. *County of Fairfax* 19 FEP Cases 753 (E.O., Va. 1979).

SELECTED READINGS

Milton Friedman, *Price Theory: A Provisional Text* (Chicago: Aldine Publishing Company, 1962). See the chapter entitled, "The Supply of Factors of Production."

Adam Smith, *Wealth of Nations* (New York: Modern Library, 1937), Book I, Chapter 10.

Robert S. Smith, "Compensating Wage Differentials and Public Policy: A Review," *Industrial and Labor Relations Review* 32 (April 1979): 339–52.

Robert S. Smith, *The Occupational Safety and Health Act: Its Goals and Its Achievements* (Washington, D.C.: The American Enterprise Institute for Public Policy Research, 1976).

W. Kip Viscusi, *Employment Hazards: An Investigation of Market Performance* (Cambridge, Mass.: Harvard University Press, 1979).

Chapter 8

INVESTMENTS IN HUMAN CAPITAL: EDUCATION AND TRAINING

Chapters 6 and 7—on the decision to work and on job choice—have emphasized the effects of *current* wages and psychic income on worker decisions. However, many labor-supply choices require a substantial initial *investment* on the part of the worker. Recall that investments, by definition, entail an initial cost that is then recouped (hopefully) over some period of time. Thus, for many labor-supply decisions, *current* wages and working conditions are not the only deciding factors. To model these decisions, one needs to develop a framework that incorporates investment behavior.

Workers undertake three major kinds of investments: (1) education and training, (2) migration, and (3) search for new jobs. All three investments involve an initial cost, and all three are made in the hope and expectation that the investment will pay off well into the future. To emphasize the essential similarity of these investments to other kinds of investments, economists refer to them as investments in *human capital*—a term that conceptualizes workers as embodying a set of skills that can be "rented" out to employers. The knowledge and skills a worker has—which come from education and training, including the training that experience yields—generate a certain *stock* of productive capital. However, the *value* of this amount of productive capital is derived from how much these skills can earn in the labor market. Job search and migration are activities that increase the value of one's human capital by increasing the price (wage) received for a given stock of skills.

Society's total wealth should therefore be thought of as a combination of both human and nonhuman capital. Human capital includes accumulated investments in such activities as education, job training, and migration, whereas nonhuman wealth includes society's stock of land, buildings, and machinery. Total wealth in the United States was estimated at $15.6 trillion in 1973, or about $75,000 for every man, woman, and child. Of this, 52 percent—or $39,000 per capita—took the form of *human* wealth.[1] Thus, investments in human capital are enormously important in our society.

The expected *returns* on human capital investments are, as noted, a higher level of earnings, greater job satisfaction over one's lifetime, and a greater appreciation of nonmarket activities and interests. Generally speaking, the investment *expenditures* can be divided into three categories:

1. *Out-of-pocket* or *direct* expenses include: tuition and books (education), moving expenses (migration), and gasoline (job search).
2. *Forgone earnings* are another source of cost because during the investment period it is usually impossible to work, at least full-time.
3. *Psychic losses* are a third kind of cost incurred because education is difficult and often boring, because job search is tedious and nerve-wracking, and because migration means saying good-by to old friends.

This chapter will analyze educational investments and their labor-market implications. Because most such investments are closely related to the supply of labor to a particular occupation or set of occupations, this aspect of human-capital theory adds more depth to the analysis of occupational choice begun in the last chapter. Chapter 9 deals with turnover and migration; other aspects of job search are treated in Chapter 18.

Demand for Education by Workers

There are many ways in which workers—or potential workers—can enhance their earning capacity through education. They can attend high school, junior college, or a university. They can go to a trade school or technical institute. They can enter an apprenticeship program, or they can acquire skills on the job. The analysis of the demand for any of these types of education or training is essentially the same. Therefore, this section will analyze the demand for a college education as an illustration and application of human-capital theory.

People will want to attend college when they believe they will be better off by so doing. For some, the benefits may be short-term: they like the courses or the lifestyle of a student. Students attending for these reasons regard college as a *consumption good*—that is, they are going to college primarily for the satisfaction it provides during the period of attendance. Others, however, are attending college because of the *long-term* benefits it provides. These benefits are partly in the form of higher earnings, partly in the form of gaining access to more interesting, challenging, or pleasant jobs, and partly in the form of prestige or enhanced

---

[1]U.S. Congress, Joint Economic Committee, *Economic Growth and Total Capital Formation* (Washington, D.C.: U.S. Government Printing Office, February 18, 1976).

enjoyment of nonmarket activities. Attendance for the long-term benefits—or *investment behavior*—is the behavior this chapter seeks to analyze.

An Overview of the Benefits and Costs of an Educational Investment

Calculating the benefits of an investment over time requires the progressive discounting of benefits lying farther into the future (see Chapter 5). Benefits that are received in the future are worth less to us now than an equal amount of benefits to be received today, for two reasons. First, if people plan to consume their benefits, they will prefer to consume earlier than later. (One is relatively sure of being able to enjoy such consumption now, but the uncertainties of life make future enjoyment problematic.) Second, if people plan to invest the monetary benefits rather than use them for consumption, they can earn interest on the investment and enlarge their funds in the future. Thus, no matter how people intend to use their benefits, they will discount future receipts to some extent.

As Chapter 5 explained, the present value of a stream of yearly benefits (B) over a time horizon (T) can be calculated as follows:

$$\text{Present Value} = \frac{B_1}{1 + r} + \frac{B_2}{(1 + r)^2} + \frac{B_3}{(1 + r)^3} + \ldots + \frac{B_T}{(1 + r)^T}, \quad (8.1)$$

where the interest rate (or discount rate) is r. As long as r is positive, benefits into the future will be progressively discounted. For example, if $r = 0.06$, benefits payable in 30 years would receive a weight that is only 17 percent of the weight placed on benefits payable immediately ($1.06^{30} = 5.73$; $1/5.73 = 0.17$).

The costs of going to college are normally incurred over a relatively short period of time. These costs include 1. the direct costs of tuition, fees, and books; 2. the forgone earnings attendant to being a full-time student; and 3. the psychic costs of studying and being examined. The total costs of going to college are thus very high, with the monetary costs alone (direct costs plus forgone earnings) in the range of $10,000–15,000 per year in 1983.

A person considering college has, in some broad sense, a choice between two streams of income over his or her lifetime. Stream A begins immediately but does not rise very high; it is the earnings stream of a high-school graduate. Stream B (the college graduate) has a negative income for the first four years (owing to college tuition costs), followed by a period when the salary is less than what the high-school graduate makes, but then it takes off and rises above stream A. Both streams are illustrated in Figure 8.1. (Why these streams are *curved* will be discussed later in this chapter.) The streams shown in the figure are stylized so that we can emphasize some basic points. Actual earnings streams are shown later in Figures 8.7 and 8.9.

Obviously, the earnings of the college graduate would have to rise above those of the high-school graduate in order to induce someone to invest in a college education (unless, of course, the psychic or consumption-related returns are

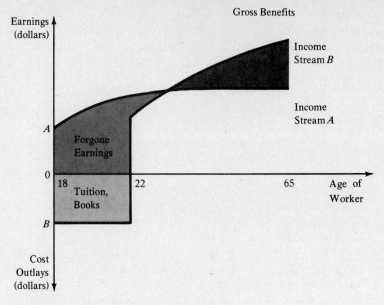

Figure 8.1   Alternative Income Streams

large). The gross benefits—the difference in earnings between the two streams—must total much more than the costs because such returns are in the future and are therefore discounted. For example, if it costs $12,000 per year to obtain a four-year college education, and if the interest rate is 6 percent, the after-tax returns (if they are the same each year) must be $3200 for 40 years in order to justify the investment on purely monetary grounds. These returns must be so high because $48,000 invested at a 6 percent interest rate can provide a payment (of interest and principal) totaling $3200 a year for 40 years.[2]

A Formal Model of Choice and Its Implications

The preceding discussion emphasized that investing in a college education is worthwhile if the present value of the benefits (monetary and psychic) are at least as large as the costs. In mathematical terms this criterion can be expressed as:

$$\frac{B_1}{1 + r} + \frac{B_2}{(1 + r)^2} + \cdots + \frac{B_T}{(1 + r)^T} \geq C, \qquad (8.2)$$

---

[2]This calculation is made using the *annuity formula:*

$$Y = X \frac{1 - [1/(1 + r)^n]}{r},$$

where Y equals the total investment ($48,000 in our example), X = the yearly payment ($3200), r = the rate of interest (0.06), and n = the number of years (40). In this example, we treat the costs of a college education as being incurred all in one year rather than being spread out over four—a simplification that does not alter the magnitude of required returns much at all.

where C equals the total costs of a college education and B_t equals the differences in earnings between college and high-school graduates in year t.

There are two ways one can measure whether the criterion in equation (8.2) is met. Using the *present-value method,* one can specify a value for the discount rate, r, and determine if the present value of benefits is greater than or equal to costs. Alternatively, one can adopt the *internal-rate-of-return-method,* which asks, "How large could the discount rate be and still render college profitable?" Clearly, if the benefits are so large that even a very high discount rate would render college profitable, then the project is worthwhile. In practice, one calculates this internal rate of return by setting the present value of benefits equal to costs and solving for r. The internal rate of return is then compared to the rate of return on other investments. If the internal rate of return exceeds the alternative rates of return, the investment project is considered profitable.[3]

In deciding whether to attend college, no doubt few students make the very precise calculations suggested in equation (8.2). Nevertheless, if they make less formal estimates that take into account the same factors, four predictions concerning the demand for college education can be made:

1. Present-oriented people are less likely to go to college than forward-looking people (other things equal).
2. Most college students will be young.
3. College attendance will increase if the costs of college fall (other things equal).
4. College attendance will increase if the gap between the earnings of college graduates and high-school graduates widens (again, other things equal).

Present-orientedness. Psychologists use the term *present-oriented* to refer to people who do not weight future events or outcomes very heavily. While all people discount the future with respect to the present, those who discount it more than average—or, at the extreme, ignore the future altogether—could be considered present-oriented. In terms of equations (8.1) and (8.2), a present-oriented person is one with a very high discount rate (r).

Suppose one were to calculate investment returns using the *present-value method.* If r is large, the present value of benefits associated with college will be lower than if the discount rate being used is smaller. Thus, a present-oriented person would impute smaller benefits to college attendance than one who is less present-oriented, and those who are present-oriented would be less likely to attend college. Using the *internal-rate-of-return method* for evaluating the soundness of a college education, one would arrive at the same result. If a college education earns an 8 percent rate or return, but the individuals in question are so present-oriented that they would insist on a 25 percent rate of return before investing, they would likewise decide not to attend.

---

[3]For our purposes here, the present-value and internal-rate-of-return methods may be considered interchangeable in evaluating investment alternatives. In *some* circumstances, however, the two methods would not provide identical rankings of investment opportunities. *See* J. Hirshleifer, "On the Theory of Optimal Investment Decision," *Journal of Political Economy* 66 (August 1958): 329–52.

The prediction that present-oriented people are less likely to attend college than forward-looking ones is difficult to substantiate or disprove. The rates of discount that people use in making investment decisions are rarely available, because the decisions are not made as formally as equation (8.2) implies. However, the model does suggest that people who have a high propensity to invest in education will also engage in other forward-looking behavior. Certain medical statistics tend to support this prediction.

In the United States there is a strong statistical correlation between education and health status.[4] People with more years of schooling have lower mortality rates, fewer symptoms of disease (such as high blood pressure, high cholesterol levels, abnormal X-rays), and a greater tendency to report themselves to be in good health. This effect of education on health is independent of income, which appears to have no effect of its own on health status except at the lowest poverty levels. Is this correlation between education and health a result of better use of medical resources by the well educated? It appears not. Better-educated people undergoing surgery choose the same doctors, enter the hospital at the same stage of disease, and have the same length of stay as less-educated people of equal income.

What *may* cause this correlation is a more forward-looking attitude among those who have obtained more education. People with lower discount rates will be more likely to attend college, and they will *also* be more likely to adopt forward-looking habits of health. They may choose healthier diets, be more careful of health risks, and make more use of preventative medicine. This explanation for the correlation between education and health is not the only plausible one, but it receives some direct support from British data on cigarette smoking.[5] From 1958–75, the proportion of men in the most highly educated groups who smoked fell by 50 percent. During the same time period, the proportion of smokers in the more poorly educated class remained unchanged. It is unlikely that the less-educated group was uninformed of the smoking dangers revealed during that period. It is more likely that they were less willing to give up a present source of pleasure for a distant benefit. Thus, we have at least some evidence that people who invest in education also engage in *other* forward-looking behavior.

Age. Given similar *yearly* benefits of going to college, young people have a larger present value of *total* benefits than older workers simply because they have a longer remaining work life ahead of them. In terms of equation (8.2), T for younger people is greater than for older ones. We would therefore expect younger people to have a greater propensity than older people to obtain a college education or engage in other forms of training activity. This prediction is parallel to the

---

[4]The analysis of the correlation between education and health status is taken from Victor Fuchs, "The Economics of Health in a Post-Industrial Society," *The Public Interest* (Summer 1979): 3–20.

[5]It could be, for example, that healthy people, with longer life spans, are more likely to invest in human capital because they expect to experience a longer payback period. Alternatively, one could argue that the higher incomes of college graduates later in life mean they have more to lose from illness than do non-college graduates.

predictions in Chapter 5 about which employers will decide to invest in when they make decisions about hiring or specific training.

Costs. A third prediction of our model is that human-capital investments are more likely when costs are lower. The major monetary costs of college attendance are forgone earnings and the direct costs of tuition, books, and fees. (Food and lodging are not always opportunity costs of going to college, because much of these costs would have to be incurred in any event.) Thus, if forgone earnings or tuition costs fall, other things equal, we would expect an increase in college enrollments.

The costs of college attendance offer an additional reason why we observe older people attending less often than younger people. As workers age, they acquire levels of experience and maturity that employers are willing to reward with higher wages. Because older workers thus command higher wages (on average), their opportunity costs of college attendance are higher than those for younger students. Older people are thus doubly discouraged from attending college: their forgone earnings are relatively high and the period over which they can capture benefits is comparatively short.

The psychic costs of going to college cannot be ignored. While these costs cannot be easily observed, they are likely to be related to ability. People who learn easily and who do well in school settings have an easier and more pleasant time in college than people who do not.

In any set of market transactions, some people are *at the margin*—which means that they are close to the point of not transacting. For example, consider a downward-sloping demand curve for education, where the number of people attending college is drawn as a function of its money costs (see Figure 8.2). If the money costs were X_0, we would observe that N_0 people would go to college. If the costs were raised to X_1, only N_1 would decide to attend. The people deciding to drop out when costs rise to X_1 are those who were closest to not going when they were X_0. They are the ones who had the hardest time making up their minds at X_0 —in other words, those who came closest to deciding not to go when costs were X_0.

Who are the people closest to the margin regarding the decision to go to college? In part, they are people for whom the psychic costs of studying and being examined are relatively high—people who do not especially like school. This group—who, we have argued, might consist to a large extent of less able students —is thus likely to be the most responsive to changes in the money costs of education. Studies that have analyzed the effects of college location on college attendance show that males of moderate ability are much more responsive to college location than those of high ability. That is, whether a college is available in one's hometown seems to matter a lot more to moderate-ability students than it does to high-ability students.[6]

---

[6]C. A. Anderson, M. J. Bowman, V. Tinto, *Where Colleges Are and Who Attends* (New York: McGraw-Hill, 1972). Given that loans to attend college often are not readily available, the financial resources of the investor are an important factor in the decision to invest. Thus, people in families with modest wealth are closer to the margin regarding the educational decision.

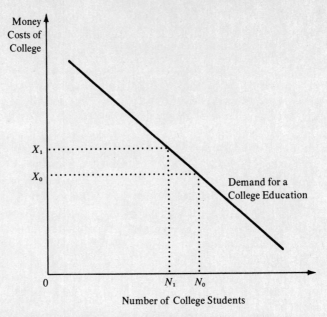

Figure 8.2   The Demand for a College Education

Earnings differentials. The fourth prediction of human-capital theory is that the demand for education is positively related to the *returns*—that is, to the increases in lifetime earnings or psychic benefits that a college education allows. In practice, this prediction can be tested only with reference to money returns, since psychic returns are unobservable.[7] This prediction has been used to explain the sharp fall in college enrollments that occurred in the early 1970s.[8]

Beginning around 1970, the labor market for college graduates began to exhibit signs of a surplus. Jobs in the professional fields where college graduates have typically found employment began to dwindle relative to the supply, and more and more college graduates had to take jobs as sales, clerical, or blue-collar workers. For example, in 1958 only 10.5 percent of recent female college graduates and 13.8 percent of recent male college graduates were employed in nonprofessional, nonmanagerial jobs—such as sales, clerical, or blue-collar work. For 1970–71 college graduates, these percentages had more than doubled to 24.4 percent for women and 30.5 percent for men. The deterioration in employment prospects for college graduates was also manifest in the starting salaries for graduates with bachelor's degrees. Table 8.1 tells the story for men, for whom

---

[7]There is evidence, although it is somewhat weak, that better-educated workers are more likely to describe themselves as "satisfied" with their jobs. [See Daniel Hamermesh, "Economic Aspects of Job Satisfaction," in *Essays in Labor Market Analysis,* eds. Orley Ashenfelter and Wallace Oates (New York: John Wiley and Sons, 1977), pp. 53–72.] *Quantifying* job or nonjob psychic benefits, however, is still not possible.

[8]The analysis in the succeeding paragraphs relies heavily on Richard Freeman, "Overinvestment in College Training?" *Journal of Human Resources* 10, 3 (Summer 1975): 287–311.

Table 8.1. Compound Annual Changes in the Starting Salaries of Male Bachelor's Graduates, 1961–69 and 1969–74

	1961–69 Period of Relative Market Boom		1969–74 Period of Relative Market Bust	
	Annual Percent Change in Salaries	Annual Percent Change Minus Change in CPI[a]	Annual Percent Change in Salaries	Annual Percent Change Minus Change in CPI
Accountant	6.0	3.4	4.0	−2.2
Business-general	5.7	3.1	2.4	−3.8
Humanities and social science	5.3	2.7	1.1	−5.1
Aeronautic engineering	4.8	2.2	3.1	−3.1
Chemical engineering	5.8	3.2	3.8	−2.4
Civil engineering	5.7	3.1	3.9	−2.5
Electrical engineering	5.1	2.5	3.2	−3.0
Mechanical engineering	5.3	2.7	3.5	−2.7
Industrial engineering	4.7	2.1	3.3	−2.9
Physical sciences, mathematics	4.8	2.2	2.1	−4.1
Changes in annual earnings of year-round full-time workers	4.7	2.1	6.6[b]	+0.4

[a]CPI = Consumer Price Index

[b]1974 estimated by percentage change in average hourly earnings of all private industry production workers from March 1973 to March 1974.

SOURCE: Reprinted from Richard Freeman, "Overinvestment in College Training?" *Journal of Human Resources* 10, 3 (Summer 1975): 288.

comparative data over time are more available and reliable than are the data for women. From 1961–69, starting salaries for male college graduates increased faster than wages and prices in general—indicative of a pre-existing *shortage* of college graduates (see Chapter 2 for a review of the concepts of *shortage* and *surplus*). From 1969–74, starting salaries for male bachelor's graduates increased more slowly than both average wages and the price level, which is what one would expect in sectors where labor surpluses exist.

In analyzing the potential effects of this surplus of college graduates on college enrollments, however, one must not ignore the fact that our model stresses the discounted stream of benefits *over a lifetime,* while the data just presented refer mainly to employment prospects *immediately after graduation.* Nevertheless, there are two reasons to believe that immediate post-college prospects are of crucial importance in the decision to go to college. First, being closer to the present, earnings immediately after graduation are less heavily discounted than earnings later on. Second, in the absence of any better information, people may use current employment trends for college graduates as estimates of what prospects in the more distant future will be like. If there is a surplus now, people may assume it will last long enough to render college a poor investment.

Associated with the surplus of college graduates was a decline in the proportion of young males going to college. Among males—for whom labor-market conditions appeared to change most in the early 1970s—the percentage of high-school graduates going to college fell from 58 percent (1969) to 50 percent (1973).

EXAMPLE 8.1

Do Unskilled Jobs Cause Poor Mental Health?

It is frequently asserted that the mental health of low-skilled workers is poorer than it is for higher-skilled workers of the same age. For example, a study of factory workers in the automobile industry found that 56 percent of middle-aged, *skilled* workers had "high" mental health, while only 26 percent of middle-aged workers in repetitive, semi-skilled jobs exhibited "high" mental health. The figures were 58 percent and 10 percent, respectively, for younger workers—and for both age groups there was a steady downward fall in the percentages of those with "high" mental health as one moved down the skill ladder in between skilled and repetitive semi-skilled jobs. The conclusions generally drawn from such findings are that the boring, uncreative nature of less skilled jobs causes workers to lose self-esteem and to adopt negative attitudes toward life.

It is entirely possible, however, that the causal connection between skill level and mental health is the reverse! For example, in the above-mentioned study of automobile workers, the following characteristics were included (with others) as indicative of poor mental health: a "live for today" attitude, a belief that success is due to luck and pull, a belief that one can't do much to shape one's future, and a lack of optimism. People with these characteristics are probably much less likely to undertake costly human capital investments with distant payoffs; lack of self-esteem raises the perceived costs of education or training, while a lack of optimism and/or a present-orientation limits the expected benefits. Thus, workers with these aspects of mental health are much less likely to undertake human capital investments and become skilled! While human capital theory cannot be used to *prove* that causation runs from "poorer mental health" (as defined by the researchers) to lower skill levels, it *can* be used to raise questions about the standard interpretation of the observed association between skill level and measures of mental health.

Sources: Arthur Kornhauser, *Mental Health of the Industrial Worker* (New York: John Wiley and Sons, Inc., 1965), p. 57. Kornhauser, p. 76 and George Strauss and Leonard R. Sayles, *Personnel: The Human Problems of Management* (Englewood Cliffs, N.J.: Prentice-Hall, Inc., 1972), p. 21.

Further, the proportion of 18- to 24-year-old males going to college, after rising almost steadily since 1950, fell from 35 percent (1969) to 27 percent (1973).

Among females, the enrollment response was an abrupt cessation of growth in the proportion of young women enrolled in college rather than a decline. Nevertheless, this response did represent a significant departure from the trend in growing college attendance during the 1960s. (The failure of enrollments to fall can possibly be explained—at least in part—by the tremendous increase in the propensity of women to seek work outside the home that has occurred in recent years. The longer one expects to work outside the home, the greater are the benefits of college attendance.) One might also argue that the differential response of men and women in terms of college attendance was due to changes during the early 1970s in the draft laws—which effectively removed the incentives for men to attend college in order to avoid the draft. While the draft-law changes did have an effect, the timing of the decline in enrollments makes it clear that such changes can only explain part of the decline in demand for college education among males. Declining returns to a college education were clearly a major stimulus for the changed patterns of college-attendance in the early 1970s.

Earnings Differences and the Demand for Education

As we have just seen, the demand for education is influenced by the differences in earnings made possible by an educational investment. However, the returns to education are themselves affected by the number of people who attend school. To obtain an overall picture of how enrollments and returns are interrelated, it is necessary to return briefly to our simple model of the labor market.

Figure 8.3 shows the labor market demand for, and supply of, college graduates. We know why the demand curve for labor slopes downward, but why does the supply curve for college graduates in Figure 8.3 slope upward? The reason, discussed earlier in this chapter, is that college is costly. If college graduates typically earn relatively low wages, few people will want to attend college. If the earnings of college graduates were to rise, more would want to attend college. If they were to rise still more, even greater numbers would enroll.

What would happen if the demand for college graduates were to shift outward, so that more such graduates were demanded at any given wage? Figure 8.3

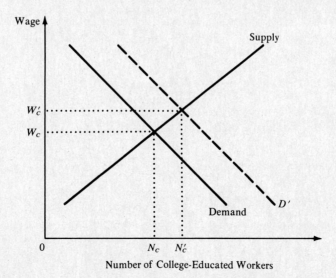

Figure 8.3   The Market for College Graduates with a Shift in Demand

illustrates that if the demand curve shifts to D′, the wages of college graduates would rise from W_c to W'_c. This increase in the wages of college graduates would serve as an incentive for more people to attend college, and the number of college graduates would rise.

What would happen if, on the other hand, the supply of college graduates were to shift to the right—indicating that more people want to attend college for any given wage level that can be attained by graduates. Such a shift might occur, for example, if the government were to subsidize students in college or to exempt students from the military draft. Figure 8.4 shows that the outward shift in the supply of college graduates drives wages down to $W''c$, a reduction that serves to moderate the increase in enrollments (as W_c falls to W''_c, the movement along S′ suggests that fewer people decide to attend).

Unfortunately, the adjustment of college enrollments to changes in the returns to education is not always smooth or rapid—particularly in special fields, like engineering and law, that are highly technical. The problem is that if engineering wages (say) were to go up suddenly in 1985, the supply of graduate engineers would not be affected for three or four years (owing to the time it takes to learn the field). Likewise, if engineering wages were to fall, those students enrolled in an engineering curriculum would understandably be reluctant to immediately leave the field. They have already invested a lot of time and effort and may prefer to take their chances in engineering rather than devote more time and money to learning a new field.

The inability to respond immediately to changed market conditions can cause *boom-and-bust cycles* in the market for highly technical workers. If educational planners in government or the private sector were unaware of these cycles, they might seek to stimulate (or reduce) enrollments at a time when they should be doing exactly the opposite, as illustrated below.

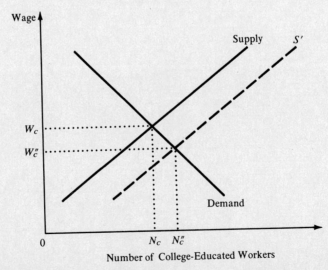

Figure 8.4   The Market for College Graduates with a Shift in Supply

Suppose the market for engineers is in equilibrium, where the wage is W_0 and the number of engineers is N_0 (see Figure 8.5). Let us now assume that the demand curve for engineers shifts from D_0 to D_1. Initially, this increase in the demand for engineers does *not* induce the supply of engineers to increase beyond N_0, because it takes a long time to become an engineer once one has decided to do so. Thus, while the increased demand for engineers causes more people to decide to enter the field, the number available for employment at the moment is N_0. These N_0 engineers, therefore, can *currently* obtain a wage of W_1 (in effect, there is a vertical supply curve, at N_0, for a few years until the supply of engineering graduates is increased).

Now W_1, the *current* engineering wage, is above W_e—the new *long-run* equilibrium wage caused by the intersection of D_1 and S. The market, however, is unaware of W_e—observing only W_1. If people are myopic and assume W_1 is the new engineering wage, N_1 people will enter the engineering field (see Figure 8.6). When these N_1 all graduate, there will be a *surplus* of engineers (remember W_1 is *above* long-run equilibrium).

With the supply of engineers now temporarily fixed at N_1, the wage will fall to W_2. This fall will cause students and workers to shift *out* of engineering, but that effect will not be fully felt for a few years. In the meantime, note that W_2 is below long-run equilibrium (still at W_e). Thus, when supply *does* adjust, it will adjust too much—all the way to N_2. Now there is another shortage of engineers, because at W_2, there is greater demand than supply. This causes wages to rise to W_3, and the cycle repeats itself. Over time, the swings become smaller, and

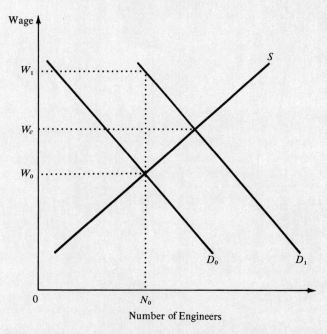

Figure 8.5 The Labor Market for Engineers

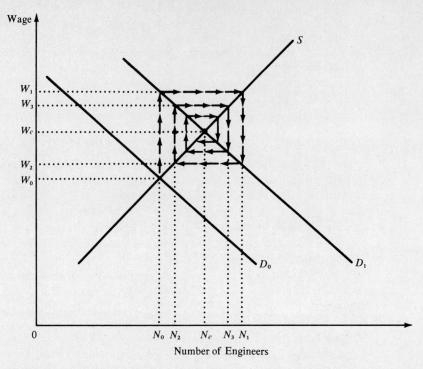

Figure 8.6   The Labor Market for Engineers: a Cobweb Model

eventually equilibrium is reached. Because the adjustment path in Figure 8.6 looks like a cobweb, the adjustment process described above is sometimes called a *cobweb model.*[9]

Any market characterized by a cobweb adjustment process will experience alternating shortages and surpluses—and any educational institution training students for these fields will also experience booms and busts. Engineering appears to be one such field.[10] In the early 1950s people were talking of a surplus of engineers. In the late 1950s and early 1960s the discussion was of shortages. In the late 1960s there was again a surplus, followed in the 1970s by another shortage. Engineering enrollments fluctuated likewise, clearly reacting to the changed state of the market for engineers.

The lesson to be learned from the cobweb model should not be lost on government policymakers. If the government chooses to take an active role in dealing with labor shortages and surpluses, it must be aware that, because supply

---

[9]Critical to cobweb models is the assumption that suppliers—in this case, workers—have static or myopic expectations about prices. In our example, they first assume that W_1 will be the prevailing wage, ignoring the possibility that the behavior of others will in 4 years drive the wage below W_1. One might expect that they would learn of their errors over time; however, as long as they assume the future prevalence of wages that oscillate above and below W_e, cobweb-type behavior will result.

[10]Richard B. Freeman, "A Cobweb Model of the Supply and Starting Salary of New Engineers," *Industrial and Labor Relations Review* 29 (January 1976): 236–46.

adjustments are slow in highly technical markets, wages in those markets tend to *overadjust.* For example, at the initial stages of a shortage when wages are rising toward W_1 (in our example), the government should be pointing out that W_1 is likely to be *above* the long-run equilibrium. If instead it attempts to meet the current shortage by *subsidizing* study in that field, it will be encouraging an even greater *surplus* later on. The moral of the story is that a rather complete knowledge of how markets adjust to changes in demand or supply is necessary before one can be sure that government intervention will do more good than harm.

The Education/Wage Relationship

The theory outlined in this chapter so far indicates that workers generally need the expectation of higher earnings to induce them to undertake costly educational investments. Put differently, because educational programs can be very costly, people will invest in them only if they can reasonably expect to receive a return on this investment. While a level of earnings higher than they would otherwise receive is not the only benefit of an educational investment, it is certainly an important one for many workers. Thus, to induce workers to invest in human capital, higher earnings generally will have to be received by those who do invest.

Higher earnings for better-educated workers, however, will be received only if employers are willing to pay them. Theory suggests that firms would be willing to pay greater wages to workers with more schooling *if* these workers were in fact more productive. After all, if workers were of different productivities yet received the *same* wage, the more productive ones would be preferred by all employers, and their wages would naturally rise above those paid to the less productive workers. While some economists assert that schooling *causes* workers to become more productive, and others contend that schooling is a screening device that just *certifies* who is already more productive,[11] the ultimate effect on the firm is the same; more highly-schooled people *are* likely to be more productive.

The relationship between education and earnings is well documented and can be observed graphically in Figure 8.7. This figure presents (for males) *age/earnings profiles*—or lifetime earnings patterns—for five different levels of schooling. Two conclusions are immediately obvious:

1. Better-educated males have higher earnings than less-educated males at each post-schooling age level—as predicted by our theory. Note, however, from the (dashed) earnings profile of men with education beyond the bachelor's degree, that earnings while in school are lower than they would otherwise be (a graphical representation of the concept of forgone earnings).
2. The age/earnings profiles for workers with more education are steeper than the profiles of workers with less education. That is, the differences in

---

[11]This issue will be discussed at greater length later in this section.

earnings associated with education tend to widen as workers grow older. In the early years the earnings gap is small. Workers who have gone to college have not had a chance to acquire the work experience of their colleagues who have been working rather than attending college. Later, after they have had a chance to gain experience, their earnings rise much more sharply. (A more detailed discussion of *why* age/earnings profiles are steeper for more educated workers will be presented later in this chapter.)

While it is well-established that workers with more education tend to earn higher wages, it is natural to ask whether the earnings of college graduates are *enough* higher to render profitable an investment in college. An individual deciding whether to go to college would naturally ask, "Will I increase my monetary and psychic income enough to justify the costs of going to college?" Further, government policymakers trying to decide whether to expand educational facilities or subsidize increased enrollments must ask, "Will the benefits of improved

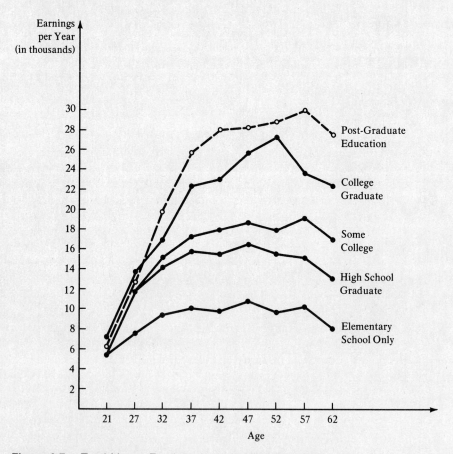

Figure 8.7   Total Money Earnings (mean), All Males, 1977

SOURCE: U.S. Bureau of the Census, *Money Income in 1977 of Families and Persons in the United States.* Current Population Reports, Series P-60, No. 118 (March 1979), Table 48.

productivity outweigh the costs?" The next two subsections deal with the issue of individual and social returns from educational investments.

Is Education a Good Investment for Individuals?

Individuals about to make an investment in a college education are committing themselves to costs of at least $10,000 per year. Is there evidence that this investment pays off for the typical student? Several studies have tried to answer this question by calculating the internal rates of return to educational investments. While the methods and data used vary, these studies normally estimate benefits by calculating earnings differentials at each age from age/earnings profiles such as those in Figure 8.7. (*Earnings* are usually used to measure benefits because higher wages and more stable jobs are payoffs to more education.) The *rate of return* is that discount rate which equates the present value of benefits to the cost of acquiring the level of education in question. It should be stressed that all such studies have analyzed only the monetary—and not the psychic—costs and returns to educational investments.

The rates of return typically estimated in the above studies generally fall in the range of 5–15 percent (after adjusting for inflation). These findings are interesting, because many other investments generate returns in the same range. Thus, it appears—at least at first glance—that an investment in education is about as good as an investment in stocks, bonds, or real estate. This conclusion must be qualified, however, by recognizing that there are systematic biases in the estimated rates of return to education. These biases—which are of unknown size —work in opposite directions.

The upward bias. The typical estimates of the rate of return to further schooling overstate the gain an individual student could obtain by investing in education because they are unable to separate the contribution *ability* makes to higher earnings from the contribution made by *schooling.* The problem is that (a) people who are smarter, harder-working, and more dynamic are more likely to obtain more schooling, and (b) such people may be more productive, and hence earn higher-than-average wages, even if they did not complete more years of schooling than others. When measures of ability are not observed or accounted for, the studies attribute *all* of the earnings differentials associated with college to college itself and none to ability—even though *some* of the added earnings college graduates typically receive would probably be received by an equally able high-school graduate who did not attend college.

Most studies attempting to identify the separate effects of ability and schooling have concluded that the effects of ability are relatively small—accounting for, at most, one fifth of observed earnings differentials.[12] However, these studies have used aptitude-test scores—such as IQ or mathematical reasoning—as measures

[12]See, for example, Gary Becker, *Human Capital* (New York: National Bureau of Economic Research, 1975); Zvi Griliches and William M. Mason, "Education, Income, and Ability" and John C. Hause, "Earnings Profile: Ability and Schooling," both in *Journal of Political Economy* 80, 3 (May/June 1972).

of ability, and these measures are primarily designed to predict success in school, not in the workplace. Success in the world of work is also affected by interpersonal skills, work habits, motivation, and resourcefulness—attributes that are not easily measured by a test.

One interesting attempt to control for all the unmeasured aspects of ability used data on twins.[13] When the researcher first calculated rates of return to an added year of education ignoring any controls for ability, the estimated return was 8 percent. When he looked only at earnings differences between identical twins—people with a common *genetic and environmental* background—with different levels of schooling, he found that the rate of return to schooling dropped to 3 percent. While no one study is conclusive, the results do suggest that part —and perhaps a large part—of earnings differentials associated with higher levels of schooling are due to inherently abler persons obtaining more schooling.

The downward bias. By focusing only on the earnings differentials associated with an educational investment, the studies of returns to educational investments ignore other aspects of the returns to schooling. First, some benefits of college attendance are not necessarily reflected in higher productivity, but rather in an increased ability to understand and appreciate the behavioral, historic, and philosophical foundations of human existence. While these benefits may be difficult to measure, they exist nonetheless.

Second, most rate-of-return studies fail to include fringe benefits; they measure money earnings, not total compensation. Because fringe benefits as a fraction of total compensation tend to rise as money earnings rise, ignoring fringe benefits tends to create a downward bias in the estimation of rates of return to education. The size of this bias is largely unknown at present.[14]

Third, some of the job-related rewards of college are captured in the form of psychic or nonmonetary benefits. Jobs in executive or professional occupations are probably more interesting and pleasant than the more routine jobs typically available to people with less education. While executive and professional jobs do pay more than others, the total benefits of these jobs are probably understated when just earnings differences are analyzed.

An interesting example of the role nonmonetary costs and benefits play in schooling decisions can be seen in the fact that there is near-universal agreement that conventionally calculated rates of return fall as educational level rises. That is, the rate of return to a high-school education is higher than for a college education, and higher yet than the average returns from going to graduate school. This fact can be understood when psychic benefits and costs are accounted for, because students who acquire the most education are, on average, the ones who dislike school the least. They may also be the ones who, because of their higher learning abilities, derive the most psychic benefits from

---

[13]Paul Taubman, "Earnings, Education, Genetics, and Environment," *Journal of Human Resources* 11, 4 (Fall 1976): 447–61.

[14]Greg J. Duncan, "Earnings Functions and Nonpecuniary Benefits," *Journal of Human Resources* 11, 4 (Fall 1976): 462–83.

college. They thus require a smaller monetary incentive to attend college than do their less able colleagues.[15]

It is difficult to summarize the findings on the question of whether education is a sensible investment for an individual. Considering only monetary costs and benefits, rates of return to educational investments are modest (once ability is accounted for)—but not out of line with the "real" returns on many other types of investments. Moreover, if benefits other than money earnings were measured, the estimated returns to education would probably be higher.

Is Education a Good Social Investment?

The United States spends 6 percent of its gross national product—or $181 billion in 1981—on formal education (primary, secondary, and college). If forgone earnings of high-school and college students were included, this figure would rise to 9 percent.[16] In part, these expenditures are justified by our need for a literate citizenry, speaking a common language and sharing a common culture. In part, however, education—especially at the secondary and college levels—is justified on the grounds that it enhances worker productivity. Interestingly, an early Soviet economist—S. G. Strumilin—wrote in 1929 that:

> a long time ago we had already arrived at the conclusion, that the expenditure of the state budget to raise the cultural level of the country ought to be considered along with the expenditures on technical reconstruction of production as capital expenditures and as equal in terms of their importance to our economy.[17]

There are some fields, such as mechanics and engineering, where education clearly has a social payoff in the form of increased productivity. Recently, however, some critics have suggested that, to a large degree, education acts merely as a "sorting device." They argue that rather than making workers more productive, the educational process is merely a screening device that reveals to employers the productive characteristics *already inherent* in prospective workers (we touched on this issue earlier in the discussion of the relationship between education and ability).

Employers—as noted in Chapter 5—are faced with the problem of ascertaining the quality of their job applicants. If they hire people for a trial period to see how they work out, they may face the costs of terminating low-quality employees and of the losses associated with their mistakes. An alternative pro-

---

[15]It may also be true that students from poor families, who lack the financial resources to obtain much education, require a higher rate of return to their educational investments than do students from families where wealth is more abundant.

[16]The forgone earnings of high-school and college students have been estimated to equal 60 percent of the *direct* cost outlays at those schooling levels. *See* Theodore Schultz, *The Economic Value of Education* (New York: Columbia University Press, 1963).

[17]Arcadius Kahan, "Russian Scholars and Statesmen on Education as an Investment," in *Educational and Economic Development,* eds. C. A. Anderson and M. J. Bowman (Chicago: Aldine Publishing Co., 1965), p. 10.

cedure is to screen applicants through interviews, evaluations from previous employers, or work-related tests. These procedures themselves are costly, of course. They take time and money—and may still give imprecise readings of applicant quality.

Employers may also use data on applicant education as a screening tool. To do well in school requires both a capacity to learn and a willingness to work. The intellectual abilities required to succeed in school are obviously more closely correlated with the requirements for success in some jobs than others; however, it is probably true that workers better able to learn in school are easier to train and more flexible in the workplace than others. The discipline required in school —promptness, willingness to follow directions, adherence to deadlines—is very similar to the discipline required to perform well in most jobs. In a real sense, schooling is the "work" of youth and may well be a good test of ability to succeed later on.

The argument of those who regard education *only* as a sorting device goes beyond the argument that employers use educational attainment to screen applicants. Such critics of education assert that schooling does *nothing* to alter productive characteristics, that it does not increase knowledge of the kind useful to employees, and that it does not impart useful attitudes or work habits. In short, they say, nothing happens to students while in school that affects productivity later on. The educational system is seen as simply a filter that has the effect of *signaling* which people are likely to be most productive.[18]

It should be recognized that even if schooling is only a screening device, it could have social, as well as private, value. Employers need a reliable method through which to select employees. Obviously, sorting millions of workers into various categories of ability is an enormous job for any society to accomplish, and schooling may be a very efficient means of doing this. The people most likely to acquire more schooling are the ones for whom schooling entails the least psychic cost—and, as we have argued, this group will tend to be heavily populated by the most able people. Investment in schooling, then, sends a *signal* to the labor market that one has a certain level of ability. The costs of investing in schooling purely for its signaling value generate net *private* benefits if the increased wage a graduate can obtain outweighs the costs. Schools in this case would have net *social* value if the decision to attend and the success one attains in school send accurate signals about productive characteristics to employers in the least costly way.

Whether schooling is purely a sorting device or whether it adds to productivity is not a particularly important question for individuals. Whatever role schools play, additional schooling does enhance one's lifetime income. Where the issue of screening is important is at the social level. If the only purpose of schools is to screen, why encourage the expansion of schooling? If 40 years ago being a

---

[18]If this was all schools did, it must be noted that they would not do much to alter the influences of family background—and thus would not be terribly useful in breaking down existing class distinctions or providing a vehicle for social mobility.

high-school graduate signaled above-average intelligence and work discipline, why incur the enormous costs of expanding college attendance only to find out that now a bachelor's degree signals above-average intelligence and work habits? The issue is of even more importance in less developed countries—where mistakes in allocating extremely scarce capital resources could be disastrous (see Example 8.2).

EXAMPLE 8.2

The Socially Optimal Level of Educational Investment

In addition to asking whether schooling is a good social investment, we could also ask, What is the socially optimal *level* of schooling? The general principle guiding our answer to this question is that society should increase or reduce its educational investments until the marginal rate of return (to society) equals the marginal rate of return on other forms of capital investment (investment in physical capital, for example).

The rationale for the above principle is that if society has some funds it wants to invest, it will desire to invest them in projects yielding the highest rates of return. If an investment in physical capital yields a 20 percent rate of return, and the same funds invested in schooling yield (all things considered) only a 10 percent return, society will clearly prefer to invest in physical capital. As long as the two rates of return differ, society could be made better off by reducing its investment in low-yield projects and increasing them in those with higher rates of return.

The text has discussed many of the difficulties and biases inherent in estimating rates of return to schooling. However, the general principle of equating the rates of social return on all forms of investments is still a useful one to consider. It suggests, for example, that capital-poor countries should only invest in additional schooling if the returns are very high —higher, in all probability, than the rates of return required for optimality in more capital-rich countries. Indeed, it is generally true that the rates of return to both secondary schooling and higher education appear to be higher in less developed countries than in developed countries. One study estimated that the rate of return on secondary schooling investments was 9.5 percent to a developed country (on average), while to a less-developed country it was 15.2 percent. Comparable rates of return to investments in higher education were 9.4 percent and 12.3 percent, respectively.

SOURCE: George Psacharopoulos, *Returns to Education* (San Francisco: Jossey-Bass, 1973), p. 67.

Unfortunately, direct evidence on the role schooling plays in society is almost impossible to obtain. Advocates of the screening viewpoint, for example, assert that the fact that rates of return to college *graduates* are higher than for college *dropouts* is evidence that schooling is a screening device.[19] They argue that what is learned in school is proportional to the time spent there and that an added bonus (rate of return) just for a diploma is proof of the screening hypothesis. Advocates of the view that schooling enhances human capital counter that one who graduates after four years probably has learned more than four times what the freshman dropout has learned. They argue that dropouts are more likely to be poorer students—the ones who overestimated their returns to schooling and quit when they discovered their mistake. Thus, their relatively low rate of return is not *because* they dropped out but is associated with the *reason* for dropping out.[20]

To take another example, proponents of the human-capital view of education sometimes argue that the fact that earnings differentials between (say) college and high-school graduates continue to grow is evidence supporting their view. They argue that if schooling is just a screening device employers would rely on it *initially* but that as they accumulate direct information from experience with their employees schooling would play a smaller role in determining earnings. Screening advocates could counter that continued growth in earnings differentials and the continued association of schooling and earnings only illustrates that educational levels are a *successful* sorting device; in other words, workers with higher levels of attainment in school do in fact make more productive workers.

Finally, it has been argued that the 1940–65 change in skill requirements for a large number of jobs was very small, yet the educational requirements for obtaining those jobs rose dramatically.[21] Thus, while shoe salespeople in 1965 performed the same job as in 1940, they were required to have more education because of the general inflation in levels of educational attainment. While this seems like persuasive evidence in favor of the screening hypothesis, it ignores the fact that the real earnings of sales personnel have risen. While the job requirements are the same—fitting and selling shoes—the salesperson of the 1960s must have a higher marginal product than his or her counterpart of the 1940s. This higher marginal productivity could be achieved by harder work and improved store layout or it could be the result of more knowledgeable sales personnel. Exactly how the increase has been obtained is unknown, but one cannot rule out improvements in human capital as a partial cause.

Thus, just about any evidence offered to support one side of the argument can be accomodated by the other side. Perhaps the best resolution of this issue is one that relies on economic reasoning. We know that college, for example, is

---

[19]Dropouts naturally have lower incomes than graduates, but because they have also invested less it is not clear that their *rates of return* should be lower.

[20]*See* Barry Chiswick, "Schooling, Screening, and Income," in *Does College Matter?* ed. Lewis Solomon and Paul Taubman (New York: Academic Press, 1973).

[21]*See* Ivar Berg, *Education and Jobs: The Great Training Robbery* (New York: Praeger Publishers, 1970).

very expensive and that to induce students to attend requires a reasonable return on their investment. Thus, to obtain college graduates, employers must pay them wages high enough to compensate them for their investment. If their investment costs are $40,000, employers must pay them a lifetime stream of wages whose present value is at least $40,000 higher than if they did not attend. In short, to get a college graduate costs an employer at least $40,000 more than a high-school graduate, in present-value terms, in the long run.

Now the college graduate may in fact be worth $40,000 more because of his or her productive characteristics. However, if these characteristics existed prior to college—and were unaffected by college—it would pay the firm to find its own method of sorting high-school graduates in order to find the best potential workers. As long as the methods it used were as reliable and cost less than a college education ($40,000 per worker), it would be profitable to adopt them. The firm could pay lower wages to their workers, because these workers would be spared the expense of college.

The fact that firms have not generally substituted their own screening devices for the educational requirements widely used suggests one of two things. Either education *does* enhance worker productivity, or it is a *cheaper* screening tool than any other firms could use. In either case, the fact that employers are willing to pay a high price for an educated work force *seems* to suggest that education produces social benefits.

Government Training Programs

Questions about the social benefits and costs of educational investments can be extended from general schooling to *particular* job-training programs—where the questions are generally easier to answer.

Beginning in the early 1960s, the federal government was rather heavily involved in programs designed to increase worker skills. In 1978, for example, 856,000 workers were enrolled in federally funded classroom or on-the-job training programs—at a cost of close to $2,000 per trainee on the average. One need not be a hard-bitten cynic to ask the question, "Are these programs worth their cost?" At times the answer seems to be a clear-cut "No."

During the 1960s, one government training program was aimed primarily at blacks in the poverty-stricken Mississippi-delta area. When delta training programs were geared to produce more than 8,000 trainees a year, available jobs for trainees were opening up at a rate of 3,000 per year.[22] Given this lack of job openings the programs became, in effect, welfare programs—valued for the stipend they paid trainees rather than their future benefits. Trainees had no incentive to graduate and tried to stay in the program as long as possible.

While it can be argued that enhancing the incomes of poor delta blacks is itself a worthy enterprise, it must be pointed out that training programs are not

[22]Michael J. Piore, "Negro Workers in the Mississippi Delta: Problems of Displacement and Adjustment," in *Perspectives on Poverty and Income Distribution,* ed. James G. Scoville (Lexington, Mass.: D.C. Heath, 1971), pp. 151–57.

an efficient means of doing this. They require society to pay the salaries of instructors (who are not poor) and to purchase capital equipment—funds which might better be used if they were given directly to the poor.

The intent of a properly conceived job-skills training program is to enhance private and social productivity by training workers to do jobs that are in demand. Some policymakers have followed a *personnel planning* approach in deciding how many workers—in what fields—to train. This personnel-planning approach asks employers how many persons with certain kinds of qualifications they will need, projects the numbers likely to be supplied by other sources, and recommends filling the gap with government training programs. While this method, if successfully used, should avoid the problems mentioned in the case of delta trainees, it does suffer the fatal flaw of ignoring *costs:*

> The manpower planner who plans supply to match demand asks the *wrong* questions. He asks, "What is the absorptive capacity of the economy for persons with different skills and educational attainments?" and does not consider the costs of schooling at all. If employers say (or his calculations lead him to believe) that an extra graduate would be hired, the manpower planner directs the education system to produce an extra graduate. He does not ask, "What is the nature of the work the graduate will perform and what benefits will he confer on society?" Nor does he ask, "How much will it cost society to educate another graduate? Do the benefits justify the costs?"[23]

The only way in which one can be sure that investments in training programs are socially productive is to weigh their costs against the increases in productivity they permit. Since theory implies that marginal productivity and wages are roughly equal, one can look at the wage increases of trainees to obtain an approximation of productivity increases. For example, if a worker would have earned $8,000 per year had she not had training, and earns $8,600 a year after training, the program has pretty clearly increased her productivity by $600 per year. This yearly benefit to her (and society) must then be weighed against the cost of training in order to see if the rate of return is as large as it would be if the funds had been invested elsewhere.

Weighing costs against returns is not an easy job, primarily because one must find some way of estimating what trainees would have earned in the absence of the program. One way to make such an estimate is to project the earnings based on past earnings trends, taking note of earnings trends among comparable workers who did not enter the training program. A comprehensive study of 13,000 people who received training in 1964 under the federal Manpower Development and Training Act (MDTA) found that, for males, yearly increases in earnings were in the $150–$500 range, with the effects declining by half over a five-year post-training period. For females, the gains were in the $300–$600 range, with no decline over time.[24]

[23]Gary S. Fields, "Private and Social Returns to Education in Labour Surplus Economies," *Eastern Africa Economic Review* 4, 1 (June 1972): 43.

[24]Orley Ashenfelter, "Estimating the Effect of Training Programs on Earnings," *Review of Economics and Statistics* 60, 1 (February 1978): 47–57.

Do these returns justify the costs? The costs per student in this program were $1,800. If a 10 percent rate of return on this investment were to be earned indefinitely, the gains would have to amount to $180 a year. The results for males roughly meet this standard, while those for females clearly exceed it. Thus, the MDTA program appears to have been a good investment in 1964, although the results do indicate that training for females was a better investment and should, therefore, have been expanded. (Later classes of trainees, it should be pointed out, did not experience as high a rate of return as did the 1964 class.)

Applications of Human-Capital Theory

The theory of human capital can be used to explain several interesting phenomena found in the labor market. This section will apply the theory to post-school investments in training and the labor-force behavior of women.

EXAMPLE 8.3

Communists or (Human) Capitalists?

The concepts of human-capital theory are neither unknown nor ignored in the Soviet Union. A study of wages in the American, German, Dutch, Italian, and Russian steel industries, for example, found that the wage premiums skilled workers in Russia command over unskilled workers are much larger than in the other countries. In fact, the range of wages paid to blast-furnace and open-hearth workers in the Soviet Union is roughly twice the range paid to comparable American workers. Why do these large wage differentials exist in a country supposedly dedicated to the ideal of equality?

According to the Soviet managers, the Soviet Union places extraordinary emphasis on the education and training of their workers:

The Soviet government recognizes that such training costs the individual effort and time, and it is willing to reward him by promotion to distinctly higher-paying jobs. . . . In other words . . . the big wage-rate differentials are part and parcel of a tremendous effort to raise the qualifications and performance of workers in the Soviet iron and steel industry.

SOURCE: M. Gardner Clark, "Comparative Wage Structures in the Steel Industry of the Soviet Union and Western Countries," *Proceedings of the Thirteenth Annual Meeting, Industrial Relations Research Association* (Madison, Wis.: IRRA, 1961), pp. 266–88.

Post-Schooling Investments and Age/Earnings Profiles

Schooling is largely a full-time, formally organized activity. However, there are less formal kinds of human-capital investments that are more difficult to observe. These investments take the form of training that normally occurs in the workplace. Some of this "training" is *learning-by-doing* (as one hammers nails month after month, one's skills naturally improve), but much of it takes place on the job, under close supervision, or consists of a formal program in the workplace. All forms of training are costly in the sense that the productivity of learners is low, and all represent a conscious *choice* on the part of the employer to accept lower current productivity in exchange for higher output later. It has been estimated that the average worker acquires the equivalent of at least two years of college in on-the-job training and that the annual cost of such training amounts to 3 percent of gross national product.[25]

Who bears the cost of on-the-job training? You will recall that Chapter 5 argued that the cost of *specific training*—training of use *only* to one's employer —would be shared by the worker and firm. The employee might be paid a wage greater than marginal product *(MP)* during the training period, but after training the employee's wage is below *MP* (but above what the employee could get elsewhere). In the case of general training, where employees acquire skills they can use elsewhere, it is they alone who pay for the training costs.

How do employees pay the costs of general training provided by their employer? They work for a wage lower than they would get if they were not receiving training. Their wage is less than their *MP* (which is, itself, decreased during the training period when trainees make mistakes or require time off the job to engage in classroom learning) by an amount equal to the supervisory or instructional costs to the firm associated with training. Why do employees accept this lower wage? They accept it for the same reason that some decide to obtain schooling: in the expectation of improving the present value of their lifetime earnings. In other words, employees incur current investment costs (lower wages) in order to obtain increased earnings later.

The timing of post-schooling investments. This chapter has demonstrated that if people are going to invest in themselves they will tend to undertake most of the investment at younger ages for two reasons:

1. Investments made at younger ages have a longer period over which to capture returns and thus will tend to have higher total benefits.
2. One big cost of investing in education and training is forgone earnings— and this cost rises as one gets older and earnings become higher (if, for no other reason, because of learning-by-doing).

Consequently, putting off human-capital investments will lower the returns to such investments.

---

[25]Jacob Mincer, "On-the-Job Training: Costs, Returns, and Some Implications," *Journal of Political Economy* (Supplement 1962): 50–79.

It is not surprising to find, then, that schooling—largely a full-time activity —is followed by on-the-job training, which is normally a part-time activity. Further, we should also find that job training declines with age, being most heavily concentrated in one's early years on the job when opportunity costs are lower. However, in the case of job training, where scholarships and loans are not available and where the training is part-time, investment will not take place all at once. Too much current consumption would have to be forgone by the ordinary worker if one's entire lifetime amount of job training were acquired completely in the first two years (say) of one's career. Thus, employees will tend to parcel out their job training over a number of years but will gradually reduce such training as time goes by.

The timing of investment and age/earnings profiles. The above theory of post-schooling investments helps to explain why age/earnings profiles are concave: rising more rapidly at first, then flattening out, and ultimately falling (see Figure 8.8). Earnings, low at first because of training investments, rise quickly as new skills are acquired. However, as workers grow older, the pace of training investment slows and so does the rate at which productivity increases. At the end of one's working life skills may have depreciated—due to lack of continued investment and the aging process—to the extent that retirement, semiretirement, or a change in jobs is necessary for many workers. This depreciation contributes to the downturn in *average* earnings near retirement age.

The fanning out of age/earnings profiles by education. As noted earlier in this chapter, the differences in average earnings between people of the same age, but with different educational levels, increase over time (see Figure 8.7). This phenomenon is also consistent with what human-capital theory would predict.

The answer to the question, "Who will invest most in post-school training?" should be familiar by now. Those who expect the highest benefits and workers who learn most quickly will do the most investing in job training. The fact that they learn rapidly shortens the training period, which both reduces investment costs and increases the duration of benefits. But who are these fast learners? They

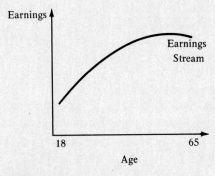

Figure 8.8   Age/Earnings Profile

are most likely the people who, because of their abilities, were best able to reap benefits from formal schooling! Thus, human-capital theory leads us to expect workers who invested more in schooling to also invest more in post-schooling job training.

The tendency of the better-educated workers to invest more in job training explains why their age/earnings profiles start low, rise quickly, and keep rising after the profiles of their less-educated counterparts have leveled off. Their earnings rise more quickly because they are investing more heavily in job training, and they rise for a longer time for the same reason. In other words, people with the ability to learn quickly select the ultimately high-paying jobs where much learning is required and thus put their abilities to greatest advantage.

Women and the Acquisition of Human Capital

The career pattern of many married women tends to consist of distinct stages. First, there is a period of employment preceding childbirth. Following the birth of the first child is a period of nonparticipation in the labor force, and then there is a return to labor market participation, often on a part-time or temporary basis. A study conducted on data collected in the 1960s found that the first stage of participation usually lasted 3–4 years and that the second stage of nonparticipation usually lasted 7 years,[26] although since the 1970s it is likely that the former lengthened and the latter shortened.

The interrupted nature of many women's careers has profound implications for the acquisition of education and training. First, because women's careers are usually shorter than men's, they have less time over which to reap the rewards of investments in human capital. This lowers the benefits of such investments as schooling and training, rendering women less likely than men to invest.

Second, the interrupted nature of women's work experience adds additional incentives to avoid costly investments. The period of nonparticipation in the labor market is one in which skills depreciate and the continuity of experience is broken. Previous investments in human capital may become almost useless—especially in highly technical, ever-changing fields such as law, medicine, engineering, and research. Thus, many women in the prematernal years will avoid investments that will lose their value during the years of child rearing, thereby taking themselves out of occupations that require continuity of experience or training to be successful.

Human-capital theory therefore predicts that women will acquire less schooling and less training than men. The evidence is consistent with these predictions, as we shall see below. Before reviewing the evidence, however, we must point out that these predictions of human-capital theory are for a "traditional" woman—one who has, *and expects to have,* an interrupted labor-market career. The predic-

---

[26]These data are taken from Jacob Mincer and Solomon Polachek, "Family Investments in Human Capital: Earnings of Women," *Journal of Political Economy* 82, 2 (March/April 1974): S76–S108.

tions do not apply to women who expect to have uninterrupted lifetime careers in the labor market—whose behavior (if we had good enough data to observe it) would be expected to parallel that of the typical male.

Women and schooling. When one considers the reduced benefits women typically receive (compared with men), it is not surprising to find that a lower percentage of women have tended to enroll in college. For example, in 1979 29.6 percent of all female high-school graduates between the ages of 18 and 24 were enrolled in college compared to 32.9 percent of males the same age. Moreover, females of high ability are apparently much more responsive than males of similar ability to the availability of a hometown college in deciding whether or not to attend.[27] As argued in the first section of this chapter, this greater responsiveness to cost considerations—seen also in males of moderate ability—is indicative of a greater likelihood of being "at the margin" (closer to deciding not to go).

Note: The percentage of women high-school graduates attending college is rising very quickly, while that of men is falling. It appears that in the mid-1980s the percentages may equalize—a circumstance undoubtedly influenced by the lengthening expected career lives of women and by associated changes in their choice of occupations. Thus, the generalizations about women and schooling made above hold only as long as a significant number of women expect substantially shorter careers than men; as expected durations of work life equalize, so will college enrollment behavior.

Women and job training. Besides reduced incentives to invest in schooling, women have fewer incentives than men to invest in job training. As a result, women do not typically find themselves in jobs with steep age/earnings profiles. While we lack the data necessary to track the earnings of individual women through time, we can plot (as we did for males) average earnings of each age group. As Figure 8.9 shows, the age/earnings profiles for women are very flat: older women do not appear to earn much more than younger women. We can conclude from this that experience-related increases in productivity are not a big influence on women's wages—which implies that the acquisition of job training is not very widespread among women.

One reason for the lack of job training among women may be their shorter and more interrupted careers, which reduces both their incentives and the incentives of their employers to engage in such training. Another reason, however, may be various forms of discrimination (see Chapter 11, for further discussion of discrimination and women's earnings). Nevertheless, at least some of the differences between the earnings of men and women are due to differences in the acquisition of human capital. The magnitude of these differences will be addressed in Chapter 11.

---

[27]Anderson, Bowman, and Tinto, *Where Colleges Are and Who Attends.*

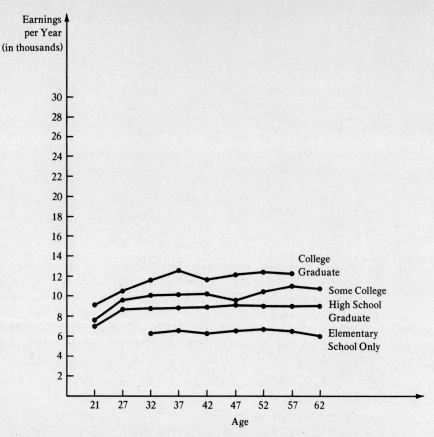

Figure 8.9   Total Money Earnings (mean), Full-Time Females, 1977

SOURCE: U.S. Bureau of the Census, *Money Income in 1977 of Families and Persons in the United States,* Current Population Reports, Series P-60, No. 118 (March 1979), Table 48.

REVIEW QUESTIONS

1. Why do women receive lower wages, on average, than men of equal age? Why does the discrepancy between male and female earnings grow with age?
2. How would college enrollments be affected if
   a. income-tax rates were substantially cut for higher-income workers but only modestly reduced for lower-income employees?
   b. the real rate of interest increased?
   c. government subsidies for college students were reduced?
   d. young people became more present-oriented?
   e. the *work* life of employees became longer (that is, if people retired at a later age)?
3. Many crimes against property (burglary, for example) can be thought of as acts that have immediate gains but that entail long-run costs (sooner or later the criminal may be caught and imprisoned). If imprisoned, the criminal loses income from both criminal and noncriminal activities. Using the framework for occupational choice in the long run,

analyze what kinds of people are most likely to engage in criminal activities. What can society do to reduce crime?

4. Suppose education provides no *social* benefits of any kind; that is, it does not enhance worker productivity and it does not accurately "signal" who is already more productive. What conditions would have to hold for there to be a positive *individual* return to education in this circumstance?

5. Why do those who argue that more education "signals" greater ability believe that the most able people will obtain the most education?

SELECTED READINGS

Gary Becker, *Human Capital* 2nd ed. (New York: National Bureau of Economic Research, 1975).

Ivar Berg, *Education and Jobs: The Great Training Robbery* (New York: Praeger Publishers, 1970.)

Mark Blaug, "Human Capital Theory: A Slightly Jaundiced Survey." *Journal of Economic Literature* 14 (September 1976):827–55.

Richard B. Freeman, *The Overeducated American* (New York: Academic Press, 1976).

Jacob Mincer, "On-the-Job Training: Costs Returns, and Some Implications." *Journal of Political Economy* (Supplement 1962): 50–79.

Jacob Mincer, *Schooling, Experience and Earnings* (New York: National Bureau of Economic Research, 1974).

Jacob Mincer, "The Distribution of Labor Incomes: A Survey with Special Reference to the Human Capital Approach." *Journal of Economic Literature* (March 1970): 1–26.

Jacob Mincer and Solomon Polachek. "Family Investments in Human Capital: Earnings of Women." *Journal of Political Economy* 82 (March/April 1974): S76–S108.

Theodore Schultz, *The Economic Value of Education* (New York: Columbia University Press, 1963).

Michael Spence, "Job Market Signaling." *Quarterly Journal of Economics* 87 (August 1973):355–74.

Chapter 9

WORKER MOBILITY: TURNOVER AND MIGRATION

A salient fact about the U.S. economy is the high degree of mobility among its workers. As noted in Chapter 7, the monthly quit rate in manufacturing industries is 1–2 percent per *month*—which implies a yearly turnover rate of 12–24 percent. Chapter 7 also noted that 20 percent of male, semiskilled workers over age 25 in 1965 were employed in a *completely different* occupation by 1970 —and the figure jumps to 43 percent for *all* males over 20. Roughly 25 percent of all workers change the industry in which they work over a three-year period.[1] Moreover, in many cases job mobility is accompanied by geographic mobility. Between 1975 and 1978, for example, 9 million people over 20 years of age—6.4 percent of the total—moved between states; 11 million more (7.6 percent) moved to a different county within a state. Thus, one seventh of the adult population made a major move in just a three-year period—and the fraction rises to one fourth when focusing only on those in their twenties. Finally, the United States receives roughly 400,000 legal immigrants each year—and the discrepancy between the numbers who want to come and the numbers permitted by law is so great that thousands more enter illegally. As of 1980, most experts believed that there were at least 4 million illegal immigrants living permanently in the country.

The mobility cited above is not without its costs. There is sometimes a temporary loss of income that occurs between the time one job is given up and a new one—perhaps in a new place—is obtained. There are direct moving costs

---

[1]Lowell E. Gallaway, *Interindustry Labor Mobility in the United States, 1957 to 1960*, Social Security Administration Research Report No. 18 (Washington D.C.: U.S. Government Printing Office, 1967), p. 29.

when migration occurs. There are the psychic costs of leaving a familiar job or a familiar place and having to become acquainted with a new environment. There can be no doubt, then, that rather large monetary and psychic costs are borne each year by large numbers of people wanting to improve their lot in life. In this sense mobility represents a significant investment in human capital. Costs are borne in the short run in order that benefits will be possible in the long run. The human-capital model of mobility described in this chapter offers some clear-cut implications about who invests in mobility and where they go.

The basic human-capital model of mobility is a model of "voluntary" mobility undertaken by workers who perceive mobility to be in their self-interest. The factors influencing employer-initiated mobility—layoffs, for example—are quite different, as discussed in Chapter 5. The determinants of voluntary mobility are discussed first, and later in the chapter the testable implications of human-capital theory for both migration and job-quitting behavior are analyzed. The chapter will conclude with an economic analysis of immigration and its implications for national policy.

The Determinants of Mobility

The human-capital model presented in Chapter 8 can be used to understand and predict worker-initiated mobility. This model views voluntary mobility as an investment, wherein costs are borne in some early period in order to obtain returns over a longer period of time. If the present value of the benefits associated with mobility exceeds the costs—both monetary and psychic—we assume that people will decide to change jobs or move or both. If the discounted stream of benefits is not as large as the costs, then people will decide against such a change.

What determines the present value of the net benefits of mobility—that is, the benefits minus the costs—determines the mobility decision. These factors can be better identified by writing out the formula one would use if one were to precisely calculate these net benefits:

$$\text{Present Value of Net Benefits} = \sum_{t=1}^{T} \frac{B_{jt} - B_{ot}}{(1 + r)^t} - C, \tag{9.1}$$

where:

B_{jt} = the utility derived from the new job (j) in the year t;
B_{ot} = the utility derived from the old job (o) in the year t;
T = length of time (in years) one expects to work at job j;
r = the rate of discount;
C = the utility lost in the move itself (direct and psychic costs); and
Σ = a summation—in this case the summation of the yearly discounted net benefits over a period running from year 1 to year T.

EXAMPLE 9.1

Job Satisfaction: An Alternative View

In the last decade or so, managers and researchers have expressed much interest in job satisfaction—and most are inclined to view dissatisfaction as a result of *employer* policies concerning job tasks, working conditions, or compensation. Economists, however, view the phenomenon of job satisfaction somewhat differently. Workers are viewed as making choices of jobs and employers from among competing alternatives; if they are unhappy in a particular occupation or with a particular employer, they will be motivated to seek other employment. Moreover, as noted in Chapter 7, pecuniary and nonpecuniary aspects of jobs are viewed as substitutes for each other; higher wages, for example, might compensate for poor working conditions and lead to overall satisfaction with one's job. Thus, economists tend to view job satisfaction as an outcome of the employer-worker *matching* process and not solely as the result of employer policies. If the matching process is impeded by factors inhibiting mobility, workers may be "stuck" in jobs they dislike. If workers are aware of alternatives and are able to leave jobs they view as unsatisfactory, they should eventually find something close to their best option.

A survey of job satisfaction around 1970 found that 47 percent of all workers were "very satisfied" with their jobs, roughly 38 percent were "somewhat satisfied," while only 15 percent were either "not too satisfied" or "not at all satisfied." A more sophisticated statistical analysis of job-satisfaction responses in this survey found that workers were more likely to indicate a feeling of satisfaction as they became older and as their *actual* earnings exceeded an estimate of their *alternative* earnings.

Taken together, the above results offer some support for economists' views. The small number of people who report themselves even mildly dissatisfied, coupled with the finding that dissatisfaction falls with age, suggests that job mobility may be an antidote for dissatisfaction. It appears that, on the one hand, employees "try out" occupations and employers, and that they are able to leave situations they dislike. On the other hand, if they realize that the job they have is, on the whole, better-paying than their alternatives, they express greater satisfaction and are presumably less likely to leave it. Thus, a "trial-and-error" process, fueled by information about one's alternatives, may well be at work, producing generally satisfactory matches between workers and jobs in the long run.

Source: Daniel S. Hamermesh, "The Economics of Job Satisfaction," Technical Analysis Paper No. 22, Office of the Assistant Secretary for Policy, Evaluation and Research, U.S. Department of Labor (May 1974), Appendix. A revised version of this paper, without the appendix, was published with the same title in Orley Ashenfelter and Wallace Oates, eds., *Essays in Labor Market Analysis* (New York: John Wiley and Sons, 1978).

Clearly, the present value of the net benefits of mobility will be larger (a) the greater the utility derived from the new job, (b) the less happy one is in the job of origin, (c) the smaller are the immediate costs associated with the change, and (d) the longer one expects to be in the new job or live in the new area (that is, the greater is T). These observations lead to some clear-cut predictions about which groups in society will be most mobile and about the *patterns* of mobility one would expect to observe. These predictions are analyzed in the following sections on migration and quit behavior.

Geographic Mobility

When people are asked about the reasons for their geographic-mobility decisions, about 75 percent mention job change as a *critical* factor, and 60 percent mention it as the *exclusive* factor motivating their move. This emphasis on job change suggests that the implications of the human-capital theory for migration can be tested in the labor market.

Comparing Wages and Employment Opportunities

If job changes are the most dominant factor motivating mobility, then we should observe people migrating from areas where wages and employment opportunities are relatively poor to areas where they are relatively good. Three interrelated patterns of internal migration can be observed in the United States over the recent decades: (1) rural-to-urban shifts, (2) the movement of blacks, and (3) the interregional flows of people.

Rural-to-urban movements. Huge movements of people from rural to urban areas have occurred in this century as farming jobs have diminished in number.[2] In 1910, 54 percent of the U.S. population lived in rural areas—that is, areas with fewer than 2500 inhabitants. In 1970 this percentage had fallen to 26 percent. In the 1960s alone, farming employment fell by 40 percent, and the rural areas of California, the Dakotas, Nebraska, and Kansas experienced population losses of 10–16 percent. Interestingly enough, the *overall* rural population fell by only 0.3 percent during the 1960s because of rural population increases in New England, the mid-Atlantic states, and the eastern north-central states. This growth reflects, to a large degree, the extension of suburban areas into neighboring rural counties and thus does not contradict our observation that people move to where the jobs are.

---

[2]Data in this section are from the *Manpower Report of the President* (Washington, D.C.: U.S. Government Printing Office, 1974), pp. 77–78.

Migration of blacks. A dramatic characteristic of rural-urban migration in this century has been the massive movement of blacks out of the rural South to urban areas in the non-South.[3] This movement began during World War I, when war-time production created jobs in the urbanized, industrial states in the North. In the 1920s this migration continued as 800,000 blacks left the South, headed primarily for big cities in the North. This flow was cut in half during the 1930s, when the Great Depression diminished job opportunities in the industrial sector, but it rose to 1.6 million during the war-dominated 1940s. In the essentially prosperous decades of the 1950s and 1960s, 2.9 million more blacks left the South.

Undoubtedly part of the migration of blacks reflects the decline in farming employment. Many southern states have also experienced outflows of whites. More whites left the states of Alabama, Kentucky, Oklahoma, and West Virginia during the 1950s and 1960s than entered them, while Arkansas, the Carolinas, Georgia, Mississippi, and Tennessee experienced out-migration of whites in the 1950s but net in-migration of whites during the 1960s.

That the migration of blacks out of the South is not completely due to the decline in agricultural jobs is clearly indicated by the fact that while blacks were *leaving* the South during the 1960s, whites were, on balance, *flowing into* the South as jobs there expanded. Because basic federal civil-rights laws concerning segregation and voting were not passed until the mid-'60s and programs aimed at eliminating job discrimination were not implemented until the late '60s, it is not farfetched to speculate that much of the black migration out of the South was induced by perceptions of greater freedom and opportunities elsewhere. As discrimination lessened in the 1970s, however, and as blacks began to share in the general economic expansion in the South, there has been, on balance, a movement of blacks *into* the South. Between 1970 and 1975 there was a net influx of 44,000 blacks into the South—the first time this has occurred in the twentieth century.

Regional migration. Further evidence that tends to support the view that people move from regions where opportunities are poor to regions where they are better can be found by examining regional migration. The older, slow-growing industrial states of New York, Pennsylvania, Ohio, Illinois, and Michigan are experiencing out-migration, while the faster-growing states in the South and West are the recipients of an influx of migrants. During 1975–78, for example, the northeast and north-central states had a net outflow of 1.4 million people, while the South and West had net inflows of 1 million and 400,000 respectively. The net inflow to the South is a complete turnaround from the 1950s, when the region was largely rural and offered relatively few job opportunities. As the South has industrialized and opportunities have improved, it has become the region with the most net in-migration.

Human-capital theory predicts that people will tend to move from areas of

---

[3]Data in this section were obtained from the *Manpower Report of the President,* 1974, pp. 90–97 and U.S. Bureau of the Census, *Statistical Abstract of the U.S.,* 99th ed. (Washington, D.C.: U.S. Government Printing Office, 1978), Table 26.

relatively poor earnings possibilities to places where opportunities are better. While the general regional flows of people support this prediction, it is important to note that the prediction can also be tested by looking at the characteristics of more specific areas from which and to which people move. In general, the results of such studies suggest that the "pull" of good opportunities in the areas of destination are stronger than the "push" of poor opportunities in the areas of origin. In other words, while people are more attracted to places where earnings are expected to be better, they do not necessarily come from areas where the opportunities are poorest.

The most consistent finding in these detailed studies is that people are attracted to areas where the real earnings of full-time workers are highest. One might also expect that the chances for obtaining work in the new area would also affect that area's attractiveness. One way to measure job availability in an area is to use the unemployment rate, but the studies find no consistent relationship between unemployment and in-migration—perhaps because the number of people moving with a job already in hand is three times as large as the numbers moving *to look* for work.[4] If one already has a job in a particular field, the *overall* unemployment rate is irrelevant.

Most studies have found that, contrary to what human-capital theory implies, the characteristics of the place of origin do not appear to have much influence on migration. One reason for this finding is that while those in the poorest places have the greatest *incentives* to move, the very poorest areas also tend to have people with lower levels of education and skills—the very people who seem least *willing* (or able) to move. To understand this last phenomenon, we must turn from the issue of *where* people go to a discussion of *who* is most likely to move.

Personal Characteristics of Movers

Migration is highly selective in that it is not an activity in which all people are equally likely to be engaged. To be specific, mobility is much higher among the young and the better-educated—as human-capital theory would suggest.

Age. Age is the single most important factor in determining who migrates. The peak years for mobility are the ages 22–24, when nearly 20 percent of the population migrates across county or state lines. By age 32, the rate of migration is half what it was in the early twenties, and by age 42 migration is only one fourth as likely as it was in the twenties.

There are two explanations for the fact that migration is an activity primarily for the young. First, the younger one is, the greater the potential returns from any human-capital investment. As noted earlier, the longer is the period over which benefits from an investment can be obtained, the larger is the present value of these benefits.

---

[4]John B. Lansing and Eva Mueller, *The Geographic Mobility of Labor* (Ann Arbor, Mich.: Survey Research Center, University of Michigan, 1967), p. 37.

Second, a large part of the costs of migration are psychic—the losses associated with giving up friends, community ties, and the benefits of knowing one's way around. When one is starting out as an adult, these losses are comparatively small because one is not well-established in the adult world. However, as one grows older, community ties become stronger, and the losses associated with leaving loom larger—thus inhibiting mobility. This line of reasoning is underscored by the fact that, within age groups, unmarried people are more likely to migrate than married ones, and that married people without children are more mobile than those with children.[5]

Education. While age is probably the best predictor of who will move, education is the single best indicator of who will move *within* an age group. As can be seen from Table 9.1, strictly speaking, more education does not make one more likely to move; it is a *college* education that makes migration more likely. The labor markets for college-educated workers are more likely to be regional or national in character than are the labor markets for those with less education.

One of the costs of migration is that of ascertaining *where* opportunities are and *how good* they are likely to be. If one's occupation has a national labor market, for example, it is relatively easy to find out about opportunities in distant places. Jobs are advertised in national newspapers. Recruiters from all over visit college campuses. Employment agencies make nationwide searches. In cases such as these, people usually move with a job already in hand.

However, if the relevant labor market for one's job is localized, it is difficult to find out where better opportunities in other areas might be. For a janitor in Beaumont, Texas, to find out about employment opportunities in the north-central region is like looking for the proverbial needle in a haystack. That such

Table 9.1. Migration Rates for Men and Women 25–29 by Educational Level, 1965–71

| Educational Level (in years) | Percent Moving Each Year | | | |
| | Between Counties within States | | Between States | |
	Men	Women	Men	Women
0–7	6.7	4.9	5.2	4.3
8	6.9	4.9	5.7	6.3
9–11	6.4	4.3	5.2	4.8
12	5.5	4.8	5.2	5.2
13–15	6.1	6.4	6.9	8.0
16	9.2	7.0	11.3	11.0
17 or more	8.3	8.1	15.6	13.5

SOURCE: *Manpower Report of the President,* 1974, p. 84.

---

[5]*See* Jacob Mincer, "Family Migration Decisions," *Journal of Political Economy* 86,5 (October 1978): 749–73.

moves occur at all, let alone in reasonably large numbers, is testimony to the fact that people are able to acquire information despite the obstacles.

The Role of Distance

Human-capital theory clearly predicts that as migration costs rise, the flow of migrants will fall. The costs of moving increase with distance for two reasons. First, as noted above, for people in local labor markets, acquiring information on opportunities elsewhere can be very difficult (costly). Surely it is easier to find out about employment prospects closer to home than farther away: newspapers are easier to obtain, phone calls are cheaper, friends and relatives are more useful contacts, and knowledge of employers is greater. Second, the money costs of transportation—both for the move and for trips back to see friends and relatives—obviously rise with distance. Thus, one would clearly expect to find that people are more likely to move short distances than long distances.

In general, people *are* more likely to move shorter than longer distances. One study published in the late 1960s found that 34 percent of all moves were of less than 100 miles and 51 percent were of less than 200 miles. In contrast, only 17 percent were of distances between 200–400 miles and only 10 percent were between 400 and 600 miles in length.[6] Thus, moves over 600 miles accounted for only 22 percent of all moves. Clearly, the propensity to move far away is smaller than the propensity to stay close to home.

Related to the desire to minimize psychic and informational costs is the fact that people tend to migrate to areas where friends or relatives have previously migrated. This *chain migration* is especially evident in the stream of migration from Puerto Rico to the mainland: most Puerto Ricans go to Chicago and to the tristate area of New York-New Jersey-Connecticut.

The Individual Returns to Migration

The previous section discussed the fact that the people most likely to move are the ones with the most to gain and the least to lose by migration—and that they move to areas where their net gains are likely to be largest. Another way to test our human-capital theory of migration is to see if the incomes of people who migrate are higher than they would have been in the absence of migration.

One interesting study that analyzed the earnings of foreign-born males found that these immigrants had, on the average, fewer skills and less education than native men, and initially earned much less than Americans of comparable skills and education.[7] After five years they still earned 10 percent less, but after 10–15 years their earnings were equal to comparable native males. Interestingly, after

---

[6]Lansing and Mueller, *The Geographic Mobility of Labor,* p. 28. Some of the moves of less than 100 miles may not have been accompanied by a job change; the explanation for these moves lies outside the realm of human-capital theory.

[7]Barry Chiswick, "The Effect of Americanization on the Earnings of Foreign-Born Men," *Journal of Political Economy* 86 (October 1978): 897–921.

20 years foreign-born males earned 6 percent more than native men. This earnings pattern suggests that hiring newcomers is regarded as a risky proposition by employers, either because they find it hard to evaluate their background or because their productivity is lowered by language and cultural problems. During this period, in effect, immigrants are investing heavily in themselves by acquiring experience in the culture and facility in the language.

Eventually, however, immigrants surpass the average native-born male (of the same educational background) in earning ability—primarily because immigrants are not average people. They are people with enough drive to accept the high costs of immigration in order to "get ahead." Interestingly, the high ability and work motivation of immigrants is also seen in the fact that white native-born sons of immigrants have earnings that are 5 percent higher than white sons of native-born parents with the same educational characteristics living in the same area.[8]

Given the poverty of the countries from which less skilled immigrants generally come, the fact that they do well here clearly implies eventual gains from immigration for them as individuals. Can the same conclusion be reached concerning migrants *within* the United States? Studies have found that, as a general rule, migrants do earn more than they would have earned if they had not moved. The exact size of the typical earnings differential is unclear, but earnings increases in the 10–20 percent range have been found for blacks moving out of the South.[9] There may be no *immediate* increases in income for migrants within the United States, but increases after five years are found and turn out to be large—a finding more or less consistent with the finding for foreign-born migrants. Thus, the studies of returns accruing to *individual* moves confirm the findings of research on the relationship between area-wide incentives and the *general flow* of migrants.

One other finding regarding the individual returns to migration is that the gains to *wives* from migration are much lower than the gains to husbands. For example, one study of husband-wife families who moved across state lines in 1971–72 found that the changes in present value of earnings over the next four years were $4254 for husbands and −$1716 for wives. (These figures compare to increases of $1648 and $160, respectively, for nonmovers.)[10] The reason for this disparity between husbands and wives is found in the way that family migration decisions have traditionally been made. The husband's earnings opportunities have probably been given primary weight in the decision about whether (and where) to move. The husband is thus free to move where his earnings potential is best, and it would only be by coincidence that this same place would be optimal for his wife (in terms of earnings). Thus, while *family* income seems to rise after a move, it is the husband's income that increases the most. The wife's earnings, as shown by this one study, may actually decline when migration takes place.

[8]Barry Chiswick, "Immigrants and Immigration Policy," in *Contemporary Economic Problems,* ed. William Fellner (Washington, D.C.: American Enterprise Institute, 1978).

[9]Michael J. Greenwood, "Research on Internal Migration in the United States: A Survey," *Journal of Economic Literature* 8, 2 (June 1975): 397–433.

[10]Solomon W. Polachek and Francis W. Horvath, "A Life-Cycle Approach to Migration: Analysis of the Perspicacious Peregrinator," in *Research in Labor Economics,* ed. Ronald Ehrenberg (Greenwich, Conn.: JAI Press, 1977), pp. 128–29.

EXAMPLE 9.2

The New Economics of Job Rotation

It is the practice of many large employers to systematically rotate employees through positions in various plant or office locations. These employers believe that such rotation creates employees with broad, flexible, company-wide perspectives who bring fresh points of view to each job. Often, however, an employee who accepts a new position (usually because it is perceived as a path to success) must also move to a new geographical location, so these transfers are accompanied by the costs of uprooting one's family.

In families where one spouse is considered the "primary" earner, locational decisions are not normally influenced much by job considerations of the "secondary" earner. Typically, this has meant that wives "follow" their husbands in geographical moves, and many of the jobs dominated by women are ideally suited to people in a "follower" role. For example, unlike many occupations, the occupations of teacher, nurse, and secretary—all heavily female—can be found in virtually every community in which one might move. Moreover, because all three occupations require little firm-specific training, human-capital losses are not imposed on employers if the employee must leave the area; thus, employers do not have great incentives to discriminate against people in a "follower" status when hiring in these jobs.

Despite the occupational adaptation of most wives to their "follower" status, the economic losses they sustain from a move may be significant. For example, the wives of military personnel (who are required to move to a new duty station every 4 years or so) are just as likely to work as other wives, but they are much more likely to work in part-time jobs. It is also clear that in the year of a move, most of the military wives who normally work throughout the year are employed for only part of the year. Nevertheless, when wives' earnings are small and only supplementary to the "primary" earnings of their husbands, the changes in overall *family* income from a potential move usually correspond relatively closely to changes in just the *husband's* earnings. Thus, as was found in a study mentioned on p. 240 of this chapter, the mobility-related gains in husbands' incomes far exceeded the corresponding losses sustained by wives—a situation that reinforces the "traditional" decision-making process concerning geographical location.

Recently, however, more women have begun to seek *careers* in higher-paying management or professional occupations with four important consequences. First, if women pursuing these careers marry, their earnings may well equal or exceed the earnings of their husbands. Second, many managerial and professional jobs are not ubiquitous; employment for chemical engineers, for example, is not normally found in small communities and may not exist in many larger cities. Third, it may not be possible to change geographical locations without sustaining large losses even when one has an occupation with ubiquitous alternatives. Employment of lawyers and doctors exists in all communities, for example, but changing communities means losing one's clientele. Fourth, family locational decisions are enormously complicated if both spouses are pursuing *careers,* because a geographical area ideal for one career may not be optimal for the other. One of the marriage partners must normally compromise his or her "best" location, and more often than not it is the wife who does. One study of wives pursuing professional careers in small cities, for example, estimated that their earnings were 8 percent less than they would be if women chose their optimal location and their husbands compromised.

For wives pursuing higher-paying managerial or professional careers, then, the costs of being in a "follower" role can be high. Further, as wives' earnings approach equality with those of their husbands, the losses they sustain from a "follower" status have a greater effect on overall *family* income. Once having found a satisfactory geographical area in which to pursue dual careers, the family will be very reluctant to leave. Thus, to the extent that *both* spouses pursue these careers, their willingness to move from area to area will be reduced—and employers' reliance on job rotation as a managerial or developmental tool will undoubtedly have to be curtailed.

Sources: Louis Jacobson, "Research to Quantify the Effect of Permanent Change of Station Moves on Wives' Wages and Labor Supply," Center for Naval Analyses, Alexandria, Virginia, December 1982; Solomon W. Polachek and Francis W. Horvath, "A Life-Cycle Approach to Migration: Analysis of the Perspicacious Peregrinator," in *Research in Labor Economics,* ed. Ronald Ehrenberg (Greenwich, Conn.: JAI Press, 1977), pp. 128–29; Robert Frank, "Why Women Earn Less: The Theory and Estimation of Differential Overqualification," *American Economic Review* 68 (June 1978): 360–73; Jacob Mincer, "Family Migration Decisions," *Journal of Political Economy* 5 (October 1978): 749–75, demonstrates the reduction in family mobility associated with the wife's attachment to the labor force.

Return Migration

To say that, on average, migration is a good investment for those who decide to undertake it does not imply that it is a good investment for all. Clearly, most people *do not* migrate in any given year—presumably because they believe that, for them, it would not be a good investment. It is equally clear, however, that some migrants find out they have made a mistake. What they thought would be a good investment may turn out not to be. In these cases people will seek to leave where they are and move elsewhere—and it is understandable that they might seek to minimize costs by moving back to an area with which they are familiar.

Twenty percent of all moves are to an area in which the person had *previously* lived—and half of these are back to one's birthplace.[11] Thus, *return migration—*

---

[11]Lansing and Mueller, *The Geographic Mobility of Labor,* p. 34.

migrating to a place from which one originated in some sense—is an important phenomenon of geographic mobility. Not all of return migration may be the result of a failed investment. After all, people do leave home to acquire training or experience with the intent to return. However, much of return migration may be a response by those who find that job opportunities were not what they had expected or that the psychic costs of living in strange surroundings are higher than they had anticipated. Return migration, then, serves to remind us that—as with other forms of investments—investments in human capital can also fail to be profitable.

Voluntary Turnover

While most workers who experience geographical mobility also change jobs (although perhaps not employers), these migrants are but one part of a wider group of workers who change jobs each year with or without a change of residence. Some of this job changing is "voluntary" in the sense that it is initiated by the employee; the remainder is said to be "involuntary" because it is employer-initiated. Voluntary separations are defined as *quits* and involuntary separations as *layoffs.* Layoffs can be temporary separations for economic reasons or permanent discharges—whether for cause (firing) or for economic reasons.

The human-capital model outlined in this chapter focuses on *worker-initiated* mobility and contains the same types of implications for this wide class of voluntary job mobility as it did for geographical mobility. This section will focus on *voluntary* turnover—deciding whether or not to quit; some of the major determinants of employer-initiated turnover have already been discussed in Chapter 5. The related decision of *how long to search* for a new job once one has quit his or her former job is discussed in Chapter 18.

Human-capital theory predicts that, *other things equal,* a given worker will have a higher probability of quitting a low-wage job than a higher-paying one. That is, workers employed at lower wages than they could obtain elsewhere are those most prone to quitting. Indeed, a very strong and consistent finding in virtually all studies of worker quit behavior is that, holding worker characteristics constant, employees in industries with lower wages have higher quit rates.[12]

Another implication of the theory is that workers will have a higher probability of quitting when it is relatively easy for them to obtain a better job quickly. Thus, when labor markets are *tight* (jobs are more plentiful relative to job seekers) one would expect the quit rate to be higher than when labor markets are *loose* (few jobs are available and many are being laid off). This prediction is confirmed in studies of time-series data.[13] Quit rates tend to rise when the labor market is tight and fall when it is loose. One measure of tightness is the unemployment rate;

[12]Donald O. Parsons, "Models of Labor Market Turnover: A Theoretical and Empirical Survey," in *Research in Labor Economics,* ed. Ronald Ehrenberg (Greenwich, Conn.: JAI Press, 1977), pp. 185–223.

[13]Parsons, "Models of Labor Market Turnover," pp. 185–223.

the negative relationship between the quit rate and unemployment can be readily seen in Figure 9.1. Another measure of labor-market conditions is the layoff rate, which tends to rise in recessions and fall when firms are expanding production. It, too, is inversely correlated with the quit rate (see Figure 9.1).

Finally, while human-capital theory predicts that, on average, workers will flow from jobs with lower wages to those with higher wages (other things equal), it does not imply that mistakes are never made. Like other investments, human-capital investments involve a substantial element of risk. A person might quit a job thinking better opportunities are abundant only to find out that he or she was misinformed. The risk of turnover, however, can be decreased if a worker who intends to quit lines up another job first. One study of "quitters" in 1966–67 found that those who quit only after another job had been obtained—about 50–60 percent of all quitters—increased their wages by 10.7 percent on average.[14] This same study found that for those who quit one job and were unemployed for a while, the average wage increase was almost nil. While the utility of the latter group of "quitters" could still have been increased by *nonwage* factors, it does seem likely that at least some of this group received returns below what they expected.

Earlier, this chapter argued that people tend to invest more heavily in human

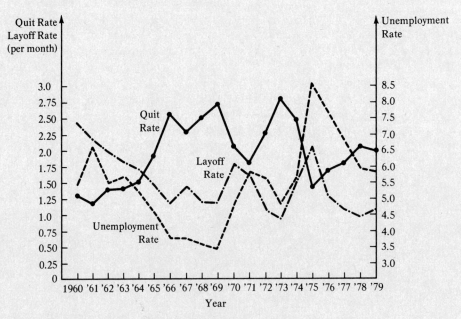

Figure 9.1   The Quit Rate and Labor Market "Tightness"

SOURCE: U.S. Department of Labor, Bureau of Labor Statistics, *Handbook of Labor Statistics,* Bulletin 2070 (Washington, D.C.: U.S. Government Printing Office, December 1980).

---

[14]J. Peter Mattila, "Job Quitting and Frictional Unemployment," *American Economic Review* 64 (March 1974): 235–39.

capital early in their careers. In many cases younger people have lower opportunity costs, and they have a longer period over which to recoup such costs. The data on all forms of job mobility clearly indicate that turnover falls as age rises, but is this true for *voluntary* mobility? The answer appears to be yes. Studies that have investigated the differences in quit rates among various industries have generally found that, other things (wages, for example) equal, quit rates are higher where the proportion of younger workers is greater.[15]

Another prediction of human-capital theory is that quit rates will be higher when the costs of quitting are lower. For example, workers in rural areas who change employers may well have to move their residence if they want to find a job in the same industry or occupation. Job changers who live in large cities have a much wider choice of jobs in their field and have a much lower probability of having to move. Because job changing is thus less costly for residents of large cities, one would expect turnover to be higher in these large cities. Indeed, we do find that industries in which employment is more concentrated in larger cities have higher quit rates, other things (wages and age of worker, for example) equal.[16]

EXAMPLE 9.3

A Positive and Normative Theory of Quitting in Nineteenth-Century Japan

Is modern labor economics, in both its positive and normative modes, culture-bound? Does the theory presented in this book pertain only to circumstances as they now are in the United States? Despite our emphasis on the analysis of current American policy issues, economic behavior is so general, and the need for markets so pervasive, that the theory presented here as *modern labor economics* is neither American nor necessarily modern.

For example, in the years just before 1900 when Japan was just beginning to industrialize, labor turnover rates (as noted in Example 5.2) were very high owing to persistent labor shortage. In 1898 a conference of business and government leaders was held to discuss the problems underlying this high turnover and the need for legislation concerning it. In the course of those discussions, Shoda Heigoro, a Mitsubishi executive, articulated the "modern" theory of job quitting behavior—in both its positive *and* normative aspects:

Since it is the nature of man to be tempted by better opportunities, it is impossible to keep workers without adequate provisions. That is, if a worker

---

[15]Parsons, "Models of Labor Market Turnover," p. 209; Farrell E. Bloch, "Labor Turnover in U.S. Manufacturing Industries," *Journal of Human Resources* 14 (Spring 1979): 236–46.

[16]Parsons, "Models of Labor Market Turnover"; Bloch, "Labor Turnover in U.S. Manufacturing."

desires to go to another factory because of better pay there, his present employer should allow him to go. If the employer wanted to keep the worker, he should raise wages so that the worker would see no reason to move. Were I censured for this statement on the ground that the competitive spiraling of wages would damage the profits of factory owners and retard industrial progress, I would rebut by calling attention to the simple logic of demand and supply in the market. Factory operatives, engineers, machinists, and other workers in modern industries are scarce in Japan today, because these occupations unlike the traditional crafts emerged only recently. It is true that their relative scarcity enables them to command relatively higher wages than other types of labor. But this very fact of high wages also induces more workers to flow into these occupations. . . .

Therefore, if the forces of demand and supply worked normally, the increase in their number would in time reduce their wages. But this subsequent decrease in their wages would spell no hardship for them, because workers would move into these occupations only insofar as the advantages there were sufficient to make them willing to move. . . . Thus, in my opinion, it is highly necessary that factory owners should acquiesce in the economic motives of workers in seeking high wages and better occupations. . . .

SOURCE: Koji Taira, *Economic Development and the Labor Market in Japan* (New York: Columbia University Press, 1970), p. 118.

National Immigration Policy

Nowhere are the analytical tools of the economist more important than in the area of immigration policy; the lives affected by immigration policy number in the millions each year. After a brief outline of the history of U.S. immigration policy, this section will analyze in detail the consequences of illegal immigration—a problem currently attracting widespread attention.

U.S. Immigration History

The United States is a rich country—a country whose wealth and high standard of living make it an attractive place for immigrants from nearly all parts of the world. For the first 140 years of our history as an independent country, the United States followed a policy of essentially unrestricted immigration (the only major immigration restrictions were placed on Orientals and convicts). The flow of immigrants was especially large after 1840, when industrialization here and political and economic upheavals in Europe made immigration an attractive investment for millions. As one can see from Table 9.2, officially recorded immigration peaked in the first decade of the 20th century, when the *yearly* flow of immigrants was more than 1 percent of the population.

In 1921, however, Congress adopted the Quota Law, which set annual quotas on immigration on the basis of nationality. These quotas had the effect of reducing immigration from eastern and southern Europe. This act was followed by other laws in 1924 and 1929 that further restricted immigration from southeastern

Table 9.2. Officially Recorded Immigration: 1820 to 1979

Period	Number (in thousands)	Annual Rate (per thousand of U.S. population)	Year	Number (in thousands)	Annual Rate (per thousand of U.S. population)
1820–1979	49,124	3.5			
1820–1830	152	1.2	1965	297	1.5
1831–1840	599	3.9	1966	323	1.6
1841–1850	1,713	8.4	1967	362	1.8
1851–1860	2,598	9.3	1968	454	2.3
1861–1870	2,315	6.4	1969	359	1.8
1871–1880	2,812	6.2	1970	373	1.8
1881–1890	5,247	9.2	1971	370	1.8
1891–1900	3,688	5.3	1972	385	1.8
1901–1910	8,795	10.4	1973	400	1.9
1911–1920	5,736	5.7	1974	395	1.9
1921–1930	4,107	3.5	1975	386	1.8
1931–1940	528	0.4	1976	399	1.9
1941–1950	1,035	0.7	1977	462	2.1
1951–1960	2,515	1.5	1978	601	2.8
1961–1970	3,322	1.7	1979	460	2.0

SOURCE: U.S. Immigration and Naturalization Service, *Annual Report.*

Europe. These various revisions in immigration policy were motivated, in part, by widespread concern over the alleged adverse impact on native employment caused by the arrival of unskilled immigrants from eastern and southern Europe.

In 1965, the passage of the Immigration and Nationality Act abolished the quota system based on national origin that so heavily favored northern and western Europeans. Under this new law, overall ceilings were established for the eastern and western hemisphere, with no more than 20,000 coming from any one country. Within these limits, however, first preference is given to family reunification (74 percent of all immigrant visas). Sixteen percent of visas are reserved for professionals or artists of exceptional ability and for workers in occupations for which labor is scarce. Immigrants in the latter categories must obtain a labor certificate approved by the U.S. Department of Labor after an investigation to verify that the applicant is qualified for the job, to verify that there is a shortage of workers for that job in the area, and to verify that the terms of employment are average or better.

While the 1965 change in immigration policy did achieve its goal of making immigration less overtly discriminatory, the policy still imposes a ceiling on immigrants that is far below the numbers who wish to come. The fact that immigration to the United States is viewed as a very worthwhile investment for many more people than are allowed to take advantage of it has created incentives for people to enter the country illegally.

One way in which entry is made is for the immigrant to come to this country as a student or visitor. Once here, the foreigner can look for work—although it is illegal to work at a job under a student's or visitor's visa. If the "student" or "visitor" is offered a job, he or she can apply for an "adjustment of status" to become a permanent resident (based on the existence of a labor certificate). Emigrants from the eastern hemisphere are allowed to remain in the United States while their adjustment-of-status application is being evaluated. Because *employers* of illegal immigrants are not subject to punishment (as of 1983), many are able to find jobs during the interim period.

Residents from the western hemisphere are required to return home while their adjustment-of-status application is being processed. The backlog of people awaiting entry is such that, as of the late 1970s, the delay in re-entering the United States as a legal permanent resident was two and a half years. Since most job offers will not wait that length of time, the affected immigrants understandably take the jobs and work here illegally while awaiting approval of their status change.

Roughly 7 million people enter the United States every year under nonimmigrant visas. Since many leave without informing U.S. officials, it is impossible to say how many of these 7 million overstay their period of admission, but government officials believe that the numbers range from 10 to 20 percent.[17] If (say) half of these visa abusers intend to immigrate illegally, the number of illegal immigrants would at least be equal to—and perhaps double the size of—the number of legal immigrants.

Moreover, there are other ways of illegally immigrating to the United States. Immigrants from the Caribbean often enter through Puerto Rico, whose residents are U.S. citizens and thus allowed free entry to the mainland. Others walk across the Mexican border. Still others are smuggled into the United States or use false documents to get through entry stations. The value of immigration as a human-capital investment is indicated by the fact that *coyotes,* people who help illegal aliens to cross the border and to find jobs, could command $300 per head in 1978[18] —or roughly 8 months pay for the average Mexican peasant.

No one knows how many illegal immigrants are in the United States. In 1977, the Immigration and Naturalization Service apprehended and deported more than 1 million illegal aliens, and many believe that for every person apprehended two make it into the country successfully.[19] The report of the Select Commission on Immigration and Refugee Policy submitted in 1981 places the total number of illegal residents at below 6 million, possibly in the range of 3.5–5 million.[20] While not all "illegals" are in the labor market, the profile of the typical illegal alien is that of a young, unattached male who is seeking work and unaccompanied by nonworking family members.

Despite the lack of precise knowledge about the dimensions of illegal immigration, the fact remains that by the early 1980s it had become a very prominent

---

[17]Walter Fogel, "Illegal Alien Workers in the United States," *Industrial Relations* 16, 3 (October 1977): 250.

[18]Edwin P. Reubens, "Aliens, Jobs, and Immigration Policy," *Public Interest* 51 (Spring 1978): 126.

[19]Reubens, "Aliens, Jobs, and Immigration Policy," p. 126.

[20]Select Commission on Immigration and Refugee Policy, *U.S. Immigration Policy and the National Interest* (Washington, D.C.: U.S. Government Printing Office, 1981), p. 36.

policy issue. The Secretary of Labor estimated in late 1979 that if only *half* of the jobs held by illegal aliens were given to U.S. citizens, the unemployment rate would drop from 6 percent to 3.7 percent. Similar beliefs have, in part at least, led the Select Commission on Immigration and Refugee Policy to recommend that the *hiring* of undocumented workers be made illegal and that offending employers be punished.[21] Some advocate allowing foreign workers in on a temporary, *guest-worker* basis only, while still others claim that permitting the flow of illegals to continue is both rational for us and humane for them. It is important to stress that the policies people advocate are based on their beliefs about the consequences of immigration. Nearly everyone with an opinion on this subject has an economic model implicitly or explicitly in mind when addressing these consequences; the purpose of the remainder of this chapter is to make these economic models explicit and to evaluate them.

Naive Views of Immigration

There are two opposing views of illegal immigration that can be considered naive. One view, which is widely held in the government, is that every illegal immigrant deprives a citizen or legal alien of a job. For example, a Department of Labor official told a House committee studying immigration, "I think it is logical to conclude that if they are actually employed they are taking a job away from one of our American citizens."[22] According to this view, if *x* illegal aliens are deported and others kept out, the number of unemployed Americans would decline by *x*.

At the opposite end of the policy spectrum is the equally naive argument that the illegals perform jobs no American citizen would do:

> You couldn't conduct a hotel in New York, you couldn't conduct a restaurant in New York . . . if you didn't have rough laborers. We haven't got the rough laborers anymore. . . . Where are we going to get the people to do that rough work?[23]

Both arguments are simplistic because they ignore the slopes of the demand and supply curves. Consider, for example, the labor market for the job of "rough laborer"—any job that most American citizens find distasteful. Without illegal immigrants the restricted supply of Americans to this market would imply a relatively high wage (W_1 in Figure 9.2). N_1 citizens would be employed. If illegal aliens enter the market, the supply curve would shift outward and perhaps flatten (implying that immigrants were more responsive to wage increases for rough laborers than citizens). The influx of illegals would drive the wage down to W_2, but employment would increase to N_2.

Are Americans unwilling to do the work of rough laborers? Clearly, at the

---

[21]Select Commission on Immigration and Refugee Policy, *U.S. Immigration Policy and the National Interest,* pp. 61–69.

[22]Elliott Abrams and Franklin S. Abrams, "Immigration Policy—Who Gets In and Why?" *Public Interest* 38 (Winter 1975): 25.

[23]Abrams and Abrams, "Immigration Policy—Who Gets In and Why?" p. 26.

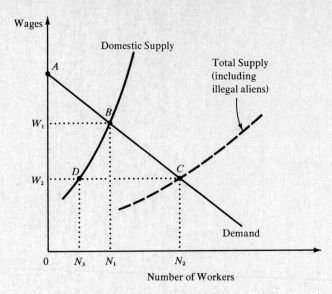

Figure 9.2   Demand and Supply of Rough Laborers

market wage of W_2, many more aliens are willing to work at the job than U.S. citizens. Only N_3 citizens would want these jobs at this wage, while the remaining supply (N_2-N_3) is made up entirely of aliens. If there were no immigrants, however, N_1 Americans would be employed at wage W_1 as rough laborers. Wages would be higher, as would the prices of the goods or services produced with this labor, but the job would get done. The only "shortage" of American citizens is at the low wage of W_2; at W_1, there is no shortage (see Chapter 2 for further discussion of labor shortages).

Would deporting those illegal aliens working as rough laborers create the same number of jobs for U.S. citizens? The answer is clearly no. If the N_2-N_3 aliens working as laborers were deported—and if all other illegal aliens were kept from the market—the number of Americans employed as laborers would rise from N_3 to N_1, and their wages would rise from W_2 to W_1 (Figure 9.2). N_2-N_1 jobs would be destroyed by the rising wage rate associated with deportation. Thus, while deportation would increase the employment and wage levels of Americans in the laborer market, it would certainly not reduce unemployment on a one-for-one basis.

There is, however, one case where deportation *would* create jobs for American citizens on a one-for-one basis: the case where the federal minimum-wage law creates a surplus of labor. Suppose, for example, that the supply of American laborers is represented by ABS_1 in Figure 9.3, and the total supply is represented by ACS_2. Because an artificially high wage has created a surplus, only N of the N' workers willing to work at the minimum wage can actually find employment. If some of them are illegal aliens, sending them back—coupled with successful efforts to deny other aliens access to these jobs—would create jobs for a compara-

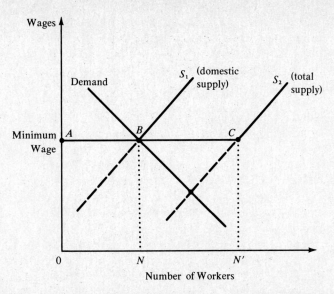

Figure 9.3 Demand and Supply of Rough Laborers with a Minimum Wage

ble number of Americans. However, the demand curve would have to intersect the domestic supply curve (ABS_1) at or to the left of Point B to prevent the wage level from rising (and thus destroying jobs) after deportation. In addition, all laborers would have to be paid the minimum wage—an unlikely eventuality given the lack of compliance noted in Chapter 3.

An Analysis of the Gainers and Losers

Some claim that, while perhaps not reducing citizen-held jobs one-for-one, large immigrant flows are indeed harmful to American workers. This view is probably the dominant force behind our restrictive immigration policy and behind the consequent concern about illegal immigration.

The argument is based primarily on a single-market analysis like that contained in Figure 9.2, where only the effects on the market for rough labor (say) are examined. As far as it goes, the argument is correct. When immigration increases the supply of rough laborers, both the wage and the employment level of American citizens working as laborers are reduced. The total wage bill paid to American laborers falls from W_1ON_1B in Figure 9.2 to W_2ON_3D. Thus, some American workers leave the market in response to the reduced wage, and those who stay earn less. If the Americans employed as laborers are, for example, minorities or members of some other group that is the target of antipoverty efforts, the influx of immigrants could substantially frustrate such efforts.

It would be a mistake, however, to conclude from the above analysis that because immigration is harmful to domestic *laborers* it is therefore necessarily harmful to Americans as a *whole*. First, immigration of "cheap labor" clearly benefits consumers using the output of this labor. As wages are reduced and employment increases, the goods and services produced by this labor are increased in quantity and reduced in price.

Second, employers of rough labor (to continue our example) are obviously benefited, at least in the short run. In Figure 9.2, profits are increased from W_1AB to W_2AC. This rise in profitability, however, should serve to attract more people to become employers—which in the long run will reduce profits back down to normal levels. As employers or managers become more numerous, opportunities for workers who would have been neither in the absence of immigration are expanded. (For example, a supply of cheap labor may induce a cook to open up his own diner or a janitor to open her own cleaning service.)

Third, our analysis of the market for laborers assumed that the influx of immigrants has had no effect on the demand curve (which was held fixed in Figure 9.2). This is not a bad assumption when looking at just one market, because the fraction of earnings immigrant laborers spend on the goods and services produced by rough labor is probably small. However, immigrants do spend money in the United States, and this added demand may create job opportunities or higher wages (or both) for the more skilled workers (see Figure 9.4). Thus, workers who are not close substitutes for unskilled immigrant labor may benefit from immigration because of the increase in consumer demand attendant to this addition to our working population.

(Note: Recall from Chapter 3 that if the demand for skilled workers increases when the wage of unskilled labor falls, the two grades of labor would be *gross complements.* Assuming skilled and unskilled labor are substitutes in the produc-

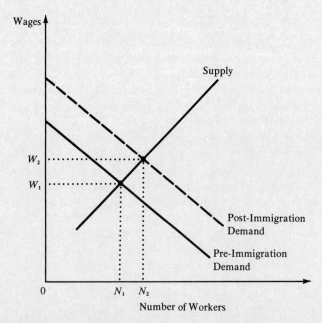

Figure 9.4   Market for All Labor Except Unskilled

tion process, the only way they could be gross complements is if the *scale effect* of a decline in the unskilled wage dominated the substitution effect. In the case of immigration one may suppose the scale effect to be very large, because as the working population rises, aggregate demand is increased. While theoretical analysis cannot *prove* that the demand for skilled workers is increased by unskilled immigration if the two grades of labor are substitutes in the production process, it can offer the above observation that an increase in demand for skilled workers remains a distinct possibility. Of course, for any type of labor that is *complementary* with unskilled labor in the production process—supervisory workers, for example—immigration does represent a clear-cut gain.)

The Effect of Immigration on the "Native" Population

Thus far we have concluded that illegal immigration is harmful to the interests of native unskilled workers but increases the real incomes of owners and possibly of skilled workers as well. However, it is also interesting and important to inquire whether the *aggregate income of native Americans* is increased. If it is, the gainers (skilled workers and owners) gain more than the losers lose. There would thus be large enough gains that the losers could be compensated for their losses—by income-maintenance or job-training programs—and the gainers would still come out ahead. In this case, policymakers might choose to pursue a policy of ignoring illegal immigration.

If immigrants are paid a wage equal to the value of their marginal product *(MP)* and if they are not subsidized by native taxpayers, then the aggregate income of U.S. citizens *will* increase as a result of the immigration. Recall that total product—the area under the marginal product curve—is greater than wages paid. Only for the last unit of labor employed, where MP = Wage, is there no surplus or profit generated. Thus, as long as immigrants get paid a wage equal only to their *MP,* the aggregate income of the native-born population cannot be reduced.

One way in which the native-born population, taken as a whole, *can lose* from immigration is if the immigrants obtain government services or payments in excess of the payroll, income, sales, and property taxes they pay. Because many government programs are essentially aids to the poor—public health, welfare, and unemployment insurance, to name just three—there is a distinct possibility that legal immigrants could be receiving net subsidies. On the other hand, *illegal* immigrants tend to be young, unattached males—people without children in school who do not generally qualify for other government programs because they are undocumented. Moreover, the taxes these workers do pay, directly or indirectly, also serve to reduce the burden of certain "overhead" expenses to U.S. citizens—expenses, like those of national defense and road maintenance, which the presence of immigrants does not increase. Thus, illegal immigration is likely to increase the aggregate income of the native-born populace.

If the aggregate income of the resident population is increased by immigration, then the gainers gain more than the losers lose. You will recall from Chapter 1 that when the gains are larger than the losses a mutually beneficial transaction is possible. The immigrants gain from their move to this country and, on balance,

EXAMPLE 9.4

Indentured Servitude and Human Capital Investments

Obtaining the funds necessary to make an investment is a common problem for would-be investors. The problem is especially formidable for those who would invest in human capital, because loans for human-capital investments are not widely made. Unlike loans for investments in physical capital (cars, homes, machines)—which can be secured by the asset purchased—loans for human-capital investments must generally be unsecured and thus are more risky to the creditor.

In the colonial days, indentured servitude was an institution that permitted poor immigrants to obtain passage to the New World using funds provided by a creditor and to secure this "loan" with all they had: their labor. British emigrants would sign an indenture with a British merchant or sea captain that specified the colony to which they would be sent and the length of time they would be bound to their master. The merchant or sea captain was then responsible for feeding, clothing, and transporting the servant to the colony. Upon arrival at the colony, the contract would be sold to a colonial farmer or planter, and the servant would be bound to this employer for the specified length of time—a length of time presumably long enough to pay back the expenses connected with immigration, plus interest.

The market for indentures was apparently competitive. There were enough British agents selling these indentures, and the potential servants were well-enough informed, that genuine bargaining took place. The "price" of an indenture was its length, which varied from 2 to 10 years. A long indenture was obviously costly to the servant, but it could bring a high price in the colonies to the agent. A short indenture was less profitable to the agent and a better deal for the servant.

Looking at the length of British indentures during the period 1718–1759 offers striking confirmation of the general implications of human-capital theory presented in Chapter 8. Literate and experienced workers were able to obtain the shortest indentures—while younger, less experienced, or illiterate workers had to sign for longer periods of indenture. (Women were able to obtain slightly shorter indentures than men, other things equal—a fact that the reader is free to interpret.) There is also evidence of compensating differentials. Indentures to be sold in the West Indies were shorter than those to be sold in the mainland colonies, where environmental conditions were more healthy and post-servitude opportunities were considered better.

SOURCE: David Galenson, "Immigration and the Colonial Labor System: An Analysis of the Length of Indenture," *Explorations in Economic History* 14 (1977): 360–77.

the resident population gains. In fact, the gains are large enough that the beneficiaries could compensate those who lose from immigration and *still* be better off.

Whether one would in fact favor a policy of unrestricted immigration would probably depend on

1. the possibility that those hurt by it could actually receive compensation,
2. the probability that immigrants would remain unsubsidized, and
3. the desirability of programs designed to reduce or deny subsidies to immigrants.

Since many social programs are aimed at the poor, compensation to unskilled workers for their losses associated with immigration of the unskilled may be fairly automatic—coming in the form of unemployment compensation, public housing, food stamps, job retraining, and welfare payments. Compensation to skilled workers (if the immigrants are predominantly skilled) would be less automatic and might have to take the form of a special program.[24]

The reservations many have about unrestricted immigration center on points 2 and 3, especially as they relate to immigration of those most likely to receive public subsidies: the unskilled. Illegal immigrants *are* denied access to certain public-welfare programs because of their undocumented status, but they also represent what some view as an "under class" who cannot vote and who do not have full citizenship rights. An alternative used in Europe—"guest worker" programs—also denies permanent residence and citizenship rights to immigrants; in addition, these workers can be required to leave the country at the government's will. Thus, ensuring that poor, unskilled immigrants remain unsubsidized means denying them the rights of other citizens and legal aliens. While the immigrants themselves are obviously willing to pay the price when they immigrate, some worry that they may not be willing to pay this price indefinitely.

The Consequences of Emigration

The consequences of emigration are generally the reverse of those for immigration. The country loses a productive resource, and those remaining are deprived of the surplus (total product less wages) produced by the emigrants. The groups most competitive with the emigrants are helped by their departure, but the aggregate income of the residents who remain will be smaller—with two important exceptions.

First, if the emigrants are owners of capital and are forced by the government to leave this capital behind, the remaining population could benefit (in much the same way the Black Death benefited the survivors, as pointed out in Chapter 2).

---

[24]Such a program already exists for those hurt by foreign imports. The Trade Adjustment Assistance Program identifies those hurt and compensates them through job retraining, subsidies to move to other areas, and special unemployment-insurance payments. While this program has been criticized as generally unsuccessful in several respects, it does serve as an example of a program specifically designed to compensate those who lose as a consequence of a public policy.

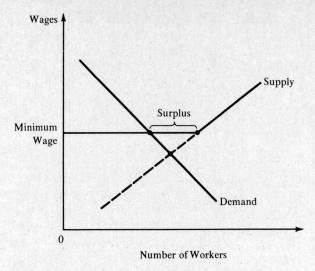

Figure 9.5 A "Labor-Surplus" Market

Some governments—most notably, Cuba—have permitted middle-class workers to leave under these conditions. A drawback, however, is that workers (such as doctors) with sizable amounts of financial capital may also have sizable amounts of *human* capital that *does* leave with them—making it necessary for those remaining to invest in programs to train replacements.

The second exception applies to economies where there is a permanent labor surplus. Many believe that in very poor countries the supply of labor is so large relative to demand that the equilibrium wage is below a socially acceptable minimum (perhaps the subsistence level). If the minimum must be paid, a labor surplus is created (see Figure 9.5). If surplus workers leave, the country obviously gains. These workers were not producing anything, but they had to be kept alive by transfer payments from others. Emigration is a clear-cut help to those who remain.

It should be noted that labor surpluses in less developed countries can also be created by the high wages paid in the industrial, urban sector. These wages are high in order to attract foreign labor with the requisite skills and must by law be paid to native workers also. Hoping to be lucky enough to obtain these jobs, migrants flock to the cities where they form a sizable group of unemployed, surplus workers. If the country were not willing to let the industrial wage for native workers fall to the point of market equilibrium, emigration would be an attractive solution to the resulting problem of a labor surplus.

REVIEW QUESTIONS

1. The following four paragraphs were taken from an Associated Press story on December 8, 1979:

WASHINGTON (AP)—Treasury Secretary G. William Miller said Friday that the Senate Banking Committee version of the Chrysler aid bill is "unworkable," in part because the automaker might lose many of its best workers.

Miller said the most objectionable feature of the committee bill is a requirement that Chrysler workers accept a three-year wage freeze in exchange for $1.25 billion in federal loan guarantees for Chrysler.

"Under the proposed bill, efforts to aid Chrysler would fail, because conditions of the bill simply could not be met," he said, adding that the wage freeze would impose "a disproportionate financing burden on the workers of the company."

"The terms of the bill would substantially impair the operations of the Chrysler Corporation, risk loss to the company of many of its most able employees, and seriously damage the morale and productivity of the workers essential to the company's future success," he said.

Suppose you are a staff worker for an important Senator trying to evaluate Secretary Miller's contention that a wage freeze would cause Chrysler to lose its best employees. Write an essay evaluating Miller's contention. Start with a coherent statement of the theory relevant to Miller's assertion and then analyze all the conditions necessary for Miller's assertion to be true.

2. As you know, thousands of illegal immigrants are working in the United States. Suppose the United States increases the penalties for illegal immigration to include long jail sentences. Analyze the effects of this increased penalty on the wages and employment levels of *all* affected groups of workers.

3. Suppose there are two nations, *M* and *U*. The government of *U* is having a problem with illegal immigration of unskilled workers from *M* and wants your advice on the best way to handle the problem. There are three options:

a. The government could fine a firm that employs unskilled workers from *M*. (For example, the fine could be $1,000 per worker and could be collected every year.)

b. The government could beef up border patrols in an effort to reduce migration from *M* to *U*.

c. The government could introduce a wage subsidy to be paid only to workers from *U*.

   The government's goals are to both reduce migration from *M* to *U* and to raise the amount of income that unskilled workers in *U* obtain from an hour of work. The government of *U* doesn't really care what happens to workers in *M*—that is *M's* problem. Given these goals and the following six assumptions, rank the options from best to worst, giving reasons for your ranking. Assume that at present (before any policy change):

a. market wages of unskilled labor in *U* are higher than market wages of unskilled labor in *M*. Thus, by migrating from *M* to *U* one is able to obtain a higher wage.

b. demand for unskilled labor in *U* is perfectly inelastic (the demand curve is vertical).

c. supply curves of unskilled labor from both *M* and *U* are upward-sloping (higher market wages lead to greater labor supply).

d. unskilled workers from *M* and *U* are perfect substitutes.

e. when workers in *M* migrate to *U* they must pay a fee to a guide. If border patrols are beefed up, these fees will rise.

f. when in *U*, unskilled workers from *M* receive the same wage as unskilled workers from *U*.

SELECTED READINGS

Barry Chiswick, "The Effect of Americanization on the Earnings of Foreign-Born Men." *Journal of Political Economy* 86 (October 1978: 897–921.

Barry Chiswick, "The Economic Progress of Immigrants: Some Apparently Universal Patterns." In *Contemporary Economic Problems,* edited by William Fellner (Washington, D.C.: The American Enterprise Institute for Public Policy Research, 1979).

Michael J. Greenwood, "Research on Internal Migration in the United States: A Survey" *Journal of Economic Literature* 8, 2 (June 1975): 397–433.

Donald O. Parsons, "Models of Labor Market Turnover: A Theoretical and Empirical Survey." In *Research in Labor Economics,* edited by Ronald Ehrenberg (Greenwich, Conn.: JAI Press, 1977), pp. 185–223.

John Pencavel, *An Analysis of the Quit Rate in the Manufacturing Industry* (Princeton, N.J.: Industrial Relations Section, Princeton University, 1970).

Michael J. Piore, "The 'New Immigration' and the Presumptions of Social Policy." *Proceedings of the Industrial Relations Research Association* (1974), pp. 350–58.

Melvin Reder, "The Economic Consequences of Increased Immigration." *Review of Economics and Statistics* 45, 3 (August 1963): 221–30.

Chapter 10

ECONOMIC ISSUES IN COMPENSATION

Chapter 6 examined factors influencing the decision to work for pay and the desired hours of work. Chapters 7 and 8 analyzed the day-to-day and human-capital aspects, respectively, of occupational choice. Chapter 9 discussed human-capital aspects of voluntary job and geographical mobility. We now turn to a discussion of yet another set of factors influencing job-choice and work-effort decisions; namely, employer compensation policies.

What ultimately matters to workers in making labor-supply decisions is the total compensation they receive per hour or month for their work. This total compensation paid to employees consists of far more than hourly, weekly, or monthly pay for time worked. There are numerous *fringe benefits* offered in varying combinations by employers, which have value to employees but are not paid to them in the form of currently spendable cash. Employers can also offer —explicitly or implicitly—different bases for computing or timing pay over one's career. These various forms of compensation affect employee behavior and labor-market outcomes in interesting ways.

This chapter will begin by describing and analyzing the consequences of fringe benefits. Of particular policy importance is the issue of pension-fund regulation by the federal government. The chapter will also discuss various ways to arrange compensation in order to provide strong incentives for employees not to be absent, not to shirk their duties, and not to perform other acts that are damaging to company interests. These forms of compensation offer different ways to *compute* current pay, but they also include a certain element of choice in *timing* a worker's pay over his or her career with a firm—choices that are particularly available in the context of an internal labor market.

The Economics of Fringe Benefits

As noted in Chapter 5, the proportion of total compensation coming in the form of cash payments to workers has fallen over time as the use of fringe benefits has risen. According to the data presented in Table 10.1, the most common fringe benefits are paid vacations, medical insurance, maternity leaves, pensions, life insurance, and paid sick leave. Less common, but still available to large numbers of workers, are company-paid education or training; discounted meals, merchandise, or work clothing; dental care, eye care, or legal benefits; stock options or savings plans; and maternity leave with pay. In addition to these private fringes, there are also publicly mandated benefits that employers must fund: Social Security, workers' compensation, and unemployment insurance.

One way to grasp the growth and composition of fringe benefits is to look at their cost to employers. Table 10.2 contains two sets of data on employer cost for specific benefits as a percentage of total compensation for workers in manufacturing industries. One set of data derives from Chamber of Commerce surveys,

Table 10.1. Fringe Benefits Available to Workers

Fringe Benefit	Percentage of Workers Reporting the Availability of the Benefit in 1977[a]
Paid vacation	80.8
Medical, surgical, or hospital insurance that covers any illness or injury that might occur *off* the job	78.1
Maternity leave will full re-employment rights	74.5
A retirement program	67.4
Life insurance that would cover a death occurring for reasons *not* connected with job	64.1
Sick leave and full pay	62.8
A training (or education) program to improve skills	49.0
Thrift or savings plan	39.8
Free or discounted merchandise	34.3
Dental benefits	29.4
Maternity leave with pay	29.4
Eyeglass or eye-care benefits	21.8
Profit sharing	19.8
Stock options	17.6
Work-clothing allowance	16.8
Free or discounted meals	16.3
Legal aid or services	10.3
Day-care facilities	2.2

[a]Includes only wage and salaried workers.

SOURCE: Robert P. Quinn and Graham L. Staines, *The 1977 Quality of Employment Survey: Descriptive Statistics, with Comparison Data from the 1969–70 and the 1972–1973 Surveys.* Research Report Series, Survey Research Center, Institute for Social Research, University of Michigan, 1979, pp. 58–59.

Table 10.2. Comparisons of Employer Expenditures for Compensation, 1959–1977

	Percentage of Employer's Total Compensation Expenditures			
	(a) Production and Related Workers in Manufacturing		(b) All Employees in Larger Manufacturing Firms	
Categories of Compensation	1959	1976	1959	1977
Pay for working time	85.4	75.2	82.2	72.8
Pay for leave time (vacations, holidays, sick leave, personal days)	5.4	7.4	7.7	9.3
Private pension plans	2.2	4.1 ⎫	5.1	9.4
Life, accident, and health insurance	2.0	5.3 ⎭		
Government-required contributions to Social Security, workers' compensation, and unemployment insurance	4.1	7.3	3.7	6.8
Other	0.7	0.7	1.3	1.7
Total fringe benefits	14.6	24.8	17.8	27.2
Total compensation	100.0	100.0	100.0	100.0

SOURCES: (a) U.S. Department of Labor, Bureau of Labor Statistics, *Handbook of Labor Statistics 1978,* Bulletin 2000 (Washington, D.C.: U.S. Government Printing Office, 1979).

(b) U.S. Chamber of Commerce, *Fringe Benefits and Employee Benefits* (1959, 1977).

which are heavily weighted with larger firms.[1] The other data were obtained from a more representative sample of manufacturing firms.

Table 10.2 provides a number of insights. First, the proportion of total compensation devoted to fringe benefits rose about 10 percentage points from 1959 to 1976/1977 in each data set. Second, the most costly fringes are paid leave time and the government-mandated benefits, which together account for 59 percent of all fringe-benefit costs. Life and health insurance and private pension plans account for roughly 35 percent of fringe-benefit costs. Third, it is clear from the data in Table 10.2 that fringe benefits are a greater proportion of total compensation in large firms than in small ones.

Table 10.3, which compares office and nonoffice employees of all but the smallest firms in the private sector, illustrates another interesting fact: fringe benefits as a percentage of compensation are slightly, but not markedly, higher for office than nonoffice workers. Further, government-required fringes and pay for nonworking time comprise the largest two components of the fringe package in both cases.

What accounts for the growth and size of fringe benefits? What are the consequences of this growth and size? To answer these questions we must examine both the employee and employer sides of the market.

---

[1]These data are based on information contained in Table 5.2 (see p. 106). The data in Table 5.2, however, calculated fringe benefits as a percentage of *wage and salary* payments; the data in Table 10.2 state fringes as a percentage of *total compensation.*

Table 10.3. Employee Compensation for Private, Nonagricultural Workers, 1976 (in percent)

	Percentage of Employer's Total Compensation Expenditures	
	Office Workers	*Nonoffice Workers*
Pay for working time	75.7	77.4
Pay for leave time (vacations, holidays, sick leave, personal days)	7.9	6.3
Private pension plans	5.1	3.7
Life, accident, and health insurance	3.6	4.4
Government-required contributions to Social Security, workers' compensation, and unemployment insurance	5.2	7.4
Other	2.5	0.8
Total compensation	100.0	100.0

Note: The data are for workers in plants with 20 or more employees.

SOURCE: U.S. Department of Labor, Bureau of Labor Statistics, *Handbook of Labor Statistics 1978,* Bulletin 2000 (Washington, D.C.: U.S. Government Printing Office, 1979).

Employee Preferences

The distinguishing feature of all fringe benefits is that they compensate workers in a form *other* than currently spendable cash. In general, there are two broad categories of such benefits. First and largest are *payments-in-kind*—that is, compensation in the form of some commodity. As we have seen, it is very common for employers to buy, or at least partially buy, insurance policies of one kind or another on behalf of their employees. Slightly less obvious as payments-in-kind are paid vacations and holidays. A woman earning $15,000 per year for 2,000 hours of work can have her hourly wage increased from $7.50 to $8.00 by either a straightforward increase in current money payments or by a reduction in her working hours to 1,875 with no reduction in yearly earnings. If her raise comes in the form of an increase in money payments she will receive $1000 (before taxes) more in yearly income that she can use to buy a variety of things (she could even buy time off by giving money back to her employer in exchange for days off). However, if she receives her raise in the form of paid vacation time she is in fact being paid in the form of a commodity: leisure time.

The second general type of fringe benefit is *deferred compensation*—compensation that is earned now but that will be paid in the form of money later on. Pension benefits are the largest proportion of these fringes.

Payments-in-kind. It is a well-established tenet of economic theory that, *other things equal,* people prefer receiving $X in cash to receiving a commodity that costs $X. The reason is simple. With $X in cash the person can choose to buy the particular commodity, but he or she can also buy a variety of other things. Cash is thus the form of payment that gives the recipient the most discretion and the most options in maximizing utility. In-kind payments are inherently more restrictive, and while they generate utility, they do not ordinarily generate as much as cash payments of equal monetary value.

As might be suspected, however, "other things" are not equal. Specifically, in-kind payments offer employees a sizable tax advantage because, for the most part, they are not taxable under current income-tax regulations. The failure to tax important in-kind payments is a factor that tends to offset their restrictive nature in affecting employee demand for in-kind payments. A worker may prefer $1000 in cash to $1000 in some in-kind payment, but if his or her income- and payroll-tax rates total 25 percent, the comparison is really between $750 in cash and $1000 in the in-kind benefit.

Deferred compensation. Like payments-in-kind, deferred compensation schemes enjoy a tax advantage as compared to current cash payments. With deferred payments the tax advantage is that the compensation is not taxed until it is received by the worker. In the case of pensions, for example, employers contribute currently to a pension fund, but employees do not obtain access to this fund until they retire. Neither the pension fund *contributions* made on behalf of employees by employers nor the *interest* that compounds when these funds are invested are subject to the personal income tax. Only when the retirement benefits are received does the ex-worker pay taxes, but because of lower income and special tax advantages given to the elderly, the tax rates actually paid are relatively low.

Because of the above-noted tax advantages accorded to pension-fund contributions, employees wishing to save for old age have incentives to do so through a pension fund rather than receiving cash payments and saving from that. In this latter case, all of their compensation would be taxed at the relatively high rates that prevail during their working years, as would the interest they earn on their *savings* toward retirement. Saving through a pension fund defers the taxation of part of one's compensation (the pension-fund contributions) until old age and permits funds for retirement to accumulate on a tax-free basis. What one *loses* with saving through a pension fund is the ability to currently control one's assets: by putting money into a pension fund, one is forgoing the ability to use that money now for routine or emergency needs.

Again, then, two opposing forces are at work on the demand for fringe benefits by employees. With both kinds of benefits there is a loss of discretion in spending one's total compensation—which tends to render fringes inferior to cash payments in generating utility. On the other hand, special tax advantages are accorded to both kinds of benefits as compared with cash payments, which tends to increase the demand for fringes.

Employer Preferences

Suppose employers are totally indifferent to spending $X on wages or $X on fringes. Both expenditures are of equal sums of money and both are equally deductible as a business expense. If so, the composition of total compensation is a matter of indifference to them; only the level of compensation is of concern.

To analyze the employer side of the market let us assume that a firm offers a certain type of job for which it must pay at least $X in total compensation in order to attract workers. Let us also suppose that the firm operates in a competitive product market and cannot earn a profit if it pays more than $X. Thus, it must compensate its workers $X per year in order to remain competitive in both the labor and product markets. However, if the *composition* of total compensation is a matter of indifference to the firm, it will be willing to offer any combination of wages and fringes that totals $X in value. The various compensation packages a firm is willing to offer fall along the "offer curve" drawn between wages and fringes (see Figure 10.1).

Any combination of wages and fringes along the offer curve shown in Figure 10.1 would yield the firm equal profits (assuming it could recruit workers). Thus, it is willing to offer $X in wages and no fringe benefits, fringes that cost (say) $300 and wages that equal $(X − 300), or any other combination totaling $X in cost. The slope of the curve is *negative,* reflecting the fact that the firm can only increase fringes if it reduces wages (again, because of competitive pressures). Further, in this case the offer curve has a slope of −1, which reflects employer indifference about the composition of compensation. If employees want a health-insurance policy costing $300, it will cost them $300 in wages.

There are some reasons to expect that firms might offer fringe benefits to their employees on something other than the dollar-for-dollar basis assumed above. One of the more obvious reasons is that by increasing compensation in the form of fringes rather than wages employers can often avoid taxes and required insurance payments that are levied as a fraction of payroll. Social Security taxes and

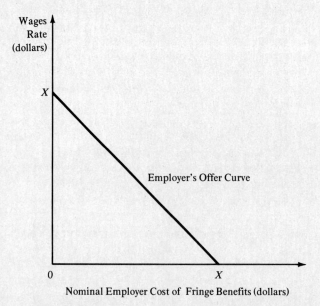

Figure 10.1   Offer Curve, Showing the Wage/Fringe Offers a Firm Might Be Willing to Make to Its Employees: A Unitary Trade-off

workers' compensation premiums are examples of costs that generally increase with salaries and wages but not with fringe benefits—thus making it more costly for an employer to increase compensation by increasing salaries than to do it by increasing benefits.[2] Payroll taxes thus tend to flatten the offer curve shown in Figure 10.1 (a $300 increase in fringes could be accompanied by only a $280 reduction in wages, say, and the firm would be equally profitable).

There are also more subtle factors that might cause firms to offer fringes to their employees on something other than the dollar-for-dollar basis in Figure 10.1. Some fringe benefits allow firms to attract a certain kind of worker in situations where the use of wage rates would be of questionable legal validity. For example, suppose a firm prefers to hire mature adults, preferably those with children, in the hopes of acquiring a stable, dependable work force. An employer attempting to attract these people by offering them higher wages than single, younger, or much older adults would risk charges of discrimination. Instead, the firm can accomplish the same effect by offering its employees fringe benefits that are of much more value to the group it is trying to attract than to others. For example, offering *family* coverage under a health-insurance plan has the effect of compensating those with families more than others, because single or childless people cannot really take advantage of the full benefit. Offering dental insurance covering orthodontic work —or tuition assistance for children who attend college—accomplishes similar purposes. Thus, at times fringe benefits allow the firm to give preferential treatment to a group it wants to attract without running afoul of discrimination laws.

The preferential treatment given to some groups of workers, however, has become of increasing concern to employees as fringes have grown in importance. Many families, for example, have dual earners—and have no need of two family medical-insurance policies. In a move to take into account employee dissatisfaction concerning the biases in fringe benefits, some firms have adopted a *cafeteria plan* whereby workers are free to elect their own fringe benefits up to some dollar limit. Instead of receiving a redundant medical insurance policy, for example, a worker already covered by a spouse's insurance policy could elect to receive a longer paid vacation. One firm implementing such a plan found that only 10 percent of its employees elected to receive the same benefits offered by its old program.[3]

Another subtle reason why a firm may prefer to put an extra dollar of compensation into fringe benefits rather than wages (and thus have a flatter offer curve than is shown in Figure 10.1) is found whenever the government regulates profits or controls wages. Regulated monopolies, for example, fearing that the granting of large wage increases would call forth an investigation or outrage public opinion, could hide an increase in compensation by granting increases in fringe benefits that are difficult to cost out: a nicer work environment, shortened days in the summer, time off for religious observances, top quality food in the

---

[2]The argument that the presence of Social Security taxes levied on the employer increases the costs of granting salary increases holds only for workers who earn less than the maximum taxable earnings base—which in 1983 was $35,700. Earnings beyond $35,700 in 1983 were not subject to the Social Security tax.

[3]"Making Job Benefits Flexible," *The New York Times*, March 13, 1981, pp. D1, D3.

company cafeteria for bargain prices, low-cost loans to employees for buying a home, and so forth.[4] Similar behavior will occur among firms that are having trouble recruiting employees during a period when the government is attempting to control wages for the purposes of fighting inflation. Wages are easy to observe and measure. Many fringe benefits are very difficult to observe and quantify, and they can thus be used to increase compensation without violating wage controls.[5] Examples of fringes that are difficult for wage-control boards to monitor are increased rest times on the job, rules increasing crew sizes in dangerous activities, and better recreational facilities for employees.

On the other hand, as noted earlier in Example 6.1, some fringe benefits could conceivably increase absenteeism—thus reducing, rather than increasing, the firm's profitability. Life insurance, health insurance, and pensions, for example, are all awarded to current employees regardless of their actual hours of work during the year (assuming they work enough to keep their jobs). If an increase in compensation comes in the form of increasing one of these benefits, workers' *incomes* are increased—in the sense that they need to save less for "rainy days" and are thus freer to spend their cash income. However, this increase in income is accomplished without an increase in the price of leisure, because the hourly wage has not risen. Recall from Chapter 6 that an increase in income with no change in the price of leisure causes people to want to work less. In this case, workers will not quit their jobs, but they may be absent from work more often.[6] The connection between absenteeism and a fringe benefit is even more obvious in the case of paid sick leave.[7]

Aside from the possibility of contributing to absenteeism, some fringe benefits compress the differentials in compensation between skilled and unskilled workers, thereby reducing the incentives of employees to obtain training for skilled positions.[8] Fringes such as medical insurance and free or discounted merchandise are of equal value to people of similar-sized families, no matter how much they earn. Because their value thus represents a larger percentage of a low-wage worker's compensation, such benefits tend to compress earnings differentials between skilled and unskilled workers.

---

[4]For further arguments along this line *see* Armen Alchian and Reuben Kessel, "Competition, Monopoly, and the Pursuit of Money," *Aspects of Labor Economics,* ed. H. G. Lewis (Princeton, N.J.: Princeton University Press, 1962).

[5]For a brief discussion of the difficulties inherent in controlling fringe benefits, *see* John Dunlop, "Wage and Price Controls as Seen by a Controller," *Proceedings of the Industrial Relations Research Association,* May 1975, pp. 457–63.

[6]Although there has not been much empirical work on this issue, a study of absenteeism in the paper-and-box industry found it was positively related to pensions and negatively related to wage rates. *See* Steven G. Allen, "Compensation, Safety, and Absenteeism: Evidence from the Paper Industry," *Industrial and Labor Relations Review,* 34 (January 1981): 207–18. *See also,* his "An Empirical Model of Work Attendance," *Review of Economics and Statistics* 63 (February 1981): 77–87.

[7]For evidence on teacher absenteeism, *see* Donald R. Winkler, "The Effects of Sick-Leave Policy on Teacher Absenteeism, *Industrial and Labor Relations Review* 33, 2 (January 1980): 232–40.

[8]See Chapter 8 for the complete argument on how wage differentials affect the incentives of workers to acquire human capital.

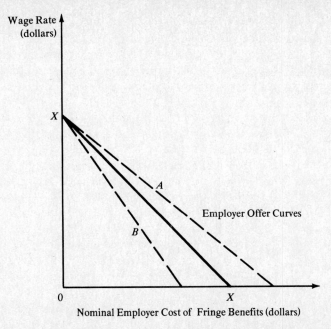

Figure 10.2   Alternative Offer Curves, Showing the Wage/Fringe Offers a Firm Might Be Willing to Make to Its Employees: Nonunitary Trade-offs

The major point of our analysis of fringes from the employer's perspective is that a dollar spent on fringes could cost employers more or less than a dollar nominally spent on wages or salaries.[9] In cases where fringes enhance productivity more than a similar expenditure on wages would, the offer curve in Figure 10.1 will flatten. Figure 10.2 shows this as offer curve *A*. In cases where fringes increase other costs or reduce productivity, the offer curve will steepen. In this case—curve *B* in Figure 10.2—a $300 fringe benefit would have to be accompanied by a $320 fall in wages, say, to keep profits constant.

The Joint Determination of Wages and Fringes

Unless a firm is a monopsonistic buyer of labor, it must pay the "market rate" for the quality of worker it is seeking to hire—meaning that the *size* of the compensation package is more or less out of the firm's control once it determines the quality of worker it wants to attract. However, the *composition* of the compensation package is still subject to choice by the firm, because it could offer a number of equal-cost combinations of wages and fringe benefits to its workers. In actuality, of course, each employer selects *one* compensation package and offers it to prospective employees. How do firms decide what package to offer, and what are the consequences of their decisions?

[9]Many fringe benefits, like pensions and paid vacations, become more generous as the worker's tenure with the firm increases. In fact, in most firms, workers are not even eligible to receive retirement benefits unless they have worked at least 10 years for the firm. These policies are clearly designed to reduce costly turnover, but they are more a matter of the *timing* of compensation than anything else. We will discuss issues regarding the timing of compensation later in this chapter.

If there are a number of employers seeking workers in a given labor market, and each offers a different compensation package with a total value of $X (which we assume to be the going rate in this market), a "market" offer curve can be traced out. One such market offer curve is illustrated in Figure 10.3, and the only difference between this curve and the one in Figure 10.1 is that the latter traced out *hypothetical* offers one firm could make, while this one traces out the *actual* offers made by firms in this labor market. (The offer curves in both Figures 10.1 and 10.3 have a unitary slope, reflecting an assumption, for illustrative purposes, that $X in wages alone or $X in fringe benefits alone are equally costly to firms, all things considered. If fringe benefits have effects on absenteeism or generate payroll tax savings, the offer curve in Figure 10.3 might be steeper or flatter than unity, respectively, as illustrated in Figure 10.2.)

Employees seeking work in the labor market depicted in Figure 10.3 are thus confronted with a variety of wage-fringe combinations, all of which cost the employer roughly $X. Those employees (like *Y* in Figure 10.3) who attach relatively great importance to the availability of currently spendable cash will choose to accept offers where total compensation comes largely in the form of wages. Other employees, who may be less worried about current cash income but more interested in the tax advantages of fringe benefits, will accept offers where fringe benefits form a higher proportion of total compensation (see the curve for Worker Z in Figure 10.3).[10] Thus, employers will tailor their compensation packages to suit the preferences of the workers they are trying to attract. If their employees tend to be young, poor, or present-oriented, for example, their compensation packages may be heavily weighted toward wages and include relatively little in the way of pensions and insurance. On the contrary, if they are trying to attract people in an area where family incomes are high and fringe benefits offer relatively large tax savings, firms may offer packages where fringe benefits constitute a larger proportion of the total.

Figure 10.3 shows that workers receiving more generous fringe benefits pay for them by receiving lower wages, other things being equal. Further, if market offer curves have a unitary slope, a fringe benefit that costs the employer $1 to provide will cost workers $1 in wages. In other words, economic theory suggests that workers pay for their own fringe benefits!

Actually observing the trade-off between wages and fringe benefits is not an easy matter. Because firms that pay high wages usually also offer very good fringe benefits, it often appears to the casual observer that wages and fringes are *positively* related. Casual observation in this case is misleading, however, because it does not allow for the influences of *other factors*—such as the demands of the job and the quality of workers involved—that influence total compensation. The other factors are most conveniently controlled for statistically, and the few statis-

---

[10]The indifference curves in Figure 10.3 are drawn with the typical convexity. One assumption underlying this convexity is that as *fringes* increase, the decrease in currently spendable cash that one is willing to bear declines owing to the loss of discretionary control in spending one's income. The other assumption is that as *current wages* increase and workers advance into higher income-tax brackets, the tax advantages offered by fringe benefits become ever more attractive (which causes the indifference curves to steepen).

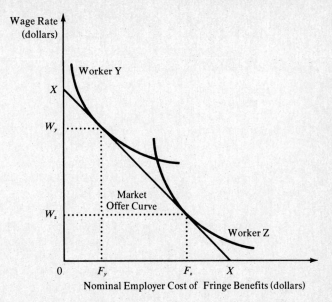

Figure 10.3
Market Determination
of the Mix of Wages
and Fringes

tical studies on this subject *do* tend to support the prediction of a negative relationship between wages and fringe benefits.[11]

The policy consequences of a negative wage/fringe trade-off are enormously important, because government legislation designed to improve fringe benefits might well be paid for by workers in the form of lower future wage increases.

Policy Application: Pension Reform Legislation

Pension plans provided by employers are of two general types: 1. the *defined-contribution* plans and 2. the *defined-benefit* plans. The least common are *defined-contribution* plans, where the employer merely promises to contribute a certain amount each year to a fund to which the employee has access upon retirement. The fund is increased each year by employer—and also perhaps by employee—contributions and by returns from investments made by the fund's managers. One's retirement benefits depend solely on the size of the fund at the age of retirement.

More common are *defined-benefit* pension plans where the employer pro-

---

[11]Empirical studies of the trade-offs between wages and pensions are as yet few in number. Many of the studies that do exist indicate workers pay—perhaps dollar-for-dollar—for their pensions in the form of lower wages. For a review of these studies, *see* Ronald Ehrenberg and Robert Smith, "A Framework for Evaluating State and Local Government Pension Reform," in *Public Sector Labor Markets*, eds. Peter Mieszkowski and George E. Peterson (Washington, D.C.: The Urban Institute, 1981). However, not all of the studies done in this area have found the predicted trade-offs, perhaps because of data problems. For a discussion of data requirements for estimating these trade-offs, *see* Robert Smith and Ronald Ehrenberg, "Estimating Wage-Fringe Trade-offs: Some Data Problems," in *The Measurement of Labor Cost*, ed. Jack E. Triplett. *National Bureau of Economic Research, Conference on Research in Income and Wealth, Studies in Income and Wealth*, vol. 48 (Chicago: University of Chicago Press, 1983).

mises employees a certain benefit upon retirement. This benefit may be a fixed sum per month or it may be a fixed fraction of one's earnings prior to retirement. In either case, employers guarantee the size of the pension benefit—and it is up to them to make sure the funds are there when the promised benefits need to be paid.

The *vesting* provision of any pension plan is the rule about who becomes eligible to receive a pension. If a plan is unvested, any worker who quits the company before retirement age loses all rights to a pension benefit. If workers are vested, they can receive a pension from Company X even if they quit X before retirement age and work elsewhere. How much they receive from X at retirement, of course, depends on their length of service with X and their preretirement earnings; however, the point is that they receive *something* from X upon retirement if they are vested.

In 1974 Congress passed the Employee Retirement Income Security Act (ERISA) that, among other things, required private-sector employers to adopt liberalized vesting rules. The intent of the legislation was to help employees by making it more likely that they will receive pensions in their old age. However, as we have seen with other programs designed to help workers, good intentions can sometimes be undone by unintended side effects. What are the side effects of ERISA's vesting provisions?

From the employees' perspective, rules that entitle them to become vested, or vested sooner, enhance their welfare if nothing else in the compensation package is changed. They are not penalized as much for voluntarily leaving an employer—nor are they as economically vulnerable to being fired. However, the value different workers attach to liberalized vesting may vary widely. Suppose ERISA forced a plant to vest its employees after 10, rather than 15, years of work. Employees who plan on working for a given employer less than ten years do not benefit at all from the liberalized vesting mandated by ERISA; neither do workers who have more than 15 years of service with the company. On the other hand, workers who might want to change employers after 10–15 years of service—or who might be fired during that period—stand to gain from liberalized vesting.

From the employers' perspective, ERISA's vesting rules impose costs, because they make it possible for more workers to qualify for pensions. For example, it was estimated that the pension costs of nonvesting employers would rise by 3–26 percent as a result of ERISA's vesting rules.[12] Will firms simply absorb these costs, or will they force workers to pay for their more liberal pension benefits in the form of lower wages?

Our theory suggests that employers will not—and in a competitive market, cannot—absorb the added pension costs. Those firms for which pension costs are increased will have to hold the line on future wage increases in order to remain competitive in the product market, and over time the wages will fall below the level they would have paid had it not been for the pension-reform legislation.[13]

---

[12]Norman True, *The Future of Private Pension Plans* (Washington, D.C.: The American Enterprise Institute for Public Policy Research, 1976), p. 89.

[13]The two studies that have looked at the effects of vesting on wages have both found that nonvesting (public) employers pay higher wages, other things equal, than ones who vest. *See* Ehrenberg and Smith, "A Framework for Evaluating State and Local Government Pension Reform."

Unfortunately the decline in wages that will occur in the firms affected by ERISA's vesting rules does *not* simply mean that worker welfare is unchanged. Indeed, it can be shown (see Figure 10.4) that *if* the workers employed by firms with illiberal vesting are both *informed* and *mobile,* their utility will be negatively affected by the ERISA vesting regulation. Suppose, for example, that before ERISA Person A worked for a nonvesting employer, receiving the relatively high wage of W_1 and a low level (P_0) of expected retirement benefits owing to the slim chances of receiving a pension. Person B, who obviously cares more than A about pensions—as can be seen by the different-shaped indifference curve—takes a job promising a relatively large and secure pension (P_1) but paying a lower current wage (W_0). Suppose also that ERISA in effect makes all levels of expected pension benefits below P_1 illegal by forcing employers with pension plans to provide vesting after 10 years.

Competitive pressures force all wage/pension offers to lie along the market offer curve, *XX,* in Figure 10.4. Thus, when the pension promises of A's employer are forcibly increased to P_1, the wage offer in that firm will eventually fall to W_0. For Person A—a person who is not willing to give up much in the way of current compensation to obtain a better pension—utility is reduced from A_1 to A_0. In other words, the effect of a law that increases pension benefits may well be to reduce wages—with the consequence that it reduces the utility of people who have the strongest preferences for current, as opposed to deferred, income.

Under certain circumstances, however, the ERISA vesting rules would enhance worker welfare. For example, take the case where people with preferences like Person C in Figure 10.5 *thought* they were working for an employer who, while perhaps not vesting their pension rights, would in fact employ them until they retire. Later, they find out that this employer is likely to fire them before retirement and that, if so, they will lose their entire pension. These people *believed*

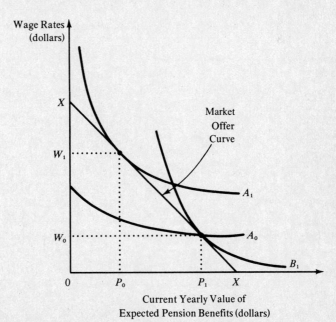

Figure 10.4
The Effects of
ERISA in a Properly
Functioning Market

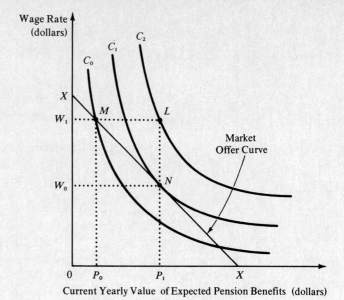

Figure 10.5
Effects of ERISA in
an Uninformed
Market

themselves to be at point L, receiving P_1 in expected pensions, W_1 in wages, and C_2 in utility. In actuality, they are, at point M, receiving P_0 in pension benefits and C_0 in utility. If ERISA forces the expected pension level to rise to P_1 by requiring vesting, their *actual* utility will increase from C_0 to C_1, despite the fact that their wages fall from W_1 to W_0 (they move in actuality from point M to N in Figure 10.5). ERISA would also improve the welfare of people like C if they were at point M and, because of a lack of mobility, could not find a job with another employer that would place them at point N.

The major point of this discussion is that if product markets are competitive, workers will pay for ERISA-mandated increases in pension benefits in the long run. Workers immobilized by ignorance or lack of choice may be better off with government-mandated floors on pension benefits, despite the downward pressure on their wages. However, there are also circumstances in which workers would be made worse off by the mandated increases in expected pension benefits. Careful study in advance of reform legislation may be desirable to avoid hurting the people government is intending to help.

Motivating Workers: Incentive Pay

Beginning in Chapter 1, this book has repeated the theme that unless workers are ignorant or immobile, the contracts they make with employers represent a mutually beneficial transaction. However, as in any transaction, each side will try to get the most it can while giving as little as it must. Employees may find that supervisors who were pleasant to them during job interviews are not quite as pleasant or easygoing after they take the job, that overtime is expected of them on a regular basis, or that their duties include more than they were told. If things get too bad they can quit—or, if they are in a union, they can protest through union channels. However, because both of these courses of action entail time and effort, employees may just decide to put up with unexpected disadvantages if they are not too serious.

Employers are faced with another set of problems. Work, by its very nature, is unpleasant to one degree or another. Some employees will try to do as little of it as possible, while still retaining their jobs. This behavior, called *shirking,* may take the form of not putting forth maximum work effort, doing poor quality work, or being absent a lot. Shirking can be minimized by close supervision, but it is not always easy to closely monitor the work of employees. Thus, it is often necessary to find other ways to induce workers not to shirk. Several kinds of compensation schemes have been designed to motivate employees to work industriously.

Firms can offer financial rewards for hard work in two ways. (1) They can offer *incentive pay*—that is, they can pay workers directly for the desired outcome; or (2) they can reward those employees who have been consistently industrious and reliable with high future compensation.

The Basis of Pay

The agreements between employers and employees concerning job duties and compensation can be considered as *contracts,* whether or not they are formally written. As mentioned briefly in Chapter 1, there are two basic types of pay provisions in labor contracts. One rewards employees for the *time* they work, and the other rewards them for some *result* of their work.[14] Some contracts, however, contain a hybrid system of rewards.

The most common reward structure is payment for time worked, with about 86 percent of U.S. employees paid either by the hour or by the month. When employees are paid for time at work, it becomes management's challenge to motivate them not to shirk during that time. An alternative that would appear to alleviate the problem of shirking is payment by results, or incentive pay. In some industries—particularly the garment industry—workers are paid for each piece of output produced. In other firms, a *standard time*—60 minutes, say—is allowed for a given task. If the task is completed *within* that time the employee is paid for the full 60 minutes regardless of the actual time spent on the task; however, if the worker takes longer than 60 minutes to complete the job, he or she is paid for the *actual* time spent. In still other instances, workers share in the profits of the firm or receive a fraction of the value of the items they sell *(commissions).* In all these cases, workers are paid at least somewhat proportionally to their output or to the degree their employer prospers. Because such payment

---

[14]This distinction concerning labor contracts is analyzed in Herbert A. Simon, "A Formal Theory of the Employment Relationship," *Econometrica* 19, 3 (July 1951): 293–305; and more recently in Joseph E. Stiglitz, "Incentives, Risk, and Information: Notes Towards a Theory of Hierarchy," *Bell Journal of Economics* 6 (Autumn 1975): 522–79.

schemes serve as an obvious incentive to work industriously, one is led to wonder why only 14 percent of U.S. workers are paid on an incentive basis. Selecting the basis for pay is ultimately a matter of satisfying the interests of both employer and employee.

Employee Preferences. If employees were told that their average earnings over the years under a time-payment system would be equal to their earnings under an individual incentive-pay scheme, they would probably choose to be paid on a *time* basis. Why? Earnings under a piece rate or commission system depend on the thought and energy one is able to bring to the job. There are days and even weeks in any person's life when one is depressed, preoccupied, tired, or otherwise distracted from maximum work effort. There are other periods when one is exceptionally productive. If employees are paid on a piece-rate basis, their earnings could be highly *variable* over time because of the somewhat uncontrollable swings in productivity. The variability in their income could cause anxiety owing to the possibility that several low-productivity months could be strung together, making it difficult to meet mortgage payments and other obligations.

Because of this anxiety about less productive periods of time, employees may prefer the certainty of time-based pay to the uncertainty of piece-rate pay if both schemes pay the same average wage over time. In order to induce employees to accept piece-rate pay, employers would have to pay higher average wages over time—that is, a compensating differential would have to exist to compensate workers for the anxiety associated with variations in their earnings. Conversely, to obtain more certainty in their stream of earnings, employees would probably be willing to accept a somewhat lower average wage.

Employer Considerations. The willingness of employers to pay a premium in order to induce employees to accept piece rates depends on the costs and benefits to employers of incentive-pay schemes. If workers are paid on a *time* basis, the *employer* accepts the risk of variations in their productivity. When they are exceptionally productive, profits increase; when they are less productive profits decline. Employers, however, may be less anxious about these *variations* than employees are. They typically have more assets and can thus weather the lean periods more comfortably than can individual workers. More important, perhaps, employers usually have several employees, and the chances are that not all will suffer the same swings in productivity at the same time (unless there is a morale problem in the firm). Thus, employers may not be as willing to pay for income certainty as are workers.

Employers must also consider, however, that incentive-pay schemes—such as piece rates—may reduce the variations in profits over time, but they will also increase the *level* of productivity. Because workers directly benefit from their own diligence in a piece-rate system, they may work much harder. A full analysis of these productivity-related incentives and costs of implementing them must take into account differences between *individual* and *group* incentive-pay plans.

Individual Rewards: Piece Rates and Commissions

The Bureau of Labor Statistics found in 1973 that nearly half of the production workers in U.S. auto-repair shops were paid incentive rates.[15] Roughly one-quarter received some fraction of the labor costs charged to the customer (they were paid by *commission,* in essence), and the other quarter were paid a flat rate *(piece rate)* for each kind of repair performed. The big advantage of these compensation schemes from the employer's perspective is that they induce employees to adopt a set of work goals that are consistent with those of their employer. Employees paid a piece rate are motivated to work quickly, while those paid by commission, are induced to very thoroughly evaluate the serving needs of the firm's customers. Moreover, these inducements exist without the need for, and expense of, close monitoring by the firm's supervisors. Auto-repair shops, however, provide a specific example of several general disadvantages to individually based incentive-pay schemes. These general problems include (1) maintaining quality standards, (2) misusing equipment, (3) setting the rate, and (4) measuring output.

Maintaining Quality Standards. Workers paid by the job are motivated to work quickly, but they are also motivated to have minimal regard for quality. Workers paid by commission are motivated to be so thorough in ferreting out servicing needs that they may fix things that are not broken. Both bases for compensation thus create a need for close supervisory attention to the quality of work performed —a need and an expense that in many cases will offset the supervisory savings associated with incentive pay.

Equipment Misuse. Allied to the problem of work quality is the problem of equipment misuse. Workers receiving incentive pay are motivated to work so quickly that machines or tools are often damaged or otherwise misused. It is often asserted, for example, that piece-rate workers disengage safety devices on machinery in their desire to maximize output. This problem is mitigated to the extent that equipment damage causes *downtime* that results in lost employee earnings.

Setting the Rate. A third problem, probably more associated with piece rates than with commissions, is setting the rate. For example, it may be standard practice in the auto-repair industry to assume that an engine tune-up will require two hours of work and to translate this time requirement into a "per job" piece rate. Suppose, however, some new tool or electronic device is adopted that reduces the time required for a tune-up. A new piece rate will have to be adopted, but how do the shop's owners determine the standard time requirement for tune-ups now? The best way may be to observe mechanics using the new devices, but if these workers know they are being observed for purposes of setting a new rate they will deliberately work slowly so that the time requirement is overestimated—in order

[15]Sandra King, "Incentive and Time Pay in Auto Dealer Repair Shops," *Monthly Labor Review,* 98, 9 (September 1975): 45–48.

to drive up the piece rate. The problem is compounded in industries facing frequent changes in products or technology. In the women's apparel industry around the turn of the century, for example, it was common to have seasonal strikes—coinciding with seasonal changes in fashions—over piece rates.[16]

Measuring Output. A fourth reason why individual incentive-pay schemes are not more widely used is the problem of measuring and motivating individual *output.* The output of an auto mechanic, salesperson, or a dressmaker is relatively

---

EXAMPLE 10.1

Incentive Pay and Output—or "You Get What You Pay For"

Paying workers for a given output can lead to unexpected uses of employee resources and time. As noted in this chapter, piece rates tend to induce workers to emphasize quantity over quality, but the total effects of piece-rate schemes also depend on just what "output" is being paid for.

There is a (probably apocryphal) story that when Soviet farm labor was compensated according to the number of acres planted, plowing was done too hastily and seeds were sown too far apart for high productivity. In an effort to improve output, the Soviet Union began to compensate farm workers on the basis of yield per acre. This caused farmers to invest too many resources (time, fertilizer) per acre and not plant extensively enough, and costs rose. Only when they seized upon the idea of paying farmers on the basis of the difference between the value of output and the costs of production (that is, *profit*) did farmers have the incentives to take into account output and costs.

Another example of the importance of understanding how incentive pay can affect output comes from Great Britain. Instead of compensating dentists on the basis of "contact hours" with patients, the British National Health Service decided (for a while) to compensate dentists on the basis of cavities filled. The result was that the incidence of tooth decay identified by dentists increased substantially and the time it took to fill cavities dropped from 18 minutes to six minutes per filling! It is obvious that this new basis for compensation was of questionable benefit to the patient.

SOURCES: Assar Lindbeck, *The Political Economy of the New Left* (New York: Harper & Row, 1971), p. 71; John Pencavel, "Piecework and On-the-Job Screening" (Stanford, California: Department of Economics, Stanford University, June 1975), p. 4.

---

[16]Louis Levine, *The Women's Garment Workers* (New York: B. W. Huebsch, 1924), p. 42. The observation that a stable technology is important for the success of an incentive-pay system is also made by Sumner H. Slichter, James J. Healy, and E. Robert Livernash, *The Impact of Collective Bargaining on Management* (Washington, D.C.: The Brookings Institution, 1960), p. 519.

easy to measure in terms of quantity, but what about that of an office manager or auto assembly-line worker? The manager has a number of duties and deals with a multitude of problems—combining them into a single index of output would be next to impossible. Assembly-line workers, on the other hand, may have an easily counted output, but this output is not individually controlled. In both cases, *individual* incentive pay would be arbitrary or useless; however, *group* incentives might be attractive in these situations.

Group Incentive Pay

In situations where individual output is hard to monitor or control, group incentive-pay schemes have sometimes been adopted. Their intent, like that of individual incentive-pay systems, is to bring the interests of workers in line with those of the employer. The form these systems take are analogous to the schemes discussed above. In some cases, work groups will be paid by the piece for output produced *by the group*. In other cases, the employees will share in the profits each year—a close analogue to the commission basis for individual pay. In still other cases, the workers might *own* the firm and split the profits among themselves.[17]

The drawback to group incentives is that groups are composed of individuals, and it is at the individual level that decisions about shirking are ultimately made. A person who works very hard to increase group output or firm profits winds up splitting the fruits of his or her labor with everyone else in the firm. Very little of the person's extra efforts are captured by him or her—most go to other persons, who may not have put out extra effort. Group incentives, then, are sometimes no incentive at all. People come to realize that they can reap the rewards of someone else's hard work without doing any extra work of their own, and that if they do put out extra work, the rewards mainly go to others. Such schemes thus give workers incentives to cheat on their fellow employees by shirking.

In very small groups, however, cheating may be easy to detect, and group punishments—such as ostracism—can be effectively used to eliminate it. In these cases, group incentive-pay systems can accomplish their aims (subject, of course, to all the drawbacks of individual incentive-pay systems noted above). However, if the group of workers receiving incentive pay is large, cheating (shirking) probably cannot be effectively handled. Group incentive-pay schemes thus become less effective as size increases.

Earnings Under Piece and Time Rates

Two observations lead to the prediction that workers on incentive pay earn more per hour than comparable workers paid on a time basis. First, if workers have a preference for being paid on a time basis, employers will have to pay a premium

---

[17]For a detailed treatment of worker-owned enterprise—the most widespread example of which is in Yugoslavia—*see* Jaroslav Vanek, *The General Theory of Labor-Managed Market Economies* (Ithaca, N.Y.: The Cornell University Press, 1970).

—a compensating wage differential—to induce them to accept an incentive-pay scheme. This earnings differential would compensate workers for accepting the risks associated with incentive pay. Second, the workers most likely to accept a job with incentive pay are those most likely to be successful at it: the fastest, most intense workers.

Although there are few studies of this issue, the prediction that incentive-pay workers earn more appears to hold up. A 1960s study of punch-press operators in Chicago found that piece-rate workers earned about 9 percent more per hour of work than did those paid an hourly wage.[18] More recent research by the Bureau of Labor Statistics found that auto-repair workers paid on an incentive basis earned 20–50 percent more per hour than those paid on a time basis.[19]

Other Kinds of Incentive Pay

Although used relatively infrequently, firms have also devised incentive-pay schemes other than piece rates, commissions, and profit sharing in order to solve particular production problems. These plans usually provide for the payment of some kind of bonus if a desired outcome is achieved. For example, a firm attempting to induce employees to avoid injuries on the job might give a quarterly bonus to any worker who remains uninjured during that quarter.

Some of the most imaginative incentive pay systems have been directed at the problem of absenteeism. There are two in particular that have achieved notice in the oral tradition of labor economics. A manufacturing plant during the 1940s coped with absenteeism by holding a daily raffle. The prizes were various consumable and durable items of special value to householders during those shortage-prone years. However, to have a chance to win, a worker had to be present. Absenteeism apparently fell dramatically.

Another scheme to reduce absenteeism was adopted by an automobile manufacturer. This involved awarding daily points to each employee who was present for work—points which could be accumulated and redeemed for prizes, such as tickets to popular vacation attractions. The wrinkle in this plan was that the points were not given to the worker, but were instead given to the worker's spouse! With the spouse helping to monitor work behavior it is said that absenteeism problems were greatly reduced.[20]

---

[18]John Pencavel, "Work Effort, On-the-Job Screening, and Alternative Methods of Remuneration," in *Research in Labor Economics,* vol. 1, ed. Ronald Ehrenberg (Greenwich, Conn.: JAI Press, 1977), pp. 225–58.

[19]King, "Incentive and Time Pay in Auto Dealer Repair Shops," p. 46.

[20]We are grateful to Walter Oi for this example. This fringe benefit is an excellent illustration of how such benefits can be tailored to attract certain groups of workers. Giving points to spouses is only of benefit to married workers—and if married workers tend to be more dependable, absenteeism could be reduced by attracting members of this group to the plant.

EXAMPLE 10.2

Compensation Schemes to Modify Worker Behavior in Other Times and Places

Employers, like psychologists, confront the problem of whether positive or negative incentives—rewards or punishments—are the better approach to changing behavior. Farmers in colonial America, for example, faced the problem of inducing their indentured servants not to run away before the end of their contractual period (and thus before the farmers' investment costs had been recouped). They adopted several negative incentives for runaways; extension of the indenture period or corporal punishment were the most common forms of penalty. However, they also used the positive incentive of *freedom dues*—a lump-sum payment of cash or property paid to servants at the end of their indenture period—that would be forfeited if the servant ran away. The use of freedom dues illustrates how deferred compensation can be used to motivate employee cooperation over long periods of time.

The same dilemma of whether to use positive or negative incentives also confronted Japanese employers in the early 1900s, when they were faced with the vexing problem of absenteeism. At times, absent employees were sought out and subjected to physical torture; in other cases, wages were confiscated unless a certain consecutive number of days were worked. As argued in Chapter 7, however, employers offering disagreeable conditions of employment will have more difficulties attracting workers in a competitive labor market than will employers offering comparable jobs without the unpleasant conditions. Thus, harsh penalties for *unwanted* behavior are not costless for employers, which has often led them to adopt positive rewards for *wanted* behavior. In Japan, for example, payments in addition to regular wages were frequently made to workers who had worked without absence for an entire month. Sometimes the bonuses were sent to the workers' families in an attempt to induce parents to encourage regular work attendance among their children. At other times the bonuses were paid to *groups* of workers with good group attendance records; often these bonuses took the form of improved worker dormitory facilities for the work group.

These compensation schemes in other times and other places indicate that the careful structuring of pay for the purpose of changing worker behavior is not the exclusive invention of modern management science.

SOURCES: David Galenson, "The Market Evaluation of Human Capital: The Case of Indentured Servitude," *Journal of Political Economy* 89, 3 (June 1981): 446–67; Koji Taira, *Economic Development and the Labor Market in Japan* (New York: Columbia University Press, 1970), pp. 120–21.

Internal Labor Markets and the Time Pattern of Compensation

Given the difficulties and disadvantages of implementing the common forms of individual or group incentive pay, firms have generally sought methods of motivating workers using a time-based pay system. Time-based approaches to motivation usually offer delayed rewards to workers only *after* diligent effort has been expended by the worker and observed by the employer over a long period. The prospect of these rewards gives workers incentives to work hard. The rewards may come either in the form of a bonus after years of loyal effort or in the form of a promotion. However, a common requirement for both forms of rewards is a *long-term relationship* between employer and employee. One way to encourage a long-term relationship is for firms to adopt *internal labor markets,* wherein promotions are exclusively or primarily done from within the organization.

Internal Labor Markets and Delayed Rewards

Recall from Chapter 5 that firms sometimes create an *internal labor market,* wherein hiring is done only at certain *entry-level jobs,* and all other jobs are filled from within the firm. This hiring and promotion system serves in part as a substitute for the careful screening of job applicants. Workers are hired at low levels of responsibility and then observed over time to determine their actual productive characteristics. Internal labor markets, however, can also be useful in constructing a system of deferred compensation for the purpose of motivating employees. The long-term association between employer and employee fosters opportunities for both deferred payments and the long-term monitoring of employee behavior necessary to make the system work.

If employees are hired with the expectation that they will spend an entire career with a firm—an expectation that is certainly encouraged by a policy of promoting only from within—then the critical element in their choice of an employer is the *present value of their career earnings.* That is, they will be concerned about their likely earnings over their entire *career* and not just the pay on the job for which they are initially hired. A firm with an internal labor market must offer a *stream* of earnings over time whose overall present value is equivalent to that offered by other firms competing in the same labor market.

To say that the present value of an earnings stream must be equivalent to that paid elsewhere does *not* imply that the wages offered for each job or at each stage in one's career must be exactly equal to those paid by other firms. Firms that pay low wages initially, but offer high earnings later on, may be very competitive with firms offering initially higher wages but not raising them much over time.

For example, suppose a firm offered a 10-year job sequence where the workers were paid $15,000 in each of the first five years and $18,000 for the next five years. Using a discount rate of 7 percent, an income stream with the same present value could be achieved by a labor-market competitor who offered $10,000 for each of the first five years and paid $25,000 per year for the last five! Thus it should be clear that firms offering workers *careers,* and not just jobs, have a fairly wide latitude in the way they sequence compensation within the constraint of having to offer career earnings whose present value is comparable to that paid by other firms for the same type of worker. It is this latitude, of course, that allows these firms to defer some of a worker's compensation until the end of his or her career.

The advantages of being able to defer rewards to the worker are captured by both employer and employee. The employer need not devote as many resources to supervision each year as would otherwise be the case, because the firm has several years in which to identify shirkers and withhold from them the reward. Workers are less likely to take chances and shirk their responsibilities because the penalties for being caught and fired are forfeiture of a large reward. Because all employees work harder than they otherwise would, their total compensation tends to be higher also.

Employment Contracts and the Sequencing of Pay

We have just argued that employers with internal labor markets have options for *sequencing* workers' pay while still offering jobs with the same *present value* of career compensation as paid by the market generally.[21] In such a setting, it may be beneficial to both employer and employee to arrange workers' pay over time so that employees are "underpaid" early in their careers and "overpaid" later on. This sequencing of pay will increase worker productivity and enable firms to pay higher present values of compensation than otherwise.

A company that pays low to begin with but pays well later on increases the incentives of its employees to work industriously. Once in the job, an employee has incentives to work diligently in order to qualify for the overpayment later on. One feasible compensation sequencing scheme would pay workers *less* than their marginal product early in their careers and *more* than their marginal product later on. This scheme, however, must satisfy two conditions. First, the present value of the earnings streams offered to employees must at least be equal to alternative streams offered to workers in the labor market; if not, the firm cannot attract the workers it wants. Since pay that is deferred into the future is discounted, deferred sums must be larger the higher is the discount rate (or *present-orientedness*) of workers (see Chapter 8). Second, the scheme must also satisfy the equilibrium conditions that firms maximize profits and do not earn supernormal profits. If profits are not maximized the firm's existence is threatened; if firms make supernormal profits, new firms will be induced to enter the market. Thus, in neither case would equilibrium exist.

The above two conditions will be met if hiring is done until the present value of one's career-long marginal product *(MP)* equals the present value of one's career earnings stream. (This career-long condition is the multiperiod analogue of the single-period profit conditions discussed in Chapter 3 and the two-period profit-maximization criteria discussed in Chapter 5.) Thus, for firms choosing the

---

[21]Our discussion here draws on Edward Lazear, "Why Is There Mandatory Retirement?" *Journal of Political Economy* 87, 6 (December 1979): 1261–84.

"underpayment now, overpayment later" compensation scheme to be competitive in both the labor and product markets, the present value of the yearly amounts by which *MP exceeds* compensation early on must equal the present value of the later amounts by which *MP falls short* of pay.

The above compensation plan is diagrammed in Figure 10.6. We assume that *MP* rises slightly over one's career but that in the first *t** years of employment, compensation remains below *MP*. At some point in one's career with the firm—year *t** in the diagram—compensation begins to exceed *MP*. From *t** onward are the years in which diligent employees are rewarded by receiving compensation in excess of what they could receive elsewhere (namely, their *MP*). For the firm to be competitive in both the labor and product markets, the *present value* of area *A* in the diagram must equal the *present value* of area *B*. (Area *B* is larger than area *A* in Figure 10.6 because sums received farther in the future are subjected to heavier discounting when present values are calculated.)

To be sure, there are risks to both parties in making this kind of agreement. Employees agreeing to this compensation scheme take a chance that they may be fired without cause or that their employer may go bankrupt before they have collected their reward in the years beyond *t**. It is easy to see that employers will have some incentives to renege since older workers are being paid a wage that exceeds their immediate value (at the margin) to the firm.

On the other hand, employers who do not wish to fire people face the risk that older, "overpaid" employees will stay on the job longer than is necessary to collect their reward—that is, they will stay on longer than time *r* in Figure 10.6. Knowing that their current wage is greater than the wage they can get elsewhere

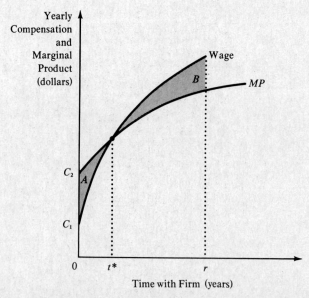

Figure 10.6 A Compensation Scheme Designed to Increase Worker Motivation

—since it reflects payment for more than current output—older employees will have incentives to keep working longer than is profitable for the firm.

A partial solution to these problems of risk is to agree on a formal employment contract that has two elements. One element protects older employees from arbitrary discharge by (a) stipulating the grounds under which employees can be discharged and (b) guaranteeing "seniority rights" for older workers. According to these seniority provisions, workers with the shortest duration of employment with the firm are usually laid off first when the firm cuts back its work force. Without these seniority rights, firms might be tempted to lay off older workers, whose wage is greater than *MP,* and keep the younger ones (who are paid less than *MP* at this point in their career).

The second element of a formal employment contract designed to reduce the risk inherent in this compensation plan is some form of retirement clause. Unless firms can induce workers to retire before the present value of area *B* in Figure 10.6 exceeds that of *A*—or unless they can force older employees to accept wage cuts so that after year *r* their wage equals *MP*—employers will not agree to the compensation-sequencing plan under discussion.

In some instances, formal employment contracts have included a mandatory retirement age, which prior to 1978 was normally set at age 65. Under these agreements, employees would have to retire at age 65 whether they wanted to or not. In other cases there may be inducements offered for voluntary early retirement. For example, the 1965 contract between the automakers and the United Automobile Workers permitted workers to retire as early as age 55—assuming they had 30 years of service. Moreover, the monthly pension benefit before age 65 was much larger than after 65, yielding an average present value of early retirement benefits equal to $18,365—compared to a present value of $9,700 associated with retirement at age 65.[22]

In making an early retirement decision, one must compare the utility generated by one's income and leisure streams if retirement occurs at 65 (say) with that generated by early retirement and its associated streams of leisure and pension income. When the stream of pension income associated with early retirement is increased in some way, the utility associated with early retirement is enhanced. Inducing early retirement by essentially bribing people to retire makes economic sense in the case where older employees are paid more than they are currently worth.

Formal agreements cannot remove risks altogether, however. There is, on the employee side, no assurance that the firm will be in business during the employee's older years. Even large, once-profitable firms go bankrupt, close down plants, or are bought out by other firms—all of which can have the effect of reducing jobs or wage opportunities for older workers in the firm. Whereas most *pension* promises are backed up by a separate fund that remains even if the employer goes bankrupt, there is really nothing to back up a promise of future pay increases. On the employer side, mandatory retirement agreements can be,

---

[22]See Richard Burkhauser, "The Pension Acceptance Decision of Older Workers," *Journal of Human Resources* 14 (Winter 1979): 63–75.

and have been, voided by federal legislation. Amendments made to the Age Discrimination in Employment Act in 1978, for example, outlawed agreements that contained age 65 as the minimum age of mandatory retirement. Age 70 is now the earliest anyone can be forced to retire.

Thus, *formal* contracts safeguarding the deferral of earnings to late in one's career are not riskless. Even more risky are *implicit contracts*—contracts that are understood to exist but that have not been formally written and signed by both parties. In these contracts, the employee is protected from arbitrary dismissal only by the need for the employer to recruit *other* workers. If a certain employer gains a reputation for firing older workers, despite an implicit agreement not to do so, that employer will have trouble recruiting new employees (as noted earlier) —which is some incentive to adhere to the implicit contract. However, if the company is in permanent decline, if it faces an unusually adverse market, or if information on company employment policies is not easily or accurately available to applicants, the incentives to renege on implicit contracts are probably very strong.

Pensions as Deferred Payments

One way to assure employees of receiving their delayed reward is to provide a pension. According to statistics published by the American Council of Life Insurance, the average yearly retirement benefit paid by private pension plans in 1978 was $1,752.[23] While this sum does not strike one as overwhelmingly large, a yearly payment of this size beginning at age 65 and lasting 15 years (the average life expectancy of a 65-year-old) requires a fund of $16,000 to finance it at a 7 percent rate of interest. Thus, giving pensioners $1,752 per year from age 65 until death is equivalent to giving the average retiree a lump-sum payment of $16,000. If the pension benefits were more generous, the lump-sum equivalent increases proportionately. For example, the average city employee in Pennsylvania received $3,800 per year in retirement benefits in 1976, implying a lump-sum equivalent of $34,700 (at a 7 percent interest rate).

It is obvious, then, that pensions represent the equivalent of a deferred payment paid to workers at the end of their careers. Under ERISA, the money to finance this payment must be set aside each year by the employer in a separate fund so that employees have some assurance of receiving their reward even if the firm goes bankrupt. As discussed in this chapter, firms offering their employees pensions must pay lower wages, other things equal, in order to remain competitive. Thus, pensions offer a mechanism whereby spendable pay is "low" during one's working years but a reward is received later on.

The strongest incentives for diligence under a pension scheme would exist if the pension were not vested. Nonvested employees can be threatened with loss of a pension up to the day before retirement. Vesting, however, modifies the incentive effects of this compensation scheme somewhat. Most private-sector

---

[23]American Council of Life Insurance, *Pension Facts 1978–1979* (Washington, D.C.: American Council of Life Insurance, 1979), p. 15.

employees with pensions become vested after 10 years, so that the threat of losing all rights to their pension is, strictly speaking, only there for the first 10 years. This in itself may be a long enough time to motivate and observe reliable work habits, but even being fired after becoming vested entails loss. A vested worker fired by Firm X may be able to obtain a pension from X at retirement, but this pension will be smaller to the extent that one's tenure with X is shorter. To receive a *full* pension benefit would require the worker to qualify for a pension with *another* firm—a process that will normally take 10 more years in itself. Thus, while vesting softens the threat of being fired for cause after 10 years, it does not remove all of the incentive to work honestly and diligently throughout one's career.

Promotion Lotteries

Another form of worker motivation within the context of internal labor markets might best be called a *promotion lottery.* Suppose a group of entering management trainees were hired with the expectation that *one* of them would become a high-ranking corporate officer and make an extraordinary sum of money each year. The employees who did not make it to the top would be guaranteed a spot in the firm somewhere, but they would not achieve such high earnings.

Now if everyone knew in advance who would be promoted, this scheme would be neither incentive-producing nor would it have aspects of a lottery. However, if no one knew in advance who would "win", but all were told that winning the top job depended on hard work, then all would be attracted by the large salary (or prestige) and work hard to get it. Here, as in the previous schemes, the prospect of obtaining large sums towards the end of one's career offers incentives for diligent work throughout earlier years.

In this scheme, however, not all diligent workers get the prize at career's end; only the winner does. Further, once the prize has been awarded and the losers are known, they no longer have the same strong incentives to work hard. Moreover, the employer—knowing the "losers" have reduced incentives—has every reason to want to get rid of them. Dangling a lucrative job in front of everyone increased the incentives of all—even the eventual losers—to work hard; once the prize has been awarded, the losers are of substantially less value to the firm.

The problem for the employer is that employees may not be willing to enter this lottery unless even the losers are treated relatively well. A firm known for firing older mid-level managers may not be able to attract a large enough group of young management trainees from which to produce an excellent corporate officer in the future. For this reason, a firm may be tempted to agree to essentially guarantee the losers a job somewhere in the organization.

Since workers whose wages are less than or equal to their marginal product do not need any guarantee of job security, it is most likely true that the losers of promotion lotteries have wages or salaries that *exceed* marginal product. If this is the case, the employer will obviously want to offer strong incentives for these employees to retire at a certain point. Again then, a mandatory retirement clause may be an essential ingredient in the running of a promotion lottery.

Hypothesizing that promotion lotteries exist helps explain three phenomena that are widely observed in the labor market. First, it helps explain why—after carefully considering a number of candidates for a top executive job—one is selected and paid perhaps three times what the others receive. Is it because he or she is three times as productive as the others? If so, the others would not have been serious contenders for the job. The huge pay differential most likely exists to serve as an incentive for younger employees to work hard so they can win the next lottery.[24]

Second, the existence of promotion lotteries helps explain why corporations sometimes tolerate *deadwood*—the older employee who obviously is not going to be promoted and who clearly is not as productive as he or she used to be—in the ranks. Such deadwood is the unfortunate cost to the firm of running a successful lottery. Third, because deadwood can be tolerated for a while but not indefinitely, there have arisen mandatory-retirement rules or other inducements for employees to retire before they might otherwise decide to do so.

Federal Policy on Mandatory Retirement Reconsidered

This chapter has argued that "underpaying" employees in the early stages of their careers and "overpaying" them later serves as an incentive for employees to work industriously. Because workers are more productive, employers can offer them an income stream whose present value is increased over what it would otherwise be. While employees can command more compensation because they, as individuals, work harder, they benefit *additionally* by a system that causes *other* employees to also work more diligently.

As we have pointed out, however, overpaying workers is something a firm cannot tolerate indefinitely. Thus, for this payment scheme to work—and it must work for both parties in order for each to have incentives to agree to it—firms must be able to terminate the overpayment at the point where it is no longer profitable in the long run.

One way to end the overpayment is to reduce the wage rate of older workers after a certain age to a wage that more closely corresponds to their marginal product. Reducing the wage rate in this way would almost surely raise charges of age discrimination—reflecting a prevailing social value that workers' nominal wages should not be reduced under any but the most extraordinary circumstances. Why society has adopted this particular value is an interesting—and open—question.[25]

A social "rule" against wage cutting suggests that the "underpay now, overpay later" scheme will be adopted only if older workers can be fired—or, more politely, subjected to mandatory retirement—by their employers. In most cases such retirement will mean no work at all; in other cases, the employees might be

---

[24]This argument is advanced by Edward Lazear and Sherwin Rosen, "Rank-Order Tournaments As Optimum Labor Contracts," *Journal of Political Economy* 89 (October 1981): 841–64.

[25]Chapter 18 discusses the related question of why employers react to decreases in demand by laying off workers rather than cutting their wages.

able to find work at a lower wage rate with some other employer. In either case, the affected employees have absorbed wage cuts, and because these cuts—when seen from the workers' perspective in old age—have been forced on them they are likely to feel worse off. They may even ask for and support legislation to outlaw mandatory retirement—which is exactly what happened with the 1978 amendments to the Age Discrimination in Employment Act, which raised the minimum age for mandatory retirement from 65 to 70.

Who gains and who loses from this mandated increase in the age for mandatory retirement? It is clear that employers lose, but is it equally clear that employees gain? Surely people who are currently near retirement gain. However, their gain lies in the fact that governmental authority has been used to break a key element of a contract from which they benefited in the past. The fact that firms can no longer enforce a critical element of their old contracts removes from them the incentive to agree to future contracts of the same type. Thus, younger employees may be harmed by the provisions of the 1978 Act. In fact, the gains to older employees only occur *once*—to the group that is allowed to break its contract. Future generations of older workers do not gain, since their employment contracts and compensation schemes will be made under the new rules of the game.[26]

REVIEW QUESTIONS

1. There is a law saying that compensation of federal-government employees must be comparable to that of private-sector employees of similar skills who perform similar duties. Suppose that comparing pay in the two sectors is done by measuring salaries or wages of a "typical" worker in each sector (one, say, with 10 years of experience). In what respects would this approach be deficient?

2. The President's Commission of Pension Policy has proposed that every employee in the country be covered by a Minimum Universal Pension (MUP). This pension would vest immediately and would be fully *portable*. (That is, all workers would qualify for a pension no matter how many employers they worked for in their lifetime or how long they worked for each. Currently, employees are not eligible to receive any private-pension benefits at age 65 unless they work for an employer 10 years.) What impact would an MUP have on labor costs and productivity in this age of inflation?

3. Suppose mandatory retirement laws were abolished and firms undertook various strategies to induce *voluntary* retirements at age 65. Some of these possible strategies are listed below. The firm's objectives are to increase unambiguously the incentives for people over 65 to retire, but to do so in a way that offers the strongest incentives to the *least productive* of the older workers to retire. (For our purposes, the least productive will be defined as the workers no other firm would want at anything close to their current wage. Productive workers, even though elderly, could get jobs elsewhere at close to their current wage.) Evaluate each of the following strategies to determine whether it will accomplish the firm's objectives:

---

[26]For further analysis of the winners and the losers, see Ronald G. Ehrenberg, "Retirement Policy, Employment, and Unemployment," *American Economic Review* 69, 2 (May 1979): 131–36.

a. Cut the wages of all workers after the age of 60.

b. Provide a large lump-sum payment to anyone who quits his or her employment *at the firm* at age 65.

c. Increase the monthly pension benefit of anyone who *retires* (and does not work elsewhere) at age 65.

SELECTED READINGS

Armen Alchian and Reuben Kessel, "Competition, Monopoly, and the Pursuit of Money." In *Aspects of Labor Economics,* edited by H. G. Lewis (Princeton, N.J.: Princeton University Press, 1962).

Steven G. Allen, "Compensation, Safety and Absenteeism." *Industrial and Labor Relations Review* 34 (January 1981): 207–18.

Peter Doeringer and Michael Piore, *Internal Labor Markets and Manpower Analysis* (Lexington, Mass.: D. C. Heath and Company, 1971).

Ronald Ehrenberg and Robert Smith, "A Framework for Evaluating State and Local Government Pension Reform." In *Public Sector Labor Markets,* edited by Peter Mieszkowski and George E. Peterson (Washington, D.C.: The Urban Institute, 1981).

Edward Lazear, "Why Is There Mandatory Retirement?" *Journal of Political Economy* 87 (December 1979): 1261–84.

John Pencavel, "Work Effort, On-the-Job Screening, and Alternative Methods of Remuneration." In *Research in Labor Economics,* Vol. 1, edited by Ronald Ehrenberg (Greenwich, Conn.: JAI Press, 1977), pp. 225–58.

Herbert A. Simon, "A Formal Theory of the Employment Relationship." *Econometrica* 19 (July 1951): 293–305.

Joseph E. Stiglitz, "Incentives, Risk and Information: Notes Toward a Theory of Hierarchy." *Bell Journal of Economics and Management Science* 6 (Autumn 1975): 552–79.

Chapter 11

THE ECONOMICS OF DISCRIMINATION

We have learned that wages differ across individuals or jobs for numerous reasons. They vary with the amount of general or specific training, with job and locational characteristics, and with age. They also vary with fringe benefits and compensation schemes, and, of course, they vary with the extent of unionism. Many of these sources of wage differentials may be regarded either as necessary in the allocation of labor or as socially legitimate on other grounds. There are, however, sizable wage differentials that appear to be associated solely with race and sex, and these differentials are often thought to be synonymous with widespread discrimination against minorities—especially blacks and Hispanics—and women. This chapter discusses the evidence and theories of discrimination and concludes with an analysis of government policy in this area.

What Is Discrimination?

The term *discrimination* is often used imprecisely because the relationship between *prejudice* and discrimination often is unclear. One might assert, for example, that a firm with two racially segregated branch offices is discriminating by failing to integrate both offices, even if workers in both branches are paid the same wages and have the same opportunities for advancement. This assertion raises the question of whether discrimination is always present where there is prejudice or just when some harm comes from this prejudice. Conversely, some people allege discrimination exists in cases where prejudice may not. For example, a firm offering specific training may prefer to hire younger workers who will stay with the firm long enough for it to recoup training costs. Is this age discrimination or good business?

Another confusing issue is whether discrimination can be identified by inequality of *achievement* or inequality of *opportunity*. Is an accounting firm located in a small, mostly white town guilty of discrimination if it has no black auditors on its staff? Would the answer change if the firm could show it had advertised job openings widely and had made the same offers to blacks as to whites but that the offers to blacks had been rejected?

Finally, just what standards are to be used to judge equality? Consider the data on college teachers in the humanities contained in Table 11.1. The overall average salary paid to black professors is slightly below the salaries paid to whites for at least two reasons. First, a lower proportion of blacks have received doctorate degrees, and, of those who have, fewer were obtained at distinguished universities. The relatively lower levels of educational attainment among blacks thus holds down their average salary. Second, among those teachers without doctorates, blacks receive lower salaries than whites. However, if one looks at salaries among professors with doctorates in the humanities from distinguished universities, we see that blacks earn *more* than whites. The same is true among those with doctorates from less distinguished universities.

Do the data in Table 11.1 suggest that blacks in academia are discriminated against? One could answer yes, because they earn less overall, because they have lower levels of preparation for their jobs, or because there are so few blacks in college teaching (2.5 percent of college professors are black, whereas blacks constitute about 8 percent of the overall employed population at large). Others might argue that there is no evidence of discrimination against blacks with doctorates, once one controls for the quality of preparation.

It is obvious from the questions raised by Table 11.1 that discrimination can occur in many forms and places. If it occurs in the labor market, workers with equal preparation and productivity receive different wages. If it occurs among educational institutions, students of equal ability are treated differently and emerge from formal schooling with unequal educations. If it occurs in childhood, young children with equal potential are raised with quite different aspirations and attitudes. Discrimination can also occur in a variety of other places: the housing market, various product markets, and treatment under the law.

Table 11.1. Mean Annual Salaries of Full-Time College Faculty in the Humanities, 1972 and 1973

	Black		White	
	Number	Salary (dollars)	Number	Salary (dollars)
All full-time faculty	2,177	15,034	85,904	15,572
Doctorate from distinguished university	89	20,259	9,765	16,832
Doctorate from other universities	173	17,262	17,894	15,790
No doctorate	1,915	14,590	58,245	15,293

SOURCE: Thomas Sowell, *Affirmative Action Reconsidered: Was It Necessary in Academia?* (Washington, D.C.: The American Enterprise Institute for Public Policy Research, 1975), p. 20.

The kind of discrimination this chapter will analyze in most depth is discrimination in the labor market. This emphasis should not imply that other forms of discrimination are unimportant or unrelated to labor-market discrimination. Indeed, *past* labor-market discrimination may have been instrumental in causing the poverty or attitudes that are *now* manifest in child-rearing practices, school-achievement levels, and career or sex-role aspirations. However, since the focus of our analysis is on *current labor-market discrimination,* we will lump all *other* forms of discrimination into a more general category we will call *premarket differences.*

An operational definition of *current labor-market discrimination* is "the valuation in the labor market of personal characteristics of the worker that are unrelated to productivity."[1] This definition recognizes that one's value in the labor market depends on all the demand and supply factors affecting marginal productivity. However, when factors that are *unrelated* to productivity acquire a positive or negative value in the labor market, discrimination can be said to occur. Race and sex are currently the most prominent of these factors alleged to be unrelated to productivity, but physical handicaps, religion, sexual preferences, and ethnic affiliations are also on the list.

Three points should be noted about the above definition. First, the emphasis in identifying discrimination is on measurable market outcomes, such as earnings, wages, occupational attainment, or employment levels. While prejudicial attitudes may be felt by members of one group toward those of another, these feelings must be accompanied by some *action* that results in a different market outcome for us to assert that discrimination is present.

Second, we are not concerned with the routine random differences in outcomes that are matters of luck. Rather, the concept of discrimination encompasses only those differences that are so systematic that they do not cancel each other out within large groups.

Finally, our definition of labor-market discrimination suggests an operational way to distinguish between *labor-market* and *premarket* factors that cause earnings differentials. Differentials that derive from differences in average *productivity* levels across race or sex groups, for example, can be categorized as *premarket* in nature. Differentials that are attributed to race or sex, *holding productivity constant,* can be said to be evidence of labor-market discrimination.

It is very important for policy purposes to measure the relative size of labor-market and premarket factors that lead to systematic earnings differences among various population groups. Any attempts to combat discrimination must be grounded in accurate information concerning the *source* of that discrimination; otherwise, effective antidiscrimination programs cannot be formulated. If the evidence points to a significant amount of labor-market discrimination, programs aimed at employers and the hiring/promotion process may be effective. If, however, most of any systematic earnings differences related to race or sex appear to be rooted in premarket factors, then programs aimed at education, training, and the process of socializing children will be required.

---

[1] Kenneth J. Arrow, "The Theory of Discrimination," *Discrimination in Labor Markets,* eds. Orley Ashenfelter and Albert Rees (Princeton, N.J.: Princeton University Press, 1973), p. 3.

Earnings Disparities by Race and Sex

There have been, and continue to be, strikingly large income disparities between most minorities and whites and between men and women. These differences are a cause of widespread social concern about discrimination, its sources, and possible remedies. This chapter will analyze various theories and their consequences for antidiscrimination policies after first describing the race and sex differences in earnings that actually exist.

Racial Differences

Blacks. In 1981, the earnings of the typical male, year-round black worker were 71 percent of his white counterpart. While this disparity in incomes is large and has varied considerably in the recession-plagued years after 1975, there is a gradual trend toward greater equality over time. As indicated in Table 11.2, the 1981 ratio was 5–7 percentage points higher than in the 1960s, and 3–4 points higher than in the early 1970s. At no point since 1974 has the ratio fallen below what is was before 1974.

Similar patterns for females can be observed from the data in Table 11.2, although much greater equality has been achieved among women. Black and white women who worked full-time at year-round jobs had virtually the same income ratios as did men in the early 1960s (around .65). However, in the mid-1960s the ratio for women began to rise until by 1981 black women who worked full-time earned, on average, 90 percent as much as full-time white women workers.

Table 11.2. Black/White Ratio of Median Income for Full-Time, Year-Round Workers

| | Black/White Income Ratio | |
Year	Males	Females
1959	0.61	0.66
1961	0.66	0.67
1963	0.66	0.64
1965	0.64	0.71
1967	0.64	0.74
1969	0.66	0.80
1971	0.68	0.88
1973	0.67	0.85
1974	0.70	0.91
1976	0.72	0.93
1977	0.69	0.93
1978	0.77	0.93
1980	0.70	0.93
1981	0.71	0.90

SOURCES: U.S. Bureau of the Census, *Current Population Reports: Consumer Income,* Series P-60 (relevant years). Data before 1980 refer to persons aged 14 or older; data for 1980–81 refer to ages 15 or older.

While these ratios and their trends are very interesting and important, they do not help us identify the immediate *source* of the disparities. Are the differences primarily due to *current labor-market discrimination,* or are they the result of *premarket factors?* Blacks, for example, tend to be younger and less educated, on average, than whites.[2] Further, it may well be that the average *quality* of schooling received by blacks is lower than the average for whites.[3] We know that earnings rise with both education and experience, so that *some* of the black/white earnings differences are surely attributable to these characteristics. How much of the overall differential in average earnings is due to differences in the characteristics that affect productivity, and how much is due to labor-market discrimination?

To measure the extent of market discrimination one must answer the following question: "What would be the black/white earnings ratio if blacks and whites had the same productive characteristics?" In other words, if blacks (on average) had the same education, training, experience, turnover rate, health and marital status, and region of residence as whites, what would be the ratio of their earnings to those of whites? One study that asked this question for males in 1966 found that 67–75 percent of the overall black/white disparity in wage rates was attributable to premarket differences;[4] another study found that 53 percent of the disparity was due to premarket factors;[5] a third estimated that 60 percent of the wage differences were rooted in premarket differences.[6] Thus, it would appear that from half to three quarters of the disparity in black/white earnings can be attributed to premarket differences.

The finding that from 50–75 percent of the difference in average earnings can be explained by differences in productive characteristics implies that current labor-market discrimination *may* account for 25–50 percent of the overall differential—suggesting a rather significant role for antidiscrimination programs or policies in the labor market. However, the figures of 25–50 percent are really upper-bound estimates of the extent of labor-market discrimination, because researchers simply do not have complete data on the productive characteristics of individuals or groups. Researchers can measure age, education, and, in many cases, experience, but they rarely have data on school quality, work habits, aspirations, degree of alienation, and other intangibles that clearly affect one's productivity. These intangibles, moreover, *may* vary across race (or sex) owing to such premarket factors as social treatment, socioeconomic status of one's parents, and cultural background. If the unmeasured characteristics tend to

---

[2]As noted in Chapter 8, one's choice of education is influenced by expected labor-market earnings over the life cycle. Hence, ensuring that market discrimination against blacks is reduced or eliminated should serve as an incentive for blacks to stay in school longer.

[3]*See* Finis Welch, "Education and Racial Discrimination," in *Discrimination in Labor Markets,* eds. Orley Ashenfelter and Albert Rees, pp. 43–81.

[4]Robert J. Flanagan, "Labor Force Experience, Job Turnover, and Racial Wage Differentials," *Review of Economics and Statistics* 56 (November 1974): 521–29.

[5]Mary Corcoran and Greg Duncan, "Labor History, Labor Force Attachment, and Earnings Differences Between the Races and Sexes," *Journal of Human Resources* 14, 1 (Winter 1979): 3–20.

[6]A. S. Blinder, "Wage Discrimination—Reduced Form and Structural Estimates," *Journal of Human Resources* 8 (Fall 1973): 436–55.

depress the productivity of minorities or women relative to white males, attributing all of the unexplained difference in average earnings to current labor-market discrimination will clearly overstate the extent of that discrimination. *Some* of the unexplained 25–50 percent may be the result of unmeasured productive characteristics and thus more appropriately labeled *premarket* in nature.

After estimating the portion of the *average* race/sex earnings differential that is explained by differences in average productive characteristics, one is left with a residual, or unexplained, portion. One part of the residual may be the result of current labor-market discrimination, but the effects of any unmeasurable (or at least unmeasured) differences in average productive characteristics show up in the residual also. Because of this methodological defect—which is mainly the result of the difficulties of measuring all characteristics that affect productivity—accurate measures of the extent of labor-market discrimination do not exist. Assuming *all* of the unexplained residual is due to discrimination, we can make estimates of the *maximum possible* effects discrimination might have; however, we are unable to say if actual labor-market discrimination is close to this maximum or not.

Hispanics. Labor-market discrimination against Hispanic workers has not been extensively studied. To control for differences in productive characteristics requires, in addition to the usual data on education and experience, information on proficiency in English—and such information is rarely available. A recent study that did make use of language proficiency data, however, suggests that discrimination against Hispanics is not as severe as against blacks.[7]

In 1975, ratios of the average earnings of male Hispanics to those of non-Hispanic white males were as follows:

—Mexicans: 0.72
—Puerto Ricans: 0.76
—Central and South Americans: 0.83
—Cubans: 0.89

However, differences in productive characteristics accounted for about 80 percent of the earnings gap for Mexicans, 50 percent for Puerto Ricans, and 15 percent of the gap for Central and South Americans. Thus, if differences in average productive characteristics were eliminated, the foregoing earnings ratios would rise to approximately 0.94, 0.88, and 0.85 for Mexicans, Puerto Ricans, and Central/South Americans, respectively. The earnings of Cuban males do not appear to be adversely affected by labor-market discrimination; if they acquired

---

[7]The findings in this section are from Cordelia W. Reimers, "Labor Market Discrimination Against Hispanic and Black Men," *Review of Economics and Statistics* (Nov. 1983). The findings are generally corroborated by an earlier study by James D. Gwartney and James E. Long, "The Relative Earnings of Blacks and Other Minorities," *Industrial and Labor Relations Review* 31 (April 1978): 336–46. *See* also Geoffrey Carliner, "Returns to Education for Blacks, Anglos, and Five Spanish Groups," *Journal of Human Resources* 11 (Spring 1976): 172–84.

the same measured productive characteristics, on average, as non-Hispanic white males, it is estimated that they would earn about 6 percent more.

Sex Differences

Differences in earnings between female and male workers are large. The average white, female, full-time worker earns roughly 60 percent of what her male counterpart earns. As one can see from Table 11.3, this ratio is down from what it was in 1955 and essentially unchanged since 1964. Further, women earn substantially less than men in each of the major occupational categories, with the ratios running from 42 percent in sales work to 76 percent among professionals. Not

Table 11.3. Ratio of Female/Male Wage and Salary Income for Year-Round, Full-Time, White Workers

Year	Ratio of Female/Male Income
1955	0.65
1964	0.59
1967	0.58
1970	0.59
1973	0.56
1977	0.58
1978	0.59
1980	0.59
1981	0.60
Private sector (1977):	
Professional-technical workers	0.76
Managerial	0.52
Sales	0.42
Clerical	0.64
Craft	0.59
Operatives	0.58
Laborer	0.64
Service	0.63
Government workers (1977):	
Federal—public administration	0.66
Federal—professional	0.68
State and local—public administration	0.60
State and local—professional	0.70
Self-employed, nonagricultural (1977)	0.38

SOURCES: 1955: U.S. Bureau of the Census, *Current Population Reports, Consumer Income,* Series P-60, No. 22 (September 1956), Table 7; 1964: U.S. Bureau of the Census, *Current Population Reports: Consumer Income, Income in 1964 of Families and Persons in the United States,* Series P-60, No. 47 (September 1965), Table 18; 1967–1973: U.S. Bureau of the Census, *Current Population Reports, Consumer Income: Money Income in 1973 of Families and Persons in the United States,* Series P-60, No. 97 (January 1975), Table F; 1977: U.S. Bureau of the Census, *Current Population Reports, Consumer Income: Money Income in 1977 of Families and Persons in the United States,* Series P-60, No. 118 (March 1979), Table 55. 1978: U.S. Bureau of the Census, *Current Population Reports, Consumer Income: Money Income in 1978 of Families and Persons in the United States,* Series P-60, No. 123 (June 1980), Table 59. 1980: U.S. Bureau of the Census, *Current Population Reports, Consumer Income: Money Income of Households, Families, and Persons in the United States: 1980,* Series P-60, No. 132 (July 1982), Table 58. 1981: U.S. Bureau of the Census, *Current Population Reports, Consumer Income: Money Income and Poverty Status of Families and Persons in the United States: 1981,* Series P-60, No. 134 (July 1982), Table 11.

even in government work do female incomes rise above 70 percent of male incomes, and among the self-employed the ratio is at its lowest (38 percent).

There are several factors other than labor-market discrimination that could cause these large disparities. First, because the market work-life of a woman is normally shorter than that of a man, women have fewer incentives to invest in schooling and post-schooling training that is specifically oriented to the labor market. (They, in essence, prepare for two careers—one at home and one in the labor market—and are thus typically less specialized than men.) The lack of on-the-job training, as noted in Chapter 8, is one reason why the age/earnings profiles for women are so flat, creating a greater disparity between female and male earnings as they grow older. Shorter working lives also mean that within each occupational grouping, women are likely to be less experienced than men. One survey, for example, found that in 1966 the average male, aged 30–44, had 19.4 years of work experience; the average work history for married women of the same age was 9.6 years.[8]

Second, because of traditional home responsibilities, women are less likely than men to work overtime or to choose occupations that offer jobs with high pay but long hours.[9] Home responsibilities also mean that women usually work closer to home than do men, a fact (as argued in Chapter 7) that implies lower wages.

Finally, historically women have tended to "follow" husbands when the husbands decided on the geographical location of their jobs (a fact noted in Chapter 9 and more explicitly in Example 9.2). Husbands, in effect, have been relatively free to choose their best offer, while wives have usually done the best they can *given* their geographical location. This sort of family decision-making behavior has also tended to reduce female earnings.[10]

While the above *premarket* differences are not immediately generated by *labor-market* discrimination, they will be *affected* by the presence of such discrimination. If current market discrimination exists, the resulting lower wage for women strengthens incentives for them to be the ones who engage in *household production.* The expectation that women will be the ones to stay home with children, for example, is probably the major reason behind each of the three premarket forces above. Anything that reduces the disproportionate share of women in household production will tend to increase their incentives to acquire human capital, work longer hours for pay, and select their jobs from a wider area. Thus, even though premarket differences are clearly important and deeply rooted

---

[8]*See* Jacob Mincer and Solomon Polachek, "Family Investments in Human Capital: Earnings of Women," *Journal of Political Economy* 82 (March/April 1974): S76–S108.

[9]"Protective" labor legislation at the state level until recently often limited the maximum hours per week a woman could work—thus closing women out of overtime opportunities available to men.

[10]Evidence that geographic migration usually causes husbands' earnings to rise but wives' earnings to fall was cited earlier (Chapter 9) based on Polachek and Horvath, "A Life Cycle Approach to Migration," *Research in Labor Economics* (Greenwich, Conn.: JAI Press, 1977). Other articles on the same topic are Robert H. Frank, "Why Women Earn Less: The Theory and Estimation of Differential Overqualification," *American Economic Review* 68 (June 1978): 360–73; and Mincer and Polachek, "Family Investments in Human Capital." Of course, increased female labor-market attachment suggests that such patterns will not necessarily persist in the future.

in factors other than current labor-market discrimination, measuring the extent of labor-market discrimination and taking steps to end it is of obvious importance.

One way to obtain a sense of the extent of market discrimination is to look at the relative earnings of women who have never married. These women are not engaged in raising children and, unless involved in caring for a parent or sibling, do not have the household duties that usually befall married women. They tend to work almost as many hours per year as the average man, and they also exhibit concave age/earnings profiles.[11] Despite these closer similarities to men, however, the average income of never-married women aged 25–64 is just 65 percent of that earned by the average man in that age group (as compared to 56 percent for married women).[12]

Before concluding that market discrimination is immediately responsible for most of the earnings gap between men and women, however, it is important to remember that the typical never-married person, aged 25–64, is probably younger and thus less experienced than the typical married person. It is also important to realize that human-capital decisions are based on *expected* career life—and many never-married women may have expected to become married when basic schooling or occupational decisions were made. In short, previously prevailing social expectations about women's roles in household production may also have influenced the human-capital decisions of women who ultimately decided not to marry, causing their earnings to be lower than otherwise. Finally, the group of never-married adults is likely to contain a higher proportion of disabled persons than is found in the married group. Thus, while *some* of the 35 percent earnings differential for never-married women may be due to current labor-market discrimination, it is unlikely that *all* of the difference can be so attributed.

The best way to estimate the upper-bound effects of market discrimination on the basis of sex is to perform the same kind of analysis reported earlier for black and white males. Thus we must ask, "What would the female/male earnings ratio be, on average, if women had the same education, training, experience, hours of work, commuting distance, turnover rate, and other productive characteristics as their male counterparts?" Studies that have attempted to answer this question have generally concluded that differences in education, training, turnover, and experience—but primarily experience—account for one-third to two-thirds of the earnings differences between men and women.[13] Thus it appears that *labor-market* discrimination can account for no more than two-thirds of the earnings gap between men and women.

---

[11]Victor Fuchs, "Differences in Hourly Earnings Between Men and Women," *Monthly Labor Review* 94, 5 (May 1971): 9–15.

[12]These ratios are for full-time, year-round whites, aged 25–64 in 1977. *See* U.S. Bureau of the Census, *Current Population Reports: Money Income in 1977 of Families and Persons in the United States,* Series P-60, No. 118 (March 1979), Table 45.

[13]Corcoran and Duncan, "Work History, Labor Force Attachment, and Earnings Differences Between the Races and Sexes"; Mincer and Polachek, "Family Investments in Human Capital: Earnings of Women;" and Sharon P. Smith, *Equal Pay in the Public Sector: Fact or Fantasy* (Princeton, N.J.: Industrial Relations Section, Princeton University, 1977).

One aspect of alleged labor-market discrimination against women is *occupational segregation*—the reservation of some jobs for men and others (mostly lower-paying ones) for women. Some dimensions of this segregation and its effects can be seen in Table 11.4, which presents for 1970 the share of women in a variety of high-paying and low-paying occupations. Very few of the high-paying occupations employed women to an extent even close to their overall proportion among all employed workers (37.7 percent in 1970). On the other hand, women were heavily *over-*represented in the low-paying occupations.

How much of the market discrimination against women takes the form of occupational segregation and how much takes the form of different wages *within* given occupations? A crude answer to this question can be obtained by estimating the wage women would make if they had productive characteristics similar to the average male. Comparing this estimated wage to the average male wage will yield an upper-bound estimate of overall market discrimination. If we then estimate the wage women would receive if they had the same productive characteristics *and* the same *occupational* distribution as men, we can calculate the wage disparities caused solely by occupational differences. The most widely quoted study of the effects of occupational segregation suggests that equalizing the occupational

Table 11.4. Representation of Women in Ten High-Paying and Ten Low-Paying Occupations, 1970

Occupation	Percent Female 1970
High-Paying:	
Stock and bond sales agents	8.6
Managers and administrators, n.e.c.[a]	11.6
Bank officials and financial managers	17.4
Sales representatives, manufacturing	8.5
Real-estate appraisers	4.1
Designers	23.5
Personnel and labor-relations workers	31.2
Sales representatives, wholesale	6.4
Computer programmers	22.7
Mechanical-engineering technicians	2.9
Low-Paying:	
Practical nurses	96.3
Hairdressers and cosmetologists	90.4
Cooks, except private household	62.8
Health aides, except nursing	83.9
Nurses' aides	84.6
Sewers and stitchers	93.8
Farm laborers	13.2
Dressmakers and seamstresses	95.7
School monitors	91.2
Childcare workers, except private household	93.2
All occupations	37.7

[a]The initials n.e.c. mean "not elsewhere classified."

SOURCE: Sharon Smith, "Men's Jobs, Women's Jobs and Differential Wage Treatment," *Job Evaluation and EEO: The Emerging Issues,* papers presented at the Industrial Relations Counselors Colloquium, September 14–15, 1978, Atlanta, Georgia (New York: Industrial Relations Counselors, 1979), pp. 67–84.

distribution of men and women with the same education and years of experience would reduce the earnings gap by 9 percentage points.[14]

It would appear, then, that perhaps half of the overall 40 percent differential between the earnings of men and women is due to premarket factors. Of the remaining 20 percent—which could be due to current market discrimination—roughly half again (9 percentage points) appears to be the consequence of occupational segregation. The effect of occupational segregation *could* be larger than this, however, because the "occupations" referred to in the study are very general categories, such as professional-technical worker, manager, clerical worker, skilled craft worker, and so forth. Not captured in the analysis, then, are the effects of segregation *within* these broad groupings. For example, an insurance company that was later the object of a sex-discrimination lawsuit had, between 1964 and 1970, hired men and women with college degrees to be "claims adjustors" and "claims representatives." The educational requirements for each job were the same, but only men were hired as "adjustors," and almost all "representatives" were women. Claims adjustors received $2,500 more in yearly salary to begin with, and only adjustors could be promoted to higher-level supervisory positions. Both positions are in the same general occupational class, but both pay and future opportunities were much better for the male workers.[15]

One study of professional-technical employees in a large corporation found that men and women with the same job level and the same characteristics received equal pay. However, in most cases women were assigned to lower job levels than equally qualified men. While one cannot generalize from the experience of a single corporation, the results of *this* study suggest that most of sex discrimination may be due to occupational segregation.[16]

Note, however, that not all occupational segregation is the result of current employer practices that exclude qualified women from higher-paying jobs. Premarket forces, beginning early in childhood, instill beliefs among women and men alike that some occupations are "women's work" and some are "men's work." These beliefs keep women out of many low-paying laborer jobs and exclude them from high-paying jobs as well. It is probably true that these notions will change over time as alternative role models become available, but not *all* of these feelings can be attributed to *current* employer practices.

Theories of Market Discrimination

As argued in the previous section, one cannot rule out the presence of substantial discrimination against women and minorities in the labor market. Before one can design policies to end discrimination, one must understand the *sources* and *mech-*

---

[14]Ronald Oaxaca, "Male-Female Wage Differentials in Urban Labor Markets," *International Economic Review* 14, 3 (October 1973): 693–709.

[15]Barbara Bergmann, "Reducing the Pervasiveness of Discrimination," in *Jobs for Americans,* ed. Eli Ginzburg (Englewood Cliffs, N.J.: Prentice-Hall, Inc., 1976).

[16]Burton G. Malkiel and Judith A. Malkiel, "Male-Female Pay Differentials in Professional Employment," *American Economic Review* 63 (September 1973): 693–705.

anisms causing it. The goal of this section is to lay out and evaluate the different theories of discrimination proposed by economists.

Three general sources of labor market discrimination have been hypothesized, and each source suggests an associated model of how discrimination is implemented and what its consequences are.[17] The first source of discrimination is *personal prejudice,* wherein employers, fellow employees, or customers dislike associating with workers of a given race or sex.[18] The second general source is *statistical prejudgment,* whereby employers project onto *individuals* certain perceived *group* characteristics. Finally, there are models according to which the desire for, and use of, *monopoly power* is the source of discrimination. While all of the models generate useful, suggestive insights, none has been convincingly established as superior.

Personal Prejudice

Employer discrimination. Let us suppose that (white male) *employers* are prejudiced against women or blacks but that (for the sake of simplicity) customers and fellow employees are not prejudiced. This prejudice may take the form of aversion to associating with women or blacks, it may be manifest as a desire to help fellow white males whenever possible, or it may be motivated by status considerations and take the form of occupational segregation. In whatever form, this prejudice is assumed to result in the discriminatory treatment of women or minorities. Further, we assume for the purposes of this model that the women and minorities in question have the same productive characteristics as white males. (This assumption directs our focus to market discrimination by putting aside premarket factors.)

If employers have a decided preference for hiring white males in high-paying jobs despite the availability of equally qualified women or minorities, they will act *as if* the latter were less productive than the former. By virtue of our assumption that the women and minorities involved are in fact equally productive in every way, the devaluing of their productivity by employers is purely subjective and is a manifestation of personal prejudice. The more prejudicial an employer is, the more actual productivity will be discounted.

Let us suppose that *MP* stands for the actual marginal productivity of all workers in a particular labor market and that *d* represents the extent to which this productivity is subjectively devalued for minorities and women. In this case, market equilibrium for white males is reached when their wage (W_M) equals *MP:*

$$MP = W_M. \tag{11.1}$$

---

[17]Two of the three general models were labeled by Kenneth Boulding, "Toward a Theory of Discrimination," in *Equal Opportunity and the AT & T Case,* ed. Phyllis Wallace (Cambridge, Mass.: The MIT Press, 1976).

[18]The models of personal prejudice are based on Gary S. Becker, *The Economics of Discrimination,* 2nd ed. (Chicago: University of Chicago Press, 1971).

For the women and minorities, however, equilibrium is achieved only when their wage (W_F) equals their *subjective* value to firms:

$$MP - d = W_F, \text{ or} \tag{11.2}$$

$$MP = W_F + d. \tag{11.2a}$$

Since the actual marginal productivities are equal by assumption, equations (11.1) and (11.2a) are equal to each other, and one can easily see that W_F must be less than W_M:

$$W_M = W_F + d, \text{ or} \tag{11.3}$$

$$W_F = W_M - d. \tag{11.3a}$$

What this says algebraically has a very simple economic logic: if the actual productivity of women and minorities is devalued by employers, workers in these groups must offer their services at lower wages than white males in order to compete for jobs.

This model of employer discrimination has two major implications—as illustrated by Figure 11.1, which is a graphical representation of equation (11.2a). Figure 11.1 shows that a discriminating employer faced with a wage rate of W_F for women and minorities will hire N_0, for at that point $MP = W_F + d$. *Profit-maximizing* employers, however, will hire N_1; that is, they will hire until $MP = W_F$. The effects on profits can be readily seen in Figure 11.1 if one

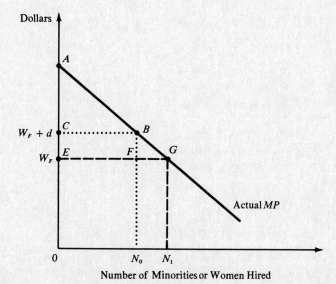

Figure 11.1 Equilibrium Employment of Women and Minorities in Firms that Discriminate

remembers that the area under the *MP* curve represents total product (or total revenues) of the firm, with capital held constant. Subtracting the area representing the wage bill of the discriminating employer *(OEFN₀)* yields profits for these employers equal to the area *AEFB*. Profits for a nondiscriminating employer, however, are *AEG*. These latter employers hire women and minorities to the point where their marginal product equals their wage, while the discriminators end their hiring short of that point. Discriminators thus give up profits in order to indulge their prejudices.

The second implication of our employer-discrimination model concerns the size of the gap between W_M and W_F. The determinants of this gap can best be understood using a graph of the supply of jobs to women or minorities (see Figure 11.2). In a given labor market wherein workers of equal productivity are seeking jobs, the supply of job opportunities for women and minorities will be a function of the gap $(W_M - W_F = d)$ between their wages and those of white males. As shown in Figure 11.2, some employers will hire women or minorities even if their wages equaled $W_M(d = 0)$. These are the nondiscriminating (profit-maximizing) employers, and supply curve $0m_1A$ assumes they account for m_1 jobs in the market. If there are less than m_1 minorities or females seeking employment in that labor market (m' say), they would all be hired by the nondiscriminators, and no discrimination would be evident. W_F would equal W_M, and women and minorities would not have to deal with those who devalue their services.

If the supply of women and minorities were greater than the number that could be absorbed by the nondiscriminating employers (m^*, say), then a wage gap would have to arise for all of them to become employed. Curve $0m_1A$ shows that if the number of women and minorities seeking jobs were to increase from m' to m^*, the required gap would rise from zero to d_2. Thus, the gap depends in part

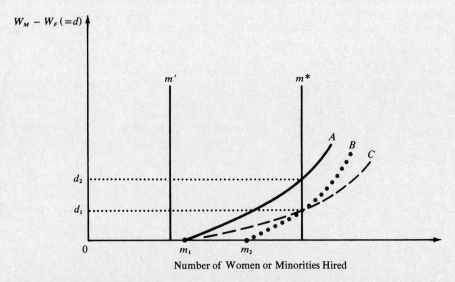

Figure 11.2 The Supply of Jobs to Women and Minorities

on the sheer size of the groups against whom there is personal prejudice. If the number of women or minorities seeking jobs were to rise beyond m^*, the difference between W_M and W_F would become greater than d_2.

The equilibrium gap between W_M and W_F, however, also depends on the distribution and extent of employer prejudice against women or minorities. If the number of nondiscriminatory employers grows (or if the number of jobs offered by such employers were to grow), the supply-of-jobs curve in Figure 11.2 would shift to the right from $0m_1A$ to $0m_2B$ (say). This shift would reduce the observed wage disparity at m^* from d_2 to d_1. The same reduction in market discrimination could also occur if the number of nondiscriminators stayed constant but the *discriminatory preferences* of the others were *reduced*. If this were to happen, discriminatory employers would require less of a wage disparity to hire a given level of women or minorities, and the supply-of-jobs curve would shift to something like $0m_1C$ in Figure 11.2.

The most disturbing implication of the employer-discrimination model is that discriminators seem to be maximizing *utility* (satisfying their prejudices) instead of *profits*. This practice should immediately raise the question of how they survive. Firms in competitive labor markets *must* maximize profits just to make a normal rate of return on invested capital. Those who do not make this return will find they can earn a better return by investing some other way—a way, perhaps, that does not involve hiring workers. Conversely, since profit-maximizing (non-discriminating) firms would normally make more money from a given set of assets than would discriminators, we should observe nondiscriminatory firms buying out others and gradually taking over the market. In short, if competitive forces are at work, employers who discriminate would be punished, and discrimination should gradually disappear.

An implication of the employer-discrimination model, then, is that wage disparities will lessen naturally over time—an implication that appears to be contradicted by the facts. The figures on race and sex wage disparities in Tables 11.2 and 11.3 show a great stability over many years; recent improvements for blacks can be seen, but these improvements are coincident with the adoption of various *governmental* programs aimed at ending poverty and discrimination.

Does this apparent inconsistency with the facts mean that the employer-discrimination model is inappropriate or wrong? Some have suggested that the model really applies only to monopolistic or oligopolistic employers who are shielded from market forces. It is argued that these firms do not have to maximize profits in order to survive, so they are freer to indulge in the "luxury" of discrimination. There is some evidence that blacks are disproportionately employed in industries that are competitive and are not very well represented in large, higher-paying, oligopolistic firms.[19] However, very large firms tend to have higher skill requirements than competitive firms anyway, and that alone could explain the

[19]Becker, *The Economics of Discrimination,* p. 48; Ray Marshall, "The Economics of Racial Discrimination: A Survey," *Journal of Economic Literature* 12 (September 1974): 864; and David P. Taylor, "Discrimination and Occupational Wage Differences in the Market for Unskilled Labor," *Industrial and Labor Relations Review* 21 (April 1968): 375–90.

underrepresentation of blacks in those firms. Further, the sector most insulated from the pressures of costs and competition is the government, and, as Table 11.3 showed for women, wage disparities in this sector are less than in the private sector. Thus, serious questions must be raised about how applicable this model of employer discrimination is in explaining labor-market discrimination.

Customer discrimination. A second personal-prejudice model stresses *customer* prejudice as a source of discrimination. Customers may have preferences to be served by white males in some situations and by minorities or women in others. If their preferences for white males extend to jobs requiring major responsibility —such as physician, stock broker, or airline pilot—and their preferences for women and minorities are confined to less skilled jobs—nurse or flight attendant, say—then occupational segregation that works to the disadvantage of women and minorities will occur. Further, if women or minorities are to find employment in the jobs for which customers prefer white males, they must either receive *lower wages* or be *more qualified* than the average white male. The reason for this is that their value to the firm is in fact lower than that of an *equally qualified* white male because of customers' preferences for white males.

A major implication of the theory of customer discrimination is that women or minorities in jobs that have no customer contact or who work for employers who have no competition should face very little, if any, discrimination. Those with the most customer contact are the most vulnerable to discrimination, as manifested by unequal wages for equally qualified people, occupational segregation, or both. The evidence to support this model is somewhat ambiguous. For example, the overall ratio of black-to-white earnings for full-time male workers in the private sector was 0.67 in 1977. Operatives—most of whom are factory workers with little public contact—fare better than average in the private sector (0.81), while there are so few blacks in sales jobs that comparable black/white ratios are not even published! Self-employed black males earn incomes that are 41 percent of self-employed whites.[20] Table 11.3 tells much the same story for women. Operatives and government workers do better than self-employed or sales workers; however, operatives do slightly worse than other occupations that may have more public contact.

There are obviously serious drawbacks to the above figures as measures of discrimination. Self-employed white males may own retail stores or electronics factories, and self-employed minorities or women may own magazine stands or janitorial services. Women in the sales field may be department-store clerks, while men may be involved with higher-technology sales. Black operatives may be much more heavily unionized than average.[21] It is thus obvious that the gross ratios given above do not take into account human capital or other important differences.

[20]The ratios quoted are for 1977 and are obtained from U.S. Bureau of the Census, *Current Population Reports, Consumer Income: Money Income in 1977 of Families and Persons in the United States,* Series P-60, No. 118 (March 1979), Table 55.

[21]Orley Ashenfelter, "Discrimination and Trade Unions," in *Discrimination in Labor Markets,* eds. Orley Ashenfelter and Albert Rees.

Studies that *do* take into account individual productive characteristics have been done for federal-government and private-sector employees of different races and sexes. These studies find that differences in productive characteristics between white males and other workers do not explain all of the earnings differentials that exist in either sector. However, as one might expect if customer discrimination is present, the "unexplained" differential tends to be smaller in the federal sector (which has no competitors and is not run for profit).[22]

The existence of unexplained race and sex earnings differentials in the federal sector, despite their smaller size than in the private sector, suggests the *possibility* of labor-market discrimination in the federal sector. Interestingly, the racial *composition* of federal employment follows a pattern that is also consistent with the *customer* discrimination model. Agencies that serve heavily minority-oriented constituencies hire greater fractions of minorities than agencies whose constituents are mainly white: employment with the Department of Housing and Urban Development is 27 percent minority, while that with the Department of Agriculture is 10 percent minority.[23] Whether this political version of the customer-discrimination hypothesis will stand up under further testing remains to be seen. While federal administrators may be sensitive to voter prejudices, the issues on which their elected superiors run are so diverse that one may legitimately wonder just how voter prejudices are communicated and enforced. At the moment, though, the existence of customer discrimination in the labor market cannot be ruled out on logical or empirical grounds.

Employee discrimination. A third source of discrimination based on personal prejudice might be found on the supply side of the market, where white male workers may be averse to situations in which minorities or women fill certain jobs they consider inappropriate. For example, they may be averse to taking orders from a woman, sharing responsibility with a minority, or working where women or minorities are not confined to menial or low-status jobs.

If white male workers have these discriminatory preferences, they will tend to quit (or avoid) employers who employ women or minorities on a nondiscriminatory basis. Employers, if they wish to hire or retain white males, will have to pay them more than they would if they confined women and minorities to their "traditional," lower-status jobs. In some cases employers may be able to avoid the higher cost of employing white males by running racially or sexually segregated plants. Segregated plants, however, are not always feasible because of the wide range of occupations required and the fact that workers of different races and sexes are not evenly distributed in each occupation.

It is interesting to note that this model of employee discrimination predicts that white males working in integrated environments will receive higher wages than those with exactly the same productive characteristics who work in segregated environments. If we could observe areas where there were no minority

[22]Smith, *Equal Pay in the Public Sector;* and James E. Long, "Employment Discrimination in the Federal Sector," *Journal of Human Resources* 11, 1 (1976): 86–97.

[23]For an analysis of this subject, see George J. Borjas, "The Politics of Racial Discrimination in the Federal Government," *Journal of Law and Economics* 25 (October 1982): 271–99.

workers, say, we would expect to find that white male wages in these areas would be pretty much the same for people embodying comparable human capital. However, in areas where blacks are found in sufficient numbers that many whites must work in integrated plants, we should observe that the wages received by white males of equal human capital will *vary* according to whether they work in segregated or integrated firms. Thus, the theory suggests that the wages received by white males within any given human-capital category will show *greater similarity* when integrated work forces are rare than when some whites work in integrated environments and some do not. When one looks at U.S. data one does in fact find that, other things equal, white male wages are more similar in states where the minority population is small—and where, presumably, few whites work in integrated plants—than they are where the minority population is large. Moreover, this finding seems to be true of both northern and southern states considered separately.[24]

The interesting thing about the above finding is that neither the employer nor the customer models of discrimination predict that *white male* wages will become *less similar* if discrimination exists. If white males are preferred for particular, higher-paying jobs, their wages will be higher than if discrimination were nonexistent. However, the fact that their wages are *higher* does not imply they are more *dissimilar.* White males who, in the absence of discrimination, would have wages clustering around some lower level instead have wages clustering around some higher level. The point is that their wages continue to cluster. However, the above finding offers only indirect support of the employee discrimination model, and it is also consistent with predictions of the "monopoly power" model outlined below. Hence, convincing evidence for the existence of employee discrimination cannot be claimed.

Statistical Discrimination

Another source of discrimination might be the kind and quality of information used in making hiring decisions.[25] Employers must try to *guess* the potential productivity of applicants, but rarely will they know what actual productivity will be. The only information available to them at the time of hire is information that is thought to be *correlated* with productivity: education, experience, age, test scores, and so forth. These correlates are imperfect predictors of actual productivity, however, and employers realize this. To some extent, then, they supplement

---

[24]Barry R. Chiswick, "Racial Discrimination in the Labor Market: A Test of Alternative Hypotheses," *Journal of Political Economy* 81, 6 (November 1973): 1330–52. It should be noted that the inequality of *minority* earnings does not vary according to their proportion in the population—a finding that seems to rule out the existence of some other, unmeasured force causing greater inequality in high-minority states.

[25]The considerations developed in this section are more formally and completely treated in Dennis J. Aigner and Glen G. Cain, "Statistical Theories of Discrimination in Labor Markets," *Industrial and Labor Relations Review* 30, 2 (January 1977): 175–87. A similar theory is developed in M. A. Spence, "Job Market Signaling," *Quarterly Journal of Economics* 87, 3 (August 1973): 355–74.

information on these correlates with a subjective element in making hiring decisions, and this subjective element could *look* like discrimination even though it may not be rooted in personal prejudice.

Statistical discrimination can be viewed as a part of the *screening problem,* which arises when observable personal characteristics that are correlated with productivity are not perfect predictors. By way of example, suppose there are *in fact* two types of workers who apply for a secretarial job: those who can type 70 words per minute (wpm) over the long haul and those who can type 40 wpm. These actual productivities are unknown to the employer, however. All the employer observes are the results of a 5-minute typing test administered to all applicants. What are the problems created by the use of this test as a screening device?

The problems relate to the fact that some typists who can really type only 40 wpm on the job will be lucky and score higher than 40 on the test. Others who can really type 70 wpm on the job will be unlucky and score less than 70 on the test. The imperfection of the test as a predictor will cause two kinds of errors in hiring decisions: 1. some "good" applicants will be rejected, and 2. some "bad" workers will be hired.

The above screening problem is illustrated in Figure 11.3, which shows the test-score distributions for both groups of workers. Those who can actually type 70 wpm score 70 on average, but half score less. Likewise, half of the other group scores better than 40 on the test. If an applicant scores 55, say, the employer does not know if the applicant is a good (70 wpm) or bad (40 wpm) typist. If those scoring 55 are automatically rejected, the firm will be rejecting some good workers, and if it needs workers badly, this policy will entail costs. Likewise, if it accepts those scoring 55, some bad workers will be hired.

In an effort to avoid the above dilemma, suppose the employer does some research and finds out that applicants from a particular business school are specifically coached to perform well on 5-minute typing tests. Thus, applicants who can actually type X words per minute over a normal day will tend to score *higher* than X wpm on a 5-minute test due to the special coaching (that is, they

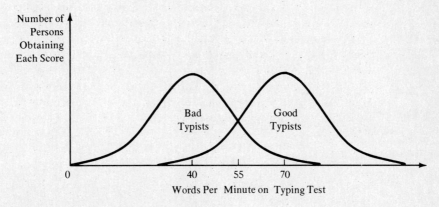

Figure 11.3   The Screening Problem

will appear better than they really are). Recognizing that students from this school are likely to have test scores above their long-run productivity, the firm might decide to reject all applicants from this school who score 55 or below (on the grounds that, for most, the test score overestimates their ability) even though some who score less than 55 really can do better.

The general lesson of this example is that, in effect, firms will use both *individual* data (test scores, educational attainment, experience) and *group* data in making hiring decisions when the former are not perfect predictors of productivity. However, this use of group data can give rise to market discrimination, because people with the same *measured productive characteristics* (test scores, education, etc.) will be treated differently on a systematic basis depending on *group* affiliation.

The relevance of the above discussion to the problem of discrimination against minorities and women is that race and sex may well be the group information used to supplement individual data in making hiring decisions. If the group data bear no relationship, on average, to actual productivity, then we really have a case of discrimination rooted in personal prejudice or monopoly power. However, we have shown that the use of group data to modify individual information may be based on nonmalicious grounds. Might these grounds legitimately apply from an employer's perspective to minorities and women?

Suppose that, *on average,* minorities with high-school educations are discovered to be less productive than white males with high-school educations owing to differences in schooling quality. Or suppose that because of shortened career lives, women with a given educational level are, *on average,* less valuable to firms than men of equal education (refer back to our discussion of women and job training in Chapter 5). Employers might employ this group information to modify individual data when making hiring decisions, just as they did in our hypothetical example of the business school above. The result would be that white males with given measured characteristics would be systematically preferred over women or minorities with the same characteristics—a condition that would be empirically identified as labor-market discrimination.

One unfortunate side effect of using group data to supplement individual data is that, while it could lead employers to the correct hiring decisions on average, it assigns a group characteristic to people who may not be typical of the group. There are women who will have long, uninterrupted careers, just as there undoubtedly would be graduates from the business school mentioned above who do not test well and thus perform more poorly on tests than they could do on the job. There will also be minority high-school graduates of substantial ability who would have gone to college had not family poverty intervened. These atypical group members are stigmatized by the use of group data. They may have actual productivity equal to those who get hired but because of the group association do not get the job.[26]

---

[26]The discussion here has obvious relevance to the "signaling" issue discussed in Chapter 8. Minorities, for example, may be *too poor* to acquire the necessary "signal" in many cases where their ability would indicate they should.

Thus, *statistical discrimination* could lead to a systematic preference for white males over others with the same *measured* characteristics, and it could also create a situation where minorities or women who are the equals of white males in *actual* productivity are paid less due to the above-mentioned group stigma. Both problems are caused by the use of group data in making hiring decisions, but we have emphasized that this use need not be motivated by prejudice. The results, however, have the same appearance and effects as if prejudice were present.

An important implication of this model of statistical discrimination is that the use of group data will become a more costly screening device as members of each group become more dissimilar. For example, as greater proportions of women desire to work in full-time, year-round careers—and do not intend to drop out of the labor force to raise children—employers using sex as a handy index of labor-force attachment will find themselves making costly mistakes. They will reject many female applicants who have a permanent labor-force attachment (in whom an investment in specific training would be very worthwhile), and they may accept male applicants who are less productive. Thus, as *premarket* differences between the races or sexes narrow, the use of race or sex *group* data should lessen, and statistical discrimination should gradually disappear.

Monopoly Power Models

The persistence of large race/sex earnings disparities has led some labor economists to wonder whether the above models are really appropriate. These economists are dissenters from the orthodox view that labor markets are essentially competitive; instead, they advance *monopoly power theories* of discrimination. Inherent in these more radical views of the labor market is the assertion that discrimination exists and persists because it is *profitable* for the discriminators.

While monopoly-power theories of discrimination vary from each other in their emphasis, they tend to share the common feature that race or sex is collectively used to divide the labor force into *noncompeting* groups, creating or perpetuating a kind of worker caste system. This view clearly denies that competitive forces are at work either in the labor market or among owners.[27]

Those who view labor-market discrimination as the result of noncompeting groups assert that a *dual labor market* exists.[28] These economists believe that a *secondary* labor market exists along side a *primary* labor market. Unlike the primary labor market, the secondary market offers low-wage, unstable, dead-end jobs. Workers relegated to these secondary jobs are tagged as unstable, undesirable workers and can never have much hope of acquiring a job in the primary sector. Since a large number of minorities and women are in the secondary

---

[27]For a summary of these views, *see* Glen G. Cain, "The Challenge of Segmented Labor Market Theories to Orthodox Theory: A Survey," *Journal of Economic Literature* 14 (December 1976): 1215–57.

[28]Michael J. Piore, "Jobs and Training: Manpower Policy," in *The State and the Poor,* eds. S. Beer and R. Barringer (Cambridge, Mass.: Winthrop Press, 1970).

market, discrimination against them tends to be perpetuated. Minorities and women, it is argued, are discriminated against because they tend (as a group) to have unstable work histories (which are passed on to their children), but these histories are themselves a result of being unable to break into the primary labor market.

The dual labor market description of discrimination does not really explain what initially caused women and minorities to be confined to secondary jobs. Rather, it offers an explanation of why discrimination *persists*. It calls into question the levels of competition and mobility that exist and suggests that the initial existence of noncompeting race/sex groups will be self-perpetuating. In short, the dual labor market hypothesis is consistent with any of the models of discrimination analyzed above; what it does suggest is that if any of these theories *are* applicable, we cannot count on natural market forces to eliminate the discrimination that results.

Other nonorthodox theories claim that white employers collude and become monopsonists with respect to the hiring of minority labor. Minorities are subjugated and held immobile while monopsonistic wages are forced on them.[29] One of the more cogent and complete *power theories* of discrimination argues that prejudice and the conflicts it creates are inherent in a capitalist society because they serve the interests of owners.[30] Even if the owners of capital did not conspire to *create* prejudice, they nevertheless find that if it continues they can enhance their profits. Workers divided by race or sex are harder to organize, and if they *are* unionized, are less cohesive in their demands. Further, antagonisms on the shop floor deflect attention from grievances related to working conditions. Hence, it is argued that owners of capital gain, while *all* workers—but particularly minorities and women—lose from discrimination.

Two pieces of evidence are cited to support this theory. First, in areas where black/white earnings differentials are largest, the income inequality among *whites* is greatest, other things equal (the greater inequality of white incomes is attributed to *owner/worker* income disparities). This kind of finding was mentioned above when we discussed employee discrimination, and there the greater inequality among whites was attributed to wage differences among white *workers*. Thus, this first piece of evidence seems more or less consistent with a theory of employee discrimination as well as the power model.[31]

---

[29]Lester Thurow, *The Economics of Poverty and Discrimination* (Washington, D.C.: The Brookings Institution, 1969).

[30]Michael Reich, "The Economics of Racism," in *Problems in Political Economy: An Urban Perspective,* ed. David M. Gordon (Lexington, Mass.: D. C. Heath and Company, 1971), pp. 107–13.

[31]A major difference between the Chiswick study of employee discrimination and Reich's test of the power model is that the former related white income inequality to the percentage of nonwhites in the population while the latter related it to the ratio of nonwhite to white earnings. Which is the more appropriate test is a matter beyond the scope of this text; however, we should note that observed earnings ratios can reflect human-capital differences as well as current discrimination. This issue illustrates the importance of *theoretical* analysis in both the execution and interpretation of empirical studies.

The second piece of evidence cited to support this power theory is that where black/white earnings differences are greatest, the percentage of the labor force that is unionized tends to be smallest. The strength of this argument decreases, however, when one realizes that the *causation* might be *reversed*. Rather than more racism causing less unionization, it could be that more unionization causes race discrimination to diminish. Evidence on this point is discussed later in this chapter and in Chapter 17.

Like the orthodox theories of discrimination, then, the monopoly power theories can muster only weak empirical support. They also share with the orthodox theories problems of logical consistency or completeness. If discrimination is created or at least perpetuated by capitalists, how does one account for its existence in precapitalist or socialist societies? It may be true that if all white employers conspire to keep women and minorities in low-wage, low-status jobs, they can all reap monopoly profits. However, if Employers A through Y adhere to the agreement, Employer Z will always have incentives to *break* the agreement! Z can hire women or minorities cheaply because of the agreement among *other* employers not to hire them, and Z can enhance profits by hiring these otherwise equally productive workers to fill jobs that A through Y are staffing with high-priced white males. Since each and every other employer has the same incentives as Z, the conspiracy will tend to break down unless cheaters can be disciplined in some way. The dual and power theorists do not tell us how the conspiracy is maintained and coordinated among the millions of U.S. employers. Thus their theories, like the orthodox ones, are less than completely satisfactory.

Evaluation of Discrimination Theories

Our analysis of the different theories of discrimination suggests that if discrimination persists, it is the result of forces that hinder *competition* or labor-market *adjustments* to competitive forces. Some theories—the "power" models—postulate the existence of noncompetitive or monopoly elements at the outset. The "orthodox" theories do not, but they have trouble explaining why discrimination *would* persist. The market should punish employers who discriminate or who fail to change their screening methods as the average characteristics of minorities or women change. A competitive market should drive employers to adopt *segregated* workplaces if employee discrimination exists; if customer discrimination exists, customers who discriminate will be punished by having to pay the higher prices associated with being served only by white males.

It would thus appear that all models of discrimination agree on one thing: any persistence of labor-market discrimination would be the result of forces or motivations that are blatantly noncompetitive or very slow to adjust to competitive forces. While no one model can be demonstrated superior to the others in explaining the facts, the various theories and the facts they seek to explain do suggest that government intervention could be useful in eliminating the noncompetitive (or sluggish) influences.

State Fair-Employment-Practice Legislation

Since the 1930s, about thirty nonsouthern states have enacted *fair-employment-practice laws* prohibiting discrimination in employment on the basis of race, creed, color, or national origin. (Unlike the federal legislation discussed below, the state laws did not address employment discrimination by sex.) These state laws normally established enforcement commissions and provided for fines and/or imprisonment for violators of the law.

Under state fair-employment-practice legislation, it is normally illegal for an organization to do at least one of the following: (1) refuse employment or discharge employees because of race; (2) discriminate in compensation or other terms of employment by race. Our discussion of theories of market discrimination earlier in the chapter suggests that if a law contains only one of these provisions, it is likely to be ineffective in reducing labor-market discrimination. That analysis predicted that even prejudiced employers would hire minority workers if they could be "compensated" by paying minorities less than their marginal product. Therefore, a state law that contains (1) but does not address discrimination in compensation permits prejudiced employers to comply with the law by hiring minorities but paying them less than other workers of comparable quality. On the other hand, an equal-pay-for-equal-work law that only forbids wage discrimination is likely to reduce the relative employment of minorities (and increase their relative unemployment and/or reduce their rate of labor-force participation) unless it is accompanied by a requirement forbidding employment discrimination, since prejudiced employers will be less willing to hire minorities if they are unable to practice wage discrimination. With sufficient enforcement, laws which forbid both employment and wage discrimination may reduce discrimination in the labor market by raising the cost of such actions to violators.

How effective have state fair-employment-practice laws been in reducing discrimination? Some studies have found that after accounting for differences in human capital between whites and nonwhites, the relative wage and the relative occupational position of nonwhites is higher in states with fair-employment-practice laws than in states which have not passed such laws. However, such findings raise a basic question of causality when they do not consider the way in which legislation is established. Fair-employment-practice laws are passed by the vote of legislators who must represent the preferences of their constituencies in order to remain in office. When we find that the relative earnings of minorities are higher in states with fair-employment-practice laws, does that represent the impact of the law or a tendency of such laws to be passed in states where prejudice is relatively low (reflected in part by the higher relative wages received by minorities)? There is some evidence that it is the latter. A measure of prejudice independent of earnings differentials is clearly needed to sort out the issue of causation; one measure used is electoral support for political candidates who are known to oppose civil rights or equal opportunity legislation. Alternatively, unions have been shown to increase the relative earnings of minorities, and because fair-employment laws tend to be found in states with above-average levels of unionization, studies attempting to find the separate effects of fair-employment-practice laws must filter out the effects of unions on earnings differentials.[32] When these adjustments have been made, state fair-employment-practice legislation appears to have little or no effect on racial earnings differentials.

Federal Programs to End Discrimination

The federal government has enforced two sets of rules in an attempt to eliminate market discrimination. One is a *nondiscrimination* requirement made of almost all employers. The other is a requirement that federal contractors engage in *affirmative action*—that is, actively seek out minorities and women to staff their vacancies.

Equal Pay Act of 1963

Over the years prior to the 1960s, sex discrimination was officially sanctioned by so-called *protective labor laws,* which limited women's total hours of work and prohibited them from working at night, lifting heavy objects, and working during pregnancy. Not all states placed all these restrictions on women, but the effect of these laws was to limit the access of women to many jobs. These laws were overturned by the Equal Pay Act of 1963, which also outlawed separate pay scales for men and women using similar skills and performing work under the same conditions.

The act, however, was seriously deficient as an antidiscrimination tool because it said nothing about equal opportunity in hiring and promotions. This flaw can be easily understood by a quick review of our theories of discrimination. If there is prejudice against women from whatever source, employers will treat female employees as if they were less productive or more costly to hire than equally productive males. The market response is for female wages to fall below male wages, because otherwise women cannot hope to be able to successfully compete with men in obtaining jobs. The Equal Pay Act took a step toward the elimination of wage differentials, but by so doing it tended to suppress a market mechanism that helped women obtain greater access to jobs![33] The act failed to acknowledge that if labor-market discrimination is to be eliminated, legislation must require *both* equal pay *and* equal opportunities in hiring and promotions for people of comparable productivity.

---

[32]*See* William M. Landes, "The Economics of Fair Employment Laws," *Journal of Political Economy* 76 (August 1968): 507–52.

[33]Some critics of the Equal Pay Act of 1963 argued that its motivation was to help men compete with lower-paid women. *See* Nancy Barrett, "Women in the Job Market: Occupations, Earnings, and Career Opportunities," in *The Subtle Revolution,* ed. Ralph E. Smith (Washington, D.C.: The Urban Institute, 1979), p. 55.

Title VII of the Civil Rights Act

Some of the defects in the Equal Pay Act of 1963 were corrected the next year. Title VII of the Civil Rights Act of 1964 made it unlawful for any employer "to refuse to hire or to discharge any individual, or otherwise to discriminate against any individual with respect to his compensation, terms, condition, or privileges of employment, because of such individual's race, color, religion, sex or national origin." Union practices were also addressed by the new legislation. Historically, it had been very difficult for racial minorities to obtain admission into certain craft unions representing workers in the skilled trades—an exclusion which denied minorities access to both the skills-training provided through union apprenticeship programs and the employment opportunities dispensed through union hiring halls. Unions representing workers in large industries were generally more integrated, although in a few unions, the quality of representation in collective bargaining and in the administration of the labor agreement varied by race. Title VII made it unlawful for any labor organization to exclude individuals from membership, to segregate membership, to refuse to refer for employment, or to discriminate in admission to apprenticeship programs on the basis of race, color, religion, sex, or national origin.

This broad statement of a national policy favoring nondiscriminatory employment practices was qualified in certain respects, however. First, Title VII is not retroactive; it was written to apply to acts of discrimination occurring after its effective date of July 1, 1965. Second, the law permits exceptions to its general requirement of nondiscrimination "where religion, sex, or national origin is a bona fide occupational qualification reasonably necessary to the normal operation of a business." In practice this applies to a limited number of situations (for example, certain jobs in religious organizations, nursing homes in which the patients are of predominantly one sex, and so forth). Third, Title VII permits an employer to differentiate wages and other employment conditions "pursuant to a bona fide seniority system . . . provided that such differences are not the result of an intention to discriminate." Finally, no party subject to the statute is required to grant preferential treatment to any group because of existing imbalances in the work force. As will become clear below, the last two qualifications have raised difficult issues for the application of the law.

Title VII applies to all employers in interstate commerce with at least 25 employees and is enforced by the Equal Employment Opportunity Commission (EEOC)—which has the authority to mediate complaints, encourage lawsuits by private parties or the U.S. Attorney-General, or (since 1972) bring suits itself against employers that have violated the law. In order to expand the impact of the law, the courts permitted individual plaintiffs to expand their suits into "class actions" in which the potential discriminatory impact of an organization's employment practices on an entire group of workers is assessed by the courts.

Over the years, the federal courts have fashioned two standards of discrimination that may be applied when discriminatory employment practices are alleged —*disparate treatment* and *disparate impact.* Disparate treatment occurs under Title VII if individuals are treated differently (for example, paid different wages or benefits) because of their race, sex, color, religion, or national origin, and if it can be shown that there was an intent to discriminate. While this is probably the more obvious approach to defining discrimination, it is not the definition that the courts have relied on most frequently. The difficulty raised by this standard is that personnel policies that appear to be neutral in the sense that they ignore race, sex, and so forth, may nevertheless perpetuate the effects of past discrimination. For example, word-of-mouth recruiting (a seemingly neutral policy) in a plant with a largely white work force would be suspect under Title VII even if the selection of new employees from the applicants was done on a nondiscriminatory basis, since the racial composition of the applicants is likely to be influenced by the recruiting method.

The concern with addressing the present effects of past discrimination led to the disparate impact standard. Under this approach it is the result, not the motivation, that matters. Personnel policies that appear to be neutral but which lead to different impacts by race, sex, and so forth, are prohibited under Title VII unless they can be related to job performance.[34] Employers, for example, may use tests and educational standards to screen applicants, but these tests must be validated against job performance. In the words of the Supreme Court, "Tests must measure the person for the job; not the person in the abstract." Job application forms may ask about *convictions* but not *arrests* (arrest rates among minorities tend to be higher, but the courts reason that it is conviction that is important to the employer). Marital status cannot be used as a screening device unless it is applied uniformly to both sexes and is clearly a job-related requirement. In interpreting Title VII, the federal courts have generally taken the position that neutral (for example, colorblind or sexblind) personnel practices that carry forward the effects of past discrimination constitute present discrimination. As a result, plaintiffs, employers, and the courts have become interested in how closely the race or sex composition of individuals selected for employment, promotion, training, or termination accords with the race or sex composition of the pool of workers available for selection.

The adoption of the disparate impact standard by the courts as a standard of discrimination has mounted a significant challenge to employer personnel-screening devices. As noted in Chapter 5, employers have an incentive to rely on screening devices, which sort job applicants on the basis of the "average" characteristics of a group rather than according to individual merit, when it is extremely costly to ascertain the qualifications of individual applicants. While the use of screening devices often results in lower costs of personnel administration, it also gives rise to the statistical discrimination discussed earlier in this chapter. In taking the position that workers must be judged on the basis of their individual abilities rather than average group characteristics, the courts have launched a strong assault against mechanisms of statistical discrimination which has as one consequence higher costs of human resource management.

In certain instances, the application of the disparate impact standard and

---

[34]*Willie S. Griggs* v. *Duke Power Company* 401 US 424 (1971).

other efforts to combat labor market discrimination have been limited by some of the express qualifications written into Title VII. In recent years three particularly difficult issues have arisen in the application of the law: the treatment of seniority arrangements perpetuating the effects of past discrimination, comparable worth, and preferential treatment of minorities and women (sometimes referred to as reverse discrimination). The first two issues are discussed below; the last in the following section.

Seniority. Most unionized firms and many nonunion firms use seniority as a consideration in allocating promotion opportunities. Moreover, employees are frequently laid off in order of reverse seniority—the least senior first—in a recession. It was partially in recognition of the historically important role of seniority in American personnel arrangements that Congress appeared to exempt seniority systems from challenge under Title VII. Yet seniority systems have the strong potential for perpetuating the effects of past discrimination. We have seen how occupational segregation—the tendency of women or minorities to be restricted to relatively low-wage jobs despite qualifications for higher positions—has been one historical mechanism of discrimination in the labor market.

In many instances, particularly in the South, job segregation was accompanied by departmental seniority arrangements. That is, seniority was computed as the time employed in a department, not as time employed in the plant or company. When companies sought to break down historical patterns of job segregation in order to comply with Title VII, two types of adjustments occurred: (1) women and minorities were moved within a company from low-wage jobs to higher-wage jobs in other departments; (2) women and minorities were hired by companies into some jobs for the first time. Under either mechanism, women and minorities ended up with relatively low seniority under departmental seniority systems.

Many of these adjustments occurred during the late 1960s when the general demand for labor was high. With the less favorable economic circumstances of the 1970s, however, firms began to lay off workers, and under departmental seniority arrangements, a disproportionate number of the layoffs were minorities and women. In many of these cases, individuals with very little departmental seniority had more *plant* seniority than workers who retained their jobs in the high-wage departments and might have been able to retain their jobs if they had the seniority that they had accrued in their former departments. Departmental seniority arrangements resulted in a disparate impact on women and minorities and were operating to perpetuate the effects of past discrimination. The resulting Title VII litigation presented the courts with a quandry: Under the disparate impact standard, the seniority systems were discriminatory, but the language of Title VII explicitly permitted "bona fide seniority systems." The lower courts tended to resolve the quandry by taking the position that a seniority system was not "bona fide" if it discriminated, and that under the prevailing definition of discrimination, only plant-wide seniority systems were "bona fide." When the Supreme Court considered the issue, however, it reversed the appellate courts and held that the language in Title VII permitted even departmental seniority systems that perpetuated the effects of discrimination.[35]

Minorities and women who were hired for the first time following passage of Title VII were susceptible to layoff under either plant or departmental seniority. In some cases, these were individuals who had been victims of hiring discrimination prior to the passage of the law or who did not apply for employment because the company had a reputation for discriminating. In litigation arising out of these cases, plaintiffs often argued that the appropriate remedy was an award of seniority, retroactive to the date when the individual would have been hired if the company had not practiced discrimination. (This is sometimes referred to as "fictional seniority.") On this issue, the Supreme Court has ruled that fictional seniority is an appropriate remedy for individuals who can demonstrate that they actually applied for a job but were rejected for discriminatory reasons.[36] However, no court has argued that it is appropriate to dismiss current employees as part of the remedy for past discrimination.

Comparable worth. We have noted earlier in the chapter how women are disproportionately employed in certain jobs and occupations in which wages are relatively low. Some have argued that the wages in these jobs are low because they are filled to a large extent by women who are the victims of market discrimination. To the extent that the labor market is biased against women, it is argued further that discrimination is perpetuated by using the market as a basis for paying, say, clerical workers (a job historically filled largely by women) less than, say, maintenance workers (a job historically filled largely by men). The remedy proposed is to pay women or minorities their "comparable worth"—that is, intrinsic value of their job. However, the intrinsic value of the job would be established by comparison of its importance to some other (presumably more highly paid) job predominantly held by males, rather than by reference to market wages.

The comparable-worth idea has proved difficult to define precisely. How much of the wage difference between two jobs can be attributed to the fact that one is largely staffed by women and the other by men? The evidence reviewed earlier in this chapter indicates that a significant portion of the wage difference between men and women reflects differences in human capital investments and other qualifications. The amount of the difference that might be attributed to discrimination is likely to vary from job comparison to job comparison. Another important influence on wage differences between jobs was discussed in Chapter 7—nonpecuniary conditions of work. To the extent that working conditions vary substantially between jobs held predominantly by men or women, one would expect the wages to vary as well. These factors illustrate some of the difficulties that would be encountered in assuming that all of the wage differential between "male" jobs and "female" jobs was the result of market discrimination. A further

---

[35]*International Brotherhood of Teamsters* v. *United States* 431 U.S. 324, 14 FEP 1514 (1977).

[36]*Franks* v. *Bowman Transportation* 424 U.S. 747, 12 FEP Cases 549 (1976).

difficulty in trying to construct an operational approach to the proposed comparable-worth remedy is evaluating the intrinsic worth of different jobs. Existing job evaluation procedures are not free of bias in the weights that they assign to different job characteristics.

In addition to the operational difficulties with the comparable-worth concept, there is a more fundamental policy question of whether it is likely to be more effective to use the law to take direct action against discriminatory job segregation rather than to develop a compensation scheme that may leave the segregation unchanged. As of the early 1980s, the federal courts have been reluctant to assess the value of "male" and "female" jobs and adopt the remedy proposed under the comparable-worth idea.

The Federal Contract-Compliance Program

In 1965 the Office of Federal Contract-Compliance Programs (OFCCP) was established to monitor the hiring and promotion practices of federal contractors (firms supplying goods or services to the federal government). OFCCP requires contractors above a certain size to analyze the extent of their under-utilization of women and minorities and to propose a plan to remedy any such under-utilization. Such a plan is called an *affirmative-action plan.* Contractors submitting unacceptable plans or failing to meet their goals are threatened with cancellation of their contracts and eligibility for future contracts, although these drastic steps are rarely taken.

Affirmative-action planning is intended to commit firms to a schedule for rapidly overcoming unequal career opportunities afforded women and minorities. Such planning affects both *hiring* and *promotion* practices, but it also raises numerous philosophical and practical questions that tend to make the planning process highly controversial.

Suppose an insurance company is attempting to construct an affirmative-action plan with regard to secretaries. Its first step in setting hiring goals is to decide on what number of minorities are "available" and what fraction they constitute of all available workers. If blacks, say, constitute 9 percent of the labor supply available to the firm, then it might seem to be a simple matter of setting a goal of 9 percent. However, the planner must resolve some serious questions.

First, should the pool of black secretaries be estimated based on the firm's *actual applicant* pool? The answer is probably no, since any discriminatory practices in the past will discourage black applicants currently. Further, affirmative-action planning is intended to force companies to *change* their hiring practices. On the other hand, as was pointed out in Chapter 7, a firm's location within a city can attract more or less black applicants, depending on how far away from the firm blacks live and what the wages offered are. Thus, to some extent the potential pool of *interested* applicants is a legitimate consideration.

Should the potential pool be estimated from the fraction of all *trained secretaries* in the area who are black? If we are interested in eradicating *market* discrimination, this may be the logical measure, since it would force firms to hire black secretaries in the same proportion as they are found in the labor market.

However, years of discrimination may have induced blacks to avoid training for this occupation, with the result that blacks may be substantially underrepresented in the secretarial labor market.

Should firms then be compelled to hire black secretaries in proportion to their numbers in the adult *population* of the city at large? This goal implicitly sets out to eliminate all discrimination, both market and premarket, but if blacks are underrepresented in the occupation, the attainment of this goal is impractical in the short run. Firms attempting to hire more black secretaries than are available would have two choices. They could hire black high-school graduates and train them in secretarial skills. Remember, however, that such training is *general* in nature, so that the firms would not offer it unless the workers involved paid for it in some way. Without training as an option, firms would simply try to bid against each other for the services of existing black secretaries, which would drive up their wage. The higher wage rates would induce more blacks to seek secretarial training, and their underrepresentation in the occupation would disappear in the long run.

While population-based goals would appear to fight both kinds of discrimination, they might in fact fight neither. It stands to reason that if hiring goals are set beyond the immediate reach of firms, each will individually fail to meet them. Can the government reasonably punish firms for failing to hire beyond the numbers currently available? If it cannot, then failure to meet goals will not result in punishment—which seems to remove the incentive for firms to take energetic steps to integrate their work force.

A final issue in hiring has to do with how the goals are applied. If black secretaries, to continue our example, are 9 percent of the available pool, does that mean that 9 percent of all *newly hired* secretaries should be black? This goal might seem reasonable from a firm's point of view, but if labor turnover is low it would take a very long time for the 9 percent of *new hires* to accumulate to the point where blacks were 9 percent of the firm's total secretarial work force. Since the Civil Rights Act of 1964 prohibits workers of one race from being fired to make room for those of another, getting rid of employment imbalances (by race or sex) must occur through new hiring. However, only if aggrieved groups are *favored* in hiring can the effects of past discrimination be eradicated quickly.

EXAMPLE 11.1

How Fast Can Discrimination Be Eradicated?

To illustrate the possible rate of progress in minority employment within a firm, let us take a numerical example. Suppose there is a job group that contains 1600 employees, 100 (6.25 percent) of whom are minorities. Suppose, further, that this is an entry-level job group (so that all replacements come from new hires) and that the yearly turnover rate is 20 percent. Finally, assume that blacks represent 12 percent of the firm's available labor pool for this job.

The firm in question must hire 320 new workers for this job group each year. If 12 percent (about 38) of those hired each year are black, how long will it take before 12 percent (192) of the 1600-person work group is black? Another, perhaps more significant, question is how fast will the racial composition of the work group change? These questions have no obvious answers, because if blacks and whites have the same turnover rate (of 20 percent), the organization is both losing and hiring blacks each year.

One way to answer the above questions is to simulate employee turnover each year. The accompanying table shows that in the first year 20 blacks quit and 38 (12 percent of the 320 new hires) are hired. The net gain in blacks raises their level of employment in the group to 118 and their percentage of employment to 7.37 (from 6.25). In year 2, 38 blacks are again hired and about 24 quit—representing a net gain of 14—and by the end of the year the work group is 8.25 percent black. As this process continues, there are net additions to the black component of the work force each year, but these additions get smaller and smaller.

Of special interest in this example is that it takes about 10 years of *nondiscriminatory hiring* for the percentage of blacks in the work group to get close to the goal of 12 percent. (The rate of progress would be approximately cut in half if the turnover rate were 10 percent instead of 20 percent.) Thus, if the proportion of blacks among new hires is equal to their proportions in the available labor pool, and if their turnover rates are no lower than those of whites, the long-run goal of employment equality will take many years to achieve once nondiscriminatory hiring is begun. This mathematical fact illustrates why those charged with administering antidiscrimination programs are simultaneously besieged by shouts of frustration and calls for patience.

Change in the Racial Composition of a 1600-Person Job Group (20% Yearly Turnover Rate)

	Year						
	0	*1*	*2*	*3*	*4*	*5*	*10*
Number of Blacks							
Loss		20	24	26	29	31	36
New Hires		38	38	38	38	38	38
Net Gain		18	14	12	11	7	2
Cumulative Level	100	118	132	144	155	162	181
Percent Black	6.25	7.37	8.25	9.00	9.69	10.12	11.31

Favoritism in hiring not only raises the issue of *reverse discrimination*—wherein whites or males can assert they are being discriminated against because of race or sex—it also raises again the issue of how firms, as a whole, can hire women or blacks in proportions greater than their current availability. As of 1983, the courts have yet to resolve the considerable tension between Title VII's standard of nondiscrimination, which protects all groups from disparate treatment, and the OFCCP's standard of affirmative action. (See Example 11.2.)

It is testimony to these difficult questions raised about affirmative-action planning that (as of 1983) the government's requirements for calculating "availability" are rather vague. The OFCCP has proposed that, for purposes of affirmative-action planning, federal contractors compute availability of minorities and women using either of two methods: the "civilian labor force" method or the "four-factor" method.[37] Under the former alternative, availability is estimated from the percentages of women and minorities in the *metropolitan area's* civilian labor force. The "four-factor" alternative would require the contractor to devise estimates by taking into account the following considerations:

1. The percentage of minorities and women in the civilian labor force in the *immediate labor area* (defined as the geographic area for which employees and applicants may reasonably commute to the establishment);
2. The percentage of minorities and women with requisite skills in the *immediate labor area;*
3. The percentage of minorities and women with requisite skills in the *relevant recruitment area* (defined as the geographic area from which the contractor may reasonably recruit its employees, including areas not contiguous to the immediate labor area);
4. The percentage of minorities and women among those promotable or transferable within the contractor's organization.

Contractors can assign weights of their own choosing (including weights of zero) to each of the four factors, as long as the weights are justified in writing and sum to 100 percent.

A brief analysis of the above requirements will show that they raise several questions. First, the civilian labor force method differs from factor 1 of the "four-factor" method in the definition of geographic area over which to calculate populations. Which is the less arbitrary definition for availability purposes: the metropolitan area or the "immediate labor area" (which may be larger or smaller than metropolitan area)? Also, given the various costs of commuting discussed at the end of Chapter 7, should everyone in the defined area be assumed equally "available" for work at a given plant?

Second, factors 1 and 2 under the "four-factor" alternative differ in the

---

[37]Bureau of National Affairs, Labor Relations Reporter, *Fair Employment Practices Manual* 401:5005. OFCCP's proposal is a revision of its 1974 guidelines for federal contractors, under which eight factors were considered. As of October 1983, the revised guidelines had not yet been implemented.

EXAMPLE 11.2

Is Affirmative Action Consistent with Equal Employment Opportunity?

One of the more difficult problems facing the implementation of public policy against discrimination is the difficulty of overcoming the present effects of past discrimination. One purpose in efforts to get employers to take "affirmative action" to increase the representation of minorities and women at all levels of the occupational structure is to overcome the residual effects of past discrimination. However, affirmative-action efforts raise the potential for conflict with a law such as Title VII of the Civil Rights Act that sets a general nondiscrimination standard. By the mid-1970s, the Supreme Court held that whites, males, and other "majority" groups are protected from race or sex discrimination by Title VII.* But does this mean that affirmative-action plans are generally prohibited under Title VII? The Supreme Court addressed this question in the following case.

The Kaiser Aluminum and Chemical Corporation operated a plant in Gramercy, Louisiana, an area in which, in the early 1970s, about 39 percent of the labor force was black. Prior to 1974, Kaiser hired only workers with previous craft experience to fill the craft positions in the plant. This employment practice virtually restricted the craft positions to white workers, since blacks had historically been excluded from the craft unions, which were sources of training through apprenticeship programs. As a result, only 5 out of 273 skilled craft employees (less than 2 percent) at the Gramercy plant were black.

In 1974, Kaiser signed a collective-bargaining agreement with the United Steelworkers of America that included an affirmative-action plan designed to eliminate these racial imbalances. As a part of the plan, Kaiser agreed to train its production workers to fill craft positions (rather than hiring from the outside). Selection for the training program was on the basis of seniority, subject to the provision that at least half of the trainees would be black until the percentage of black craft workers in the plant was similar to the percentage in the outside labor force. (See the previous example for an indication of how long this process might take.) In 1974, 7 black and 6 white production workers at Kaiser were selected for the training program, but some of the white workers whose applications for the program were rejected had more seniority than some of the blacks who were selected. One of the white workers, Brian Weber, filed a legal action alleging that the affirmative-action plan violated Title VII of the Civil Rights Act because the plan discriminated against (white) workers on the basis of race. The lower courts agreed with Weber, and the company and the union appealed the case to the U.S. Supreme Court.

In a controversial decision, the Supreme Court held that Title VII does not forbid "private employers and unions from voluntarily agreeing upon bona fide affirmative-action plans that accord racial preferences in the manner and for the purpose" provided in the Kaiser plan. Yet the court did not rule out the possibility that some affirmative-action plans might favor minorities to an extent that violated Title VII and refused to "define a line of demarcation between permissible and impermissible affirmative-action plans." It found instead that while Title VII does not require *preferential treatment,* it permits such treatment when arrived at voluntarily. Moreover, in the Kaiser case, the purpose of the affirmative-action plan was to break down historical patterns of occupational segregation by race—clearly an objective of Title VII—and the plan did not "trammel the interests of white employees," since none were discharged and some were admitted to the training program. While it is true, as the Court noted, that a broad prohibition on such plans would bring about a result at variance with the purpose of Title VII, the extent to which affirmative-action plans can grant preferential treatment without violating Title VII was far from certain in the early 1980s.

*McDonald v. *Santa Fe Trail Transportation Co.,* 427 US 273 (1976).

Source: *United Steelworkers* v. *Weber,* 443 US 193 (1979).

attention given to *existing* skills—raising the issue discussed above concerning the goals of the contract-compliance program. Is the aim of the program to eliminate only current *market* discrimination against those already in a given skill group, or should it directly address the issue of *premarket* differences in skill acquisition among race or sex groups?

Third, factor 3 is intended to apply to firms hiring in occupations that have regional or national labor markets. However, if contractors are required to adopt, as a matter of course, nontraditional hiring practices that are likely to yield more female or minority applicants, is it unreasonable to expect them to recruit regionally or even nationally for workers they normally recruit locally?

Finally, several questions can be raised about factor 4. If few minorities or women are at the office-manager rank in an organization, is the firm obliged to offer special managerial-training courses for them? Should such training be equally available to interested white males? What if the interest in managerial positions varies by race or sex? Are companies supposed to promote on a nondiscriminatory basis, with the result that imbalances in its *higher*-level jobs will remain for years into the future? Instead must employers hurry women and blacks along the promotional ladder faster than normal so that these higher-level imbalances will go away more quickly? These are the dilemmas inherent in the government's contract-compliance program.

Effectiveness of Federal Antidiscrimination Programs

A question of obvious interest is just how effective the two federal antidiscrimination programs have been in increasing the relative earnings of minorities and women. The question is not easy to answer because we must make some guess as to what earnings differentials *would have been* in the absence of these programs.

As we have seen, the ratio of black to white incomes has risen since 1960 (see Table 11.2), most especially in the mid-1970s. Has this rise in the ratio been a result of government efforts, or have other forces been working to accomplish this same result? Three other forces are commonly cited. First, an improvement in the educational *attainment* of black workers relative to whites during this period is thought to have played an important role in raising the ratio of black to white income.[38] Second, the evidence that the *quality* of schooling received by blacks improved from 1960 to 1970 more than it did for whites lends further impetus to the increase in relative earnings.[39] Finally, blacks have historically experienced relative gains in periods of low unemployment and suffered disproportionately in periods of economic distress. The late 1960s was a period of very full employment, which could have helped increase the black/white earnings ratio from 1960 to 1970. However, general business conditions in the 1970s were not as good as in the late 1960s, so the continued improvement in that decade is unlikely to be solely the result of overall business conditions.

Two types of studies have attempted to distinguish the effects of the government programs from the other factors that affect relative earnings: (1) time-series studies and (2) the analysis of federal contractors.

Time-series studies. There seems to have been a significant upturn in the black/white earnings ratio after the EEOC was created in 1964—an upturn that is independent of both the effects of *educational* gains by blacks and changes in the *unemployment rate.*[40] However, it also appears to be true that the labor-force participation rate of blacks fell relative to whites after 1964—a year in which many income-maintenance programs began to become more generous.[41] If, as seems likely, the blacks with the lowest wages were the ones who left the labor market, their exit would increase the average wage paid to blacks and give the *appearance* of improvement. Some—probably less than half—of the post-1964 improvement is due to this latter factor.[42] Thus, there seems to be at least *some*

---

[38]Orley Ashenfelter, "Changes in Labor Market Discrimination Over Time," *Journal of Human Resources* 5, 4 (Fall 1970): 403–30; Richard Freeman, "Changes in the Labor Market for Black Americans, 1948–72," *Brookings Papers on Economic Activity,* No. 1 (1973), pp. 67–120; Barry R. Chiswick and June A. O'Neill, eds., *Human Resources and Income Distribution: Issues and Policies* (New York: W. W. Norton, 1977), pp. 20–21.

[39]Finis Welch, "Black-White Differences in Returns to Schooling," *American Economic Review* 63, 5 (December 1973): 893–907.

[40]*See* Freeman, "Changes in the Labor Market for Black Americans," and (a study which updates Freeman) Richard Butler and James Heckman, "The Government's Impact on the Labor Market Status of Black Americans: A Critical Review," *Equal Rights and Industrial Relations* (Madison, Wis.: Industrial Relations Research Association, 1977), pp. 235–80.

[41]Butler and Heckman, "The Government's Impact on the Labor Market Status of Black Americans."

[42]Charles Brown, "Black/White Earnings Ratios Since the Civil Rights Act of 1964: The Importance of Labor-Market Drop-Outs" (Cambridge, Mass.: National Bureau of Economic Research, Working Paper No. 617, 1981), forthcoming in the *Quarterly Journal of Economics.*

evidence that the post-1964 government efforts to lessen discrimination have helped blacks.

Analysis of federal contractors. If the contract-compliance program administered by OFCCP is effective, we should observe that the economic status of blacks improves faster among federal contractors than noncontractors. Several studies have tested this hypothesis, and some have even distinguished whether or not the contractors involved had been subjected to a compliance review by the government (the government does not have the resources to inspect the affirmative-action plans of *all* its contractors). The results suggest that blacks have made faster gains in contractor firms, although the gains are relatively small.[43]

One problem in assessing the *overall* effects of OFCCP, however, is that because the contract-compliance program relates only to *some* employers (contractors), the gains in black employment among these firms may come at the expense of losses among noncontractors. Eligible blacks may just be bid away from noncontractors—although it should be pointed out that anyone successfully bid away from a former employer must have experienced an expected gain in utility. Perhaps more serious is the problem that becoming or remaining a federal contractor is a voluntary decision. Firms that perceive the costs of affirmative action to be high may simply choose not to be contractors. The contract-compliance program may end up concentrating its efforts toward the firms within which discrimination is a relatively small problem.

A final reason to temper optimism about the government's efforts to end discrimination is that it appears that the gains of blacks among contractors have come at least partially at the expense of white women. The growth of white female employment relative to total employment has been slower among federal contractors than among noncontractors, both in the early 1970s (before women were a focus of the contract-compliance program) and later.[44] The reasons for this finding have not yet been convincingly explained.

In summary, it appears that some of the gains registered by blacks since 1964 may be due to efforts by the EEOC and OFCCP, but the effects of these programs on women and other minorities have not been extensively studied. What evidence there is concerning the effects of the contract-compliance program on targeted groups other than blacks does not generate optimism about what future studies may find.

---

[43]For a summary of the four studies done in the early 1970s, *see* Butler and Heckman, "The Government's Impact on the Labor Market Status of Black Americans." For generally comparable results in a study of the late 1970s, *see* Jonathon S. Leonard, "Employment and Occupational Advance Under Affirmative Action," (mimeo, School of Business Administration, University of California at Berkeley, January 1983).

[44]Morris Goldstein and Robert S. Smith, "The Estimated Impact of the Antidiscrimination Program Aimed at Federal Contractors," *Industrial and Labor Relations Review* 29, 4 (July 1976): 523–43; and Leonard, "Employment and Occupational Advance Under Affirmative Action."

EXAMPLE 11.3

Age and the End of Discrimination

Our discussions of investments in human capital, presented in Chapters 5, 8, and 9, suggest that if discrimination diminishes over time, it will diminish first with young adults. Job training—whether it is specific or general, whether it is on-the-job or given formally—takes place most often in one's young-adult years, so that it is this group that will be favored by any expansion of occupational opportunities. Young adults are also the group most likely to adjust to new opportunities by paying for their own education or training. Thus, human-capital theory suggests that the eradication of discrimination's effects may be a long process that will tend to favor each successive generation of new workers over their older counterparts.

Tests of the notion that young adults are helped the most by antidiscrimination programs must take into account the fact that the age/earnings profiles of women and minorities tend to be flatter than those for white males—reflecting the smaller amounts of on-the-job training offered (or induced among) these groups. Thus, the ratio of earnings among these groups to similar-aged white males tends to fall as age increases. The fact that the black/white earnings ratios in both columns of the table fall with experience reflects the more steeply sloped age/earnings profile for white male high-school graduates—not the effects of antidiscrimination efforts.

The pattern of reductions in earnings disparities can best be seen by comparing *changes* in the earnings ratios between 1960 and 1970 in the table. These comparisons can be made in two ways. First, let us follow the same groups of workers over time to see how their earnings ratios change. For example, males with 1–5 years of experience had a black/white earnings ratio of 0.714 in 1960. In 1970, this same group—then having 11–15 years of experience—had an earnings ratio of 0.749. Following the arrows in the table we can see that each age group of black males experienced improvement relative to white males as they aged over the decade of the 1960s. Although those with 1–10 years of experience in 1960 gained to a greater extent than those with 11–20 years, those with 21–30 years of experience in 1960 gained to an even greater degree. Looked at this way, the young adults do not appear to have been the biggest group of gainers among black male high-school graduates.

Male Black/White Earnings Ratios for High-School Graduates of Various Experience, 1960 and 1970

Years of Experience	Black/White Ratio of Average Weekly Earnings	
	1960	*1970*
1–5	0.714	0.806
6–10	0.714	0.791
11–15 }		0.749
16–20 }	0.685	0.750
21–30	0.648	0.698
31–40	—	0.690

SOURCE: James P. Smith and Finis R. Welch, "Black-White Male Wage Ratios: 1960–70," *American Economic Review* 67 (June 1977): 323–38 (Table 1).

There is a second way of looking at the changes from 1960 to 1970, however. Instead of following the same group of workers over time, we could look to see how groups with the same experience in the two years fared. Beginning workers, for example, had an earnings ratio of 0.714 in 1960, but 0.806 in 1970. Those with 6–10 years of experience had a ratio of 0.714 in 1960, while the group 10 years behind them (with 6–10 years of experience in 1970) had a ratio of 0.791. This method suggests that the relative earnings position of the youngest blacks did improve the most.

What we can conclude from our two ways of comparing 1960 and 1970 is that while each group of black males improved in its own economic status from 1960 to 1970, the improvements were even larger for the groups 10 years their junior. To see this, look at those with 1–5 years of experience in 1960. The 1960 ratio for this group was 0.714, and in 1970 it had risen to 0.749 for the same group. However, the ratio for new workers (1–5 years of experience) in 1970 was an even higher 0.806. For those with 21–30 years of experience in 1960, the earnings ratio rose from 0.648 to 0.690; for those 10 years their junior (having 21–30 years of experience in 1970), however, the 1970 earnings ratio was 0.698.

Thus, it appears that while each age group of black males experienced relative improvement in their earnings in the 1960s, the gains made by the groups that *followed* them were larger. A sobering aspect of the way in which these changes are taking place is that overall wage equality between blacks and whites will occur some 40 years after wage parity for *new* workers is attained. (It requires 40 years to "flush" the system of discrimination's victims if discrimination is first ended among younger workers.)

REVIEW QUESTIONS

1. Assume that it is a fact that women live longer than men, on the average. Suppose an employer hires men and women, pays them the same wage for the same job, and contributes an equal amount per person toward a pension. However, the promised monthly pension after retirement is smaller for women than men (because the pension funds for them have to last longer). According to the *Manhart* decision by the Supreme Court, the above employer would be guilty of discrimination because of the unequal monthly pension benefits after retirement.
   a. Comment on the Court's implicit definition of discrimination. Is it consistent with the definition normally used by economists? Why or why not?
   b. Analyze the economic effects of this decision on men and women.
2. Assume there is a central-city school district where the student population is predominantly black. Surrounding the central city are separate, predominantly white suburban school districts. Together, the central-city and suburban school districts can be thought of as a local labor market for teachers. Other things being equal, black teachers in this labor market are equally willing to work in central-city and suburban schools, but all white teachers prefer suburban schools and are reluctant to accept jobs in the central city. There are too few black teachers to completely staff central-city schools, and teachers generally have choices in the jobs they can accept.

   If federal law requires equal salaries for teachers of all races *within* a given school district—but allows salaries to vary across school districts—will black teachers earn more, less, or the same salary as they would if white teachers were not prejudiced against black students? (Note: the prejudice of white teachers extends only to students, not to black teachers as coworkers. Note also: the chain of reasoning required in this answer should be made explicit in your answer.)
3. Suppose government antidiscrimination laws require employers to disregard marital status and sex in screening and hiring workers.
   a. Disregarding the employers who are engaged in discrimination, which employers will be most affected by this ruling?
   b. What alternatives do these employers have in coping with the problems created by this decision?
   c. What are the likely consequences of each alternative on employment levels and job stability among these employers?
4. Suppose the government has two methods of awarding contracts to firms. One is competitive, with the award going to the lowest bidder (who cannot then charge more than his bid). The other is noncompetitive, with the award going to a selected contractor who is reimbursed for actual costs incurred plus a certain percentage for profits. Suppose, too, that government contractors must hire a certain quota of minorities, many of whom require general training to be fully productive. Suppose also that federal legislation prevents the employer from shifting the costs of this general training to the minority employees. If you were an already-trained minority worker, which method of contract award would you prefer? Why?

SELECTED READINGS

Dennis J. Aigner and Glen G. Cain, "Statistical Theories of Discrimination in Labor Markets." *Industrial and Labor Relations Review* 30 (January 1977): 175–87.

Kenneth J. Arrow, "The Theory of Discrimination." In *Discrimination in Labor Markets,* edited by Orley Ashenfelter and Albert Rees, (Princeton, N.J.: Princeton University Press, 1973).

Gary Becker, *The Economics of Discrimination,* 2nd ed. (Chicago: University of Chicago Press, 1971).

Richard Butler and James Heckman, "The Government's Impact on the Labor Market Status of Black Americans: A Critical Review." *Equal Rights and Industrial Relations* (Madison, Wis.: Industrial Relations Research Association, 1977), pp. 235–80.

Glen G. Cain, "The Challenge of Segmented Labor Market Theories to Orthodox Theory: A Survey." *Journal of Economic Literature* 14 (December 1976): 1215–57.

Barry R. Chiswick and June A. O'Neill, eds., *Human Resources and Income Distribution: Issues and Policies* (New York: W. W. Norton, 1977).

Richard Freeman, "Changes in the Labor Market for Black Americans, 1948–72." *Brookings Papers on Economic Activity,* No. 1 (1973), pp. 67–120.

Victor Fuchs, "Differences in Hourly Earnings Between Men and Women." *Monthly Labor Review* (May 1971): 9–15.

Ray Marshall "The Economics of Racial Discrimination: A Survey." *Journal of Economic Literature* 12 (September 1974): 849–71.

Ronald Oaxaca, "Male-Female Wage Differentials in Urban Labor Markets." *International Economic Review* 14 (October 1973): 693–709.

Michael Reich, "The Economics of Racism." In *Problems in Political Economy: An Urban Perspective,* edited by David M. Gordon (Lexington, Mass.: D. C. Heath and Company, 1971), pp. 107–13.

James P. Smith and Finis R. Welch, "Black-White Male Wage Ratios: 1960–1970." *American Economic Review* 67 (June 1977): 323–38.

Sharon P. Smith, *Equal Pay in the Public Sector: Fact or Fantasy* (Princeton, N.J.: Industrial Relations Section, Princeton University, 1977).

Chapter **12**

THE DEVELOPMENT OF UNIONS AND COLLECTIVE BARGAINING

Our analysis of the workings of labor markets has, for the most part, omitted any mention of the role of labor unions and collective bargaining. In doing so, the analysis has stressed labor-market processes through which workers improve their work situations through *individual* actions—particularly by changing or threatening to change employers. Workers can also seek to improve their working conditions through *collective* action, and historically, this has been an important mechanism of change. Indeed, the development of labor unions and collective bargaining has been part of the process of economic growth in virtually every country in the world.

Because many people have strong and conflicting opinions about the role of unions in our society, it is often difficult to remain objective when discussing them. Some individuals view labor unions as forms of monopolies that, while benefiting their members, impose substantial costs on other members of society. In contrast, other individuals view unions as *the* major means by which working persons have improved their economic status and as important forces behind much social legislation. In fact, we shall see that there are important economic and legal constraints on collective actions by employees. While unions play an important role in our society, their influence is probably not as pervasive as either their supporters or opponents would have us believe.

In order to analyze the process and outcomes of collective bargaining, one must first understand the objectives of employers and unions who participate in the process. The objectives of employers have already been determined as those that obtain the profit-maximizing demand for labor (in Chapters 3–5). The goals of unions are far more varied and complex. In contrast to business firms, unions may form for ideological as well as economic reasons, although historically, unions in the United States have placed more emphasis on economic objectives than their European counterparts. Even when restricted to economic considerations, the specification of union goals is complicated by the fact that unions are inherently political organizations whose members often have very different and even conflicting views of the benefits that they should receive from union representation and have methods of changing unions or union leadership if they feel they are not being represented adequately. Moreover, the security of the union as an institution is influenced by the general economic and legal environment.

In this chapter, we begin our study of collective bargaining by examining unions as organizations at both the macro and micro level. At the macro level, we examine the growth of unions in the United States and the major historical events that shaped the present structure and attitudes of unions in the private and public sectors. The chapter then presents a simple conceptual model of the forces that influence the overall level of unionization and shows how this model can be used to explain the historical pattern of union membership. We then turn to the micro level and examine models of decision-making by individual unions and the implications for a union's internal operations and collective-bargaining objectives.

Having established the nature of unions and discussed their objectives, we explore other aspects of the collective-bargaining relationship in subsequent chapters. In Chapter 13, we examine the legal regulation of union organizing and collective bargaining. In Chapters 14 and 15, we discuss the collective-bargaining process, examining first the relationship between the structure and tactics of collective bargaining and bargaining power, before turning to an analysis of labor disputes and dispute settlement. In Chapter 16, we examine the nature of collective-bargaining agreements, and in Chapter 17, we consider the apparent effect of collective bargaining on the workplace and on the economy.

The Development of the American Labor Movement

Distinctive Features

One of the most striking features of the American labor movement is its slow growth and relatively modest representation of American workers. In recent years, approximately 20 percent of all individuals in the labor force and 25 percent of all employees on nonagricultural payrolls were union members. This percentage is considerably lower than that found in most Western countries (see Table 12.1). While the extent of unionization was small in most countries at the turn of the century, the subsequent growth of unions was much more rapid abroad than in North America. In contrast to most other countries, union penetration in the United States appears to have declined slowly but steadily since the mid-1950s.

In addition, the United States is one of the few Western countries in which labor unions are not intimately and uniformly associated with one political party (such as the Labour Party in England, which is dominated by trade unionists). While most of the leaders of the American union movement are generally more

Table 12.1. Union Membership as a Percent of Potential Union Membership by Country, Selected Years, 1900–75

	1900	1930	1950	1975
Australia	9.0[a]	43.5	56.0	54.3
Canada	—	13.5[b]	32.8	34.6
Denmark	—	32.0	51.9	66.6
Germany	5.7	33.7	33.1	37.2
Great Britain	13.1	25.7	43.8	49.2[c]
Norway	3.4	18.3	n.a.	60.5
Sweden	4.8	36.0	67.7	87.2
United States	5.5	8.9	28.0	25.1

[a]1901.
[b]1931.
[c]1974.

Note: The definition of potential union membership differs slightly from the concepts of labor force and nonagricultural employment against which union membership is compared in Table 12.2 and elsewhere in this chapter.

SOURCE: George Sayers Bain and Robert Price, *Profiles of Union Growth: A Comparative Statistical Portrait of Eight Countries* (Oxford: Basil Blackwell, 1980), p. 170.

supportive of the goals of the Democratic Party than those of the Republican Party, their influence on the selection of candidates and party programs has been variable. Moreover, some union leaders regularly support the Republican Party. For years, both the teamsters' union and the carpenters' union have supported Republican candidates for president. In the 1980 presidential election, the Professional Air Traffic Controllers' Association (PATCO) broke with most of the labor movement and supported Ronald Reagan, the successful Republican candidate, hoping that their support would gain sympathy for their bargaining demands. When the union later struck illegally after negotiations reached an impasse, however, the government held firm and fired most of the union's members, eventually driving the union into bankruptcy.

The absence of a permanent affiliation with a major political party is a symptom of another distinctive characteristic of American unions—an absence of ideological objectives. Again, in contrast to the experience of some other Western countries, the growth of unions in the United States was motivated more from efforts at economic advancement than from a general belief that workers had to band together to restructure society. American unions generally accept the capitalist form of economic organization and focus instead on increasing workers' share of national income.

Labor unions have two general methods for attaining their goals—*collective bargaining* and *legislative enactment.* Given the emphasis on economic objectives and the informality of political associations, American unions historically have placed more emphasis on the method of collective bargaining than their European counterparts. Fewer fringe benefits are provided by legislation in the United States and more by collective bargaining agreements, for example. While unions seek legislative support for improvements in the environment of collective bargaining and in the work environment (for example, through their support for laws regulating health and safety conditions at the workplace), they prefer to minimize government involvement in the bargaining process itself.

Finally, the process of collective bargaining is highly decentralized in the United States. While a few large negotiations in major companies and industries receive significant attention in the media, there are, in fact, about 200,000 collective bargaining agreements in force in the United States. Most collective-bargaining activity occurs unheralded in thousands of negotiations in individual plants and companies. This structure of collective bargaining contrasts sharply with negotiations in Europe, which are frequently conducted at the industrywide or nationwide level. It bears more similarity to the structure of collective bargaining in Japan, where negotiations occur most frequently at the plant or company level. (Detailed discussions of collective bargaining and dispute resolution in Europe, Japan, and Australia appear in examples in Chapter 14.)

Union Growth in the Private Sector

Table 12.2 presents data on a century of union membership, from 1880 through 1980. While data on union membership are notoriously poor, the table nevertheless yields some striking patterns. First, union membership, in both absolute terms and as a percentage of the labor force (and of nonagricultural employment), grew slowly and somewhat erratically prior to the mid-1930s. Second, membership growth accelerated dramatically during the late 1930s and through World War II. The former result was somewhat surprising to analysts, since prior to the 1930s periods of high unemployment were typically associated with declining union strength.[1] After a slight dip in the immediate postwar period, union strength reached a peak of 25 percent of the labor force in the mid-1950s. However, since that time, the share of union members in both total nonagricultural employment and the labor force has declined steadily. Indeed, by 1980, union membership stood at about 20 percent of the labor force—a 30-year low.

In order to interpret the historical circumstances behind these developments and their relevance for the shape of the present-day labor movement in the United States, it is important to appreciate certain characteristics of unions. *Labor unions* are collective organizations whose primary objectives are to improve the pecuniary and nonpecuniary employment conditions of their members. Unions can be organized along two different lines: (1) an *industrial* union represents most or all of the workers in an industry or firm regardless of their occupations; and (2) a *craft* union represents workers in a single occupational group. Examples of industrial unions are the unions representing automobile workers, steel workers, bituminous coal miners, and rubber workers; while examples of craft unions are those representing printers, dock workers, and the various building trades (for example, carpenters and plumbers).[2]

---

[1] For evidence and a discussion of the pre-1930s view, *see* John R. Commons, *The History of Labor in the United States,* vol. III (New York: Macmillan, 1918).

[2] For reasons that will become apparent later in the chapter, many unions that originally organized on a "craft" basis now represent workers on an "industrial" basis. For example, the Internationaly Brotherhood of Electrical Workers often represents all employees of unionized electrical machinery firms. Likewise, many industrial unions have expanded their organizing efforts beyond their original industry. Both the United Autoworkers and the Teamsters, for example, now organize university employees.

Table 12.2. Union and Association Membership in the United States, 1880–1980

Year	Union Membership Only			Union and Association Membership		
	Total (in thousands)	Percentage of Labor Force	Percentage of Nonagricultural Employment	Total (in thousands)	Percentage of Labor Force	Percentage Nonagricultural Employment
1880	200	n.a.	2.3			
1890	372	n.a.	2.7			
1900	791	n.a.	5.2			
1910	2,116	n.a.	9.8			
1920	5,034	n.a.	18.3			
1930	3,401	6.8	11.6			
1932	3,050	6.0	12.9			
1934	3,088	5.9	11.9			
1936	3,989	7.4	13.7			
1938	8,034	14.6	27.5			
1940	8,717	15.5	26.9			
1942	10,380	17.2	25.9			
1944	14,146	21.4	33.8			
1946	14,395	23.6	34.5			
1948	14,300	23.1	31.9			
1950	14,300	22.3	31.5			
1952	15,900	24.2	33.3			
1954	17,022	25.4	33.7			
1956	17,490	25.2	33.2			
1958	17,029	24.2	33.2			
1960	17,049	23.6	31.5			
1962	16,586	22.6	29.9			
1964	16,841	22.2	28.9			
1966	17,940	22.7	28.1			
1968	18,916	23.0	27.9	20,721	25.2	30.5
1970	19,381	22.6	27.3	21,248	24.7	30.0
1972	19,435	21.8	26.4	21,657	24.3	29.4
1974	20,119	21.7	25.8	22,809	24.5	29.1
1976	19,634	20.3	24.5	22,662	23.4	28.3
1978	20,246	19.7	24.0	22,757	22.2	26.2
1980	n.a.	n.a.	n.a.	22,366	20.9	24.7

Note: Data for 1880–1920 include Canadian membership in U.S. unions. In 1910 and 1920 Canadian membership was probably between 100 and 200 thousand workers.   n.a. not available

SOURCE: U.S. Bureau of Labor Statistics, *Directory of National Unions and Employee Associations, 1979,* Bulletin 2079 (Washington, D.C.: U.S. Government Printing Office, 1980) for 1958–1978 data; U.S. Bureau of the Census, *Historical Statistics of the United States: Colonial Times to 1970* (Washington, D.C.: U.S. Government Printing Office, 1975) for 1900–1956 data. Lloyd Ulman, "American Trade Unionism Past and Present" in *American Economic History* ed. Seymour E. Harris, (New York: McGraw-Hill, 1961) p. 393, for 1880–1890 data. Bureau of National Affairs, *Directory of U.S. Labor Organizations,* 1982–83 Ed. (Washington, D.C.: Bureau of National Affairs, Inc., 1982), Table 2 for 1980 data.

To an important degree, the extent and form of union organization is influenced by the underlying economics of the labor markets in which unions operate. In this respect, some of the tools developed in previous chapters enable us to interpret the pattern of union growth observed in the United States. Union growth can also be significantly influenced by another factor that has not been discussed yet—the legal environment in which unions operate. An analysis of the economic and legal environment facing unions helps to explain why prior to the mid-1930s the American labor movement was relatively small and consisted almost exclusively of craft unions.

The Early economic environment. With respect to the general economic environment, the major influences on labor-market conditions prior to the 1930s were the general scarcity of labor in the United States, large immigration flows, and periodic recessions. During most of this period, land and capital were in abundant supply relative to labor. As a result of the labor scarcity, real wages and the general standard of living of even unskilled workers were high relative to the European countries from which most U.S. workers emigrated. This aspect of the economic climate may have reduced the interest of some workers in unions as a vehicle of economic change.

More importantly, the prospects of relatively high wages and living standards helped induce large immigration flows into the United States. Immigration provided a flood of largely unskilled, manual labor until 1920 when the immigration laws became more restrictive. (Review the immigration statistics in Table 9.2.) During the years of peak immigration in the late nineteenth and early twentieth century, the supply of unskilled labor effectively became infinitely elastic at the prevailing real wage (that is, the labor-supply curve was essentially horizontal; additional labor could be recruited without raising wages). Under these conditions, efforts by unions to organize and raise the wage of any group of low-skilled workers above the market level were likely to be undercut by the flow of new, unorganized workers willing to take jobs at the market wage. The challenge to early unions presented by immigration is an example of the broader problem of organizational security that all unions face. As a labor-market monopoly, a union's security as an institution depends importantly on the same factor that determines the durability of monopolies in product markets—barriers to entry. When a union is unable to prevent the entry of unorganized workers to perform the work being done by its members, the union's efforts to raise wages and improve working conditions above market levels will be undercut. Unions thus must seek to organize and police their entire jurisdiction. This objective is difficult to achieve with unrestricted immigration, which explains the handicap that early unions faced in trying to organize the unskilled and why unions generally oppose open immigration policies.

Even with the substantial flow of immigrant labor, the increases in labor demand that accompanied the geographic expansion of markets and the growth of large industry exceeded the expansion of the labor supply. Demand grew more rapidly than supply, labor remained relatively scarce, and real wages continued to rise.

How did unions adapt to an environment that was both relatively prosperous and also discouraged the organization of low-skilled workers? It is clear from our earlier labor-market analysis that only craft unions were likely to survive under these conditions. First, the security of craft unions was less likely to be threatened by the flood of unskilled immigrants because significant training was required to acquire skill in a particular craft. The union's strategy was then to acquire control of the training process, usually by setting up apprenticeship programs under which unskilled workers spent a period of years learning the skills of a trade, and to limit entry into the program. The simple analytics of apprenticeship-restriction are illustrated in Figure 12.1. Under normal labor market conditions, the supply of skilled workers *(SS)* would rise as the skilled wage increased, and the equilibrium wage and employment of skilled workers would be W_S and E_S respectively. When training is provided only through an apprenticeship program, and the union limits entry to E_u individuals, labor supply becomes inelastic at E_u and the wage for skilled workers becomes W_u. When a craft union is able to control the training programs, it can raise the wages of workers in the craft without even bargaining *if* employers make no defensive response! The union simply increases the scarcity of skilled workers (by limiting entry into apprenticeship) and lets market forces do the rest. Thus, craft unions had a tool (apprenticeship) not available to industrial unions, and during the nineteenth century, groups of skilled workers formed exclusive organizations to protect their own bargaining power.

The actual advantage derived from this tool by craft unions depends on the response of employers. The analysis traced in Figure 12.1 applies if a union is able to deal with each employer separately. However, the union's tactics provide an incentive for employers to band together to resist union pressures for higher wages. The formation of such multiemployer bargaining arrangements creates a situation of *bilateral monopoly* in the labor market, because both the sale of labor and the purchase of labor are regulated by single decision-making units (the union

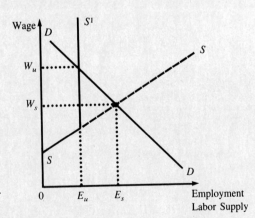

Figure 12.1   Restriction of Labor
Supply by Craft Unions

and the multiemployer bargaining association, respectively). A complete discussion of the outcome of bargaining under bilateral monopoly, which is less predictable than the outcome described in Figure 12.1, is postponed until our discussion of bargaining structures in Chapter 14. For the moment, the important point is that in analyzing labor-relations situations, one should consider *both* the strategic move by a party *and* the likely strategic response to the move by that party's opponent.

The second advantage that craft unions had over industrial unions can be appreciated by recalling the conditions governing the wage elasticity of the derived demand for labor. The laws of derived demand discussed in Chapter 4 imply that the derived demand for union labor will be relatively inelastic if it is difficult to substitute other inputs for union labor; if price elasticities of demand for the final product are relatively inelastic; if the supply schedules of substitute inputs are unresponsive to their prices; and, under certain conditions, if union labor is a relatively small proportion of total cost. There are obviously fewer substitutes for skilled labor than for unskilled labor, and in many instances, the work performed by members of a single craft union may constitute a relatively small proportion of the total cost of a product. It may be, then, that the trade-off between employment and wages faced by the members of skilled craft unions is much smaller than the trade-off faced by the members of industrial unions. Therefore, even if craft unions bargained for wages in excess of W_u in Figure 12.1, the negative employment consequences were likely to be modest.

These inherent economic advantages to craft unions drove skilled workers in the direction of forming rather exclusive organizations, in order to protect their bargaining power. These advantages were not unappreciated by many unskilled workers, and there were sporadic and ultimately unsuccessful attempts to develop more broadly based unions combining both skilled and unskilled workers, on the theory that the inherent bargaining power of the skilled could be used to improve the wages of the unskilled. Skilled workers recognized that such collaborations in industrial unions would result in a dilution of their power and generally remained aloof from such efforts. The net result was that prior to the 1930s, organized labor in the United States was to a large extent a movement of the skilled elite in the labor force.

The development of national unions. There were several forces, however, that led local craft unions to coordinate their efforts across the country. First, even a craft union that effectively organized and controlled entry into one local labor market could be threatened by the spread of markets as the country expanded, and by the emergence of large multiplant companies. If new markets remained unorganized, or were organized by local unions that negotiated markedly lower terms and conditions of employment, the security of unions in other markets would be threatened. Similarly, the rise of multiplant companies gave management a "whipsaw" advantage over local unions. Efforts to raise wages in one plant could be thwarted by shifting production to other plants (usually in other locations). The threat to unions is easily seen by again recalling the determinants of the wage elasticity of the demand for labor. The elasticity is high when it is easy for consumers to substitute for the product that the members of a local union are producing. Since the best substitute for any one group's product is the identical product being produced at lower cost in another location, there was a powerful incentive for unions to develop an institutional response that would effectively take labor costs out of competition by coordinating the bargaining of local unions in different areas. Second, in some areas, union standards were threatened by the in-migration of skilled labor, and some local unions sought a mechanism to regulate the conditions under which craftsmen from other locals could work in their area. Finally, some locals needed support from other unions simply to muster the resources necessary to counter successfully a large employer.

Following the Civil War, the institutional response that evolved in an effort to standardize the terms and conditions of employment across locations was the national union (often referred to as an "international" union when there are Canadian members), an umbrella organization of all the locals of a particular union. National unions acquired considerable power over the activities of local unions in order to coordinate bargaining activities in a way that would tend to standardize the terms and conditions of employment across locations. In particular, the national unions used economic leverage in the form of large strike-funds (accumulated from per capita dues paid by the local unions) to coordinate the activities of the locals. Funds were allocated to those local unions whose strikes were sanctioned by the national union and were withheld from locals engaging in unauthorized strikes. The authorization process frequently led national union officials to provide assistance in the negotiations between locals and employers and to direct efforts to organize nonunion workers in the union's jurisdiction.[3]

Early legal environment. The economic impediments to widespread union organization during the nineteenth and early twentieth centuries were reinforced by a legal environment that was unfavorably disposed toward unions and collective bargaining. Generally speaking, the legal environment for institutional behavior is conditioned by the common law and statutory law as interpreted by the judiciary. *Common law* consists of general principles and the accumulation of decisions over time, developed by the judiciary without the aid of explicit legislation. *Statutory law,* on the other hand, is established by legislation and can modify the common law. Prior to the 1930s, the legal environment of unions in collective bargaining was mainly set by the common law, and the frequent use of judicial discretion in interpreting the common law to thwart the activities of unions left the American labor movement with a deeply rooted opposition to substantial reliance on the courts in the institutional arrangements surrounding collective bargaining.

In considering the status of unions and union activity, the judiciary applied a number of doctrines from the common law.[4] The earliest unions encountered

[3]Lloyd Ulman, *The Rise of the National Labor Union* (Cambridge, Mass.: Harvard University Press, 1954).

[4]For an extensive review of the early legal treatment of unions in the United States, *see* Charles O. Gregory, *Labor and the Law,* 2nd revised edition with 1961 supplement (New York: Norton, 1961), Chapters I–VI.

the high water mark of judicial emphasis on the freedom of contract, and were treated as criminal conspiracies. Under the *criminal conspiracy* doctrine, individual actions to raise wages or otherwise alter the terms and conditions of employment were permissible (on the grounds that they had no general impact on the economy), but group actions to achieve identical ends were unlawful, because of the purported economic power accruing from combinations of workers. What was legal for an individual was illegal for a group. (Some judges developed a curious double standard in applying the criminal conspiracy doctrine by permitting combinations of employers—which raised the possibility of monopsony power as discussed in Chapter 3—on the grounds that such combinations constituted defensive efforts to force wages down to their competitive level.)

The conspiracy doctrine was supplanted by the *illegal purpose doctrine,* which held that while the formation of unions by workers was lawful, the ends of such an organization might be illegal. While this doctrine established the legality of some of the more traditional union activities, such as strikes for improved wages and working conditions, it left the legitimacy of many other union objectives in doubt and a matter of judicial discretion. By the late nineteenth century, however, employers began to rely increasingly on the *labor injunction.* An injunction is a court order directing an individual or group to take or to refrain from taking a particular course of action. As a technique for restricting union activities, it is direct and to the point: failure to obey an injunction constitutes contempt of court and can be punished summarily with a jail sentence or fine. The issuance of labor injunctions was a matter of judicial discretion, but employers usually were able to locate a willing judge. While the general purpose of injunctions is to protect property from irreparable damage, U.S. courts had extended the concept of "property" to include intangible items (such as the right to run a profitable business) as well as tangible property. As a result, virtually any prospective union effort to organize and enforce demands for better wages and working conditions could be construed as a threat to "property."[5]

The final legal restraint on unions came from a statutory law that was not obviously directed at unions and collective bargaining. The Sherman Antitrust Act, enacted by Congress in 1890, provided that "every contract, combination, . . . or conspiracy, in restraint of trade or commerce among the several States, . . . is . . . illegal," but made no mention of unions. Nevertheless, the act was used for many years to curb certain union practices. The treatment of unions under antitrust law is discussed more extensively in Chapter 13.

Structure of authority within the American labor movement. The remaining threat to those craft unions that managed to develop a toehold in the precarious economic and legal environment of the nineteenth and early twentieth centuries was from rival union organizations. The rivals were usually more broadly based efforts to establish industrial unions by mixing craft workers, with their superior bargaining power, with unskilled and semiskilled workers. Some of the rival

---

[5]One study estimated that by 1931 employers had obtained 1845 injunctions against unions while unions had obtained only 43 against employers. Edwin D. Witte, *The Government in Labor Disputes* (New York: McGraw-Hill Book Company, 1932) pp. 231–34.

organizations also had a distinctly different ideological position regarding the place of labor in society. Inevitably, the rival unions attempted to organize workers who the established craft unions viewed as working in their jurisdiction. While none of the alternative movements that arose during the nineteenth century survived for any appreciable period of time, the interorganizational rivalry challenged the institutional security of established craft unions and eroded their ability to present a united front to employers.

The challenges arose because the nature of industrial development left the craft form of union organization increasingly inappropriate for large groups of workers. With the growth of large-scale manufacturing enterprises came the widespread introduction of machines, which eliminated or diluted many skills, created a few others (for example, machinists), but on balance increased the ratio of semiskilled and unskilled jobs to skilled jobs in industry. With the westward economic expansion, skills also broke down on the frontier where it became more important for a worker to be a jack-of-all-trades than a master-of-one. Despite the growth of employment outside of the traditional craft occupations, however, early attempts to form industrial unions proved unable to survive periodic recessions when unions were generally unable to defend their members against wage cuts by employers.

Some of the tensions between the craft and industrial philosophies of union organization are illustrated by the experience of the Knights of Labor, which represented the first large-scale attempt to adopt the industrial-union principle of organization. Originally founded in 1869 as a secret society in the Philadelphia area, the Knights abandoned secrecy in the early 1880s to openly pursue political and social objectives. They shared with organizations of farmers and small shop-keepers an opposition to what was perceived at the time as the growing monopoly power of banks and railroads. In addition, the leadership of the Knights saw the established craft unions as labor market monopolists with, from their perspective, rather limited objectives. By uniting workers at all skill levels in one union, the Knights hoped to break down the divisions that they believed were associated with the craft approach to union organization and to use the bargaining power of the skilled workers to secure economic gains for all workers.[6] To this end, they organized workers of all skills into "assemblies." Unlike most unions, the Knights of Labor initially favored arbitration and consumer boycotts over strikes as a method of settling bargaining impasses. However, the inability to enforce arbitration decisions increasingly led the Knights to use the strike weapon.

The Knights of Labor were bitterly opposed by the established craft unions with whom they competed for the allegiance of skilled workers. Several craft unions had established the Federation of Organized Trades and Labor Unions in 1881, and the Federation regarded skilled workers as being exclusively in their "jurisdiction" for the purpose of organizing. The Federation proposed a treaty under which the Knights would abandon the assemblies in trades organized by

---

[6]The Knights of Labor also pursued a number of political objectives including the establishment of a federal bureau of labor statistics, a prohibition of child labor, an end to sex discrimination, and the establishment of an eight-hour day.

established craft unions, and would agree not to organize skilled workers without the permission of the Federation. Since this would have involved a total capitulation to the craft unions, the Knights refused. Following a surprisingly successful railroad strike in 1885 their membership grew from around 100,000 to almost a million. However, the Knights had developed only loose control over their assemblies, and a year later, another railroad strike, initiated by a local assembly without the approval of the leadership, was lost, and the Knights went into decline as an organization.

In an effort to resolve issues of union rivalry and to coordinate action on issues of interest to the labor movement as a whole, the members of the Federation of Organized Trades and Labor Unions, in 1886, formed a loose umbrella organization for the national craft unions, the American Federation of Labor (AFL). The principles on which this federation was established a century ago are important in understanding the behavior of its successor organization (the AFL-CIO) today. Although the Federation is on the top of the hierarchy of union organization, it is not the center of power within the American labor movement and has rather circumscribed authority relative to labor federations in many western European countries. The national unions that established the Federation insisted that it be founded on two broad principles—*exclusive jurisdiction* and *national union autonomy.*

The first principle, exclusive jurisdiction, addressed the problem of union rivalry by providing that only one union would be accorded the right to organize workers of a particular skill or performing a particular type of work. In order to implement this principle, the AFL was granted the authority to issue a charter to each national union, defining the jurisdiction or categories of workers within which the union was authorized to organize workers. New unions could not be given jurisdictions that overlapped with those of existing national unions. From the perspective of the national unions, the Federation therefore had an important role to play in awarding jurisdictions and in resolving jurisdictional conflicts between affiliated national unions. (In practice, conflicts appeared to be resolved in favor of the more powerful contestant. Since the Federation was financed by per capita payments from member unions, larger unions were more important to its economic well-being.) While subsequent developments have greatly modified the authority of the Federation with respect to jurisdiction, the notion of exclusive jurisdiction has been an important influence on the behavior of American unions.

The principle of national union autonomy also continues to have an important influence and constraint on behavior of the Federation. Under this doctrine (which is embedded in the Federation's constitution), the Federation has no authority over the internal affairs of its constituent national unions or their membership. In fact, workers are not permitted to belong to the Federation. Instead, they belong to a national union and the membership of the Federation consists of national union organizations that choose to affiliate. Thus, the AFL (and now the AFL-CIO) is constitutionally forbidden from interfering in national union practices regarding admissions to unions, apprenticeship programs, discipline of the membership, and internal government. In recent decades, this constitutional limitation on the Federation's authority has made it very difficult for it to respond actively to some of the more trenchant criticisms of unions with respect to discrimination and union corruption. As the organizational pinnacle of the labor movement, the Federation is a natural target for public criticism of union behavior. Yet, even when such charges were restricted to the activities of a few national unions, the national autonomy doctrine limited the extent to which the Federation was able to respond.

Furthermore, the Federation was given no real role in collective bargaining. The national unions were sufficiently determined to retain all decisions with respect to collective bargaining, so that the Federation was not given the authority to maintain a strike fund. To this day, the Federation has very little leverage over the bargaining policy or tactics of its constituent national unions. The net result of the relationship between the Federation and the national unions is that despite the organizational hierarchy, the real locus of economic power resides in the national unions. The Federation needs them more than they need the Federation. Indeed, when a national union chooses or is forced to disaffiliate, the Federation loses the dues payments (which can be substantial) that it received from the national union, while the union loses the Federation's protection from "raids" by other unions on its jurisdiction (something that has become a less consequential threat, particularly to large unions, in the twentieth century).

The other main function of the Federation is to represent the labor movement politically. In contrast to the situation abroad, the development of labor unions in the United States has been marked by a clear precedence of economic over political objectives. In fact, many European unions are formed with explicit political objectives, and many visitors to the United States are surprised by the lack of class consciousness in American unions. As noted earlier, American unions have emphasized the method of collective bargaining over the method of legislative enactment to a much greater extent than unions in most European nations. Rather than adopting any particular ideological stance or affiliating with any party, the AFL took the pragmatic stance of "rewarding one's friends and punishing one's enemies" in its quest to obtain legislation that improved the general climate of collective bargaining. For years, however, its legislative objectives were surprisingly limited. Until the 1930s, for example, the Federation opposed legislative proposals to establish minimum wages, Social Security, and other benefits on the grounds that these were tasks for collective bargaining. Since the 1930s, the Federation has been a major supporter of legislation in favor of these and other workplace benefits, such as regulations aimed at improving occupational health and safety.

Challenges to the American Federation of Labor. The American Federation of Labor's emphasis on the interests of skilled workers, its limited demands on the political system, and its general acceptance of the capitalist economic system left it vulnerable to criticism from groups who believed that the economic position of workers could only be advanced through a more radical restructuring of society. The main radical challenge to the prevailing political and economic philosophy of the American Federation of Labor came from the Industrial Workers of the World (IWW), formed in 1906 by an alliance of western metal miners and socialist trade union leaders. Contrary to the AFL, the IWW rejected the idea that workers and employers had sufficient common interests to resolve their differences through collective bargaining. The stark philosophical difference between the two organizations is clear from the opening lines of the preamble to the IWW constitution, which state that "The working class and the employing class have nothing in common. . . . Between these two classes a struggle must go on until workers of the world unite as a class . . . and take possession of the machinery of production and abolish the wage system."

The IWW was equally opposed to the craft principle of organization that characterized unions in the AFL on the grounds that it led to competition rather than solidarity between different crafts in an industry. Interestingly, the IWW also saw a conflict between normal collective-bargaining arrangements and the goal of worker solidarity. If different groups of workers in an industry were represented by different unions or for other reasons worked under collective-bargaining agreements with different expiration dates, then some workers could be forced to continue working while others struck. In the view of the IWW, the sanctity of the contract took second place to worker solidarity. Few AFL unions shared this view. The difference in the authority granted the respective leadership of the AFL and the IWW reflected the difference in the philosophies of the organizations. In contrast to the limitations on the authority of the officers of the AFL, the leadership of the IWW could order all member unions to give financial or other assistance (including sympathetic work stoppages) to aid striking subordinates.

Nevertheless, this basic philosophical challenge to the trade-union organization under the AFL was accompanied by a footloose, anarchic style that rendered the IWW more colorful than effective. Despite a few successful strikes between 1906 and 1914, it proved unable to attract the durable allegiance of a large fraction of American workers. The same conclusion concerning the influence of radical political ideas on American workers can be drawn more generally. One reason for this may be the high standard of living of American workers relative to their European counterparts. Moreover, radical appeals could not be based on the political disenfranchisement of workers. Even in the nineteenth century, workers in the United States had the ballot. As with the Knights of Labor, the main aspect of the IWW philosophy that was to survive was the attack on the craft-union basis of early American organized labor.

Union growth in the modern period. In the face of the difficult economic and legal environment and the determined opposition of employers, unions established little more than a toehold in the United States until World War I, when at the behest of the government, a period of cooperation between labor and management was accompanied by a period of union growth (see Table 12.2). This was followed at the conclusion of the war by a sharp employer counter-offensive to restore a nonunion environment. In the absence of statutory support for collective bargaining, unions could be established by the voluntary consent of an employer or by striking an employer in an effort to compel recognition. Under prevailing employer attitudes toward unions, the first option was effectively ruled out. The second option was frequently countered by the use of the labor injunction, as noted previously. Where an injunction was not used, the techniques of employer-opposition were often less delicate. Espionage, private detectives, and strikebreakers were employed to thwart union activities, and efforts to establish unions were frequently accompanied by violence.

In other situations, employers also required employees to sign "yellow dog" contracts—contracts in which potential employees had to agree *not* to join a union as a condition of employment. If a union then attempted to organize the employees, the union could be sued for inducing breach of contract. During the 1920s, employers also established "company unions" as a representational device for workers. While such organizations could discuss some terms and conditions of employment with employers, they were not independent employee organizations. Typically, the company union was financially supported by the employer, its officers were chosen by the company, and the agenda for its meetings was set by the company. Nevertheless, it provided a semblance of representation and was sometimes used to convince workers that they did not really need representation from an outside union. Employers also developed and introduced a number of innovative fringe-benefit plans as a way of maintaining the allegiance of employees during this period. The net result of these developments was that during the 1920s, unions lost most of the ground that they had gained during World War I.

However, some of the difficulties encountered by the American labor movement were traceable to its own internal structure. While most of the employment growth was occurring in large mass-production factories staffed by largely semi-skilled, operative work forces, the American Federation of Labor remained, with a few exceptions such as the United Mine Workers, an organization of skilled craft unions. Since skilled workers constituted a small proportion of employment in the mass-production industries, no single craft union or group of unions had the resources to mount a successful organizing campaign. As a result, workers in the automobile, steel, rubber, and other large industries remained unorganized. Moreover, the craft unions within the AFL opposed attempts to charter industrial unions, which structurally would have been more suited to organizing in such industries, on the grounds that the minority of skilled workers found in the industries were within traditional craft-union jurisdictions and hence could not be organized by newly chartered industrial unions. Despite the efforts of John L. Lewis, the president of the United Mine Workers, and a few other leaders of AFL unions to get the Federation to charter new industrial unions to organize the mass-production industries, the internal stalemate in the AFL on this issue persisted into the mid-1930s.

These tensions within the labor movement and between employees and employers came to a head during the 1930s in the wake of the Great Depression. To many, the extraordinary losses in production and employment in the early 1930s signaled the failure of the *laissez-faire* theory of economic organization that formed the basis of the freedom-of-contract approach to public policy toward labor markets. This set the stage for the passage of two major pieces of legislation that established an explicit statutory policy toward unions and collective bargaining and significantly altered the legal environment of industrial relations. The first of these, the Norris-LaGuardia Act, passed in 1932, provided the first statutory statement that American public policy sanctioned unions and collective bargaining, and broadened the definition of a legally permissible labor conflict from a dispute between employers and employees (a standard developed in earlier court decisions) to a dispute between those having an economic interest at stake. This extension effectively freed strikes over union recognition from legal restraint. The act also went much further by forbidding the issuance of injunctions in most labor disputes and by declaring that "yellow dog" contracts were unenforceable in the federal courts. The basic effect of the statute was to remove the courts and judicial value judgements from labor disputes and to introduce a period of roughly equivalent legal rights and status for unions and management.

This brief period ended in 1935 with the passage of the National Labor Relations Act (NLRA), often referred to in this original version as the Wagner Act, which tipped the support of public policy toward unions. Support for this legislation within the Roosevelt Administration stemmed more from the view that the spread of collective bargaining would stimulate recovery from the Depression than from any inherent commitment to the idea of unionization. To the extent that unions were successful in raising the wages and purchasing power of workers, it was believed that the growth of collective bargaining would increase demand. A second objective of the Act was to reduce labor disputes and the associated disruptions of production.

The Wagner Act provided a fuller statutory guarantee than the Norris-LaGuardia Act of the basic rights of employees to organize, to bargain collectively, and to engage in strikes or other concerted activity in order to secure their objectives. It established two broad mechanisms to secure and enforce these rights. First, the law established a government-supervised election procedure to determine which union, if any, should represent employees in collective bargaining with their employers. By substituting an administrative procedure for the use of force in determining bargaining status, the NLRA sought to reduce strikes over recognition. A union receiving the support of a majority of the employees in an election became the *exclusive bargaining representative* of all employees in the bargaining unit.

The concept of an exclusive bargaining representative is a unique feature of American labor law. It imposes on the union the duty to represent and bargain for all employees in the unit, including those who voted against it. At the same time, employers are required to deal with employees through the union rather than individually. On the one hand, the legal requirement is advantageous to unions because it reduces competition in the supply of labor to the bargaining unit in which the union wins an election. Rival unions are excluded, and the employer is prevented from hiring nonunion workers at lower wages in an effort to undermine the union's position. Exclusive representation effectively protects the monopoly position of a union within the bargaining unit. On the other hand, the legal requirement raises a *free rider* problem for the union—employees who do not support the union nevertheless receive the benefits of union activities. This has encouraged unions to develop *union security* arrangements, which are discussed more fully later in this chapter.

Second, while the Norris-LaGuardia Act had removed major judicial impediments to union organization, the Wagner Act sought to remove several employer-techniques of union resistance by proscribing a number of employer unfair-labor-practices because they constituted interference with or restraint of employees seeking to exercise their rights under the act. (The specific unfair labor practices and their impact on modern American labor relations are discussed more extensively in Chapter 13.) In order to implement these provisions, an administrative agency of the federal government, the National Labor Relations Board (NLRB), was established to conduct elections for union representation and to investigate, prosecute, and adjudicate unfair labor-practice charges.

The passage of the NLRA, and its aftermath, had major consequences for the size and structure of the American labor movement. With union representation decided by NLRB elections, the AFL lost the only major power that it had with respect to the national unions—the awarding of jurisdiction. Under the NLRA, the appropriate bargaining unit was to be decided by the NLRB (if the union and employer could not agree), and the choice of union depended on a vote of employees in the unit rather than an award by the AFL. More generally, the entire notion of exclusive jurisdiction,[7] which was of such importance to the craft unions, was eroded under a system in which the majority of workers decided who would represent them. Also, once majority rule rather than relative power became the criterion for establishing a bargaining relationship, unorganized employees rather than employers became the "targets" of union organizing efforts.[8] This raises a number of interesting questions concerning why workers join (vote for) unions that are discussed more fully in Chapter 13.

Most importantly, the passage of the NLRA brought the internal debate within the AFL over the structure of the labor movement to a head by providing procedures that effectively reduced the cost of organizing large industries. As the craft unions continued to oppose the principle of industrial unionization, John L. Lewis and a few other leaders of national unions affiliated with the AFL formed a Committee on Industrial Organization in 1935. Since this move was viewed by the craft unions as an attempt to set up rival union organizations (because there were a few craft workers in the mass-production industries), the unions involved were thrown out of the AFL. Subsequently, these unions formed a rival labor federation, the Congress of Industrial Organizations (CIO), with the avowed purpose of organizing workers in the mass-production industries into new industrial unions.

With the formation of the new federation and its assault on the mass-production industries, the American labor movement went through a period of extraordinary growth beginning in 1937 (see Table 12.2). Although the new statutory support for collective bargaining undoubtedly helped to persuade some workers to join unions, it must be said that this explosion of new union membership did

---

[7]Recall that the concept of "exclusive jurisdiction" is different from the concept of "exclusive representation." The former refers to a founding principle of the AFL under which only one union was given the right to organize a particular group of workers; the second refers to the legal concept that the union winning a representation election under the NLRA is the sole representative of all workers in the bargaining unit.

[8]Some of the coercion that unions had formerly practiced against employers in efforts to secure recognition were at times even exercised against employees.

not come about through the relatively civilized election procedures that had been established in the NLRA. Sitdown strikes, violence, and the use of force (mitigated only by an occasional secret negotiation over recognition) dominated efforts to gain union recognition during the period, but by 1940, the CIO had made major inroads into the automobile, rubber, steel, and electrical manufacturing industries.[9] Unionization was also extended during World War II when most unions adhered to a no-strike pledge, and the War Labor Board, which was charged with regulating employment conditions to aid the war effort, encouraged resisting employers to establish collective-bargaining relationships with unions.

Following World War II, the public-policy pendulum shifted decidedly in an antiunion direction. The most immediate stimulus was a sharp increase in strike activity as unions attempted to press demands that had been muted during the wartime no-strike pledge. Although work time lost to strike activity amounted to only 1.4 percent of employee hours in 1946, it represented a record high, and inspired demands to protect neutral third parties—particularly the public at large —from the consequences of disputes between major unions and major employers. There was also concern over the potential use of coercive actions by unions against employees. The growing concern with the consequences of union power culminated with the passage in 1947 of the Taft-Hartley Act, which altered the National Labor Relations Act by amending it in significant ways.

While the new legislation maintained the basic rights to organization and collective bargaining that had been established in the Wagner Act, it sought to protect the individual's right to belong or *not* to belong to a union, to rehabilitate the employer's freedom of expression, and to protect neutral third parties from the consequences of major labor disputes. The legislation sought to achieve these objectives by adding a list of union unfair labor-practices (discussed at greater length in Chapter 13) to the list of employer unfair-labor-practices in the Wagner Act, by providing for decertification elections in which employees could vote on whether a union should be removed as their bargaining agent, and by establishing a set of emergency dispute procedures that could be invoked under certain circumstances in major labor disputes. (The latter procedures are examined in Chapter 15 on disputes and dispute settlement.) It also includes the famous "Section 14B," which permits individual states to pass so-called *right-to-work laws.*[10] These laws prohibit contractual requirements that a person become, or promise to become, a union member as a condition of employment. By 1980, some twenty states, located primarily in the South, Southwest, and Plains areas, had passed such laws.

The increasing hostility of public policy toward unions and collective bar-

---

[9]For a detailed history of this period, *see* Walter Galenson, *The CIO Challenge to the AFL* (Cambridge, Mass.: Harvard University Press, 1959).

[10]Federal labor legislation permits the negotiation of union security arrangements. Technically, when both federal and state legislation address the same issue, the provisions of the federal legislation take precedence. Section 14B of the Taft-Hartley Act creates an exception to this general convention for cases in which states have passed statutes forbidding the negotiation of union security clauses in collective bargaining agreements.

gaining contributed to an interest on the part of the AFL and the CIO in exploring the possibility of an alliance. In addition to their common interest in improving the general public-policy climate for collective bargaining, some of the earlier philosophical differences between the two labor federations had dissipated by the early 1950s. In competing for membership, the AFL had overcome its initial craft orientation and established some industrial unions. For its part, the CIO had not been bashful about organizing new craft unions. That continued jurisdictional competition could be counterproductive seemed to be confirmed when a joint study by the federations showed that, when an AFL union competed with a CIO union in an NLRB representation election, the most frequent outcome was that workers voted for "no union." Following a period of negotiations, the two federations signed an agreement in which they agreed not to raid each other's memberships. Subsequently, in 1955, a merger of the two federations into the present American Federation of Labor-Congress of Industrial Organizations (AFL-CIO) was completed, with George Meany, the president of the AFL, as president of the merged federations, and Walter Reuther, the president of the CIO, as vice-president.

The merger occurred at about the time when union membership peaked. (Refer again to Table 12.2.) With the rise of industrial unionism, failures to advance unionization were no longer attributable to structural limitations in the labor movement. During the postwar period, most of the employment growth occurred outside of the occupational and industrial sectors in which unions of any type had been successful. Attempts to unionize white collar—particularly professional—employees, public employees, workers in the service industries, and workers in the South were relatively unsuccessful.

Further evidence of the increasing difficulty faced by unions in their efforts to extend union membership can be found in the National Labor Relations Board union election and decertification vote data for the decade of the '70s, which are found in Table 12.3. These data indicate that while the number of elections in

Table 12.3. Results of Representation Elections and Decertification Polls Supervised by the National Labor Relations Board

Fiscal Year	Union Elections	Percent Won By Union	Decertification Votes	Percent Lost By Union
1970	8,074	55.2	301	69.8
1971	8,362	53.2	401	69.6
1972	8,923	53.6	451	70.3
1973	9,369	51.1	453	69.5
1974	8,858	50.0	490	69.0
1975	8,577	48.2	516	73.4
1976	8,638	48.1	611	72.8
1977	9,484	46.0	849	76.0
1978	8,240	46.0	807	73.6
1979	8,043	45.0	777	75.0
1980	8,198	45.7	902	72.7

SOURCE: *Annual Report of the National Labor Relations Board,* Appendix Tables (various years).

which unions have sought to win the right to represent unorganized workers has fluctuated between 8000 and 9500 a year, the *share* of the elections that the unions actually won has fallen steadily during the period, from 55 to 45 percent. Furthermore, the annual number of *decertification votes*—votes in which union claims to represent a majority of workers in a firm were challenged—more than doubled, with the share of these votes lost by unions increasing slightly to more than 70 percent during this period.

In addition, new public policy toward unions continued to diminish union power. Developments in the late 1950s, however, were not fundamentally directed at labor-management relations as were the Wagner and Taft-Hartley Acts. After a series of Congressional hearings that developed evidence of serious official corruption, mismanagement of financial resources, and undemocratic procedures in a few unions, Congress passed the Labor-Management Reporting and Disclosure Act (also known as the Landrum-Griffin Act after its chief sponsors) in 1959. This act marked a shift in legislative emphasis from union-management relations toward the regulation of internal affairs of unions to an extent not observed for corporations. The act provided a "bill of rights" for union members, required unions to file annual financial reports with the U.S. Department of Labor, limited the extent to which national unions could place local unions in trusteeship and take over their operations, imposed standards of fiduciary responsibility on union officials, and, perhaps most importantly, provided that the Department of Labor can set aside and rerun elections for union office when there is evidence of irregularities in the original election. These new procedures have increased the effective degree of democracy in unions by making it easier for union members to challenge union leaders through the internal election process. They also made it easier for the government to take corrective action in situations in which the pension funds of union members were placed in investments of dubious value. As argued in Chapter 15, such provisions may also have had the side effect of increasing the level of strike activity in the economy.

Union Growth in the Public Sector

The development of unions in the public sector has followed a much different course than in the private sector. Although a few unions of public employees were formed as early as the nineteenth century, for years public policy toward collective bargaining in the public sector rested on the view that the government's authority to act in the public interest was absolute. Collective bargaining by public employees, a process that implied a sharing of such authority with respect to the determination of the terms and conditions of employment, was held to be inconsistent with this "doctrine of sovereignty." Thus, in the mid-1930s, President Roosevelt could simultaneously support the rights of private employees to organize and bargain collectively (in the National Labor Relations Act) but invoke the doctrine of sovereignty to oppose the extension of similar rights to public employees, who to this day are not covered by the NLRA. In particular, most public employees still do not have the right to strike that was guaranteed private-sector employees by the labor relations legislation of the 1930s.

During the period of rapid union growth in the private sector, public-sector unions were virtually moribund. During the 1960s and 1970s, however, the expansion of unions in the public sector has been the main source of union membership growth in the United States. While the fraction of private-sector workers who are union members has been declining, union membership is growing rapidly in the public sector in both absolute and percentage terms. For example, between 1963 and 1977, the proportion of federal employees in the executive branch covered by collective-bargaining agreements rose from 48 to 88 percent.[11] Similarly, the proportion of state and local government (SLG) employees belonging to unions rose from 7.7 percent in 1964 to 17.4 percent in 1978 (see Table 12.4). If one includes membership in bargaining organizations—which include professional organizations such as the National Education Association (NEA)—an even higher membership level is seen. The primary purpose of employee associations historically has not related to collective bargaining; for example, the NEA has long been primarily concerned with professional standards and improving the quality of education. Many of these associations have become increasingly involved in the collective-bargaining process in the public sector however. As Table 12.4 indicates, the percentage of SLG employees who belong to bargaining organizations rose from 27 to 36 percent, while their absolute

Table 12.4. State and Local Government Employees Belonging to Unions or Bargaining Organizations or Covered by Union Contracts

Year	*SLG Employees Belonging to Unions* Number (in thousands)	Percent	*SLG Employees Belonging to Bargaining Organizations* Number (in thousands)	Percent	*Percentage of SLG Employees Covered By a Formal Contract*
1964	556	7.7			
1966	664	7.8			
1968	804	8.8	2,466	27.1	
1970	947	9.6	2,668	27.1	
1972	1,105	10.4	3,137	29.4	
1974	1,529	13.4	3,911	34.1	
1976	1,710	14.0	4,521	37.0	27.7
1978	2,243	17.4	4,674	36.2	
1980	n.a.	n.a.	3,956	32.9	

n.a. not available

SOURCE: John F. Burton, Jr., "The Extent of Collective Bargaining in the Public Sector" in *Public Sector Bargaining* eds. Benjamin Aaron *et. al.* (Washington, D.C.: Bureau of National Affairs, 1979), Tables 2 and 4; U.S. Bureau of Labor Statistics. *Directory of National Union and Employee Associations* (Washington, D.C.: U.S. Government Printing Office, 1980); and Bureau of National Affairs, *Directory of U.S. Labor Organizations* 1982–83 Edition (Washington, D.C.: Bureau of National Affairs, Inc., 1982), Table 14.

---

[11]John F. Burton, Jr., "The Extent of Collective Bargaining in the Public Sector," in *Public-Sector Bargaining,* eds. Benjamin Aaron *et al.* (Washington, D.C.: Bureau of National Affairs, 1979), Table 3.

membership increased from 2.5 to 4.7 million between 1968 and 1978. (Inclusion of employee association members earlier in Table 12.2 also raises the estimates of *total* union membership somewhat, but it does not alter the underlying overall union-membership trend in recent years.)

As in the private sector, union representation is unevenly distributed by occupation and geography. By the late 1970s, for example, the most rapid growth of union membership among full-time public employees had occurred among teachers and fire and police protection personnel (Table 12.5). Unionism in the public sector also varied geographically, with the more rapid gains occurring in the larger and older cities. In 1979, 86 percent of state governments but only 17 percent of local government units had developed a labor relations-policy toward their employees. Local governments in southern states, where private-sector unions are weakest, are least likely to have developed a labor-relations policy.[12]

One factor that continued to affect this growth in public-sector unionization was changing public attitudes and legislation governing bargaining in the public sector. Given the early influence of the doctrine of sovereignty, laws governing collective bargaining in the public sector are of recent vintage. For example, Executive Order 10988, issued by President John F. Kennedy in 1962, legitimized collective bargaining in the federal sector for the first time, providing federal workers with the rights to join unions and bargain over working conditions—but *not* wages. While this executive order has been modified several times since then, in the early 1980s most federal employees' wages were still not determined by the

Table 12.5. Percent of Organized Full-Time Employees, by Function and Level of Government, 1979

Function	State and local governments	State governments	Local governments
Total	47.9	38.7	51.4
For selected functions:			
Education	55.2	29.0	61.1
Teachers	64.5	36.1	67.5
Other	38.2	25.4	44.9
Highways	43.6	50.7	37.0
Public welfare	40.8	40.3	41.3
Hospitals	39.5	48.4	29.6
Police protection	52.6	50.3	52.9
Local fire protection	70.5	—	70.5
Sanitation other than sewerage	43.8	—	43.8
All other functions	36.7	37.8	36.1

—Represents zero.

SOURCE: U.S. Bureau of the Census, *Labor-Management Relations in State and Local Governments:* 1979 State and Local Government Special Studies No. 100 (Washington, D.C.: U.S. Govt. Printing Office, Oct. 1980)

---

[12]U.S. Bureau of the Census, *Labor-Management Relations in State and Local Government, 1979* State and Local Government Special Studies No. 100 (Washington, D.C.: U.S. Government Printing Office, 1980) pp. 2–3.

collective-bargaining process, and the bargaining rights of federal employees did not include the right to strike.[13]

Instead of bargaining over wages, *comparability legislation* was passed at the federal level in 1962 and tied the wages of federal white-collar workers to those of private workers found "comparable" in a survey, subject to possible presidential or congressional modification.[14] Federal blue-collar workers' wages are also determined, in the main, by the comparability process, with comparisons in this case being made at the local labor-market level. The influence of federal unions on wages operates, then, primarily through the political pressure they can exert on the President and Congress to approve wage increases that the surveys suggest they deserve. The wage-determination process under collective bargaining in the federal sector clearly differs in many ways from wage determination under collective bargaining in the private sector.

Favorable state legislation for SLG-employee collective bargaining began with a 1959 state law in Wisconsin; prior to that date, collective bargaining was effectively prohibited in the state and local sector. By the early 1980s, most industrial states had adopted statutes that permitted SLG employees to participate in the determination of their wages and conditions of employment, although very few states permitted strikes by public employees.[15] Nevertheless, by 1976, 27.7 percent of all SLG employees were covered by a formal union contract (Table 12.4).

At the same time as employment and unionization were growing in the SLG sector, SLG employees' earnings started to rise relative to the earnings of private-sector employees; from the mid-1950s to 1970, for example, the relative-earnings position of SLG employees improved by some 15 to 20 percent. The growth in the relative-earnings position of SLG employees during the 1960s, coupled with the growing strength of public-employee unions, their increased militancy, and the trend towards allowing SLG employees to bargain over wage issues, led to fears that inflationary wage settlements would continue in the sector and aggravate the financial problems faced by state and local governments. These fears were explicitly based upon the belief that many public services are both essential and produced under monopoly conditions, which implies that the wage elasticity of

[13]There were some major exceptions—namely, postal workers and employees of federal-government authorities, such as the Tennessee Valley Authority (TVA). In each of these cases the prices of the products or services produced (mail delivery, hydroelectric power) can be raised to cover the cost of the contract settlement, unlike other federal agencies where salaries are paid out of general revenues.

[14]*See* Sharon Smith, *Equal Pay in the Public Sector: Fact or Fantasy* (Princeton, N.J.: Princeton University, 1977) for a more complete description of the comparability process in the federal sector. For an interesting analysis of some of the anomalies and incentive problems presented by the current federal pay-comparability procedures, *see* Robert Hartman, *Federal Employees Pay and Retirement Benefits: The White Collar Waiting Game* (Washington, D.C.: The Brookings Institution, 1983).

[15]*See* discussion of public sector labor relations law in Chapter 13 and B. V. H. Schneider, "Public-Sector Labor Legislation: An Evolutionary Analysis" in *Public-Sector Bargaining* eds. Benjamin Aaron *et al.* (Washington D.C.: Bureau of National Affairs, 1979) for a more complete discussion of the evolution of legislation governing bargaining in the public sector.

demand for public employees is very inelastic and that unions in the public sector are therefore potentially very powerful. To many, the logical conclusion was that, in the absence of market constraints that would limit the wage demands of public employees, limitations should be placed on the collective-bargaining rights of these groups.[16]

Although, by the late 1970s, eight states did grant the right to strike in one form or another to selected public employee groups, most continued historic prohibitions against strikes. The states that prohibited strikes, however, often provided assistance to local governments and unions in settling contract disputes, with a number of states adopting forms of binding arbitration as the terminal stage in their impasse procedures. (The nature and implications of modern techniques of dispute resolution are discussed more extensively in Chapter 15.) Some of the fears concerning public sector unionism began to diminish in the late 1970s as the earnings of SLG workers rose less quickly than those of workers in the private sector.

A Model of the Level of Unionization

A simple model of the demand and supply of union activity can be used to help explain the forces that influence union strength.[17] On the demand side, employees' demand to be union members will be a function of the "price" of union membership; this price includes monthly dues, initiation fees, the value of the time an individual is expected to spend on union activities, and the expected costs of collective bargaining, including possible wage loss if a strike occurs. Other things being equal, the higher the price, the lower the fraction of employees who will want to be union members—as represented by the demand curve D_0 in Figure 12.2.

It is costly to represent workers in collective-bargaining negotiations and to supervise the administration of union contracts. Moreover, union-organizing campaigns require resources, and as unions move from organizing workers who are the most favorably inclined towards unions to those who are the least favorably inclined, the cost of making a sufficiently strong case to win a union-representation election increases. As such, it is reasonable to conclude that, other things being equal, on the supply side of the market the willingness of unions to provide union services is an upward-sloping function of the price of union membership—as represented by the supply curve (S_0) in Figure 12.2. The intersection of these demand and supply curves yields an equilibrium percentage of the work force that is unionized (U_0) and an equilibrium price of union services (P_0).

What are the forces that determine the *positions* of the demand and supply

[16]*See,* for example, H. Wellington and R. Winter, "The Limits of Collective Bargaining in Public Employment," *Yale Law Journal,* 69 (June 1969): 1107–27.

[17]This model is based upon the approach found in Orley Ashenfelter and John Pencavel, "American Trade Union Growth, 1900–1960," *Quarterly Journal of Economics* 83 (August 1969): 434–48; and John Pencavel, "The Demand for Union Services: An Exercise," *Industrial and Labor Relations Review* 24 (January 1971): 180–91.

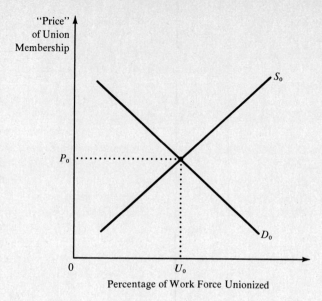

Figure 12.2   The Demand and Supply of Unionization

curves? Anything that causes either the demand curve *or* the supply curve to shift to the right will increase the level of unionization in the economy, other things being equal. Conversely, if either of these curves shifts to the left, other things being equal, the level of unionization will fall. Identifying the factors that shift these curves enables one to explain *changes* in the level of unionization in the economy over time.

On the demand side, it is likely that individuals' demand for union membership is positively related to their perceptions of the *net benefits* from being union members. For example, the larger the wage gain they think unions will win for them, the further to the right the demand curve will be and the higher the level of unionization. Another factor is worker preferences; if individuals' tastes for union membership increase—perhaps because of changes in social attitudes or the introduction of labor legislation that protects the rights of workers to join unions —the demand curve will also shift to the right.

On the supply side, anything that changes the *costs* of union-organizing activities will affect the position of the supply curve. Introduction of labor legislation that makes it easier (harder) for unions to win representation elections will shift the supply curve to the right (left). Changes in the industrial structure that make it more difficult to organize the work force will shift the curve to the left and reduce the level of unionization.

The rapid growth in unionization that took place in the private sector during the 1930s was a product of both the changing legal environment (Norris-LaGuardia and Wagner Acts) and changing social attitudes towards unions induced by the Great Depression—changes that shifted both the demand and supply curves to the right.[18] The growth continued during the World War II years as low unemployment rates reduced workers' fears of losing their jobs if they indicated pro-union sentiments (shifting the demand curve to the right). Unemployment increased after the end of World War II, shifting the demand curve back to the left, while the passage of the Taft-Hartley Act placed restrictions on union organizing tactics and shifted the supply curve further to the left. Both of these shifts served to decrease the percentage unionized.

The decline in private sector union membership since the mid-1950s can be at least partially explained by two factors, already discussed in earlier chapters. First, the fraction of the labor force that is female has increased substantially (see Chapter 6), and females historically have tended not to join unions. The benefits from union membership are a function of individuals' expected tenure with firms; seniority provisions, job-security provisions, and retirement benefits are not worth much to individuals who expect to be employed at a firm for only a short while. *In the past,* females tended to have shorter expected job tenure than males and to have more intermittent labor-force participation. As a result, their expected benefits from joining unions were lower; an increase in their share in the labor force would shift the aggregate demand curve for union membership to the left.[19]

The second factor in the decline of union membership is the shift in the industrial composition of employment, discussed in Chapter 2. The last 25 years have seen a substantial decline in the relative employment shares of manufacturing, mining, construction, transportation, and public utilities, and conversely, a substantial increase in the share of employment in wholesale and retail trade, finance, insurance, real estate, and the service industries. Indeed, the former group fell from 48.7 percent of nonagricultural payroll employment in 1955 to 32.3 percent by 1982. During the same period the latter group rose from 37.7 to 50.1 percent.[20] As Table 12.6 indicates, the industries in the latter group are the ones that are least unionized. The shifting industrial composition of employment has led to a distribution that is weighted more heavily towards industries that are not heavily unionized.

Why does the latter set of industries tend not to be unionized? These industries tend to be highly competitive ones, with high price elasticities of demand. As discussed in Chapter 4, other things being equal, industries with high price elasticities of product demand will also have high wage elasticities of demand for labor. High wage elasticities limit unions' abilities to increase their members'

---

[18]It is difficult to identify the effect of the laws *per se,* as they are determined by societal attitudes themselves. However, as noted both above and also below, prior to and after the Depression, periods of high (low) unemployment have been associated with weakening (growing) union membership, which leads one to suspect that the changing legal environment induced by the Depression, which reduced employees' fears of being fired for union activities, did have a substantial effect on union growth during the 1930s.

[19]We emphasize "in the past" here. Changing labor-force patterns, with a greater share of females now having permanent attachment to the labor force, will likely increase their propensity to become union members in the future.

[20]U.S. Bureau of Labor Statistics, *Employment and Earnings* 30 (March 1983) Table B–1, p. 65.

Table 12.6 Union and Association Membership by Industry in 1978

Industry	Number of Union Members (in thousands)	Number of Employees on Payrolls (in thousands)	Percentage of Employees that Are Union Members
Manufacturing	8,119	20,476	39.7
Mining	428	851	50.3
Construction	2,884	4,271	67.5
Transportation and public utilities	2,651	4,927	53.8
Wholesale and retail trade	1,713	19,499	8.8
Finance, insurance, and real estate	51	4,727	1.1
Service	1,824	16,220	11.2
Federal government	1,383	2,753	50.2
State and local government	2,243	12,723	17.4

SOURCE: U.S. Bureau of Labor Statistics, *Directory of National Unions and Employee Associations,* Bulletin 2079 (Washington, D.C.: U.S. Government Printing Office. 1980). Table 16; U.S. Bureau of Labor Statistics, *Handbook of Labor Statistics,* 1980, Bulletin 2070 (Washington, D.C.: U.S. Government Printing Office, 1979).

wages without substantial employment declines also occurring. As such, the net benefits individuals perceive from union membership may be lower in these industries, and an increase in their importance in the economy would shift the demand for union services to the left in Figure 12.2, thereby reducing the percentage of the work force that is unionized.[21]

These factors should be kept in mind when we consider two controversial features of the legal environment of labor relations that are said to influence union membership trends. The first, discussed later in this chapter, is the passage of so-called "right-to-work" legislation in several states during the post-World War II period. The second, examined in Chapter 13, is the legal regulation of the union organizing process and the alleged increase of "union avoidance" tactics by employers within the regulatory framework surrounding labor relations.

This simple demand-and-supply model of union membership can also be used retrospectively to provide some insight into why unionization in the public sector has grown so rapidly since the 1960s. On the one hand, changing public attitudes and the evolution of labor legislation relating to collective bargaining in the public sector, which we described earlier in the chapter, reduced the costs of organizing public employees (shifting the supply of union services to the right) and probably increased the benefits public employees perceived from union membership (shifting the demand for union membership to the right). Both forces would lead to

[21]These industries tend to be populated by small establishments. The demand for unionization is thought to be lower for employees who work in small firms, since they often feel less alienated from their supervisors. Similarly, since it is more costly to try to organize 1000 workers spread over 100 firms than it is to organize 1000 workers at one plant, it is often thought that the supply of union services would shift left as the share of employment going to small firms increases. Both of these factors tend to suggest (in terms of Figure 12.2) that unionization will decline as the share of employment occurring in small establishments increases, providing another reason why the shift in the industrial distribution of employment has affected the extent of unionization.

an increase in union strength. On the other hand, the decline in the relative-earnings position of state and local government employees that occurred in the mid-1970s, along with the slowdown in the rate of growth of employment and the imposition of expenditure- and tax-limitation legislation in several states, may have strengthened the desires of public employees to turn to unions in the hopes of regaining their former relative-earnings positions and winning job-security clauses in their contracts. Because these forces all increased the net benefits public employees perceived from union membership, they shifted the demand for unions further to the right.

Current Union Structure and Finances

Union Structure

The present structure and operation of the American labor movement reflects the main historical developments reviewed above. Figure 12.3 describes the general organization of the AFL-CIO as of the early 1980s. Out of 196 labor organizations counted by the Bureau of Labor Statistics, 162 were affiliated with the Federation in 1980. Those that were not affiliated included two of the three largest unions in the United States—the Teamsters' union (1,924,000 members), which had been expelled for corrupt activities in 1958, and the United Auto Workers (1,499,000 members) which left the Federation over policy differences in 1968 but rejoined in the early 1980s. While the supreme governing body of the AFL-CIO is the biennial convention, most of the Federation's business between conventions is guided by the Executive Council and the General Board. There are a number of staff departments that assist in developing the Federation's legislative positions and assist in general organizing activities. In addition to the central office there are various state offices of the Federation as well as local labor councils of AFL-CIO affiliates.

The relationship of each of these bodies to the constituent national unions is much as it was when the Federation was founded in 1886. At all levels of the organization the real power over collective bargaining and the governing of union organizations remains lodged in the national unions and in their local units, while the Federation's activities remain more in the nature of advocacy of labor's political objectives and support for the movement in general. The Federation continues to have no direct bargaining role in the negotiations conducted by the national unions.

The limitations on the Federation's power with respect to the national unions is also evident from the nature of the financial relationships between the AFL-CIO and the unions, and from the distribution of financial resources through the union structure. Per capita payments from the constituent national unions form a major part of the Federation's annual revenues, whereas there is no comparable flow of revenues from the Federation to the unions. A similar picture emerges from a review of the assets of union organizations. When compared to national unions, the AFL-CIO ranked 17th in size of assets

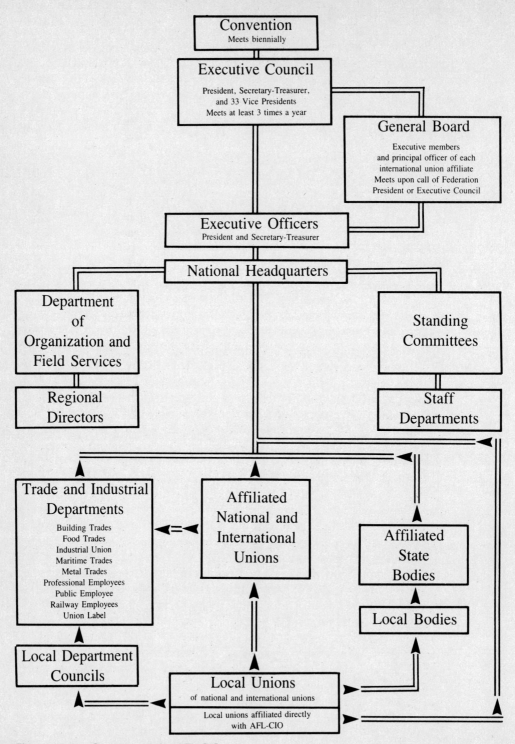

Figure 12.3 Structure of the AFL-CIO

($24.0 million) in 1976.[22] Individual national unions with substantially larger assets in 1976 included the International Brotherhood of Electrical Workers (with assets of $326.3 million), the United Automobile Workers ($233.9 million), the United Steelworkers ($144.9 million), the International Brotherhood of Teamsters ($112.0 million), the International Ladies Garment Workers ($105.1 million), and the United Mineworkers ($77.0 million).[23] Three of these unions, the Autoworkers, Teamsters, and Mineworkers, were not affiliated with the AFL-CIO at the time (although the autoworkers have since reaffiliated).

Financial Resources of Unions

What are the financial resources of labor organizations in the United States, and how do these resources compare with those of other economic institutions? In 1976, the consolidated assets of all levels of union organization were in the neighborhood of $4 billion, up from over $2.5 billion in 1970 (Table 12.7). The liabilities were much lower than assets, leaving unions in a strong net asset position. While the level of assets is larger than for unions in other countries, they are quite modest in comparison to the corporate world. If all the unions whose assets are represented in Table 12.7 belonged to a single, centrally-directed organization, that organization would have ranked 34th among the Fortune 500 corporations in 1976 and 31st in 1970. But our review of the historical development of organized labor in the United States has shown that unions are anything but a single, centrally-

Table 12.7. Assets and Liabilities of Unions and Percent Distribution of Assets by Type of Union, 1970 and 1976 (dollars in millions)

	1970		1976	
Assets	*($)*	*(%)*	*($)*	*(%)*
All unions	2,574	100	3,931	100
AFL-CIO		1		1
National unions		40		46
Local unions		59		53
Liabilities				
All unions	254		609	
Net assets				
All unions	2,320		3,322	

Note: Data are for unions required to file financial reports under the Labor-Management Reporting and Disclosure Act of 1959. This includes essentially all labor organizations except those whose members are not engaged in interstate commerce, most unions of state, county and municipal employees, and state and local units of the AFL–CIO. Unions of federal workers are only included in the 1976 data. Local unions include intermediate regional bodies.

SOURCE: U.S. Labor-Management Services Administration, *Union Financial Statistics 1976* (Washington, D.C.: U.S. Department of Labor, 1980) p. 6.

---

[22]If the assets of the Federation's Industrial Union Department and Building and Construction Trades Department are included,. the AFL-CIO would rank 12th with $32.5 million in assets.

[23]Data are from U.S. Labor-Management Services Administration, *Union Financial Statistics 1976* (Washington, D.C.: U.S. Department of Labor, 1980), p. 37.

directed organization. In addition to the constitutional limitations on the authority of the AFL-CIO, the data in Table 12.7 show that the financial resources at the Federation's command are small relative to those of the labor movement generally. By itself, the AFL-CIO accounts for about one percent of the assets of union organizations—not enough to place it in the Fortune 500.

The data in Table 12.7 also show that over half of organized labor's financial assets are held by local unions. In part, this reflects the needs of the relatively decentralized collective-bargaining structures that have emerged in the United States and that will be discussed more fully in Chapter 14. This significant concentration of wealth at the local union level, in many instances, can place limitations on the authority of national union headquarters over their local units. Underlying these averages, however, there is substantial inequality in the distribution of assets across unions. For example, ninety-nine percent of all national union assets were held by the 50 percent of national unions that reported total receipts of $1 million or more in 1976.

In what forms are these assets held by unions? A small number of unions— most notably the Teamsters—have been accused of using union funds to finance investments of very questionable quality. The impression obtained from data on the distribution of assets held by most labor organizations in the United States, however, is that unions are generally quite risk-averse in their financial policies. In particular, their assets tend to be held in highly liquid form. For example, fully half of the assets of local unions tend to be held as cash in standard bank accounts and hence earn relatively low interest (Table 12.8). Only about 14 percent of the assets of local unions go into higher yielding (and somewhat riskier) investments in marketable securities and mortgages. On the other hand, almost half of the assets of national unions go into the "other investment" category that generally offers higher yields, and only about thirty percent of the assets are kept as cash or relatively liquid, low-risk, U.S. Treasury securities.

Why do so many local unions persist in following investment strategies that impose such a high opportunity cost on their organizations in terms of forgone opportunities to increase the growth of their financial resources? Unions fre-

Table 12.8. Structure of Union Assets, 1976 (percent distribution)

Asset	All Unions	National Unions	Local Unions
Total assets	100%	100%	100%
Cash	32	12	50
Loans receivable	3	4	3
U.S. Treasury Securities	13	19	7
Other Investments[a]	30	48	14
Other Assets[b]	22	17	26

See note to Table 12.7.

[a]Marketable securities, mortgage investments, and investments in subsidiaries.

[b]"Other Assets" include land, buildings, office furniture, office equipment, and automotive equipment.

SOURCE: U.S. Labor-Management Services Administration, *Union Financial Statistics 1976* (Washington, D.C.: U.S. Department of Labor, 1980).

quently argue that an important potential use of their resources is to provide strike benefits to their members in the event of a work stoppage, and that they must keep their assets liquid in order to make the strike weapon a credible threat.[24] However, this overlooks the fact that most collective-bargaining agreements have an explicit expiration date, so that the time at which strike benefits might be needed is known well in advance. In addition, there is an array of financial instruments available with different maturity dates. It would not be difficult to place a larger percentage of union assets in investments (with higher yields than bank accounts) that matured at times when unions might need access to cash. One is left with the impression that the resources of labor unions could be significantly larger if unions were more imaginative in their use of the financial instruments now available in capital markets.

As a partial result of the high liquidity of their assets, most of the revenues of local unions come from dues (70 percent in 1976) and various fees, fines, assessments, and charges for work permits (8 percent). The main categories of expenditures are for affiliation payments (30 percent of expenditures), salaries for union officers and employees (25 percent),[25] and administration (10 percent). Because they follow different investment policies, national unions receive a larger proportion of their revenues (and disbursements) from the turnover of relatively short-term securities. Only about 30 percent of their receipts were from dues, per capita taxes, and fees in 1976.

Union Decision Making at the Micro Level

Many theories of union behavior attempt to formalize the view that unions are organizations seeking to maximize some well-defined objective function.[26] A classic debate took place more than thirty-five years ago over whether it was more meaningful to use standard maximization models or political models of union

---

[24]For a discussion of this point, *see* Leo Troy, "American Unions and Their Wealth," *Industrial Relations* 14 (May 1975): 134–44 and Neil Sheflin and Leo Troy, "Finances of American Unions in the 1970s, *Journal of Labor Research* IV (Spring 1983): 149–57.

[25]The salaries of most major union leaders are considerably lower than the salaries of presidents of corporations of similar size. In 1983, for example, the president of the AFL-CIO and several national union presidents earned salaries in the range of $100,000 to $140,000, but the president of the United Automobile Workers received about $75,000. The exception at the high end of the scale was the president of the International Brotherhood of Teamsters, who received salaries and expenses totaling over $550,000; the exception at the low end was the president of the United Farm Workers, whose salary was just under $7,500. Data are from the U.S. Department of Labor as reported in the *San Francisco Sunday Examiner and Chronicle,* July 3, 1983, p. A10.

[26]*See* Wallace Atherton, *Theory of Union Bargaining Goals* (Princeton, N.J.: Princeton University Press, 1973) for an extensive discussion of the various theories. Recently, several econometric studies have even attempted to estimate the parameters of such an objective function. *See* Henry Farber, "Individual Preferences and Union Wage Determination: The Case of the United Mine Workers," *Journal of Political Economy* 86 (October 1978): 923–42; and J. N. Dertouzos and J. H. Pencavel, "Wage and Employment Determination Under Trade Unionism: The International Typographical Union," *Journal of Political Economy* 89 (December 1981): 1162–81.

behavior.[27] In fact, the two approaches are not as far apart as past debates may have indicated. The relationship between a union and its members bears more resemblance to the relationship between a government and voters than to the relationship between a firm and its customers or workers. As a result, many aspects of union goals and behavior can best be understood from the perspective government decision-making models. While these may reasonably be referred to as "political" models, they do not abandon the notion that unions may adopt maximizing behavior.

A Political Model of Internal Union Decision Making

The basic fact that makes the analysis of unions and governments distinctive is not that their leadership is elected—voting processes also exist in private firms, and customers vote all the time in their choice of which products to purchase—but is the nature of the services provided. As with governments, many of the services provided by unions to their members are *public goods,* which differ importantly from the *private* goods and services produced by business firms. One distinctive characteristic of public goods is that they are "jointly consumed" and thus provide benefits to many people simultaneously. That is, one person's consumption does not reduce the amount available to another person.[28] (By way of contrast, an automobile purchased by one consumer is not available to benefit another consumer.)

Many of the benefits negotiated by unions in collective bargaining are in the nature of public goods at the workplace. Contractual rules governing the speed of a production line, safety conditions, and the amount of discretion accorded supervisors are examples of benefits that, once negotiated, are available more or less equally to all workers in the bargaining unit. The fact that one worker benefits from a contractual requirement that reduces the speed of a production line does not reduce the benefit that another worker can receive from the same rule. (Not all goods or services provided by unions have this characteristic inherently. In contrast to negotiated improvements in safety conditions, for example, it is possible in principle to vary the wage and fringe benefits received by different workers.)

A second characteristic of public goods that influences union goals and behavior is that it is usually impossible (or at least very costly) to prevent individuals who refuse to pay their share of the cost of providing a public good from enjoying the benefits of it. When the speed of a production line is reduced, it affects all workers on the line—not just those who pay union dues. This nonexclusion characteristic of public goods differs sharply from the situation for private

---

[27]The former approach is espoused in John Dunlop, *Wage Determination Under Trade Unions* (New York: Macmillan, 1944), while a political model of union behavior is articulated in Arthur Ross, *Trade Union Wage Policy* (Berkeley, Calif.: University of California Press, 1948).

[28]For example, national defense is collectively consumed; person A's consumption of it does not reduce the deterrence available to person B.

goods where possession of a good or service can be denied to those who do not pay. While unions could in principle attempt to prevent nonmembers from receiving those benefits of collective bargaining that are not jointly consumed (for example, increases in compensation, access to the grievance procedure), in practice, American labor legislation forbids this in the private sector. Once a union is certified by the National Labor Relations Board as the *exclusive* bargaining representative of workers in a bargaining unit, that union has the duty to represent *all* workers in the unit, and the benefits of collective bargaining accrue equally to members who pay dues to the union and to nonmembers who do not. Exclusive representation therefore converts even those negotiated benefits that are not inherently jointly consumed into public goods.[29] This point is less generally applicable in the public sector, because the exclusive representation feature of the NLRA has not been adopted uniformly in the various state laws governing labor relations in state and local governments.

The nonexclusion characteristic of union-negotiated public goods can give rise to a *free rider* problem; workers who automatically benefit from any work-rule change may be inclined to hang back and wait for others to bear the costs of accomplishing the change. As we shall see below, this has led unions to argue that they should be able to compel dues or service payments just as governments are able to compel tax payments to finance public goods produced for the population at large.

When public goods are an important aspect of the work environment, one can see how a collective institution, such as a union, has a comparative advantage over the actions of individuals in achieving change. The benefit to an *individual* worker of changing a particular working condition may be small relative to the total benefit received by a *group* of workers. If left to individual actions, the working condition may not be changed because the person who incurs the cost of lobbying for the change is unlikely to be compensated by others for the risk that he or she takes in confronting the employer. Since the benefit to the individual is small relative to the cost of seeking change, fighting for changes in the provision of workplace public-goods is unlikely to occur if left to individual workers. Instead, dissatisfied workers will quit. Because a union is an organization that can represent the collective will of a group of workers, it has a comparative advantage in establishing or changing the levels of workplace public-goods without workers having to quit in order to express their preferences.[30]

---

[29]Even without the legal requirement, however, there would be nothing to prevent employers from providing the benefits negotiated by unions for their members to employees who were not union members. Indeed, many employers in the United States regularly extend the benefits negotiated in collective bargaining to workers (usually white-collar) who are not in the bargaining unit in an effort to remove the incentive for more widespread unionization of their work force.

[30]Mancur Olson, *The Logic of Collective Action* (Cambridge, Mass.: Harvard University Press, 1965); Greg Duncan and Frank Stafford, "Do Union Members Receive Compensating Wage Differentials?" *American Economic Review* 70 (June 1980): 355–71; and Robert J. Flanagan, "Workplace Public Goods and Union Organizations," *Industrial Relations,* 22 (Spring 1983): 224–37.

Decision making over workplace public goods. What level of a public-goods working condition should a union bargain for? This is where the maximization aspect of union behavior enters. As we have seen, changes in working conditions often yield benefits to many workers simultaneously. At the same time, the union incurs resource costs in negotiating, possibly striking over, and then enforcing those changes. Unions maximizing the welfare of their members will seek improvements in a particular working condition until the sum of the marginal benefits ($\sum_{i=1}^{n} MB_i$) to its n members equals the marginal costs *(MC)* to the union of achieving the changes in working conditions: $\sum_{i=1}^{n} MB = MC$. This decision rule is similar to the rule that a profit-maximizing firm will produce until its marginal revenue from the last unit of production equals the marginal cost of that unit, with one important difference. Because many workers enjoy the benefits of a public-goods type of working condition simultaneously, it is the *sum* of the marginal benefits across all workers that must be balanced against the marginal cost of providing the improved working condition.[31]

Maximizing behavior by unions can be illustrated more clearly using Figure 12.4 in which the vertical axis represents the marginal benefit or marginal cost (in dollars) of a particular working condition and the horizontal axis represents the amount or level of the workplace public good. The marginal cost *(MC)* curve

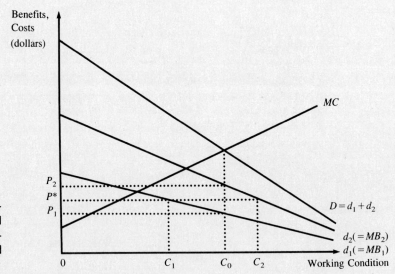

Figure 12.4 Determining the Optimal Level of and Financing of a Public-Good Bargaining Demand

describes the cost incurred by the union in establishing the working condition. The curve is positively sloped because an employer's resistance to a proposal is pre-

---

[31]Paul Samuelson, "The Pure Theory of Public Expenditure," *Review of Economics and Statistics* XXXVI (November 1954): 386–89.

sumed to increase with the level, and hence, cost of the proposal, thereby requiring more negotiating time and perhaps even a strike on the part of the union. The valuation of different levels of the working condition by different union members is represented by the d_i curves, which are preferences of union members for different levels of the working condition. (They can be thought of as the demand curve of individual members for the working condition, since they describe the marginal benefits of different levels of the working condition in terms of the maximum dues price the member would be willing to pay to obtain each level of the working condition.) In order to simplify the graphical presentation, we have limited the number of members to two, with preferences represented by d_1 and d_2.

There are two features of the d_i curves that are important. First, they are negatively sloped to express the idea that even the consumption of working conditions is subject to diminishing returns. (A union member is assumed to value negotiated changes in working conditions that reduce the risk of death or injury from 10 in 100,000 to 9 in 100,000 more than changes that reduce risk from 2 in 100,000 to 1 in 100,000.) Second, the d_i curves are at different levels, reflecting the fact that union members are unlikely to have identical preferences for a given working condition. In Figure 12.4, the union member(s) represented by d_2 prefer the working condition on the horizontal axis more strongly than the member(s) represented by d_1. As will become apparent, the dispersion of preferences among the union membership represents one of the major problems facing unions trying to maximize membership welfare and is a major source of the "political" aspects of union behavior.

Since all union members benefit simultaneously from public-good working conditions, the total marginal benefit to the union membership of negotiating one more unit of a working condition is the sum of the individual benefits. Graphically, this is represented by the D curve, which represents the sum all workers (taken together) are willing to pay for that level of the workplace public good.[32]

Membership welfare is maximized when $\sum_{i=1}^{n} MB = MC$; that is, where $D = MC$ in Figure 12.4. It should now be clear that a union will maximize membership welfare by negotiating C_0 units of the working condition, the level at which the marginal benefits to the membership equal the marginal costs of providing those benefits. If the union were to negotiate a level less than C_0, it would not be expending enough effort on the membership's behalf. If it were to negotiate more than C_0, it would be wasting union funds in the sense that the cost of additional negotiations exceeds the value received by the membership.

The role of membership preferences. It is much easier to describe C_0, the optimal level of a negotiated benefit, than to achieve it as a union leader. In particular, it is no easy task for a union leader to discover with great precision the valuation that its membership places on various working conditions (i.e., the D schedule in Figure

---

[32]In graphical terms, D (which equals $\sum_{i=1}^{n} MB_i$) is the vertical summation of the d_i curves, which describe the individual marginal benefits obtained from different levels of the working condition.

12.4). Even when preferences are known, they may be so dispersed that they are difficult to satisfy. To see this, consider the question of how a union finances the negotiation of C_0. The answer to this question is at the heart of the political problem faced by labor unions. One approach would be to charge each union member according to the benefit received from the working condition (or package of conditions) negotiated by the union. Since not all members place the same valuation on a particular working condition, this would mean that different members would be charged different amounts. In Figure 12.4, for example, the union member whose preferences are represented by d_1 would be charged a dues-price per unit of workplace public good equal to P_1 and the member whose preferences are represented by d_2 would be charged a dues-price equal to P_2.

This system would have two desirable results. First, the total cost of obtaining the improved working conditions would be covered, since the sum of P_1 and P_2 equals MC, the marginal cost of providing the working condition.[33] Second, each union member is satisfied with the outcome in the sense that the amount that they are charged is equivalent to the marginal benefit that they receive. There are some serious problems, however, with this approach to financing a union's activities. If union members know that they will be charged according to the strength of their preferences for various benefits, they will have an incentive to understate their preferences and hope that other members will bear the burden of paying. This effort to "let the other members pay for it" is familiar free-rider behavior. In addition, the idea of differentiating dues payments among workers according to these criteria is contrary to the egalitarian principles of most labor unions.

Instead, most unions adopt an approach that is easy to administer and consistent with their egalitarian philosophy—they charge each individual an equal amount as union dues, for example, the amount P^* in Figure 12.4. As with the first approach, charging equal dues solves the financial issue, but unlike the first approach it leaves the union with an internal political problem. This can be seen by considering how satisfied each member is with the union's activities when everyone is charged P^* as dues. Suppose the working condition under negotiation is a pension plan. Normally this type of fringe benefit holds more appeal for older workers than younger workers. Younger workers, whose preferences for the pension plan might be represented by d_1 are unhappy because at price P^* they would prefer a more limited pension plan, C_1. Their marginal valuation of C_0 units of the pension plan is less than the P^* that they are required to pay for it. The opposite is the case for older members whose preferences might be represented by d_2. At level C_0 the price P^* is low relative to their valuation of additional units of the benefit, and they would prefer that the union negotiate a more extensive pension plan (i.e., C_2). Therefore, with a substantial dispersion of membership preferences a union can be in the paradoxical situation of making no group of members happy when it negotiates a contract that provides the optimal level of benefit from the standpoint of the membership as a whole. Some members may think it should have negotiated more, and some may think that it should have

---

[33]Note, however, that the net benefits received by a union member are positive. The total benefit is the sum of the marginal benefits (graphically, the area under the worker's d curve), while the total cost is the price per unit, P_i, multiplied by the number of units, C_j.

negotiated less. Generally, the internal political stability of unions is probably directly related to the homogeneity of preferences among the union's members.

Trade-offs faced by unions. The difficulty of meeting membership expectations is increased by the fact that there are inherent trade-offs unions must face in collective bargaining. We have seen several examples of these trade-offs in earlier chapters in the book. The best-known is the one between wages and employment summarized in the demand curve for labor, which was first introduced in Chapter 2. Even seemingly powerful unions do not press for the highest wage rate that is potentially possible because of the adverse effects of such a policy on the employment prospects of union members. Instead, as we shall see in Chapter 14, unions frequently try to secure legislation or bargaining structures that alter the terms of the trade-off. Even these activities, however, indicate that unions recognize that such trade-offs exist and form a constraint on their objectives.

Most unions face other important trade-offs as well. For example, we noted in Chapter 7 how demands for greater safety and other changes in nonwage working conditions often are costly to implement and therefore tend to be provided at lower wages. A union may try to use its bargaining power to induce an employer to provide both higher pay and better working conditions, but if this raises the labor costs of the company relative to its competitors, the employment of union members will be jeopardized in the long run. Similarly, the trade-off between wages and fringe benefits that was discussed in Chapter 10 is present in union as well as nonunion employment relationships.

One of the difficulties facing a union leader is that different groups of members within the union may have different rates at which they may be willing to trade between wages and other benefits. For example, in companies in which the last person hired is the first to be fired, workers with relatively high seniority are likely to be less concerned about the employment consequences of high wages than recently hired union members. Younger members, on the other hand, are more likely than older workers to want the union to put more emphasis on negotiating high wages and less emphasis on pensions or other fringe benefits that have a payoff in the distant future. That is, they will accept a smaller sacrifice of wages for additional pension benefits. Those members who are less familiar with the basic economics of the industry than the union leadership may question whether trade-offs are necessary at all. Thus, one important task of union leaders is to ascertain what trade-offs are acceptable to a majority of the union membership from among the diverse notions of different groups.

Political Pressures on Union Leaders

Probably the most difficult job facing union leaders is accommodating the heterogeneity of interests among the membership. Indeed, when the heterogeneity is great, the task of formulating bargaining demands within the union may be more difficult than actual collective-bargaining negotiations. Union leaders who fail to accommodate membership interests sufficiently face several possible consequences.

First, the membership may fail to ratify a collective-bargaining agreement on which management and the union negotiators have tentatively agreed. This is more than a theoretical possibility; some 10 percent of tentative labor agreements are rejected in the ratification process—usually in well-established bargaining relationships. In 1966, airline mechanics affiliated with the International Association of Machinists rejected a tentative agreement that had been negotiated in the White House with the personal intervention of President Johnson, who was interested in keeping wage increases within voluntary federal "wage guideposts" that existed at the time. (The "guideposts" are discussed in Chapter 19.) In this instance, the willingness of the leadership to acquiesce in federal policy was out of step with the rank and file. More recently, efforts to negotiate wage concessions in the automobile and steel industries have received a mixed reception by the rank-and-file (see Examples 12.1 and 12.2). In these instances it has sometimes appeared that the rank-and-file and the union leadership had different views of acceptable trade-offs between wages and employment.

Ratification procedures can serve a number of useful purposes. In testing the acceptability of a proposed agreement to those who are to be governed by it, the process provides some indication of the willingness of the union membership to live by the terms of the agreement. A high degree of acceptability raises the likelihood that the contract will be self-enforcing—a factor that both the union and management are interested in.[34] The acceptability test also reduces the likelihood that union leaders will negotiate contracts that do not really benefit union members, but it may also limit their ability to negotiate provisions that are important to the long-term survival of the union when such provisions are contrary to the short-term interests of office. As noted earlier in the chapter, the Landrum-Griffin Act, which was passed in 1959, included a procedure through which the results of an election for union office could be set aside and rerun under federal supervision in the event of election irregularities. In the ensuing years several major union elections were rerun with different outcomes under this procedure, so that incumbent officers are now more susceptible to challenges from the rank-and-file than previously. At the present time the tenure of office for the principal officers of most national unions is less than ten years (although in 1979 the presidents of two unions had taken office before 1950). The turnover of union presidents is relatively high in smaller unions where elections tend to be more frequent, so that the opportunity for change is higher; however, turnover is also relatively high in the largest unions despite longer terms of office and less frequent elections.[35] The lower probability of retaining office when an election occurs in larger unions is consistent with the hypothesis that larger unions are character-

---

[34]The ratification process can also be used to a limited extent for tactical purposes during collective-bargaining negotiations. For an interesting discussion of this and other contract ratification issues, *see* Clyde W. Summers, "Ratification of Agreements," in John T. Dunlop and Neil W. Chamberlain eds., *Frontiers of Collective Bargaining* (New York: Harper and Row, 1967), pp. 75–102.

[35]U.S. Bureau of Labor Statistics, *Directory of National Unions and Employee Associations, 1979* Bulletin 2079 (Washington, D.C.: U.S. Government Printing Office, September 1980), pp. 51–52, 110–11.

ized by greater heterogeneity of interests among the membership and are therefore much more difficult to run successfully, although it may also be true that there are greater rewards to leading a large union, and therefore, more competition for the positions.

Finally, if a union is sufficiently unresponsive to membership needs, it may be decertified in a special election by the National Labor Relations Board. As the data in Table 12.3 indicated, such elections, while still small in comparison to representation elections, are increasing—as is the proportion of such elections that result in decertification of the union as bargaining agent.

Faced with the need to satisfy their members, union leaders develop *political* methods for deciding about issues of compensation and working conditions affecting their often heterogeneous membership. The adoption of a political approach to the formulation of bargaining objectives—which must be done when decisions about wages and other conditions of employment are made—can lead to employment contracts that are radically different from what would exist in the absence of unions. Prior to this chapter, virtually all of the analysis of the pricing and allocation of labor in this book has been concerned with nonunion labor markets, where workers who are dissatisfied with their employment can only "vote with their feet" by quitting. We have stressed the fact that it is the choices by the marginal workers—the workers most likely to change their place of employment or their employment status—that are crucial in the operation of nonunion labor

EXAMPLE 12.1

Wage Concessions in the Automobile Industry

In the early 1980s the U.S. automobile industry came under severe economic pressure from a combination of international competitive pressures and a deep domestic recession. The Ford Motor Company reported losses of $1.5 billion and $1.0 billion in 1980 and 1981 respectively, while General Motors reported a loss of $763 million in 1980 and a profit of $333 million in 1981. The Chrysler Corporation was near bankruptcy. By early 1982, each of the major companies had begun to close major assembly plants.

During the winter of 1981–82, the auto companies approached the United Automobile Workers (UAW), the large industrial union that represents their workers in collective bargaining, to request contract concessions so that the industry could reduce its labor-cost differential with respect to foreign auto producers. At that time, the collective-bargaining agreement between the UAW and the major automobile companies was not due to expire until September 1982, and there was a prohibition against major revisions during the term of the contract. Convinced of the seriousness of the economic problems facing the industry, the leadership of the UAW obtained permission to suspend this prohibition and to begin negotiations with the auto companies.

In fact, the membership of the UAW was seriously split over the issue of negotiating concessions in wages and other benefits. While members at Ford generally supported the move, members working for General Motors doubted the seriousness of the company's economic plight. At one point early in 1982, the UAW halted negotiations that had been initiated with GM because the margin of support for such negotiations among its members at GM was narrow, only to resume again after several plant closings by GM appeared to convince some members of the seriousness of the company's economic situation.

Eventually, the UAW concluded separate negotiations with both Ford and GM in which union members agreed to forgo some annual pay increases, to defer some cost-of-living adjustments (COLAs) for 18 months, and to give up certain holidays in exchange for participation in a profit-sharing plan, greater income security for workers with high seniority, and certain concessions on job security. The new contract was estimated to save about $2.00 per hour in labor costs or $190.00 per car over the life of the contract. One interesting feature of the concessions negotiated at Ford and GM (and those negotiated in other industries by other unions) is that they did *not* include wage *cuts.* Instead, the concessions involved the timing (for example, by deferring COLAs or other payments) and size of increases in compensation.

When the ratification vote was taken, however, it was clear that the membership remained sharply divided over the advisability of the concessions, despite the fact that the leadership was convinced that they were needed for the survival of the industry and hence the union as an organization. Normally, collective-bargaining contracts that are negotiated by the UAW receive the support of about 80 percent of the membership, and in fact 73 percent of the UAW members at Ford voted in favor of this new agreement. At General Motors, however, the agreement received the approval of only 52 percent of UAW members. The widely varying attitudes of union members on concessions was indicated by the fact that some union locals overwhelmingly endorsed the agreement while others soundly rejected it.

Why would a union leader support a proposition facing such opposition from the members who have the power to vote him out of office? One interesting aspect of the auto industry negotiations was that Douglas Fraser, the president of the UAW, was in his last term of office under rules set forth in the union's constitution. Freed from worries concerning the effects of an unpopular policy on his prospects for his survival in office, he had greater flexibility to consider concessions that improved the long-run viability of the union as an organization.

SOURCES: John Holusha, "Ford's New Contract: Who May Win, Who May Lose," *New York Times,* February 16, 1982; Robert L. Simison, "GM Workers' Narrow Vote for Concessions Might Hinder Further Cost Cuts at Plants," *Wall Street Journal,* April 12, 1982; John Holusha, "Union View: Auto Industry Sacrifices Should be Equal," *New York Times,* April 29, 1982.

markets. Nonunion employers must offer favorable enough terms to attract a work force of optimal size; thus, the workers who have the greatest effect on the content of nonunion employment packages are those "at the margin"—those potentially mobile workers closest to the point of being attracted to or leaving employment at a given plant. Building on the applications of human capital analysis in Chapter 9, it is clear that younger workers who are still willing to invest in job search and mobility will tend to have the greatest influence on nonunion employment contracts.

Union leaders, who are of course involved in collective decision making, cannot afford to base their policies on the preferences of the marginal workers. If they wish to retain their jobs, they must formulate policies that command the support of at least half of the membership. The bargaining objectives of unions are therefore more likely to reflect the preferences of the average worker, who will in general be older and less mobile than the marginal worker. Thus, not only the structure of the compensation package, but also the nature of job allocation mechanisms are likely to differ substantially between nonunion firms and unionized firms in which workers' interests are represented collectively.[36]

EXAMPLE 12.2

Wage Concessions in the Steel Industry

Efforts to negotiate wage concessions in the steel industry, where the union leadership was not free of concerns for their political future, followed a somewhat different scenario from the auto industry. The basic steel agreement, covering around 286,000 steelworkers, is negotiated every three years between the United Steelworkers of America (USW) and the eight largest steel companies. Several other companies in steel adopt the terms of the basic steel agreement on a "me too" basis without further negotiations. Unlike the procedure in the automobile industry, the rank and file of the USW do not ratify proposed contracts directly. Instead, ratification is by the Basic Steel Industry Conference, which consisted in the early 1980s of the union's executive board, district directors, and the presidents of union locals at the eight major steel companies and the "me too" firms.

Under substantial economic pressure from foreign competition and a deep domestic recession, the steel industry sought in July 1982 to renegotiate the basic steel agreement that was scheduled to run until August 1983. At the time, the agreement provided the average steelworker a wage and fringe benefit package valued at $24.40 per hour. The industry proposed a virtual freeze on wages and fringe benefits for three years and a reduction of cost-of-living-adjustment (COLA) payments; the union proposed increased aid for unemployed steelworkers. The leadership of the

[36]Differences between employment contracts in the union and nonunion sectors are discussed in Chapter 16.

USW recommended that the Basic Steel Industry Conference *reject* the employer proposals. The recommendation was promptly followed.

Subsequently, economic conditions in the industry deteriorated sharply, and by the autumn of 1982 the steel industry was operating at 40 percent of its capacity. At the biennial convention of the USW in September 1982, the leadership was authorized to reopen negotiations. In November, after several weeks of negotiations, the executive board of the union unanimously recommended approval of a tentative agreement providing for concessions amounting to about an eleven percent cut in compensation and substantial changes in the COLA arrangement in exchange for benefits for unemployed members. Despite the recommendation of the union's leadership, however, the Basic Steel Industry Conference again rejected the employer proposals.

Two months later, the executive board of the USW altered the ratification process by permitting only local union presidents from the eight major steel companies to vote on ratification (along with executive board members and district directors). Excluded were about 300 local union presidents representing workers at the "me too" companies. These officials and their members appeared to have less to lose (at least in the short run) by holding out for more favorable terms, since their companies would often continue to operate if a strike developed at the eight major companies. When yet another round of negotiations was held in late February, the revised ratification group approved an agreement providing for substantial pay concessions (including initial wage reductions that would be made up only near the end of the three-year agreement) and a commitment by the companies to invest in modernizing the industry. Given the political nature of union decision making, it was necessary to adopt a change that reduced the heterogeneity of interests among those voting in the ratification process in order to achieve changes that the leadership felt was in the long-run interest of the union.

SOURCES: Carol Hymowitz and J. Ernest Beazley, "Steel's Recovery Is Seen Set Back by Union's Vote," *Wall Street Journal* November 22, 1982, p. 2; Thomas F. O'Boyle and J. Ernest Beazley, "USW Chiefs, Backing Concessionary Pact, Slash Number Eligible to Ratify Contracts," *Wall Street Journal* January 13, 1983, p. 8; William Serrin, "Steel Union Leaders Ratify Concessions," *New York Times* March 2, 1983.

Union Security Arrangements

The public-goods aspects of union activities contribute to the intense union interest in the negotiation of *union security* arrangements. Despite the protection afforded a union by its status as exclusive representative of workers in a bargaining unit, the fact that workers in the unit who receive the benefits of union representation are not required by law to support the union financially has left unions extremely sensitive to the problem of free riders and concerned about protecting their institutional security. As a result, one of the first issues usually addressed in a new collective-bargaining relationship is the nature of the union security arrangement that will apply in the bargaining unit.

Over the years, a variety of union security arrangements have been devised in negotiations (see Table 12.9). By far the most common arrangement in labor agreements in the private sector is the *union shop,* which requires employees to become union members within a specified period of time (usually 30 to 60 days) after being hired and to remain members as a condition of employment in the firm. In contrast to a *closed shop* arrangement (now illegal in most industries), which requires the employer to hire only from among current union members, a union shop affords employers considerable freedom in hiring employees of their choice. Yet all union security arrangements contain an element of compulsion for individual employees and they have inspired opposition from some employers and politicians.

Although less popular with unions, alternative forms of union security arrangements have been devised in an effort to compromise between the interests of unions in obtaining financial support and the interests of some employers in protecting the rights of individual employees who may be philosophically or otherwise opposed to union membership. For example, a *modified union shop* exempts certain employee groups—often those long-term employees who are opposed to joining a newly-established union—but requires all other employees and all new hires to join the union. The *agency shop,* an arrangement that is used far more extensively in the public sector than the private sector, requires employees in the bargaining unit who do not join the union to pay a monthly "service charge" (usually the equivalent of the dues paid to the union by its members) as a condition of employment. *Maintenance of membership* provisions, which require employees who are members of a union when a labor agreement is negotiated (or who join subsequently) to remain members until the expiration of the agreement, have been used infrequently since World War II.

The union security issue—the question of whether unions should be able to

Table 12.9. Union Security Provisions in Major Collective Bargaining Agreements, 1980[a] (Percent Distribution)

	All Agreements	Union Shop	Modified Union Shop	Agency Shop	Maintenance of Membership	Other	Sole Bargaining[b]
All Industries	100	60	6	8	3	6	17
Manufacturing	100	55	7	7	5	7	20
Nonmanufacturing	100	64	5	9	2	6	14
Public Sector[c]	100	7	3	12	10	2	66

[a]Labor Agreements covering 1,000 workers or more in the private sector.

[b]Union recognized as bargaining agent for all employees in bargaining unit, but union membership is not required as a condition of employment. Other types of union security are discussed in the text.

[c]Data are for 1974.

SOURCE: U.S. Bureau of Labor Statistics, *Characteristics of Major Collective Bargaining Agreements, January, 1980* Bulletin 2095 (Washington: U.S. Government Printing Office, May 1981), p. 23–24. U.S. Bureau of Labor Statistics, *Characteristics of Agreements in State and Local Governments, January 1, 1974,* Bulletin 1861 (Washington, D.C.: U.S. Government Printing Office, 1975), p. 10.

compel membership and/or dues payments when they have a legal duty to represent all workers—has constituted one of the major controversies associated with the growth of unions in the United States. On the face of it, union security arrangements—particularly union-shop arrangements—appear to be popular with both unions and union members. Over 80 percent of the major collective-bargaining agreements in the private sector and about a third of the agreements in the public sector contain some form of security agreement (Table 12.9). There also appear to be few genuine conscientious objectors to unions among organized workers. At the urging of employers, Congress incorporated in the Taft-Hartley Act a provision that required a secret ballot of union members before a union-shop clause could be approved. Between 1947 and 1951, when the provision was repealed at the request of employers, well over 90 percent of the workers who cast ballots supported the union shop. Contrary to the expectations of employers and Congress, union-shop provisions do not appear to be negotiated by union leaders against the will of the rank-and-file.

As noted earlier, Section 14B of the Taft-Hartley Act also permits state laws addressing the union security issue to take precedence over federal law, which permits union security arrangements. Subsequently, some twenty states passed so-called *right-to-work* laws, which prohibit union-shop provisions, and there are periodic attempts to pass similar legislation in other states or to repeal existing legislation. The contests over right-to-work legislation inspire considerable emotion on both sides which, like the term "right-to-work", does little to clarify the underlying issues. Underlying the philosophical debates, both unions and their opponents appear to believe that they are engaged in a power struggle that will influence the future of unions in the United States.

Just what is the evidence on the influence of right-to-work legislation on the support for labor unions? Most of the laws have been passed in southern and western states. Since there has been a general movement in population and employment since 1955 from the industrial Northeast and Midwest—the "snow belt"—to the "sun belt" of the South where right-to-work legislation is more common, the effect of such laws on union membership could be of considerable consequence for the future of unions.

Table 12.10 presents data on the extent of unionization that existed in 1978 in right-to-work and other states. The data indicate quite clearly that union strength is lowest in states that have right-to-work laws. In 16 of the 20 right-to-work states, the proportion of nonagricultural employees that were union or employee-association members was less than 20 percent. In contrast, in 22 of the other 30 states, the proportion exceeded 25 percent. While right-to-work states are not uniformly identical to those in the sun belt, there is considerable overlap. As a result, between 1955 and 1978, the proportion of employees working in right-to-work states increased from 24.1 to 30.6 percent. This shifting geographic distribution of the work force undoubtedly had a depressing effect on union membership.

It is not obvious, however, that the decline in unionization occasioned by the move to the sunbelt can be attributed to right-to-work laws *per se.* The extent of unionization in right-to-work states tended to be lower than that in other states even prior to the passage of the laws. In fact, there is growing evidence that these

Table 12.10 Percent of Nonagricultural Employees That Are Union Members, 1980

Right-to-Work States	Union or Association Members (percent)	Other States	Union or Association Members (percent)
Alabama	21.8	Alaska	33.7
Arizona	16.0	California	27.0
Arkansas	16.0	Colorado	18.1
Florida	11.8	Connecticut	23.0
Georgia	15.1	Delaware	25.2
Iowa	22.2	Hawaii	28.0
Kansas	15.4	Idaho	18.4
Louisiana	16.4	Illinois	30.4
Mississippi	16.2	Indiana	30.4
Nebraska	18.1	Kentucky	24.0
Nevada	23.8	Maine	24.1
North Carolina	9.6	Maryland-D.C.	22.8
North Dakota	17.1	Massachusetts	24.9
South Carolina	7.8	Michigan	37.3
South Dakota	14.8	Minnesota	26.2
Tennessee	19.3	Missouri	27.6
Texas	11.4	Montana	29.2
Utah	17.7	New Hampshire	15.8
Virginia	15.0	New Jersey	25.7
Wyoming	18.9	New Mexico	19.0
		New York	38.8
		Ohio	31.3
		Oklahoma	15.3
		Oregon	26.1
		Pennsylvania	34.6
		Rhode Island	28.3
		Vermont	18.0
		Washington	34.4
		West Virginia	34.4
		Wisconsin	28.5

SOURCE: Bureau of National Affairs, *Directory of U.S. Labor Organizations,* 1982–83 Ed. (Washington, D.C.: Bureau of National Affairs, Inc., 1982), Table 21.

laws may only reflect attitudes towards unions that already exist in these communities.[37]

---

[37]Numerous econometric studies have sought to estimate the effect of right-to-work laws on union strength, wages, and industrial conflict. Studies concluding that these laws have little or no effect on union-membership levels include Keith Lumsden and Craig Peterson, "The Effect of Right-to-Work Laws on Unionization in the United States," *Journal of Political Economy* 83 (December 1975): 1237–48; William J. Moore and Robert Newman, "On the Prospects for American Trade Union Growth: A Cross-Section Analysis," *Review of Economics and Statistics* 57 (November 1975): 435–45; Barry T. Hirsch, "The Determinants of Unionization: An Analysis of Interarea Differences," *Industrial and Labor Relations Review* 33 (January 1980): 147–61; William J. Moore, "Membership and Wage Impact of Right-to-Work Laws," *Journal of Labor Research* 1 (Fall 1980): 349–68; and Henry S. Farber, "Right-to-Work Laws and the Extent of Unionization," (mimeo, Massachusetts Institute of Technology, March 1983).

In Conclusion

There are a number of lessons for interpreting union behavior that may be drawn from this analysis. First, there are likely to be inherent tensions between the leadership and the membership of a union. These tensions are tied to the fact that the leadership must consider the welfare of the organization as a whole and the membership as a group, while union members are more likely to act on the basis of their individual self-interest. The tensions are also related to the fact that a major role of unions is to provide for working conditions that are public goods over which different people will have different preferences. Second, while these tensions could, in principle, be resolved through an appropriate pricing mechanism for union services, there are practical barriers to implementing such a system. As a result, the internal political stability of unions is likely to be greatest when the preferences of members are similar.

Third, the absence of a pricing system that resolves these tensions forces the leadership of unions to develop political allocation mechanisms within the union, for where the preferences of individual members are diverse, there is likely to be considerable contention within the membership over specific union negotiating goals. Bargaining within a union over what its demands should be may be more difficult than the actual collective bargaining between the employer and the union. When preferences are widely dispersed, it may also be more difficult to achieve ratification of an agreement by the membership. Indeed, unions with particularly heterogeneous memberships have devised special ratification procedures to mediate sharp differences in objectives among different segments of their membership.[38]

REVIEW QUESTIONS

1. It has been said that the American Federation of Labor (AFL) was founded on two broad principles: national autonomy and exclusive jurisdiction. (a) What was the effect of these principles on the structure of authority within the U.S. labor movement? (b) How have the principles been modified in at least three instances since the formation of the AFL?
2. How would you analyze the prospects for union growth in the next decade? Based on your analysis, what are the prospects for union growth? (Consider these questions again after you have read Chapter 13 and see if there are any aspects of your answer that you would like to change.) How would you have answered this question in 1930?
3. "It is hardly surprising that craft unions have been the earliest and most durable labor organizations in most countries, for craft unions are inherently more powerful than industrial unions." Evaluate this statement, being careful to delineate conditions under which it might hold and conditions under which it might not.

---

[38]For example, skilled workers in the United Automobile Workers can veto a national contract covering the entire membership of the union if they do not approve of its provisions. This provision was an outgrowth of attempts by the skilled membership, which constitutes a minority of the union's members, to secede from the UAW and join a separate union.

4. In recent years, there have been an increasing number of union mergers. Analyze the incentives and disincentives for two unions to merge. Under what circumstances would you expect a merger to increase the effectiveness of a union? Under what circumstances might effectiveness decrease?

SELECTED READINGS

Orley Ashenfelter and John Pencavel, "American Trade Union Growth, 1900–1960." *Quarterly Journal of Economics* 83 (August 1969): 434–48.

Wallace Atherton, *Theory of Union Bargaining Goals* (Princeton, N.J.: Princeton University Press, 1973).

Richard B. Freeman and James L. Medoff, "The Two Faces of Unionism." *Public Interest* 57 (Fall 1979): 69–93.

Mancur Olson, *The Logic of Collective Action* (Cambridge, Mass.: Harvard University Press, 1965).

Lloyd Ulman, "The Development of Trades and Labor Unions," Chapter 13 in Seymour E. Harris (ed.) *American Economic History* (New York: McGraw-Hill, 1961).

Chapter 13

THE REGULATION OF UNION-MANAGEMENT RELATIONS

T he legal environment of the employment relationship has several elements: the general common law of contracts, wage, and hours legislation (discussed in Chapters 3 and 5), equal-employment-opportunity legislation (discussed in Chapter 11), laws governing health and safety at the workplace (discussed in Chapter 7), regulations pertaining to aspects of the pay package (see, for example, the discussion of pension legislation in Chapter 10), and statutes governing the relationship between unions and employers. All but the last aspect of the legal environment largely address *substantive* aspects of the employment relationship, and as noted in Chapter 12, legislation has historically played a larger role in these areas in Europe than in the United States. On the other hand, the law has been more pervasive in its impact on the *procedural* aspects of the relationship between labor and management in the United States than in any other country in the world. We now examine the effect of legal regulation on the formation of unions and the collective-bargaining process.

With the growth of unions, nations inevitably face significant questions of public policy toward unions and collective bargaining. Unions raise fairly fundamental conflicts between the right to combination and freedom of contract, between the right to group action and an employer's right to manage his or her business, between private collective bargaining and the public interest, and between majority rule and individual rights. All of these are issues over which there may be a significant conflict of values between different segments of the community. In making a choice or striking a compromise between the conflicting values, public policy must confront a number of specific issues in industrial relations. What should the stance of government be toward the process of union organizing?

Should the government mandate collective bargaining? What legal status should be accorded collective-bargaining agreements? What limits should be placed on the use of force? Does the public have an interest in the relationship between a union and its members?

Different countries have taken sometimes radically different approaches to these issues, but generally speaking, there appear to be two alternative principles that might be applied in making a choice of labor-relations policy. The first is the principle of *consensus,* in which the parties to collective bargaining (unions and employers) mutually develop and assent to a set of rules that is to govern their conduct for the duration of their collective-bargaining relationship. This approach is taken in some European countries, particularly in Scandinavia, often with the hope of keeping the government out of direct involvement in collective bargaining. It has the advantage that, when the parties to collective bargaining develop the rules governing their conduct themselves, they are more likely to bear responsibility for adhering to those rules than when the rules are imposed by third parties.

A second alternative is the principle of *majority rule,* under which the conduct of some individuals or groups is governed almost entirely without regard to their desires (that is, by the passage of legislation rather than by the negotiation of a set of rules by the parties to collective bargaining). As the broad outline of the National Labor Relations Act in the previous chapter indicates, this has been the basic approach to public policy in the United States. While the adoption of a majority-rule approach to public policy toward labor relations is understandable given the determined resistance of American employers to unions, the approach is not without its costs. If the minorities under a majority-rule system strongly dissent, they will try to circumvent the objectives of the policy by taking advantage of loopholes or engaging in activities that do not seem to be covered by the existing law. The response to these efforts at evading the law's objectives is normally additional, more detailed rule-making by legislative and/or administrative bodies in an effort to close the loopholes. This in turn encourages a search for still other loopholes and subsequent rule-making to close them. Experience with the NLRA provides a fascinating study of the evolution of regulatory activity over time from a limited amount of statutory language to a very detailed web of rules surrounding the conduct of labor relations. The result has been an extremely litigious system, which is one of several characteristics of the American approach to public policy toward labor relations that is unusual in comparison to other countries.

In this chapter, we examine some of the major consequences for unions and collective bargaining of the approach to public policy toward labor relations adopted in the United States. We begin with a review of the main objectives of the NLRA and of the employee and union unfair labor practices established by the Act. Since much of the policy is initiated in the interpretations of the NLRA by an unusual regulatory agency, the National Labor Relations Board, this is followed by a discussion of the environment in which the agency's rulings are made. Subsequently, the requirements placed by the Board on unions and management during organizing campaigns and collective-bargaining negotiations are reviewed, along with a consideration of the apparent impact of the regulations on the behavior of the various parties and the efficacy of remedies for violations of the NLRA. This is followed by a review of the main features of the legal regulations of labor relations in the public sector. We conclude with an analysis of the effect of a very different type of legislation—antitrust law—on union power and collective bargaining.

Basic Provisions of the National Labor Relations Act

The present-day *National Labor Relations Act (NLRA)* consists of the Wagner Act (passed in 1935) as amended by the Taft-Hartley Act (1947) and by certain provisions in the Landrum-Griffin Act (1959). Coverage is limited to workers in the private, nonagricultural sector engaged in interstate commerce. Workers in federal, state, and local government have never been covered by the Act. Moreover, the agricultural sector was excluded to secure votes of southern members of Congress for passage. Thus the requirements of the NLRA have not applied to unions attempting to organize farm workers or to management in its efforts to block unions. As we noted in our review of the historical development of union-management relations in the United States in Chapter 12, the Wagner Act guaranteed workers the right to engage in "concerted activities" such as collective bargaining and was passed with the explicit intention of facilitating the organization of unions and reducing the level of strife (mainly from strikes and related violence) associated with the efforts of unions to organize industry. The Norris-LaGuardia Act (1932) had already removed most judicial impediments to union activity, and the NLRA was structured to remove many of the employer impediments.

The Act set out to accomplish this in two ways. First, it provided for an election procedure to determine whether a group of employees wished to be represented by a union, and established a government agency, the *National Labor Relations Board (NLRB)* to conduct the elections and certify the results. (Previously, workers had to use strikes or other forceful means in an effort to organize a resisting employer.) Second, it limited the opposition that employers could legally mount against workers' efforts to form unions and to engage in collective bargaining, by establishing a list of employer unfair labor-practices. These are listed in the left-hand column of Table 13.1 by the section of the NLRA in which they occur. Moreover, the NLRB was given authority to investigate, prosecute, and adjudicate allegations that unfair labor practices had occurred.

The limitations placed on employers by the unfair labor practices were substantial. The first (Section 8(a)(1)) was a broad proscription against any attempts to thwart employee efforts to form unions and to negotiate an agreement. Indeed, violations of any of the other employer unfair-practices normally constitute a violation of this section as well. The second employer unfair labor-practice guideline was intended to eliminate the "company unions," which, as noted in Chapter 12, were often established and controlled by employers during

Table 13.1. Unfair Labor Practices Under the National Labor Relations Act

Unfair Labor Practice for Employers:	*Unfair Labor Practice for Unions:*
Section:	Section:
8(a)(1): To interfere with, restrain or coerce employees in the exercise of their rights to join labor organizations and to bargain collectively.	8(b)(1): To restrain or coerce employees in the exercise of their rights to join or to refrain from joining a labor organization.
8(a)(2): To dominate or interfere with the formation or administration of any labor organization or contribute financial or other support to it.	8(b)(2): To force an employer to discriminate against an employee (unless the employee refuses to pay union dues).
8(a)(3): To discriminate against individuals supporting a labor organization with respect to any term or condition of employment.	8(b)(3): To refuse to bargain collectively with an employer.
8(a)(4): To discharge or otherwise discriminate against an employee because he has filed charges or given testimony under the NLRA.	8(b)(4): To engage in a secondary boycott.
8(a)(5): To refuse to bargain collectively with the union representing his employees.	8(b)(5): To charge exorbitant initiation fees.
	8(b)(6): To force an employer to pay for services that are not performed.
	8(b)(7): To engage in "organizational" picketing to pressure an employer to recognize a union without a representation election.

the 1920s to thwart efforts by employees to form independent unions. An employee organization established for collective bargaining must be independent of the employer with which it bargains. The third employer unfair labor-practice statute forbids discrimination based on a worker's attitude toward or support of unions. Employers may not fire union supporters while retaining employees who oppose unionization. Once a union is established, employers may not pay employees in the bargaining unit who do not belong to the union more than those who do. The application of this unfair labor-practice statute also raises more subtle issues that are discussed at greater length below in the section on regulation of the union organizing process. The fourth employer unfair labor-practice statute was included to assist in the enforcement of the act. For example, one employer violated this section of the act when he reduced the paycheck of employees who testified against him by the amount of time spent in an NLRB hearing but did not similarly reduce the paycheck of those who testified on his behalf. The final employer unfair-practice statute imposes an affirmative duty to bargain in an effort to ensure that meaningful collective bargaining would begin once a union won a representation election. The issues that have arisen in applying this requirement are discussed extensively below in the section on the regulation of collective bargaining.

The NLRA also places certain obligations on both labor and management. If a union wins a representation election, it is certified as the *exclusive* bargaining representative of the group of employees who were eligible to vote. This requires the union to represent *all* employees in the bargaining unit equally—even though some may not support the union. Over the years, the exclusive representative status has been interpreted by the courts to impose on the union a "duty of fair representation." That is, the union may not discriminate in the way that it treats different union members. For example, a union may not refuse to process a reasonable grievance of a member because of the member's race or because the member may be associated with a dissident political faction within the union. The concept of exclusive bargaining representative also requires the employer to deal through the union with employees in matters affecting the terms and conditions of their employment.

Experience with the Wagner Act indicated that unions could be coercive in their efforts to organize workers, just as employers historically had been coercive in their efforts to resist unionization. The unfair labor practices established in the Wagner Act limited the coercive actions of employers, but left open the possibility for union coercion. By 1947, as noted in Chapter 12, there appeared to be considerable public sentiment for achieving a more even balance of power between labor and management, for protecting the freedom of choice of individual workers (particularly if they chose *not* to have union representation), and for protecting neutral third parties (particularly the general public) from the consequences of major labor disputes. The Taft-Hartley Act addressed the first two concerns by permitting *decertification elections* and by adding a list of union unfair-labor-practices to the employer unfair-labor-practices established in the Wagner Act. (The union unfair-practices are listed in the right-hand column of Table 13.1.)

The union unfair-labor-practices under Sections 8(b)(1) and 8(b)(3) simply parallel the employer unfair practices under Sections 8(a)(1) and 8(a)(5). They were intended to prevent unions from pressuring individuals in making a free and reasoned choice of whether or not to vote for union representation and to place a duty of bargaining on unions. There was also an effort to protect individual workers against unreasonable pressures by forbidding excessive dues requirements (Section 8(b)(5)), picketing pressures that might short-circuit the election procedure through which individual workers can express their preferences (Section 8(b)(7)), and closed shop or other preferential hiring arrangements. The latter was achieved in section 8(b)(2), which effectively precludes an employer from giving preference to individuals who already are union members (as a closed shop arrangement requires). This requirement was relaxed somewhat for the construction industry in amendments to the NLRA passed with the Landrum-Griffin Act in 1959.

The prohibition against secondary boycotts (Section 8(b)(4)) was part of the effort to protect neutral third parties. A *secondary boycott* occurs when a union tries to bring pressure against an employer with whom it is negotiating by striking a third party (for example, a supplier or customer) that is not involved in the negotiations. It is not always clear who is "neutral" in a labor dispute, however, and efforts to enforce this unfair practice have raised difficult issues that are discussed more extensively in Chapter 15. The final unfair practice listed in Table 13.1, forcing an employer to pay for services that are not performed, was included to prevent what many regarded as wasteful practices. For example, at one time, locals of the American Federation of Musicians required employers who used out-of-town musical groups to pay for an equal number of local musicians even though no local musicians were used. (The rationale was that the out-of-town groups were taking the employment opportunities of local musicians.) Section 8(b)(6)) makes these types of activities illegal. It does not, however, prohibit payments for services that are performed although not really wanted, and the response of many locals of the Musicians' Union to this law was to require local bands to precede out-of-town musical groups! Among other things, this illustrates the difficulty of addressing problems involving job security through statutory language.

The preceding paragraphs provide an overview of the general objectives and approach to regulation taken in the NLRA. However, the role and impact of the law are understood best when the law is examined in the context of the industrial relations activity that it seeks to regulate. For this reason, detailed discussions of the requirements imposed by the unfair labor practices are integrated with specific discussions of union organizing and collective bargaining activities in the remainder of this chapter and in Chapters 14 through 16. The role of the law in union-organizing campaigns and the nature of the duty to bargain are discussed later in this chapter. The role of the National Labor Relations Board in determining election units and the effect on bargaining structure are discussed in Chapter 14. The legal status of strikes, lockouts, and secondary boycotts is examined in the discussion of labor disputes in Chapter 15, and the relationship between NLRB regulation and the private institution of arbitration is discussed in Chapter 16.

The National Labor Relations Board as a Regulatory Agency

Under the National Labor Relations Act (i.e., the Wagner Act of 1935 as amended by the Taft-Hartley Act in 1947 and by portions of the Landrum-Griffin Act in 1959), an independent regulatory agency, the National Labor Relations Board, was established for two broad purposes: (1) to conduct elections to determine whether groups of employees would be represented by a union in dealing with their employer over the terms and conditions of their employment, and (2) to investigate and adjudicate charges that one or another of the parties to collective bargaining had committed one or more of the unfair labor-practices that are proscribed in the legislation. Activity in each of these two areas has expanded since the Board was established. In Figure 13.1, the annual number of union-representation election and unfair labor-practice cases filed with the NLRB is graphed for the period since the end of World War II. The number of representation cases has expanded modestly, peaking in the mid-1970s. The number of unfair labor practices filed was relatively stable through the mid-1950s. Following 1957, however, there was a sharp increase in the number of cases filed with the NLRB and the number of cases has basically doubled in every decade since 1950. At least by the evidence of unfair labor-practice charges, over forty-five years of experience under the NLRA has not produced a consensus between labor and

Source: *Annual Report of the National
Labor Relations Board*, Appendix Tables (various years)

Figure 13.1 Representation Cases and Unfair Labor-Practice Charges Filed with the National Labor Relations Board

management in the United States on the country's labor relations policy and policy goals.

Housing both the prosecutorial and the judicial functions within the same agency is somewhat unusual and presented a potential conflict of interest. The NLRB responded to this problem organizationally by establishing within the agency a separate Office of the General Counsel, which specializes in the administrative side of the Board's work: handling representation cases, conducting representation elections, investigating unfair labor-practice charges, issuing complaints, and prosecuting charges that are found to be meritorious. Much of this work is performed by the NLRB's regional offices, which are largely under the direction of the General Counsel. Most unfair labor-practice charges—85 percent in 1980—are dismissed, withdrawn, or otherwise closed before formal prosecution is initiated. After a complaint is issued, the forum shifts to the judicial side of the NLRB. A hearing is held at a regional office by an administrative law judge who issues a decision. In a minority of cases—about 5 percent of the unfair labor-practice cases closed in recent years—one of the parties will appeal the decision to the national Board in Washington, D.C. The five Board members, any three of which can constitute a panel to hear most cases, are appointed by the President of the United States to overlapping five-year terms, so that under normal circumstances, a president would not be able to appoint the entire Board during one term of office.

If a majority of the Board sustains the unfair labor-practice charge, the Board issues an order that the employer or union "cease and desist" from the activity that gave rise to the charge. The Board may also impose a remedy for the damage to labor relations done by the commission of the practice. However, the NLRB has no direct enforcement power under the law. If a cease-and-desist order is not obeyed (that is, the unfair practice is continued), the NLRB must seek enforcement of its order in the U.S. Court of Appeals. In general, the court accepts the facts developed by the Board and reviews the case to determine whether the law has been applied properly. While the Appeals Court may choose not to enforce the Board's order, if it does agree to enforce the Board's cease-and-desist order, failure to end the unfair labor practice constitutes contempt of court. Either the Board or an employer or union can appeal a decision of the Appeals Court to the Supreme Court, and many of the most far-reaching decisions concerning unfair labor practices have been made by the Supreme Court.

The NLRB's unfair labor-practice rulings are inherently controversial, for as with many regulatory agencies, it is working in an area in which there is often intense disagreement over appropriate public policy. The evidence of steadily rising unfair labor-practice charges alone seems to indicate that there has been no general acceptance of the basic principle on which the National Labor Relations Act rests—that employees have the free right to join unions and engage in collective bargaining. It seems equally clear that there is no strong agreement between unions and management on their relative spheres of influence in industrial relations.

In this environment, the Board, like other regulatory agencies, is at times accused of bias in its decision making and of "making law" through the administrative process. In response to such charges, it is not uncommon for Board members to claim that their objectives are to make impartial decisions and to promote the public interest. Upon reflection, however, it is clear that impartiality is not a realistic goal for or description of the Board's rulings on unfair labor-practice charges. One reason for this is that the Board must often work with sketchy legislative guidance. Legislators frequently are unable to agree on the exact results that they want from a particular law and may choose statutory language that is deliberately imprecise in order to secure enough votes for passage of the legislation. As a result, a regulatory agency such as the Board can rarely implement legislation as written, because the language itself may not be clear. In the NLRA, for example, the breadth of the statutory language that defines unfair labor practices does not always provide a clear guide to interpreting specific factual situations. For example, under the NLRA it is an unfair labor practice for either management or labor to refuse to bargain collectively—but the law provides little guidance on what constitutes a refusal to bargain. The answer seems clear: if one party refuses to meet with the other. But what if meetings occur and one party insists on a topic that the other does not believe is within the scope of bargaining; or one party refuses to provide information to back up its position; or one party mechanically rejects the proposals of the other? The law provides no specific guidance that the Board can follow on these issues. (The way that the Board has treated these issues is discussed below in the section on the regulation of the collective-bargaining process.)

Therefore, with only vague legislative guidance, the Board must spell out through administrative rule-making the meaning of the legislative language to specific factual situations that arise in the course of union organizing and collective bargaining. Under these circumstances, the best that a regulatory agency such as the Board can do is to attempt to choose rules that are consistent with the underlying purposes of the enabling legislation. Thus, in fashioning its decisions and rules, it is not unusual for the Board to emphasize congressional intent as much as particular legislative language.

A second difficulty of the impartiality standard is that the Board is administering public policy, which itself is not impartial. We have already noted that there are sharply conflicting values within any community concerning unions and collective bargaining. The presence of such conflicts creates a demand for some mechanism of choice or compromise between the values of different groups, and the role of public policy is to specify this choice and, in the process, define the dominant values of the community at large. Since the role of policy is to make a choice between conflicting values in the community, some groups' values will always be compromised when a policy is chosen. The same may be said of the NLRB in administering labor-relations policy. Impartiality is basically impossible because any decision helps one party obtain its objectives over the other. This may explain why, after several decades of experience under the National Labor Relations Act, there is still considerable contention over public policy toward labor relations. With respect to the bias question, the key issue is really whether the NLRB "chooses the partiality imposed by the statute."[1]

Even when the NLRB chooses a course that is consistent with the statute, however, there remains the question of how the Board's regulatory strategy influences the behavior of unions, management, and employees. In the view of Congress, "[T]he ultimate purpose of the unfair labor-practice provisions of the National Labor Relations Act is to create a climate which will encourage voluntary compliance with the prohibitions stated in the Act."[2] Judged by the general trend in unfair-labor-practice charges illustrated in Figure 13.1 and the data in Tables 13.2 and 13.3 on charges of specific unfair-labor-practice violations, the Act has not yet achieved this purpose. These data reveal two interesting features of regulatory activity under the NLRA. First, it is clear that the main task of the NLRB is to adjudicate charges of employer unfair labor-practices, which constitute over 80 percent of the charges filed. Second, at a time when union-organizing in the private sector is on the decline, unfair labor practices in several categories

---

[1]This point is made in Clyde W. Summers, "Politics, Policy-Making, and the NLRB," *Syracuse Law Review,* Second Annual Labor Law Conference, pp. 93–108.

[2]Senate Report No. 95-628, 95th Cong. 2d Sess. (1978).

Table 13.2. Unfair Labor Practice Charges Against Employers, 1950–80 (numbers in parentheses are index numbers with 1950=100)

	8(a)(1)		8(a)(2)		8(a)(3)		8(a)(4)		8(a)(5)	
1980	31,281	(699)	979	(172)	18,315	(570)	1,321	(1,347)	9,866	(754)
1970	13,601	(304)	592	(103)	9,290	(289)	331	(338)	4,489	(343)
1960	7,723	(173)	820	(144)	6,044	(188)	184	(188)	1,753	(134)
1950	4,472	(100)	570	(100)	3,213	(100)	98	(100)	1,309	(100)

Note: Since any employer unfair labor practice is also automatically a violation of Section 8(a)(1) of the National Labor Relations Act, the 8(a)(1) column is also the total column.

SOURCE: *Annual Report of the National Labor Relations Board,* Appendix Tables (various years).

Table 13.3. Unfair Labor Practice Charges Against Unions, 1950–80 (numbers in parentheses are index numbers with 1950=100)

	8(b)(1)		8(b)(2)		8(b)(3)		8(b)(4)		8(b)(5)		8(b)(6)		8(b)(7)	
1980	8,206	(1,137)	1,690	(217)	913	(537)	2,987	(876)	46	(418)	42	(124)	600	(220)
1970	4,055	(562)	1,782	(229)	620	(365)	2,290	(672)	22	(200)	25	(74)	409	(150)
1960	2,196	(304)	1,953	(251)	282	(166)	830	(243)	16	(145)	20	(59)	273	(100)
1950	722	(100)	778	(100)	170	(100)	341	(100)	11	(100)	34	(100)	—	

Note: Definitions of unfair labor practices are in Table 13.1.

SOURCE: *Annual Report of the National Labor Relations Board,* Appendix Tables (various years).

are growing at accelerating rates. The flow of annual new charges against employers, which increased 76 percent between 1960 and 1970, rose 130 percent during the 1970s, and by 1980 was seven times the level in 1950. Charges of discrimination against union supporters, the largest class of employer charges, doubled during the 1970s. Rates of increase were even greater for charges of Section 8(a)(4) (discrimination against employees who testify) and Section 8(a)(5) (failure to bargain in good faith) violations.[3]

These data suggest that the key to the volume of unfair labor-practice charges is to be found in the strong and persistent resistance of employers in the United States to unions. By way of contrast, managers in most European countries are more accepting of the presence and role of unions. The resistance of employers in the United States may in part result from the economic pressures associated with a decentralized bargaining structure. Under the NLRB representation election procedures, collective-bargaining relationships tend to be established on a company-by-company (and even plant-by-plant) basis, in contrast to Europe where bargaining is frequently conducted on an industrywide or nationwide basis. Under decentralized bargaining arrangements, employers cannot be assured that the costs that they incur will be matched elsewhere, and the incentive to resist what is perceived as a threat to their competitive position may be strong. More-

[3]For a study of the relationship of unfair labor practice cases to economic variables and industrial relations activity, see Myron Roomkin, "A Quantitative Study of Unfair Labor Practice Cases," *Industrial and Labor Relations Review* (January 1981).

over, the threat is real. American unions bargain hard, in part because in contrast to Europe, American workers are attracted to unions more on economic than ideological grounds.

Other factors contributing to the unfair labor-practice trends may be imbedded in the administration of the NLRA itself. As membership on the NLRB changes, the Board's decisions on some issues can change, and ambiguity about what the law requires may contribute to noncompliance in some instances. More importantly, the Board's rulings and the sanctions it has devised for violations of the NLRA may contribute significantly to the volume of regulatory activity. We cannot pursue this theme any further without first examining the nature of some of the Board's more important regulations and the impact on labor relations. In the remainder of this chapter we shall examine the content and impact of the Board's rule-making on two central areas of American labor relations—union organizing and collective-bargaining negotiations—before turning our attention to the relationship between unions and antitrust policy.

Public Policy Toward the Formation of Unions

There are two methods by which a union becomes established in the United States. The first method—organizing from the top down—occurs when the union and the employer mutually agree that the union will be the recognized bargaining agent of the employees. As one might surmise from the historical resistance of American employers to unions, this consensus approach to union representation is rare in the United States. Prior to the passage of the Wagner Act in 1935, organizing from the top down was the only method available to unions, and conflicts over union representation were the source of considerable strike activity. This approach to union organization remains legal under the provisions of the NLRA, but its use is largely limited to situations in which the union has enormous economic power relative to the employer. The second method—the union-representation election procedure established in the Wagner Act—has no counterpart in other countries, but was incorporated in the American labor-relations statute as an institutional mechanism to reduce the historical conflict surrounding efforts at union organizing. In fulfilling its responsibility to administer representation elections, the National Labor Relations Board seeks to ensure that employees have free choice in their legally guaranteed right to self-organization by regulating certain aspects of the organizing campaign that precedes an election.

The Union Organization Process: An Overview

In this section we review the process of union organization under the second method, which is by far the more common, and then consider the apparent impact of NLRB activity on the outcome of representation elections. While it may appear unusual to study union organizing in the midst of a discussion of the legal environment of labor relations, union organizing is largely a legal process under the administration of the NLRA, far removed from the violent confrontations that often accompanied efforts to establish unions in the early years of the century. It is a process, moreover, that is of the utmost importance to unions and management, for while there has been no discernible trend in the number of union elections in recent years (see Figure 13.1), the proportion of representation elections won by unions has declined from almost 75 percent in 1950 to under 50 percent by the early 1980s.

The union-organizing process begins when a union solicits, often surreptitiously, employee signatures on cards authorizing the union to represent the employee in collective bargaining with the employer. At some point, the union will send the employer a letter claiming to represent a majority of his or her employees and requesting an appointment to begin negotiating a binding contract that will establish the terms and conditions of employment for covered employees. When the employer invariably rejects the union's request, the union petitions the NLRB for an election and submits the signed authorization cards to satisfy the Board's requirement that at least 30 percent of the employees support the petition.

Before ordering a secret-ballot election, the Board must determine the scope of the election unit—that is, which employees will be eligible to vote in the representation election. While the unit issue is often resolved by agreement between the employer and the union, there are issues that may prevent such agreement from occurring. For example, the size of the unit may influence the likelihood that the union will win the election and may also influence the relative bargaining power of a union once it is established. If the employer and union are unable to agree, the NLRB will determine the appropriate election unit and set a date for the election that is usually 15–30 days away.[4] During this period, the union and the employer typically engage in a campaign for the employees' votes. Unlike earlier periods of American labor history, these campaigns are generally quite bloodless, although often deeply felt. The use of detectives, physical violence, and sit-in strikes to settle union representation issues has been supplanted by the use of lawyers, campaign speeches, and unfair labor-practice charges.

Essentially, the same procedures apply to decertification elections, but the process is initiated by a petition claiming that a majority of the employees in the bargaining unit do not wish to be represented by the currently certified bargaining representative. Decertification and representation elections are governed by the same rules concerning election conduct and unfair labor practices.

Regulation of the Union Organizing Process

Over the years, the NLRB has developed an elaborate set of rules governing the conduct of unions and employers during representation campaigns. The touchstone for these rules is the general statutory language defining unfair labor-practices and the general purposes of the National Labor Relations Act. Given the objectives of the NLRA,, the Board's task is to regulate elections in a manner that guarantees that employees have a free choice of bargaining representative.

---

[4]Because of the often close relationship between unit determination and bargaining structure, discussion of the NLRB's policy toward election units is postponed until Chapter 14.

This is not a simple goal to obtain, however. In the first place, the Board's task would seem to call for regulations that prevent the kinds of election campaign activity that distort employee voting-behavior. But what sorts of campaign activity are likely to distort employee voting-behavior? Throughout most of the Board's history, there has been very little information available on this fundamental issue, raising questions about the validity of the behavioral assumptions on which the Board's administrative rule-making rests. We shall return to this interesting question after reviewing the regulatory scheme that has developed over the past forty-five years as the NLRB has ruled, on a case-by-case basis, on the merits of unfair labor-practice charges arising during the course of union-representation campaigns.

The second difficulty that the NLRB faces in regulating the election campaign is that, while the NLRA guarantees workers the right of self-organization, the first amendment to the Constitution guarantees all parties, including employers, freedom of expression. The Board must somehow strike a balance that prevents employer interference with the workers' right to organize while protecting employer freedom-of-expression. The only guidance provided by the NLRA is a statement that the expression and dissemination of views on the desirability of unionization by employers is not evidence of an unfair labor practice as long as there is no threat of reprisal (if a union wins an election) or promise of benefit (if the workers vote against the union). This "threat-promise" test has been central to a number of determinations made by the Board and the federal courts. For example, employers cannot threaten to relocate their plant if a union wins and cannot promise wage or benefit increases to workers if the union loses. In fact, unexpected improvements in wages, benefits, or working conditions during a representation campaign would be viewed with suspicion by the NLRB.

On the other hand, the Board has developed a general standard for union election campaign tactics that is not required by the statute. In its own words, the Board seeks ". . . to provide a laboratory in which an experiment may be conducted under conditions as nearly ideal as possible, to determine the uninhibited desires of the employees."[5] Many observers have noted that this objective deviates substantially from the standards set for behavior in American political campaigns and have questioned whether it is either desirable or attainable given the uncertainty concerning the determinants of individual voting behavior.[6] Nevertheless, the Board maintains this standard in applying two levels of regulation to representation campaigns. The parties can file objections to campaign conduct which deviates from "laboratory conditions" but nevertheless does not constitute an unfair labor practice. If the Board sustains the objection, it will set aside the results on the grounds that they were polluted by the objectionable conduct and rerun the election. Secondly, the losing party may file unfair-labor-practice charges alleging some form of interference with free choice. If the charge has merit, the Board will issue a cease-and-desist order and set aside the election's

---

[5]*General Shoe Corp.,* 77 NLRB 124, 127 (1948).

[6]Derek Bok, "Regulation of Campaign Tactics in Representation Elections Under the NLRA," *Harvard Law Review,* 78 (November 1964): 38–141.

results. Moreover, when the Board believes that the results of a new election would be contaminated by the effects of past unfair labor practices, it may certify the union that lost the election as bargaining agent and order the offending employer to bargain. (The NLRB will take this unusual measure of reversing the outcome of a representation election only if over half of the employees in the unit had originally signed cards authorizing the union to bargain on their behalf.)

Union organizing campaigns most frequently give rise to charges under the first and third employer-unfair-labor-practices. (See Table 13.1.) Any activity that can be construed as interfering with the employee's right to join or refrain from joining the union of his or her choice is a violation of the first unfair-labor-practice. Thus, violation of any other employer-unfair-labor-practice automatically becomes a violation of Section 8(a)(1). The third employer-unfair-practice simply requires that workers who support unions be treated the same as workers who do not. Charges of employer unfair-labor-practices during an organizing campaign can also arise under Section 8(a)(2), which originally was included to prohibit company unions, which were prevalent in the 1920s and early 1930s. Under this provision an employer cannot solicit members, provide financial support, or otherwise express preference or support for a particular labor organization.

Broadly speaking, the NLRB has developed rules concerning union access to employees, campaign speech and literature, discrimination against union supporters, and the totality of conduct of an employer or union. Rulings on several specific issues are discussed below.

Access. The basic idea behind the access rules is that a union or employer should win a representation election on the merits of the case rather than because the other side lacks the opportunity to express its views on unionization to the voters. At the same time, the Board has had to be sensitive to an employer's right to operate a business in an orderly fashion. Under Board rulings, companies can keep nonemployee organizers off the premises, so long as the access policy is applied in a nondiscriminatory manner. Management can also prevent employee solicitation of union support during working hours, but cannot prevent employees from soliciting union memberships from fellow workers on company property during nonwork time (for example, lunch periods). More recently, the Board has required employers to place the names and addresses of eligible voters on file with the NLRB to facilitate union access to voters.

The form of campaign speech. The NLRB also regulates both the form and content of campaign speeches by unions and employers. Employers can address their employees on the subject of unionization during company meetings (so-called *captive audience* speeches) up to twenty-four hours before the election without providing a similar opportunity to union supporters, as long as employees will have a reasonable opportunity to hear both sides during the course of the campaign. On the other hand, the interrogation of employees regarding their support for the union, surveillance of union activities, and the use of company spies, may be a basis for setting aside the results of an election on the grounds that the ultimate purpose of such activities is to threaten employees or discriminate against union supporters.[7]

The substance of campaign speech. A more controversial area of Board rule-making concerns its regulations governing the substance of campaign speech (including written forms of "speech" such as letters and printed literature). Given the purpose of the National Labor Relations Act, the Board's objective is to develop standards to determine when employer speech goes beyond permissible limits to constitute illegal interference with the employees' freedom of choice. In regulating the substance of campaign speeches, however, the Board faces a basic difficulty of distinguishing what the speaker says or intends from what the listener hears or understands. What is understood from a particular speech is likely to depend on the time and place of the speech, the relative power of union and management, and the personal values and beliefs of the individual listener. Words that will intimidate a southern textile worker may only antagonize a Detroit truck driver. Since the meaning that listeners may place on a given speech is likely to vary from situation to situation, it is hardly surprising that the Board's regulation of campaign communications is a relatively controversial aspect of its activities.

Campaign speeches or other communications that promise benefits to employees if the union is defeated, or threaten reprisals if the union is elected, constitute unfair labor-practices. However, the boundary line between an employer threat to close down the business if the union wins an election and an employer prediction that under collective bargaining, economic circumstances may force the closure of the firm, can be very thin. In practice, the Board forbids outright threats of economic reprisal against workers taken at the employer's discretion, but permits predictions that are carefully phrased on the basis of objective fact, to convey an employer's belief concerning the probable consequences of unionism that are beyond the employer's control. If the predictions are based on economic necessity rather than anti-union animus, there is no violation of the Act.

Appeals to prejudice. The Board has also taken the position that appeals to racial and religious prejudice can be coercive and grounds for setting aside the results of an election. While the Board will tolerate election propaganda that truthfully describes the employer or union position on matters of race, it will not accept inflammatory arguments or appeals which seek to overstress and exacerbate racial feelings.[8] This area of regulation illustrates many of the basic conflicts between interference with free choice, on the one hand, and free speech on the other. Is it clear that inflammatory appeals, which are common in political campaigns, are unprotected by the First Amendment of the Constitution? Why do emotional appeals raise the question of employer *power* over employees when such appeals are not forbidden in political campaigns? Moreover, attempts to draw a line

---

[7]Case examples include *Isaacson-Carrico Mfg. Co.,* 200 NLRB 788 (1972); *Flight Safety, Inc.,* 197 NLRB 223 (1972); and *Cannon Electric Co.,* 151 NLRB 1465 (1965).

[8]*Sewell Mfg. Co.,* 138 NLRB 66 (1962).

between temperate and intemperate speech imply that the Board (or anyone) can determine the point at which such speech begins to distort voting behavior.

Factual Misrepresentations. The Board's policy toward factual misrepresentations by either the employer or the union has changed direction several times. Initially, such misrepresentations were grounds for ordering a new election. While the general principle that voting decisions should be made on the factual merits of the case is unassailable, this aspect of the Board's implementation of the principle resulted in the setting aside of some elections because of rather small factual errors in the claims of one side or the other. (For example, election results have been voided when a union made a modest misstatement of the wage rate that it had negotiated elsewhere, and when an employer misstated the union dues that employees would be required to pay if they voted for a union.) Subsequently, the NLRB abandoned this policy, later readopted it, and, in 1982, abandoned it again.[9]

Discriminatory Treatment of Union Supporters. Organizing campaigns also regularly give rise to charges of discriminatory treatment of employees who support a union. A common example is when a worker is allegedly discharged by an employer in retaliation for union activities. (See Example 13.1) A second form of discrimination is closing a plant to avoid dealing with a union that has won the right to represent employees at the plant. (See Example 13.2.) In most such cases, the Board must judge the relative merit of employer claims that a particular action was taken for sound business reasons and union claims that the action was motivated by a desire to thwart union objectives.

Application: Impact of NLRB Regulation of Organizing

The elaborate set of rules developed by the NLRB in its regulation of campaigns for union representation is unmatched elsewhere in the world and has been a source of controversy and uncertainty: controversy, because the Board's regulation undoubtedly dissuades both unions and employers from using some campaign tactics that they believe to be legitimate; uncertainty, because the Board has from time to time reversed its position on certain issues. Some of the volume of unfair labor-practice charges may be related to this latter factor, since unions and employers may be more inclined to adopt campaign tactics whose legality remains ambiguous. Both the controversy and the uncertainty may be the result of a more basic underlying difficulty: an inadequate understanding by all parties of what types of campaign behavior really exert a coercive influence on the voting behavior of employees. Without a basic understanding of the determinants of voting behavior, unions, employers, and members of the NLRB, who are far removed from the campaign activities, may develop different beliefs about how much regulatory protection employees need in voting on union representation. But how

---

[9]See NLRB decisions in *Hollywood Ceramics,* 140 NLRB 221 (1962); *Shopping Kart Food Market,* 228 NLRB 190 (1977); and *Midland Life Insurance Co.* 263 NLRB 24 (1982).

valid are these beliefs? What effects do various unions or management campaign tactics have on voting behavior? And what can the law hope to accomplish in this voting environment?

Until recently, there was very little information bearing on either the empirical validity of the assumptions about employee behavior underlying NLRB regulation or, more broadly, what factors, legal and otherwise, lead workers to join unions. Workers face a definite choice in a union-representation election, and the history of unions in the United States indicates that the choice is more likely to be made on the basis of economic rather than ideological considerations.

To the extent that the union-representation choice is governed by rational economic decision making, workers will vote for a union only if the expected utility of their job is higher when they are represented by a union than when they are not. The expected impact of a union on wages and benefits is only one aspect of this calculus, since one consequence of negotiating higher wages and benefits through collective bargaining may be to reduce the probability of retaining one's job (as employers are forced up along their demand-for-labor curve). As a result, the availability of alternative jobs in the labor market and the utility attached to those jobs is also relevant to a worker's choice. Moreover, not all employees are likely to reach the same conclusions regarding the relative merits of union representation. To the extent that unions attempt to standardize rates and reduce wage differentials within a firm, the advantages of unionization will be inversely related to an employee's position in the firm's earnings distribution. Similarly, the substitution of a "web of rules" and a system of "industrial jurisprudence" to govern working relationships that were formerly governed by the individual discretion of supervisors will benefit those who had good relationships with supervisors less than those who did not. More generally, individuals are likely to have different subjective evaluations about their working conditions and how they expect unions to be able to change the work environment.

There is some empirical support for the view that voting decisions in union elections are made on the basis of an economic calculus. For example, one recent study found that the probability of voting for a union was inversely related to both the position of an individual in the wage distribution of a firm and concerns over job security when alternative jobs were not easily available. That is, workers with relatively high wages in their place of employment were less likely to vote for a union, as were those highly concerned about job security in markets with few opportunities. Voting behavior was also influenced by individual expectations of the effect of unions on the probability of promotion, fairness of treatment, and other nonmonetary issues of employment. In terms of personal characteristics, blacks and younger workers were more likely to vote union.[10] One implication of this research is that workers may enter a union-representation campaign with a fairly strong predisposition to vote for a union or the employer based on their knowledge of employment conditions and their expectations about how unions are likely to influence them.

---

[10]Henry S. Farber and Daniel H. Saks, "Why Workers Want Unions: The Role of Relative Wages and Job Characteristics," *Journal of Political Economy* 88 (April 1980): 349–369.

EXAMPLE 13.1

When Is a Discharge of a Union Member Discriminatory?

Section 8(a)(3) of the National Labor Relations Act prohibits employers from discriminating against workers because of their union activities. But what constitutes a discriminatory discharge? When a union supporter is discharged, the union alleges a violation of the Act, while the employer claims that the discharge was a result of poor job performance. Who is right? How does the NLRB or a court decide? The distinction between a discharge for cause and a violation of Section 8(a)(3) is illustrated in this amusing federal Appeals Court decision from 1943:

The case of Walter Weigand is extraordinary. If ever a workman deserved summary discharge it was he. He was under the influence of liquor while on duty. He came to work when he chose and he left the plant and his shift as he pleased. In fact, when a foreman on one occasion was agreeably surprised to find Weigand at work and commented upon it, Weigand amiably stated that he was enjoying it.* He brought a woman (apparently generally known as the "Duchess") to the rear of the plant yard and introduced some of the employees to her. He took another employee to visit her and when this man got too drunk to be able to go home, punched his time-card for him and put him on the table in the representatives' meeting room in the plant in order to sleep off his intoxication. Weigand's immediate superiors demanded again and again that he be discharged, but each time higher officials intervened on Weigand's behalf because, as was naively stated, he was "a representative" [that is in the company union]. In return for not working at the job for which he was hired, the petitioner gave him full pay and on five separate occasions raised his wages. . . . [F]our raises were given Weigand at times when other employees in the plant did not receive wage increases.

Shortly after Weigand disclosed his membership in a CIO union, he was discharged on grounds of poor performance. In response to the CIO's subsequent unfair labor-practice charge, the Appeals Court ruled:

It is, of course, a violation to discharge an employee because he has engaged in activities on behalf of a union. . . . [I]t is certainly too great a strain on our credulity to assert, as does the petitioner, that Weigand was discharged for an accumulation of offenses. We think that he was discharged because his work on behalf of the CIO had become known to the plant manager. That ended his sinecure at the Budd plant.

The fact that the plaintiff's relentless incompetence was tolerated by the company only until he began to support an outside union indicated to the court that the discharge was a violation of Section 8 (a)(3).

*Weigand stated that he was carried on the payroll as a "rigger." He was asked what was a rigger. He replied: "I don't know; I am not a rigger."

SOURCE: *Edward G. Budd Mfg. Co. v. NLRB,* United States Court of Appeals, Third Circuit, 1943, 138 F.2d 86, 13 LRRM 512.

EXAMPLE 13.2

Does a Plant Closure Discriminate Against Unions?

Example 13.1 indicated how an employer might illegally discriminate against an individual worker by discharging the worker for union activities. It has also been claimed that an employer can discriminate against an entire group of employees who support a union by closing a plant in which a union has won representation rights. Most charges of this nature arise in "runaway shop" situations, when an employer closes a unionized plant and subsequently opens a nonunion plant in a new location—usually in the South. In these cases, the NLRB seeks to distinguish closures that are motivated by "anti-union animus"—and hence are illegal under the NLRA —and those that are motivated by economic pressures, which are legal. But what happens if a plant goes out of business permanently after being organized by a union?

In 1956, the Textile Workers' Union initiated an organizing campaign at the Darlington Manufacturing Company in South Carolina, one of several textile mills operated by Deering-Milliken & Co., a New York textile marketing company. During the strongly contested campaign for union representation, the company threatened to close the mill in the event of a union victory. When the union did win the election, the head of Deering-Milliken called together the directors of Darlington, and they promptly voted to liquidate the corporation. The union filed unfair labor-practice charges.

The NLRB attributed the closure of the Darlington Company to the anti-union animus of the head of Deering-Milliken, found a violation of Section 8(a)(3) of the NLRA, and ordered back-pay for all terminated employees until they obtained similar work or were put on preferential hiring lists at other Deering-Milliken mills. The Board's startling proposition that under certain circumstances an employer could not go completely out of business without violating the NLRA was rejected by both a Circuit Court of Appeals and the Supreme Court. Motivation is irrelevant in the case of the liquidation of a business by an independent employer.

In its 1965 decision, however, the Supreme Court went on to make a further distinction:

On the other hand, a discriminatory partial closing may have repercussions on what remains of business, affording employer leverage for discouraging the free exercise of Section 7 rights among remaining employees of much the same kind as that found to exist in the "runaway shop" and "temporary closing" cases. . . . By analogy to those cases involving a continuing enterprise we are constrained to hold, in disagreement with the Court of Appeals, that a partial closing is an unfair labor practice under Section 8(a)(3) if motivated by a purpose to chill unionism in any of the remaining plants of the single employer and if the employer may reasonably have foreseen that such closing will likely have that effect.

Upon remand to determine the motivation for the closing, the NLRB found (and an Appeals Court agreed) that the Darlington plant had been closed by Deering-Milliken in order to deter union organization at its other plants.

In summary, a single firm can go out of business, irrespective of the owner's motivation, but if one unit of an organization shuts down, the legitimacy of the action under American labor law depends on whether or not the motivation for the shutdown is to chill unionism.

SOURCES: *Textile Workers' Union v. Darlington Mfg. Co.* 380 U.S. 263 (1965); *Darlington Mfg. Co. v. NLRB,* 397 F. 2d 760 (4th Circuit, 1968)

What then is the role of the union-representation campaign that the NLRB regulates? Both employers and unions use the campaign to try to change workers' predispositions (and persuade undecided employees) by altering expectations about what the union will achieve. Candidates for political office have a similar objective, but political scientists find that voters are often inattentive to a campaign, are unaware of issues (or even candidates), and in general, do not acquire the information necessary for rational choice among candidates. If there are also limitations on the inherent rationality of voters in union-representation elections, how important is the regulatory objective of "laboratory conditions" likely to be to the voting outcome?[11] The NLRB has rejected the political campaign analogy because of the employer's economic leverage over employees—a factor that is not present (or not as obvious) in political campaigns.[12] Like other Board positions, this rests on some untested assumptions concerning employee behavior when faced with the choice to unionize.

One recent study of voting choices in thirty-one union-representation elections reached provocative conclusions concerning the effectiveness of the NLRB regulation of campaign conduct.[13] The basic method of the study was to compare the voting intentions of employees—after the petition for a representation election had been filed with the Board but before the campaign had begun—with their actual voting behavior in the representation election at the conclusion of the campaign. The basic finding of the study was that employees vote in accord with intentions formed well in advance of the union-representation campaign, and little that occurs during the campaign itself has a significant effect on those intentions. Initial voting intentions were related to satisfaction with current job

[11]This question is raised in Derek C. Bok, "The Regulation of Campaign Tactics."

[12]Actually, the fiscal policies pursued by elected federal officials may sometimes have more influence on an individual's employment prospects than the decisions of an individual employer.

[13]Julius Getman, Stephen B. Goldberg, Jeanne B. Herman, *Union Representation Elections: Law and Reality* (New York: Russell Sage Foundation, 1976).

and employee attitudes toward unionism in general (rather than attitudes concerning the particular union(s) involved in the campaign). With this information alone, the authors were able to predict the outcome of 29 out of 31 elections. Moreover, the predictions were not improved by adding information on tactics used during the subsequent representation campaign to the information on voting intentions before the campaign began. Taken at face value, the conclusions of the study provide a powerful challenge to the assumptions that underlie the NLRB's current policy toward union-representation campaigns.[14]

Why is it that the campaign activities fail to influence the initial voting intentions of workers significantly? Largely, according to the study, because the basic behavioral foundations underlying the Board regulation are not valid. While the Board attempts to replicate laboratory campaign conditions, the majority of employees are inattentive to the campaign. When surveyed, most either could not remember many of the issues raised by either side in the campaign or remembered a few issues imperfectly. Many were already knowledgeable about unions and industrial relations from their general work experience or prior employment at unionized firms. Campaign information that is received is subject to perceptual distortion—that is, the way that workers perceive the campaign is a function of their prior beliefs. Employees who are predisposed toward the union before the campaign begins are likely to interpret an employer's speech as more threatening than workers who support the employer, but they may tend to interpret it as further evidence of the need for union representation. The general picture that emerges from the study is that misinformation, threatening behavior, and promises of benefit do not affect workers in ways that are likely to have a coercive influence on the choice of a union, and, by implication, much of the NLRB's current regulation of campaign conduct could be abandoned.

While there is very little difference between employees' original voting intentions and their final vote, the vote-switching that does occur tends to be from union to employer rather than in the opposite direction. The study finds that union and company supporters among the employees are equally familiar with the company campaign (probably as a result of "captive audience" meetings on company premises), but company supporters are much less familiar with the union campaign than are union supporters. This finding may suggest that as a matter of public policy, unions should get greater access to employees during a representation campaign, but it conflicts somewhat with the more general finding of inattentiveness noted above.

Judging by the level of resources allocated to union-representation campaigns, the provocative results of this study contrast sharply with the prevailing beliefs of both unions and management concerning employee voting-behavior. In fact, the conclusions of the study have not gone unchallenged, and there have been subse-

---

[14]Since all 31 elections took place under NLRB rulings, the study cannot tell us exactly what would happen if "no-holds-barred" campaigns were permitted; rather, it suggests that workers' decisions may not be as sensitive to many campaign tactics as the Board assumes.

quent re-analyses of the underlying data using more extensive controls for non-campaign influences on voting behavior. These analyses generally confirm the importance of voting predispositions held by workers on the likelihood of voting for a union, but they only partially confirm the earlier findings concerning the impact of campaign tactics. While many aspects of employer campaign speeches and tactics that the NLRB finds illegal do not have a statistically significant relationship to the probability of voting for a union, one study found that employer threats had a substantial and statistically significant tendency to reduce the probability that an employee would vote for a union. This finding is more supportive of the Board's prohibition of overtly threatening behavior by employers.[15]

The commission of unfair labor-practices is only one of the methods of union avoidance sometimes adopted by employers opposed to the unionization of their employees. Many employers hire consultants to plan and implement the strategy and tactics of the management side of a union-representation campaign. Such consultants often manage the flow of information to workers during the campaign and advise employers on tactics that purportedly will undermine the success of the union campaign. The increasing use of such consultants during the 1970s has been opposed by the labor movement and led to proposals that their activities be subject to legal restrictions.

As with the use of unfair labor-practices for union avoidance, however, recent research indicates that the use of consultants is not the major reason for the declining success of private-sector unions in representation elections.[16] Why, then, has the use of consultants in representation campaigns become an important issue for both unions and management? It is possible that neither side realizes that among the confluence of factors influencing a worker's decision to vote for a union, the impact of consultant activities is small. It is also notable, however, that most union-representation elections nowadays involve relatively small employee units and are often decided by very few votes.[17]

---

[15]William T. Dickens, "Do Campaigns Affect the Way Workers Vote In Union Representation Elections," ((processed), Dept. of Economics, University of California, Berkeley, November 1981). *See also,* William T. Dickens, *Union Representation Elections: Campaign and Vote,* Ph.D. dissertation, Dept. of Economics, MIT (October 1980).

[16]One study of 130 representation elections in a sample of retail grocery stores in seven states in the 1970s found that the use of consultants had a weak tendency to reduce the probability of a union victory, but this result was only marginally significant in a statistical sense. John J. Lawler, "The Impact of Management Consultants on Union Victories in NLRB Certification Elections," *Industrial and Labor Relations Review* (forthcoming).

[17]For example, one study found that a change of voting intention by as few as eight workers is sufficient to change the outcome of the average union-representation election. As is often the case, the behavior of the *marginal* workers, that is, those most prone to change their behavior, is more crucial to the outcome than the average behavior of all employees. Myron Roomkin and Richard Block, "A Preliminary Analysis of the Participation Rate and the Margin of Victory in NLRB Elections," *Proceedings of the Industrial Relations Research Association* (1982):220–26.

Remedies for Unfair Labor Practices

Since its inception, the National Labor Relations Board has faced the problem of developing corrective measures for violations of the unfair labor-practice provisions of the NLRA. The array of sanctions that the Board has adopted has been limited by decisions of the U.S. Supreme Court that hold that the purpose of the NLRA is remedial rather than punitive. Under this concept, whatever sanctions the Board designs are supposed to restore the *status quo* in labor relations at the time of a violation, but they are not supposed to impose any additional penalty on the employer or union responsible for the violation.

Current remedies applied by the NLRB attempt to meet this standard. In response to modest violations of "laboratory campaign conditions," the Board may set aside election results that it views as tainted by illegal campaign conduct and rerun the election. For serious violations of unfair labor-practices, the Board may order an employer to bargain with a union that lost an election, if a majority of the employees in the bargaining unit had originally signed cards authorizing the union to bargain for them. (Here the Board assumes that the *status quo* that existed at the time the authorization cards were signed was later distorted by unfair labor practices.)[18] The use of authorization cards for this purpose has been controversial, on the grounds that what workers do in the privacy of a voting booth is likely to be a more reliable guide to their preferences than what they may say (or sign) to get a union organizer to leave them alone. However, one study found that authorization cards did reflect worker voting intentions accurately.[19] In instances where illegal forms of employer resistance to unionization occur before a union has obtained enough signed authorization cards to file an election petition with the NLRB, the Board may certify the union as the bargaining representative and issue an order to bargain *even though an election has not been held,* on the belief that, but for the employer's unfair labor-practices, the union would have acquired the signed cards and won the election.

In the case of a discrimination discharge, the Board tries to compensate the employee for wage losses incurred as a result of the unfair labor-practice; however, if the employee receives more than was lost, the corrective measure would be punitive. Therefore, the typical remedy is reinstatement with back pay (or back pay alone if the worker does not wish reinstatement).[20] Back pay due the employee

---

[18]In *NLRB v. Gissel Packing Co.,* 395 U.S. 575 (1969), the Supreme Court ruled that while the results of a representation election were the preferred indication of employee preferences for union representation, authorization cards could be accepted as reliable indicators of employee voting intentions when extensive unfair labor practices by an employer were believed to have polluted the results of a representation election. A union with authorization cards signed by a majority of the employees could be certified as bargaining agent. Absent unfair labor practices, however, an employer has a right to an election even when the union has authorization cards from a majority of the employees in a unit.

[19]Getman, Goldberg, and Herman, *Union Representation Elections,* Chapter 6.

[20]Back pay awards include fringe benefits, forgone interest, and wages including adjustments for expected promotions (based on the employment history of similarly situated workers within the firm). It does not include compensation for losses—such as repossession of car or eviction—that a worker might incur as a result of being unable to meet financial obligations while illegally discharged.

by the employer responsible for the discharge is reduced by any interim earnings or unemployment compensation received by the worker, so that the total amount received since discharge from all sources does not exceed what the employee would have earned from the employer if the discharge had not occurred. Clearly, the back pay for which the employer is liable can be very small when a discharged worker immediately finds another job.

How well do these remedies restore the *status quo* in labor relations at the time of an unfair labor-practice? One factor bearing on this question is the long delay in reaching decisions. Over a year typically passes between the filing of a charge and a Board decision. If that decision is appealed, another 1–2 years will be required before a U.S. Circuit Court of Appeals reaches a decision. With such delays, workers who have been discharged because of their union activities frequently have taken other jobs long before their case is resolved. While they may accept the back pay, few return to resume their career with the former employer.[21] It is by no means clear that this procedure restores the *status quo*. From the perspective of the employees who remain with the employer, an individual who supported unions was discharged and never reappeared. The loss of leaders and supporters will directly reduce union support and it may have indirect effects as well. The jeopardy in which other union supporters may find themselves seems clear. From the perspective of the employer, the back-pay liability can be very small when the discharged worker takes a job soon after being dismissed— possibly much less than the costs of additional compensation that might be negotiated in a collective-bargaining contract after a successful organizing campaign. Some employers behave as if they believe that the expected costs of compliance with unfair labor-practice provisions of the NLRA exceed the expected costs of violations, a situation that raises doubts about how well the remedial objective of the NLRA is being attained in union-representation campaigns.

Several of the above issues concerning procedures and remedies were addressed in a labor-law reform bill that was sent to Congress in 1978. The bill provided for alterations in some NLRB procedures to cut down time delays and encouraged the use of temporary injunctive relief for employees (for example, the immediate reinstatement of a discharged worker) pending the resolution of unfair labor-practice charges. It also sought to raise the expected cost of violating the NLRA by providing for awards of up to double back pay for workers who had been discharged illegally and by barring companies that willfully violate NLRB orders from participating in federal contracts for a period of three years.[22] Nevertheless, after an intensive lobbying campaign, the legislation failed to secure passage in Congress.

---

[21]A study of 217 reinstatement orders issued by one NLRB regional office in 1971 and 1972 found that 129 of the individuals refused reinstatement, largely because of fear of further mistreatment by the company. Only 5 percent of those offered reinstatement 6 months or more after they were discharged accepted the remedy. Of those who did accept, only a third remained with the company for more than six months. Elvis C. Stephens and Warren Chaney, "A Study of the Reinstatement Remedy Under the NLRA," *Labor Law Journal* 25 (January 1974): 31–41.

[22]Experience with a similar provision regarding federal contracts in American equal-employment-opportunity policy suggests that the government is reluctant to enforce remedies of this nature.

EXAMPLE 13.3

Union Avoidance and Labor Law

In 1963, the Textile Workers' Union of America (TWUA) began a drive to organize J.P. Stevens & Company, the second largest textile company in the United States, with some 39,000 hourly workers and 80 plants located primarily in southern states. Over the next 12 years the union lost 11 of 12 representation elections held at Stevens' factories and was certified as the bargaining agent for some 3,000 textile workers in the single election that it won. However, the election campaigns were accompanied by massive unfair labor practices on the part of the company. The NRLB ruled against the company in 22 out of 23 unfair labor-practice cases, finding that Stevens had fired or otherwise discriminated against 289 workers for their union activities. In some cases, where the union lost an election, the Board concluded that Stevens' unfair labor practices had distorted workers' freedom of choice and ordered the company to bargain with the TWUA. The company ignored the orders and also refused to bargain with the TWUA at the plant where the union won the representation election. The federal courts upheld the Board in 13 of the 16 cases that were appealed when cease-and-desist or bargaining orders were ignored. In the 17 years following the beginning of the TWUA organizing campaign, J.P. Stevens violated more labor laws than any other company in the history of the National Labor Relations Act and had become a symbol of the use of union avoidance tactics by employers.

Given the company's resistance to legal remedies, and the failure of an attempted nationwide boycott of J.P. Stevens' products initiated by the labor movement, the TWUA devised an unusual strategy to induce the company to sign an agreement: it began to bring pressure on companies that had business or financial dealings with the J.P. Stevens Company or that had officials of Stevens on their boards of directors. By generating unfavorable publicity and suggesting that unions should shift their pension funds and other financial assets from financial institutions that had dealings with J.P. Stevens, the TWUA appeared to force the chairman of Stevens to resign from the board of two companies. Its most successful tactic, however, was to threaten to run two dissident candidates to oppose the official nominees for the board of directors of the major life-insurance company that held over 40 percent of J.P. Stevens' long-term debt. Faced with the unappealing and unusual prospect of a contested board-of-directors election that could cost between $5–7 million to conduct, the insurance company met with Stevens' officials and, after seventeen years of union avoidance, Stevens recognized the union and signed an agreement with the TWUA. (As part of the agreement the union agreed not to restrict "the availability of financial or credit accommodations to Stevens.")

The J.P. Stevens case is interesting in part because it illustrates the limitations of legal procedures and remedies in guaranteeing workers their statutory rights to union representation and collective bargaining in the face of determined employer resistance. Ultimately, the struggle between J.P. Stevens and the TWUA was determined by economic power. For plants where the union was not able to win a representation election, the case also raises several of the policy issues considered earlier in this chapter and in the discussion of "right-to-work" legislation in Chapter 12. Did workers vote against the union because of the employer's unfair labor practices or because of personal preferences to remain nonunion? Do employer unfair labor-practices dissuade workers from voting for a union or convince them of the need for a union to protect them from arbitrary exercise of employer power? Some of the research cited in this chapter indicates that the answers to these questions are not as obvious as is sometimes supposed.

SOURCES: Terry W. Mullins and Paul Luebke, "Symbolic Victory and Political Reality in the Southern Textile Industry: The Meaning of the J.P. Stevens Settlement for Southern Labor Relations," *Journal of Labor Research* III (Winter 1982): 81–88; and Gail Bronson and Jeffrey H. Birnbaum, "How the Textile Union Finally Wins Contracts at J.P. Stevens Plants," *Wall Street Journal* October 20, 1980.

Alert readers may have noticed a tension between this discussion of remedies for unfair labor practices and the discussion of the impact of NLRB regulation on the outcome of union election campaigns in the preceding section. If many of the activities that the Board regulates have no important effect on the outcome of the campaign, as indicated by some of the evidence that was reviewed in the previous section, then the *status quo* may be preserved even in the absence of remedies. That is, particular election results may have occurred independently of the behavior that the Board regulates and hence would not have been affected by the nature of the remedies available. Obviously, the intensity of the lobbying surrounding the relatively modest reforms proposed in the Labor Law Reform Bill of 1978 indicates that this is not a view that is widely held among representatives of union and management.

Even if NLRB regulations have no effect on the vote, there may still be a case for remedies. For example, firing union leaders may not affect the vote, but it allows the employer to get rid of those employees he or she finds to be the most onerous and who might be the most militant if the employees gained collective-bargaining rights. In this case, the remedy of back pay and reinstatement serves to protect the "right" of nonunion employees not to be arbitrarily discharged *and* if a union wins the election, it protects the workers in place *prior* to the election (subject to normal turnover).

The NLRB also has the authority to remedy unfair labor practices by unions, although these constitute a relatively small proportion of its work load. The main remedy for a union unfair labor-practice is the injunction. One section of the NLRA permits the Board to seek an injunction against mass picketing accompanied by violence, efforts to induce an employer to discriminate against individuals who are not union members, and other unfair practices. (The NLRA also permits the Board to enjoin employer unfair labor-practices, but this occurs rarely.) Another section of the Act requires the NLRB to seek a temporary injunction if the union is charged with secondary boycott activity (a violation of Section 8(b)(4)), strikes in support of work assignment demands, or unusually long picketing for the purpose of obtaining union recognition.

Regulation of the Collective-Bargaining Process

In addition to establishing procedures for the selection of unions, Congress wished to assure, in drafting the NLRA, that workers would actually receive some of the benefits of a collective-bargaining relationship and sought to implement this intention by imposing a duty to bargain on employers and unions. At the same time, it appears that the legislation was not intended to give the government a substantive role in the collective-bargaining process. (One Senator stated that the government would lead the parties to the door of the bargaining room but "would not go one step beyond.") That there is a real tension between these two objectives can be seen from the way in which the legal environment of collective bargaining has developed under the NLRA.

Once a union has won a representation election, the National Labor Relations Act imposes certain obligations on both the union and the employer with whom it will bargain. These obligations are tied to the concept of *exclusive representation,* which is a unique feature of American labor law, and the duty to bargain established by the unfair labor practices in Section 8(a)(5) and 8(b)(3) of the Act (see Table 13.1). A union which wins a representation election is certified by the National Labor Relations Board as the exclusive bargaining agent for all employees in the bargaining unit. This status imposes on the union the duty to represent *all* employees in the unit—even those who may have opposed representation by the union. At the same time, an employer may not work out contractual relations with individual employees once a union has been certified. Nor may an employer deal with other organizations (for example, those of employees who voted against the union) on matters of employment conditions. In each instance, the employer must deal with the employees through their union. The principle of exclusive representation also prohibits an employer from taking unilateral action with respect to employment conditions until after the employer has bargained with the certified union to a point of impasse.

Exactly what constitutes collective bargaining and how does one know when a bargaining impasse has been reached? The legislative guidance on bargaining and impasse is provided by Section 8(d) of the National Labor Relations Act, which elaborates the meaning of the duty to bargain:

> ". . . to bargain collectively is . . . [the] mutual obligation to meet at reasonable times and confer in good faith with respect to wages, hours, and other terms and conditions of employment, or the negotiation of an agreement . . . and the execution of a written contract incorporating any agreement reached if requested by either party, but such obligation does not compel either party to agree to a proposal or require the making of a concession."

EXAMPLE 13.4

How Well Are Workers Protected by the Duty To Bargain?

The original case for including the duty to bargain in the National Labor Relations Act was to assure that meaningful collective bargaining commenced once a union won a representation election. Yet, as we have seen, Section 8(d) of the act qualifies the duty by not requiring either side to concede. One outcome of collective bargaining under these legal provisions is illustrated by the following case. The language is that of the U.S. Court of Appeals after considering an employer's appeal of an NLRB decision:

Refusal to bargain in good faith [may] be sustained solely by reference to the terms of the employment contract which management finally says it is willing to sign if such proposed contract could fairly be found to be one which would leave the employees in no better state than they were without it. . . . [W]e may assume that the Board could find that [by] the terms of the contract insisted on by the company the union is in no better position than if it had no contract. It is perfectly apparent that the company representatives approached the bargaining table with a full understanding of their obligations to meet with, and discuss with, representatives of the employees any terms and conditions of employment that either put forward; that they must at least expose themselves to such argument and persuasion as could be put forward, and that they must try to seek an area of agreement at least as to some of the terms of employment; that if they were able to arrive at such agreement they must be willing to reduce it to writing and sign it. . . . The question is: Can the company's insistence on terms overall favorable to it in net result be taken as proof that it did not approach the bargaining table in good faith? . . . [T]he Board is saying that although the statute says no concession need be made and no item need be agreed upon, if a company fails to concede anything substantial, then this is too much, and such failure amounts to bad faith. The language of the Courts is not . . . entirely clear, but we find no case which precisely supports the proposition here asserted by the Board. . . . A careful study of the record before us . . . leaves us with the clear impression that the Board erred in finding adequate proof of a failure to bargain in good faith.

Note that a similar situation could arise if a powerful union simply presented a contract proposal to a weak employer on a take-it-or-leave-it basis. Indeed, instances of such behavior led Congress to extend the duty to bargain to unions in the 1947 Taft-Hartley amendments. But, in either case, what difference does this legal duty make to the outcome of collective bargaining? What factor(s) ultimately determine the content of the labor agreement signed by the union and management?

SOURCE: *White v. NLRB,* United States Court of Appeals, 5th Circuit, (1958). 255 F.2d 564.

In determining when a legal bargaining impasse has occurred, the NLRB as a matter of policy must determine what constitutes "good faith" and what constitutes "other terms and conditions of employment." In order to resolve these issues, the NLRB and the courts have had to review the reasonableness of the positions of the negotiating parties in an effort to assess the "state of mind" of the negotiating parties.

Over the years the NLRB and the courts have developed a set of standards or rules for what constitutes good faith bargaining that has some impact on the tactics and behavior used by unions and management in collective bargaining. First, there are a set of *per se* violations of the duty to bargain that pertain to behavior at the bargaining table. A violation of the duty to bargain in good faith will generally be found if either party simply listens to and rejects the other party's proposals, if counter-proposals are not made (although, as Section 8(d) specifies, neither party is required to make concessions), if stalling tactics are used, or if either party suddenly shifts position when agreement is near. The Supreme Court has also held that good-faith bargaining requires that the parties provide data in support of their bargaining claims. For example, if a company claims it is unable to pay the costs that would be imposed by union demands, it must provide the financial data to support that claim if the union requests it.[23]

In addition to the tactical issues raised by the legal duty to bargain, the Board and the courts have been confronted with issues involving the substance of collective bargaining. The NLRA requires labor and management to bargain over "wages, hours, and other terms and conditions of employment." Is the NLRA violated when one party refuses to bargain with the other over a proposal that would violate other laws (for example, equal-employment-opportunity legislation)? Just what are "other terms and conditions of employment"? Is the NLRA violated when one party refuses to bargain with the other over an issue that it does not believe to be a "term and condition of employment" under the meaning of the law? In one important case, for example, an employer refused to bargain with a union over subcontracting decisions, on the grounds that such decisions were in the scope of management prerogatives.[24] These questions must ultimately be answered by the NLRB and the courts, but in the process, these institutions end up "defining" many of the issues that *must* be bargained under the law.

The NLRB has addressed these issues by developing a three-way classification of substantive bargaining issues: *illegal* issues, which should not be a topic of negotiations because they violate some other law; *mandatory* issues, which fall within the definition of "other terms and conditions of employment" and therefore must be bargained; and *voluntary* issues, which, although legal, do not fall within the definition of "terms and conditions of employment." Refusal to bargain over voluntary conditions does not constitute a violation of the legal duty to bargain.

---

[23]*NLRB v. Truitt Mfg. Co.* 351 U.S.149 (1956).

[24]In this case, the Board and the courts agreed with the union that the employer was required to bargain over this issue. *See Fibreboard Paper Products Corp. v. NLRB,* 379 U.S. 203 (1964).

The implications of this classification scheme for bargaining issues were expanded with the Supreme Court decision in the Borg-Warner case in 1958.[25] This case grew out of collective-bargaining negotiations in which the company insisted that two clauses be incorporated in a new labor agreement: recognition of the local (rather than the national) union and a "last offer ballot"—that is, a requirement that employees be polled on whether or not they supported the employer's last bargaining offer before a strike was called. The union refused to bargain over these demands on the grounds that they were internal union matters and not subject to collective-bargaining negotiations. When the company continued to insist on the two clauses a strike was called, but the union eventually lost the strike and filed unfair labor-practice charges, alleging that Borg-Warner had violated the duty-to-bargain provision of the NLRA. At the same time, Borg-Warner alleged that the union had violated the same provision by refusing to bargain over the issues. The Board and the courts found that the two proposed clauses were voluntary subjects of bargaining and, consistent with past policy, the union's refusal to bargain was therefore not an unfair labor practice. However, the duty-to-bargain concept was then extended by the further ruling that the company's insistence on bargaining a voluntary issue to the point where a bargaining impasse and strike occurred constituted bargaining in bad faith.

At first glance, this ruling may appear unusual. Although the company's bargaining conduct may be perfectly legal, its insistence on a voluntary topic of collective bargaining to the point of impasse is a violation of the duty to bargain. On the other hand, insistence on bargaining over a mandatory topic to the point where a strike or lockout occurs is not a violation of this duty. What is behind this distinction? Recall that Section 8(d) of the NLRA does not require that agreement be reached in bargaining over "wages, hours, and other terms and conditions of employment" so that work stoppages over these issues are consistent with the Act. On the other hand, a general objective of the NLRA was to reduce the general level of industrial conflict, and rulings that prohibit work stoppages resulting from refusals to bargain over issues that seem peripheral to the key issues in union-management relations are consistent with this.

But which issues are central to collective bargaining and which issues are peripheral? How do employers and unions know whether a proposal is mandatory or voluntary? If the Board has not ruled on a similar issue in a previous case, they do not know. Therefore, one result of the ruling is that as new issues are introduced into collective bargaining, the party opposing change can adopt the strategy of refusing to bargain over the new proposal in the hope that when the NLRB considers the unfair labor-practice charge normally following such a stance, it will rule that the proposal is voluntary and need not be bargained. Increases in the number of issues introduced into collective bargaining can therefore contribute to the increase in duty-to-bargain unfair labor-practice charges noted earlier in the chapter.

More fundamentally, rulings by the NLRB and the courts on the classifica-

---

[25]*NLRB v. Wooster Division of Borg Warner Corp.,* 356 U.S. 342 (1958).

tion of bargaining issues can alter the relative bargaining power of unions and management in collective bargaining. Consider the Borg-Warner case. The union lost a strike and had to accept the company's proposals. The ruling by the NLRB and the Supreme Court (on appeal) effectively restored to the union a contractual position that it was unable to achieve by standard collective-bargaining methods. On this issue, the ruling effectively increased the bargaining power of the union relative to management and through legal intervention altered the outcome of the collective-bargaining process. At the same time, application of the Borg-Warner rule tends to influence the scope of collective bargaining. Topics that the NLRB labels "mandatory" are more likely to end up in collective-bargaining agreements than topics that are labeled "voluntary," simply because the ability to use force to back up the former demands raises the probability that they will be accepted. Therefore, while the original intention of the NLRA may have been to keep the government out of the substance of collective bargaining, the intervention of the Board and courts in determining mandatory and voluntary topics of bargaining can have considerable impact on the outcome and scope of collective bargaining.

Application: Good Faith and General Electric's Labor Relations

The labor-relations policy practiced by the General Electric Company for almost twenty years provides an interesting review of the issues raised by the duty-to-bargain requirement in the National Labor Relations Act. Following a serious strike in 1946, GE's vice-president of labor relations, Lemuel R. Boulware, devised a new labor-relations policy for the firm that became known as "Boulwareism." Under the new plan, GE solicited considerable information on the benefits and working conditions desired by its employees, formulated specific proposals on the basis of this information, and then tried to sell the package of proposals to the employees and the general public through a massive marketing campaign that included bulletins to GE employees and newspaper advertising.

GE had a collective-bargaining relationship with the International Union of Electrical, Radio, and Machine Workers (IUE), and the new approach to labor relations became part of the company's overall bargaining strategy. Most companies enter collective-bargaining negotiations offering less than they can afford (or less than they believe they will have to settle for) in order to have something to trade during the negotiations process. GE objected to this approach on the grounds that the union typically received credit from the workers for any concessions that were received from the employer during negotiations, and the company's credibility with its employees was diminished. Instead, under Boulwareism, GE announced that its initial offer was proper and final and would not be altered unless it were faced with information that had not been considered in the research underlying the company's offer. This aspect of the strategy was an effort to deny the union a political victory in collective-bargaining negotiations, for the company was unwilling to alter its proposal solely because the union disagreed with it. It was the company's position that its extensive research left it at least as well apprised of what workers wanted out of a labor agreement as the union was, and it generally adopted a patronizing attitude toward union counterproposals.

Following negotiations in 1960, the IUE filed unfair labor practices alleging that GE had violated the duty-to-bargain provision of the NLRA. During those negotiations, GE had attempted to institute unilaterally a personal accident insurance benefit for employees, refused to release certain details (including the cost of the package of company proposals), and generally adopted the take-it-or-leave-it bargaining stance that was a feature of Boulwareism. After protracted legal proceedings, the Board and the Courts sustained the unfair labor-practice charge. The difficulty with the effort to institute the insurance proposal is that once a collective-bargaining relationship is established, under the NLRA, neither party to the relationship can terminate or modify the contract without giving 60 days notice and offering to renegotiate. Even unilateral modifications that may *increase* the value of the contract (as GE's insurance proposal would have) cannot be instituted without bargaining, since the union may have other priorities and prefer that the cost of the modification be allocated to a different purpose. Generally, the Courts took the position that the union's ability to serve as an effective bargaining agent is impaired by unilateral offers by an employer. Likewise, the NLRB and the courts had long held that employers and unions have a duty to provide information in support of their bargaining claims, and GE's failure to do so constituted a violation of the duty to bargain.

Fundamentally, the federal courts also ruled that the entire pattern of collective-bargaining conduct developed by GE under its policy of Boulwareism was inconsistent with good-faith bargaining. Part of the courts' rulings were based on GE's conduct at the bargaining table and included the company's refusal to furnish information, its patronizing attitude, its refusal to comment specifically on union proposals, and its reluctance to offer counterproposals (that would have differed from its initial offer). The courts also took exception to the company's emphasis on selling its proposal through marketing techniques rather than collective bargaining. In the words of the Circuit Court of Appeals: ". . . The aim, in a word, was to deal with the Union through the employees, rather than with the employees through the Union" as is required by the NLRA.[26]

Remedies for Refusal To Bargain

Violations of the duty-to-bargain are inherently difficult to remedy. When an employer simply refuses to negotiate with a union that has been certified by the NLRB, the union can only file an unfair labor practice and wait out the several years until the various appeals are exhausted. At that point, the remedy is an order to bargain, but from the perspective of the employees and the union this hardly restores the *status quo,* since several years of possible increases in benefits through collective bargaining have been forgone while the employer's refusal to bargain was being litigated.

---

[26]*NLRB v. General Electric Co.* 418 F.2d 736 (2d Circuit, 1969).

Unions have urged that under the concept of adopting remedies that restore the *status quo* of labor relations, workers should be "made whole" for the benefits that were lost during the period of litigation. But what were those benefits? To determine what workers were owed would be to prejudge the outcome of the collective-bargaining process, for the Board would have to effectively decide what benefits would have been negotiated if collective bargaining had occurred over the period of litigation. This would constitute an even more intrusive impact on the substance of collective bargaining than the indirect influence that the Board now has in its determinations of whether certain issues are mandatory or voluntary topics of bargaining. As a result, the Board has refused to adopt "make-whole" remedies for violations of the duty-to-bargain requirement.[27] The Labor Law Reform Bill of 1978, which was defeated in Congress, provided that when an employer refused to bargain for a first contract, employees would be "made whole" for their losses over the period on the basis of the average wages received by workers in companies where bargaining had occurred. Although the implication that newly established unions typically negotiate wages equal to the average union scale in their area is not well-established, the passage of the proposed remedy would have substantially altered the bargaining power of new unions relative to employers. By raising the expected gains from union membership, the remedy presumably would have influenced the outcomes of union-representation elections.

Labor-Relations Policy in the Public Sector

Public policy toward union-management relations is more varied and unsettled in the public sector than in the private sector. As noted in Chapter 12, a "doctrine of sovereignty" pervaded thinking about the rights of public employees to negotiate the terms and conditions of their employment. Public employees were therefore excluded from coverage under the NLRA, and even as late as the early 1980s, some states and major cities did not have legislation specifying labor-relations policy beyond a general prohibition on strikes by public employees. At the other extreme, a few states had laws that accorded some public employees the right to strike. Our purpose in this section is to summarize the main features of labor policy in the public sector and note important differences from policy in the private sector. A discussion of one of the most important issues, the question of the right-to-strike by public employees, is postponed until the discussion of labor disputes in Chapter 15.

Public employees along with private employees have a constitutional right to join unions. The differences between policy in the public and private sectors is in the scope of activities that unions can engage in. However, in developing policy the same general issues are presented in each sector: procedures for recognition, the scope of the collective-bargaining rights that a union receives with recogni-

---

[27]*Ex-Cell-O Corp.*, 185 NLRB 107 (1970).

tion, permissible forms of labor-management conflict, and other dispute-settlement mechanisms.

In the federal government sector, labor-relations policy was initially specified in Executive Order 10988 issued by President Kennedy in 1962. The federal policy toward recognition bears some resemblance toward private-sector policy under the NLRA in that a union that receives majority support from employees in a bargaining unit is granted *exclusive recognition,* which carries with it a right to negotiate agreements. Unlike the NLRA, however, the executive order also provides other levels of recognition. Unions representing up to ten percent of the members of a bargaining unit receive *informal recognition,* which entitles them to be heard on employment issues by the management of a federal agency. Unions representing 10 to 50 percent of employees in a unit receive *formal recognition,* which entitles them to be consulted by management on changes in employment policy.

While the executive order seeks to guarantee the rights granted to employees and managers by proscribing certain unfair labor practices, it does not establish an independent agency to judge the merit of charges arising under the policy. Instead, charges are appealed to higher levels of federal management. However, the most substantial limitation of federal policy, both in comparison to policy in the private sector and in most states and localities, is the limitations on the topics appropriate for collective bargaining. Not only wages (which are set through the legislative process with reference to pay comparability studies, as described in Chapter 12), but also the methods of work, technology, mission of an agency, and many other issues affecting employment are excluded from bargaining.

Strikes are forbidden and strikes by federal employees have carried severe penalties. In 1982, for example, a strike by the Professional Air Traffic Controllers resulted in the dismissal of all striking workers, fines and jail sentences for several leaders of the strike, and ultimately, the bankruptcy of the union. While the courts recognize the right to belong to unions as a *constitutional* right, they have held that the right to strike is not a constitutional right and must be provided by statute. While such rights are now provided by the NLRA to private workers and, in a few instances, by state legislation to certain categories of public workers, federal workers do not have the right to strike.

While there is considerable variation in the policies pertaining to state and local government (SLG) employees, certain central tendencies have emerged. Recognition is normally established on the basis of representation elections similar to those that occur in the private sector and many of the rules followed by the NLRB are adopted. SLGs vary, however, in the rights accorded to recognized unions. In some jurisdictions, the public employer is authorized only to *meet and confer* with representatives of public employees. Under "meet-and-confer" legislation, the parties may sign a memorandum of understanding if some agreement is reached, but the public employer is not legally obligated to follow it. In other jurisdictions, the law permits collective negotiations in which labor and management are equal legal parties, and the outcome of negotiations can be a mutually binding labor agreement, as in the private sector. Moreover, the scope of permissible bargaining issues is typically not as constrained as in the federal sector.

With the difference in collective-bargaining rights between the public and private sectors, unions in the public sector generally prefer legislation imposing a legal duty to bargain in good faith. In the absence of a right to strike, the legal duty may be important to compel bargaining by recalcitrant public employers.

Unions and the Antitrust Laws

When Congress passed the Sherman Antitrust Act—the nation's basic antitrust statute—in 1890, it established a national policy in favor of competition and its effects, including productive efficiency and a decentralization of economic decision making. The statute provided that "every contract, combination, . . . or conspiracy in restraint of trade or commerce among the several states . . . is illegal. . . . Every person who shall monopolize, or attempt to monopolize, or combine or conspire with any other person or persons, to monopolize any part of the trade or commerce among the several states . . . shall be guilty of a misdemeanor"; treble damages were provided in the event of a violation. In the years since the passage of the act, firms that have acquired a dominant position in an industry or have engaged in price-fixing or other anti-competitive practices have often been found to be in violation of the statute.

Over the same period, antitrust law has been applied infrequently to unions, despite the fact that unions in general advance the welfare of their members by monopolizing the sale of labor in a bargaining unit and otherwise reducing wage competition among workers. Some members of the public are often puzzled as to why certain union practices that appear to have an anticompetitive impact—for example, restrictive work practices and industry-wide collective-bargaining negotiations—and even unions themselves are not the target of antitrust enforcement. The Sherman Act itself contains no specific reference to unions and the intent of Congress concerning the application to unions is unclear from the legislative history. It is hardly surprising that unions stressed that they were not included in the statute while employers stressed that unions were not excluded.

Matters were not clarified with the passage of the Norris-LaGuardia Act in 1931 and the National Labor Relations Act in 1935. In providing statutory support for unions and collective bargaining, Congress established a policy that sanctioned large-scale labor organizations, despite the capacity of such organizations to interfere with the competitive objectives of the antitrust laws. This presented the federal courts with a significant policy dilemma: how are the national policies favoring competition, on the one hand, and unionization and collective bargaining, on the other, to be reconciled? Since the policy on unions and collective bargaining was established more recently, it is unlikely that Congress intended that it should be completely subordinated to antitrust policy. Yet neither the Norris-LaGuardia Act nor the NLRA contains language addressing the relationship between the newer labor legislation and the older antitrust legislation. Over the years, the federal courts have had considerable difficulty in accommodating the two policy objectives. Since almost any variety of union activity constitutes some sort of restraint on competitive market behavior, the problem faced by the courts has been to determine which types of market restraints resulting from union behavior are illegal under the antitrust statutes and which restraints are protected under the labor-relations statutes.

Even prior to the passage of the labor-relations statutes in the 1930s, the Sherman Act was not used against the more obvious signs of union monopoly power, such as efforts to organize all of the firms in an industry under the terms of a single collective-bargaining agreement. Instead, the act was used to thwart "bad practices" such as the use of secondary boycotts.[28] In one early Sherman Act case,[29] an action that became popularly known as the *Danbury Hatters'* case, the United Hatters of North America instituted a nationwide consumer boycott against an employer's products *and against individuals who purchased the employer's products,* after the failure of an organizing strike. Because the union's action was not limited to the employer, it constituted a secondary boycott, and the Supreme Court ruled that this was a violation of the Sherman Act. Subsequent efforts by the labor movement to reverse this application of antitrust legislation culminated with the passage of the Clayton Act in 1914. Section 6 of the act provided that, "Nothing contained in the antitrust laws shall be construed to forbid the existence and operation of labor organizations from lawfully carrying out the legitimate objects thereof; nor shall such organizations, or the members thereof, be held or construed to be illegal combinations or conspiracies in restraint of trade, under the antitrust laws."[30] Although unions hailed Section 6 as an exemption from antitrust, the language of the statute was clear only on the point that the existence of union organizations was not by itself an antitrust violation. Section 6 said very little about the basic issue raised by the Danbury Hatters' decision—the tactical freedom permitted unions under the antitrust laws—and left it to the federal courts to interpret the key words *lawfully* and *legitimate.*

The limitations of Section 6 became clear with a 1921 Supreme Court decision in the *Duplex Printing Press* case.[31] The facts of the case were similar to those in the Danbury Hatters' case. A union of machinists that had organized all but one of the producers of a certain type of printing press instituted a secondary boycott of the lone holdout after a strike for recognition failed. The employer, Duplex Printing Press, alleged an antitrust violation, and the Supreme Court agreed. To the consternation of the unions, the court held that the secondary boycott was not a "lawful" and "legitimate" activity, in large measure because it did not involve the direct relationship between an employer and his employees. From a legal perspective, the decision clearly indicated that the exemption of unions from antitrust was limited. From an economic perspective, the decision is of interest because of what it did *not* say. In the Duplex Printing Press decision, as in earlier decisions, the courts raised no objections to the scope of union organization or to the specific objective of extending union control over an entire

[28]For an extensive discussion of this point, *see* Bernard D. Meltzer, "Labor Unions, Collective Bargaining, and the Antitrust Laws," *Journal of Law and Economics* 6 (October 1963):152–223.

[29]*Loewe v. Lawlor,* 208 U.S. 274 (1908).

[30]*Clayton Antitrust Act* 6, 38 Stat. 730 (1914).

[31]*Duplex Printing Press v. Deering,* 254 U.S. 443 (1921).

industry. Even prior to the labor-relations legislation of the 1930s, applications of antitrust law were limited to questionable practices and the courts raised no antitrust barriers to union objectives of developing monopolistic market structures.

With the labor-relations legislation of the 1930s, the courts had to adopt a new approach to the relationship between unions and the antitrust laws. The Norris-LaGuardia Act broadened the definition of a legal labor dispute beyond the position taken in the Duplex case and freed most union tactics, including the secondary boycott, from judicial regulation. Nevertheless, the courts still faced a difficult issue in trying to decide when union activity violated antitrust law. It was not enough to restrict the application of antitrust to those union activities that have a product-market impact, since virtually all union labor-market activity with respect to wages, hours, fringe benefits, and so forth, is naturally linked to the product market so long as production costs influence prices. But these activities are basic to the existence of unions and are at the core of protected activity under the NLRA. The problem facing the courts is to determine the limits of labor's antitrust exemption when union activities have a serious noncompetitive impact on product markets.

The court's struggle to resolve these conflicting national policies is still evolving, but certain tests that the court applies in its efforts to balance conflicting interests are gradually becoming clear. With its power to inquire into the legitimacy of union activities apparently circumscribed by the Norris-LaGuardia Act and the NLRA, the Supreme Court in the early 1940s adopted the position that unions were exempted from the antitrust statutes so long as they acted in their self-interest and did not combine with nonlabor groups (usually businesses) to obtain their objectives. Combination with nonlabor groups was to be the main exception to labor's general exemption from the antitrust statutes. The application of this test seemed clear enough in situations like a case in which a local of the International Brotherhood of Electrical Workers formed an alliance with an electrical contractors' association to preclude the purchase of equipment that was not made by members of the local, and the Supreme Court found an antitrust violation.[32] On the other hand, if the union had achieved the same result alone, rather than in combination with a business group, there would not have been an antitrust violation. Generally, almost any interaction between a union and an employer in normal collective bargaining will have an impact on the product market. Contractual provisions influencing wages, fringe benefits, and the efficiency of production will all influence a firm's marginal costs and hence its market price. Since the bargaining that results in these effects involves a union in "combination with nonlabor interest", this test did not provide the clearest guide to the range of union behavior that was exempted from antitrust regulation.

In 1965, the Supreme Court modified this test in the *Jewel Tea* decision.[33]

---

[32]*Allen-Bradley v. IBEW, Local 3,* 325 U.S. 797 (1945).

[33]*Local 189, Amalgamated Meatcutters v. Jewel Tea Company,* 381 U.S. 676 (1965).

This case grew out of a collective-bargaining proposal by the butchers' union in Chicago that no meat sales occur in grocery stores after 6:00 P.M., despite the fact that most of the stores in the multiemployer bargaining unit remained open until 9:00 P.M. The owners of the Jewel Tea stores were opposed to the proposal, but when the other stores in the bargaining unit agreed to accept the rule, Jewel Tea realized that if it held out for its position in collective bargaining after the other stores signed the labor agreement, it alone would face a strike by the union while its competitors were operating. Instead, Jewel Tea signed the new collective-bargaining agreement and then filed an antitrust action against the union.

There are two aspects of the case that are particularly interesting. First, the "combination with nonlabor interests" standard is not relevant. Instead, the case involves an attempt by the butchers' union to impose, unilaterally, a practice that would reduce competition. Second, the case illustrates how the treatment of unions under the antitrust statutes may affect strategic behavior in collective bargaining. In this instance, Jewel Tea gave ground in collective bargaining that they hoped to regain later through an antitrust action. Therefore, the stance taken by the courts toward the union's antitrust vulnerability inevitably will feed back into behavior at the collective-bargaining table.

Recognizing that the "combination with nonlabor interests" standard was not relevant to the case, the Supreme Court ruled that the key question was whether the union's hours restriction was "intimately related" to the issues of "wages, hours, and other terms and conditions of employment" that are protected by the National Labor Relations Act, and, hence, are exempt from antitrust action. Although the court found that in this instance the union's demand did meet the "intimately related" test and did not constitute a Sherman Act violation, it clearly indicated that under the new standard, a union could lose its antitrust exemption by pursuing actions that did not meet the test. In the future, the Supreme Court would evaluate alleged union violations of the Sherman Act by balancing the relative impact of a union practice on the product market against the interests of union members in the practice on a case-by-case basis. At the present time, however, the Supreme Court has not been very specific on the criteria that should be applied in establishing this balance.[34]

REVIEW QUESTIONS

1. Evaluate the advantages and disadvantages of removing the duty-to-bargain from the National Labor Relations Act. Would a duty-to-bargain obligation play a different role in the public sector? Explain.
2. "History here and abroad demonstrates the futility of trying to legislate good labor relations. There is much to be gained and little to be lost if we repeal all federal and state labor-relations statutes." Agree or disagree, and support your position.

---

[34]In many respects, this involves making the same judgments that are made under the NLRA in evaluating whether unions and employers have a duty to bargain over novel collective bargaining proposals.

3. As a member of a special commission, you are given authority to design a labor-relations statute to cover state and local employees in a state which has had only a public-sector strike prohibition in the past. You are instructed to develop a law that specifies the basic collective-bargaining rights that public employees are to have, prevents abuses of those rights, minimizes industrial strife, and is not too complex to administer well. What elements of labor-relations legislation governing the private sector (i.e., the NLRA) would you include in your bill? What elements would you exclude? Why?

4. Although labor-relations policy (law) might be expected to increase agreement concerning generally acceptable labor-management relations, this does not appear to be the case in the United States, where the volume of unfair labor-practice charges continues to increase substantially each year. What aspects of the policy do you feel contribute to this result?

SELECTED READINGS

Derek Bok, "Regulation of Campaign Tactics in Representation Elections Under the NLRA," *Harvard Law Review,* 78 (November 1964): 38–141.

Julius G. Getman, Stephen B. Goldberg, and Jeanne B. Herman, *Union Representation Elections: Law and Reality* (New York: Russell Sage Foundation, 1976).

William B. Gould, *A Primer on American Labor Law* (Cambridge, Mass.: The MIT Press, 1982).

Bernard D. Meltzer, "Labor Unions, Collective Bargaining, and the Antitrust Laws," *Journal of Law and Economics* 6 (October 1963): 152–223.

Harry H. Wellington, *Labor and the Law* (New Haven, Conn.: Yale University Press, 1968).

Chapter 14

COLLECTIVE BARGAINING: STRUCTURE AND TACTICS

Much of the early part of this book developed the economic analysis of labor markets. In the past two chapters we have reviewed the main features of labor unions and have noted how the development and form of unions were constrained by or related to market forces and the legal environment. We now move into the study of the behavior and tactics of unions in their efforts to advance the economic position of union members. Later, in Chapter 17, we shall examine their actual impact.

Unions have always had two general methods for achieving their objectives —*legislative enactment and collective bargaining*. While unions in the United States use both methods, they rely less on legislative enactment than unions in other western countries, and their use of the political process is more frequently to influence the general environment of collective bargaining and union power than to secure specific benefits. We first examine some of the politically attained methods through which unions pursue their objectives and then turn to the collective-bargaining process. The actual power that unions and management bring to the bargaining table is influenced by both the *structure* of bargaining and the specific bargaining *tactics* that each party can adopt. We begin the analysis, however, with a general discussion of market constraints faced by unions.

Market Constraints Facing Unions

The variety of membership interests that a union is called upon to represent require unions to play many roles in addition to negotiating wage rates for their members; hence, it is not surprising that there is no widespread agreement as to the specific objectives of unions. Nevertheless, it is generally agreed that in most cases unions value (1) the wage and fringe benefits they can achieve for their members[1] *and* (2) their members' employment levels. Therefore, the position and wage elasticity of the labor-demand curve are the fundamental market constraints that limit the ability of unions to accomplish their objectives.

Figure 14.1 shows two demand curves, D_e^0 and D_i^0, that intersect at an initial wage W_0 and employment level E_0. Suppose a union seeks to raise the wage rate of its members to W_1. To do so would require employment to fall to E_e^1 if the union faced the relatively elastic demand curve D_e^0, or to E_i^1 if it faced the relatively inelastic demand curve D_i^0. Other things equal, the more elastic the demand curve for labor, the greater the reduction in employment that will be associated with any given increase in wages.

Suppose now that the demand curve D_i^0 shifts out to D_i^1 while the negotiations are underway, due perhaps to growing demand for the final product. If the union succeeds in raising its members' wage to W_1, there will be no absolute decrease in employment in this case. Rather, the union will have only slowed the

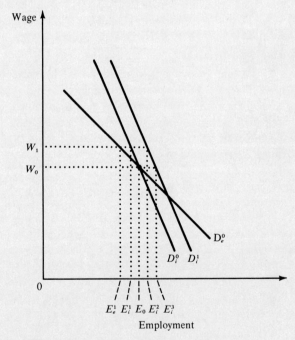

Figure 14.1   Effects of Demand Growth and Wage Elasticity of Demand on Market Constraint Faced by Unions

---

[1]As noted in Chapter 12, unions also negotiate important "workplace public goods", such as health, safety conditions, and limitations on managerial discretion. Since these firms often incur costs in providing these "nonmonetary" benefits, they can produce the same trade-off with employment as wages and fringe benefits.

growth rate of employment to E_i^2 instead of E_i^3. Generally, the more rapidly the labor demand curve is shifting out (in), the smaller (larger) will be the reduction *in employment* or the reduction *in the rate of growth of employment* that will be associated with any given increase in wages. Hence, the unions' ability to raise their members' wages will be strongest in rapidly growing industries with inelastic labor-demand curves. Conversely, unions will be weakest in industries in which the wage elasticity of demand is highly elastic and in which the demand curve for labor is shifting in.

Many actions that unions take are direct attempts to relax the market constraints that they face: either to increase the demand for union labor or to reduce the wage elasticity of demand for their members' services. The laws of derived demand discussed in Chapter 4 implied that four important determinants of the wage elasticities of demand were the price elasticity of demand for the final product, the ease of substituting other inputs for union members in the production process, the importance of labor compensation in total costs, and the responsiveness of the supply of other inputs to their prices. If price elasticities of demand for the final product are less elastic, if it is difficult to substitute other inputs for union labor, if labor costs constitute a small percent of total costs, or if the prices of other inputs rise considerably if the demand for the inputs increases, a more inelastic demand for union labor will result.

As noted in Chapter 4, the wage elasticity of demand for labor is more elastic in the long run than in the short run. In the short run, for example, there may be only limited foreign competition in a given output market. However, as American automobile manufacturers realized in the late 1970s and early 1980s, in the long run, foreign competition may increase, and the increased availability of foreign substitutes will raise the price elasticity of demand for domestic output. Likewise, production technologies may be fixed in the short run, while, in the long run, labor-saving technologies may be introduced. Finally, in the short run, the supplies of alternative inputs (for example, nonunion labor) may be fixed; in the longer run—due to immigration, or the training of other nonunion workers—supplies will tend to increase, providing more alternative inputs at lower cost to the employer. As a result, the market constraints unions face are more severe in the long run than in the short run; large wage gains won today may lead to substantial employment losses in the future. Such constraints often limit the economic gains that unions are able to win for their members.

Legislative Enactment: Altering the Demand for Union Labor

Attempts by unions to shift the demand curve for union labor to the right and to reduce the wage elasticity of demand have taken many forms. Many of these attempts have *not* occurred through the collective-bargaining process *per se*. Rather, they have occurred through union support of legislation that, at least indirectly, achieved union goals and through direct public-relations campaigns to increase the demand for products made by union members.

EXAMPLE 14.1

Legislative Enactment to Retain Union Jobs

Many of the factors influencing union jobs are not within the scope of normal bargaining structures or may involve factors that unions do not have the power to obtain through collective bargaining. In such situations, unions often turn to the legislative process to protect their interests. In addition to using legislation to shift the demand for union services to the right or to reduce the elasticity of demand for union labor, unions may also seek legislation that prevents the shift in demand for union services to the left.

For example, during the Congressional debate over proposed tax legislation in 1982, the Hotel Employees and Restaurant Employees International Union, which represents some 450,000 restaurant employees, lobbied extensively in the House of Representatives to block a provision passed in the Senate that would have eliminated half of the previous tax deduction for many business-related meals. By allowing only half of the price of such meals to be deducted from taxable income, the legislation effectively would have increased the price of the meals, led to a reduction in the number of meals consumed, and led to a reduction in the derived demand for the services of the members of the union. The union estimated that between 55,000 and 150,000 jobs held by union members would be lost if the legislation passed. Yet it was an issue that could not be addressed through the normal collective-bargaining process in the industry. Indeed, in this instance, the union of restaurant employees, restaurant owners (who would suffer a loss of business if the proposal was passed), and many business groups (who stood to lose a valuable tax deduction) were of one mind in opposing the proposed change.

SOURCE: Edward Cowan, "Meal Tax Bill Fought by Union," *New York Times*, July 27, 1982.

Policies to Shift the Product Demand Curve

Turning first to policies to *shift* out the demand curve for the final product, unions have lobbied for quotas or tariffs on foreign-produced goods that would limit the amount of these goods sold in the United States. Both the steel workers and the automobile workers sought such forms of protection during the late 1970s and early 1980s.

Other unions have opposed tax and deregulation policies that would reduce the demand for the services of their members (see Example 14.1). For example, with the deregulation of the airline industry in the United States in the late 1970s, competition between airlines increased substantially, stimulating mergers and other structural changes that threatened the employment of some union members in the industry. Rather than address the issues of job protection or compensation for displaced union members in collective-bargaining negotiations with individual airlines, the airline unions sought legislation requiring compensation for employees who lost their jobs as a result of economic adjustments in the industry. Officials in the industry argued that the cost of the proposal would retard the economic adjustments set off by deregulation.[2]

Union support of legislation is not the only way to shift product demand. Some unions have sought to directly influence people's tastes for the products they make. The International Ladies Garmet Workers' Union (ILGWU) continually seeks to encourage people to "Buy American," featuring the song "Look For the Union Label" in some of its television ads. Unions in the printing trades encourage people to buy stationery and other printing products that carry a union "bug"—a small printed emblem signifying that the printing work was done in a union printing shop.

Policies to Limit Substitution of Other Inputs

Unions have also sought, by means of legislation, to pursue strategies that either directly restrict the use of other inputs that are potential substitutes for union members or increase the costs of using such inputs. (See Example 14.2.) For example, as noted in Chapter 3, labor unions have been among the primary supporters of higher minimum wages.[3] While such support may be motivated by their concern for the welfare of low-wage workers, increases in the minimum wage *do* have the effect of increasing the relative costs to employers of low-skilled nonunion workers, thereby increasing the costs of the products they make and reducing employers' incentives to substitute (perhaps by moving their plants) nonunion workers for more skilled union workers.

Another example of a legislative strategy to discourage the substitution of cheaper inputs is union support for the Davis-Bacon Act. This act, a form of "prevailing wage" legislation, requires that wages paid to construction workers on projects that are federally financed, federally assisted through loans, or whose financing is insured by the federal government, be set at least equal to the prevailing wage in the area as determined by the Secretary of Labor. Since, typically, the prevailing wage has been set equal to the union wage scale, the net effect is to eliminate any cost advantage that nonunion construction workers

[2]Albert R. Karr, "Airlines, Unions Mount Lobbying Battle As Senate Nears Vote on Bill to Protect Jobs," *Wall Street Journal,* August 11, 1982, p. 42.

[3]For evidence that union support for minimum-wage legislation is often transformed into pro-minimum wage votes by members of Congress, *see* James Kau and Paul Rubin, "Voting on Minimum Wages: A Time-Series Analysis," *Journal of Political Economy* 86 (April 1978): 337–42; Jonathan Silberman and Garey Durden, "Determining Legislative Preferences on the Minimum Wage," *Journal of Political Economy* 84 (April 1976): 317–30; and James Cox and Ronald Oaxaca, "The Determinants of Minimum-Wage Levels and Coverage in State Minimum-Wage Laws" in *The Economics of Legal Minimum Wages* (Washington, D.C.: American Enterprise Institute for Public Policy, 1981).

EXAMPLE 14.2

Domestic Content Legislation

One approach to reducing the elasticity of demand for union services is to reduce the scope of substitution for union labor available to employers. In some instances, this is done by negotiating restrictive work practices in collective bargaining. In many instances, however, producers may seek to minimize costs by having some of the production done abroad at a lower labor cost. Some unions have sought a legislative defense against such practices in the form of *"domestic content" legislation* (that is, legislation requiring a certain proportion of products to be domestically produced).

Since 1890, for example, the Copyright Act has included a clause that books written in English by authors living in the United States must be printed in the United States or Canada in order to receive full copyright protection. This clause has been supported by unions in the printing trades to prevent the printing of such books abroad in countries with lower labor costs. In 1982, the U.S. Department of Labor estimated that in the absence of this provision, between 78,000 and 172,000 jobs in the printing trades would be lost to low-wage printing facilities in Asia.

Recently, the United Automobile Workers (UAW), historically a proponent of free international trade, has been concerned about the impact of foreign automobile production on the employment prospects for American autoworkers. A growing fraction of automobiles sold in the United States is produced in foreign countries and an increasing proportion of the components of automobiles sold by American manufacturers is made abroad. During 1982, the UAW supported legislative proposals to require both domestic and foreign automobile manufacturers with substantial sales in the United States to increase the share of their production in the United States. One proposal, for example, would have required firms with annual sales in the United States of 100,000 automobiles in 1986 to produce domestically or purchase auto components worth 10 percent of the value of sales. The "domestic-content" requirement would rise with the level of sales, reaching a maximum requirement of 90 percent of sales for producers with sales of 900,000 or more. If this proposal were to be enacted, what would you expect the impact to be on employment and auto sales in the United States?

SOURCES: "Copyright Act Rule Cleared by Congress," *AFL-CIO News,* July 10, 1982, p. 5. "Auto Jobs Bill Pushed in House," *AFL-CIO News,* September 25, 1982, p. 1.

might have, thereby discouraging the substitution of nonunion for union labor.[4]

---

[4]John Gould, *Davis-Bacon Act: The Economics of Prevailing Wage Laws* (Washington, D.C.: American Enterprise Institute, 1971) and Armand Thieblot, Jr., *The Davis-Bacon Act* (Philadelphia, Pa.: Industrial Research Unit, Wharton School, 1975) contain more complete descriptions of the act and its administration.

Since the Davis-Bacon Act was passed in 1931, almost 100 similar "prevailing wage" statutes have been passed in fields such as education, health, housing, and transportation—and 35 states have passed "little Davis-Bacon statutes" covering state construction projects.

A third example of how unions can use legislative means to influence the demand for union labor (by reducing substitution possibilities) is the union position on immigration policy. The AFL-CIO has been quite explicit, both historically and in recent years, about its concern that immigrants depress wages and provide competition for unionized American workers. Indeed, with respect to the problem of illegal immigration in the early 1980s, the AFL-CIO asserted that

> while the nation should continue its compassionate and humane immigration policy, it is apparent that large numbers of illegal immigrants are being exploited by employers, thus threatening hard-won wages and working conditions. U.S. immigration policy should foster reunification of families and provide haven for refugees from persecution, while taking a realistic view of the job opportunities and the needs of U.S. workers.[5]

It is not surprising then, that unions have historically supported legislation restricting immigration, especially during recessionary periods.[6]

Finally, there are several ways in which unions or employee associations can seek legislatively to restrict entry into an occupation. One way is to control the accreditation of outside institutions that provide training; the American Medical Association's accreditation of medical schools is an example of this. Another way to restrict the entry of potentially cheaper substitutes into an occupation is to lobby for state occupational licensing laws, which limit the practicing of a given occupation to only those who meet certain standards.[7] Finally, some cities— usually reacting to the political influence of unions—have adopted codes that require union labor to be used in any construction or building-repair projects within their jurisdictions.

The Structure of Collective Bargaining

Despite the importance of legislative influences on the environment in which unions operate, most union achievements are obtained through the process of *collective bargaining.* Indeed, unions often use collective-bargaining approaches to accomplish the very same goals of restricting the substitution of other inputs for union labor. Some unions, notably those in the airline, railroad, and printing

[5]*The AFL-CIO Platform Proposals: Presented to the Democratic and Republican National Conventions 1980* (Washington, D.C.: AFL-CIO, 1980), p. 14.

[6]F. Ray Marshall, Allan King, and Vernon Briggs, *Labor Economics: Wages, Employment, and Trade Unionism* 4th ed. (Homewood, Ill.: Richard D. Irwin, 1980), p. 196.

[7]*See,* for example, Alex Maurizi, "Occupational Licensing and the Public Interest," *Journal of Political Economy,* 82 (March/April 1974): 399–413.

industries, have sought and won guarantees of minimum crew sizes. (For example, at least three pilots are required to fly certain jet aircraft.) Such *staffing requirements* prevent employers from substituting capital for labor.[8] Other unions have won contract provisions that prohibit employers from *subcontracting* for some or all of the services they provide. For example, a union representing a company's janitorial employees may win a contract provision preventing the firm from hiring external firms to provide it with janitorial services. Such provisions may limit the substitution of nonunion for union workers. Craft unions, especially those in the building and printing trades, often negotiate specific contract provisions that restrict the functions that members of each individual craft can perform, thereby limiting the substitution of one type of union labor for another. Finally, craft unions also limit the substitution of unskilled union labor for skilled union labor by establishing rules about the maximum number of *apprentice* workers—workers who are learning the skilled trades—that can be employed relative to the experienced *journeymen* workers.

Collective bargaining consists of negotiations between representatives of labor and management over the terms and conditions of employment to which both parties will be bound for the duration of the labor agreement that normally results from such negotiations. This process drastically alters the determination of the employment relationship. Under the market mechanisms that we have examined earlier in the book, the employment relationship emerges from the interaction of many buyers (firms) and sellers (workers), or through the interaction of a single employer and many workers (monopsony).[9] Under collective bargaining, the employment relationship is established through the interaction of a single representative of employee interests (the union) and a single representative of employer interests—a market structure known as *bilateral monopoly*.[10] How are wages and employment determined under this market structure?

Consider the interests on each side of the bargaining table. We have seen in Chapter 3 that when there is only one employer or employer organization in a labor market, profit maximization will lead that employer to behave as a monopsonist, tending to reduce both the level of wages and the level of employment below their competitive levels. In Figure 14.2, employer profits will be maximized when the marginal labor cost equals the marginal revenue product of labor (given by the labor demand curve). Therefore, the employer will want a wage of W_m at which E_m workers will be hired. (These are lower than the competitive wage

---

[8]In cases in which these requirements call for the employment of workers whose functions are redundant—for example, fire stokers in diesel-operated railroad engines—*feather-bedding* is said to take place. For an economic analysis of this phenomenon, *see* Paul Weinstein, "The Featherbedding Problem," *American Economic Review* 54 (May 1964): 145–52.

[9]See discussion in Chapter 3.

[10]As will become apparent, there may be several employers or unions participating in negotiations. The key feature of bilateral monopoly is that each side adheres to a single set of bargaining demands.

(W_c) and employment (E_c) levels that would be determined by the intersection of the labor demand and labor supply schedules.) The union, which now monopolizes the sale of labor, will wish to use its power to raise wages above the

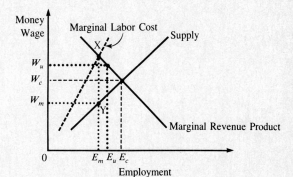

Figure 14.2 Bilateral Monopoly

competitive level, say to W_u. This would result in employment of E_u, which is also less than the competitive employment level. Higher wages would imply a greater employment loss than the union is willing to accept.[11]

Neither labor nor management will want more than W_u, and neither party will want less than W_m. Therefore, W_u and W_m denote the upper and lower limits of a *contract zone,* or range in which the final collective-bargaining agreement must lie.[12] Where, exactly, will the final solution lie? Unfortunately, the analysis of bilateral monopoly cannot tell us. Instead, it describes how the respective interests of labor and management determine the location of the contract zone. Where the final settlement ends up depends on the bargaining power and negotiating skills of *each* side. That is, the interests of *both* parties must be considered in determining the final outcome of bargaining. Some theoretical analyses using diverse assumptions that do not always correspond well to the realities of collective bargaining conclude that labor and management will "split the difference" and end up in the middle of the contract zone,[13] but the limited empirical evidence on this question reaches a different conclusion. (See Example 14.3.)

---

[11]As discussed in Chapter 12, union objectives are difficult to formulate as precisely as those of employers because unions must adopt political methods of accommodating the often diverse goals of their individual members. Nevertheless, the final result will reflect the wage-employment trade-off that the union is willing to make.

[12]The range may in fact be narrower, since a union is unlikely to insist on W_u if it will bankrupt an employer, and an employer is unlikely to insist on W_m if a union is willing to strike indefinitely rather than accept that wage. These issues are explored in Chapter 15.

[13]Frederick Zeuthen, *Probléms of Monopoly and Economic Warfare,* Reprints of Economic Classics Series (Fairfield, N.J.: Augustus M. Kelley, 1968); John Nash, "The Bargaining Problem," *Econometrica* 18 (April 1950): 155–62.

EXAMPLE 14.3

Do Labor and Management Split the Difference?

Where do negotiators end up in the contract zone? Does one party or the other tend to "dominate" in collective bargaining, or do the parties simply "split the difference" and settle halfway between their respective preferred positions? It is very difficult to obtain the data needed to answer these interesting questions, but two studies have made a start.

Each study compared data on the initial wage demands of labor and management in collective bargaining with the final wage increases agreed to. One study examined data from negotiations with the Tennessee Valley Authority (TVA), while the other used data from negotiations in the public sector involving unions of teachers, police, and firefighters. In each case, unions made larger concessions during negotiations than did management. In the TVA negotiations, unions demanded wage increases averaging 11 percent, employers offered increases averaging 3 percent, and the final settlements averaged 6 percent. The comparable figures for the public-sector negotiations were 23 percent, 8 percent, and 12 percent. Taken at face value, the data seem to suggest that collective-bargaining settlements tend to be closer to the employer's end of the contract zone.

Unfortunately, it is not clear that these data can be extrapolated "at face value" to collective-bargaining negotiations generally. In contrast to negotiations in the private sector, strikes were illegal in both the TVA and public-sector samples used in the studies. Unions may have bluffed—demanded more than their preferred amount—more than management in an effort to compensate for their reduced power.

SOURCES: Roger Bowlby and William Shriver, "Bluffing and the 'Split the Difference' Theory of Wage Bargaining," *Industrial and Labor Relations Review* 31 (January 1978): 161–71; Daniel S. Hamermesh, "Who 'Wins' in Wage Bargaining?" *Industrial and Labor Relations Review* 26 (July 1973): 1146–49.

Where the parties to bargaining end up in the contract zone depends on bargaining power, but a precise operational definition of this concept has proved elusive over the years. Bargaining power reflects the ability of either party to secure a labor agreement on one's own terms. One party's inducement to agree with another's proposal in negotiations depends on the cost of disagreeing with the proposal relative to the costs of agreeing with it.[14] The larger the costs of disagreeing relative to the costs of agreeing, the more likely one party is to accept the other's proposal. These costs are influenced to a significant degree by the structure and tactics of collective bargaining. In the private sector, these costs are influenced to a large extent by the factors governing the elasticity of the derived demand for labor, which has an important influence on the ability to strike (in

---

[14]This is the approach developed in Neil W. Chamberlain and James W. Kuhn, *Collective Bargaining,* 2d ed. (New York: McGraw-Hill, 1965): 162–90.

the case of unions) or to take a strike (in the case of employers). In the public sector, these considerations apply to a certain extent (since there have been many work stoppages despite the general illegality of the strike), but factors affecting the political influence of labor relative to management also have an important bearing on bargaining power. These factors are discussed below.

Bargaining Structure in the Private Sector

Bargaining structure refers to the scope of worker and employer interaction in an issue of labor relations. In any given industry, however, the bargaining structure consists of a spectrum of units defined by an often complicated set of economic, legal, and social relationships. Most bargaining structures have at their base *informal work groups*—groupings of the rank and file defined by technology and the organization of production—whose aspirations help to define a union's goals and the acceptability of a collective-bargaining agreement. An *election unit* (a group of jobs whose incumbents are eligible to vote in a union-representation election) typically consists of several informal work groups, and its scope is formally determined or endorsed by the National Labor Relations Board (NLRB) as part of the process of running a union-representation election. The unit for which collective-bargaining negotiations actually take place is called the *negotiation unit,* and, in many instances, this will be larger than the election unit, owing to industrywide or multiplant agreements. In some instances, emulation or pattern-following may result in a *unit of direct impact* that exceeds the scope of the negotiating unit.[15] We discuss the election and negotiation units below.

Election unit. When a union petitions the NLRB for a representation election, the National Labor Relations Act (NLRA) requires the Board to conduct the election in "a unit appropriate for such purposes"—the election district. Often the district is jointly agreed to by the union and the employer involved, but when there is disagreement between them, the NLRB has the authority to determine a group of jobs that constitute an appropriate unit. Individuals employed in those jobs are entitled to vote in the representation election. In requiring the NLRB to choose *an* appropriate unit, the law recognizes that there may be several potentially appropriate units (for example, an occupational group within a plant, an entire plant, a group of plants within a company, an entire company). The board may therefore face considerable choice in its unit determination activities.

These determinations can have a significant influence on the ultimate power relationships in the industry for several reasons. First, the scope of the unit may determine whether or not an election is held (since unions must show evidence of support from at least 30 percent of the employees in the unit before an election can occur), and if it is, whether the union wins the representation election. The scope of the unit can therefore determine whether employment conditions in an industry will be subject to collective bargaining. When there is a disagreement

---

[15]These distinctions were suggested in Arnold R. Weber, "Stability and Change in the Structure of Collective Bargaining," in Lloyd Ulman, ed., *Challenges to Collective Bargaining* (Englewood Cliffs, N.J.: Prentice-Hall, Inc., 1967).

between an employer and a union over the scope of an election unit, the employer typically argues for a larger unit, since unions tend to have more difficulty winning elections in relatively large units, where there is likely to be more diversity of skills, interests, and objectives among employees.

Second, when more than one union is campaigning for representation rights, the unit that the NLRB determines to be appropriate for the purposes of the election may influence *which* union wins the election. A craft union that specializes in representing workers performing a particular occupation will find it easier to win an election if the unit is confined to the set of jobs in that occupation than if the unit is plantwide or companywide.

Third, the scope of the unit can also influence the effectiveness of a union's representation if it wins. We noted in Chapter 12 that the task of running a union organization effectively is enhanced if the preferences of the membership are relatively homogenous. Larger units often include employees with rather diverse skills, interests, and objectives—raising the possibility that the union will encounter conflicts of interest among its members and internal opposition to its efforts to negotiate and administer a collective-bargaining agreement that is viewed as fair by a majority of the membership. Smaller, more homogenous units are likely to increase the effectiveness of union representation and to accord individual members a greater opportunity to have their views on union policy heard.

Finally, to the extent that the election unit becomes the negotiating unit, the scope of the election unit will also influence the cost of labor relations to the employer. From the perspective of an employer, fragmented bargaining structures in which employees are distributed among many small bargaining units and often represented by different unions raise the costs of negotiating and administering labor agreements. More time goes into multiple negotiations, there are more opportunities for negotiations to break down and a strike to occur, and there is often the possibility that a strike in any one bargaining unit will influence operations in other units. Fragmented bargaining units represented by different unions also increase the likelihood of jurisdictional disputes between different unions over the right to represent employees performing new work or whose status may otherwise be uncertain. Employers must balance these considerations against the threat of a much larger work stoppage when bargaining is conducted in broader units.

For all of these reasons, the determination of an appropriate election unit can be a matter of substantial importance in labor relations. Yet the language of the NLRA provides the NLRB with little guidance concerning the criteria or standards for such determinations. Section 9(b) simply states that ". . . the unit appropriate for the purposes of collective bargaining shall be the employer unit, craft unit, plant unit, or subdivision thereof. . . ."[16] Over the years the NLRB has

---

[16]The NLRA also does not permit the Board to include plant guards in a unit with other employees, forbids the inclusion of professional and nonprofessional employees in a single unit "unless a majority of the professional employees vote for inclusion", and permits craft employees to establish a separate unit even if they were at one time included in a broader unit (for example, in an election establishing representation rights for an industrial union).

articulated a standard of *community of interest,* in which proposed units would be evaluated according to the extent to which they included workers sharing common interests and excluded groups of workers whose interests would be in conflict. But what determines the community of interest? The NLRB considers factors that include the similarity of work performed, similarity of compensation and working conditions, skill-levels, geographic proximity, integration of production processes, common supervision or labor-relations policy, history of collective bargaining, desires of employees, and extent of union organization. But the variety of factors considered—as well as the fact that when considered separately they may not all give consistent guidance on the appropriate unit size—highlights the lack of precision in the determination of election units.

As we noted above, negotiating units are often larger in scope than the election unit. Nevertheless, the NLRB's policies in determining election units have undoubtedly contributed to the fact that collective bargaining in the United States is generally decentralized, with over 200,000 labor agreements in force in the private and public sectors combined. When the interests of labor and management concerning unit size conflicted during the early years of the NLRA, the Board tended to give more weight to the preferences of unions for relatively small units in order to encourage the formation of unions and the spread of collective bargaining. In the Taft-Hartley Act amendments to the NLRA, Congress prohibited the NLRB from using the extent of employee support for unions as the sole criterion for determining an election unit. Subsequently, the Board (supported by the federal appeals courts) has held that extent of organization is nevertheless one of the factors that may be considered in determining which employees are eligible to vote in a representation election. After leaning toward the establishment of multiplant election units during the 1950s, the NLRB has increasingly permitted single-plant election units, even when the "plant" may be one of several stores operated with a common personnel policy by a single company in a single metropolitan area. In some cases a group of employees within a store may be found to be an appropriate election unit.

Negotiation unit. The outcome of collective bargaining can depend importantly on the structure of negotiating units—the size and scope of the units that conduct collective bargaining. The sheer number of agreements, noted above, is suggestive of the decentralization of the collective-bargaining structure in the United States. This decentralization is one of the more distinctive differences between the industrial relations system in the United States and in Europe, where collective bargaining is more frequently conducted at the industry, regional, and even national level. (See Example 14.4.) This difference, in part, reflects the public policy toward election units discussed in the previous section. Because so many election units are proposed and accepted at the plant and company level, collective bargaining tends to occur much closer to the workplace in the United States than in many European countries. For different reasons, negotiations also tend to occur at the plant or company level in Japan (see Example 14.5). However, a more complete analysis of collective bargaining in the United States requires that we look beyond the election unit to the forces that influence the size and power of negotiating units.

EXAMPLE 14.4

Centralized Collective-Bargaining Structures in Europe

European negotiating units are typically much broader than those in the United States, and, as a result, collective bargaining is more centralized. In most countries, collective bargaining occurs at the industry or regional level, and in some Scandanavian countries, bargaining normally occurs between the labor *federation* (that is, the equivalent of the AFL-CIO in the United States) and a management federation at the national level—with one agreement determining the employment conditions for all workers who belong to unions that are members of the federation. Centralized collective-bargaining agreements change the character of labor agreements and labor relations in interesting ways.

First, as a general proposition, the scope of labor agreements resulting from relatively centralized collective-bargaining negotiations tends to be more limited than the scope of most agreements negotiated in the United States. The basic reason for this is that it is very difficult for the language of a single collective-bargaining agreement to cope effectively with the wide variety of labor-relations problems faced by the many plants or industries covered by the agreement. On issues pertaining to work rules and safety, for example, a single contractual rule is unlikely to address the underlying heterogeneity of circumstances adequately. As a result, negotiators tend to restrict their attention to issues, such as wages and hours of work, that have a common meaning and method of application across companies. As a result, many topics that are of considerable concern to workers, but which vary in nature across firms, are not addressed by the official labor agreements.

Second, although this need not be the outcome of a central collective-bargaining structure, collective bargaining in Europe tends to produce contractual wage rates that are set sufficiently low to keep the least efficient firms covered by an agreement in business. (Historically, American unions have been willing to let a few firms that are unable to meet their wage standards go out of business.) One result of this is a phenomenon known as *wage drift*—the tendency of the actual earnings received by workers to increase at a more rapid rate than the contractual wage rates established in the collective-bargaining agreement. As a result, in many European countries, contractual wage rates are often not a reliable indicator of the true path of wage costs. Drift appears to result, in part, from decisions by employers in high-productivity firms to pay higher wages than the labor agreement requires in order to attract or retain a high quality work force. (With decentralized collective bargaining, as in the United States, the wage provisions of labor agreements are more likely to reflect the economic circumstances of individual companies.) Since drift commonly increases when the demand for labor is high and decreases in recessions, it appears to be a mechanism through which wages are brought into equilibrium irrespective of the contractual provisions of labor agreements.

The relationship between the wage provided for in a collective-bargaining agreement and the wage actually paid in Europe contrasts sharply with the situation in the United States where, under the National Labor Relations Act, unionized employers cannot unilaterally raise wages without first bargaining with the union. In some cases in the United States, unions that have been concerned with the internal political difficulties raised by altering traditional relative-wage relationships between different groups of members have refused to permit employers to voluntarily grant wage increases to selected groups of workers in order to increase the supply of workers with relatively scarce skills.

Third, workers tend to develop alternative institutional mechanisms to seek representation for issues that are not addressed by the labor agreements produced by centralized negotiating units. In the United Kingdom, for example, a second and decidedly unofficial tier of bargaining has developed at the plant level. Shop stewards frequently bargain with British plant management over issues (such as the pace of work, safety, and work assignments) that either are not addressed or are not addressed adequately in the official agreements (usually negotiated at the industry or regional level). Pressure at the second tier of bargaining can also be a source of wage drift. In Sweden, a country generally known for its record of labor peace, there was an outbreak of "wildcat" (unofficial) strikes in the late 1960s protesting the modest wage settlements resulting from centralized collective bargaining and demanding independent bargaining rights. More importantly, over the past twenty-five years, unions representing white-collar and professional employees have broken away from the main federation and formed separate federations that represent their interests more effectively.

SOURCES: Everett M. Kassalow, *Trade Unions and Industrial Relations: An International Comparison* (New York: Random House, 1969); T.L. Johnston, *Collective Bargaining in Sweden* (London: George Allen & Unwin, 1962).

With such a large number of separate collective-bargaining situations, one might wonder about the source of the monopoly power that is sometimes attributed to unions. In fact, union membership is not distributed evenly. Almost half of all unionized employees in the private sector work under the relatively small number of agreements (approximately 1550) that cover at least 1,000 workers and are henceforth referred to as major agreements. Moreover, the content of these major collective-bargaining agreements in the United States are determined in a wide array of bargaining structures. (Table 14.1) Thirty percent of the major contracts are determined in *single plant* negotiations between an employer or plant manager and a union at the plant level; another 30 percent are established through *multiplant* negotiations with an employer that will affect

Table 14.1. Structure of Major Bargaining Units, by Industry, 1980[a] (percent distribution)

	All Agreements		Single Employer			Multi Employer
	Number	Percent[b]	Total	Single Plant	Multiplant	
All Industries	1,550	100%	60%	30%	30%	40%
Manufacturing	750	100	86	53	33	14
Food	79	100	63	37	27	37
Apparel	31	100	19	6	13	81
Chemicals	36	100	100	89	11	—
Primary metals	88	100	99	55	44	1
Machinery	81	100	98	68	30	2
Electrical machinery	83	100	97	66	31	3
Transportation equipment	112	100	96	40	56	4
Nonmanufacturing	800	100	35	8	27	65
Communications	80	100	100	5	95	—
Construction	327	100	1	c	1	99
Hotels and restaurants	31	100	10	3	6	90
Retail trade	123	100	53	11	41	47
Services	66	100	29	14	15	71
Utilities	81	100	96	26	70	4

[a]Labor Agreements covering 1,000 workers or more, January 1, 1980.
[b]Columns may not add to 100 percent because of rounding error.
[c]Less than 0.5%.

SOURCE: U.S. Bureau of Labor Statistics, *Characteristics of Major Collective Bargaining Agreements, January 1, 1980,* Bulletin 2095 (Washington, D.C.: U.S. Government Printing Office, May 1981), p. 19.

several plants of the same company; and some are conducted at the company level and will affect all of the operations. (The tens of thousands of agreements covering less than a thousand workers are largely the outcome of negotiations at the plant or company level.) The most prevalent bargaining structure among the "major" units, however, is *multiemployer* bargaining, in which a group of employers negotiate jointly with a union or group of unions to reach an agreement that will cover all workers in an industry. Over 40 percent of major collective-bargaining agreements (Table 14.1), covering about half of the workers included in major contracts (and about a quarter of all union workers in the private sector), are negotiated in the context of multiemployer bargaining structures.

In order to evaluate alternative bargaining structures, it is useful to analyze the factors that tend to determine structure. In fact, bargaining structures tend to be affected by a complex of legal determinations (discussed in the previous section), market forces, technological factors, representational factors, and even the nature of bargaining issues.[17] Of particular importance in collective bargaining is the fact that different bargaining structures imply different degrees of bargaining power. For this reason, changes in bargaining structures are among the most bitterly contested issues in labor relations.

---

[17]These factors are discussed extensively in Weber, "Stability and Change in the Structure of Collective Bargaining."

EXAMPLE 14.5

Bargaining Structure and Labor Relations in Japan

On the surface, the structure of collective bargaining in Japan bears some resemblance to bargaining in the United States. The degree of unionization is about the same—around 22 percent of the labor force in the early 1980s—and bargaining is highly decentralized. Over 90 percent of the unions and union members in Japan are organized on an enterprise (company or plant) basis; bargaining on a craft or industrial basis is unusual.

Two factors appear to account for the enterprise-based bargaining structure. First, production support organizations, which were formed in each enterprise during World War II, served as a preliminary union structure and evolved into unions following the war. Second, an enterprise-based bargaining structure was consistent with a distinctive feature of Japanese personnel practice in larger companies—lifetime employment commitments. Contrary to practice in the United States and other Western countries, it is not unusual for Japanese workers at all occupational levels to spend their entire work life in a single company. The company effectively assumes much of the risk of employment uncertainty in exchange for which the worker may be more committed to the goals of the organization. One consequence of this personnel system is that layoffs and quits are much lower in Japanese companies than in most Western companies; another is that there is much less mobility during the course of the average worker's work life. In forming unions, then, workers have been most concerned with negotiations that affect their company or plant, which is their effective labor market under this unusual personnel system. Indeed, there is a general resistance on the part of both employers and employees to the intervention of central or industrial unions whose members are not all part of a particular enterprise, and like the AFL-CIO in the United States, Japanese labor federations are not directly involved in collective bargaining.

All employees in an enterprise, irrespective of skill or occupational position, are members of the enterprise union. It is unusual to find, as one does in the United States and Europe, several unions in a company representing workers with different skills. In fact, the enterprise unions in Japan have worked to eliminate many of the distinctions between manual and nonmanual workers in terms of wages and social status, and have institutionalized seniority-based wage systems.

One apparent advantage of the enterprise-based bargaining structure is that Japanese unions are apparently better able to address issues relating to the operation of the enterprise and technical innovation than are their American and European counterparts. On the other hand, wages and other working conditions are less likely to be consistent throughout an industry or the economy. We have seen how the operation of a competitive labor market will tend to equalize the wages paid across firms and industries for a given skill, and how many unions in the United States and Europe form their bargaining objectives on the basis of what similar workers are paid in other industries. In Japan, however, bargaining objectives are formed on the basis of enterprise-specific criteria, such as ability to pay. As a result, there can be considerable dispersion *across* enterprises in the wage paid for a given skill (although the Japanese labor federations are trying to stimulate some coordination of wage demands within a given industry).

One other feature of the enterprise-basis of unionization is that unions generally lack the power to mount a large-scale offense or defense against employers at the industrial or national level. This is illustrated by the unusual nature of strike activity in Japan. Most contracts expire annually, and each spring a "Shunto" or spring wage campaign is organized by the federations. A target for wage demands is set and a timetable of warning strikes by different unions is scheduled to occur from mid-April to mid-May. Each union performs for about a day on schedule. Rather than being used as a weapon to counteract a bargaining deadlock, strikes in Japan therefore tend to be used to signal or symbolize the seriousness of the unions in their bargaining demands. In the end, however, the actual wage agreements are determined by each enterprise, so that the exercise does not necessarily succeed in coordinating conditions between enterprises.

SOURCES: Japan Institute of Labor, *Labor Unions and Labor-Management Relations* (Tokyo: Japan Institute of Labor, 1979); Tadashi Mitsufuji and Kiyohiko Hagisawa, "Recent Trends in Collective Bargaining in Japan," *International Labour Review* 105 (1972): 135–53; Koji Taira, *Economic Development and the Labor Market in Japan* (New York: Columbia University Press, 1970).

In order to analyze what lies behind the preferences for different bargaining structures by unions and employers, one must appreciate the main economic considerations underlying bargaining power. For management in the private sector, the main consideration is to reduce the risk of losing business to competitors, both in the short run (during a strike) and in the long run (because other firms have lower labor costs). Therefore, in the short run, an employer's bargaining power (that is, the ability to take a strike) depends on the extent to which consumers are able to shift to substitute products or services. In the long run, when an employer must live with the consequences of a settlement, bargaining power will depend on the ease with which nonunion competitors can enter the market and offer consumers lower-price substitutes.

The objectives of a union are more complex, as discussed in Chapter 12, but most unions seek to raise the wage of their members, to take the wage "out of competition" (that is, reduce the wage dispersion between employers for a given skill of worker, in order to minimize competition between employers on the basis of labor costs), and to prevent a substantial reduction in the employment of union members. As discussed earlier, these objectives are most easily arranged when the demand for labor is relatively inelastic; that is, when it is relatively difficult to find technical substitutes in production for the skills of the union members, when substitutes exist but their supply can be increased only at increased cost, when labor is a relatively small proportion of total cost (in most situations), and when there are relatively few substitutes for the products that union members help to produce. (Note that reducing product-demand elasticity is desired by *both* unions and management.) In any particular set of negotiations, a union's bargaining power will also be influenced by its ability to finance a strike.

Multiemployer bargaining. Many employers must choose between bargaining alone or joining a multiemployer bargaining association—a group of employers in the same industry who join together for the purpose of negotiating with a union or group of unions that represent employees in each company. On the one hand, negotiations between a single employer and one or more unions provide a company with considerable flexibility in devising a bargaining strategy best suited to its particular needs, rather than the average needs of a group of employers. On the other hand, many employers recognize that in industries in which competition in the product market is strong, a labor agreement establishing common labor costs insures them against some of the risks of competition.[18] In addition, the weakest management position may be to bargain as a single firm, since the best substitute for one company's product is the same product produced by another firm.

In the event of a bargaining impasse and strike, a firm bargaining alone would lose its market share to its competitors. At the same time, however, the union could be in a relatively strong position—for even if the struck firm lost a share of the market to its competitors, total employment in the industry would not necessarily fall by much. (Jobs would open up at the plants of competitors, but to obtain them those union members on strike might have to move and/or be willing to accept jobs with less seniority.) Moreover, by striking only one firm, the union would be able to finance a longer strike, since only a fraction of the total membership would qualify for strike benefits. When employers in a competitive product market have been organized by a single union, they are thus susceptible to *whipsaw* tactics, in which the union strikes or threatens to strike one employer (usually the weakest) and then extends the (relatively generous) agreement reached with that employer to others in the same industry. It is the threat of whipsaw tactics that provides a particularly strong incentive to employers in competitive product markets to form multiemployer bargaining structures.

Indeed, it is interesting to note from Table 14.1 that it is precisely in the most competitive industries that multiemployer bargaining occurs most frequently. Multiemployer bargaining structures are not characteristic of industries where individual firms have substantial market power—for example, the oligopolistic

---

[18]For a discussion of this point, *see* Wallace E. Hendricks and Lawrence M. Kahn, "The Demand for Labor Market Structure: An Economic Approach," 1984, forthcoming in the *Journal of Labor Economics.*

market structures in durable goods manufacturing. They are most prevalent in nonmanufacturing industries characterized by substantial competition between small to medium size firms in local or regional product markets (for example, construction, hotels and restaurants, supermarket chains, etc.).

The advantage of a multiemployer bargaining structure comes from reducing the potential for consumer substitution. Employers can offer a united front and at the same time be assured that the ultimate agreement will impose the same labor costs on all participants in the negotiations. Multiemployer negotiating units also permit both employers and unions to take advantage of economies of scale in negotiating labor agreements. Where there are many relatively small firms in an industry, a multiemployer negotiating unit also permits more expert representation in negotiations. In addition, if a strike occurs, it involves a much larger proportion of union membership, so that the financial resources of the union are depleted more rapidly and the union is unlikely to sustain as long a strike as if only one employer were struck.

One might think that by increasing the bargaining power of employers, multiemployer bargaining structures would reduce the size of settlements as compared to what would be agreed upon under a single-plant bargaining structure. This is not necessarily the case, however, because reducing the elasticity of product demand is also favorable to workers, who can now attain wage increases with less loss of employment. (Remember that while total employment in an industry may change little if one plant is struck, job *locations* may change, so that the members of any one bargaining unit may be unwilling to demand too much.)

Put differently, if the union negotiated with a single firm, it would be equivalent to a labor-market monopolist negotiating with a product-market competitor, and the expectation might be that the ultimate wage would be higher than under competition. The formation of a multiemployer bargaining association effectively supplants this labor-market structure with bilateral monopoly, where, as we have seen, the ultimate outcome depends on the relative bargaining skills of labor and management. A multiemployer bargaining association may use its additional market power to resist the union's bargaining demands or it may accept the demands and try to pass the costs along to consumers.[19] As a result, *a priori* we cannot predict what the effect of having this bargaining structure on contract outcomes will be. The empirical evidence, however, indicates that after controlling for the characteristics of industries and workers, wages tend to be *higher* under multiemployer bargaining units in local product markets that in single employer units.[20]

---

[19]Recall that the analysis in Chapter 3 shows that in most situations it is not possible to pass the entire increase in costs (here a result of a wage increase rather than the imposition of a payroll tax) on to consumers.

[20]Hendricks and Kahn, "The Demand for Labor Market Structure"; Wallace Hendricks, "Labor Market Structure and Union Wage Levels," *Economic Inquiry* 13 (September 1975): 401–16; and Peter Feuille, Wallace E. Hendricks, and Lawrence M. Kahn, "Wage and Nonwage Outcomes in Collective Bargaining: Determinants and Tradeoffs," *Journal of Labor Research* 2 (Spring 1981): 39–53.

In so-called "casual" labor markets, a worker typically works for more than one employer in the course of a year (for example, construction, longshoring, maritime, music). In these industries both unions and management typically prefer a multiemployer bargaining unit. The assignment and payment of workers is then regulated through a "hiring hall" into which employers indicate their employment needs on a given day and the union assigns the requisite number and skill of workers.

Recent econometric analyses of the determinants of bargaining structures in the United States and in the United Kingdom confirm the importance of the degree of competition in the product market in determining the structure of negotiating units.[21] Although restricted to the manufacturing sector (thereby excluding many of the industries which are shown in Table 14.1 to be characterized by multiemployer bargaining), these studies also find that multiemployer bargaining units are more likely in industries with a relatively large number of firms and relatively small plant size, and in industries in which labor constitutes a large percentage of total costs. All of these features describe markets in which wage increases would lead to significant competitive pressures for a company bargaining alone. The tendency toward multiemployer bargaining is reduced to the extent that there are different unions at different companies in the industry.[22]

Multiemployer labor agreements infrequently extend beyond local or regional product markets. Among industries in which employers compete in much broader product markets, industrywide agreements are found only in the basic steel, bituminous coal, and trucking industries. An important reason for this is that multiemployer bargaining structures are inherently unstable. The stability of national, industrywide, bargaining associations of several employers is threatened by the greater potential for the emergence of nonunion firms and by the same general factors that were seen in Chapter 12 to threaten the stability of union organizations. As the number of members of an employer's association grows, the heterogeneity of the membership generally increases, and it may become more difficult to formulate a bargaining position that is agreeable to all of the members of the association. In some instances, one or more members of an employer bargaining-association may not be affected by an issue that most companies in the association are willing to take a strike over. In a nationwide steel strike in 1959, brought about by employers' efforts to revise work rules in the industry, the Kaiser Steel Company, is a relatively new company that did not have the work-rule problems that troubled the other steel companies, pulled out of the joint negotiations and settled two months before the other companies reached agreement with the union.

---

[21]*See* Wallace E. Hendricks and Lawrence M. Kahn, "The Determinants of Bargaining Structure in U.S. Manufacturing Industries," *Industrial and Labor Relations Review* 35 (January 1982): 181–95; D.R. Deaton and P.B. Beaumont, "The Determinants of Bargaining Structure: Some Large Scale Survey Evidence for Britain," *British Journal of Industrial Relations* 18 (July 1980): 101–16.

[22]*See* Thomas A. Kochan and Richard N. Block, "An Inter-industry Analysis of Bargaining Outcomes: Preliminary Evidence from Two-Digit Industries," *Quarterly Journal of Economics* 91 (August 1977): 431–52; Wallace E. Hendricks, "Labor Market Structure and Union Wage Levels."

Generally, when there are wide variations in internal efficiency among members of the employer bargaining-association, each member company may have a different "acceptable concession" that it is willing to make. The more efficient firms may be willing to make relatively large concessions (which they are better able to absorb) than less efficient firms in order to avoid the costs of a strike. In seasonal industries, such as construction, some contractors may be anxious to settle in periods of relatively high demand in order to avoid losses during the limited production season that would exceed the additional labor costs incurred from an early settlement. Not all members may be willing to hold out for the same period of time in support of their bargaining position. If they are unable to persuade other members of a multiemployer bargaining association to conclude an agreement, they may bolt the association, leading to a weakening or breakdown of the association and possible restoration of whipsaw tactics by unions.

National industrywide agreements can raise serious problems for unions as well. It is usually more difficult for unions to maintain organization over all firms in a national market. The security of both the employer and union sides of a national, industrywide agreement is threatened by the emergence of new, nonunion firms paying lower wages and charging lower benefits.[23] Import competition is one such challenge, but challenges to market share from domestic firms are possible as well. One of the most interesting illustrations of the possibilities and perils of a multiemployer bargaining association is provided by the development over a period of years of a national collective-bargaining agreement in the over-the-road trucking industry (see Example 14.6).

Single-employer bargaining. In oligopolistic product markets in which most production is done by a few large companies (for example, the automobile, rubber, and meatpacking industries), single employer (companywide) bargaining predominates. Bargaining typically occurs between the union and a "target" company selected for each bargaining round. Until the late 1970s, the terms established at the target company became the "pattern" and were typically extended to other companies in the same industry. If a strike occurs, only a fraction of the union's membership (those employed at the target company) will draw strike benefits, and the union's financial resources will therefore support a longer strike than if the union faced a multiemployer bargaining unit. At the same time, the target company may be in a relatively vulnerable position. The target company's ability to take a long strike is normally undermined by the continued production and sale by unstruck competitors. By taking a strike the firm risks a permanent loss of market share, since whatever terms are agreed to at the first company will simply be extended to the others in the industry.

---

[23]One empirical study of union wages concludes that in national product markets, union bargaining power (as indicated by the union wage level) is higher when the market is organized into company-level bargaining units than when it is organized into industrywide units. *See* Hendricks, "Labor Market Structure and Union Wage Levels." That is, the value of multiemployer bargaining units to unions appears to be greater in *local* product markets than in *national* product markets.

EXAMPLE 14.6

Multiemployer Collective Bargaining in the Trucking Industry

The trucking industry is a complicated array of local, regional, and national markets served by thousands of employers. Over the years the International Brotherhood of Teamsters, largely under the leadership of James Hoffa, developed a network of multiemployer bargaining arrangements in the various markets. By 1964, Hoffa succeeded in establishing a single, nationwide Master Freight Agreement covering all over-the-road truckers (those not operating solely in a local market) by combining the various regional employers' associations into a national association for the purposes of collective bargaining. The national agreement offered advantages to the union in terms of establishing uniform wages and working conditions on a nationwide basis, but there was considerable diversity among the hundreds of trucking firms that authorized Trucking Management Inc. (TMI) to bargain with the Teamsters on their behalf. In particular, the national trucking companies were typically in a stronger financial position than most of the smaller regional companies.

The Teamsters knew how to exploit such diversity in the multiemployer association to their advantage. During a strike that arose during the 1976 negotiations, for example, the union permitted employers who were willing to temporarily accept the union's last offer to operate during the strike with the understanding that when a new agreement was reached, the companies would only be subject to the terms of that agreement. This seemed like an attractive offer to financially pressed trucking companies. They could earn some money immediately and ultimately would suffer no competitive disadvantage, because they would be subject to the same terms and conditions of employment as their competitors. As fewer and fewer employers arrived at the bargaining table each day, the position of the employers became increasingly weak, and a settlement was rapidly reached. This was only the beginning of the troubles facing the multiemployer unit, however.

Although the structure of the trucking industry is essentially competitive, it had been subject to considerable regulation by the Interstate Commerce Commission (ICC) since 1935. The ICC effectively reduced price competition (by fixing freight rates), limited entry into the industry, and issued regulations that established excess capacity in the industry. By the late 1970s, however, there was increasing recognition that the regulation of industries with competitive market structures was detrimental to consumers, and the ICC began to deregulate the industry. Trucking companies came under intense competitive pressures, because as regulatory barriers to entry were dropped, new firms, many of them nonunion, entered the industry, and extensive rate-cutting developed. These pressures were further increased by the deep recession of the early 1980s.

In early 1982, the Teamsters and the TMI negotiated a new 37-month

Master Freight Agreement, in which there were significant wage concessions in recognition of the economic pressures facing the industry. Under the agreement, over-the-road truckers agreed to annual rather than semiannual cost-of-living adjustments or COLAs (the significance of the frequency of COLA adjustments is discussed further in Chapter 16) and to relax certain work rules. Moreover, part or all of the COLA payments could be diverted, if needed to meet cost increases for maintaining benefits in the health and welfare and pension plans. Nevertheless, the increased product-market competition had served to increase conflicts of interests among regional and national trucking companies. With nonunion firms taking over some of the full-truckload business from national firms, the latter successfully entered the market for less-than-truckload business that had been the main activity for regional trucking companies. Large national firms, with networks of terminals at which partial loads could be reassembled into full-truck loads for delivery to other terminals, were able to compete more effectively than the regionals in this market. As a result, when it came time to negotiate the new National Freight Agreement, many regional trucking companies declined to authorize TMI to negotiate with the Teamsters on their behalf. The number of trucking companies authorizing TMI to represent them dropped from 487 in 1979 to only 284 in 1982.

The trucking companies that abandoned the multiemployer bargaining arrangement argued that they needed more extensive concessions than were negotiated in the Master Freight Agreement in order to meet competitive pressures. Most argued that the national multiemployer arrangement was not appropriate to the competition spawned by deregulation, since the extent of nonunion competition varied. Moreover, the TMI was dominated by the larger national companies whose interests were in conflict with the smaller regional companies. For example, it was in the interests of the larger companies to have a high labor cost agreement imposed on the regional firms with whom they now competed for business.

The regional trucking companies wished to negotiate separately with the Teamsters for a contract that provided lower labor costs and hence increased their prospects for survival. At the same time, the larger companies who had been represented by TMI made it clear that they would abandon the Master Freight Agreement if any breakaway companies negotiated a more favorable contract with the Teamsters. Faced with the dissolution of the national multiemployer arrangement, the Teamsters initially insisted that the breakaway companies accept the terms of the Master Freight Agreement, and struck firms that insisted on negotiating an alternative arrangement. Several trucking firms went out of business. Eventually, however, the union negotiated further wage concessions for workers whose jobs were most threatened by nonunion competitions.

SOURCE: Agis Salpukas, "Regional Truckers Debate Labor Costs," *New York Times,* February 24, 1982; Agis Salpukas, "Dilemma for Union Truckers," *New York Times,* June 22, 1982. Robert S. Greenberger, "Teamsters Chief Offers Plan to Reduce Pay of Union Drivers Hauling Full Truckloads," *Wall Street Journal,* June 27, 1983.

Other companies in the industry will never be in a worse competitive position than the target company, and until the terms of the new agreement are actually extended to them, they may be in a better competitive position, either because the target company is not producing (if a strike occurs), or because there is a temporary period (after the target company signs a new agreement but before the terms of that agreement are extended to the other companies in the industry) when the target company is producing at higher cost. On the other hand, the sooner the target company signs, the sooner it will be in an equivalent competitive position with other firms in the industry and the lower the risk of a loss of market share. While market shares may be protected, the average product price is likely to be relatively high and the level of sales and production relatively low. The limited empirical evidence available indicates that unions achieve more generous contracts in company-wide bargaining units than industrywide bargaining units, at least in national product markets.[24]

There are long-run dangers with bargaining arrangements that result in relatively high labor costs. For the most part, such arrangements work to the union's advantage so long as the main substitutes available to consumers are produced under essentially the same union contract. Eventually, labor costs and product prices may become sufficiently high so that new producers entering the industry are not part of the bargaining arrangements and therefore can produce the product or service at lower cost, so that the exercise of union power implies a serious loss of employment to union members. The most dramatic recent example of this process occurred in the automobile industry in the United States in the late 1970s, as sales by foreign automobile producers captured an increasing share of the American market. The Chrysler Corporation was brought to the verge of bankruptcy, and the United Automobile Workers, the union that represents workers in the automobile industry, was forced to grant concessions to the company in order to protect its members' jobs. Unions in other industries in which product-market competition increased were also forced to abandon traditional patterns and negotiate concessions in order to protect the job opportunities of their members.

Multiplant bargaining units. In multiplant companies, bargaining structures may be influenced by technological factors. When several plants of a company produce the same product, the union will normally prefer a bargaining unit that includes all of the plants, while the employer is likely to prefer a unit that is less broad —perhaps even plant-level negotiations. In each case, the reason is the same. If one plant is struck, it may be possible for the employer to reduce the costs of the strike substantially by shifting production to other plants that are not a part of the negotiating unit. The employer would balance this tactical advantage against

[24]See references in footnote 20.

the increased costs associated with negotiating separate contracts at each plant or at several groups of plants. On the other hand, if different plants carry out different stages of a vertically-integrated production process, a company will prefer companywide bargaining, since plant-level bargaining would create the potential for shutting down the company's entire production process, given the interdependence of the production conducted at different plants. Unions may also see an advantage in a multiplant bargaining unit in this situation, since a strike at any one plant would induce unemployment among union members at other plants that were forced to shut down.

Influence of bargaining issues. The structure of negotiating units can also be influenced by the scope of the issues that are subject to collective bargaining. The product and labor-market influences that have been stressed in the preceding discussion have a particularly important impact on collective bargaining over issues such as wages, hours of work, and employment conditions that have a marketwide impact. Some issues cannot be addressed sensibly in small units, however, even when the labor and product market served by union labor is relatively small. Pension and insurance plans, which for actuarial reasons often need large numbers of participants, provide examples of issues that may not be handled effectively in plant-level or local labor-market negotiations.

On the other hand, there are many issues that arise in collective bargaining which may be unique to a plant, firm, or local labor market. Work rules, job safety, and job security are common examples. In most instances, the exact nature of the issues varies from plant to plant (for example, the nature of restrictive work practices or safety problems are likely to vary by place of employment), and efforts to settle these issues in a relatively large negotiating unit are rarely successful. For example, an epic strike in the steel industry during 1959 and 1960 was attributable in part to an effort to resolve work rules in industrywide collective bargaining.

One solution to this problem is to develop a more flexible bargaining structure in which different categories of bargaining issues are negotiated at different levels. In the automobile industry, for example, negotiations at the national company level establish wages, fringe benefits, seniority policies, a grievance procedure, and many other provisions that have a marketwide impact or pertain to company-wide personnel policies. The national agreement is then supplemented by negotiations between local units of the United Automobile Workers and management representatives at individual plants of the company over "local issues" including work rules and safety. Much the same procedure was used in the telephone industry prior to deregulation.

Since the acceleration of union growth in the United States in the late 1930s, the trend has been toward larger negotiating units, as unions and management have adjusted to spreading markets, the emergence of potential substitute products, and the growing importance of fringe benefits in collective-bargaining agreements. Yet the expansion of negotiating-unit size, which may increase the bargaining power of unions, is not costless to unions or employers. In particular, as the scope of a negotiating unit expands, the diversity of interests of workers encompassed by the unit grows. Disputes may emerge between younger workers and older workers concerning whether collective bargaining should emphasize immediate wage gains or more generous pension provisions. Skilled workers may have a conflict of interest with unskilled workers concerning the form of wage increases: uniform cents-per-hour wage increases erode the relative wage differentials that uniform percentage increases protect. The analysis of the union as a provider of public goods developed in Chapter 12 is pertinent here. As the heterogeneity of the membership covered by a collective bargaining-agreement increases, it becomes more difficult for the union to represent the preferences of its membership. Any agreement that is negotiated will leave a larger proportion of the membership dissatisfied than if the union were negotiating for a smaller, more homogenous membership.[25]

As a result, gains in bargaining power tend to be offset by loss in the ability to represent many of the interests embedded in the membership. Moreover, it may become increasingly difficult for individuals or even groups of members to influence union policy. With the increased heterogeneity of expanding negotiating units comes increased pressure on the union from membership groups who feel that their interests are not being adequately represented. Unions increasingly face a problem of how to reconcile pressures for market control and tactical striking power with membership demands for effective representation. As noted in Chapter 12, when union members are dissatisfied with the quality of representation, they have methods of expressing their dissatisfaction, including the election of new officers, refusal to ratify labor agreements that their leadership has negotiated, and wildcat strikes.

Bargaining Structure in the Public Sector

Although labor unions in the public sector share most of the objectives of private-sector unions, collective bargaining in the public sector occurs in a very different legal and economic environment, and the structure and tactics of public-sector collective bargaining differ accordingly. One basic fact facing unions in the public sector is the inherent tendency for unit labor costs to increase more rapidly in the public sector than in the private sector, quite independently of the presence or absence of unions and collective bargaining. This tendency arises because the rate of growth of labor productivity in the public sector (and in service industries generally) is low relative to that experienced by goods-producing industries in the private sector. Yet most public-sector organizations must increase wages and benefits in line with the growth of compensation in the private sector in order to attract and retain their work force. To the extent that the growth of real compensation in the private sector is in line with the (higher) growth of labor productivity in private industry, wages in the public sector will tend to increase more rapidly

---

[25]For a discussion of the consequences of expanding negotiating units for local unions and special groups within unions, *see* George Brooks, "Unions and the Structure of Collective Bargaining," in Arnold R. Weber, ed., *The Structure of Collective Bargaining* (Chicago: Graduate School of Business, 1961), pp. 123–40.

than the productivity of public workers, and the labor costs of providing a given level of public services will rise steadily.[26] Since 50-75 percent of local government expenditures are for wages and benefits, the inherent upward pressure of labor costs on budgets in the public sector would occur even in the absence of collective bargaining.

Federal, state, and local governments are differentiated from most (but not all) private-sector employers in that profit maximization is unlikely to be an objective of governmental units.[27] In addition, governments generally operate in a nonmarket environment. Many of the services provided by the governments are *public goods,* consumed jointly by all members of the community, and most government activities are not conducted under the normal exchange relationships that characterize the private sector. Most governments are effectively monopolists in the production of public services for a particular political jurisdiction and are not subject to the direct competitive pressures raised by the possibility of new entrants. Individual government services are not generally sold at explicit prices, as are private goods and services.

From the perspective of collective-bargaining strategies in the public sector, it is also notable that the flow of revenues to a public employer is not closely tied to the flow of service as it is in the private sector. As indicated in Table 14.2, most government revenues are from taxes levied on individuals, businesses, and property, and from intergovernmental transfers (mainly transfers from the federal

Table 14.2. Sources of Revenue of Federal, State, and Local Governments, 1980–81 (percent distribution)

Source	Federal	State	Local
Intergovernmental revenue			
From federal govt.	0	21.8	7.8
From state govt.	0.3	0	30.9
From local govt.	0	0.9	0
Individual income tax	43.2	13.2	1.9
Corporation income tax	9.3	4.6	0
Property tax	0	0.9	25.0
General sales tax	0	14.9	3.2
Selective sales tax	6.1	8.5	1.4
Misc. taxes	2.8	6.1	1.4
Charges and misc. general revenue	12.4	12.1	17.7
Utility revenue	0	0.6	8.6
Liquor store revenue	0	0.9	0.2
Insurance trust revenue	25.9	15.5	1.9

SOURCE: U.S. Department of Commerce, Bureau of the Census, *Government Finances in 1980–81* (Washington, D.C.: U.S. Government Printing Office, 1982), Table 4, p. 17.

---

[26]*See* William Baumol and William Bowen, "Macroeconomics of Unbalanced Growth: The Anatomy of Urban Crisis," *American Economic Review* 57 (June 1967): 415–26.

[27]For interesting analyses of the *private* not-for-profit or voluntary sector, *see* Burton Weisbrod, *The Voluntary Non-profit Sector: An Economic Analysis* (Lexington, Mass.: Lexington Books, 1977) and Henry Hansmann, "The Role of Nonprofit Enterprise," *Yale Law Journal* 89 (April 1980): 835–901.

government to the states and municipalities). Only a minute portion of government revenues are tied to fees in which payment depends on delivery of service (for example, charging admission to a municipal zoo). While collective bargaining in the public sector may not be subject to the kinds of market pressures that are present in the private sector, there are clearly political forces that can influence the revenue sources reported in Table 14.2. During the late 1970s and early 1980s, voters in several states placed limits on the extent of property taxation, an important element of local government revenues, and changes in federal policies reduced the scale of transfers of revenues collected by the federal government to the states and the cities. Both of these developments reduced the growth in demand for public employees and served to increase the resistance of public employers in collective bargaining.

The fact that governments operate in a nonmarket environment does not mean that they are completely shielded from market forces and need not be concerned with market like pressures when negotiating with public-sector unions. While individual public services do not carry a price, the package of services provided by a government carries a price in the form of the taxes noted in Table 14.2. When this tax-price becomes too high, a city or state may be faced with a market like response as individuals or businesses exercise their option to "exit" and move to other cities or states where the package of taxes and government services are more appealing.[28] (This is the public-sector analogy to a loss of market share in the private sector.) Alternatively, disaffected taxpayers can exercise their "voice" by voting political leaders out of office. A second market like response to generous wage settlements can come through the capital markets, as Cleveland, New York, and other major cities discovered during the 1970s. When investors become concerned about the financial soundness of a city or state, the quality rating of that government's debt is likely to be downgraded so that it becomes more expensive, or in very extreme cases (such as New York City in the mid-1970s), impossible to borrow in private capital markets. Thus, the fact that governments generally operate in a nonmarket environment does not eliminate the economic pressures that public-sector managers and unions must consider in collective bargaining; however, these pressures may operate less directly and with greater time lags than market pressures on private producers.

There are also important differences in the structure of authority in private and public organizations that influence the structure and tactics of collective bargaining. In most private-sector organizations, management authority usually flows down from the top of the organization. This tends to facilitate the formulation of an organization's labor-relations policy, for when the policy is determined at the top, the interests of only a limited number of parties need be considered. In the public sector, authority flows from the bottom up through the electoral process. Political leaders are ultimately responsible to the voters that elect them. As a result, a more heterogeneous set of interests must be considered in determining labor-relations policy.

Some of this heterogeneity is reflected in the greater extent to which manage-

---

[28]Charles M. Tiebout, "A Pure Theory of Local Expenditures," *Journal of Political Economy* 64 (October 1956): 416–24.

ment power is shared in the public sector. The executive branch obviously shares power with the legislative branch at all levels of government, but power is also shared within the executive branch. Moreover, the goals of managers in different parts of the executive branch may be in conflict. For example, since few agencies have the ability or authority to raise the money to finance their activities directly, the revenue and expenditure functions of government are usually managed centrally in a budget agency. The head of an operating agency may be more willing to conclude a collective-bargaining agreement providing for large increases in compensation than the head of the budget agency for the city or state. What the head of the budget agency is willing to approve may in turn be determined by the size of the budget that the city council or state legislature is willing to approve. The limits on what management negotiators can agree to may be further constrained by Civil Service requirements, which are established on a citywide or statewide basis.

Generally, collective bargaining by public employees becomes an element in the political process that determines the leadership and activities of government. Unlike the situation in the private sector, the ultimate public employers are the citizens who purchase and use public services and who elect public officials. Therefore, officials in the public sector are likely to be as sensitive to the effects of labor-relations policies on their share of the votes as private-sector managers are to the effects on their share of the market. Citizen-voters who are not employees share an interest in obtaining their public services at the lowest possible price, much like consumers in the private sector. But unlike the situation of workers in the private sector, citizen-voters who are also public employees are able to vote on decisions that may affect their conditions of employment. While public employees typically constitute a minority of the voters in any public-sector jurisdiction, they may find it easier than nonemployee voters to organize and direct pressure at political leaders. This becomes true when public employees organize into unions.[29] Interestingly, political efforts to require public employees to live in the cities in which they work (motivated by a desire that employees be more sensitive to the concerns of the community) can have the effect of increasing the amount of pressure that public employees are able to mount against public employers through the voting process.[30]

The political context of public-sector activities as well as the historical-legal opposition to collective bargaining have influenced the structure of collective bargaining. As in the private sector, bargaining structures in the public sector tend to be highly decentralized; in fact, there is an even greater tendency for

---

[29]Clyde W. Summers, "Public Employee Bargaining: A Political Perspective," *Yale Law Journal* 83 (1974): 1156–1200; Paul Courant, Edward Gramlich, and Daniel Rubinfeld, "Public Employee Market Power and the Level of Government Spending," *American Economic Review* 69 (December 1979): 806–17.

[30]The use of political leverage through the voting process is sufficiently important to public employees that there have been reports from several cities of groups of public employees maintaining their voting registration at addresses in the cities in which they work, although they live in other communities.

single-employer collective bargaining in the public sector than in the private sector. The tendency toward single-employer bargaining reflects a reluctance among different governmental jurisdictions to give up some decision-making discretion for the purpose of maintaining a multiemployer bargaining arrangement. It also reflects the problem that confronts efforts to establish multiemployer arrangements in the private sector—the financial condition and the political pressures on elected officials differ considerably across states and cities, and as a result it can be difficult for different jurisdictions to agree on the degree of resistance or extent of concessions to be offered in collective bargaining.[31] As a result, collective bargaining in the public sector generally occurs between a single public employer and an individual union.

But it is also true that in many states and municipalities, there has been a proliferation of bargaining units so that a single public employer faces more unions than a typical employer in the private sector. For example, by the early 1970s, the state of Massachusetts had some two hundred bargaining units in which employees were represented by more than 40 labor organizations. In the early 1970s, the city of New York had over 200 bargaining relationships with about 90 labor organizations; some bargaining units had as few as two employees. In the mid-1970s, Detroit had 78 separate bargaining units. While many governmental jurisdictions had succeeded in reducing or limiting the number of negotiating units by the late 1970s, public employers in 23 states and 82 municipalities, including some of the largest cities in the country, each faced over ten bargaining units (Table 14.3). Almost 40 percent of the bargaining units at the state level and 50 percent of the units in municipalities contained fewer than 25 employees.[32]

Table 14.3. Public Sector Bargaining Units, by Level of Government, October 1979

	Number of Governments	Percent with Bargaining Units	Percent of Employees Represented by a Bargaining Unit	Number of Units		
				1–2	3–9	10+
State and Local Governments	79,928	16.3	38.0	9,081	3,743	220
State	50	68.0	25.8	3	8	23
Local	79,878	16.3	42.8	9,078	3,735	197
Counties	3,040	22.6	30.9	350	291	45
Municipalities	18,878	13.0	45.6	1,270	1,099	82
Townships	16,827	6.0	35.6	618	353	41
Special Districts	26,010	3.1	28.9	695	108	7
School Districts	15,123	53.2	48.5	6,145	1,884	22

SOURCE: U.S. Bureau of the Census, *Labor-Management Relations in State and Local Governments: 1979*, State and Local Government Special Studies No. 100 (Washington, D.C.: U.S. Government Printing Office, 1980) p. 148.

---

[31]Thomas A. Kochan, *Collective Bargaining and Industrial Relations: From Theory to Policy and Practice* (Homewood, Ill.: Richard D. Irwin, Inc., 1980), pp. 457–58.

[32]Note that the data in Table 14.3 also indicate that whereas the majority of states and school districts had established collective-bargaining relationships by the late 1970s, the likelihood of a bargaining unit declines with the size of the governmental unit. As in the private sector, there may be economies of scale in organizing unions in the public sector.

The proliferation of bargaining units in many sections of government is traceable to a combination of political and legal factors and to historical accidents. Many of the units were permitted as rewards for political support during periods in which there was little cost of another collective-bargaining unit, since strikes were forbidden and unions appeared unwilling to strike in violation of the law. In this climate new bargaining units could effectively be ignored. Moreover, the public sector is not covered by the National Labor Relations Act, and under the prevailing legal climate in most public-sector jurisdictions, there were no formal unit-determination procedures during the 1960s and the early 1970s; further, the range of issues over which unions were legally permitted to negotiate was quite circumscribed prior to legislative changes during the 1970s. In short, neither party had much incentive to give a great deal of attention to the appropriateness of a particular bargaining unit. With the growing professionalism of labor relations in the public sector during the 1970s and 1980s, collective-bargaining agencies established by law at the city or state level of government increasingly moved to consolidate and reduce the number of units into more manageable numbers.

The fragmented bargaining structures mentioned above present severe problems for the management of labor relations. Public employers must allocate considerable resources simply to the negotiation and administration of a plethora of labor agreements. Collective bargaining itself may be uncoordinated if the expiration dates of different labor agreements are staggered. Multiple units can also give rise to unstable compensation structures as a result of "coercive comparisons" of wages and benefits between different groups. At one time, for example, the separately negotiated labor agreements covering police officers and firefighters in New York City provided (1) that the ratio of the wage of a police patrolman to a police sergeant be 3/3.5, (2) that the ratio of wages of a firefighter to a fire lieutenant be 3/3.9, and (3) that the wages of police sergeants and fire lieutenants be equal. This unstable formula, a product of uncoordinated collective-bargaining negotiations, yielded no equilibrium! Once either service received a wage increase, the contract of the other provided it with a case for an increase, which in turn would trigger a claim for an increase from the first service, etc.

The Tactics of Collective Bargaining

In the previous section we discussed how bargaining structure, the level at which negotiations are conducted, could be related to bargaining power. Within a given bargaining structure, however, the outcome of collective bargaining can also be influenced by the general environment of collective bargaining and the tactics adopted by the parties. In this section we discuss environmental and tactical factors influencing collective bargaining in the private and public sectors.

Bargaining Tactics in the Private Sector

Business fluctuations. One important determinant of the relative bargaining power of labor and management is largely beyond their influence. Business fluctuations, which reflect the monetary and fiscal policies of the federal government, influence the costs incurred by both parties in the event of a work stoppage. In general, the relative bargaining power of unions varies cyclically, increasing in business expansions with growth of demand in product markets and decreasing in recessions. When product demand is relatively weak, for example, an employer may have little to lose by offering stiff resistance to a union's demands. In the event that the resistance results in a bargaining impasse and strike, the employer may be able to meet orders from inventories, which are often relatively large anyway as a result of the slack demand. Alternatively, if the employer wishes to continue to operate by hiring replacements for striking workers, there are likely to be many individuals willing to accept work, even as strikebreakers, when unemployment is high. Conversely, when demand expands and inventories are low, the employer risks a loss of orders and potentially a permanent loss of market share in the event of a work stoppage. The cost of a strike will also be relatively high to management because it is likely to be difficult or relatively expensive to hire replacements for strikers during periods when unemployment is low.

Contract expiration date. Unions have developed a number of tactics aimed at increasing the cost of a strike to management. One of the more common tactics is to try to time the expiration date of a labor agreement to a period when labor services are particularly crucial. In the automobile industry, for example, the major union contracts expire in early autumn at about the time that the auto companies expect their production and sales to build in response to the introduction of new models. Newspapers are particularly vulnerable to strikes called in the periods preceding the Christmas and Easter holidays when advertising revenues are particularly large. Strikes by farmworkers at harvest time would be particularly damaging to farmers. As these examples indicate, unions have an incentive to try to establish contract expiration dates during periods in which a work stoppage would impose relatively large costs on management. Employers, of course, have an incentive to resist such efforts.

Since an expiration date is itself established in collective bargaining, it is likely to reflect more basic underlying determinants of the relative bargaining power of the two parties. In situations in which a union is unable to negotiate an expiration date that places the employer under considerable pressure to settle, the union may achieve the same result by working without a new contract after the expiration date and continuing to negotiate until a time when the costs of a strike to an employer are relatively high. However, union control over the timing of work stoppages has been weakened in recent decades by the increasing latitude of the courts and the National Labor Relations Board toward the use of lockouts by employers. As discussed in Chapter 15, employers are free to use a lockout once a bargaining impasse has occurred and therefore have some control over the timing of a work stoppage.

Inventory build-ups. A common management tactic in manufacturing industries is to build up inventories in advance of a contract expiration to anticipate a possible strike. In some cases, the company itself holds the inventories if it is able to ship during a strike. In other cases, the company's customers may stockpile goods in advance of a potential strike date. During a long strike in the rubber industry in 1979, for example, automobile manufacturers were able to supply cars, initially by using tires that they had stockpiled in advance of the strike, and later by omitting the spare tire from new cars until the strike concluded. As a result, there was much less pressure from customers on tire manufacturers to settle the strike than the union had anticipated.

Bargaining with multinational corporations. During the 1960s and 1970s, there was an unprecedented expansion into other countries of the operations of corporations based in the United States, Western Europe, and Japan. While earlier examples of multinational enterprise had primarily involved the vertical integration of a corporation with foreign sources of raw materials, the recent growth of multinational corporations (MNCs) has largely consisted of a horizontal extension of companies into new product markets.

Since many MNCs make the same product in several countries, unions bargaining in any one country face the possibility that production will be shifted across national borders during a labor dispute. "Production-switching" of this nature increases the corporation's bargaining power by increasing its ability to take a strike. The risk of a serious loss of market share during a strike is reduced when production can be increased in other countries. (This is similar to the problem faced by a union bargaining at one plant of a multiplant firm.) Unions also complain that it is frequently difficult to pin down the locus of decision-making authority for industrial relations issues in many MNCs.

European and American unions have developed different strategies for addressing the collective-bargaining issues raised by the growth of MNCs.[33] Some European labor organizations have attempted to develop *transnational collective bargaining*—the coordination of collective-bargaining demands among workers of different nations in the same industry. As with the development of national unions discussed in Chapter 12, this particular institutional response represents an effort to develop a bargaining structure that reduces the elasticity of demand for the services of the workers of an MNC involved in negotiations in a particular country by limiting the scope for substitution of production activities to other countries. In particular, it represents an effort to prevent the bargaining objectives of unions in one country from being undermined by the activities of unions in

---

[33]The strategies are discussed at greater length in Robert J. Flanagan and Arnold R. Weber, eds., *Bargaining Without Boundaries: The Multinational Corporation and International Industrial Relations* (Chicago: The University of Chicago Press, 1974) and B.C. Roberts, "Multinational Collective Bargaining: A European Prospect?" *British Journal of Industrial Relations* 11 (March 1973): 1–19.

other countries. As a result of these efforts, a few groups of workers have refused overtime or additional work resulting from attempts by an MNC to shift production from a struck plant in another country.

However, this tactical coordination has not been widespread to date, and efforts to counter MNCs through transnational collective-bargaining arrangements face more imposing barriers than the development of a national union structure within a particular country. Labor organizations in different countries frequently have very different mixes of economic and political objectives, and the timing of strikes or other job actions to secure political objectives may not correspond well with the timing that is best for securing economic objectives. Moreover, the bargaining structures differ between countries, and labor federations are often fractured along political or religious lines (see discussion in Example 14.4), with the result that a particular plant or industry may employ workers represented by different federations and having diverse objectives.

Impressed by these barriers, unions in the United States have taken the position that the transnational collective-bargaining strategy is too slow to accommodate the immediate problems that they associate with the growth of MNCs. Viewing the MNC as the modern equivalent of the runaway shop, they have instead pressed for protectionist legislation to reduce the incentives for American corporations to establish subsidiaries in other countries. American unions may also view protectionist legislation as a bargaining position from which to achieve reductions in trade barriers erected by foreign countries. To the extent that MNCs establish foreign subsidiaries to get around such barriers, the ultimate effect of reducing such barriers could be to increase the extent to which foreign markets are supplied by exports from the source country rather than by production by subsidiaries—a development that would increase jobs in the source country. On the other hand, there is an inherent conflict between the approaches espoused by American and European unions: to the extent that the American unions are successful in obtaining protectionist legislation, the job opportunities of European union members are reduced.

The ratification procedure. As noted in Chapter 12, most union constitutions call for some form of ratification of a tentative collective-bargaining agreement by the union membership or by a representative body elected by the membership. Effectively, the ratification procedure means that union negotiators do not have the final authority to bind the union to a proposed agreement. The authority of management negotiators may similarly be limited to the extent that an agreement must be approved by an executive or board that is not participating directly in the negotiations. There is sometimes a temptation to use the ratification procedure tactically. Either side may try to obtain more from the other by returning to the bargaining table claiming that their principals refused to approve the agreement without further concessions. Negotiators may even influence whether ratification occurs by the manner in which they portray a proposed agreement to their principals.

While the above use of the ratification procedure may appear to be a clever method of extracting further concessions, it rarely works more than once. In subsequent bargaining rounds, the party that was a victim of the tactic may simply hold back the best offer initially, anticipating the rejection of tentative agreements. To the extent that both parties adopt the strategy, the tactical use of a ratification procedure may ultimately reduce the concession that either side is willing to make initially and therefore raise the possibility of a strike. Yet the tactical use of the ratification procedure may be tempting because a failure to ratify need not be costly initially (see Example 14.7).

Strike insurance. Many industries provide products or services that have time value and cannot feasibly be placed in inventory for use during a strike. In several of these industries—notably newspapers, railroads, and the airlines—*strike-insurance* arrangements have been used at various times to reduce the cost of strikes to management. In the event of a strike, an employer participating in a strike-insurance plan is entitled to receive payments from other employers in the plan according to a pre-established formula, which typically differs from plan to plan. Although the details of various plans differ, their objectives are similar—to reduce the costs of a strike to an employer by restoring some of the revenues that would otherwise be lost, as customers shift to nonstruck firms in the industry. To the extent that they are successful, strike-insurance plans will increase the ability of employers to take a strike.

Strike-insurance arrangements are not free of problems for employers, however. Although strike insurance will maintain some of the revenues of a firm during a strike, it does not guarantee that customers will return when the strike is over. Employers can still suffer permanent losses of market share to their competitors. In this sense, strike insurance provides less protection to individual employers than a multiemployer bargaining arrangement. Secondly, since strike insurance rests on the ability of firms that are operating to subsidize a struck firm, the development of a strike-insurance plan provides a strong incentive for unions in the industry to press for industry-wide strikes or bargaining structures, which would remove the value of the insurance arrangement.[34]

A broader difficulty presented by strike-insurance arrangements stems from the incentives set up by the mere existence of the insurance. Insurance generally works best when the events which are insured against are random events. But not all contingencies for which insurance is desired are random. Many such events (for example, fires, automobile accidents) are to some extent influenced by the behavior of the individuals who are insured. The mere existence of insurance may create a problem known as *moral hazard,* whereby the behavior of the insured is altered in ways that raise the likelihood that the event that is insured against occurs. (For example, fire insurance may lead insured individuals to be less careful about fire prevention.) The main defenses against moral hazard that have been devised by insurance companies are varieties of *coinsurance* which require the insured party to pay a either a fixed amount (a "deductible") or a fixed proportion of the loss. While this reduces the moral hazard incentive, it does not completely eliminate it.

---

[34]Unions also argued (unsuccessfully) that strike-insurance arrangements violated federal antitrust laws.

EXAMPLE 14.7

Contract Ratification in the Automobile Industry

Although collective bargaining in the automobile industry is conducted at the company level, the industry historically has provided an example of "pattern bargaining," wherein the terms of the contract that are established in negotiations with a "target" company in each bargaining round are extended to other companies. In 1980 and 1981, however, the Chrysler Corporation came close to insolvency, and the United Automobile Workers (UAW), the union representing most Chrysler employees, agreed in 1980 to a contract that included significant wage concessions by union workers at Chrysler. As a result of these concessions, by the summer of 1982, when a new round of collective-bargaining negotiations began, autoworkers at Chrysler had not received a wage increase for almost two years and were earning an average of $2.50 an hour less than workers represented by the UAW at the General Motors Corporation and at the Ford Motor Company.

After several weeks of negotiations, the UAW and Chrysler reached a tentative agreement in September restoring cost-of-living adjustments that had been dropped as part of the earlier concessions and providing for wage increases later if Chrysler attained certain levels of profitability. Although the union leadership urged ratification, workers at Chrysler, who wanted a labor agreement that included an immediate raise, voted 70 percent to 30 percent to reject the tentative agreement. Negotiators for Chrysler maintained that the company did not have the economic resources to improve their offer. One month later, Chrysler workers voted, also by a 70 percent to 30 percent margin, *not* to strike, but to work under the terms of the old contract that had expired in September 1982 until new negotiations over immediate wage increases could be resumed in early 1983.

To many outsiders, the scenario seemed bizarre: a union rejects a tentative contract and then agrees to continue working under an old contract rather than striking the company to obtain an improvement over the rejected agreement! In many respects, however, the outcome reflects the fact that contract-ratification procedures in the automobile industry, as in many other industries, do not impose any costs on union members who reject a contract. In most unions, a failure to ratify a contract is not simultaneously a pledge by the union membership to strike in support of demands for a better contract. Strike votes are usually taken separately. Moreover, some unions require two-thirds of the membership to approve a strike but only one-half of the membership to reject a contract. As a result, union members often do not have to balance the consequences of taking action to obtain better contract terms against the contents of the proposed contract. A failure to ratify is no more than a statement that the membership would like more to come out of the negotiations, and as such, can be used, as in the Chrysler case, as an expression of frustration over the workers' economic position.

SOURCES: Dale D. Buss, "UAW to Ask Chrysler Workers Tuesday: Strike or Work Under Old Pact Until '83," *Wall Street Journal* October 22, 1982; Dale D. Buss, "Chrysler Corp. Workers Vote to Stay on Job," *Wall Street Journal* October 27, 1982. John Holusha, "Auto Workers Overwhelmingly Reject Strike Against Chrysler," *New York Times* October 27, 1982.

Strikes are not random events; they are influenced by the behavior of the parties to collective bargaining. As such, a strike-insurance arrangement that reduces the net cost of a strike may increase the probability that a strike occurs, since the employer will have a smaller incentive to take costly actions that might avoid a strike than if there were not insurance payments to cushion the losses from a strike. Even in a coinsurance arrangement, which imposes some of the costs on the company that takes the strike, there is still a smaller incentive to reach agreement than would exist without strike insurance. Strike insurance therefore presents a moral hazard problem. Its existence may increase employer resistance in collective bargaining, but it may also provide a subsidy for inept labor relations.

In the case of strike insurance, the presence of moral hazard can give rise to a problem of *adverse selection,* which can undermine the risk-sharing function of the insurance. Adverse selection occurs when only those parties with a relatively high risk of suffering a loss purchase insurance. The cost of participating in an insurance arrangement tends to be based on the average loss experience for the group that is insured. Yet, individual participants are likely to differ in their risk of loss. Participants that know their risk of loss is high will see the insurance cost as a bargain, while participants who know that their risk of loss is relatively low will find that the insurance cost exceeds their expected loss and will decide not to purchase insurance. Over time, people with low risk will drop out of the insurance market and only individuals with a high risk of loss will want to purchase insurance.

Adverse selection is a real possibility in the case of strike insurance, because most strike-insurance arrangements have no screening procedure that can be used to identify poor risks and deny them insurance. Payments made by participants in a strike-insurance arrangement are not varied on the basis of participants' strike experiences. In fact, in some arrangements, the size of the payment may depend on the size of the losses suffered by other members of the insurance pact. Yet the individual members of a strike-insurance arrangement may differ in the quality of their labor relations, and hence, the likelihood that they will experience a strike. If firms that developed relatively good labor relations found themselves regularly making payments to firms that experienced many strikes as a result of poor labor relations, the former set of firms would rationally lose interest in participating in a strike-insurance arrangement. By remaining in the arrangement, they might be subsidizing the inept labor-relations practices of their competitors.

Application: airline strike insurance. For 20 years, the airline industry in the United States maintained a mutual aid agreement, which provided a form of strike insurance for participants in the arrangement. The agreement was established in 1958 by six of the largest airlines and initially provided that each member airline would make "windfall" payments to the struck member. Each member's windfall payment was "an amount equal to its increased revenue attributable to the strike during the term thereof, less applicable direct expenses."[35] In effect, if all of the business lost by a struck airline shifted to other airlines, the windfall payments would have fully indemnified the struck airline for any losses suffered as a result of the strike.

In fact, airlines faced considerable uncertainty concerning the level of compensation that they would receive in the event of a strike. During periods, such as major holidays, when nonstruck airlines normally operated at full capacity, there would be no increase in revenues attributable to the strike. A similar problem confronted airlines flying routes on which there was no competition from other members of the Mutual Aid Agreement. In the event of a strike, consumers would either shift to nonmember airlines or to other means of transportation, neither of which would provide compensation for the struck airline. Also, if a union broadened a strike to include all members of the agreement flying on parallel routes, none of the members would receive strike benefits. As a result, some airlines chose not to join in the arrangement, since they saw little prospect of benefiting from it (given their route structures), and the windfall-payments approach meant that airlines that did become members of the agreement would benefit by different amounts in the event of a strike.

In an effort to solve these problems, the Mutual Aid Agreement was later amended twice, and by late 1969 provided that a struck airline would receive 50 percent of its normal operating expenses during the first two weeks of a strike, 45 percent during the third week, 40 percent during the fourth week, and 35 percent for the remaining weeks of the strike. Payments were made irrespective of the windfall gains to other airlines during a strike. The share of each nonstruck airline in the strike payments was equal to its share of the operating revenues of members of the agreement during the previous year up to a maximum liability of one percent of revenues. The actual burden on nonstruck airlines depended on the extent to which they made windfall earnings when a member of the agreement was struck.

The revised Mutual Aid Agreement substantially reduced the net costs of a strike to the point where some member airlines actually earned operating profits

---

[35]S. Herbert Unterberger and Edward C. Koziara, "The Demise of Airline Strike Insurance," *Industrial and Labor Relations Review* 29 (October 1975): 27. The discussion here draws on this study and its sequel by the same authors, "The Demise of Airline Strike Insurance," *Industrial and Labor Relations Review* 34 (October 1980): 82–89.

during long strikes. For example, when National Airlines was struck for 114 days by the Airline Employees' Association in 1970, it earned an operating *profit* of $1,590,000. Without the benefits from the Mutual Aid Agreement it would have experienced an operating *loss* of $26,396,000. (Under the earlier windfall payments approach, it would have experienced a loss of $7,673,000.) At the same time, the revised agreement was in effect a coinsurance arrangement—the operating profits of National Airlines, while positive, were lower than they would have been in the absence of a strike. National incurred some of the costs of the strike in the form of forgone profits. With the reduction in the net costs of a strike, strikes in the airline industry lengthened significantly under the Mutual Aid Agreement.

Over time, there was evidence that the pact was running into the moral hazard, and ultimately, the adverse selection problems discussed in the previous section. Some airlines, such as Northwest, had a pattern of repeated and often lengthy strikes while participating in the Mutual Aid Agreement, while others experienced few, if any, work stoppages. As a result, some companies were regularly required to pay benefits and others regularly collected benefits. The pattern of payments and receipts by major airlines is summarized in Table 14.4. By the 1970s, some of the airlines who were the largest net contributors to the plan began to lose interest in regularly subsidizing the operations of a few strike-prone rivals. Pan American, which had paid in about $64 million under the agreement but received only about $5 million, gave notice in 1975 that it was withdrawing from the Mutual Aid Agreement. The announcement came at a time when Pan American was financially pressed and negotiating for wage concessions with the Airline Pilots' Association, but the management of Pan Am noted that the plan had not been advantageous financially to the company. Subsequently, Eastern Airlines, which had paid almost $90 million but received only around $26 million, announced that it would leave the Mutual Aid Agreement.

Table 14.4. Net Receipts by Major Airlines Under the Mutual Aid Agreement: October 1958–October 1978 (in thousands)

Airlines	Net Receipts[a]
American	−$83,181
Braniff	−18,711
Continental	−11,171
Eastern	−63,021
National	120,124
Northwest	187,906
Pan American	−58,782
Trans World	37,134
United	−88,912
Western	−26,310
Total Major Airlines	−$ 4,924[b]

[a]Negative figures indicate the amount by which an airline's payments under the Mutual Aid Agreement exceeded its receipts.

[b]There was a net transfer over the period from major airlines to local service airlines.

SOURCE: S. Herbert Unterberger and Edward C. Koziara, "The Demise of Airline Strike Insurance," *Industrial and Labor Relations Review* 34 (October 1980): 84.

Unions in the airline industry were understandably opposed to the Mutual Aid Agreement, since by reducing the cost of a strike to the airlines it increased the bargaining power of employers in the industry. They were unsuccessful in their efforts to get the agreement overturned by the Civil Aeronautics Board (CAB), the federal regulatory agency whose approval was necessary before the arrangement could be implemented, or by the federal courts, which rejected claims that the agreement violated antitrust law.

The demise of the agreement came in late 1978 with the passage of federal legislation to deregulate the airline industry. In an effort to reduce the opposition of the labor movement to the legislation, Congress included a provision in the Airline Deregulation Act of 1978 that permits the CAB to approve only those strike-insurance plans that meet conditions which greatly limit the attractiveness of such plans to employers. Under the new law, an airline cannot receive strike insurance during the first 30 days of a strike, and once payments begin (for strikes that exceed 30 days), they are limited to a duration of eight weeks and a maximum amount of 60 percent of the direct operating expenses of an airline *during the strike period* (rather than the 60 percent of *normal* expenses during a nonstrike period permitted under the Mutual Aid Agreement). In addition, the Airline Deregulation Act requires airlines to submit the issues in a collective-bargaining dispute to binding arbitration if requested to do so by employees.[36]

Bargaining Tactics in the Public Sector

As discussed earlier in the chapter, collective bargaining in the public sector occurs in an environment in which power is dispersed between appointed public managers and elected officials, economic pressures are often less immediate than in the private sector, and the law restricts the use of traditional union weapons. Some of the tactics of collective bargaining in the public sector resemble those in the private sector. For example, some of the ratification tactics discussed above may surface when professional negotiators have to bring a proposed agreement back to a mayor, commission, or school board for final approval. But it is hardly surprising that in the decidedly political atmosphere of the public sector, unions and management have frequently developed tactics that are quite different from those commonly observed in negotiations in the private sector. If unions in the private sector adopt tactics that threaten resistant employers with a loss of market share, unions in the public sector are attracted to tactics that threaten resistant public employers with a loss of vote share.

The most direct influence that public-sector unions have on their employers is through the votes of members who live or maintain a voting residence in the city or state in which they work. While it is often illegal for public employees to take political positions as individuals, unions or other *organizations* of public employees are free to lobby for improved working conditions. Through their unions and through their votes, public employees are likely to support ballot issues, political leaders and, where they are elected, judges who are likely to

---

[36]U.S. Congress, "Airline Deregulation Act of 1978," Public Law 95-504 Sec. 29(e)(2) (1978).

advance their cause. The contrast with the activities of private-sector unions is perhaps greatest with respect to the election of judges. Given the restrictive legal environment facing public-sector unions, judicial interpretations of the law and legal doctrine can have a substantial influence on the scope of activities open to public-sector unions. Unions representing public employees are therefore likely to be as concerned about certain state and municipal judgeships as the AFL-CIO and private-sector unions are about appointments to the National Labor Relations Board.

Some efforts by public employees at the ballot box have been strikingly effective. In some cities unions have succeeded in establishing their notions of equity through the political process. In San Francisco, for example, the city charter specified that the pay of certain groups of public employees had to equal the highest pay for similar jobs elsewhere in the state or in the country. Such criteria for wage-setting generally have little connection with conditions in the labor market for such employees, but it is achieved through the exercise of political power rather than bargaining power or negotiating skill. As in collective bargaining, however, political power is subject to alteration, and the voters can retract what they once provided (as they did in San Francisco in late 1975). Generally, the objectives of public employees often imply higher taxes, which are unlikely to appeal to the majority of voters.

With the professionalization of labor relations in the public sector, bargaining for state and local governments has increasingly been conducted by professional negotiators rather than elected officials. When confronted with a management negotiator who is taking a tough stance, unions in the public sector have frequently adopted the tactic of the "end run" around the negotiator to an elected official or legislative body in an effort to obtain their objectives. To the extent that elected officials or representatives offer concessions, the authority of the official negotiators is obviously undermined.

That the tactic pays off at all reflects the fact that power over employment conditions is widely shared in the public sector. In fact, some union representatives claim that while a successful "end run" may undermine the authority of the official management negotiators, the "end run" usually occurs because little authority is vested in the official negotiators in the first place. A tentative agreement may have to be approved by a school board, a mayor, a budget director, or a legislative body before it is binding. As with any ratification process, this extra step of approval can be used tactically to send a negotiator back for further concessions. In situations such as this, unions prefer to deal directly with the management body that has the authority to commit to a contract, and this can stimulate "end runs" when the political leadership is reluctant to grant full authority to its negotiators. The result is a greater tendency toward *multilateral bargaining*—in which three or more groups may be involved in negotiations—in the public sector than in the private sector. Demands for a different type of multilateral bargaining may also arise if a community interest group seeks to be involved in collective-bargaining negotiations over an issue that concerns them (for example, with teachers over the quality of schooling).

One difficulty that collective bargaining presents managers in the public sector is that its timing may not correspond well with the timing of the budget cycle. In most political jurisdictions there are statutory requirements for the submission and approval of budgets for future government expenditures. While the expiration dates of collective-bargaining agreements covering public employees ideally ought to precede the budget submission, this is not always the case, and even when it is, a settlement may occur some time after the formal expiration of the contract. The conflict between bargaining and budgeting is potentially serious, given that labor comprises a large percentage of costs in the public sector.

In the short run, the above budgetary conflict has not seemed very great in many bargaining relationships. In some cases, managers have "padded" their budgets by including amounts that they anticipate will have to be paid as a result of the outcome of collective bargaining. Union negotiators in the public sector have a strong incentive to develop expertise in the budgeting practices of states and cities, however, and efforts to hide anticipated future wage increases can usually be detected by skilled union negotiators. Once the wage concessions that employers are willing to make have been revealed (in the budget), there is then the danger that the anticipated amounts will become the floor rather than the ceiling on union wage demands. Generally, there is considerable flexibility in both the budgeting process (for example, unanticipated wage increases can be offset by reductions in other budget categories such as capital expenditures) and in the way in which public funds are raised (for example, new bond issues or grants from a higher level of government may cover some of the unanticipated expense).

By the mid-1970s, however, it was becoming clear that many of the short-run expedients used to reconcile bargaining and budgeting had extremely serious long-run consequences for the financial viability of cities and states. One illustration of the short-run measures sometimes used to balance public budgets is provided by the extent to which many public-employee retirement systems are underfunded (that is, these systems lack the assets to meet their accrued liabilities). Although most public-sector pension systems nominally require advance funding, the typical public-employee pension fund had only *half* of the assets it should have had to be fully funded in 1975. While some of the short fall was attributable to inappropriate actuarial assumptions and a failure to take account of the fact that pension benefits will increase as salaries increase, the simple refusal of employers to contribute sufficient funds to the pension systems also constitutes a major source of underfunding. Underfunding is clearly used as a means of balancing current operating budgets, suggesting that short-term considerations take priority over long-run consequences when government employers put together compensation packages.[37] Another illustration of this same general point is provided in Example 14.8.

---

[37]U.S. House of Representatives, *Pension Task Force Report on Public Employee Retirement Systems* (Washington, D.C.: U.S. Government Printing Office, March 15, 1978) and the *Report of the Permanent Commission on Public Employee Pension and Retirement Systems—Financing the Public Pension Systems, Part I: Actuarial Assumptions and Funding Policies* (New York, 1975).

EXAMPLE 14.8

Labor Relations and Fiscal Crisis in New York City

Developments in collective bargaining in New York City since 1965 illustrate many observations in this chapter about factors influencing bargaining structure and tactics in the public sector. Collective bargaining was formally introduced in the late 1950s during the administration of Mayor Robert Wagner, who limited its scope to salaries and a few fringe benefits and who, by his regular personal involvement in bargaining, made it a highly political process. With the limited scope of collective bargaining and seemingly few economic constraints (given a substantial flow of tax revenues and intergovernmental transfers from the federal government), wage increases for city workers ran ahead of increases in the private sector. Moreover, bargaining units were approved readily, and at one point, 85 different unions had established a total of 405 bargaining units to represent the city's 250,000 employees. By the mid-1960s, municipal unions formed a major political interest group in the city.

Beginning with the administration of Mayor Lindsay in the late 1960s, there was an effort to reduce the political element by delegating collective bargaining and other aspects of the city's labor relations to professionals. In 1967, the City of New York passed a collective-bargaining law establishing an Office of Collective Bargaining to bring the city's labor relations under central administration. Among other achievements, this office reduced the number of bargaining units to approximately 100 by 1975, and it established a city-wide bargaining unit for the negotiation of certain benefits that had to be uniform for employees covered by the city's career and salary plan. Nevertheless, the political element in the city's labor negotiations was never entirely removed, and despite the city's claims of increasing financial difficulties brought about by the recession of the early 1970s, and a reduction in federal grants-in-aid, unions continued to negotiate as if there were no serious economic constraints on the city. They obtained substantial increases in compensation throughout the first half of the 1970s.

Suddenly, in March 1975, with an operating deficit of $2 billion and a need to refinance $6 billion of outstanding short-term debt, the city was unable to market its securities and faced the prospect of imminent default. When it became clear that the city would not be able to manage the crisis itself, the State of New York took two actions. In an effort to address the immediate financial problems of the city, the state legislature created the Municipal Assistance Corporation (MAC) in June of 1975, and it authorized the agency (1) to sell securities to finance the short-term debt and operating expenses of New York City and (2) to impose certain limits on the city's budgeting and accounting practices. In September, in an effort to address more basic management problems in the city government, the legislature established a state Emergency Financial Control Board (EFCB) with authorization to intervene in city management in an effort to develop long-term solvency. The net impact of these extraordinary measures was to increase the influence of the state and of private investment interests in running New York City at the expense of the city's political leaders and groups, such as the unions representing public employees (who previously had considerable influence with the local leaders).

The public-employee unions adopted several equally unusual strategies in an effort to maintain their influence despite the shift in power. Faced with hostile public opinion and the possibility that a freeze might be imposed by the mayor (at the request of the MAC) on a scheduled wage increase, virtually all of the public unions altered their former bargaining structure to form a coalition that negotiated a more favorable wage deferral agreement with the city and MAC officials than would have been imposed on them. In particular, they were able to preserve their cost-of-living increases and to obtain a promise from the city to pay their previously negotiated (but frozen) wage increases after the fiscal crisis was over if productivity increases allowed for it. In the autumn of 1975, when the city again seemed on the brink of default, the unions extended their influence in the discussions of the city's rescue by committing their pension funds, whose assets exceeded $7 billion, to the purchase of MAC securities. (This played an important role in helping the city qualify for federal loans.) Given the shift of power to the state and federal government, and to private investors, brought about by the financial plight of New York, the only way for the unions to be major players in the negotiations over the fiscal rescue of the city was by altering traditional tactics and becoming major financiers of the city.

In subsequent negotiations, the public-employee unions further altered their traditional bargaining arrangements in order to adjust to the new economic environment of collective bargaining. Under a two-tier bargaining arrangement adopted in 1976, a coalition of the unions first established the general guidelines for a two-year agreement. Subsequently, individual unions in the coalition negotiated separate agreements which could differ in detail, but stayed within the basic economic limits of the framework established by the coalition.

SOURCES: Raymond D. Horton, "Economics, Politics, and Collective Bargaining: The Case of New York City" in David Lewin, Peter Feuille, and Thomas A. Kochan, eds., *Public Sector Labor Relations: Analysis and Readings* (Glen Ridge, N.J.: Thomas Horton & Daughters, 1977), pp. 205–17; David Lewin and Mary McCormick, "Coalition Bargaining in Municipal Government: The New York City Experience," *Industrial and Labor Relations Review* 34 (January 1981): 175–90.

REVIEW QUESTIONS

1. Critics of centralized bargaining units have argued that the best way to reduce the power of unions is to require that all contracts be negotiated at the plant level. Explain why you agree or disagree with this proposal.

2. A few American industries have adopted strike-insurance plans to reduce strike pressures. Why only a few? What may be the barriers to more widespread adoption of such plans?

3. Unionized plumbers are in unions that control the size of their membership. Wages are kept high by keeping membership highly qualified and therefore small. Employers needing or wanting to employ union labor must hire from the ranks of union membership. Suppose there is a plumbers' union in each of two cities. City A has an ordinance that states that all plumbing installations and repairs must be performed by union members. City B has no such ordinance. Analyze as completely as you can the effects of City A's ordinance on workers, consumers, and the general well-being of society. (*Hint:* you can gain insight into this question by comparing Cities A and B.)

4. The Jones Act mandates that at least 50 percent of all U.S. government-financed cargo must be transported in American-owned ships and that any American ship leaving an American port must have at least 90 percent of its crew composed of American citizens. What would you expect the impact of this act to be on the demand for labor in the shipping industry and the ability of unions to push up the wages of their members?

5. Suppose that a proposal for tax reductions associated with the purchase of capital equipment is up for debate. Suppose, too, that union leaders are called upon to comment on the proposal from the perspective of how it will affect the welfare of their members as workers (not consumers). Will they all agree on the effects of the proposal? Explain your answer.

SELECTED READINGS

A.H. Raskin, "The New York Newspaper Strike," *The New Yorker,* Part I (January 23, 1979): 41–87; Part II (January 29, 1979): 56–85.

Richard E. Walton, and Robert B. McKersie, *A Behavioral Theory of Negotiations* (New York: McGraw-Hill, 1965).

S. Herbert Unterberger and Edward C. Koziara, "Airline Strike Insurance: A Study in Escalation," *Industrial and Labor Relations Review* 29 (October 1975): 26–45.

Arnold R. Weber, "Stability and Change in the Structure of Collective Bargaining," in Lloyd Ulman, ed., *Challenges to Collective Bargaining* (Englewood Cliffs, N.J.: Prentice-Hall, Inc., 1967).

Arnold R. Weber, ed., *The Structure of Collective Bargaining* (Chicago: Graduate School of Business, 1964).

Chapter 15

LABOR DISPUTES AND DISPUTE RESOLUTION

Work stoppages and dispute resolution procedures are at the heart of the collective-bargaining process. Collective bargaining only works as a method of fixing the terms and conditions of employment, because a failure to agree can result in significant losses of income for both sides. The mere existence of the threat of a costly work stoppage or of an uncertain resolution of a labor dispute by a third party provides unions and management with a range of potential settlements—sometimes referred to as a *contract zone*—that are preferable to the losses associated with a work stoppage. It is the incentive to avoid such losses that induces labor and management to reach agreement without a work stoppage in the vast majority of collective-bargaining negotiations.

Unions are able to win management concessions at the bargaining table because of their ability to impose costs on management. These costs typically take the form of work slowdowns and strikes, but they may also come from having "outsiders" make decisions about the terms of a labor agreement (a point that we will fully discuss later in this chapter). A *strike* is a concerted refusal by union members to work. Termination of a strike is usually contingent on the granting of certain union demands by management, and without the strike weapon or the threat of binding arbitration, there would be little need for employers to take union demands very seriously. As noted in the previous chapter, however, employers are also able to impose costs on unions to the extent that employers have the capacity to endure or "take" a strike. Under certain circumstances, employers may also lock out their employees in the course of a labor dispute. A *lockout* is a refusal by an employer to let union members work. Conceptually, there may seem to be little practical difference between a lockout and taking a strike, but, as will be discussed, there are occasions when a lockout may have certain strategic advantages.

This chapter begins with a review of the basic trends in work stoppages in the United States and a discussion of how these trends relate to strike activity in other countries. One of the most notable features in the data is the different level of work-stoppage activity in the private and public sectors. We consider the public policy influences on this difference and then use elementary tools of labor-market analysis to evaluate the rationale for maintaining different public policies toward strikes in the private and public sectors.

Work stoppages do not occur randomly; in the aggregate, the level of strike activity varies systematically with economic events. Later in this chapter, we build on the political nature of union behavior discussed in Chapter 12 to consider some theories that link strike activity with economic developments. Because work stoppages can impose significant costs on society, most countries have, as a matter of public policy, considered other methods of resolving impasses. This has been particularly true in the United States with the rapid expansion of collective bargaining in the public sector. The final part of this chapter introduces several dispute-settlement procedures and considers the effect of these procedures on collective-bargaining behavior.

Profile of Strike Activity

Strike Frequency and Duration

While only a few major work stoppages are reported in the media, strikes are in fact a fairly common experience in industrial life. Table 15.1, for example, shows that in recent years, between 1 and 3 million workers have been involved in the 4,000 to 6,000 strikes occurring each year.[1] On the other hand, there are approximately 200,000 labor agreements in force in the United States, so that most collective-bargaining negotiations are concluded without a strike. In comparison to other countries, the United States has a relatively high *strike frequency* (usually measured as the number of strikes per thousand workers) and *strike duration* (usually measured as the number of working days lost per thousand workers), despite the fact that union membership is less extensive and less politically motivated than in most other countries.[2] One of the main reasons for this is that under the decentralized system of collective bargaining there are more negotiating situations in the United States and, hence, more opportunities for negotiations to break down. Therefore, the relatively high level of strike activity is related, in

---

[1]The data in Table 15.1 enumerate work stoppages, which include lockouts of employees by employers. However, employer lockouts occur infrequently, so that the figures in the table mainly reflect strike activity.

[2]Royal Commission on Trade Unions and Employer Associations, *Written Evidence of the Ministry of Labour* (London: HMSO, 1965), p. 69; Hugh Clegg, *Trade Unionism Under Collective Bargaining: A Theory Based on a Comparison of Six Countries* (Oxford: Basil Blackwell, 1976), p. 69.

Table 15.1. Work Stoppages in the United States, 1953–1979

Year	Number of Strikes	Workers Involved		Estimated Percentage of Working Time Lost	Unemployment Rate
		Number (in thousands)	As Percentage of Employed		
1953	5,091	2,400	4.7	0.22	2.9
1954	3,468	1,530	3.1	0.18	5.5
1955	4,320	2,650	5.2	0.22	4.4
1956	3,825	1,900	3.6	0.24	4.1
1957	3,673	1,390	2.6	0.12	4.3
1958	3,694	2,060	3.9	0.18	6.8
1959	3,708	1,880	3.3	0.50	5.5
1960	3,333	1,320	2.4	0.14	5.5
1961	3,367	1,450	2.6	0.11	6.7
1962	3,614	1,230	2.2	0.13	5.5
1963	3,362	941	1.1	0.11	5.7
1964	3,655	1,640	2.7	0.15	5.2
1965	3,963	1,550	2.5	0.15	4.5
1966	4,405	1,960	3.0	0.15	3.8
1967	4,595	2,870	4.3	0.25	3.8
1968	5,045	2,649	3.8	0.28	3.6
1969	5,700	2,481	3.5	0.24	3.5
1970	5,716	3,305	4.7	0.37	4.9
1971	5,138	3,280	4.5	0.26	5.9
1972	5,010	1,714	2.3	0.15	5.6
1973	5,353	2,251	2.9	0.14	4.9
1974	6,074	2,778	3.5	0.24	5.6
1975	5,031	1,746	2.2	0.16	8.5
1976	5,648	2,420	3.0	0.19	7.7
1977	5,506	2,040	2.4	0.17	7.1
1978	4,230	1,623	1.9	0.17	6.0
1979	4,800	1,700	1.6	0.15	5.8
1980	3,885	1,366	1.5	0.14	7.1

SOURCE: U.S. Bureau of Labor Statistics, *Handbook of Labor Statistics, 1980,* Bulletin 2070 (Washington, D.C.: U.S. Government Printing Office, 1980), Tables 28 and 167. U.S. Bureau of Labor Statistics, *Work Stoppages, 1980,* Summary 81-9 (Washington, D.C.: U.S. Government Printing Office, 1981), Table 1.

part, to the tendency for union-representation elections to be held at the plant level, under the unit-determination policies of the National Labor Relations Board (NLRB). In contrast, we noted in Chapter 14 that formal collective bargaining often occurs at the industry, regional, or even economywide level in Europe. The number of negotiations, or opportunities for a work stoppage to occur, is therefore much lower in countries with relatively centralized bargaining structures, although when a stoppage occurs it is likely to idle a large number of workers. What one would like to know from a careful comparison of the propensity to strike is how the probability that a negotiation will lead to a strike (that is, the number of strikes resulting from a given number of negotiations) varies across countries. Unfortunately, precise data on the total number of negotiating situations are not available.

There is, however, a second structural aspect of collective bargaining in the United States that may contribute to comparatively high strike levels. As a general rule, collective-bargaining agreements cover a wider range of issues in decentralized bargaining systems (for reasons discussed in the previous chapter), so that there is often more to resolve in American collective-bargaining negotiations and more potential for negotiations to reach an impasse. Issues of safety, production standards, and grievance procedures, for example, arise more frequently in plant-level collective bargaining in the United States than in more centralized negotiations abroad.

Besides being affected by the level of centralization in collective bargaining, the scope of bargaining may also be influenced by the presence of a labor or socialist party. Where such parties are in power, some have argued that many union goals may be achieved through legislation, and the burden placed on collective bargaining will be relatively light—causing the likelihood of strikes to be correspondingly low. It has also been argued that union-controlled labor parties discourage strikes in order to maintain a reasonably broad base of political support. Analyses of the relationship between strikes and the characteristics of political systems tend to show the opposite, however. Strikes tend to be higher when left-of-center governments are in power, perhaps because workers tend to have higher expectations concerning what they should be able to achieve.[3]

Wildcat Strikes

In addition to their frequency, a second important characteristic of strikes in the United States is that they are usually associated with officially sanctioned collective-bargaining negotiations. Unofficial, or *wildcat,* strikes that occur while a labor agreement is in effect account for less than ten percent of American work stoppages and tend to be concentrated in a few industries, such as coal. As can be seen from Table 15.2, strikes associated with attempts to negotiate an initial agreement with an employer are most frequently over issues of institutional security, while official strikes within the context of an established collective-bargaining relationship occur mainly during periods of renegotiation and are related to substantive issues of wages, hours, and employment conditions. Wildcat strikes, however, usually occur *during* the term of the contract and they often represent (a) attempts by groups within the union to secure gains that were not or could not be obtained in official negotiations or (b) protests against the manner in which certain provisions of the agreement are being administered (Table 15.2). Most collective-bargaining agreements include provisions that are designed to channel conflict into a grievance procedure (see Chapter 16) in order to avoid work stoppages during the term of the agreement, but in some cases workers seek a more rapid resolution of a complaint.[4]

---

[3]*See* Douglas A. Hibbs, Jr., "Industrial Conflict in Advanced Industrialized Societies," *American Political Science Review* 70 (December 1976): 1033–58; Martin Paldam and Peder J. Pedersen, "The Macroeconomic Strike Model: A Study of Seventeen Countries, 1948–1975," *Industrial and Labor Relations Review* 35 (July 1982): 504–21.

[4]Some labor agreements stipulate that certain issues are not subject to the normal dispute-resolution procedures, such as arbitration, that apply during the term of an agreement. Strikes over these issues while an agreement is in effect do not violate the contract.

Table 15.2. Strikes by Contract Status and Issue, 1961–1972 (in percent)

	Strikes with Given Issue				Workers Involved in Strikes with Given Issue			
	First Agree-ment	Renego-tiation	During Term	Other	First Agree-ment	Renego-tiation	During Term	Other
Wages, hours, and other contractual matters	31.1	89.6	10.8	60.6	39.1	81.2	13.7	61.1
Union organization and security	61.7	3.6	3.9	6.3	51.5	5.3	2.4	3.7
Job security, plant administration	5.1	5.1	49.9	24.6	4.5	12.4	63.5	26.6
Inter and intra union	1.5	0.2	27.7	4.4	4.3	0.3	13.5	4.1
Other work conditions	0.6	1.5	7.8	4.2	0.6	0.8	6.9	4.5
All	100	100	100	100	100	100	100	100

Note: Some columns may not add to 100 because of rounding error

SOURCE: P. K. Edwards, *Strikes in the United States 1881–1974* (New York: St. Martin's Press, 1981) p. 183.

One important reason for the relatively low level of wildcat-strike activity is the fact that the labor agreement is a legally binding contract between a union and an employer, so that if a strike occurs during the term of the agreement, the union as an organization may be liable for damages along with the individuals responsible for the strike. (For example, the United Mine Workers has been fined several times for unofficial strikes that occurred in the coal fields.) For this reason, it is not unusual to see both the employer and the officers of a national union attempting to end an unofficial strike. By way of contrast, in the United Kingdom where the labor agreement is not a binding legal document, unofficial strikes are common.

Public-Sector Strikes

A third feature of American work stoppages is that the level of strike activity is distinctly lower in the public sector than in the private sector. Strikes in the public sector were almost nonexistent until the mid-1960s, but have increased substantially since then as union organization has spread, particularly at the state and local level. Despite the significant increase in public-sector strike activity, however, the general level (adjusted for numbers employed) remains considerably lower. One reason for this is the distinctly different legal status of strikes in the private and public sectors, an issue to which we now turn.

Legal Status of Strikes

The difference in the legal treatment of strikes in the private and public sectors is easily explained: there is no constitutional right to strike in the United States, so that whatever rights exist must be provided by statute. Federal labor-relations statutes guarantee the right to strike in the private sector, but most state and federal government legislation actually prohibits strikes by public employees.

This legal stance raises three general issues concerning the collective withholding of labor services to support collective-bargaining demands: (1) what is meant by the right to strike; (2) what limitations, if any, are placed on the right to strike in the private sector; and (3) should public policy toward strikes differ in the private and public sectors? We will address each of these issues as we examine the legal status of strikes in the private and public sectors separately.

Legal Status of Strikes in the Private Sector

Employee rights. The first statutory source of public policy toward strikes in the private sector was the Norris-LaGuardia Act of 1932, which basically immunized from injunction peacefully conducted strikes. One consequence of the statute was that federal judges lost the power to decide whether or not the purposes of a particular strike were lawful. This general right-to-strike was extended by Section 7 of the National Labor Relations Act (NLRA), which provided that "employees have the right . . . to engage in other concerted activities for the purpose of collective bargaining or other mutual aid or protection. . . ."

Taken literally, the language of the NLRA seems to provide a broad protection to almost any action taken by a group of workers; it might also be viewed as drastically circumscribing employer anti-strike actions, since almost any action that an employer might take could be interpreted as interfering with the rights provided by Section 7. In fact, the courts have not provided such broad protection to strikers or applied such broad restrictions to employers. While the legal right-to-strike in the private sector prohibits employers from discharging or disciplining employees who strike, the key to a statutory right-to-strike is the replacement rights accorded to striking employees. Employees *always* have a constitutional right to quit their jobs—individually or in groups—to protest disagreeable working conditions. A strike occurs when a group of workers temporarily leave their jobs in an effort to change the terms of employment. The difference lies in the expectation that striking employees will be reinstated at the end of the strike. Yet, even in the private sector, the reinstatement right is not absolute.

Shortly after the passage of the NLRA, the Supreme Court held that in a normal economic strike, the employer has a right to hire permanent replacements for striking employees.[5] Once the strike is over, however, strikers who have been replaced must be given preference for employment as vacancies occur. Moreover, strikers who have been replaced retain a right to vote in an NLRB election to determine the union's status at the plant for a year after their replacement. Without such a right, an employer might simply replace striking employees with workers who were not sympathetic to unions in order to reduce support for the union in the plant.

Not all employers in the private sector take advantage of their legal right to replace striking employees, however, since it may be difficult to find replacements with the specific skills needed. Moreover, attempts to bring in replacements

---

[5]*Mackay Radio and Telegraph Co.*, 304 U.S. 333 (1938). Employers may also replace workers who exercise their legal right to refuse to cross a picket line during a strike.

during the course of a strike often create considerable tension and even violence. For similar reasons, employers in the public sector often do not exercise their legal right to discharge or discipline public employees who strike. Overall, when viewed in terms of the implications for job security, the difference between the right to strike in the private and public sectors is not as great as is frequently thought.

In contrast to reinstatement rights pertaining to normal economic strikes, if a strike occurs as a result of an employer unfair labor-practice, the employees who went out on strike have an absolute right to reinstatement, even if it means displacing replacements that the employer hired during the course of the strike. If the law did not make a distinction between economic and unfair labor-practice strikes, an employer could eliminate a union from the plant by violating the law —that is, by provoking a union into a strike by committing unfair labor practices and then replacing the union strikers with new nonunion employees.

The fact that the reinstatement rights of striking workers rest on whether the employer has committed an unfair labor practice creates an incentive for the union to file unfair labor-practice charges during negotiations, and even to try inducing the employer into committing an unfair labor practice in order to protect the reinstatement rights of its members. If an employer does not commit an unfair labor practice, he or she can replace all strikers. If an employer violates the act, however, employees who have struck must be reinstated. In 1982, for example, the players in the National Football League went on strike when team owners refused to bargain over certain pay proposals. The players argued that the owners' refusal to bargain was an unfair labor practice (see discussion in Chapter 13) giving the players full reinstatement rights. This obviously introduces an important element of gamesmanship into bargaining.

Limits on employees' right to strike. The seemingly broad rights accorded concerted pressure activities by employees by the language of Section 7 of the NLRA may also be limited because of (1) the method used, (2) the purpose of the activity, or (3) the activity being taken separately from a certified union. With respect to methods, violent strikes are illegal, as are nonviolent harassment tactics such as intermittent strikes or disparagement of the employer's product. With respect to illegal purposes, we noted above the proscription against wildcat strikes (that is, strikes in violation of a no-strike clause in a labor agreement). Strikes intended to force an employer to violate a law are also illegal, as are strikes in support of union-organizing activities, which could threaten the NLRA principle of employee free-choice by either coercing employees to join (or employers to recognize) a union.

As we noted in our discussion of union unfair labor practices in Chapter 13, "secondary" strikes or boycotts—that is, strikes against neutral firms that are not a party to the collective-bargaining agreement—are also forbidden. This has been a difficult area for public policy. A moment's reflection reveals one reason— virtually all strikes have harmful effects on firms that are not a party to the collective-bargaining agreement! If a strike curtails or shuts down production at a company (the "primary" employer), that company's suppliers ("secondary" employers) lose orders and often have to lay off workers. Similarly, the company's customers (who also are secondary employers) suffer harm unless substitutes for the struck good are readily available. If the struck good is used in the production processes of other industries (for example, steel), the secondary effects of the strike may be quite substantial as the struck company's customers curtail production and employment.

Nevertheless, these secondary effects of a union's strike do not constitute an illegal secondary boycott because the union's action is not aimed directly at neutrals. A secondary boycott arises when, in addition to (or instead of) striking the primary employer, a union also strikes or otherwise brings direct pressure against a neutral employer. For example, an illegal secondary boycott normally occurs if a union strikes a supplier of the primary employer in order to induce the latter to settle on its terms.

In certain important situations, however, direct action against a secondary firm does not constitute illegal activity. One exception occurs if secondary employers take actions that effectively make them a party to the primary dispute. For example, if employers are found to be *allies* of a struck employer, they lose their neutrality; unions are permitted to strike an ally even though the ally is not directly involved in the labor dispute. Allies include firms with common ownership or management, as well as independent companies who knowingly accept work that otherwise would have been performed by the struck employer.[6] An example of this situation arose when a typewriter company, Royal, which normally maintained machines that it leased to outside companies, was struck by a union representing some of its employees. During the strike, the company gave the maintenance work normally performed by its employees to another company. When the union proceeded to picket the second company, it was charged with conducting a secondary boycott. The Supreme Court rejected the charge, however, ruling that the second firm had injected itself into the dispute as an ally when it accepted the work from Royal.

A second exception to the proscription against secondary boycotts has been "common situs" picketing, which has been one of the more prominent labor policy disputes involving secondary boycott issues over the past few years. Common situs picketing problems arise when both primary and secondary employers perform duties at the same location—for example, a general contractor and several subcontractors at a construction site. In this situation, one or more unions might picket the unionized general contractor at a construction site in an effort to induce him to cease doing business with a nonunion subcontractor. If there is no direct dispute between the general contractor and the union, the Supreme Court has ruled that this constitutes illegal secondary activity, since the object of picketing is to use an "innocent" third party to bring pressure to bear on the party with which the union has a dispute.[7] An entire worksite cannot be shut down legally because of a dispute between a union and one subcontractor. On the other hand, legal picketing can occur at a common situs if a reserve gate is established for workers who are not involved in the dispute and there is no picketing or interference with that gate.

---

[6] *AFL-CIO Brewery Workers' Union (Adolph Coors Co.),* 121 NLRB 35 (1958).
[7] *NLRB* v. *Denver Building Trades,* 341 U.S. 675 (1951).

Construction unions have been deeply opposed to this interpretation of the law, particularly since the substantial growth of nonunion construction work during the 1970s. To date, however, they have not been successful in obtaining legislation that would permit broader common situs picketing.

A third exception occurs if unions picket peacefully at a secondary establishment in an effort to persuade consumers not to buy *a particular product* sold by that establishment. The Supreme Court has ruled that this is legal activity.[8] However, if the picket signs, handbills, or any other aspect of the union's communications urge consumers not to patronize the establishment, the activity becomes an illegal secondary boycott. This issue arises most frequently in the picketing of retail stores. In the campaign to organize the J. P. Stevens Company (discussed previously in Example 13.3) the labor movement launched a nationwide consumer boycott of the *products* of the company. Interestingly, when the United Farm Workers were organizing in the California grape fields during the late 1960s, they were legally able to urge consumers to boycott *stores* selling nonunion grapes—because agriculture is not covered by the NLRA!

Actions by other than certified unions, taken at unionized locations, are also not protected by the NLRA. Such actions include strikes by unions that do not represent a majority of the workers in a bargaining unit (that is, unions that have lost an NLRB union-representation election) and actions taken by groups of employees independently of their union. (For an example of the latter, see Example 15.1.) These actions are unprotected because they are inconsistent with the principle of exclusive representation that forms the core of a union's rights and duties under American labor law. Efforts by other unions or groups of employees to determine employment conditions in the bargaining unit independently of the certified bargaining representative would undermine the legal effort to establish a single voice for employees with respect to employment conditions.

EXAMPLE 15.1

The Emporium Case: Can Workers Bring Action Independently of Their Union?

To what extent can a group of union members take action independently of the union to secure rights that they believe are guaranteed to them by public policy? The following case provides an interesting review of the issues raised by such activity. The language describing the situation is that of the U.S. Supreme Court:

This case presents the question whether, in light of the national policy against racial discrimination in employment, the National Labor Relations Act protects concerted activity by a group of minority employees to bargain with their employer over issues of employment discrimination. . . .

The Emporium Capwell Company (the Company) operates a department store in San Francisco . . . [and] was a party to the collective-bargaining

---

[8]*NLRB* v. *Fruit and Vegetable Packers, Local 760* ("Tree Fruits"), 377 U.S. 58 (1964).

agreement negotiated by . . . the Department Store Employees' Union (the Union). The agreement, in which the Union was recognized as the sole collective-bargaining agency for all covered employees, prohibited employment discrimination by reason of race, color, creed, national origin, age, or sex, as well as union activity. It had a no-strike or lockout clause, and it established grievance and arbitration machinery for processing any claimed violation of the contract, including a violation of the antidiscrimination clause.

On April 3, 1968, a group of Company employees covered by the agreement met with the Secretary-Treasurer of the Union, Walter Johnson, to present a list of grievances including a claim that the Company was discriminating on the basis of race in making assignments and promotions. . . . [The union investigated the charges of discrimination,] concluded that the Company was discriminating, and [announced] that it would process every such grievance through to arbitration if necessary. . . .

[Later some employees] expressed their view that the contract procedures were inadequate to handle a systemic grievance of this sort; they suggested that the Union instead begin picketing the store in protest. Johnson explained that the collective agreement bound the Union to its processes. . . .

[Subsequently,] several . . . dissident employees held a press conference . . . at which they denounced the store's employment policy as racist, reiterated their desire to deal directly with "the top management" of the Company over minority employment conditions, and announced their intention to picket and institute a boycott of the store. . . . [Later,] employees picketed the store throughout the day and urged consumers not to patronize the store. Johnson encountered the picketing employees, again urged them to rely on the grievance process, and warned that they might be fired for their activities. The picketers, however, were not dissuaded, and they continued to press their demand to deal directly with the Company president. . . . When the conduct was repeated . . . the two employees were fired.

When the case reached the Supreme Court, the Court ruled against the employees on the grounds that their activity undermined the union's status as the exclusive representative of employees within the bargaining unit. If the union had refused to represent the interests of minorities within the bargaining unit, legal remedies were available, but this was obviously not the case in this situation. An employer facing demands from each of several groups is unlikely to be able to satisfy each simultaneously and still fulfill the contractual obligations. Similarly, a union, as an organization for collective action, has a legitimate interest in presenting a united front and "in not seeing its strength dissipated and its stature denigrated by subgroups within the unit separately pursuing what they see as separate interests. . . . The policy of industrial self-determination as expressed in Section 7 does not require fragmentation of the bargaining unit along racial or other lines in order to consist with the national labor policy against discrimination."

SOURCE: *Emporium Capwell Co.* v. *Western Addition Community Organization,* 420 U.S. 50 (1975).

Employers' rights. What actions can employers take during a labor dispute in defense of their interests? This question has raised difficult issues for the NLRB and the courts, for while an employer has a right to operate a business effectively, almost any action taken by an employer in the course of a labor dispute technically involves discriminating against employees on the basis of their union membership. For many years the use of the employer *lockout*—closing a plant in the course of a labor dispute—was restricted by the courts to situations where (1) the timing of a strike by a union could create unusual hardship for the employer because of the perishable nature of the product or the seasonal nature of production, and (2) a multiemployer bargaining unit existed and the union struck only one member of the unit. In this case, a lockout might be required to defend and preserve the multiemployer nature of the contract.

With a ruling in 1965, however, the Supreme Court permitted employers to use the lockout offensively in situations where a labor agreement with a union had expired and a bargaining impasse had developed over mandatory bargaining issues.[9] The Court held that the right to strike in the private sector provided by the NLRA did not carry with it the presumption that the unions have the exclusive right to determine the timing and duration of work stoppages. At the same time, the Court ruled that the use of lockouts must be in defense of a legitimate bargaining position rather than an effort to discourage unionization. One important difference between a strike and a lockout is that workers who are locked out by an employer have a right to be reinstated at the end of the dispute, whereas workers who strike do not. Since the hiring of permanent replacements is legal if the union initiates a work stoppage but is not legal if the employer does, some employers may try to enhance their long-term bargaining position by waiting for the union to strike rather than using their legal right to lock out employees once an impasse has been reached.

Legal Status of Strikes in the Public Sector

Perhaps the most critical issue concerning public policy toward labor disputes in the past 25 years has been raised by the rapid growth of unions and strike activity in the public sector. The recent growth of public-sector unions was analyzed in Chapter 12, and the broad outlines of the increased militancy among public employees is described by the data in Table 15.3. In particular, it can be seen that, after years of relatively placid labor relations in the public sector, 1966 marked a transition to a higher level of strike activity.

While the growth of work stoppages has increased more rapidly among public employees than private employees since the mid-1960s, the level of strike activity among government employees remains low relative to the private sector. In 1978, for example, 0.04 percent of working time at all levels of government was lost as a result of work stoppages, as against 0.17 percent of working time in all industries. Public-sector strikes tend on average to be shorter but to involve

---

[9]*American Ship Building* v. *NLRB,* 380 U.S. 300 (1965).

Table 15.3. Work Stoppages by Level of Government, 1958–1979 (workers in thousands)

	All Levels of Government		Federal Government		State Government		Local Government	
	Number of Stoppages	Workers Involved	Number of Stoppages	Workers Involved	Number of Stoppages	Workers Involved	Number of Stoppages	Workers Involved
1958	15	1.7	—	—	1	a	14	1.7
1959	25	2.0	—	—	4	0.4	21	1.6
1960	36	28.6	—	—	3	1.0	33	27.6
1961	28	6.6	—	—	—	—	28	6.6
1962	28	31.1	5	4.2	2	1.7	21	25.3
1963	29	4.8	—	—	2	0.3	27	4.6
1964	41	22.7	—	—	4	0.3	37	22.5
1965	42	11.9	—	—	—	—	42	11.9
1966	142	105.0	—	—	9	3.1	133	102.0
1967	181	132.0	—	—	12	4.7	169	127.0
1968	254	201.8	3	1.7	16	9.3	235	190.9
1969	411	160.0	2	0.6	37	20.5	372	139.0
1970	412	333.5	3	155.8	23	8.8	386	168.9
1971	329	152.6	2	1.0	23	14.5	304	137.1
1972	375	142.1	—	—	40	27.4	335	114.7
1973	387	196.4	1	0.5	29	12.3	357	183.7
1974	384	160.7	2	0.5	34	24.7	348	135.4
1975	478	318.5	—	—	32	66.6	446	252.0
1976	378	180.7	1	a	25	33.8	352	146.8
1977	413	170.2	2	0.4	44	33.7	367	136.2
1978	481	193.7	1	4.8	45	17.9	435	171.0
1979	593	254.1	—	—	57	48.6	536	205.5
1980	536	223.6	1	.9	45	10.0	493	212.7

aFewer than 100.

SOURCE: U.S. Bureau of Labor Statistics, *Work Stoppages in Government, 1980* Bulletin 2110 (Washington, D.C.: U.S. Government Printing Office, October 1981) p. 4.

larger bargaining units than private-sector strikes. While there are many small bargaining units, there are also many that are huge. In 1979, 12,000 Chicago transit workers left their jobs for 4 days. In 1970, there was a nationwide strike by postal workers. In Detroit, 19,300 teachers struck for 13 days in 1979, and, three years later, 11,000 teachers struck for three weeks. Also in 1982, a nationwide strike by some 12,000 air-traffic controllers resulted in the dismissal of the union's membership—an unusual event in the public sector. However, the average number of days that a worker is on strike in the public sector is about half as long as in the private sector.

Eighty to ninety percent of all government strike activity involves employees of local-government units (cities, counties, or special districts), and virtually all of the remainder is at the state level. Over half of the strikes by government employees are in the education sector. While strikes by police and firefighters are usually highly publicized, they accounted for less than 10 percent of strike activity in the public sector in the late 1970s.

The remarkable fact about the surge of strike activity in the public sector since the mid-1960s is that it is virtually all illegal. Although unions representing public-sector employees have long claimed a constitutional right to strike, the federal courts have not supported this claim. Any right to strike must be provided by statutes, such as the Norris-LaGuardia Act and the National Labor Relations Act in the private sector. In general, no comparable legislation exists in the public sector. While most states have passed legislation permitting collective bargaining by public employees, only a few states have also accorded public employees the right to strike. Those that have passed such legislation have not extended the right to strike to police officers or firefighters.

Why should public policy toward unions in the public sector differ from policy toward private-sector unions? If the strike weapon is necessary to compel collective bargaining in the private sector, why is it not equally necessary in the public sector? These questions, which have been under debate for decades, came under intense re-examination during the 1970s. One argument advanced for not extending the right to strike to the public sector is that collective bargaining in the public sector is less necessary to eliminate inequalities of bargaining power between labor and management.[10] It is argued that if inequalities of bargaining power are unlikely in the first place, providing labor groups with the right to strike will *create* inequalities that will place public employers at a disadvantage. The case against allowing public employees to strike is usually based on two assertions: (a) the demand for labor is less elastic in the public than in the private sector, and (b) the political power of unionized public employees, when buttressed by the economic power inherent in the right to strike, would distort the overall influence of public employees beyond their numbers in a community.

Wage elasticity of demand for public employees. It is often argued that the costs to society of collective bargaining are greater in the public sector than in the private sector, because the economic restraints on collective bargaining are much weaker in the nonmarket environment of government. We have seen how the demand for labor in the private sector is derived, in part, from the demand for a product or service, which itself is closely related to the product's price. Therefore, unions in the private sector face a difficult trade-off between the wages they negotiate (which influence product prices) and the employment of union members. In contrast, the argument runs, government typically does not sell a product for which there are close substitutes, or for which demand is very responsive to price. In short, the "conventional wisdom" has been that, because many forms of public services are both monopolized and "essential," the demand for public employees is wage inelastic (relative to the demand for labor in the private sector), so that the wage demands of unions representing public employees are less likely to be tempered by concern over potential loss of employment by union members.

Generally speaking, this argument is not strongly supported by the evidence. At the conceptual level, government services do carry a price—taxes. When consumers of government services feel that the tax-price has become too high,

---

[10]This view has been developed most forcefully by Harry H. Wellington and Ralph K. Winter, Jr., in *The Unions and the Cities* (Washington, D.C.: The Brookings Institution, 1971).

they have several options. Individuals and businesses can and do move to other cities or states where the taxes they pay for comparable services are lower. In so doing, they reduce the tax base of the jurisdiction that they leave, thereby reducing the ability of that jurisdiction to provide the same level of government services and government employment. Taxpayers may also adopt tax-limitation legislation or constitutional amendments that roll back taxes and drastically limit the ability of all levels of government in a state to increase future tax revenues, and they may vote out of office political leaders who do not keep taxes down. Also, as unions in New York and in several other major cities faced with fiscal crises discovered during the 1970s, the unseen parties at the bargaining table are often the investors in a city's bonds. When there are difficulties in floating a bond issue, cities have financial incentives similar to those faced by private employers to keep wage costs down and seek greater efficiency in the utilization of labor. Moreover, public sector jurisdictions can go bankrupt. In June 1983, for example, the San Jose, California, Unified School District declared itself insolvent and filed for bankruptcy when it ran out of funds to pay teachers and other employees of the District.

It is also important to keep in mind that the elasticity of demand for labor is affected by more than the characteristics of product demand. First, labor costs in the public sector form a very large proportion of total costs, which tends to make the demand for labor more elastic than it would otherwise be. Second, public employers who are faced with financial pressures have more opportunities for factor and product substitution than is commonly recognized. One can easily think of substituting capital for labor in the provision of public services. For example, police patrol cars could be substituted for officers on the beat, thus making it possible for the same area to be patrolled by fewer officers. Snowblowers could be substituted for snow-removal workers with shovels, and school buildings can be redesigned to hold larger classes. Further, private firms can provide the same services now provided publicly: garbage pick-up, towing of parking violators, and street repair work could be subcontracted to private employers, or private companies could be hired to handle janitorial services in public buildings. Further, given the limited resources that state and local governments can command, an increase in the relative price of one service should lead a government to substitute other services that would be relatively cheaper (for example, minimally supervised playground programs could be substituted for summertime instructional programs in sports or crafts). In other words, while a local government does not have the option of moving its plant to a nonunion area, it can substitute capital for labor, change its services, or subcontract with private firms if it feels its labor costs are too high. Hence, it is *not* obvious *a priori* that the economic constraints on collective bargaining are weaker in the public sector than in the private sector.

The operational question raised by these observations is whether the wage elasticities of demand for state- and local-government employees are inelastic. Three studies have presented estimates of the wage elasticities of demand for eleven functional categories of state- and local-government employees, and these studies are summarized in Table 15.4.[11] In the main, these estimates suggest that demand curves for labor in state and local government *are* generally inelastic. The estimates also indicate that the scope for substitution for labor varies among the government functions. As expected, the services of police, fire, and public health workers appear to be most essential (that is, the wage elasticity of these groups of workers is lowest), while there appears to be greater scope for substitution for employees in education, streets and highways, and public welfare. Nevertheless, the estimated elasticities do not appear substantially lower in absolute value than the private-sector wage-elasticities of demand that were summarized in Table 4.1. Regardless of these estimates, one should recall, as stressed in Chapter 14, that public employees are also voters and, through the political process, seek to increase (shift) the demand for their own services.[12] To the extent that they are successful, the employment loss that would be associated with any wage increase would be smaller than if the demand curve had not been shifted out.

Table 15.4. Estimates of Wage Elasticities of Demand for Labor in the State and Local Sector

Category	(1)	(2)	(3)
Education	−1.06	−0.08 to −0.57	−0.57 to −0.82
Noneducation	−0.38		
Streets and highways	−0.09	−0.44 to −0.64	
Public welfare	−0.32	−0.33 to −1.13	
Hospitals	−0.30	−0.30 to −0.51	
Public health	−0.12	−0.26 to −0.32	
Police	−0.29	−0.01 to −0.35	
Fire	−0.53	−0.23 to −0.31	
Sanitation and sewage	−0.23	−0.40 to −0.56	
Natural resources	−0.39	−0.39 to −0.60	
General control and financial administration	−0.28	−0.09 to −0.34	

SOURCES:
(1) Orley Ashenfelter and Ronald Ehrenberg, "The Demand for Labor in the Public Sector" in *Labor in the Public and Nonprofit Sectors,* ed. Daniel Hamermesh (Princeton, N.J.: Princeton University Press, 1975), Table 6.
(2) Ronald G. Ehrenberg, "The Demand for State and Local Government Employees," *American Economic Review* 63 (June 1973): 366–79.
(3) Robert J. Thornton, "The Elasticity of Demand for Public School Teachers," *Industrial Relations* 18 (Winter 1979): 86–91.

[11]Orley Ashenfelter and Ronald G. Ehrenberg, "The Demand for Labor in the Public Sector," in *Labor in the Public and Nonprofit Sectors,* ed. Daniel Hamermesh (Princeton, N.J.: Princeton University Press, 1975); Ronald G. Ehrenberg, "The Demand for State and Local Government Employees," *American Economic Review,* 63 (June 1973): 366–79; and Robert Thornton, "The Elasticity of Demand for Public School Teachers," *Industrial Relations* 18 (Winter 1979): 86–91.

[12]For a recent treatment of this point *see* Paul Courant, Edward Gramlich, and Daniel Rubinfeld, "Public Employee Market Power and the Level of Government Spending," *American Economic Review* 69 (December 1979): 806–17.

Distortions of influence. A second line of argument advanced in opposition to extending the right to strike to public employees concerns potential distortions of the political process. This view begins with the observation that what a mayor, governor, or other chief executive gives unions must be taken away from some other group, and that political chief executives are inclined to allocate resources among different groups on the basis of their relative power. It is then argued that with the economic power that comes with the right to strike, public-sector unions would have an advantage over other groups who could rely only on political power. The result would be that the public would pressure government officials to settle labor disputes quickly and that this pressure would lower employer resistance in the public sector.

The main difficulty with this view is that it exaggerates the distinction between economic and political power in the context of public-sector collective bargaining. While elected officials are often attentive to the number of votes a group may be able to deliver (a type of political power), the political leverage of groups other than unions frequently appears to rest on economic considerations. For example, lobbying activities are frequently tied to the economic support of political figures via campaign contributions. As noted earlier, businesses can threaten to reduce the tax and employment base by moving to another political jurisdiction if a city does not keep down taxes (a large fraction of which are driven up by labor costs). Investors may be unwilling to acquire a city's debt if the city government appears to have weak control over its labor costs and productivity.[13] It is difficult to draw a clear distinction between these methods of bringing political pressure against a public-sector employer and the use of a strike by unions. In recent years, the popularity of tax-limitation movements in several states suggests that far from bringing pressure on a public employer to settle a labor dispute rapidly, the voting public may be more supportive of political leaders who offer considerable resistance to union bargaining-demands.

Theories of Strike Activity

It is obvious that strikes can impose serious losses of income on both workers and firms. If strikes involve costs to both union members and employers, why do they ever occur? It would seem that if both parties were aware of these costs, they would have an incentive to reach a settlement before a strike results. In fact, as we have seen earlier in the chapter, only a small fraction of collective-bargaining negotiations result in strikes in any one year. Nevertheless, strikes do occur even in experienced collective-bargaining relationships, and students of labor relations have long been interested in the reasons for the significant variations in strike activity over time and across industries. Despite the apparent irrationality of

---

[13]For a discussion of these considerations and a generally skeptical view of the argument that the political process would be distorted if public employees had the right to strike, *see* John F. Burton, Jr., and Charles Krider, "The Role and Consequences of Strikes by Public Employees," *Yale Law Journal:* 79 (January 1970): 418–40.

strikes between well-informed negotiators, the variations in observed strike behavior appear to be too strong to be attributed to accidents or miscalculations.

Most models of the collective-bargaining process focus on the likely division of the spoils between management and employees and ignore the determinants of strike activity. The first, and also simplest, model of strikes in the bargaining process was developed by Sir John Hicks.[14] Suppose that management and labor are bargaining over only one issue—the size of the wage increase to be granted. How would the percentage increase that the union demands and the increase that the employer is willing to grant vary with the expected duration of a strike?

On the employer side of the market, the longer a strike lasts, the more costly it becomes in terms of lost customers. As noted in Chapter 14, struck firms may suffer a permanent loss of market share to the extent that former customers are able to find other suppliers or substitutes for their work. This increasing cost suggests that, as a strike progresses, an employer should be willing to increase the wage offer; this willingness is denoted by the upward-sloping *employer-concession schedule, EC,* in Figure 15.1.

On the employee side of the market, union members' attitudes may be hardened by a feeling of solidarity in the initial phases of a strike, and they may actually increase their wage demands during the early part of a strike. However, after some point, the loss in income that union members are individually suffering begins to color their attitudes, and they should begin to reduce their wage demands. This reduction is indicated by the *union resistance curve, UR,* in Figure 15.1, which eventually becomes downward-sloping.

As the strike proceeds, then, the union's demands decrease and the employer's offer increases until at strike duration (S_0) the two coincide. At this

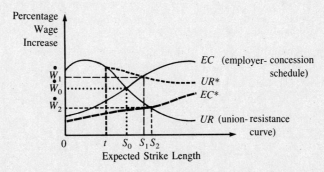

Figure 15.1 Hicks' Bargaining Model and Expected Strike Length

point, a settlement can be reached, the parties agree upon a wage increase of $\dot{W}_0$, and the strike will be terminated.

---

[14]John R. Hicks, *The Theory of Wages,* 2nd ed. (New York: St. Martin's Press, 1966), pp. 136–57.

It is interesting to note, however, that *if* each party were aware of the position and shape of the other party's curve, each would know in advance both the strike length and the size of the ultimate settlement. Thus, it would make sense for each party to agree to a settlement of $\dot{W}_0$ *prior* to the strike so that they *both* could avoid incurring the costs associated with the strike.

If such a settlement could be made in advance, why would strikes ever occur? One reason is that information is imperfect; one or both sides in the negotiation could fail to convey the true shape and position of their schedule to the other party.[15] A second reason is that to enhance their bargaining positions and retain the credibility of the threat of a strike, unions may have to periodically use the weapon; a strike may be designed to influence *future* negotiations.[16] Finally, strikes may be useful devices by which the internal solidarity of a union can be enhanced against a commonly perceived adversary—the employer.[17]

The major problem with these explanations of when a strike will occur is that they do not enable one to predict whether a strike will occur in a particular contract negotiation and, more important, they do not offer any insights about why the aggregate level of strike activity should vary over time.

Despite the fact that the Hicks model seems to emphasize strikes as the result of faulty or incomplete information, this simple model of the bargaining process can be useful in predicting the effects of changes in the bargaining environment on the outcome of collective bargaining. That is, it provides a description of how factors that influence the bargaining environment may influence the final settlement, even if it does not provide a good description of when strikes are likely to occur. For example, consider the effects of permitting strikers to collect unemployment insurance after some waiting period, *t.* By increasing the financial support of striking union members, this policy should raise the union resistance curve to the right of point *t* in Figure 15.1 to *UR**. The model therefore predicts that the effect of permitting strikers to collect unemployment insurance is to raise the final wage increase to $\dot{W}_1$ unless the waiting period, *t,* is greater than S_0.[18]

As a second example, consider the effects of a strike-insurance arrangement among employers, similar to those discussed in the previous chapter. With the revenues from strike insurance available to defray at least partially the costs of a strike, employers will be under less pressure to make concessions and will, therefore, be willing to hold out longer before agreeing to a union wage proposal.

---

[15]In the words of Hicks, "The majority of strikes are doubtless the results of faulty negotiations," Hicks, *The Theory of Wages,* p. 146.

[16]Lest one carry this "rusty weapon" argument too far, the reader should consider its implication for the use of nuclear weapons.

[17]Richard Walton and Robert McKersie, *A Behavioral Theory of Labor Negotiations* (New York: McGraw-Hill, 1965), p. 32.

[18]Thus, it is often alleged—although there is no strong empirical evidence as yet—that the level of strike activity is higher in the two states, New York and Rhode Island, that allow workers on strike to collect (after a waiting period) unemployment-insurance benefits. This example implicitly assumes that the unemployment benefits paid out have no effect on the unemployment-benefits tax paid by the employer.

In terms of Figure 15.1, the employer-concession schedule will shift downward to *EC** and this will tend to reduce the size of the final collective-bargaining settlement (to $\dot{W}_2$ in Figure 15.1).

The limitations of the Hicks model can be illustrated with reference to Table 15.1, which presents data on work stoppages in the United States during a recent 27-year period. These data suggest that strike activity, as measured either by the percentage of workers involved in strikes or the percentage of estimated working time lost, is cyclical, increasing when unemployment rates are low and decreasing when unemployment rates are high. To be useful, a model of strike activity should be able to explain this and other observed relationships between strike activity and economic and social events. One such model is discussed in the following section.

A Political Model of Strike Activity

Although there is no universally accepted model of strike activity, Orley Ashenfelter and George Johnson have recently built upon Arthur Ross's earlier work and developed what is essentially a political model of strike activity.[19] Their approach illustrates how the maximization models of economists can be generalized to incorporate noneconomic variables and allows us to analyze the effects of the Landrum-Griffin Act on the level of strike activity.

The Ashenfelter-Johnson model is based upon the premise that it is inappropriate to view the collective-bargaining process as involving only two parties, an employer and a union. Rather, they acknowledge that different members of the union will have different, and sometimes conflicting, objectives (as noted in the model of internal union decision-making in Chapter 12 above). Their focus is on the divergence in objectives between union members and union leaders. While union members are concerned primarily with their pecuniary and nonpecuniary conditions of employment, union leaders are also concerned about the survival and growth of the union and their own personal political survival.

Union leaders, who have been actively involved with management in the bargaining process, may have much better information than rank-and-file union members about the employer's true financial position and the maximum wage settlement the union will be able to extract. If this settlement is smaller than the membership wants, the union leaders face two options.

On the one hand, union leaders can return to their members, try to convince them of the employer's true financial picture, and recommend that management's last offer (the maximum that they know they can achieve) be accepted. The danger they face with this option is that the members may vote down the recommendation, accuse the leaders of selling out to management, and ultimately vote them out of office.

---

[19]Arthur Ross, *Trade Union Wage Policy* (Berkeley, Calif.: University of California Press, 1948), and Orley Ashenfelter and George Johnson, "Bargaining Theory, Trade Unions, and Industrial Strike Activity," *American Economic Review* 59 (March 1969): 35–49. A more recent test of the model is found in Henry Farber, "Bargaining Theory, Wage Outcomes, and the Occurrence of Strikes," *American Economic Review* 68 (June 1978): 262–71.

On the other hand, union leaders can return to their members and recommend that the members go out on strike. This recommendation will allow them to appear to be strong, militant leaders, even though the leaders themselves know that the strike will not lead to a larger settlement. However, after a strike of some duration, in accordance with the notion of the union-resistance curve in Figure 15.1, union members will begin to moderate their wage demands, and ultimately, a settlement—for which the union leaders will receive credit—will be reached. Since the latter strategy is the one that is more likely to maintain the union's strength *and* keep the leaders in office, it is the strategy leaders may opt for, even though it is clearly not in their members' best interests in the short run (the members have to bear the costs of the strike).

The above model can provide insights about the forces that affect the frequency and duration of strike activity. In panel (a) of Figure 15.2, curve *UR*

(a) Union Members' Acceptable Wage Increase

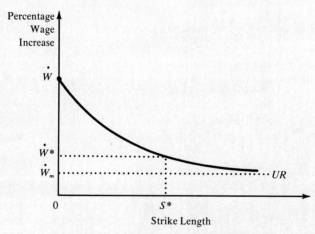

(b) Employer Present Value of Profit Function

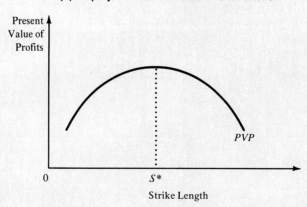

Figure 15.2   Graphic Representation of Ashenfelter-Johnson Model of Strike Activity

represents union members' minimum acceptable percentage wage increase ($\dot{W}$) as a function of the length of a strike; this curve is nothing more than the Hicks union-resistance curve. To simplify the discussion, we have assumed that curve *UR* always declines with strike length. In this diagram, $\dot{W}$ is the union members' initial wage demand (the amount they would settle for without a strike), and $\dot{W}_m$ is the minimum amount they would ever settle for. Depending upon economic conditions and the members' hostility to management, $\dot{W}_m$ may be positive, zero, or even negative—the last possibility would occur if union members felt that they had to take a pay cut to preserve their jobs.

Panel (b) of Figure 15.2 plots the employer's present value of profits *(PVP)* as a function of the length of a strike. An increase in strike duration has two offsetting effects. In the immediate period, the employer loses profits because the firm loses some sales. However, in the future, the firm's profits may be higher because the longer strike means that the employees will be willing to settle for smaller wage increases (from panel [a] of Figure 15.2). In panel (b), initially the second effect dominates and then, ultimately—since the union demands fall less rapidly (in absolute terms) and lost sales begin to mount up—the first effect dominates. That is, the employer's present value of profits first increases and then decreases with strike duration.

Suppose the employer's goal is to maximize the firm's present value of profits, and suppose the employer knows the position and shape of the curves in Figure 15.2. The employer can maximize the firm's present value of profits by offering the union a wage increase of $\dot{W}^*$ after a strike of length S^*. At that point, the union members will accept the offer and the strike will end. If the *PVP* curve in Figure 15.2 were always negatively sloped, the employer would either settle prior to a strike or go out of business if paying $\dot{W}$ would cause the firm to suffer losses.

If factors underlying the curves in Figure 15.2 change, the probability of occurrence and expected duration of a strike will be affected. For example, if the union's initial wage demand ($\dot{W}$) increases, but other factors stay the same, a strike will have a greater payoff to the employer and the expected duration will increase. Similarly, an increase in the rate at which the union's wage demands decline over time, other things equal, will increase the employer's payoff from prolonging the strike. In contrast, an increase in the union members' minimum acceptable wage demand $\dot{W}_m$ (sometimes called the union's *resistance point)* will reduce the employer's gain from incurring a strike, and will reduce the probability of a strike occurring.

The Ashenfelter and Johnson model—which assumed that $\dot{W}$, $\dot{W}_m$, and the steepness of the *UR* curve in Figure 15.2 are influenced by the unemployment rate in the economy (as well as by past changes in wage rates and prices, and by the profit rates of corporations)—is able to explain why strike activity tends to be reduced when the unemployment rate is high.[20] In the context of their model, an increase in the unemployment rate reduces the initial wage demands of unions

---

[20]Ashenfelter and Johnson, "Bargaining Theory . . . ," pp. 42–46.

($\dot{W}$), since the wages of other groups are rising more slowly and because there are fewer alternative job opportunities. Thus it is less likely that either side will see much to be gained by a strike.

Ashenfelter and Johnson also found that after statistically controlling for the unemployment rate, profits, and past wage and price changes, the level of strike activity (as measured by the number of work stoppages per year) tended to decline during the period they studied (1952–1967). However, the decline took a particular form: while the pattern was downward from 1952 to 1959, the number jumped up in 1959 before resuming its downward trend (see Figure 15.3).[21]

The general decline in strike activity in the American economy has been attributed by many observers to the maturation of industrial relations in the United States; fewer strikes are now caused by the parties misunderstanding each other's intentions or by the need to use a strike today to enhance bargaining power tomorrow.[22] The increase in 1959 coincided with the passage of the Landrum-Griffin Act. By increasing union democracy, this act increased the chances that union leaders would be voted out of office if they failed to satisfy union members' expectations at contract-negotiation time. In the context of the model presented here, making union leaders more accountable to membership would increase the

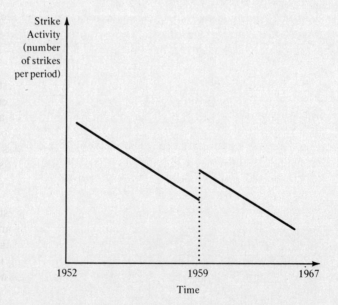

Figure 15.3 Ashenfelter and Johnson's Estimated Time Trend in Strike Activity

---

[21]Ashenfelter and Johnson, "Bargaining Theory . . . ," p. 47.

[22]It is hard to discern a trend in any of the measures of strike activity over the 1953–79 period in the *raw* data presented in Table 15.1. One must remember, however, that during the period, all of the other variables (unemployment, wage and price changes, and profits) were changing. The trends Ashenfelter and Johnson observed are found after one statistically controls for these other factors.

probability that leaders would recommend going on strike, rather than trying to sell the rank-and-file an unacceptable contract. To return to a previous theme, social programs and legislation often have unintended side effects; the Landrum-Griffin Act may well have unintentionally led to an increase in the level of strike activity in the economy.

The model presented in this section does not pretend to be the ultimate model of strike activity. It focuses only on strikes that result from disagreements over economic issues and ignores strikes that may result from conflict over recognition procedures, grievance procedures, unsafe working conditions, and the like. It also makes certain assumptions that, while sometimes plausible, are unlikely to be true always.[23] For example, in essence, this model suggests that union leaders and management implicitly collude to the detriment of union members. Union leaders are assumed to be willing to recommend a strike that will impose costs (in the form of lost income) on members, even though they may know that the strike will not increase management's ultimate wage offer. Management is assumed to know fully union members' resistance curves. Finally, union members are assumed to be ignorant, in the sense that they never learn how the bargaining process is actually working. Nonetheless, the model provides useful insights into the bargaining process and an explanation of why the Landrum-Griffin Act and the unemployment rate should be expected to influence the level of strike activity.

Interindustry Strike Activity

Persistent differences in the level of strike activity also exist across industries. In 1979, for example, the Bureau of Labor Statistics reported that two industries (tobacco and ordnance) each had only two work stoppages while two other industries (trade and government) each had over 500 stoppages.[24] While some of the wide interindustry variation in the number of strikes can be explained by interindustry differences in the number of bargaining units, substantial differences in the extent of strike activity between industries remain even after adjustment for this factor.

What explains this phenomenon? It has been suggested that variations in worker militancy and/or employer resistance by industry are the explanation, but these assertions simply raise the question of why militancy and/or resistance varies by industry. Moreover, the level of strike activity in an industry can be influenced by institutional arrangements that the negotiating parties devise. (See Example 15.2.)

---

[23]A comparative study of aggregate strike experience in seventeen countries found that the United States was the *only* country in which there was a negative relationship between strikes and real wage changes, and that higher unemployment rates rarely had a depressing effect on strike activity outside the United States. *See* Paldam and Pedersen, "The Macroeconomic Strike Model: A Study of Seventeen Countries, 1948–1975."

[24]U.S. Bureau of Labor Statistics, *Analysis of Work Stoppages, 1979* Bulletin 2092 (Washington, D.C.: U.S. Government Printing Office, April 1981).

EXAMPLE 15.2

The Steel Industry's Experimental Negotiating Agreement

Uncertainty concerning the outcome of major collective-bargaining negotiations can have a significant influence on industrial patterns of output and employment. In the steel industry, negotiations between the United Steelworkers of America and major steel producers occur every three years, and effectively establish terms and conditions of employment for the industry. While there has not been an industrywide strike in steel since the 1959 negotiations, the *possibility* that a strike might occur led most substantial purchasers of steel to build up inventories in advance of the contract expiration date in the steel industry, so that they could continue to operate in the event of a steel strike. When negotiations were completed without a strike, the steel industry would fall into a slump with plant shutdowns and layoffs as the industry's major customers worked off their inventories. The cycle also produced permanent losses for the steel industry: foreign steel producers who assisted American firms in building up inventories of steel and who were not subject to the same collective-bargaining cycle were often able to sign long-term contracts to supply former customers of American steel producers.

In April 1973, the major steel companies and the United Steelworkers' union signed a pact known as the Experimental Negotiating Agreement (ENA) that subsequently applied to negotiations in 1974, 1977, and 1980. The Agreement effectively provided insurance against the uncertainties formerly faced by the steel union, the steel industry, and steel consumers. Under the ENA, the union agreed not to strike over national bargaining issues, thus guaranteeing uninterrupted steel production. Issues that were not resolved in negotiations were referred to an arbitration board consisting of one union-appointed member, one company member, and three members appointed with the approval of both sides; only the three impartial members could vote. In return for forgoing the right to strike over national bargaining issues, union members were given a one-time bonus of $150, a guaranteed wage increase of 3 percent per year, and cost-of-living adjustments (COLAs). The union retained a limited right to strike over local issues.

This innovative agreement was retained for three rounds of national negotiations but was dropped in the early 1980s as a result of employer opposition. The opposition stemmed from two factors. First, while the ENA succeeded in eliminating national strikes, steel companies continued to face local strikes. Moreover, employers argued that some national issues were being redefined as local issues so that the union could bring the strike weapon to bear. In 1977, for example, several thousand steelworkers in the Minnesota iron-ore range struck over incentive pay on the grounds, disputed by employers, that it was a local issue. To the extent that national issues were "transformed" into local issues, some of the uncertainty that the ENA was designed to remove remained. Second, the pact proved to be expensive, particularly as the inflation of the late 1970s and early 1980s resulted in large COLA payments. By the early 1980s, imported steel still accounted for a large share of the American market, and the strategy of the steel industry shifted from buying a reduction in conflict to seeking wage concessions (see Example 12.4).

SOURCES: National Academy of Arbitrators, *Arbitration of Interest Disputes: Proceedings of the 26th Annual Meeting,* pp. 79–80, 88; Michael Drapkin, "Steel Union Backs Arbitration Plan to Avoid Strike," *Wall Street Journal,* March 29, 1973; and Douglas R. Sease, "Fate of Steel Industry's No-Strike Accord in 1983 Depends on Three Major Factors," *Wall Street Journal,* April 28, 1980.

One recent study argued that the level of strikes in an industry should reflect (1) the prior learning and experience of the bargainers and (2) the costs of strikes. We discussed the first factor earlier: it is hard to see why a strike would occur if both union and management negotiators were well informed about their adversary's strength and seriousness. Misinformation and miscalculation are most likely in new bargaining relationships, and the study found that there tend to be more strikes in industries with a relatively large number of new bargaining relationships. As the parties gain negotiating experience with each other, however, the number of strikes attributable to these factors should decline. For a given degree of bargaining experience, each party still must decide whether or not to adhere to a negotiating position that may induce a strike. If the parties act rationally, this decision will be related to the relative cost of a strike, and the study found evidence that strikes are less likely in manufacturing industries in which strike costs are relatively high.[25]

Methods of Dispute Settlement

Bargaining impasses typically develop into strikes or lockouts that can impose significant costs on individuals who are not involved in a particular labor dispute. As a result, most societies have, as a matter of policy, attempted to devise methods of dispute settlement in an effort to reduce the likelihood that a bargaining impasse will occur. The development of such procedures is a delicate matter, since the objective is to reduce the probability of an impasse while maintaining collective bargaining as the main route to a settlement. Moreover, the nature of the procedure may itself influence the probability that an impasse will develop.

The most widely adopted approach to dispute settlement is to introduce *third-party procedures* into the collective-bargaining process. Third-party procedures inject one or more individuals who are not directly involved in the labor

[25]Melvin W. Reder and George R. Neumann, "Conflict and Contract: The Case of Strikes," *Journal of Political Economy* 88 (October 1980): 867–86.

dispute into the bargaining process. Some procedures are available as a matter of course in virtually all collective-bargaining situations, while others are reserved for special situations, such as national emergency disputes or disputes in the public sector where strikes are forbidden. Paradoxically, the most effective third-party procedures in collective bargaining are those that are not used frequently; their function is to provide incentives for labor and management to reach agreement without resorting to the procedure. To the extent that such procedures are able to reduce the likelihood of a bargaining impasse, it is by improving the information between the parties on settlement possibilities, or by potentially imposing costs that labor and management seek to avoid. That is, third-party procedures may either seek to minimize the misunderstandings and lack of information that were stressed as a source of strikes in the Hicks model of bargaining, or they may create a contract zone (as would the threat of a strike) by imposing costs on parties who cannot come to an agreement on their own. The potential effectiveness of alternative dispute-settlement procedures can be assessed in terms of their ability to improve information or impose such costs.

There are three third-party procedures that are commonly used, and these will be discussed in the order of increasing intrusiveness into the collective-bargaining process. *Mediation* involves the use of a third party in the negotiations to facilitate the fashioning of an agreement by labor and management. Mediators have no authority to impose a solution to a dispute, however. *Fact-finding* is simply a search for the basic facts and issues in a labor dispute by a neutral individual or panel of individuals. *Arbitration* involves the use of a third party to actually determine the terms and conditions of a labor agreement.

Mediation

Perhaps the most common form of third-party intervention in labor disputes is *mediation,* in which an experienced neutral joins union and management negotiators in an effort to resolve the differences that remain between them. Unlike an arbitrator, however, a mediator has no authority to impose a settlement on the parties. His or her role is to facilitate the search for an agreeable compromise between the two parties. Most mediation in the private sector is conducted by members of the Federal Mediation and Conciliation Service (FMCS), who see more collective bargaining in the course of a year than many union and management negotiators see in a lifetime.[26] Many states also have mediation agencies or public employment relations agencies that, among other functions, provide mediation services to help resolve labor disputes in the public sector.

Why might mediation work to achieve a settlement? Unlike a strike, mediation does not directly impose costs on the parties or otherwise provide any particular

---

[26]By the early 1980s, the FMCS was involved in 20,000 labor disputes annually. About half of the disputes required only informal mediation while the other half involved joint mediation activities with labor and management. About 10 percent of the disputes requiring joint mediation were in the public sector. The FMCS also provides training and other technical assistance to negotiators and neutrals in dispute settlement. Federal Mediation and Conciliation Service, *Thirty-fourth Annual Report, Fiscal Year 1981* (Washington, D.C.: U.S. Government Printing Office, 1982), p. 37.

incentive to avoid the procedure by settling their dispute. Instead, the main role of mediation is to facilitate a settlement by increasing the flow of information between labor and management. One of the limitations of mediation as a technique of dispute settlement is that it is unlikely to succeed in situations where a contract zone—a range of potential agreement between labor and management—does not exist because the parties to collective bargaining hold mutually inconsistent expectations. Only in situations where a mediator is able to suggest alternatives that the parties had not thought of themselves is mediation likely to facilitate agreement by creating a contract zone where none existed before.

More frequently, where a contract zone does exist, the role of mediation is to guide the parties to a settlement by facilitating the flow of information and concessions. Many professionals feel that mediation is a complement to, rather than a substitute for, strike activity. That is, labor and management may be more responsive to mediation efforts when faced with the threat of a strike if mediation fails. From this perspective, mediation may be more successful in the private sector than in the public sector, where there generally is no legal right to strike. Even in collective-bargaining situations in which a strike is possible, mediation can fail because of poor timing. Unless negotiations are sufficiently far advanced that the parties can feel the pressure of a failure to agree, they may be relatively unresponsive to efforts to mediate the dispute.

The mediator's task is generally to cut through the formally stated bargaining positions of union and management negotiators to discover what the essential goals of each side are and where the resistance points that could trigger a strike lie. Sophisticated mediators also have to recognize that negotiators for both sides may be constrained by a need to satisfy different political factions within their own organizations. There is no set format for handling this task, and different mediators develop different styles and procedures. Most mediators listen, at least briefly, to an initial statement of the issues by each side in a joint meeting of the negotiating teams. Even though such sessions are likely to be marked by considerable posturing and are unlikely to reveal the real resistance points of either side, they clarify the nature of the conflict and can reveal internal political tensions that may have an important influence on the bargaining.

Real progress in mediation is usually achieved only after the parties are separated and the mediator begins to shuttle between them in a series of private discussions. During this more private part of the process, the mediator attempts to get the parties to reveal their fundamental goals and to determine possible trades that might form the basis for an agreement. This part of the process is particularly delicate, since the parties are well aware of the mediator's objectives and may wish to release information selectively in order to advance their own causes. Yet a relentlessly self-serving use of a mediator by each side would probably result in a breakdown of mediation and create consequences that might be quite costly. It is easily seen that when those consequences are severe, as when strikes are permitted, the parties have more inclination to treat the mediation process seriously. As noted above, an able mediator may be able to suggest alternatives or compromises that the parties had not thought of themselves.

A mediator may also propose to both parties an alternative that they had thought of but were unwilling to propose, for fear of losing ground (if the other side rejected it) or face (if it involved withdrawing from an earlier position). Proposals advanced by a mediator may also relieve the negotiators of some political pressures—they can always claim that an unpalatable result was the mediator's idea. In smaller bargaining units in the public sector, for example, it is not unusual for the parties to use "outside negotiators" (that is, teachers may bring in a regional representative of their national union or professional association, and the board of education may hire an attorney from a major law firm). Often these experienced professionals may agree on a settlement but need a way to "sell it" to their respective sides. The mediator becomes a "seller" of the settlement to the negotiators' principals, overcoming unrealistic expectations about what is possible from the negotiations.

It is not easy to evaluate the performance of mediation as a technique of dispute resolution. While the basic objective of all professional mediators is to obtain a collective-bargaining settlement, a determination of the number of strikes avoided as a result of mediation would understate the effectiveness of the process. Even when mediation is followed by a bargaining impasse and strike, the mediator may have narrowed the range of issues under contention and, as a result, shortened the duration of the strike.

Professional mediators are single-minded in their efforts to secure an agreement between the parties to collective bargaining. In order to do this, they must remain acceptable to both labor and management; their usefulness is over when either party lacks confidence in them. Most mediators feel that the acceptability that is fundamental to their success would be jeopardized if they were to pursue goals other than achieving a settlement. As a result, they avoid becoming involved in some of the key issues that are raised by the presence of collective bargaining in society. Contrary to arbitrators, for example, mediators are generally unconcerned with the fairness or equity of a collective-bargaining settlement. Their task is to prevent breakdowns of negotiations, not to rectify inequalities in bargaining power. Similarly, mediators are unwilling to enforce laws or public policy, on the grounds that it would undermine their acceptability to labor and management. Therefore, if the parties were to negotiate a clause in a collective-bargaining agreement that violated a federal law—for example, a clause that discriminated against women or racial minorities—a mediator might inform the parties of the conflict with federal law, but not take further action. During the periodic experiments with incomes policy in the United States since the early 1960s, there has been an interest among some federal policy makers in having the FMCS enforce the guidelines for wage increases in such policies during their mediation efforts. The FMCS has successfully resisted such suggestions on the grounds that the effectiveness of mediators would be undermined if their primary responsibility was perceived to be the enforcement of an administration's wage policy.

Fact-Finding

Under fact-finding the individual or panel that is chosen to determine and report on the issues at stake in a dispute does not intervene in the bargaining process directly. Instead, the publication of a fact-finding report, it is argued, may cut through the bluff and exaggerated claims of a bargaining situation. Supporters of fact-finding procedures hope that informing the public of the objective issues in a labor dispute will help muster public opinion in favor of an appropriate settlement and bring its weight to bear against the recalcitrant party. Particularly in public-sector negotiations, however, fact-finders may attempt to devise an acceptable compromise settlement; to that end, the fact-finding report may have the flavor of "advisory arbitration."

While fact-finding procedures have been available for many years for use in "national-emergency disputes" in the private sector (discussed more extensively below) and have more recently been adopted in the public sector, they have generally fallen short of expectations in promoting the resolution of bargaining impasses. In part, the fact-finding reports fail to muster public opinion. The ambivalence of many fact-finding reports is not well suited for focusing public opinion in a way that a recalcitrant negotiator might find costly. This is due to the fact that in many disputes the fact-finder also acts as a mediator and is torn between (a) trying to help arrange a solution and (b) trying to state "objectively" what the solution should be. These two objectives are not always consistent. Even in the absence of such ambivalence, it appears that the public does not accord much attention to such reports. Finally, even if public opinion were more focused as a result of a fact-finding report, there is little cost imposed on the negotiators. Thus, fact-finding appears to offer weak inducements for ending a bargaining impasse, because it is a technique that is unlikely to introduce new information into the bargaining process or to threaten significant costs for labor and management that they could avoid by reaching agreement among themselves.

Evidence from the public sector indicates that the effectiveness of fact-finding procedures has declined over time. Their availability has generally not been effective in preventing strikes in the event of a bargaining impasse and, over time, labor and management in public-sector jurisdictions with fact-finding procedures have become less willing to accept the recommendations of fact-finders. In some states, arbitration procedures covering public employees have been adopted to provide another stage in dispute-settlement in case a fact-finding report is not accepted.[27]

Interest Arbitration

The final third-party procedure that is often invoked to settle labor disputes is *arbitration,* in which an individual or a panel selected by the parties to collective bargaining (or appointed by a governmental body) actually determines the outcome of the labor dispute.[28] Arbitration procedures tend to take on the character-

---

[27]For an extensive review of evidence on the performance of fact-finding and other third-party procedures in the pub_ sector, *see* Thomas A. Kochan, "Dynamics of Dispute Resolution in the Public Sector," in *Public-Sector Bargaining,* eds. Benjamin Aaron, Joseph R. Grodin, and James L. Stern (Washington, D.C.: Bureau of National Affairs, 1979), pp. 150–90.

[28]Arbitration is also used extensively outside the field of labor relations—for example, to resolve disputes over obligations under commercial contracts and in developing divorce settlements.

istics of a trial with the arbitrator serving as judge. Only those cases in which the parties are unable to develop "out-of-court" (negotiated) settlements "go to trial" (an arbitration hearing). Labor and management may present their cases to the arbitrator through their respective attorneys, and witnesses may be called to give testimony. Some time after the hearing, the arbitrator will hand down a written decision. Unlike most court hearings, however, there is generally no formal appeals mechanism.

Arbitration is therefore the most intrusive of the third-party procedures because it imposes the judgment of an outside individual on the union and management parties who must live with and implement the decision. Since even an experienced outsider is less likely to understand an industry and a particular collective-bargaining relationship as well as the parties themselves, it is often argued that arbitrated settlements are less likely to be self-enforcing than settlements achieved through normal collective-bargaining procedures. When negotiating parties do not shape the standards that are to govern their conduct during the period of the contract, they may be less apt to accept the responsibility for enforcing those standards.

There are two other ways in which arbitration may be incompatible with collective bargaining. First, arbitration may have a *chilling* effect on collective bargaining if labor and/or management believe that concessions made during a collective-bargaining period preceding arbitration may result in an arbitration award that is less favorable to their positions. Second, arbitration may have a *narcotic* effect on collective bargaining if the parties forgo the rigors of bargaining in favor of an arbitrator's award.

For these reasons, *interest arbitration,* the use of arbitration to determine the terms and conditions of a collective-bargaining agreement, is used very rarely and only in rather special circumstances in the private sector, where the parties have the right to strike or lockout in support of their bargaining positions. In addition, the parties find it difficult to agree on the selection of the arbitrator empowered to determine the terms and conditions of employment in the industry. Regular use of interest arbitration might also lead workers to question the value of union representation. In recent years, the main private-sector examples of interest arbitration have been the use of arbitration in national-emergency disputes (discussed later in the chapter) and the resolution of salary disputes between professional baseball players and the owners of baseball clubs.

On the other hand, *grievance arbitration,* or the use of arbitration to resolve disputes over the interpretation and application of a collective-bargaining agreement is very common in the private sector. One important distinction between interest arbitration and grievance arbitration is that in the latter case, the parties to collective bargaining have the opportunity to limit the scope of the arbitrator's authority in advance through the language that they incorporate in the collective-bargaining agreement. (This and other aspects of grievance arbitration are discussed in the following chapter.)

The situation is much different in the public sector, as we have seen. Most states permit collective bargaining but prohibit strikes by state- and local-government employees, so that the traditional method of exerting leverage in support of bargaining demands is not available to unions. In the absence of a right to strike, most state and local governments have adopted alternative forms of impasse resolution, and some states have adopted binding interest arbitration as a final stage in their procedures, to be used after mediation and/or fact-finding have failed.[29]

The growing use of interest arbitration in the public sector and, to a limited extent, in the private sector raises two broad questions about the effects of arbitration procedures. First, to what extent do the decision-rules that arbitrators use influence the likelihood of a negotiated settlement? Second, to what extent does arbitration influence the size of the final agreement?

Interest arbitration and the likelihood of settlement. As we noted earlier, the most effective dispute-settlement procedures may be those that are least likely to be used. That is, given the advantages of a mutual agreement between management and labor over the terms and conditions of employment, the most desirable arbitration procedures are those that provide the greatest incentive for the parties to collective bargaining to avoid arbitration by concluding a negotiated agreement.

Does the presence of an arbitration procedure provide the incentives to conclude such an agreement? At the beginning of the chapter we noted that the threat of a strike provides such incentives in the private sector to the extent that the cost of making concessions in collective bargaining is less than the costs of incurring a strike. The possibility of a strike, in effect, creates a "contract zone" or range of potential settlements that both parties consider preferable to a strike.

While the parties using arbitration incur some direct costs (for example, the arbitrator's fee, fees for attorneys who may represent labor and management at an arbitration hearing, the costs of preparing for a hearing, etc.), these are not likely to be equivalent to the costs associated with a strike, except in the smallest bargaining units. Therefore, if arbitration provides an incentive to labor and management to settle, it must be mainly through different mechanisms. The characteristic of arbitration most often thought of as an inducement to settle is *uncertainty* concerning the arbitrator's award. Faced with this, risk-averse negotiators will be willing to forgo some of the expected gains from an arbitrated settlement in order to avoid uncertainty.

Consider a situation in which there is no uncertainty concerning the behavior of the arbitrator. That is, both labor and management can forecast with certainty what the arbitration award in a particular dispute will be. It is easy to see that there is little incentive to bargain in this situation, because the party faced with an outcome more adverse than it could obtain through arbitration would hold out to the point of impasse. Suppose that one party, labor, attempted to obtain more through collective bargaining than it would receive in the arbitration award. Then the sensible strategy for management would be to refuse to agree so that a bargaining impasse developed and the dispute moved into arbitration, where the award was known to be more favorable. When each party knows with certainty

---

[29]Arbitration is now used to settle labor disputes for some categories of public employees in Alaska, Connecticut, Iowa, Maine, Massachusetts, Michigan, Minnesota, New Jersey, New York, Oregon, Pennsylvania, Rhode Island, Washington, Wisconsin, and Wyoming.

what the arbitrator will award, neither party can obtain more than the arbitrator's award in collective bargaining. Collective bargaining may flourish in a mechanical sense (if only so that labor and management can avoid the costs of arbitration), but it cannot flourish in any substantive sense, because the outcome will be predetermined by the parties' advance knowledge of the arbitrator's award.[30] Arbitration procedures that are structured in ways that make the arbitrator's award highly predictable—for example, requiring that an arbitrator use only the criterion of recent cost-of-living increases in determining the appropriate wage increase—will therefore tend to be destructive of meaningful collective bargaining.

In fact, the behavior of arbitrators in the real world is rarely so predictable. Arbitrators may use a variety of criteria as well as their own judgments concerning what is "fair" in fashioning an award, and different arbitrators may use different criteria or accord different weights to alternative criteria. As a result, both labor and management may be uncertain that an arbitrator will make an award more or less favorable to what they could obtain by negotiating a settlement themselves. If the parties are risk-averse or risk-averse on balance, they will prefer the certainty of a negotiated settlement, even though it may result in a contract that is somewhat lower in value than the expected value of an uncertain arbitration award. It is the existence of uncertainty that creates a contract zone, (in which risk-averse labor and management may prefer to negotiate a solution) analogous to the contract zone created in the private sector by the threat of incurring costs from a strike or lockout. Therefore, any procedure that increases the amount of uncertainty concerning the outcome of an arbitration award will widen the contract zone and provide a stronger incentive for the parties to negotiate a solution. Because this incentive rests on the interplay of uncertainty and risk aversion, however, negotiated settlements will tend to be less favorable to the more risk-averse party than will settlements reached through the arbitration process.

One might wonder why arbitration would ever be used to establish the terms of a collective-bargaining agreement if labor and management would be willing to avoid the uncertainty by reaching a negotiated agreement. One reason is that the parties may simply have different information and expectations concerning the outcome of the arbitration process. Whether an arbitration procedure is used initially depends on how labor and management expect an arbitrator to rule relative to what they expect to achieve in negotiations without arbitration. If at least one party believes the arbitrator will award more than they will get out of negotiations, then the dispute will go to arbitration. If labor and management each expect that the arbitrator's award will be more favorable to their position than the outcome of negotiations, then the dispute will reach impasse and go to arbitration. A second reason, reminiscent of one of the incentives to use mediation, is that either party may wish to place the blame for an unpalatable but inevitable outcome on a third party. (It would be easier, for example, for a labor leader to report that a wage concession had been imposed by an arbitrator than

---

[30]This situation is analyzed in Vincent P. Crawford, "On Compulsory-Arbitration Schemes," *Journal of Political Economy* 87 (February 1979): 131–60.

to defend the acquiescence of union negotiators in such a proposal.) In this case, the parties may prefer an arbitration award even when they know what the award is likely to be.[31]

A third possibility is that the uncertainty associated with arbitration may decline. Over time, labor and management learn more about the behavior of arbitrators as they acquire more experience with arbitration proceedings. Most of the information that they receive tends to reduce their uncertainty concerning an arbitrator's award. They have their direct experience in arbitration proceedings to rely on. Moreover, because many arbitration decisions are published in reporting services, the previous track record of experienced arbitrators can be checked out. The standards that arbitrators rely on in fashioning their decisions become clearer, and there is less uncertainty concerning an arbitrator's ruling on a particular situation in the future.

One interesting question posed by the increased presence of interest-arbitration procedures in the public sector is whether the reduction in uncertainty that accompanies greater use is likely to reduce the incentives to bargain over time. In answering this question, one must remember that it is unlikely that uncertainty concerning the results of arbitration can ever be eliminated completely. Different rounds of arbitration may be held before different arbitrators, who weight various criteria differently. Moreover, as economic and social conditions change, different criteria may become important. Compensation for increases in the cost of living is only introduced as an argument for wage increases during periods of inflation. The financial condition of a city may receive more weight from an arbitrator during a period of fiscal crisis than in more normal times. In general, then, it appears that uncertainty concerning the likely results of arbitration will be reduced, but not completely eliminated, as interest arbitration is more widely used. Since the major incentive to bargain is uncertainty concerning the arbitrator's award, there may be a tendency for arbitration procedures to be invoked more frequently over time, although not to the point where meaningful collective bargaining collapses.[32]

---

[31]A study of dispute-resolution procedures in the public sector in New York State found that almost all decisions by a tripartite arbitration board were *unanimous,* suggesting that the arbitration procedure may have been a "cover" for bargaining. *See* Thomas A. Kochan, Mordechai Mironi, Ronald G. Ehrenberg, Jean Baderschneider, and Todd Jick, *Dispute Resolution Under Factfinding and Arbitration: An Empirical Analysis* (New York: American Arbitration Association, 1979).

[32]There have been a number of studies that have attempted to test for the existence of a so-called narcotic effect from arbitration procedures in the public sector. Efforts to estimate whether the probability of going to an impasse requiring arbitration in one negotiation is positively related to the extent to which arbitration procedures were used by the parties in previous negotiations, raise relatively advanced issues of statistical methodology, and not all studies have been sufficiently attentive to the statistical issues. As a result, the tests for a narcotic effect of arbitration to date are inconclusive. For a discussion of the methodological issues and a sample of the results, *see* the exchange between Richard J. Butler and Ronald G. Ehrenberg, "Estimating the Narcotic Effect of Public Sector Impasse Procedures," *Industrial and Labor Relations Review* 35 (October 1981): 3–20; and Thomas A. Kochan and Jean Baderschneider, "Estimating the Narcotic Effect: Choosing Techniques That Fit the Problem," *Industrial and Labor Relations Review* 35 (October 1981): 21–28.

EXAMPLE 15.3

Compulsory Arbitration in Australia

Australia provides the leading example of the use of compulsory arbitration as a means of preventing strikes. Since 1904, Australia has encouraged the use of arbitration tribunals rather than work stoppages as means of resolving disputes over contract terms and over the interpretation of labor agreements. Tribunals at the federal and state level set minimum standards for pay rates, hours of work, and paid leave, usually by industry or craft, for over 90 percent of Australian workers.

In principle, the system is voluntary; unions and employers must register if they wish to participate. In practice, the substantial benefits that are tied to registration have introduced a strong compulsory element to union participation in the arbitration system. Registered unions are accorded recognition as representatives of employees in an industry, and with recognition, unions can bring issues that employers refuse to negotiate over to arbitration. In addition, the members of registered unions receive employment preferences and benefit from minimum-pay standards set by an arbitration commission. Registered unions also give up the right to strike: with registration comes an obligation to submit unsettled disputes to arbitration and forgo the use of strikes or lockouts. Many employers were initially unwilling to participate in a system that extended such institutional security to labor unions, but the possibility of resolving disputes without work stoppages and the fact that the awards of arbitration tribunals did not generally encroach on management's authority to control the operations of the firm eventually led employers to register as well.

What has been the impact of the Australian arbitration system on strikes and collective bargaining? First, the system has not eliminated work stoppages or prevented major upsurges in strike activity such as occurred in the late 1960s and early 1970s. There are several reasons for this. Not all parties to collective bargaining register with the tribunals. Moreover, the sanctions that can be effectively applied against unions that strike are modest. The major sanction is deregistration, but a well-established union may no longer need the institutional protection accorded by registration, and once deregistered, the union is outside of the influence of the arbitration system. The government can also fine unions that strike illegally, but even when imposed, such fines have rarely been collected. Another factor is that many strikes in Australia appear to have an element of symbolic protest. Most strikes end without the use of arbitration—indeed, about half end without any negotiations whatsoever!

If the arbitration system has not eliminated strikes, has it reduced the incidence of work stoppages? It is difficult to answer even this question definitively, because data on work stoppages prior to the introduction of the arbitration system are sparse. However, it does appear that while the annual number of strikes has increased since 1904 (as has the extent of unionism in Australia), the length of strikes and the time lost as a result of strikes has declined. Moreover, strikes appear to be concentrated in a few industries over issues concerning physical working conditions and grievances about the application of the agreement. Relative to other countries, there are few strikes over the issues of wages and hours that are most frequently addressed by the arbitration tribunals. The arbitration system may therefore have influenced the duration and nature of strikes in Australia.

The effect on collective bargaining is more difficult to pinpoint. Many observers feel that the possibility of an arbitrated settlement has reduced the willingness of negotiators to offer concessions at the bargaining table. On the other hand, considerable collective bargaining occurs, and when the parties reach an agreement, they can have it endorsed by a tribunal to give it the status of an arbitration award, setting industry standards. The parties may also voluntarily decide to negotiate "supplements" to an arbitration award, but these have no legal status in the arbitration system. There is some evidence that wage determination is dominated by the arbitration system when labor-market conditions are weak, but that under strong market conditions, unions may feel that they can obtain more from collective bargaining than arbitration. With the tight labor markets of the late 1960s and early 1970s, for example, there was an increase in collective bargaining and strikes that reduced the influence of the arbitration system in wage determination. It was not until a system of indexing wages to prices was introduced through the arbitration tribunals in the mid-1970s that the primacy of the arbitration system was restored.

SOURCES: Kenneth E. Walker, *Australian Industrial Relations Systems* (Cambridge, Mass.: Harvard University Press, 1970); and Russell D. Lansbury, "The Return to Arbitration: Recent Trends in Dispute Settlement and Wages Policy in Australia," *International Labour Review,* 117 (1978): 611–24.

The decision-rules of arbitrators. We have argued that it is uncertainty over the outcome of arbitration that provides the main incentive for labor and management to conclude an agreement on their own, and that mutually determined labor contracts are viewed as an objective of the industrial-relations system. As a result, one approach to reducing the probability of a narcotic effect, which in an extreme form might lead to a collapse of collective bargaining, is to develop institutional arrangements that increase the uncertainty associated with arbitration and, conversely, avoid arrangements that reduce the uncertainty associated with the procedure. For example, in some public-sector labor disputes, arbitrators have based their settlements on the reports of fact-finding that often precedes arbitration. Once labor and management come to recognize this as the arbitrator's approach, the results of arbitration become more predictable and the parties pattern their offers accordingly. The range of potential settlements becomes narrower and more gauged to the arbitrator's standards than the original objectives of labor and management. A similar flow of information between an arbitrator and the parties is generated when an arbitrator is permitted to engage in mediation as well. The presence of information concerning the arbitrator's views of a desirable settlement will tend to reduce the uncertainty costs associated with arbitration and to move the final settlement away from the range in which a negotiated solution would have fallen.

The decision-rules applied by an arbitrator can also influence the amount of uncertainty associated with the arbitration process. The actual decision-rule chosen will reflect incentives faced by the arbitrator, unless the rule is specified by law. Many arbitrators derive considerable income from their practices. At the same time, the parties to collective bargaining often have a direct input into which arbitrator is hired. Labor and management may choose an arbitrator themselves (for example, by crossing the names of arbitrators off a list with an odd number of names until only one remains), or may indicate their preferences to the state or municipal agency that appoints an arbitrator. Moreover, arbitration decisions cannot, in general, be overturned by a higher review body. As a result, arbitrators have an obvious incentive to be rehired, and to be rehired an arbitrator must be viewed as reliable by both the union and management sides of a dispute. This may require fashioning decisions that include elements that appeal to each side. It has been argued that, in order to be rehired, arbitrators will develop some form of compromise between the union and management positions, and that, at times, the compromise might take the form of splitting the difference between the union and management positions.

The central flaw of a split-the-difference approach to arbitration is that it discourages the settlement of a dispute by the parties themselves. It is hard to imagine a decision-rule that penalizes concession more. Any effort by one party to concede in the hope of encouraging settlement simply moves an award based on splitting the difference closer to the opponent's position. Compromise is penalized rather than rewarded, and the rational strategy for parties who know that an arbitrator is likely to split the difference is to take extreme bargaining positions. Another difficulty with a literal split-the-difference approach to arbitration decisions is that it would leave labor and management with very little uncertainty about the outcome of arbitration and, hence, would provide little incentive to reach a negotiated agreement.[33]

Is there a decision-rule that an arbitrator could follow which would reverse

---

[33] It seems doubtful that arbitrators literally split the difference regularly. For example, we do not normally see labor and management taking the very extreme positions that would be encouraged if arbitrators mechanically split the difference between final offers. Moreover, evidence on the question of the behavior of arbitrators is difficult to interpret. Data indicating that arbitration awards tend to be at the midpoint of the final positions of labor and management are not necessarily evidence of splitting the difference. So long as an arbitrator gives any weight to some personal or external criteria for what constitutes a fair settlement (in addition to the actual final offers of the parties), labor and management will have incentives to position their final offers around the expected award of the arbitrator. The result may appear to be the outcome of splitting the difference, whereas, in fact, the opposite is occurring. That is, the offers of each party may be influenced by their perception of the arbitrator's notion of a fair settlement rather than vice versa. *See* Henry S. Farber, "Splitting-the-Difference in Interest Arbitration," *Industrial and Labor Relations Review* 35 (October 1981): 70–77.

the incentives and encourage a convergence in bargaining positions? One proposal that has been advanced is the antithesis of splitting the difference. Under the *final-offer-selection* approach, an arbitrator would be instructed (under the terms of a labor-relations statute or collective-bargaining agreement) to select either management's final proposal or the union's final proposal—whichever was more reasonable in the arbitrator's judgment. This approach to interest arbitration has been adopted to resolve salary disputes in professional baseball and in several cities.

Since each party would face the possibility of losing everything under this decision-rule, the procedure appears to provide an incentive to offer concessions at the bargaining table by increasing the uncertainty concerning the outcome of arbitration and, therefore, raising the probability of a negotiated settlement.[34] It is also true, however, that the parties to collective bargaining can influence the probability that their position will be accepted by the arbitrator by the very offers that they submit. For example, a risk-averse bargainer can reduce the probability that an adversary's package is accepted by submitting a more moderate package. The other party can respond in kind. In the end, this direct influence may reduce the uncertainty associated with final-offer selection below that inherent in conventional arbitration.

Uncertainty is also reduced if the arbitrator is permitted to choose between final offers on an issue-by-issue basis rather than selecting the entire package offered by the union or employer. When there are several issues at stake, the arbitrator has more latitude to make trade-offs between the union and employer positions in fashioning an award. As a result, the final package may be more of a compromise than if selection were not permitted on an issue-by-issue basis.

Effects of Arbitration Statutes on Wages of State- and Local-Government Employees

Binding-arbitration legislation is typically opposed by municipal-government officials who argue that arbitration takes the final decision over public employees' wages out of the hands of elected officials and leads to inflated wage settlements. Several studies have analyzed the consequences of arbitration statutes and have concluded that (1) the use of arbitration may compress differentials across cities (since arbitrators tend to award larger increases in cities where public employees are paid relatively low wages than they do in cities where public employees' wages are relatively high), but that (2) given initially comparable pay scales, on average, the wage settlements that go to the arbitration stage are no higher than the wage settlements in otherwise comparable cities that do not go to arbitration.[35] That is, if the average percentage wage-settlement in cities that went to arbitration, $\dot{W}_A$, is compared to the average percentage wage settlement in otherwise comparable cities that did not go to arbitration, $\dot{W}_N$, the difference *(D)* is roughly zero:

---

[34]This proposal was originally advanced by Carl M. Stevens, "Is Compulsory Arbitration Compatible with Bargaining?" *Industrial Relations* 5 (February 1966): 38–52.

[35]*See,* for example, Thomas Kochan, et al., *Dispute Resolution Under Factfinding and Arbitration;* and James Stern, et al., *Final Offer Arbitration* (Lexington, Mass.: Lexington Books, 1975).

$$D = \dot{W}_A - \dot{W}_N = 0.$$

One might be tempted to conclude from such evidence that the arbitration process *per se* has had no effect on the size of the average wage settlement in the public sector. However, this conclusion assumes that the rates of wage increase in cities in which negotiations did not go to arbitration ($\dot{W}_N$) are the same as they would have been in the absence of the arbitration statute—which is not necessarily correct. The existence of the arbitration statute *per se* may well alter the size of wage settlements even in cities that do not go to arbitration, as we will soon discuss.

For example, if municipal-government negotiators fear that there is some chance that arbitrators will award settlements that are substantially more generous than would otherwise occur, they may try to induce a settlement prior to the arbitration stage by voluntarily offering their employees a wage package in excess of what they would have offered in the absence of the statute.[36] Such an action would cause the estimated differential *D* to *understate* the effect of the arbitration statute on wages. Conversely, if public employers believed, and public-employee unions concurred, that arbitrators were likely to award low settlements, management might offer—and unions might accept—an offer less than what management would have offered in the absence of the statute. While we can not ascertain *a priori* whether the existence of the arbitration statute *per se* increases or decreases the size of wage settlements in cities that do not go to arbitration, it is very likely that the presence of an arbitration statute *does* affect the negotiations in cases where the settlement is made prior to arbitration.[37]

An assessment of the impact of arbitration on wages must be clear about the wage standard against which arbitration is being compared. For example, one might be interested in the difference between wage increases under arbitration and wage increases under collective bargaining in an environment without arbitration. (Comparisons of arbitration awards with nonunion wage increases may also be of interest in determining the standards that arbitrators appear to apply to wage disputes.) Alternatively, given the presence of an arbitration statute, one might be interested in the difference between wage increases in disputes that go to arbitration and wage increases in disputes that are resolved by a negotiated settlement. These will not be the same, in general, because, as noted before, a legal requirement that bargaining impasses must be resolved by arbitration is likely to influence the size of negotiated settlements. Unfortunately, there has been relatively little reliable research on these questions.

How does the *form* of arbitration influence the effect of arbitration? Does it make any difference whether conventional arbitration or final-offer arbitration is used in dispute resolution? This raises questions about the influence of final-offer

---

[36]The union might agree to such a settlement even if it expected that, on average, an arbitrated settlement would be higher, because of uncertainty about how the arbitrator would rule (that is, there was some chance that his or her settlement would be lower). Put another way, "a bird in the hand may well be worth two in the bush."

[37]For a more complete discussion of this point in the context of a simple bargaining model, *see* Henry S. Farber and Harry C. Katz, "Interest Arbitration, Outcomes, and the Incentive to Bargain," *Industrial and Labor Relations Review* 33 (October 1979): 55–63.

selection on the bargaining proposals advanced by labor and management, as well as the comparison of the standards that arbitrators apply in selecting one or the other to the standards they would apply in a conventional arbitration situation. Some evidence on the impact of a final-offer-selection procedure is offered in Example 15.4.

EXAMPLE 15.4

Final-Offer Selection and the Wages of Police Officers

Studies of the salary determination of municipal police officers in New Jersey, where there is a statute providing for arbitration using final-offer selection in the event of impasse, indicated that, on the average, the wage increases obtained under final-offer arbitration did not differ significantly from either negotiated increases or increases determined under conventional arbitration (which the parties had the option of selecting). Yet, the pattern of the arbitration awards revealed some interesting aspects of the behavior of the parties under the final-offer-selection procedure.

Employer proposals were chosen by an arbitrator only a third of the time, but the wage increases provided for in these proposals were significantly *lower* than the average wage increases received by police officers in disputes that did not go to arbitration. Since an arbitrator is instructed to choose the most reasonable final offer, one may infer that employer offers were even further below the general wage increases for police officers in situations in which the arbitrator chose the union offer. The presence of a final-offer-selection procedure therefore was not driving employer wage offers to the center of the wage-offer distribution in New Jersey.

Union proposals, on the other hand, were selected by an arbitrator in two-thirds of the disputes that went to arbitration under final-offer selection, but the wage increases provided by the proposals were no larger than the increases received by similarly situated police officers elsewhere in the state. Unions, in effect, were winning more arbitrations because they submitted relatively conservative final offers, while employers were winning less frequently but gaining more from the arbitrations in which they did win. Judged by this evidence, the police unions were more risk-averse than public-sector employers. There is, no doubt, some real political appeal to the employer strategy, since public employers can argue that they submit proposals that are intended to keep the wage budget down, and if they lose the arbitration and a higher wage increase is awarded, they can blame it on the arbitrator.

SOURCE: David E. Bloom, "The Effect of Final-Offer Arbitration on the Salaries of Municipal Police Officers in New Jersey," Working Paper #129 (Princeton, N.J.: Industrial Relations Section, Princeton University, November 1979); Orley Ashenfelter and David Bloom, "Models of Arbitrator Behavior: Theory and Evidence," *American Economic Review* (forthcoming).

National-Emergency-Disputes Policy: An Application

While the right to strike has long been accepted as a necessary component of collective bargaining in the private sector, there has been persistent concern about the social disruption caused by strikes having widespread consequences for neutral third parties—particularly the general public—either because of the crucial nature of the product or service for consumers (for example, coal, transportation), or because of the extreme importance of the struck product as an input to crucial products and services (for example, steel and transportation). The demand for a public-policy response resulted in the inclusion of *national-emergency-disputes* procedures in the Railway Labor Act, which was originally passed in 1926 and now covers the railroad and airline industries, and the Taft-Hartley Act, passed in 1947 following a brief postwar surge in strike activity, covering most other industries involved in interstate commerce. The structure of these procedures, as well as subsequent experience with them, provides a useful introduction to the first principles of dispute settlement.

National-Emergency Procedures and Their Goals

The effort to devise national-emergency-disputes procedures presented a classic conflict of objectives for labor policy in the United States. On the one hand, there was the desire for a private system of collective bargaining, in which employers and unions would resolve their differences with a minimum of governmental intervention, and, on the other, the desire for industrial stability which seemed to imply a need for some form of intervention. In an effort to strike a balance between these objectives, Congress wished to minimize the probability of strikes in key sectors of the economy (because of the cost of such strikes to the public at-large) while maintaining collective bargaining as the main mechanism through which a settlement was to be achieved. The basic policy objective was, therefore, to exert some pressure but allow and encourage an essentially voluntary settlement.

To maintain its commitment to collective bargaining, Congress did not actually outlaw strikes in key sectors of the economy. Instead, Congress left collective bargaining as the route to a settlement, but added a set of third-party procedures which were intended to reduce the probability of a bargaining impasse. If an impasse developed, the procedures were available to delay (but not prohibit) a strike. There was some concern about the choice of procedures that would not intrude greatly into the bargaining process, but as will become apparent, this is not an easy objective to fulfill when designing dispute-settlement procedures.

Taft-Hartley procedures. The national-emergency-disputes procedures established in the Taft-Hartley Act are deceptively simple. If a labor dispute that concerns the President approaches an impasse, the President can appoint an emergency fact-finding board of inquiry to study the dispute and report back on its findings. The difficulty in trying to devise procedures that simultaneously encourage private collective bargaining while providing for a government presence may be seen in the authority accorded the fact-finding board. Although the board is, in principle, the set of neutrals with the fullest command over the facts of a dispute, it is prohibited from making recommendations for a settlement in its report. A set of public recommendations, which might have a flavor of arbitration, was viewed as too intrusive into the bargaining process. (This contrasts with the use of fact-finding in labor disputes in the public sector, where, as we have seen, public policy places more emphasis on the goal of industrial stability and less on the goal of unrestrained collective bargaining than in the private sector. In the public sector, fact-finding reports are often made public in the hope of setting a standard for a negotiated settlement.) Congress apparently hoped that the determinations of the fact-finding board would muster public opinion against an obstinate union or employer, but in three dozen applications of the emergency-disputes procedures since 1947, there have been only four occasions when the board has placed the blame for a labor dispute solely on one party to the negotiations.[38]

Having received the board's report, the President may direct the Attorney General to petition a District Court for an injunction, which under the law is limited to 80 days. Although the court is supposed to judge whether an emergency actually exists, in practice, the President's assertion of an emergency is accepted without substantial judicial examination. The parties to the collective-bargaining dispute then have a duty to bargain during this 80-day "cooling-off" period.

If no settlement has been reached after the first 60 days of the injunction, the emergency fact-finding board makes a public report on the positions of the employer and union, and within the last 15 days of the injunction, the National Labor Relations Board must poll the union membership to determine whether they favor the employer's last offer, irrespective of what their elected representatives are saying at the bargaining table. If the union members do not vote in favor of the employer's last offer—and they never have—the union is free to strike when the 80 days elapse. The President can then send a report and recommendations, if any, to Congress. Disputes have been settled during the injunction period in about half of the instances in which the procedures have been invoked.

Railway Labor Act procedures. Under the Railway Labor Act, the first step is mediation of the dispute by the railroad industry's National Mediation Board. If mediation fails, and the parties do not mutually agree to accept arbitration, the Mediation Board decides whether the dispute is of sufficient magnitude to deprive the country of essential transportation service. It informs the President, who then appoints an emergency board (which is permitted to make recommendations) to investigate. Conditions in the industry are then frozen for 30 days, after which

---

[38]In the late 1940s and 1950s, the Taft-Hartley procedures were invoked for disputes in the atomic energy, bituminous coal, meatpacking, longshore, and metals industries. More recently, the procedures have been initiated for a coal strike in 1977 and considered, but not applied, for a national trucking strike in 1979.

the parties are free to strike, unless there is some form of *ad hoc* government intervention.

While it was originally hoped that the mere existence of these procedures would reduce the likelihood of a major collective-bargaining impasse, the procedures were used quite frequently into the early 1970s, and most major disputes in the railroad industry still end up in the Railway Labor Act procedures. Increases in industrial conflict can reflect increased union militancy and/or increased employer resistance. Is there also something in the nature of dispute-settlement procedures themselves or in the way in which they are administered that encourages their use and discourages collective bargaining?

Problems with National-Emergency Procedures

The first problem one encounters in trying to analyze the wisdom of the emergency-disputes procedures is deciding when they will be used. What constitutes a national emergency in labor negotiations? The *economic* approach to defining a potential national-emergency situation would stress the availability of substitutes. A *national* strike in the telephone industry might be judged to create an emergency, since it would include telegraph service as well, but a shutdown of the airlines leaves other modes of transportation and communication available. Consideration would also be given to the geographical scope and imminence of the strike if economic factors are paramount in defining an emergency. For example, in many areas, a local strike of unionized telephone personnel might have little immediate impact on highly mechanized telephone services, since nonunion supervisors could operate the equipment.

When the foregoing economic criteria are applied, one finds that relatively few of the disputes in which the national-emergency procedures were invoked actually qualified as true economic emergencies; the procedures have been used more frequently than would seem warranted if only potential economic costs are considered. When considering procedures that are invoked at the discretion of the Chief Executive, it is natural to look for *political* influences. The difficulty with the economic approach to defining national-emergency disputes is that it fails to satisfy the political pressures generated by a major work stoppage. When political criteria are admissible in defining a national emergency, either of the parties to collective bargaining can use this to its advantage, and recourse to the procedures will be more frequent. This appears to have occurred over the years in the railroad industry, where the government has only infrequently permitted disputes to result in work stoppages.

There is also a basic paradox built into the design of the national-emergency-disputes procedures. Although collective bargaining is the only method provided for settling a dispute, the procedures themselves impede collective bargaining. In particular, management and labor know in advance the timing and consequences of government intervention in national-emergency situations. This knowledge can be relied upon by either party and, therefore, forestall settlement. In particular, too-easy recourse to government intervention leads the parties to try to use the government to secure gains which they cannot achieve through collective bargaining.

Thus, a first principle in designing dispute-settlement procedures is to avoid devices that have a built-in bias which alters the relative bargaining power of the union and the employer. When such a bias occurs, one party will have a stronger incentive to use the procedures than to engage in collective bargaining. Paradoxically, if collective bargaining is to be the main route to a settlement, then the best set of dispute-resolution procedures are those that are least likely to be used. However, to minimize the use of dispute-resolution procedures, one must find procedures that do not alter the relative bargaining strength of labor or management.

From this perspective, the current national-emergency-disputes procedures have drawbacks. The fact that the parties know, in advance, that an injunction is likely to be imposed reduces the pressure to reach agreement in advance of the contract expiration. Moreover, in preserving the status quo, the injunction tends to work to the disadvantage of labor, which, except during periods such as the early 1980s when collective bargaining in some industries was directed at wage concessions, is usually pushing to extend the terms of the current agreement; the employer, who generally desires less change, has little incentive to bargain. Most importantly, however, the presence of the injunction and cooling-off period does little to resolve the underlying dispute. While collective bargaining is left as the main route to a settlement, the injunction has the effect of weakening collective bargaining by removing the private sanctions (the strike and lockout) available to unions and management to force an agreement.

The requirement that the NLRB poll workers toward the end of the 80-day injunction on the acceptability of the employer's last offer also does not appear to contribute to the collective-bargaining process. In the period preceding the last-offer ballot, the union leadership must follow an essentially political strategy of lining up votes rather than focusing energies on the settlement of the dispute. Union members, recognizing that the employer is no doubt withholding the best offer until the end of the injunction period, have always rejected, by large majorities, the last offer—a result which serves only to reduce the union's negotiating flexibility in subsequent negotiations. Employers presume their last offers will be rejected by the membership and, therefore, withhold concessions. The net result is that paradoxically the last-offer ballot requirement tends to prolong a collective-bargaining impasse.

In practice, experience under the Taft-Hartley Act appears to have been less destructive of collective bargaining than experience under the Railway Labor Act. This is probably because, under the former legislation, the government has normally allowed strikes to occur if no settlement has been reached when the 80-day injunction expires. Under the Railway Labor Act procedures, however, the final step has increasingly been some form of governmental intervention into the bargaining process—usually in the form of arbitration by a specially appointed outside committee or by Congress itself. Indeed, experience under the act indicates that the government is unlikely to tolerate major work stoppages in the railroad industry. As indicated in the previous section, knowledge that a dispute may be settled by split-the-difference arbitration if collective bargaining fails to produce a labor agreement is likely to *reduce* the probability of a collective-bargaining agreement.

Alternative Procedures

A number of alternatives to the national-emergency-disputes procedures in the Taft-Hartley and Railway Labor Acts have been advanced.[39] One is to require *partial operation* of an industry to maintain a level of production that would meet crucial national defense, health, and safety needs. This requires some agreement on how much production is necessary to fulfill essential needs, and some mechanism for determining which union members shall work at full pay and which shall be on strike. However, some unions have voluntarily adopted a partial-operation strategy in an effort to forestall a court finding that their strike would constitute a national emergency. When a nationwide trucking strike occurred during the renegotiation of the national Master Freight Agreement in early 1979, for example, the Teamsters' union agreed to transport materials critical to the operation of hospitals and defense activities.

A second, and characteristically academic, proposal is the *non-stoppage strike* (sometimes called the *statutory strike*), under which there would not be a walkout by workers when an impasse is reached in collective bargaining. Instead, while full production continued, the economic pressures of a strike would be *simulated* by taxing management's profits and the workers' wages by the amounts that would be lost during a strike. Both parties would be left to settle the dispute themselves, and the collected taxes would go into the public treasury.[40]

The main difficulty with this proposal is the practical one of devising an appropriate tax structure to be applied against management and labor. The tax formula would be written into a statute or set by an administrative body, and centralized determinations always breed pressures for uniform rules to economize on the substantial information cost of devising a large set of tax rates. However, the relative cost of a strike to management and labor is anything but uniform across major collective-bargaining situations. With centralized determination of the tax on each party, the relative costs and the result of a strike might well differ from what would be observed without the law. One party or the other may gain from such legislation; that is, for one of the parties, the cost of the non-stoppage strike may be less than the cost of a real strike. This will then have the defect that we have noted in some other proposals: one party will have an incentive to avoid serious bargaining until an impasse develops and the simulated economic pressure begins.[41]

---

[39]For further discussion of these alternatives *see* Donald E. Cullen, *National Emergency Disputes,* ILR Paperback No. 7 (Ithaca, N.Y.: New York School of Industrial and Labor Relations, Cornell University, 1968).

[40]Stephen H. Sosnick, "Non-Stoppage Strikes: A New Approach," *Industrial and Labor Relations Review* 18 (October 1964): 73–80.

[41]The only method for devising a tax structure that is likely to reflect the relative bargaining power of management and labor is collective bargaining itself! If the parties set up the tax formula in collective negotiations, the result should reflect their relative bargaining strength at the time of negotiations. To date, labor and management in major industries have shown little inclination to negotiate such agreements. However, an example of a somewhat different arrangement, providing for an arbitrated settlement rather than a strike in the event of a bargaining impasse is discussed in Example 15.2.

A third possibility would be for the government to take over the operation of an industry when a strike was judged to create a national emergency. This approach has been used on occasion—most notably by President Truman in the bituminous coal industry in the early post-World War II period. Government seizure is largely a change in legal status. The operation of the industry normally remains in the hands of its managers rather than government personnel. Nevertheless, the procedure is intrusive, and actions that the government takes as owner may impose long-run obligations on industry management.[42]

If there are theoretical or practical difficulties with each of the main mechanisms of dispute settlement considered individually, is there any advantage to combining them into a single procedure? This is the essence of the *choice-of-procedures* or *arsenal-of-weapons* approach, which gives the Chief Executive several alternatives from which to choose when a dispute with national-emergency potential threatens. In considering this proposal, it is important to recall that, given the primacy accorded collective bargaining, the essence of any dispute-settlement procedure is to minimize its own use (that is, to maximize the incentive for private bargaining). The essence of the choice-of-procedures approach is *uncertainty.* Neither management nor labor would know which procedure would be chosen; in fact, they would not know if *any procedure would be chosen,* for one of the most important alternatives is the choice of doing nothing about the dispute.

The effect of uncertainty on private bargaining behavior is intensified by including at least one alternative in the arsenal of weapons which is distasteful to each party. When bargaining, each party must then consider the probability that the Chief Executive will choose a procedure that is distasteful to that party if an impasse develops and government intervention is required. The possibility of gaining more from government-intervention procedures than from bargaining is minimized, and the incentive to actively engage in collective bargaining therefore increases.

There has been only one major effort to revise national-emergency-disputes procedures along these lines. In 1970, the Nixon administration proposed including the railroad and airline industries under the Taft-Hartley Act procedures and amending the latter to provide the President with a choice of (1) extending the 80-day injunction for an additional 30 days; (2) partially operating the industry; (3) arbitrating with final-offer selection; or (4) referring the entire issue to Congress as is now the case if an agreement is not reached at the end of the 80-day injunction period. Opposed by the labor movement, however, the bill made no real progress in Congress.

REVIEW QUESTIONS

1. How does the general absence of the right-to-strike influence the nature of industrial relations in the public sector? To what extent are differences between the private and

---

[42]For a discussion of historical instances of the government seizure approach, *see* John L. Blackman, Jr., *Presidential Seizure in Labor Disputes* (Cambridge, Mass.: Harvard University Press, 1967).

public sectors in bargaining behavior and pressure tactics ultimately related to the right-to-strike? What differences would you expect to remain if the right-to-strike existed in both sectors?

2. What are the advantages and/or disadvantages of substituting binding arbitration for the strike or lockout as a means of resolving impasses in collective bargaining?

3. When a national trucking strike appeared imminent in 1980, the federal government indicated that it might seek an injunction under the Taft-Hartley Act emergency-disputes procedures. The Teamsters' union responded by indicating that it would permit its members to carry materials needed for health care and defense activities. Was this response in the self-interest of the union? Why?

4. "It is often argued that the availability of interest arbitration can induce negotiators to settle without using arbitration in order to avoid the uncertain results of an arbitrator's award. One way to increase the uncertainty concerning the outcome of arbitration is to instruct arbitrators to select randomly between union and management proposals." Discuss the viability of this approach to interest arbitration.

SELECTED READINGS

Orley Ashenfelter and George Johnson, "Bargaining Theory, Trade Unions, and Industrial Strike Activity," *American Economic Review* 59 (March 1969): 35–49.

John F. Burton, Jr., and Charles Krider, "The Role and Consequences of Strikes by Public Employees," *Yale Law Journal* 79 (January 1970): 418–40.

Ronald G. Ehrenberg, "The Demand for State and Local Government Employees," *American Economic Review* 63 (June 1973): 366–79.

Henry S. Farber and Harry C. Katz, "Interest Arbitration, Outcomes, and the Incentive to Bargain," *Industrial and Labor Relations Review* 33 (October 1979): 55–63.

Thomas A. Kochan, "Dynamics of Dispute Resolution in the Public Sector," in *Public-Sector Bargaining,* eds. Benjamin Aaron, Joseph R. Grodin, and James L. Stern (Washington, D.C.: The Bureau of National Affairs, 1979).

Carl M. Stevens, "Is Compulsory Arbitration Compatible with Bargaining?" *Industrial Relations* 5 (February 1966): 38–52.

Harry H. Wellington and Ralph K. Winter, Jr., *The Unions and the Cities* (Washington, D.C.: The Brookings Institution, 1971).

Chapter 16

THE COLLECTIVE-BARGAINING AGREEMENT

The outcome of collective bargaining is a labor agreement that governs the relationship between labor and management in the bargaining unit until its expiration. Such agreements cover many aspects of the employment relationship and frequently are more than a hundred pages in length. These formal labor agreements are not common in firms without unions, but the relationship between nonunion employers and their employees is often like an *implicit contract* in which each party has mutual expectations concerning the behavior of the other.[1] In such cases, employers implicitly offer the prospect of long-term employment security in exchange for reliable performance.

The task of explicit labor agreements is to establish the rights of labor and management in the employment relationship. Collective-bargaining agreements effectively establish a system of private law between employees and their employer. Specification of the benefits and conditions of employment that will apply at the time that the contract is signed is only part of this task. Most labor agreements now last for more than one year. Contracts lasting for at least three years rose from 22 to 74 percent of all major agreements in the private sector between 1956 and 1980, and in the public sector, 25 percent of the agreements were at least three years in duration and 64 percent were in effect for two or more

---

[1]Several state courts have recently recognized *de facto* implicit employment contracts between nonunion employers and employees in ruling that employers cannot necessarily terminate long-service employees "at will"—the original common-law standard for employment contracts. *See* "Protecting At Will Employees Against Wrongful Discharge: The Duty to Terminate Only in Good Faith," *Harvard Law Review* 93 (1980): 1816–44.

years by the mid-1970s.[2] Negotiators face considerable uncertainty concerning economic conditions during the later years of a multiyear agreement. As a result, an agreement may also provide mechanisms for altering benefits and employment conditions during the term of the agreement in response to unforeseen economic developments. Finally, most collective-bargaining agreements also establish procedures pertaining to the administration of the contract (specifying rules for promotions, layoffs, and disputes over contract interpretation, for example).

A collective-bargaining agreement generally covers five aspects of the employment relationship between unions and employers: the institutional security of the union, management rights, compensation, the allocation of economic opportunities within the firm, and dispute resolution during the term of the agreement. The issues raised by these aspects of the employment relationship are addressed in this chapter. In the first section, we provide an overview of a typical collective-bargaining agreement that is negotiated by labor and management. Probably the most familiar aspect of collective bargaining to the public at-large are the provisions regarding wages and fringe benefits. These provisions can influence both employment levels and the distribution of income between employers and employees. In the subsequent section, we review the distinction between these two effects of a bargaining relationship, and we consider the contractual arrangements that labor and management can develop to adjust future compensation payments to unforeseen changes in economic circumstances during the term of the agreement. In the final part of the chapter, we examine the administration of the collective-bargaining agreement, with particular attention to the role of the grievance procedure and grievance arbitration.

The Collective-Bargaining Agreement

A *collective-bargaining agreement* is the joint outcome of negotiation between labor and management. As noted in the analyses in Chapters 14 and 15, each party begins bargaining with distinct objectives that are inevitably compromised during the negotiation process. Some provisions of the final labor agreement may be closer to the objectives of labor and others closer to the objectives of management, so that the overall document will normally reflect a compromise rather than the dominance of one party. The final agreement will also reflect the relative bargaining power of the parties, and because this can vary considerably across bargaining situations for reasons discussed in Chapter 14, there is considerable variation in the size, scope, and specific contents of individual labor agreements. Nevertheless, there is considerable similarity in the general issues that are addressed in collective-bargaining negotiations, and it is possible to discuss the types

---

[2]Throughout this chapter "major" collective-bargaining agreements will refer to agreements covering 1000 or more workers. Data on the provisions of labor agreements can be found in U.S. Bureau of Labor Statistics, *Characteristics of Major Collective Bargaining Agreements, January 1, 1980,* Bulletin 2095 (Washington, D.C.: U.S. Government Printing Office, May 1981) and U.S. Bureau of Labor Statistics, *Characteristics of Agreements in State and Local Governments, January 1, 1974,* Bulletin 1861 (Washington, D.C.: U.S. Government Printing Office, 1975).

of provisions that might appear in a typical collective-bargaining agreement (Table 16.1). The general structure of labor agreements in the private and public sectors is similar, although the details of some provisions vary substantially.

Institutional Protection of Labor and Management

A collective-bargaining agreement typically opens by addressing the issues concerning the institutional security of the union. The union is recognized as the sole bargaining agent for employees in the bargaining unit (as required by the exclusive representation feature of the National Labor Relations Act), the scope of the unit represented by the union is defined (usually the election unit established by the NLRB), and the nature of the union-security arrangements, if any, are spelled out. For example, many labor agreements in the private sector provide for a *union shop* under which new employees are required to join a union within a fixed period of time following their hire. *Agency-shop arrangements,* under which employees are permitted to pay a "service charge" to a union rather than joining formally, are more common in the public sector. (There is a more extensive discussion of alternative union-security provisions and their implications in Chapter 12.) Dues-checkoff provisions, in which the employer withholds dues from employee pay-

Table 16.1. Outline of a Typical Collective-Bargaining Agreement

Article I. Recognition and Representation
  a. Recognition; definition of bargaining unit
  b. Union security
  c. Dues checkoff
  d. Rights of union stewards and other officials

Article II. Management Rights

Article III. No Strike or Lockout

Article IV. Hours of Work and Overtime
  a. Normal workday and work week
  b. Overtime premium
  c. Allocation to overtime opportunities

Article V. Wages
  a. Wage schedule by job
  b. Immediate and deferred wage increases
  c. Contingent wage increases
    • Cost-of-living increases
    • Incentive payment plans
  d. Shift premium

Article VI. Vacations
  a. Amount of vacation time
  b. Eligibility
  c. Vacation pay
  d. Scheduling

Article VII. Holidays
  a. List of recognized holidays
  b. Eligibility
  c. Holiday pay

Article VIII. Sick Leave
  a. Amount
  b. Eligibility

Article IX. Insurance
  a. Types (e.g., life, accident, health)
  b. Coverage
  c. Eligibility

Article X. Pension Plan
  a. Eligibility
  b. Benefits

Article XI. Seniority
  a. Definition
  b. Probationary period
  c. Layoff and recall procedure
  d. Promotion and transfer procedure
  e. Loss of seniority

Article XII. Grievances and Arbitration
  a. Definition of grievance
  b. Steps in procedure
  c. Provision for arbitration
    • Selection of arbitrator
    • Scope of arbitrator's authority

Article XIII. Duration of Agreement

checks when authorized to do so, are found in over 80 percent of major collective-bargaining agreements in both the private and public sectors. They are found most frequently in labor agreements that do not include a union-security arrangement, but unions also find them desirable because they permit union officials to devote more time to aspects of contract administration other than the collection of dues.

Having addressed the organizational interests of unions, most labor agreements then turn to the institutional interests of management. Two of the most important provisions for management in a collective-bargaining agreement are a management-rights clause and a clause prohibiting strikes while the contract is in effect (Articles II and III in Table 16.1). A *management-rights clause* describes the functions of running an organization that are reserved in whole or in part for the employer, and the wording of such clauses often reflects the inherent conflict of interests between labor and management that the labor agreement seeks to mediate. In the public sector, management-rights clauses often do little more than define the scope of issues that are legally subject to collective bargaining.

Management will want the broadest possible statement of its rights to run the firm, while unions will want language that makes it clear that the collective-bargaining agreement itself constrains some activities of management. Management may seek to establish language that states that its rights "include but are not limited to" a list of functions involved in directing the work force, such as hiring, scheduling production, promoting and transferring employees, and so forth. Unions will seek language that states that management's rights "will not be applied in a manner that violates other provisions of the agreement." The inherent tension between the interests of labor and management is perhaps best illustrated by a statement—typical in management-rights clauses—that permits the employer to "discharge employees for just cause." The employer is granted the right to act, but the phrase "for just cause" provides grounds for unions to protest the action and constrain the right granted to the employer.

A *no-strike provision* is simply a guarantee of labor peace during the term of the agreement that most employers seek as a *quid pro quo* for the commitments and constraints that they accept in the rest of the labor agreement. The intention is that the clause will channel disputes that arise during the term of the agreement into grievance and arbitration procedures (discussed later in the chapter) rather than work stoppages. One important consequence of including a no-strike clause in a labor agreement is that the union may be legally liable for breach of contract if some of its members initiate an unofficial or "wildcat" strike during the term of the agreement. As a result, it is not unusual to observe both the union and management trying equally hard to get wildcat strikers to return to the job.

Economic Benefits

Following provisions addressing the institutional interests of labor and management, the major part of the collective-bargaining agreement specifies economic benefits and working conditions for employees, particularly wages (Article V in Table 16.1) and fringe benefits (Articles VI–X). Wage provisions, historically the central element in a collective-bargaining agreement, raise a number of interesting issues for negotiators and for public policy that will be discussed in the following section.

Since World War II, however, fringe benefits have become an increasingly important part of the compensation package in both union and nonunion establishments, as noted in Chapters 5 and 10. The analysis in Chapter 10 stressed that both employers and employees are likely to have distinct preferences concerning the mix of wages and fringe benefits in the compensation package, and that these preferences are likely to be expressed as trade-offs that each is willing to make between wages and fringes. At times, these trade-offs become quite explicit during collective bargaining (see Example 16.1).

EXAMPLE 16.1

The Wage/Fringe Trade-Off in the Collective-Bargaining Process

At times, the wage/fringe trade-off can be directly observed in the collective bargaining process, although management and unions are usually reluctant to explicitly acknowledge that workers might be paying for their own fringe benefits. In 1950, however, the United Automobile Workers (the UAW) called a strike against Chrysler over the issue of pensions. Chrysler had promised a pension benefit to its workers for the first time, but it had not promised to put aside current funds to *guarantee* retirees that they would obtain benefits in the future. Fearing that Chrysler could become bankrupt in the future, the UAW wanted this pension promise to be backed up with current funding, and it called a strike. The union's last offer to Chrysler before the strike is an excellent illustration of a wage/fringe trade-off: it asked Chrysler either to pay six cents per hour (per worker) to a pension fund and four cents to buy medical insurance or to give workers a ten cents per hour raise in wages!

SOURCE: *The Daily Labor Report,* January 17, 1950, p. A-17.

Because of their importance in the compensation package, fringe benefits have become a significant component of labor costs and, hence, a potential source of conflict between labor and management in collective bargaining. While few managers in unionized firms would sensibly wish to eliminate fringe benefits (since even nonunion firms offer such benefits to attract qualified workers), unions may seek to raise the level and change the composition of fringe benefits beyond what managers feel that they need to pay for competitive purposes. As noted in Chapter 12, the political nature of union decision-making causes union leaders to favor benefits that appeal to the median member—that is, bargaining goals that will be supported by a majority of the membership—while employers are more likely to favor benefits that appeal to new applicants and to the workers who are most likely to leave the company for another firm if their preferences are not met. Since the median worker is likely to be older and less mobile than the marginal worker, unions generally have an incentive to negotiate for compensation items that have particular appeal to older workers; thus, collective-bargaining contracts generally call for mixes of fringe benefits and wages different from those found in nonunion companies.

A progressive income-tax system, under which higher incomes are taxed at higher rates, also may influence the composition of the union pay-package. Since union members on average receive higher rates of compensation than their nonunion counterparts (as discussed more extensively in Chapter 17), they are likely to be subject to higher income-tax rates. Union members therefore have a stronger incentive than nonunion workers to have a larger proportion of their compensation package as untaxed fringe benefits.

Collective bargaining typically focuses on several key features of fringe benefits that determine their ultimate cost to the firm and benefit to the workers. First, the parties must determine which workers will be eligible to receive the benefit. For most fringe benefits, eligibility is determined by the length of time that an employee has worked for the firm. For example, a contract may require a minimum amount of time worked in order to qualify at all for a vacation. Next, the parties must determine the level of the benefit, that is, the number of weeks of vacation and which holidays will be observed. Frequently, these are also related to tenure of employment. For example, the amount of vacation time is likely to increase with years of service to the firm. The exact formula relating job service to the level of a fringe benefit is established in negotiations. Finally, the contract must specify the rate of pay that will be applicable—usually straight time—for holidays and vacations. In the case of insurance plans, to take another example, there is often considerable bargaining over the level of contributions and the respective shares of labor and management.

Seniority and Economic Opportunity

Once the general provisions for wages and fringe benefits have been established, the welfare of employees is determined by their access to favorable economic opportunities within the firm and by the way in which the contract provisions are applied. Economic opportunities include promotions, transfers, opportunities to work overtime, and protection from layoff. In most collective-bargaining relationships in the United States, unions give employers considerable freedom to determine the level and composition of employment within a firm, but they seek to establish the criteria by which employment opportunities will be granted.

Evidence gathered in campaigns for union representation (see Chapter 13) indicates that one of the most effective appeals for support that unions make to workers is their claim that they will reduce managerial discretion and favoritism in personnel decisions. Therefore, unions seek to define the criteria for promotions, transfers, layoffs, and overtime opportunities in the collective-bargaining agreement, and to choose criteria that reduce the scope for supervisory discretion. *Seniority,* or length of service, is the criterion most commonly favored by unions because it is objective and because the application of seniority rules by management is relatively easy to monitor and enforce. In addition, unions argue that seniority is related to productivity and family need.

While seniority rules constrain managers to some extent—by reducing their discretion in hiring, layoff, and promotion decisions—the total cost of these provisions to management depends on the average relationship between productivity and compensation as workers acquire experience in an organization. We found in Chapter 8 that wages generally rise with experience in both nonunion and union employment. But does productivity rise with experience and hence with pay? Productivity and pay may rise together. Indeed, the human-capital theory reviewed in Chapter 8 assumes that the positive correlation between pay and seniority exists because workers become more productive through on-the-job training that they receive as part of their work experience.

Some recent studies, however, suggest that while pay rises with job experience, productivity does not. These studies find that while the earnings of professional and managerial workers were positively related to seniority *within a job grade,* seniority was uncorrelated with the performance ratings of individuals. Hence, the familiar relationship between earnings and experience or seniority within job grades may not be the result of increased productivity.[3]

This evidence is for white-collar workers only. There is very little direct evidence for blue-collar workers, in part because much blue-collar work occurs in team-production settings where the productivity of individuals is difficult to measure. Moreover, much of the correlation between wages and experience or seniority results from the effect of seniority on promotions into higher-paying job grades. In fact, the findings reported above may well reflect a tendency for the most able workers to be promoted most rapidly (after a relatively short time in a job grade). In addition, we have already reviewed, in Chapter 10, some reasons why profit-maximizing companies might adopt compensation systems for career employees in which earnings would rise with seniority even if productivity did not increase with seniority. Under these pay systems, a firm will be profiting in a long-run sense by paying workers less than the value of their marginal product in their early years with the firm and more than the value of their marginal product later. If a firm were to fire workers in the later years, once their value (on an annual basis) was less than their wage, the firm would be breaking the

---

[3]Katherine G. Abraham and James L. Medoff, "Length of Service and the Operation of Internal Labor Markets," *Proceedings of the Industrial Relations Research Association* (1983), pp. 308–18; James L. Medoff and Katherine G. Abraham, "Experience, Performance, and Earnings," *Quarterly Journal of Economics* XCV (December 1980): 703–36.

"implicit contract" and would be unable to get employees to agree to this compensation strategy in the future. Further, it has been argued that seniority rules promote on-the-job training by removing any disincentives for older workers to show younger workers the "tricks of the trade."

As a result, it is difficult to say what the exact costs of seniority arrangements are to management. It is easy to see that while there are a number of reasons why management negotiators might object to the use of seniority as the *sole* criterion for allocating economic opportunities, using it as *one* of the criteria might be in their best interests.

In practice, seniority is rarely established as the sole criterion for allocating opportunity in collective-bargaining agreements. In one broad sample of agreements, for example, seniority was one factor to be considered in promotion in about 70 percent of the contracts but was the sole factor in only 4 percent. In the same sample, almost half the contracts provided for some consideration of seniority in determining transfers, but it was the sole factor in only 5 percent. Overall, some reference to seniority as a factor in ranking employees for intrafirm economic opportunities appeared in over 90 percent of the labor agreements in the sample.[4] The most common factor used in conjunction with seniority is ability. For example, many contracts permit an employer to choose the most able worker available for promotion but require that seniority be used to choose from a pool of workers of equal ability. Moreover, unions will normally reserve the right to protest an employer's ability-rankings of employees.

There are several important issues regarding seniority that are typically addressed in the section of the collective-bargaining agreement that covers seniority (Article XI in Table 16.1). The first is the actual definition of seniority. Is it from the date of hire or the end of a probationary period? Is it lost in the event of layoff, unexcused absence, or failure to respond to a recall? A second set of issues surrounds the question of how seniority is to be applied. In most agreements, seniority is applied on a "last-in, first-out" (LIFO) basis; those with the highest seniority are ranked first for positive opportunities (for example, promotions) and last for negative opportunities (for example, layoffs) to the extent that seniority is used as a criterion for selection. More important is whether seniority applies on a departmental, plant, or companywide basis, for this indicates the scope of a worker's seniority rights. In departmental seniority systems, workers who transfer to a new department generally lose all seniority previously accrued in their first department, which may seriously limit their opportunities for promotion or overtime in a new department and leave them vulnerable to layoff in an economic downturn. (This has raised an important public-policy issue in the implementation of equal-employment-opportunity laws, as discussed in Chapter 11.)

The last major section of the model collective-bargaining agreement outlined in Table 16.1 concerns grievances and arbitration (Article XII). The value of a

---

[4]Bureau of National Affairs, *Basic Patterns in Union Contracts,* 8th ed. (Washington, D.C.: Bureau of National Affairs, May 1975), pp. 85–87.

contract to union members depends not only on its apparent contents, but also on how the specific provisions are interpreted and applied during the term of the agreement. Often union and management representatives have the same under-standing of a provision. When they disagree over the interpretation of a clause, however, a mechanism of dispute settlement is needed. Provisions for grievances and arbitration are included in most labor agreements for this purpose and will be discussed in detail in the final section of the chapter.

Wage Bargaining

In bargaining over wages, unions and management seek to establish a level and structure of wages by job, and changes in wages over time. Each of these dimen-sions of the wage bargain raises issues relating to the efficiency with which labor resources are allocated—the primary touchstone of the analysis in the first ten chapters of this book—and to equity, a concept of "fairness" that is much more difficult to define. Employers are likely to be motivated primarily by efficiency considerations, which leads them to stress the need to remain competitive and to provide desirable work incentives to different groups of workers. Employers would prefer that compensation be related to the productivity of their work force. Unions are not insensitive to efficiency considerations and often propose that wages be increased because a firm has been profitable. However, they are more likely than employers to stress equity considerations and propose that wages be increased even when a firm's profits are low, because prices have increased more rapidly than expected or because the wages of workers at other firms have increased. Thus, the labor agreement can have equity effects as well—it can influence the distribution of earnings between labor and capital and between union and nonunion labor.

Theoretical Analysis of Wage Bargaining[5]

The distinction between the efficiency and equity issues raised by employment and compensation relationships can be seen with the assistance of Figure 16.1, which describes the preferences of unions (in part [a]) and employers (in part [b]) between the rate of compensation and the amount of employment. As noted in the discussion of union objectives in Chapter 12, most unions are concerned with *both* the rate of compensation and the level of employment of their members.[6]

---

[5]The material in this subsection represents a higher level of technical analysis than is found in the rest of the chapter. Students who wish to skip this formal analysis of bargaining may proceed to the next subsection.

[6]Discussing a document as complex as a collective-bargaining agreement solely in terms of compensation (or wages) and employment is not as artificial as it may appear initially. The terms *compensation* and, in the subsequent discussion, *wages* are used in a broad sense to include not only wage and fringe-benefit payments but also the value or monetary costs of other provisions in the labor agreement which, while often referred to as nonmonetary, have obvious value to union members (since they wish to negotiate such provisions) and costs for employers (who frequently oppose union proposals).

That unions are willing to trade between higher wages and higher employment in order to maximize the welfare of their members was dramatically illustrated by the "concession bargaining" of the early 1980s, in which unions in several industries made wage and fringe-benefit concessions in exchange for greater job security for their members. The preferences of unions with respect to compensation and employment may therefore be represented by the curves u_i in Figure 16.1(a). Each union-indifference curve describes the combinations of wages and employment that leave the union (and its average member) equally satisfied; each

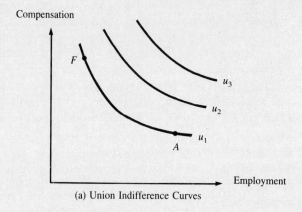

(a) Union Indifference Curves

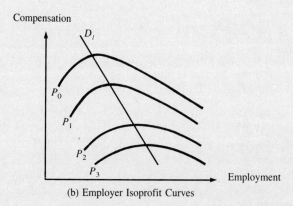

(b) Employer Isoprofit Curves

Figure 16.1   Bargaining Preferences of Unions and Employers

curve is negatively sloped (falls downward to the right) to reflect the fact that unions are willing to trade-off between compensation and employment. For a given employment level, higher indifference curves represent higher wages and therefore index greater levels of satisfaction (that is, u_2 is preferred over u_1).

The particular curvature of the u_i curves reflects the assumption that the rate at which unions are willing to trade between compensation and employment is not constant. At point *F* in Figure 16.1(a), the union is willing to sacrifice more compensation for an increase in employment than at point *A*. At *F* the relatively high rate of compensation permits employed union members to enjoy a relatively high standard of living, but the relatively low employment level may threaten the bargaining power of the union and its viability as an organization. As a result, members may be willing to "pay" a relatively large amount in terms of forgone compensation to increase the employment of union members. At point *A*, however, the opposite is the case: employment is larger, but the standard of living is considerably lower. Under these circumstances, union members would have to receive much larger employment gains in order to give up more compensation.

Consider next the interest of employers. Assuming that the objective of the firm is to maximize profits, employers will be indifferent between various compensation and employment combinations that leave profits unchanged. These employer trade-offs between compensation and employment can be graphed through the use of *isoprofit curves*—curves that show the various combinations of compensation and employment levels that yield a given level of profits (*iso* means equal). Therefore, all the points along a given curve—such as P_1 in Figure 16.1(b)—are pay and employment combinations that yield the *same* level of profits. In this sense, each isoprofit curve can be interpreted as an "indifference curve" for the firm. At any given employment level, lower isoprofit curves are associated with lower wages and therefore index *higher* levels of profits (that is, profits are higher along P_2 than along P_1).

What accounts for the shape of the isoprofit curves? The slope of each curve describes the rate at which an employer can trade between wages and employment while keeping profits constant. Recall that profits are simply revenues minus costs. For simplicity, we assume that costs are the rate of compensation times the number of employed—that is, each additional employee adds the same amount to costs. Each additional employee does *not* add the same amount to revenue, however. This is because the marginal product of labor decreases at higher levels of employment as a result of the law of diminishing returns (first discussed in Chapter 3). Now, at relatively low employment levels the marginal revenue received by the firm as a result of employing more workers (that is, the marginal revenue product) exceeds their marginal cost (that is, the rate of compensation), and profits increase when employment is expanded. Equal *(iso)* profits can only be maintained if the rate of compensation increases to offset the relatively high marginal revenue product in this range, and this accounts for the positively sloped segment of the isoprofit curve. The argument is reversed when marginal revenue product falls below the wage rate.

To summarize, the shape of an isoprofit curve reflects a basic technological condition of production—the law of diminishing returns. Over the range of employment for which the marginal revenue product *(MRP)* exceeds the marginal cost of labor, the isoprofit curve is rising; when the *MRP* is less than marginal costs, the curve is falling. Therefore, the marginal revenue product equals marginal labor cost (the rate of compensation) at the peak of the isoprofit curve. But we learned in Chapter 3 that the demand-for-labor schedule is the locus of wage-employment combinations for which this equality holds. Therefore, the firm's demand-for-labor schedule cuts the peak of each isoprofit curve (see D_l in Figure 16.1[b]).

Given the preferences of unions and employers, we can now characterize an efficient solution to bargaining between the employer and the union. The value premise underlying the concept of an efficient solution is that of *mutual benefit,* which was first discussed in Chapter 1. In the context of collective bargaining, a mutually beneficial bargain is one in which neither labor nor management loses and at least one party gains. Alternatively, an efficient bargain has been reached when it is impossible to increase either the satisfaction of labor or the profits of management without reducing the welfare of the other party.

The application of this concept of efficiency can be illustrated in Figure 16.2 in which parts (a) and (b) of Figure 16.1 have been combined. Suppose that when

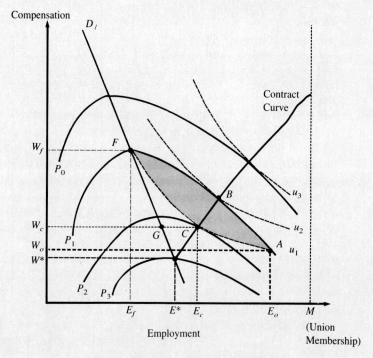

Figure 16.2   Analysis of Bargaining

bargaining begins, the wage is W_0 and the employment level is E_0 so that the parties are at point A. Position A is inefficient in the sense that there are other positions that could be reached that would improve the position of at least one of the parties without making the other any worse off. For example, bargaining that raised the wage rate and lowered the employment level could place the parties at either points *B* or *C*. At point *B*, where a relatively large wage increase is accompanied by a relatively small loss of employment, the union's satisfaction is increased and employer profits are held constant. At point *C*, where the wage increase is smaller and employment losses are larger, the union's level of satisfaction is constant and employment profits are increased. These are just extremes of the array of efficient points that could be attained through collective bargaining.

Generally, when negotiations begin at position *A*, mutual gains by both labor and management are possible to the extent that negotiations lead to any point in the shaded cigar-shaped area which represents higher levels of satisfaction and profits to the respective parties. The line running between *B* and *C* represents the locus of *efficient* preferred points in the sense that it is not possible to move from that line without reducing the well-being of at least one of the parties to collective bargaining. Each point on the line segment *BC* consists of a tangency between an employer-isoprofit curve and a union-satisfaction curve. Since the slopes of these curves must be equal for a tangency to occur, at each point on *BC*, the rate at which employers are willing to trade between wages and employment at a given profit level is identical to the rate at which the union is willing to trade between these two dimensions of the employment relationship. No further mutual gains from trade are possible. Recognizing that bargaining might start from points other than *A*, it becomes clear that the line segment *BC* is just one part of a much longer locus of efficient wage and employment combinations. This locus of efficient points is known as the *contract curve*.

Each point on the contract curve is therefore efficient in the sense described above, but each point represents a different distribution of income between the union and the firm. Unlike bargaining to reach an efficient position when the parties start away from one, collective bargaining over the distribution of income between unions and employers along the contract curve is a zero sum game— what one party wins, the other party loses. For this reason, collective bargaining over purely distributional issues is likely to be more contentious than bargaining that leads to a more efficient wage-employment combination.

Suppose now that a union specifies a rate of compensation, but allows the employer to choose the level of employment. In order to determine whether the result of this arrangement is efficient, one must consider the response of a profit-maximizing employer to a contractual wage or compensation requirement. When confronted with a contractual wage requirement, the employer will choose the level of employment that maximizes profits at that wage rate. In terms of Figure 16.2, this is reflected in the (graphically) lowest isoprofit curve that touches a horizontal line from the chosen wage. This is another way of demonstrating that the demand for labor curve of the firm, D_l, is the locus of the maximum points of the isoprofit curves of the firm. In order to clarify the effects of collective bargaining on the market, we shall define the competitive rate of compensation —that is, the supply price of labor to the firm in the absence of unions—to be

W^*. Faced with this market-determined wage, a profit-maximizing employer would choose employment level E^*.[7]

Since the employer is permitted to choose the level of employment, any wage-employment combination on the employer's demand-for-labor schedule is available to the union. Therefore, the union will choose the wage, W_f, which in combination with the employment level (E_f) chosen by the profit-maximizing employer at that wage will maximize the union's welfare. This wage-employment combination is indicated by point F in Figure 16.2 where the union-indifference curve, u_1, is tangent to the employer's demand-for-labor schedule. Any other point on that schedule will leave the union at a lower level of satisfaction (that is, on a lower indifference curve). The interesting feature of this solution is that it is *not* efficient. When the union, acting as a monopolist, simply sets the wage and allows the employer to choose the level of employment, the outcome is not on the contract curve. At point F, further mutually beneficial gains from negotiation are possible. Specifically, any point on the contract curve between points B and C would improve the welfare of at least one party while leaving the other party no worse off. In order to reach an efficient solution, the collective-bargaining agreement would have to specify the level of employment as well as the rate of compensation.[8] In specifying an efficient solution, however, the distribution of income between the union and the employer could be drastically altered from what it would be at F.

The divergence between the solution at a point such as F and an efficient solution is tied to the fact that while the union's satisfaction is determined by both employment and wages, the employer is interested only in maximizing profits. For example, while a union that negotiated W_f would be equally happy at point C where the lower wage, W_c, was offset by a higher employment level, E_c, it would never agree to a wage as low as W_c without an explicit employment guarantee written into the collective-bargaining contract. For while the firm receives higher profits at C than at F, its profits are higher still at G. Therefore, in the absence of an employment guarantee, the firm would select point G, where the employment of union members, while higher than at point F, was not sufficiently high to offset the union's loss of satisfaction from the lower wage. The lower wage induces employers to hire more workers, but not enough more to fully compensate the union for the loss in satisfaction due to the reduced wage. (The union's satisfaction level is lower at G than at C.)

---

[7]Since workers can get W^* from other employers, no contract establishing a lower rate would sensibly be negotiated in a competitive labor market, and, for this reason, the contract curve does not extend below this point in Figure 16.2.

[8]This was first pointed out by Wassily Leontief, "The Pure Theory of the Guaranteed Annual Wage Contract," *Journal of Political Economy* 54 (February 1946): 76–79; and William Fellner, "Prices and Wages Under Bilateral Monopoly," *Quarterly Journal of Economics* (August 1947): 503–32. More recent discussions and extensions include Ian M. McDonald and Robert M. Solow, "Wage Bargaining and Employment," *American Economic Review* 71 (December 1981): 896–908; and Robert E. Hall and David M. Lilien, "Efficient Wage Bargains Under Uncertain Supply and Demand," *American Economic Review* 69 (December 1979): 868–79.

Wage Bargains in Practice

How likely are American collective-bargaining contracts to produce an "efficient" solution, given the preferences of unions and employers? We saw, in the previous section, how an efficient solution would require agreement among negotiators on *both* the level of compensation and the level of employment. One of the most striking features of American collective-bargaining agreements is that they contain often elaborate provisions governing the compensation of union members but leave decisions concerning the level of employment up to the employer. A labor agreement will usually delineate whether compensation is to be on the basis of time worked (hourly, daily, or weekly rates), the amount produced (incentive-payment plans or payment-by-results), commission payments or mileage payments (used chiefly in the transportation industries) for various occupational groups in the bargaining unit. Most major agreements in the private sector specify wage rates, rate ranges, or, less frequently, minimum-wage rates along with the nature of the wage-progression plan that will apply to members of the unit. Labor agreements also spell out the nature of wage differentials for working less-preferred shifts, for hazardous work, for abnormal working conditions, and for overtime and weekend work, as well as the nature of extra payments for tools, clothing, and travel that are required as part of the job. As noted earlier in the chapter, the same sort of detail is characteristic of provisions governing fringe benefits. Contract provisions typically specify the eligibility (usually a minimum service period with the company) and pay for vacations and holidays, as well as the amount of vacation time (usually related to years of service), and the specific holidays that will be recognized.[9]

In contrast, American labor agreements are usually mute on the question of the employment level. Explicit wage-employment guarantees are infrequent (Table 16.2). In 1980, only 11 percent of major private-sector collective-bargaining agreements—mainly those in transportation, retail trade, and construction—had such guarantees. Limitations on crew size, largely in construction, printing, utilities, and transportation, are also relatively rare. Limitations on subcontracting work that was previously done by members of the bargaining unit are more prevalent but do not dominate the employer's choice of employment level. Even these provisions are virtually nonexistent in the public sector.

By default, then, the decision over employment levels in most collective-bargaining agreements in the United States is left to the catchall management-rights clause. It is not unusual for such clauses to contain language to the effect that "the right to schedule work hours, to hire, promote, demote, and transfer, discharge for just cause, or to reduce employment because of lack of work or for

---

[9]Data on the distribution of contractual provisions governing wages and fringe benefits by industry and by level of government may be found in U.S. Bureau of Labor Statistics, *Characteristics of Major Collective Bargaining Agreements, January 1, 1980,* Bulletin 2095 (Washington, D.C.: U.S. Government Printing Office, May 1981); and U.S. Bureau of Labor Statistics, *Characteristics of Agreements in State and Local Governments, January 1, 1974,* Bulletin 1861 (Washington, D.C.: U.S. Government Printing Office, 1975).

Table 16.2. Employment Provisions in Major Collective-Bargaining
Agreements, 1980

	Total Agreements	Wage-Employment Guarantees	Crew-Size Limitations	Subcontracting Limitations
Total	1550	173 (11%)	337 (22%)	900 (58%)
Manufacturing	750	59 (8%)	94 (13%)	399 (53%)
Nonmanufacturing	800	114 (14%)	243 (32%)	501 (67%)

Note: Since the contract provisions are not mutually exclusive, percentages may add to more than 100%.

SOURCE: U.S. Bureau of Labor Statistics, *Characteristics of Major Collective Bargaining Agreements, January 1, 1980,*
Bulletin 2095 (Washington, D.C.: U.S. Government Printing Office, May 1981), pp. 104, 106, 109.

other legitimate reasons are vested exclusively in the company, provided that such
rights are not applied in a manner that violates the provisions of the agreement."[10]

Bargaining over an Uncertain Future

One of the most difficult problems facing union and management negotiators is
how to structure an agreement that addresses their respective interests in efficiency and equity when facing an uncertain future. One approach to uncertainty
is to negotiate short-term contracts, possibly no longer than a year in duration,
so that contract terms can be adjusted to unexpected events through frequent
renegotiations. The renegotiation of a labor agreement is a costly process, however, and over the years, management and labor have sought to reduce negotiating
costs by lengthening the duration of collective-bargaining agreements. With long-
term labor agreements and highly imperfect economic forecasts, how can the
parties deal with uncertainty?

There are two general approaches to adapting long-term contracts to uncertainty. One is to *preset* the terms based on a forecast of what future economic
conditions will be. The second is to make certain benefits *contingent* on future
events that may or may not occur. Both devices are used in modern collective-
bargaining agreements. The data in Table 16.3, for example, show that labor
agreements in both the private and public sector make some provision for wage
adjustments during the term of the agreement. (Such adjustments are generally
more frequent in the private sector where the average duration of a collective-
bargaining agreement is longer than in the public sector.) The data also show,

---

[10]Some unions negotiate employment restrictions as well as compensation levels—an approach
that can result in an efficient contract. The results of an econometric analysis of wages and employment in newspaper composing rooms organized by the International Typographical Union suggested
that bargains negotiated by this union tended to be on the contract curve. *See* Thomas E. MaCurdy
and John Pencavel, "Testing Between Competing Models of Wage and Employment Determination
in Unionized Markets" (unpublished paper, Department of Economics, Stanford University, November 1982). Others have argued that under conditions of uncertainty, management control over
employment levels may be consistent with efficient bargaining. *See* Hall and Lilien, "Efficient Wage
Bargains . . . ."

Table 16.3. Wage Adjustments During the Term of a Collective-Bargaining Agreement

	All Agreements	Percent of All Agreements in Sector[a] with Provisions for:		
		Escalator (cost-of-living) Adjustments	Deferred Wage Increases	Contract Reopening
Private industry[b]	100	49	89	21
Manufacturing	100	64	90	16
Nonmanufacturing	100	34	88	25
State and local government[c]	100	15	52	24
State	100	8	35	32
County	100	10	44	31
Municipal	100	20	66	15
Special district	100	50	50	21

[a]Percentages may add to more than 100 because some agreements have more than one type of wage adjustment provision.
[b]Agreements covering 1,000 workers or more, January 1, 1980.
[c]Agreements in effect on January 1, 1974.

SOURCE: U.S. Bureau of Labor Statistics, *Characteristics of Major Collective Bargaining Agreements, January 1, 1980,* Bulletin 2095 (Washington, D.C.: U.S. Government Printing Office, May 1981), p. 55; and U.S. Bureau of Labor Statistics, *Characteristics of Agreements in State and Local Governments, January 1, 1974,* Bulletin 1861 (Washington, D.C.: U.S. Government Printing Office, 1975), p. 25.

however, that, in both sectors, preset deferred-wage increases, which are scheduled to be received at particular times irrespective of actual economic developments, are more common than contingent increases. Preset deferred wages are often granted in response to the union requests for an "annual improvement factor" (to reflect an implicit forecast of general productivity increases over the life of the contract) and in response to the negotiators' general forecasts of future economic events, such as inflation and unemployment. Present wage increases involve risk to both parties, because economic events may turn out more or less favorable to either party than anticipated. Because wage increases are predetermined and do not respond to *actual* economic events during the lifetime of the contract, employment fluctuations are likely to be larger than they would be if wage increases were contingent on economic performance.

Two common methods for providing for contingencies are to permit a contract to specify circumstances under which the parties can reopen negotiations prior to the scheduled expiration date of the agreement or to automatically adjust wages to changes in a general index of prices (usually referred to as "cost-of-living" adjustments). Of these, the latter is more common in the private sector and raises a number of issues that are discussed in the next section.

One interesting feature of the arrangements providing for contingent increases that have been established in collective bargaining prior to the 1980s is that wage adjustments were almost always keyed to movements in external economic indicators rather than indicators of the performance of the firm(s) that are parties to the agreement. Methods of making wage increases contingent on the performance of the firm have received far more attention during the "concession bargaining" of the 1980s, and we examine some of these methods later in the chapter.

Cost-of-Living Adjustment (COLA) Clauses

One of the major uncertainties facing both union and management negotiators is the path that prices will follow during the term of the collective-bargaining agreement. Management is interested in the likely future path of the prices for its products and services, for those prices will affect the profitability of the company. Union leaders are interested in the future path of prices in general, because the general rate of inflation will affect the real earnings that their members achieve from the collective-bargaining agreement. When the period between contract negotiations is relatively short—up to a year—each party may be able to forecast the behavior of prices with reasonable accuracy in determining the wage increases that they wish to demand or grant. If a forecast turns out to be inaccurate, a relatively brief period of time passes before the parties have the opportunity to try to adjust to the new information in another round of collective-bargaining negotiations. When the period between negotiations is relatively long, however, the forecasts of price behavior in the later years of a contract are likely to be less accurate and the consequences of inaccurate forecasts can be substantial. The future behavior of prices becomes an important contingency against which most unions require protection before they are willing to sign a long duration agreement. In some cases, labor agreements provide for reopening a contract during its term under specified circumstances. More frequently, however, unions have pressed for *cost-of-living adjustment (COLA)* provisions (sometimes referred to as "cost-of-living escalators") as a *quid pro quo* for signing a contract of long duration.

A COLA imposes a contractual obligation on an employer to adjust the wages of workers in a bargaining unit in response to changes in a general index of prices (usually the national Consumer Price Index for urban wage earners and clerical workers) according to a formula that is specified in the contract. There is considerable variation in the formulae adopted in different collective-bargaining situations. For example, COLAs that required that wage rates of all workers increase by the same percent as the price index would offer complete real-wage protection. Such formulae are the exception rather than the rule in collective-bargaining agreements, however, in part because they maintain existing relative wage differentials by skill, which many unions wish to narrow in line with their egalitarian objectives. Instead, COLA formulae take a variety of other forms that generally provide less than full compensation for price increases. In the early 1980s, for example, the compensation provided by COLAs ranged from 50 to 100 percent in major collective-bargaining agreements, with the average around 65–75 percent. Historically, the most generous COLAs—offering essentially full compensation for general price increases—were negotiated by the United Automobile Workers and the major automobile manufacturers, but these were significantly amended in bargaining over wage concessions in the early 1980s.

The most common COLA formula provides for a uniform cents-per-hour wage increase for a specified absolute change in the price index—for example, one cent an hour for every change of 0.3 or 0.4 of a point in the Consumer Price Index. In providing the same absolute wage adjustment for inflation to all workers irrespective of their wage level, this formula provides higher percentage wage increases to low-wage workers than to high-wage workers and therefore has the effect of narrowing percentage wage differentials by skill. For this reason, the formula is favored by unions that wish to achieve a more equal distribution of earnings. As wage levels change over time, however, the average compensation for price increases provided workers by a COLA based on this formula decreases, leading unions to attempt to renegotiate the parameters of the formula periodically. Employers are sometimes successful in limiting their potential obligation under a COLA by negotiating a "cap" or maximum payment to be made during a given period. Unions typically want a "floor" to the COLA so that their wages do not fall if prices fall (a very rare event in the past 35 years!).[11]

Once a formula has been agreed to, the yield of a COLA is also influenced by the frequency with which changes in the CPI are reviewed in order to determine whether payments are due. The shorter the period between reviews, the more closely will the movement of money wages track the path of prices. Moreover, COLA payments received throughout a year (that is, under a quarterly or semi-annual review) can be spent or invested and, hence, have more value for a worker than payments received at the end of a year (that is, under an annual review). Quarterly reviews are found most frequently in major collective-bargaining agreements, but annual reviews are also common.[12]

Cost-of-living escalation coverage is by no means uniform over time or across industries in the United States. Although the use of "cost-of-living" as a criteria for wage increases dates back to the beginning of this century,[13] the first major American labor contract to contain a COLA provision was the 1948 contract between General Motors and the United Automobile Workers, which also marked a shift from annual to two-year agreements. The subsequent development of COLAs has been fitful, and even after the substantial inflation of the 1970s, many union workers were not covered by COLAs (Table 16.4). Moreover, formal COLAs are rare in nonunion firms, so that the percentage of the labor force whose

---

[11]One of the few examples of pay cuts under a COLA during the postwar period was in the initial COLA between the General Motors Corporation and the United Autoworkers' Union. Shortly after the agreement was signed in September 1948, the CPI fell, requiring union members to accept money wage-cuts under the COLA in parts of 1949 and early 1950.

[12]Sixty-three percent of the COLAs in effect in major collective-bargaining agreements in 1983 provided for quarterly review, sixteen percent provided for annual review, and fifteen percent for semi-annual review. (The remaining contracts had other review procedures.) William M. Davis, "Collective Bargaining in 1983: A Crowded Agenda," *Monthly Labor Review,* 106 (January 1983): 11.

[13]For a discussion of early uses of COLAs, see Elma B. Carr, *The Use of Cost-of-Living Figures in Wage Adjustments,* Bureau of Labor Statistics Bulletin No. 369 (Washington, D.C.: U.S. Government Printing Office, 1925).

Table 16.4. Coverage of Cost-of-Living Escalator Provisions in Major Union Contracts[a]

Date	Number of Workers Covered by Major Union Contracts (millions)	Number Covered by Cost-of-Living Provisions (millions)	Percent Covered by Cost-of-Living Provisions	Annual Percent Change in the Consumer Price Index in the Previous Year
1/50	n.a.	0.8	n.a.	5.8
1/57	7.8	3.5	45	2.9
1/59	8.0	4.0	50	1.8
1/60	8.1	4.0	49	1.5
1/61	8.1	2.7	33	1.5
1/62	8.0	2.5	31	1.7
1/63	7.8	1.9	24	1.2
1/64	7.8	2.0	26	1.6
1/65	7.9	2.0	25	1.2
1/66	10.0	2.0	20	1.9
1/67	10.6	2.2	21	3.4
1/68	10.6	2.5	24	3.0
1/69	10.8	2.7	25	4.7
1/70	10.8	2.8	26	6.1
1/71	10.6	3.0	28	5.5
1/72	10.4	4.3	41	3.4
1/73	10.5	4.1	39	3.4
1/74	10.3	4.0	39	8.8
1/75	10.2	5.1	50	12.2
11/76	10.0	6.0	61	4.8
11/77	9.7	5.8	60	6.8
11/78	9.6	5.6	58	9.0
11/79	9.4	5.5	59	13.3
11/80	9.3	5.3	57	12.4
10/81	9.0	5.1	56	8.9
1/83	8.5	4.9	58	5.6

n.a. not available

[a]Contracts covering 1,000 or more workers in private industry. Prior to 1966 the construction, service, finance, and real estate industries were excluded.

SOURCES: H. M. Douty, *Cost-of-Living Escalator Clauses and Inflation,* Table 1 (Council on Wage and Price Stability, August 1975) (for data through January 1975); *Monthly Labor Review,* January issues for 1976–1983 (for data from November 1975 on); *1982 Economic Report of the President,* Table B55 (consumer price index) (Washington, D. C., 1981).

wages are formally indexed to price movements is much smaller than indicated by the data in Table 16.4.[14] The uneven incidence of COLAs is also apparent in the

---

[14]Information on COLA coverage in the nonunion sector is sparse, but one study of wages in manufacturing firms found that a maximum of four percent of nonunion workers were covered by a COLA during the 1970s. In a typical year, two percent of the workers were covered. As a result, only about a third of all workers in manufacturing were covered by COLAs during the mid-1970s. (The study also found that COLA coverage was more extensive in major bargaining units [1,000 or more workers] than in smaller bargaining units.) George Ruben, "Observations of Wage Developments in Manufacturing During 1959–78," *Current Wage Developments* 33 (May 1981): 49. A 1975 survey of a random sample of 480 private firms (both union and nonunion) found that 39 percent of the firms paid COLA wage increases to union hourly employees. The comparable percentages for nonunion employees were: nonunion hourly—10 percent; exempt salaried—nine percent; officers—four percent. David A. Weeks, *Compensating Employees: Lessons of the 1970s* (New York: National Industrial Conference Board, 1976).

data on the industrial distribution of COLA coverage in collective bargaining (reported in Table 16.5 on the next page.)

The historical evidence suggests that the prevalence of COLA provisions in collective-bargaining contracts has fluctuated over time; in particular, they appear more frequently after a period of inflation has started and tend to be dropped after a period of price stability. There was an expansion in COLA coverage in response to the increase in inflation in 1957 and 1958, but it took several years to drop the clauses when prices leveled off at the end of the 1950s and into the early 1960s. In part, this reflected the spread of long duration agreements, which reduced the speed with which contract terms could be adjusted to external events. This inertia in the response of contractual provisions to external events can be seen (Table 16.4) in the late 1960s. By the mid-1960s, coverage in major collective-bargaining agreements was low and it remained so throughout the growth of inflation in the late 1960s. By the time unions reestablished COLA protection during collective-bargaining negotiations in the early 1970s, the rate of inflation had dropped. With the persistence of high inflation rates during the late 1970s, the extent of COLA protection reached an historical high and has remained fairly stable since then.

What accounts for the variation in COLA coverage and the compensation for general price increases provided by COLAs over time and across industries? Some of the variance across industries is related to differences in contract duration. However, this itself is related to more basic underlying forces. Recent studies suggest that the extent of COLA protection is related more fundamentally to the nature of the risks firms face in different industries and to the risk preferences of employers and employees. If firms were completely risk neutral, that is, unconcerned about year-to-year variations in profits around their long-run level, they would presumably be willing to grant complete indexation, and COLAs would yield full compensation for general price increases. In fact, the data show that both COLA coverage and the degree of wage adjustment for inflation are far from complete. Workers receive only partial insurance for uncertain future price changes. Employers, too, must be risk averse. Evidence increasingly indicates that the variety in COLAs reflects patterns of risk-sharing between employers and employees in which each is partially insured for the risks incurred during a long-term labor agreement.[15]

Indexing Wages to Firm Performance

An alternative form of contingent contracting would index changes in compensation for union members to the general performance of the firm. Payment-by-results (piecework) systems, productivity bargaining, profit-sharing, and employee stock-ownership of firms are all methods by which the compensation of labor can be made to depend on the output or productive efficiency of a firm. Historically, most unions that have agreed to contingent wage increases have been

---

[15]*See* Ronald G. Ehrenberg, Leif Danziger, and Gee San, "Cost-of-Living Adjustment Clauses in Union Contracts," *Journal of Labor Economics* 1 (July 1983); David Card, "Indexation in Long Term Labor Contracts: A Theoretical and Empirical Analysis," Working Paper No. 152 (Princeton, N.J.: Industrial Relations Section, Princeton University, August 1982).

Table 16.5. Prevalence of Cost-of-Living Adjustment Clauses in Major Collective-Bargaining Agreements, October 1982 (workers in thousands)

2-digit standard industry classification (SIC)	Industry	All Contracts		Contracts with COLA Clauses		Percent of Workers Covered by COLA Clauses
		Workers Covered	Number of Contracts	Workers Covered	Number of Contracts	
	Total	8,484	1,772	4,928	687	58.1
10	Metal mining	36	12	34	10	93.2
11	Anthracite mining	2	1	2	1	100.0
12	Bituminous coal and lignite mining	160	1	—	—	0
15	Building construction general contractors	612	162	42	8	6.8
16	Construction other than building construction	435	116	105	16	24.2
17	Construction-special trade contractors	410	190	31	17	7.5
20	Food and kindred products	252	87	127	33	50.4
21	Tobacco manufacturing	22	7	20	6	90.2
22	Textile mill products	45	16	8	3	18.1
23	Apparel and other finished products	351	47	266	21	75.8
24	Lumber and wood products, except furniture	60	14	1	1	2.2
25	Furniture and fixtures	20	13	8	6	40.8
26	Paper and allied products	86	53	8	1	9.3
27	Printing, publishing, and allied industries	54	27	33	15	62.2
28	Chemicals and allied products	68	34	21	10	31.5
29	Petroleum refining and related industries	34	18	—	—	0
30	Rubber and miscellaneous plastics	66	14	59	11	90.5
31	Leather and leather products	38	13	—	—	0
32	Stone, clay, glass, and concrete products	85	35	70	26	81.6
33	Primary metals industries	437	97	421	88	96.4
34	Fabricated metal products	94	52	72	38	76.7
35	Machinery, except electrical	238	78	203	66	85.6
36	Electrical machinery, equipment, and supplies	373	77	341	60	91.4
37	Transportation equipment	1,130	94	984	73	87.2
38	Instruments and related products	28	13	8	4	29.4
39	Miscellaneous manufacturing industries	19	10	4	3	22.5
40	Railroad transportation	412	26	412	26	100.0
41	Local and urban transit	17	3	15	1	85.8

(Continued)

2-digit standard industry classification (SIC)	Industry	All Contracts		Contracts with COLA Clauses		Percent of Workers Covered by COLA Clauses
		Workers Covered	Number of Contracts	Workers Covered	Number of Contracts	
42	Motor freight transportation	442	17	442	17	100.0
44	Water transportation	89	19	34	7	38.5
45	Transportation by air	182	45	72	14	39.6
48	Communications	759	46	696	29	91.7
49	Electric, gas, and sanitary services	235	75	44	13	18.7
50	Wholesale trade—durables	10	5	3	1	25.5
51	Wholesale trade—nondurables	39	10	31	4	78.6
53	Retail trade—general merchandise	78	18	25	4	32.3
54	Food stores	517	95	197	33	38.1
55	Automotive dealers and service stations	11	8	1	1	11.5
56	Apparel and accessory stores	10	4	—	—	0
58	Eating and drinking places	66	20	—	—	0
59	Miscellaneous retail stores	16	5	15	4	93.5
60–65	Finance, insurance, and real estate	93	18	46	6	49.6
70–89	Services	353	77	25	10	7.1

Note: Because of rounding, sums of individual items may not equal totals, and percentages may not reflect shown ratios. Dashes indicate absence of cost-of-living coverage.
SOURCE: William Davis, "Collective Bargaining in 1983," *Monthly Labor Review* 106 (January 1983):10.

willing to index wages to general economic indicators (such as prices) but not to the fortunes of the firms that employ their members (Table 16.6).

In the early 1980s, this situation changed dramatically in several industries with the severe product-market pressures brought about by a deep recession, increased foreign competition, deregulation of pricing, and new firm entry. In an effort to survive, employers in these industries proposed a number of changes that

Table 16.6. Profit-sharing, Savings, and Stock-Purchase Plans by Industry (percent of all agreements in sector)

	All Agreements	Profit-sharing Plans	Savings Plans	Stock-Purchase Plans
Private industry[a]	100	2	5	2
Manufacturing	100	3	8	4
Nonmanufacturing	100	1	2	1

[a]Agreements covering 1000 workers or more, January 1, 1980.

SOURCE: U.S. Bureau of Labor Statistics, *Characteristics of Major Collective Bargaining Agreements, January 1, 1980,* Bulletin 2095 (Washington, D.C.: U.S. Government Printing Office, May 1981), p. 49.

had the effect of altering the nature of collective-bargaining agreements so that compensation (labor cost) was more directly related to the performance of the firm or industry. The fact that unions responded is a dramatic example of the fact that far from being insulated from market forces, collective bargaining can be a remarkably flexible and even innovative institution when under great pressure. We shall examine several methods of indexing wages to employer-specific contingencies that have been adopted in collective bargaining.

Indexing wages to output. The most widely used method of indexing wages directly to output in collective-bargaining agreements is *piecework* or *payment-by-results.* About a quarter of the major private-sector agreements provide for incentive payments to some employees (typically certain production workers in the manufacturing sector). While such systems can result in higher productivity, they also can have a number of undesirable consequences on production (see Chapter 10) that effectively limit their application. In particular, payment-by-results and related incentive-payment systems may be inappropriate when it is difficult to monitor the quality of output or to discern the contribution of individual workers to output. This helps to explain why payment systems that directly link wages and output are not found more widely in industry.

Unions often view incentive-payment systems with suspicion on the grounds that when misused, they can become disguised methods of production speedup. This is a particular concern when management seeks to change incentive-pay rates as a result of changes in technology, materials, or the organization of production that alter the average output expected from a worker in a given period of time. In most situations piece rates are adjusted downward (for example, to compensate for greater efficiency made possible by increased capital intensity). But if rates are adjusted downward too far, workers will have to expend more effort to maintain their prior incomes. Unions, therefore, seek language in the collective-bargaining agreement that establishes a union role in setting or protesting revisions in incentive-pay rates. Efforts to alter incentive-payment standards can be a major source of grievances in unionized firms, and this additional cost of these payment-by-results systems may be another factor that limits their use in industry.

Productivity bargaining. *Productivity bargaining* occurs when labor and management directly negotiate the terms under which specific changes in methods designed to increase production will occur. In contrast to the more or less continuous incentives for efficiency embedded in the payments-by-results systems discussed above, productivity bargaining is usually part of an effort by management to establish major once-and-for-all changes in the work environment. Productivity bargaining is most likely to arise when management wishes to introduce a major technical change, to eliminate work rules that reduce productive efficiency, or both. Either of these objectives normally constitutes a threat to the job security of union members, and the task of productivity bargaining is to explore methods of gaining the benefits of greater efficiency while minimizing concerns over job security.

There is an inherent conflict between labor and management over the question of contractual work rules that specify the number of workers required to do a job or the flexibility with which employees can be assigned to different jobs. Employers are likely to view such rules as leading to reductions in productive efficiency, and it is usually the case that labor productivity would be higher in their absence. Unions, however, often argue that the rules are required to maintain reasonable health and safety standards at the workplace for their members. Does it take three people on a modern, computerized flight deck to fly an airplane safely or only two? Chapter 7 discussed how well-informed and mobile workers would consider on-the-job health and safety risks when choosing their place of employment, and how employers offering unsafe conditions would have to pay a wage premium in order to attract workers. Unions hold the view that when information is imperfect and workers are immobile, so that the theoretical market incentives for employers to reduce unsafe working conditions are not always present, the task of providing for worker health and safety falls to collective bargaining.

In fact, some union work rules only become "restrictive" or inefficient as technology changes. Rules concerning the number of employees needed to do a job may be quite reasonable under one state of technology but quite inefficient when there is technical advance. For example, painting many surfaces with a brush is efficient until someone invents a spraygun. To take another example, a rule, negotiated long ago by railroad unions, specified that railroad workers receive a day's pay for every 100 miles traveled—a sensible requirement when it takes an eight-hour shift to travel 100 miles. However, when technological changes in railroading make it possible to travel three times that distance in an eight-hour day, the rule results in substantial inefficiency. It is the effort to maintain past work rules as technology changes that gives rise to restrictive union work practices or "featherbedding" in some industries. The most serious restrictive practices appear to have been limited to a few industries, such as construction, printing, and railroads, which are organized primarily by craft unions. In some of these industries, union concerns over the health and safety of the work environment are supplemented by the threat of some technological changes to the existence of the union itself. In industries where each craft union represents workers in a relatively narrowly defined skill, there is a danger that some innovations may eliminate the need for that skill entirely and, hence, the need for the union. Efforts to maintain past work rules are stronger when the survival of a union is at stake.

Even in industries organized by industrial unions, however, there are frequently restrictions on the flexibility with which workers can be assigned to different jobs.[16] When the work force of a plant is divided into many craft groups, and the labor agreement does not permit workers in one craft to do jobs in others,

---

[16]Restrictive work rules are commonly associated with the presence of unions. In fact, norms of work behavior that many employers would view as restrictive develop among and are enforced by workers in nonunion firms. For an early study of restrictive working norms among nonunion employees, with some interesting observations on management actions that encouraged the development of the norms, *see* Stanley B. Matthewson, *Restriction of Output Among Unorganized Workers* (New York: Viking Press, Inc., 1931). Similarly, John R. Commons, a distinguished student of unions, is said to have remarked that, "The non-unionist does not change his nature when he becomes a unionist, but merely has more power to do what he wanted to do before."

employers may have to pay workers who are idle because there is a temporary shortage of work in their craft jurisdiction. A contract that established fewer craft units and broader definitions of the jobs that each craft could perform would result in more efficient production.

How are labor agreements structured to deal with technological change or adjustment of work rules? In some situations, productivity bargaining may not be necessary. The impact of new technology on a rapidly growing firm may be to slow the rate of growth of employment rather than to reduce the number of jobs. In cases where some job loss occurs, if the introduction of new technology can be spread over time, the employment adjustment may be handled through attrition—the loss of employees through the normal turnover that every organization experiences.

Some collective-bargaining agreements require employers to provide advance notice of layoff or major technological change. The purpose of advance-notice requirements is to provide time for adjustment to the change. With sufficient advance notice, it is easier to take advantage of the attrition approach to easing employment adjustments. However, contractual provisions for advance notice are more common for layoffs (resulting from poor economic conditions, plant shutdowns, or relocation) than they are for technological change. In 1980, only about 10 percent of the major agreements in the private sector required that the union receive advance notice of technological change, whereas about 45 percent required it for layoffs.

Another approach to protecting workers from changes in technology or economic conditions is to provide for income security in the event of displacement. That is, contractual provisions are negotiated that require an employer to provide severance pay—either a fixed sum or a monthly allowance graduated by length of employment—to workers whose employment is terminated, or supplemental unemployment benefits to workers who are placed on layoff. In 1980, about a third of the major agreements provided for severance pay, and less than 15 percent provided for supplemental unemployment benefits.

A third general approach to economic change is to spread the available work opportunities by broadening seniority units or by establishing rights for workers to transfer between plants. In practice, this approach often creates severe political difficulties for the union or unions involved, since it usually grants rights to one group of members (in the threatened department or plant) to supplant or "bump" other less-senior members (in another department or plant). In effect, it shifts the problem of job—and income—insecurity from more senior workers to less senior workers.

When employers wish to achieve major changes in work rules or production methods, however, change may sometimes only occur through productivity bargaining, in which agreement by the union to specific changes is sought, in return for commitments from the employer concerning the job or income security of union members. One interesting feature of productivity bargaining is that it is not necessarily a zero sum game—gains to one side are not necessarily offset by losses to the other. If the result is an increase in the productivity of the organization, the size of the pie available for division between labor and management will be larger. This has been exactly the outcome in several important instances of productivity bargaining (see Example 16.2). Nevertheless, this outcome is not always obvious in advance, and agreement over the change often requires provisions for job or income security (as Example 16.2 also illustrates).

One characteristic of productivity-bargaining negotiations is that the union is typically concerned with the security of current members only. Therefore, where the prospective efficiency gains from technological change or an alteration of work rules are sufficiently large, employers may find income guarantees to those workers most threatened by the changes economically feasible. Even when guarantees are feasible, they do not usually provide job or income security indefinitely. (For a notable exception and its consequences, however, see the last two paragraphs of Example 16.2.) In some instances—particularly where the work force is relatively old, so that retirement places an implicit limit on the guarantee —an employer may agree to provide "lifetime" security. An agreement reached between a local of the Typographical Union and newspaper publishers and printing establishments in New York City during the mid-1970s provides a dramatic example. The parties signed 10-year agreements in which the union dropped all "manning requirements" (contractual rules requiring the use of union printers even when automated printers could do a task more efficiently) and allowed virtually unlimited introduction of automated composing techniques, in exchange for *lifetime* job guarantees for *regular, full-time* printers. Interestingly, the average age of regular, full-time printers at the time was 56, and the contract provided for mandatory retirement from the industry at age 68!

Profit-sharing and worker ownership. Another method of structuring labor agreements so that compensation is linked to the performance of the firm is through *profit-sharing arrangements* in which workers receive a share of the profits of a business in addition to their regular pay. *Employee stock-ownership plans* are a related method of linking at least some of a worker's compensation to the economic fortunes of the firm. Historically, profit-sharing arrangements have been almost unknown in collective-bargaining agreements in the United States (Table 16.6). However, profit-sharing and stock-purchase plans received increasing attention during the 1980s as union and management negotiators sought ways to adapt contracts to the severe economic pressures faced by many industries. In 1983, for example, members of the Airline Pilots Association working for Eastern Airlines, which had suffered serious financial losses, agreed to accept debentures that would later be convertible into shares of Eastern's common stock, in exchange for *deferring* some of their pay. The pilots were expected to own as much as a 21 percent share of Eastern's common stock under the arrangement. In addition, the pilots were to be given the right to name one or two members to the sixteen-member board of directors of the airline.

To the extent that profit-sharing or stock ownership is an element of the pay package, at least part of compensation is effectively contingent on *all* of the uncertainties faced by the firm—including many factors, such as shifts in product demand, that may not be controllable by union members. Even efforts to enhance employee productivity through profit-sharing or employee ownership may en-

EXAMPLE 16.2

Productivity Bargaining in the Pacific Longshore Industry

Pacific Coast longshore workers, who load and unload cargo for ships in ports such as Seattle, San Francisco, and Los Angeles, were organized by the International Longshoremen's and Warehousemen's Union in 1934, following a coastwide strike. The labor market for longshore workers was "casual"—meaning that the timing of work and one's employer varied daily, depending on the irregular arrivals and departures of cargo ships. Because the work itself was basically unskilled and many jobs lasted only a few hours, entry into the labor market was easy. While some individuals had a full-time attachment to longshore work, others worked only part-time, often "moonlighting" while holding a primary job in some other industry. Hours and earnings were erratic and unemployment was frequent.

Following the establishment of collective bargaining in the industry, several steps toward a more formal approach to the labor market were made with the assistance of a special arbitration board. A hiring hall run jointly by the ILWU and the Pacific Maritime Association (PMA), the employers' association for the industry, was established to dispatch workers to jobs. Experienced longshore workers were registered to use the hiring hall, and gradually, each port began to make a distinction between workers with a more or less full-time attachment to the industry (who were put on an "A" list) and workers with a more intermittent attachment (who were put on a "B" list and worked only after workers on the A list were dispatched to jobs).

The union also succeeded in establishing a number of restrictive work practices in an effort to offset the irregularity of hours and the extensive unemployment. In an effort to reduce the pace of work, limits were placed on the amount of cargo that could be moved between ship and shore in a sling load. The agreement required a basic work group of eight longshore workers in the hold while loading a ship, and six in the hold while unloading a ship. Typically, however, only half of each group actually worked, and the remaining members came to be known as "witnesses" of the work performed by their colleagues. Multiple handling of cargo was also common. Cargo delivered to the docks in pallet-loads prepared by workers outside the ILWU were frequently required to be unloaded from the pallet at dockside and then reloaded on pallets by ILWU members. As is frequently the case with restrictive work rules, many of these practices had some basis in worker safety—but the cumulative effect of the rules was essentially that there was no gain in the productivity of longshore workers for 25 years.

In the late 1950s, there was considerable pressure for giving up the rules. Given the inefficiencies, the West Coast ports were losing business to the East and Gulf Coast ports, where similar rules were not in effect. Moreover, there were important technological changes, including the containerization of loads, that employers wished to introduce in order to compete more effectively. Yet it was widely assumed that there would be a severe reduction in the employment of longshore workers if employers were given a free hand in their choices of technology. Longshore employment appeared threatened whether the restrictive practices were retained or given up. The challenge to collective bargaining was to find some mechanism that would permit the employers to modernize the docks while handling workers' fear for their job security.

In 1959 the ILWU and the PMA signed a seven-year Mechanization and Modernization Agreement in which the union gave up the restrictive work practices and dropped its objections to containerization, and the employers set up a $29 million fund that was to be used to guarantee job security. First, it offered incentives for early retirement in an effort to induce the substantial number of older longshore workers to withdraw from the industry. More importantly, the agreement guaranteed the earnings equivalent of 35 hours of work per week at the basic straight-time wage rate to all longshore workers on the industry's A list. If someone on the A list averaged less than 35 hours a week, the difference between the actual earnings and the guaranteed earnings would be made up from the fund.

The impact of the agreement on productivity was remarkable. After 25 years of stagnation, labor productivity increased by a third between 1960 and 1964. One careful study found that most of the productivity was attributable to the elimination of work rules, and that increased capital intensity associated with employer investments—particularly in containerization—played a significant, but secondary, role. At the same time, the expected decline in longshore employment did not materialize. With increased productivity of longshore operations, more shippers used West Coast ports, and it was found that workers on the A list never had to draw on the $29 million dollar fund in order to attain their guarantees! The fund was distributed through lump-sum payments to workers on the A list at the end of the seven-year period.

Efforts to buy out work rules that are viewed as obsolete and inefficient through productivity bargaining are not inherently successful, however. The ultimate outcome depends on the balance between the efficiency gains from eliminating work rules, on the one hand, and the size of payments to union members necessary to secure an agreement to give up the rules. That this balance may not always be favorable is illustrated by experience under an agreement negotiated in the New York City longshore industry.

In 1966, the International Longshoremen's Association (ILA) gave up practices similar to those that were eliminated in the West Coast ports in exchange for a guarantee that any longshoreman who had worked at least 700 hours in 1965 would be guaranteed 2080 hours of work (40 hours per week for 52 weeks) annually *or* the equivalent pay—*forever!* The relatively low number of hours of work required for eligibility, the relatively high number of hours for which pay is guaranteed, and the fact that the guarantee is lifetime have produced much higher costs than were experienced under similar plans on the West Coast and in other ports. As a result, the cost of the program to the steamship lines that pay for it has risen from $1.7 million in its initial year to $70 million in 1983, when the annual guarantee was $29,120. Several hundred longshoremen do not work at all under current levels of demand in the port of New York; they are only required to check in briefly each morning in order to qualify for payment.

The result is a vicious circle. The high labor costs lead shippers to use other ports. (It is estimated that the port of New York's share of all container cargo dropped from 17 percent to 10 percent during the 1970s, for example.) As demand declines, however, the number of people receiving pay for no work rises, thereby increasing the unit costs of the work that is done, which encourages more shipping to be diverted to other ports.

SOURCE: Paul T. Hartman, *Collective Bargaining and Productivity: The Longshore Mechanization Agreement* (Berkeley: University of California Press, 1969); Sam Roberts, "On the Waterfront: Cost of Labor Could Make City a Noncontender," *New York Times*, June 22, 1983, and "Economics on the Piers: Wage Guarantee Is the Crux," *New York Times*, June 23, 1983.

counter some of the risks inherent in group incentive plans, discussed earlier in Chapter 10. Chief among these is the "free-rider" problem. The benefits of increased profits are a public good—that is, they accrue to each worker, irrespective of his or her role in raising profits. Therefore, while some workers strive to improve efficiency, others may decide to take a "free ride" and collect the benefits of someone else's hard work. This is particularly easy to rationalize in a large organization in which a worker may reason that increasing his or her own individual effort would have a relatively small effect on profits. If most workers reason this way, improvements in profits and pay are unlikely. In the early 1980s, a few unions in economically distressed firms or industries began to accept limited profit-sharing arrangements in exchange for forgoing normal noncontingent wage increases, but the spread of such arrangements was slow. (In the automobile industry, Chrysler offered to grant wage increases once profits passed certain levels, for example.)

The most extreme form of profit-sharing is worker ownership of a company, wherein workers own or control a company's stock. In 1972, for example, Northwest Industries, Inc., sold the Chicago & Northwestern Railway to the railroad's employees. However, a group of independent trustees was given the authority to run the railroad, and, for ten years, the voting rights of employee-stockholders were limited to questions involving mergers and new stock issues. While only ten percent of the employees initially purchased the stock, the profitability of the railroad and the value of the stock increased substantially over the next decade. Worker ownership of a company raises most of the issues that workers and unions confront in more limited profit-sharing plans. In addition, there is an array of complicated financial and management issues; in particular, the entire question of the union's role as a representative of the employees, who are now the owners of the firm. Is the strike threat now credible? Will unions play an important role in advising employees how to vote their stock? Is the question of the distribution of the firm's earnings between labor and capital any longer an issue? Why should a worker-owned firm be inherently more profitable? A widespread movement toward worker ownership of firms would undoubtedly raise serious challenges to traditional forms of collective bargaining as we have known them. To date, the examples of worker ownership have largely been limited to situations in which companies of substantial size, are in economic distress (see Example 16.3).

Administration of the
Contract-Grievance Procedures

When representatives of labor and management reach agreement over the terms and conditions of employment that each side recognizes as preferable to the alternative of incurring or continuing a work stoppage, it is likely that each party to the negotiations will bear some responsibility for enforcing the terms of the agreement. Nevertheless, labor agreements are not inherently self-enforcing, and it is not unusual for disagreements to arise between union and management representatives over the application of various clauses while the contract is in effect. While strikes or lockouts could, in principle, be used in an effort to compel agreement over the interpretation of the contract, we have seen how management often insists on a no-strike pledge while a contract is in effect, as a *quid pro quo* for signing an agreement in the first place. Moreover, most union leaders are unwilling to precipitate a strike that will result in lost wages for large numbers of union members over an issue of contract interpretation— the application of a discharge clause, for example—that affects only one or, at most, a few workers.

Therefore, some alternative method for resolving *grievances,* disputes that arise during the term of an agreement, is necessary. Ninety-nine percent of major private-sector collective-bargaining agreements in the United States and almost 90 percent of the agreements in state and local governments include provisions for a *grievance procedure* for this purpose (see Table 16.7). Grievance procedures first provide an opportunity for labor and management representatives to work out a solution to their disagreement. If the parties fail to resolve the dispute, the vast majority of labor agreements provide for arbitration as the final stage of the grievance procedure. *Grievance arbitration* is different in important respects from interest arbitration, which was discussed in the previous chapter, and in the remainder of this chapter we discuss the role of both the grievance procedure and grievance arbitration in the administration and evolution of collective-bargaining agreements.

EXAMPLE 16.3

An Employee-Owned Steel Mill

From the early 1900s, the National Steel Corporation, the fourth largest steel producer in the United States, operated a large plant in Weirton, West Virginia. Workers at the Weirton Works were represented by the Independent Steelworkers' Union and traditionally received higher wages than workers at companies organized by the larger United Steelworkers of America (USW). The higher wages were paid in part to reduce the likelihood of organization by the USW and to guarantee that the plant would operate in the event of a national steel strike.

In the early 1980s, the steel industry in the United States was under considerable pressure from foreign competitors, who produced at lower cost, and from the general reduction in demand resulting from the deep international recession. Faced with low profits, National Steel announced in early March 1982 that it no longer intended to make substantial investments in its Weirton plant, and that it would gradually cut back operations at Weirton unless the workers chose to purchase the plant. The announcement initiated a vigorous effort by officials of the union, company, and community to find a way for the employees to buy the plant. There were significant incentives on each side to strike a bargain. The workers and the community had a stake in the jobs. Employment, which had been as high as 12,000, had fallen to about 7,000 workers by early 1983, and over 3,000 workers were on layoff. But the company also faced substantial costs, if the plant ceased operations, in the form of pension obligations to past and present workers.

A year later, the company and the union announced an agreement under which the workers would purchase the Weirton plant. Given the depressed conditions in the industry, the company was willing to sell the plant and equipment for $66 million—about 22 percent of book value. Workers agreed to pay another $300 million for raw materials and other inventory, and to assume about $185 million in liabilities. However, most of the liabilities were not due for several years, and it was assumed that the new company would be in a better position to handle them by then. As part of the agreement, workers took pay cuts of at least 32 percent—an amount that an independent study indicated was necessary to make the plant competitive—in exchange for stock in the new company. Effectively, workers were trading current wages for the uncertain prospect of higher future income that would depend on the performance of their new company. National Steel also assumed some of the risk of failure by agreeing to assume pension and other shutdown costs if the new company failed during the first five years of operations. With $1 billion of sales per year, the Weirton steel works was now the largest employee-owned company, the eighth largest steel company, and one of the 300 largest corporations in the United States.

The development of employee stock-ownership plans, such as the purchase of the Weirton Works can require unusual financial and management arrangements. In the case of Weirton, the National Steel Corporation agreed to hold notes for a large portion of the purchase price, and principal payments were not scheduled to begin until 1989, some six years after the employee-purchase agreement was completed. The principal would be paid out over the next 10 years, but interest payments would not be made until the Weirton Works had a net worth of $100 million. A board of directors, including union representatives, former company officials, and outside experts, would be responsible for major policy decisions and the selection of top management for the new company.

SOURCE: William Serrin, "Employees to Buy Huge Steel Works in $66 Million Pact," *New York Times* (March 14, 1983).

Role of Grievance Procedures

Disagreements between unions and management during the term of a collective-bargaining agreement can occur for several reasons. Frequently, disputes over the application of an agreement reflect disagreements between a union and management over the actual meaning or interpretation of a part of the agreement. The interpretive difficulties may, in turn, stem from vague or ambiguous contractual language concerning some aspects of the employment relationship. For example, labor agreements frequently permit management to discharge workers "for just

Table 16.7. Grievance and Arbitration Procedures in Collective-Bargaining Agreements (percent of all agreements in sector)

	All Procedures	Grievance and Arbitration	Grievance Only	Arbitration Only	No Reference to a Procedure
Private industry[a]	99	97	2	c	1
Manufacturing	99.7	98	2	—	c
Nonmanufacturing	97.9	95	2	c	2
State and local government[b]	87	76	11	—	13
State	94	82	12	—	6
County	83	72	11	—	17
Municipal	86	75	11	—	14
Special district	100	79	21	—	—

[a]Agreements covering 1,000 workers or more, January 1, 1980.
[b]Agreements in effect on January 1, 1974.
[c]Less than 0.5 percent.

SOURCES: U.S. Bureau of Labor Statistics, *Characteristics of Major Collective Bargaining Agreements, January 1, 1980,* Bulletin 2095 (Washington, D.C.: U.S. Government Printing Office, May 1981) pp. 112–13, and U.S. Bureau of Labor Statistics, *Characteristics of Agreements in State and Local Governments, January 1, 1974,* Bulletin 1861 (Washington, D.C.: U. S. Government Printing Office, 1975), p. 41.

cause," but what is "just cause"? Who is to decide? Often the ambiguity is deliberate. It represents the best that the negotiators could agree to in the formal collective-bargaining negotiations. When neither party is willing to permit language that endorses the other's position on an issue, and neither is willing to accept language that precludes his or her own position, the resulting contract language on the issue is likely to be ambiguous. As a result, the application of contract language to specific situations that arise in day-to-day employment relations often is unclear.

In other instances, there may be a disagreement between labor and management as to whether a violation of an agreement has occurred. In some cases, a dispute may reduce to a disagreement over the facts of a particular incident. Finally, there may be differences of opinion between labor and management over the fairness or reasonableness of a disciplinary action or some other aspect of the employment relationship. For example, if an employee initiates an altercation with a supervisor, can the firm fire the employee, or is a suspension the more appropriate discipline?

In most cases, these disagreements cannot wait to be resolved in formal collective-bargaining negotiations at some distant time. Instead, they are resolved through a grievance procedure. As a result, a labor agreement takes on much of its ultimate meaning through the interpretations of contract language that are developed during the administration of the agreement, and particularly through the resolution of grievances. In this sense, negotiations do not stop with the signing of a collective-bargaining agreement. Since it is the interpretation of the agreement that is ultimately important to the conduct of day-to-day labor relations, disputes over grievances can be seen as an extension of the collective-bargaining process. In particular, there is an obvious incentive for either party to try to obtain, through the grievance process, objectives that it failed to obtain at the bargaining table.

Because grievances represent disagreements, the flow of grievances in an organization can be an index of the quality of industrial relations in different plants. Relative to quits, absenteeism, and wildcat strikes, grievances are a relatively costless method for workers to signal discontent with working conditions. However, the filing of grievances can also be used as a political tool by unions even when worker discontent is not deep-seated. The rank and file of a union may file grievances to remind its leaders about offending clauses in the existing union contract. Unions themselves may encourage the filing of many grievances as a way of increasing the company's labor-relations costs at a time when the union is having difficulty getting the company to acquiesce on other issues.

While unions may use grievances for tactical reasons, they also have an interest in allocating their resources where they will do the most good for the membership. As a result, most unions try to screen grievances and apprise members of complaints that either cannot be handled as a grievance (because there is no applicable contract language), or are so lacking in merit that the union would prefer not to pursue the complaint as a grievance. In making these decisions, unions must be cognizant of their legal "duty of fair representation." The federal courts have held that with the right to *exclusive* representation of workers granted unions under American labor law comes the obligation to refrain from arbitrary or discriminatory treatment of union members.[17] Thus, if a union refuses to process a member's grievance, it must have good reason for its action. Moreover, if an employee proves that an employer violated the collective-bargaining agreement, and the union violated the duty of fair representation in refusing to process the employee's grievance, *both* the union and the employer may be held liable for damages awarded to the worker.[18]

Grievance Arbitration

As noted above, virtually all collective-bargaining agreements contain language discussing how disagreements over the application of the contract are to be resolved. In general, it is the task of the parties to negotiate language about the nature of the grievance procedure and of the arbitration arrangements that may apply to grievances. Most agreements also include language specifying that the grievance and arbitration procedures are the sole means of resolving disputes during the term of the collective-bargaining agreement. This reinforces the no-strike clause discussed earlier.

Typically, a collective-bargaining agreement will describe the various steps in the grievance procedure, indicate who is entitled to participate in the discussions at each step, and possibly set time limits for appeals of a decision made at each step. Each step of the procedure consists of a discussion concerning the merits of a grievance between the aggrieved individuals (usually accompanied or represented by a union official) and management. Successive steps involve discussions at higher levels of the union and the company. If the parties fail to agree at any stage of the procedure, they move onto the next stage. Initially, there will be an attempt to resolve a grievance at the level at which it occurred, perhaps by discussions between the supervisor of a grievant and a shop steward or other union representative on the shop floor. Failing agreement, the dispute may then move up to a discussion between middle management and a higher level union official, and if agreement is still not reached, the grievance may be considered by the company's top industrial-relations personnel and top union leadership. Most grievances are resolved at one of the stages that precede arbitration.

About 97 percent of major private-sector collective-bargaining agreements (98 percent of contracts with grievance procedures) and three quarters of state and local agreements now provide for arbitration as the final step in the grievance procedure (Table 16.7). The extensive use of arbitration rather than the courts as the final step in procedures to resolve disputes over the application of the collective-bargaining agreement is a feature of labor relations peculiar to the United States. (As Example 16.4 illustrates, many European countries use special courts for this purpose.) Its appeal stems from the fact that, relative to litigation, arbitration is flexible (the parties can design a system that suits their

---

[17]*Steele* v. *Louisville and Nashville Railroad,* 323 U.S. 192 (1944) and *Miranda Fuel Co.,* 140 NLRB 181 (1962).

[18]*Vaca* v. *Sipes,* 386 U.S. 171 (1967) and *Bowen* v. *U.S. Postal Service,* Case 81-525 U.S. (1983).

particular circumstances), informal, and generally more expeditious (although we shall see how grievances that go to arbitration can be costly in terms of money and time). Moreover, as we shall see, the parties to the collective-bargaining agreement can specify the standards that an arbitrator is to apply in reaching a decision.

EXAMPLE 16.4

Labor Courts in Europe

In Western European countries, arbitration is rarely used as a method of settling disputes over the interpretation of labor agreements. Instead, such disputes are referred to *labor courts,* which are usually appointed by the government but remain outside of, or as autonomous divisions of, the regular court systems. This separateness was designed to encourage cheaper and more expeditious settlement of grievances than would be possible in ordinary litigation. The actual structure and jurisdiction of the courts varies among countries, but in most countries decisions of the labor court are rendered by a tripartite panel of judges, often after some initial efforts to mediate a solution to the dispute. Under some systems the decisions can be appealed to higher courts (unlike the situation with most arbitration awards in the United States).

What accounts for this difference between the United States and Europe in the nature of the institutions that are established to resolve disputes over the interpretation and enforcement of the labor agreement? First, as we have noted, many of the terms and conditions of employment established through collective bargaining in the United States are established by legislation in European countries. It is natural to take grievances over alleged violations of legislated benefits to the courts rather than to arbitration. Second, in many European countries, the law provides for the extension of the terms of collective-bargaining agreements to firms that are not a party to the agreement and may not be unionized. Because the obligations are again imposed by law, it is more natural to grieve to an institution that is not directly established in formal collective bargaining. Finally, for reasons connected with the role of the courts in retarding the growth of unions in the United States prior to the 1930s (see Chapter 12), American unions are reluctant to have the courts involved in the actual determination or interpretation of the collective-bargaining agreement.

SOURCES: Eileen B. Hoffman, *Resolving Labor-Management Disputes: A Nine-Country Comparison,* Conference Board Report No. 600 (New York: The Conference Board, 1973); William H. McPherson and Frederic Meyers, *The French Labor Courts: Judgement by Peers* (Urbana, Ill.: University of Illinois, 1966).

Nevertheless, arbitration proceedings do have some of the characteristics of a trial. Each side presents its case and claim for relief in a hearing before the arbitrator (or arbitration panel) who has the authority to make a final determination and issue an award. Some of the informality of the arbitration arises from the fact that arbitrators generally use less stringent procedures and rules of evidence than judges. More importantly, arbitrators are not bound to past legal doctrines or the precedent of past decisions (by the courts or by other arbitrators) to the extent that judges are. Instead, arbitrators may invoke a less well-delineated "law of the shop" and interpret the contract in the light of past practice in the firm or industry and what they regard as generally accepted standards of equity. Arbitration also differs from most judicial proceedings in that there is typically no appeal of the arbitrator's decision.

In negotiating the arbitration clause of a collective-bargaining agreement, the parties typically seek to specify the nature of the arbitration panel, the means of selecting the panel, and the jurisdiction of the panel. There are a number of forms that an arbitration panel can take. Perhaps the most important is a single impartial arbitrator. In some instances, such as labor agreements between the United Automobile Workers and the major automobile manufacturers, the arbitrator may be a "permanent umpire"—a single individual who hears all of the grievances arising under a particular collective-bargaining agreement. In other instances, the parties may select an arbitrator each time a grievance goes to arbitration.[19] A potential advantage of the latter procedure is that the background of the arbitrators can be varied to suit the nature of the grievance.

A second approach to arbitration is to use a tripartite board, consisting of one representative of management, one representative of labor, and one neutral. Since the management and labor representatives are likely to vote for the positions of their sides, the outcome is basically determined by the neutral. Why, then, bother with the tripartite procedure? One appeal of the tripartite procedure to labor and management is that it reassures them that their arguments will be fully heard. It also offers some assurance that an arbitrator will not wander too far from the general standards of the contract in fashioning a decision. In some instances of tripartite grievance arbitration, the voting is anonymous. That is, the award is announced, but neither the votes of the members of the arbitration panel nor the final vote counts are revealed. Arbitrators who have operated in this system revealed to researchers that the most frequent result is unanimity! Representatives of management and labor in an organization often have fairly common views as to what constitutes appropriate workplace behavior, but unions are often under political pressure to press grievances that they may not view as meritorious. With

---

[19]The typical procedure is to obtain an odd number of names (usually five) from either the Federal Mediation and Conciliation Service or the American Arbitration Association and for the parties to alternately strike names from the list until only one name is left. The survivor becomes the arbitrator!

anonymous voting, all representatives can vote their consciences and later act as if they were outvoted on an unpopular decision.[20]

As in the case of interest arbitration discussed in Chapter 15, the incentive to resolve a grievance prior to the final step of arbitration depends on the costs associated with going to arbitration. The costs associated with grievance arbitration are largely uncertainty regarding the arbitrator's award. Unlike the situation with interest arbitration, however, with grievance arbitration the parties are able to reduce the uncertainty to a certain extent by explicitly limiting the arbitrator's authority. Most collective-bargaining agreements contain language that explicitly circumscribes the authority of the arbitrator to the contents and language of the collective-bargaining agreement and forbids the arbitrator to use other standards. That is, unlike the situation with interest arbitration, the parties are able to establish in the language of their collective-bargaining agreement the general standards under which an arbitrator will operate. For example, an agreement between the International Brotherhood of Teamsters and a midwestern manufacturing company provided that:

> The arbitrator shall have no right to amend, modify, nullify, ignore or add to the provisions of this Agreement. He shall consider and decide only the particular issue(s) presented to him in writing by the Company and the Union, and his decision and award shall be based solely upon his interpretation of the meaning or application of the terms of this Agreement to the facts of the grievance presented.[21]

In addition to costs associated with the uncertainty of outcome, there are those resulting from time delays in resolving an issue and those arising from a need to compensate the arbitrator. In recent years, there has been increasing concern with both the compensation costs and the time delays associated with arbitration. Between 1971 and 1981, the average amount charged by an arbitrator for a single arbitration doubled to over $1,100 as the amount of time spent (mainly on post-hearing study) and the daily fees increased (Table 16.8). As a guide to the time consumed and money spent on grievance arbitrations, the data in Table 16.8 are only the tip of an iceberg. In one sample of arbitrations studied by the Federal Mediation and Conciliation Service, the average time elapsed between the filing of a grievance to the date of an arbitrator's award was 242 days—about eight months. On average, cases took almost half a year to get to an arbitration hearing. Of this time, discussions in the lower stages of the grievance procedure consumed two and a half months, another month and a half was spent in appointing an arbitrator, and two more months passed before the arbitrator was able to hear

---

[20]As noted in Chapter 15, a similar outcome has been noted in the use of interest arbitration to determine the terms and conditions of employment for police and firefighters in New York State. Thomas A. Kochan, Mordechai Mironi, Ronald G. Ehrenberg, Jean Baderschneider, and Todd Jick, *Dispute Resolution Under Factfinding and Arbitration: An Empirical Analysis* (New York: American Arbitration Association, 1979).

[21]Bernard D. Meltzer, *Labor Law: Cases, Materials, and Problems* (Boston: Little, Brown and Co., 1970), Appendix, pp. 134–35.

Table 16.8. Charges for Arbitrator's Service, 1971 and 1981[a]

Days charged for by arbitrator:	1971	1981
Total	3.0	3.3
Travel	0.4	0.3
Arbitration hearing	0.9	1.0
Post-hearing study	1.7	2.0
Per diem rates	$163.88	$299.62
Total charged	$566.59	$1,132.31

[a]Average for a sample of arbitrators selected by the Federal Mediation and Conciliation Service.

SOURCE: Federal Mediation and Conciliation Service, *Thirty-Fourth Annual Report, Fiscal Year 1981* (Washington, D.C.: U.S. Government Printing Office, 1982), p. 37.

the case. Following the hearing, an average of 46 days—including the time it took union and management to prepare and submit final briefs—passed before the arbitrator issued an award.[22] In addition, both sides incurred attorneys' fees as well as the costs of their own personnel who were involved in preparing for and participating in the hearing. Small wonder that many representatives of both management and labor are interested in devising less costly methods of resolving disputes during the term of a collective-bargaining agreement!

In an effort to reduce the burden of arbitration, some unions and management have begun to experiment with amended forms of grievance resolution. Under "expedited" arbitration arrangements, which have been adopted in several industries, including steel, longshoring, and the U.S. Postal Service, the parties may agree to dispense with a transcript of the arbitration hearing, with their briefs, and even with attorneys on the understanding that the arbitrator will hear the case promptly and issue an award rapidly. In contrast to the delays under conventional grievance arbitration noted above, the elapsed time from the request for arbitration to the hearing is in the range of five to seven days under these arrangements, and the award is either issued from the bench or within two or three days of the hearing.[23] In the longshore industry, arbitrators are "on call" to report immediately to the site of a disagreement (for example, over the implementation of work rules) between labor and management. The arguments of each side are heard on the spot, and the arbitrator issues a verbal award immediately, so that work can resume. In other instances, mediation has been found useful in resolving certain types of grievances before they reach arbitration (see Example 16.5).[24]

---

[22]Data are from the Federal Mediation and Conciliation Service, *Thirty-Fourth Annual Report, Fiscal Year 1981* (Washington, D.C.: U.S. Government Printing Office, 1982), p. 39.

[23]John Zalusky, "Arbitration: Updating a Vital Process," *The American Federationist* 83 (November 1976): 1–4.

[24]Grievance mediation has been used extensively by the Labour Board in British Columbia since 1976, achieving a 71 percent settlement rate, and by several state mediation services. See *Avoiding the Arbitrator: Some New Alternatives to the Grievance Procedure,* Proceedings, 30th Annual Meeting (Washington, D.C.: National Academy of Arbitrators, 1977).

EXAMPLE 16.5

Grievance Mediation in the Coal Mining Industry

The bituminous coal mining industry in the United States has historically had a high level of grievances, wildcat strikes, and labor strife. While the three-year agreement beginning in 1974 was in effect, for example, it is estimated that there were an average of 2,700 grievance arbitrations per year resulting in arbitration costs of almost $2 million annually. From five to six months often elapsed from the time a grievance was filed until an arbitrator's decision was announced.

In late 1980, a six-month experiment in which grievance *mediation* was offered as an alternative to arbitration (after the steps in the internal grievance procedures were exhausted) was begun in two areas of the Appalachian coal fields. Under the procedure, the mediator tried to assist the parties to reach a mutually satisfactory resolution of the grievance, using the normal techniques of mediation. The parties retained the option of taking the grievance to arbitration if the mediation effort failed, however. Therefore, in a departure from normal mediation practice, the mediators involved in the experiment (who all had previous arbitration experience in the coal industry) provided the parties with an oral advisory arbitration opinion—the mediator's best judgment of what an arbitrator would decide upon hearing the case—if it appeared that no resolution of the grievance would be possible through mediation.

In an effort to reduce the cost and delays associated with resolving grievances through arbitration, the mediators scheduled three mediations per day, charged $375 per day plus travel expenses (but not for travel *time,* since there was no written decision and hence no "reflection," "study," or "writing" time), and scheduled regular dates for mediation conferences.

During the six-month experiment, mediation succeeded in resolving 86 percent of the 37 grievances presented. An advisory arbitration decision by the mediator was only needed in 30 percent of the mediations; in half of these cases the ruling became the basis for resolving the grievance—the parties did not proceed to arbitration. Of the five cases that were subsequently taken to arbitration, the decision of the arbitrator (who, by prearrangement, could not be one of the mediators) coincided with the advisory opinion in three instances. The mediation procedure also offered considerable savings in time and money over grievance arbitration. The directors of the study reported that "[t]he average time between the request for mediation and the mediation conference was 13 days compared to an average of 49 days between a request for arbitration and the arbitrator's decision. . . . The average cost (mediator's fee and expenses) of mediation was $250 per grievance, compared to an average arbitration cost (arbitrator's fee and expenses) of $1,025."

These advantages led one of the two areas participating in the experiment to adopt grievance mediation on a more permanent basis and encouraged other areas in the coal mining industry to initiate similar experiments.

SOURCE: Stephen B. Goldberg and Jeanne M. Brett, "An Experiment in the Mediation of Grievances," *Monthly Labor Review* 106 (March 1983): 23–30.

Public Policy Issues Raised by Grievance Arbitration

Despite the spread of grievance arbitration arrangements following World War II, the legal status of agreements to arbitrate was uncertain. If one party to a labor agreement refused to arbitrate an issue, could the federal courts compel arbitration? If a party refused to arbitrate on the grounds that the issue involved was not subject to arbitration, could the courts determine if the issue was subject to arbitration under the terms of the collective-bargaining agreement? Although Section 301 of the Taft-Hartley Act gives the federal courts jurisdiction over suits alleging violations of labor agreements, these questions were not decided until 1957, when the Supreme Court ruled that the federal courts could enforce provisions to arbitrate in collective-bargaining agreements.[25] The court ruled further in the famous *Steelworkers' Trilogy* cases that ". . . [t]he courts, therefore, have no business weighing the merits of the grievance, considering whether there is equity in a particular claim, or determining whether there is particular language in the written instrument that will support the particular claim. . . . The processing of even frivolous claims may have therapeutic values of which those who are not a part of the plant environment may be quite unaware."[26] In short, the Supreme Court restricted the role of the courts to deciding whether a particular employment issue could be arbitrated under the terms of the labor agreement and instructed the courts to defer to arbitration except in instances in which the contract explicitly excludes an issue from arbitration. Moreover, the Court held that federal courts should enforce an arbitrator's award without reviewing its merits as long as the award was generally consistent with the labor agreement on which it was based.

In taking this strong position in favor of arbitration, the Supreme Court noted that as a *quid pro quo* for a no-strike pledge, grievance arbitration is an institutional arrangement that advances the National Labor Relation Act's objective of increasing industrial peace. The Court further expressed particular confidence in the qualifications of arbitrators for resolving disputes over the interpretation of a labor agreement, noting at one point that:

The labor arbitrator is usually chosen because of the parties' confidence in his knowledge of the common law of the shop and their trust in his personal judgment to bring

---

[25] *Textile Workers' Union* v. *Lincoln Mills,* 353 U.S. 448 (1957).

[26] *United Steelworkers of America v. American Mfg. Co.,* 363 U.S. 564 (1960). The other cases in the *Trilogy* were *United Steelworkers v. Warrior & Gulf Nav. Co.,* 363 U.S. 574 (1960) and *United Steelworkers of America v. Enterprise Wheel & Car Corp.* 363 U.S. 593 (1960).

to bear considerations which are not expressed in the contract as criteria for judgment. . . . [t]he ablest judge cannot be expected to bring the same experience and competence to bear upon the determination of a grievance, because he cannot be similarly informed.[27]

The net effect of these decisions was to increase greatly the prestige and authority of voluntary arbitration as an institution for resolving disputes over the interpretation of the collective-bargaining agreement and to insulate arbitration awards from judicial review. As noted above, this aspect of the resolution of grievance disputes differs markedly from Europe, where the judiciary plays a much more direct role in disputes arising from the application of a labor agreement.

Not all observers would agree with the Court's perception of the value of voluntary arbitration or the unique competence of arbitrators in interpreting a collective-bargaining agreement. Many arbitrators, for example, do not appear to have any special qualifications for understanding or interpreting "the common law of the shop."[28] In addition, labor and management often appear to want an arbitrator to interpret the language of the contract much the way judges are called upon to interpret contracts outside of the employment area. Nevertheless, much of the basic deference accorded arbitration by the Trilogy decisions remains.

More recently, however, the domain of arbitration has been challenged by the passage of social legislation that has important implications for the employment relationship. Examples include equal employment legislation (discussed more extensively in Chapter 11), the Occupational Health and Safety Act (OSHA) of 1970 (discussed in Chapter 7), pension reform legislation (for example, the Employee Retirement Income Security Act of 1974 [ERISA] discussed in Chapter 10), and even aspects of the Fair Labor Standards Act ([FLSA], discussed in Chapter 3). These laws raise two general questions for the conduct of arbitration and the protection of the rights of workers at the workplace. First, should an arbitrator be bound by the language of a statute or by the language of the collective-bargaining agreement when the two are in conflict? Second, should the courts defer to arbitration—the proposition advanced by the Supreme Court in the Steelworkers' Trilogy—when both collective-bargaining agreements and statutory law address an issue that has arisen? These questions have been the source of considerable controversy within the arbitration profession, and each is discussed below.

----

[27]The quote is from the majority opinion prepared by Justice Douglas in *United States of America v. Warrior and Gulf Navigation Co.* 363 U.S. 574 (1960), 80 U.S. 1347 (1960).

[28]While information is sparse, one study of presumably favorable biographical sketches prepared by a group of 652 arbitrators revealed that other than legal training, most arbitrators in the sample did not appear to have experience that was particularly relevant to the task. Only 29 were full-time arbitrators, another 43 had experience as judges, 205 were lawyers, and 78 were law professors. Outside of the law, professors of economics (63) or industrial relations (50) were the most frequent backgrounds cited by the arbitrators. One hundred fifty-nine arbitrators did not list any experience that had relevance for arbitration. Generally, these data cast doubt on the proposition that arbitrators are likely to have more expertise for their task than "the ablest judges." Paul Hays, *The Practice of Labor Arbitration* (New Haven, Conn.: Yale University Press, 1966), pp. 51–56.

The arbitration profession is deeply divided over the question of whether it should expand the criteria to be considered in fashioning arbitration awards to include the requirements of external law as well as the language of the labor agreement. The dominant view appears to be that arbitrators should restrict their activities to interpreting the language of the agreement. It has been argued that many arbitrators may not have either the knowledge of federal statutes or the expertise to interpret them in a manner that is consistent with decisions of the federal judiciary. Therefore, efforts by arbitrators to interpret federal legislation might simply invite the judicial intervention into the arbitration process that has been absent since the Steelworkers' Trilogy decisions. On the other hand, many arbitrators feel that the institutional expertise of arbitrators ought to reflect the current realities of the employment relationship and, that by incorporating the standards of external law, the arbitration process could expedite social progress in the areas addressed by federal legislation. As of the early 1980s, the former view of the role of the arbitrator in the grievance procedure appeared to be more widely adopted.

When a labor agreement and a statute address the same issue (for example, equal employment opportunity [EEO] or occupational health and safety), an employee who has a complaint faces a choice between filing a grievance alleging a violation of the labor agreement or initiating a complaint or suit alleging a violation of the statute. Is the employee free to choose either forum—the grievance procedure or the courts? The thrust of the Steelworkers' Trilogy decisions was that the courts should defer to arbitration, which implies that unionized employees facing this choice should use the grievance procedure. Suppose an employee processes a grievance alleging discrimination to arbitration, but receives an adverse ruling. Should the employee then be permitted to file suit under EEO legislation? The question is an important one for public policy, because unions and employers—the parties who are often accused of discrimination—control the arbitration process. As we have seen, they jointly select the arbitrator and establish through contractual language the scope of the arbitrator's authority. Since arbitrators serve at the behest of both labor and management, they may be reluctant to take positions that will jeopardize their future employment. Moreover, if discrimination is the direct result of contract language, the tendency of arbitrators to interpret the contract rather than statutory law may produce a result that is at variance with public policy.

The Supreme Court recognized this conflict in holding that an employee who receives an adverse arbitration award in a grievance concerning employment discrimination is not precluded from filing a court suit on the same issue.[29] Contrary to the implications of the Steelworkers' Trilogy cases, the courts need not defer to arbitration awards on employment-discrimination issues, although the Supreme Court noted in its decision that the courts could give some weight to prior arbitration on an issue before them. Subsequent decisions indicate that the courts also need not defer to arbitration awards when workers bring suits

---

[29]*Alexander* v. *Gardner-Denver* 415 U.S. 36 (1974).

under statutes that guarantee minimum-employment standards to workers—for example, OSHA, ERISA, and the FLSA.

REVIEW QUESTIONS

1. In what specific respects would you expect the content of explicit employment contracts negotiated by unions and management in the private sector to differ from the content of "implicit" employment contracts governing the employment relationship in non-union firms? On what grounds do you expect these differences?
2. What differences would you expect between negotiated labor agreements and nonunion employment arrangements in the public sector? What general differences would you also expect between private-sector and public-sector employment arrangements?
3. What is the relationship between the collective-bargaining process and the administration of the labor agreement?
4. What is the distinction between the concepts of "equity" and "efficiency" in collective bargaining? How does the concept of efficiency in bargaining relate to the concept as it is more generally used in labor economics?
5. Some employers oppose COLA clauses on the grounds that changes in the prices of their product(s) may move differently from changes in the CPI to which wages are generally indexed. How would you expect labor and management to react to a proposal to index wages to the price of the company's product(s)? Why?

SELECTED READINGS

Bureau of National Affairs, *Basic Patterns in Union Contracts,* 9th ed. (Washington, D.C.: Bureau of National Affairs, 1979)

David E. Feller, "A General Theory of the Collective Bargaining Agreement," *California Law Review* 61 (May 1973): 663–856.

R. W. Fleming, *The Labor Arbitration Process* (Urbana, Ill.: University of Illinois Press, 1965).

Wassily Leontief, "The Pure Theory of the Guaranteed Annual Wage Contract," *Journal of Political Economy* 54 (February 1946): 76–79.

Albert E. Rees, *The Economics of Trade Unions,* 2nd. ed. (Chicago: University of Chicago Press, 1977).

Sumner H. Slichter, James J. Healy, and E. Robert Livernash, *The Impact of Collective Bargaining on Management* (Washington, D.C.: The Brookings Institution, 1960).

Chapter 17

THE EFFECTS OF UNIONS

O ur discussion of unions and collective bargaining has examined changes in the institutions and public policy influencing relations between employers and employees when workers are represented by unions. We have examined the nature and objectives of union organizations, the legal environment of union-management relations, the interaction of labor and management in collective bargaining, and the labor agreement, which is the outcome of the collective-bargaining process. For the most part, however, our discussion has not addressed the actual economic effects of unions. How do they change the patterns of compensation, employment, productivity, and profits that would be observed in a market economy without unions? This is an important question, for, as noted in Chapter 1, surface impressions of union economic effects can be misleading.

This chapter examines the effects unions have had on wage *and* nonwage outcomes. Economists have traditionally focused on estimating the amount by which unions have increased the wages of their members *relative* to the wages of comparable nonunion workers—and their conclusion that unions have a negative effect on the allocation of resources in society is based on these estimates, which will be discussed in the first part of this chapter. Recently, however, analytical labor economists have begun to rediscover the variety of roles that unions play and have concluded that unions may play many positive roles that leave society as a whole better off.[1] Therefore, in subsequent sections, we shall

---

[1]This "new" view of unions is summarized by two of its exponents in a nontechnical fashion in Richard B. Freeman and James L. Medoff, "The Two Faces of Unionism," *Public Interest* 57 (Fall 1979): 69–93.

also consider the effects of unions on productivity, labor turnover, and profitability.

Union Wage Effects

The most frequently stated economic objectives of unions are to raise the wages of union members and to take wages "out of competition." The former goal is the more commonly understood interest of unions in raising the compensation of their members relative to that of nonmembers. To the extent that unions succeed in this objective, they would seem to increase the inequality of wages among workers of comparable skill levels. Also important to unions, however, is the elimination of competition between employers on the basis of differential labor costs. This goal implies reducing the wage differences among employees performing the same job in different geographical areas and even among employees of different skills in the same area. In this section, we examine, first, union effects on *relative* compensation and, then, turn to the broader effects they have had on inequality and the distribution of income in the United States.

The Theory of Union Wage Effects

Suppose one had data on the wage rates paid to two groups of workers who were identical in every respect except for the fact that one group was unionized and the other was not.[2] Let W_u denote the wage paid to union members and W_n the wage paid to nonunion workers. If the difference between the two could be attributed solely to the presence of unions, then the *relative-wage advantage* that unions would have achieved for their members would be given, in percentage terms, by

$$R = (W_u - W_n)/W_n \qquad (17.1)$$

Contrary to what one might expect, this relative-wage advantage does *not* represent the absolute amount, in percentage terms, by which unions would have increased the wages of their members because unions both directly and indirectly affect *nonunion* wage rates also. Moreover, one can not *a priori* state whether estimates of R will overstate, or understate, the absolute effect of unions on their members' real wage levels. (This chapter, as noted before, focuses on the union effects on wage *levels;* Chapter 19 will discuss union effects on the *rate of wage change.)* Figure 17.1 presents a simple two-sector model of the labor market. Except for the fact that the labor-supply curves are upward sloping in both sectors, this model is identical to the one used in Chapter 3 to analyze the effects of the minimum wage in the presence of incomplete coverage; the analyses here will proceed along similar lines.

---

[2]Much of the discussion in this section is based upon the pioneering work by H. G. Lewis, *Unionism and Relative Wages in the United States* (Chicago: University of Chicago Press, 1963).

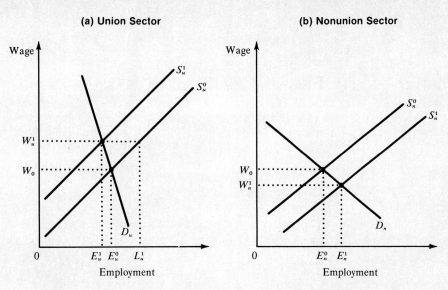

(a) Union Sector

(b) Nonunion Sector

Figure 17.1 Spillover Effects of Unions on Wages and Employment

Panel (a) is the union sector and panel (b) is the nonunion sector. Suppose initially, however, that both sectors are unorganized. If mobility is relatively costless, workers will move between the two sectors until wages are equalized between them. With demand curves D_u and D_n, workers will move between sectors until the supply curves are S_u^0 and S_n^0, respectively. The common equilibrium wage will be W_0, and employment will be E_u^0 and E_n^0, respectively, in the two sectors.

Now suppose a union succeeds in organizing the workers in the first sector and also succeeds in raising their wage to W_u^1. This increased wage will cause employment to decline to E_u^1 workers in the union sector, resulting in $L_u^1 - E_u^1$ unemployed workers in that sector. These workers have several options; one is to seek employment in the nonunion sector. If all of the unemployed workers *spill over* into the nonunion sector, the supply curves in the two sectors will shift to S_u^1 and S_n^1 respectively. Unemployment will be eliminated in the union sector; however, in the nonunion sector an excess supply of labor would exist at the old market-clearing wage, W_0. As a result, downward pressure would be exerted on the wage rate in the nonunion sector until the labor market in that sector cleared at a *lower* wage (W_n^1) and a higher employment level E_n^1.

In the context of this model, the union has succeeded in raising the wages of its members who kept their jobs. However, it has done so at the expense of shifting some of its members to lower-wage jobs in the nonunion sector and, because of this spillover effect, at the expense of actually lowering the wage rate paid to individuals initially employed in the nonunion sector. As a result, the observed union *relative-wage* advantage (R_1), computed as

$$R_1 = (W_u^1 - W_n^1)/W_n^1, \tag{17.2}$$

will tend to be greater than the true *absolute* effect of the union on its members' real wage. This true absolute effect (A_1), stated in percentage terms, is computed as

$$A_1 = (W_u^1 - W_0)/W_0. \tag{17.3}$$

The relative effect will not necessarily be larger than the absolute effect however, because there are several other responses that employees or employers can make. Employers in the nonunion sector may be concerned that unions will subsequently try to organize their employees—employers may view a union as undesirable if unionization both increases their wage costs and limits their managerial flexibility. As such, they may try to "buy off" their employees by offering them wage increases to reduce the probability that the employees will vote for a union.[3] Because of the costs associated with union membership, noted earlier, some wage less than W_u^1, but higher than W_0, would presumably be sufficient to assure employers that the majority of their employees would not vote for a union (assuming that the employees are happy with their nonwage conditions of employment).

The implications of such *threat effects*—nonunion wage increases resulting from the threat of union entry—are traced in Figure 17.2. The increase in wage in the union sector, and resulting decline in employment there, is again assumed to cause the supply of workers to the nonunion sector to shift to S_n^1. However, in response to the threat of union entry, nonunion employers are assumed to

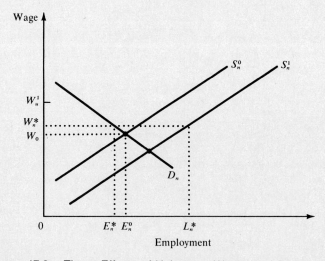

Nonunion Sector

Figure 17.2   Threat Effects of Unions on Wages and Employment

[3]For a more formal discussion of this possibility, *see* Sherwin Rosen, "Trade Union Power, Threat Effects, and the Extent of Organization," *Review of Economic Studies* 36 (April 1969): 185–96.

increase their employees' wages to W_n^*, which lies between W_0 and W_u^1. This wage increase causes employment to decline to E_n^*; at the higher wage nonunion employers demand fewer workers. Moreover, since the nonunion wage is now not free to be bid down, an excess supply of labor, $L_n^* - E_n^*$, exists, resulting in unemployment. Finally, because the nonunion wage is now higher than the original wage, the observed union relative-wage advantage,

$$R_2 = (W_u^1 - W_n^*)/W_n^*, \tag{17.4}$$

is smaller than the absolute effect of unions on their members' real wages.

One might question whether workers who lose their jobs in the union sector, as a result of the union's increasing the wage rate, will necessarily seek jobs in the nonunion sector. Even with a fixed employment level in the union sector, job vacancies occur due to retirements, deaths, and voluntary turnover (including quits to take other jobs in the same area, geographic migration, and individuals who are temporarily leaving the labor force). It may pay union members to remain attached to the union sector *and* temporarily unemployed if they believe that they will ultimately obtain a job in the union sector. Indeed, it may actually pay some employed nonunion workers to quit their jobs and move to the union sector in the hopes that they will obtain a relatively higher-paying union job in the future. Such decisions lead to *wait unemployment:* workers rejecting lower-paying nonunion jobs and waiting for higher-paying union jobs to open up.[4]

Workers will move between the union and nonunion sectors until their *expected earnings* in each are equal. If one ignores complications such as the costs of union membership, the presence of unemployment-insurance benefits for some unemployed workers, fringe benefits, and the like, expected earnings will be equal when the wage rate paid in each sector, multiplied by the fraction of each period (F) that individuals in the sector expect to be employed, are equal—or when

$$W_u F_u = W_n F_n. \tag{17.5}$$

Figure 17.3 illustrates the process. If threat effects are ignored, the consequences of an increase in the union wage to W_u^1 would be a decline in employment in the union sector to E_u^1, a shift in the supply curves to S_u^1 and S_n^1, and a resulting decrease in nonunion wages to W_n^1 and increase in nonunion employment to E_n^1. Since there is no unemployment in this situation, F_u and F_n are both equal to unity. Hence, labor-market equilibrium, as indicated in equation (17.5), would require that wages be equal in the two sectors. But they are *not;* W_u^1 is greater than W_n^1; hence, individuals' expected earnings are higher in the union sector.

The above difference in expected earnings would induce some individuals to

---

[4]*See* Jacob Mincer, "Unemployment Effects of Minimum Wages," *Journal of Political Economy* 84 (July/August 1976, Part 2): S87–S104. Although Mincer discusses minimum-wage effects, union-imposed "minimum wages" can be analyzed analogously.

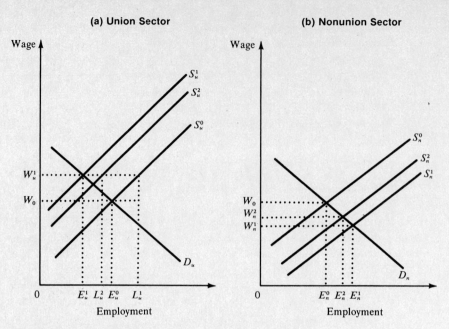

(a) Union Sector

(b) Nonunion Sector

Figure 17.3 Wait Unemployment (nonunion wage falls)

move from the nonunion sector to wait for jobs in the union sector. This movement leads to an increase in the expected earnings in the nonunion sector (as supply decreases there, wages are bid up) and a decrease in expected earnings in the union sector (as supply increases there, the probability of obtaining a job in that sector decreases). Eventually expected earnings are equalized between the two sectors by this process.

We have *assumed* that expected earnings are equalized in Figure 17.3 at the points at which the supply curves in the two sectors are S_u^2 and S_n^2, respectively. The resulting wage in the nonunion sector is W_n^2, and the resulting employment level is E_n^2. *Wait unemployment* now exists in the union sector; its level is given by $L_u^2 - E_u^1$. Finally, although W_n^2 is greater than W_n^1, W_n^2 is less than W_0. Thus, if the union relative-wage advantage is measured as

$$R_3 = (W_u^1 - W_n^2)/W_n^2, \tag{17.6}$$

it will again be larger than the true absolute effect of the union on its members' real wage levels.

Of course, we have assumed that the expected earnings would be equalized as indicated in Figure 17.3. Under certain assumptions, the equalization may not occur until after the supply of labor to the union sector has shifted to the *right* of its initial position and after the supply of labor in the nonunion sector has shifted to the *left* of its initial position. This situation is more likely to occur if the demand curve in the union sector is inelastic. An inelastic demand curve would cause *expected earnings* $(W_u^1 F_u)$ in the union sector to increase immediately after the increase in the union *wage,* because employment losses are so small. This immediate rise in expected earnings induces employees to migrate from the nonunion to union sector.[5] As Figure 17.4 indicates, supply in the union sector shifts right (to S_u^3) and supply in the nonunion sector shifts left (to S_n^3). In this situation wait unemployment would increase to $L_u^3 - E_u^1$, and the nonunion wage would increase to W_n^3, which is greater than W_0. The union relative-wage advantage in this case, which is computed as

$$R_4 = (W_u^1 - W_n^3)/W_n^3, \tag{17.7}$$

would be less than the absolute effect of unions on their members' real wages.

One final case will complete our discussion. Suppose the union increases its members' wages by means of increasing the demand for union labor—using any of the methods discussed in Chapter 14. Figure 17.5 illustrates an increase in the demand for labor in the union sector to D_u^1. If this increase comes at the expense of the demand for labor in the nonunion sector, the latter curve will fall—say, to D_n^1. Initially, the effect is to increase both wages (W_u^1) and employment (E_u^1) in the union sector and decrease wages (W_n^1) and employment (E_n^1) in the nonunion sector. The ultimate change in the nonunion wage, however, will depend upon the extent to which threat effects or wait unemployment are important. So again, estimates of the union *relative-*wage effects alone tell us little about the *absolute* effects of unions on their members' real wage levels.

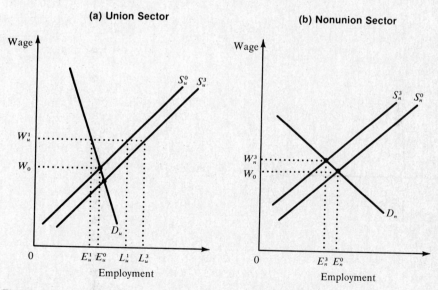

(a) Union Sector   **(b) Nonunion Sector**

Figure 17.4 Wait Unemployment (nonunion wage increases)

[5]*See* Mincer, "Unemployment Effects of Minimum Wages" and Edward Gramlich, "The Impact of Minimum Wages on Other Wages, Employment, and Family Incomes," *Brookings Papers on Economic Activity,* 1976–2, pp. 409–51, for a more complete discussion of when this is likely to occur.

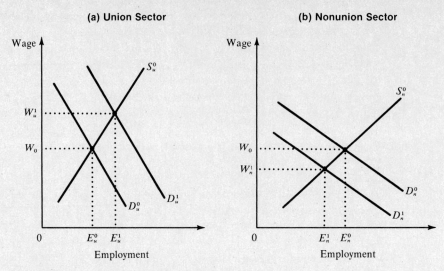

Figure 17.5 Union "Shifts" the Demand Curve

Because unions *are* present in the economy, at any point in time all one can observe are the union and nonunion wage rates (W_u and W_n). One can *not* observe the wage that would have existed in the absence of unions, W_0. Hence, direct estimates of a union's effects on the absolute level (A_1) of its members' real wages—refer back to equation (17.3)—can not be obtained. Care must be taken not to mistake relative-wage effects for absolute-wage effects.[6]

Evidence of Union Wage and Total Compensation Effects

In recent years, economists have expended considerable effort to estimate the extent to which unions have raised the wages of their members relative to the wages of comparable nonunion workers.[7] These studies have tended to use data on large samples of individuals and have attempted to separate wage differentials due to unionization from wage differentials due to differences in personal characteristics and differences in industry and occupation of employment. That is, these economists have sought to ascertain how much more union members get paid

---

[6]This discussion has assumed a partial-equilibrium model. Once one considers a general-equilibrium framework and allows capital to move between sectors, even more possibilities may exist. On this point, *see* Harry Johnson and Peter Mieszkowski, "The Effects of Unionization on the Distribution of Income: A General Equilibrium Approach," *Quarterly Journal of Economics* 84 (November 1969): 539–61.

[7]*See* H. Gregg Lewis, *Union Relative Wage Effects: A Survey* (forthcoming, 1984); C. J. Parsley, "Labor Unions and Wages: A Survey," *Journal of Economic Literature* 18 (March 1980): 1–31; George E. Johnson, "Economic Analysis of Trade Unionism," *American Economic Review* 65 (May 1975): 23–28; and Daniel J. B. Mitchell, "The Impact of Collective Bargaining on Compensation in the Public Sector," in *Public Sector Bargaining,* eds. B. Aaron et al. (Washington, D.C.: Bureau of National Affairs, 1979).

than nonunion workers, after controlling for any differences between the two groups in other factors that might be expected to influence wages.[8]

Private-sector wage studies. The various studies use several different data bases that span various years, and they often employ different statistical methodologies. As such, they do not yield a single unambiguous estimate of the extent to which union members' wages exceed the wages of comparable nonunion workers in the private sector. Perhaps the best estimate is that the union relative-wage advantage, on average, has fallen in the range of 10 to 20 percent in recent years. These union wage effects, however, are neither constant over time nor constant across groups.

A recent study by Orley Ashenfelter, summarized in Table 17.1, suggests that the estimated union relative-wage advantage in the private sector rose substantially between 1967 and 1975, from 11.6 to 16.8 percent. The year 1967 was one of low unemployment; the year 1975 was one of high unemployment. Since unionized workers' wages tend to be less responsive to labor-market conditions than nonunion workers' wages (see Chapter 19), this result is not surprising; the union relative-wage advantage tends to be larger during recessionary periods.[9]

The estimates in Table 17.1 also suggest that unions have helped improve the relative economic positions of black males. On the one hand, the estimated relative-wage effects are larger for black males than white males; being a union member enhances black males' earnings by more than it does white males' earnings. On the other hand, the percentage of black males that are union members also appears to be slightly larger than the comparable percentage for white males.

Table 17.1. Estimated Union/Nonunion Relative Wage Effects, 1967, 1973, and 1975

	Percentage Union Wage Effect			Percentage Unionized		
	1967	*1973*	*1975*	*1967*	*1973*	*1975*
All workers	11.6	14.8	16.8	23	26	25
White males	9.6	15.5	16.3	31	33	31
Black males	21.5	22.5	22.5	32	37	37
White females	14.4	12.7	16.6	12	14	14
Black females	5.6	13.2	17.1	13	22	22

SOURCE: Orley Ashenfelter, "Union Relative Wage Effects: New Evidence and a Survey of Their Implications for Wage Inflation," in *Econometric Contributions to Public Policy,* eds. R. Stone and W. Peterson (New York: St. Martin's, 1979), Tables 2.1 and 2.2.

---

[8]Some of the more ambitious studies also attempt to control for the fact that unionization and wages may be simultaneously determined; as noted earlier, workers' decisions to join a union are partially based on the expected gains from union membership. *See,* for example, Lung-Fei Lee, "Unionism and Wage Rates: A Simultaneous-Equations Model with Qualitative and Limited Dependent Variables," *International Economic Review* 19 (June 1978): 415–33.

[9]Lewis, *Unionism and Relative Wages,* provides evidence that this relationship appeared to hold during the 1930–1960 period as well.

On balance then, in spite of well-publicized conflicts between some unions and civil-rights organizations over union seniority rules and the use of racial quotas, unions appear to have improved the economic well-being of black males relative to white males.

In contrast, Table 17.1 emphasizes that female workers are considerably less likely to be union members than are male employees. Although in some years females who are union members appear to have gained as much as *white* males who are union members vis-a-vis their nonunion counterparts, on balance the *overall* effect of unions is to reduce female wages relative to male wages—perhaps by as much as 2.9 percent in 1975.[10]

Unions do not explicitly negotiate wages for demographic groups, however; they negotiate wages by job and by industry. Therefore, the patterns of union-wage impact reviewed above are to a large extent the result of the interaction between (1) the effects of unions on relative wages within industries and occupations, and (2) the employment distribution of different demographic groups by industry and occupation. Evidence from early studies of union-wage impact indicated that craft unions in the construction and transportation industries achieved the largest relative-wage effects—on the order of 20–25 percent—and the unusually large wage effects of unions in these industries appeared to hold up at least into the late 1970s. Industrial unions generally have a somewhat smaller relative-wage impact—10–15 percent in the 1950s and perhaps somewhat higher now—although an intriguing exception is the United Mine Workers' Union, the oldest industrial union in the country. In the late 1950s, workers in the bituminous coal industry represented by the United Mine Workers' Union were estimated to receive wages that were 42 percent higher than those paid nonunion miners. Finally, in a few highly competitive industries, such as textiles and apparel, unions appear to have no effect on wages.[11]

The findings from the studies cited (and many others) indicate that the wage impact of unions in the private sector is anything but monolithic. What accounts for the fact that the estimated wage effects associated with unions have varied from as little as zero to as much as 40 percent from industry to industry? One key determinant appears to be the ability of a union to maintain control of its jurisdiction—to extend its standards to all firms in a particular market. When there are few barriers to the entry or location of new firms (as, for example, when the capital requirements for an industry are low), it is often difficult for a union to keep its jurisdiction organized. Negotiating a relative-wage increase at unionized firms may simply lead to the emergence of nonunion firms paying lower

---

[10]Orley Ashenfelter, "Union Relative Wage Effects: New Evidence and a Survey of Their Implications for Wage Inflation," in *Econometric Contributions to Public Policy,* eds., R. Stone and W. Peterson (New York: St. Martin's, 1979).

[11]For a summary of early studies, *see* Lewis, *Unionism and Relative Wages,* p. 280. One recent study estimated union relative-wage effects of 46 percent in construction, 26 percent in transportation and communications, and 16 percent in manufacturing. *See* William J. Moore and John Raisian, "The Level and Growth of Union/Nonunion Relative Wage Effects, 1967–77," *Journal of Labor Research* IV (Winter 1983): 65–79. In each of the studies, the relative-wage effects may partially reflect factors that are correlated with the presence of unionism rather than the effects of union power.

wages in other areas (for example, southern states). If a union is unable to organize these newly emerged firms, their (lower) wages will attract business (and jobs) from the union firms. Thus, when a union is unable to keep its jurisdiction organized, its power to raise relative wages is limited by the availability of cheaper nonunion substitutes. (Ultimately, most explanations of union power seem to lead back to the factors governing the elasticity of the demand for labor that we have discussed in Chapters 4 and 14.)

Difficulties in maintaining jurisdictional control tend to limit the ability of unions to obtain large relative-wage gains for their members in many highly competitive industries. The textile industry, where, as noted above, there is a negligible difference between union and nonunion wages, represents an example of an industry where unions (in the north, primarily) were unable to prevent the movement of jobs to nonunion areas. In an environment where wages cannot be raised much by unions, a union's appeal stems from its ability to regularize the allocation of economic opportunities, establish a grievance procedure, and reduce the extent of supervisory discretion in personnel matters.

Interestingly, however, relatively large union/nonunion wage differentials are found in some competitive product markets, such as trucking, longshoring, and construction. How are unions in these industries able to achieve a large relative-wage impact while unions in other competitive industries may have none? Again, the key factor appears to be the union's ability to maintain its jurisdictional control. One characteristic of each of these industries (and of the bituminous coal industry in the late 1950s when the United Mine Workers had such a dramatic impact on the wages of its members) is that there are distinct geographical limitations on the area of product-market competition. Longshoring is restricted to key ports; the Teamsters could achieve considerable leverage by controlling terminal facilities in a few major cities where freight was delivered or transferred; construction sites and mines are not particularly mobile. When the product market is confined to a particular area, it is less costly for unions to organize and police their jurisdictions. [12]

As noted in Chapter 14, there is also evidence that the wage impact of unions is related, in general, to bargaining structure, so that the patterns of union wage impact by industry will reflect, in part, differences in bargaining arrangements. Another factor that can influence labor relations and union wage impacts is the economic regulation of an industry by government agencies. For many years, the government regulation of industries such as air transportation and surface transportation tended to limit the entry of new firms and thereby made it easier for unions in these industries to maintain their degree of organization. With deregulation, the union wage impact in these industries may be reduced. In the case of public utilities, which are often "natural" monopolies that are not threatened by the entry of competing firms, the regulation of utility rates may have influenced the bargaining stance of employers and the wage impact of unions (see Example 17.1).

---

[12]*See* Harold M. Levinson, *Determining Forces in Collective Bargaining* (New York: John Wiley & Sons, Inc., 1966).

EXAMPLE 17.1

Unions in Regulated Industries

A union's effect on relative wages in an industry can be influenced by government policy. For example, state commissions that regulate public utilities (such as telephone, electric, and gas companies) must decide whether all the costs that the utilities incur should be legitimately charged to consumers. Deciding whether or not labor costs should be charged to consumers raises particular difficulties. On the one hand, it is often conjectured that employers in regulated industries have less of an incentive to "bargain tough" with the unions that represent their employees than do employers in nonregulated industries, because historically, regulatory commissions have allowed utilities to pass on all labor-cost increases to consumers (in the form of higher utility prices). If such an argument is valid, it would indicate the need for commissions to carefully scrutinize utilities' wage settlements. On the other hand, it is difficult to decide upon what wage rates a commission should consider "just and reasonable."

At the very least, it is important to take into account any qualitative differences among the work forces of the utility and of other employers in the same labor-market area. By statistically controlling for such factors as education and experience, it should be easier to see if employees in a regulated industry are paid more than employees in other firms. When such a comparison was made for telephone workers in New York State, it was found that the utility's employees were paid approximately 9–12 percent more than were other employees with comparable education and experience levels in the state, in 1970.

However, these estimates can be fraught with difficulties. Part of any estimated wage premium paid to unionized workers in regulated industries may be justified as a differential to compensate them for having relatively unfavorable working conditions or more difficult jobs than employees in other industries. Wage comparisons may not accurately reflect total compensation comparisons because they ignore fringe benefits. They also may neglect the potential positive effects that the union and a high-wage policy might have (for example, reduced employee turnover and reduced strike activity). In the particular case mentioned above, the commission decided not to limit the permissible wage increase but did reserve the right to limit future wage "pass-throughs" if similar comparative studies illustrated the need for such limits. By even considering the issue, however, a commission raises interesting issues for public policy.

A commission's decision to disallow part of any collectively bargained wage settlement from being passed on to consumers would not violate the National Labor Relations Act, since it would not affect the terms of the settlement. However, it would undoubtedly affect management's willingness to grant the union large wage increases in the future; if the commission refuses to grant price increases to cover cost increases, the firms' profits must fall. In other words, the commission's intervention would affect the environment in which bargaining takes place and the relative bargaining power of the union. Thus, implicitly, the commission's action would affect future wage settlements.

We should also note, however, that commissions which uncritically allow all labor-cost increases to be passed on to consumers will also affect the environment in which bargaining takes place—by increasing the relative bargaining power of unions. This outcome, which corresponds closely to the status quo in most states, is not necessarily more desirable. In any case, it should be clear that it is difficult for government to remain neutral; its mere presence—whether or not it takes any action—affects labor markets.

SOURCE: Ronald G. Ehrenberg, *The Regulatory Process and Labor Earnings* (New York: Academic Press, 1979).

In our discussions of the elasticity of labor demand earlier in the book, we noted that demand is less elastic in the short run than in the long run. Application of this analysis suggests that even the more powerful unions might incur limitations on their ability to raise wages over time. Recent history provides many examples. The power of the UMW, for example, has been eroded in more recent times with the opening of nonunion mines as new coal deposits are discovered. A more dramatic change in fortunes occurred in the construction industry, in which negotiated wages increased relative to virtually every other group in the country in the late 1960s and early 1970s. One consequence of this increase was a significant increase in the amount of nonunion construction activity. By the mid- and late 1970s, employment opportunities for unionized construction workers had deteriorated so severely that negotiated wage increases in construction were among the smallest in the country.

The union relative-wage impact also varies by occupation, largely because most unions adopt the egalitarian strategy of negotiating equal absolute (that is, cents-per-hour) wage increases for all workers. In relative (percentage) terms, workers in lower-wage occupations achieve larger gains than more highly skilled workers. As a result, among blue-collar workers, the union wage impact is generally largest for laborers, next highest for operatives, and lowest for service workers and craft workers (in industrial unions). The union wage impact is also much higher for blue-collar workers than for white-collar workers, and higher for workers with less than a high school education than for high school graduates.[13] One reason for the disproportionately large union relative-wage impact for black males reported in Table 17.1 is that they are disproportionately employed in low-wage jobs, for which the union wage impact is largest generally.

---

[13]Much of the more recent evidence is reviewed in Lewis, *Union Relative Wage Effects . . . ,* Chapter 7.

The estimates cited above are of the relative-wage advantage *(R)* that unions in the private sector have achieved for their members in comparison to nonunion workers. These estimates do not indicate what effects unions have had on the absolute real-wage levels of their members. In other words, the estimates do not reveal how unions have influenced *nonunion* workers' wages. The limited evidence on this point, although ambiguous, suggests that unions may well depress the wages of nonunion workers; the *spillover effect* described in Figure 17.1 appears to dominate over the *threat* and *wait-unemployment effects* described in Figures 17.2 and 17.4.[14] That is, other things equal, the wages of nonunion workers are lower in cities in which the percent of workers in the city who are union members is high. Thus, estimates of the relative-wage effects of unions may well be greater than their effects on the absolute level of their members' real wages.

Private-sector total compensation effects. Estimates of the extent to which the wages of union workers exceed the wages of otherwise comparable nonunion workers may prove misleading for two reasons. First, such estimates ignore the fact that wages are only part of the compensation package. It has often been argued that fringe benefits, such as paid holidays, vacation pay, sick leave, and retirement benefits will be higher in firms that are unionized than in nonunion firms. The argument states that because tastes for the various fringe benefits differ across individuals, and because there is no easy way to communicate the preferences of the average employee to the employer in a nonunion firm, nonunion firms will tend to pay a higher fraction of total compensation in the form of money wages.[15] Recent empirical evidence tends to support this contention; fringe benefits and the share of compensation that goes to fringe benefits do appear to be higher in union than in nonunion firms.[16] Ignoring fringes may therefore understate the true union/nonunion total compensation differential.

In contrast, ignoring nonpecuniary conditions of employment may cause one to overstate the true effect of unions on their members' total compensation vis-a-vis nonunion workers. For example, recent studies have shown that for blue-collar workers, unionized firms tend to have more structured work settings, more hazardous jobs, less flexible hours of work, faster work paces, and less employee control over the assignment of overtime hours than do nonunion firms.[17] This situation may arise because production settings that give rise to interdependence among workers and the demand for specific work requirements

[14]Lawrence Kahn, "The Effect of Unions on the Earnings of Nonunion Workers," *Industrial and Labor Relations Review* 31 (January 1978): 205–16.

[15]This line of reasoning goes back at least as far as Richard Lester, "Benefits as a Preferred Form of Compensation," *Southern Economic Journal* 33 (April 1967): 488–95.

[16]Richard Freeman, "The Effect of Trade Unions on Fringe Benefits," *Industrial and Labor Relations Review* 34 (July 1981): 489–509; William T. Alpert, "Unions and Private Wage Supplements," *Journal of Labor Research* 3 (Spring 1982): 179–99.

[17]Greg Duncan and Frank Stafford, "Do Union Members Receive Compensating Wage Differentials?" *American Economic Review* 70 (June 1980): 355–71; Ronald G. Ehrenberg and Paul L. Schumann, *Longer Hours or More Jobs?* (Ithaca, N.Y.: ILR Press, 1982), Chap. 7; and J. Paul Leigh, "Are Unionized Blue Collar Jobs More Hazardous Than Nonunionized Blue Collar Jobs?" *Journal of Labor Research* 3 (Summer 1982): 349–57.

by employers also give rise to unions. That is, the decision to vote for unions may be heavily influenced by these nonpecuniary conditions of employment. While unions often strive to affect these working conditions, they do not always succeed. Part of the estimated union/nonunion earning differential may be a premium paid to union workers to compensate them for these unfavorable working conditions. Indeed, one study estimates that two fifths of the estimated union/nonunion earnings differential reflects such compensation—suggesting that the observed union/nonunion earnings differential may overstate the true union/nonunion differential in total compensation.[18]

EXAMPLE 17.2

Codetermination and Union Relative-Wage Gains in West Germany

Since the early 1950s, legislation has encouraged greater employee participation in management in West Germany. These *codetermination laws* give employees in the German iron-steel and mining industries one half of the seats on company Boards of Directors and give employees in all other industries (save for shipping and air transport) one third of the seats. The position of labor director has also been established on Management Boards in the steel and mining industries; this director cannot be approved or dismissed without a majority vote of the employee representatives to a company's Board of Directors.

German employee representatives on Boards of Directors participate in decisions about industrywide collective-bargaining agreements. One might expect that these laws have increased labor's bargaining power, especially in the iron-steel and mining industries, and have thus increased the size of observed wage differentials between unionized workers in these industries and other employees in the economy. A recent study concluded that codetermination has increased the earnings of the average unionized German iron-steel and mining employee by roughly 6.2 percent relative to the earnings of primarily nonunion employees in the textile industry. The effects of unions on relative wages clearly depend upon the prevailing institutional arrangements.

SOURCE: Jan Svejnar, ''Relative Wage Effects of Unions, Dictatorship, and Codetermination: Econometric Evidence from Germany,'' *Review of Economics and Statistics* 63 (May 1981): 188–97.

---

[18]Duncan and Stafford, "Do Union Members Receive Compensating Wage Differentials?" The true effect of unions on wages may also be overstated because some quality differences between workers in union and nonunion firms cannot be measured for statistical analyses. Portions of the relative-wage effect reported above may therefore reflect greater ability among union workers rather than union power. *See* Wesley Mellow, "Unionism and Wages: A Longitudinal Analysis," *Review of Economics and Statistics* 63 (February 1981): 43–52; and particularly Lewis, *Union Relative Wage Effects . . . ,* Chapter 5.

Public-sector studies. Several studies have attempted to estimate what the effect of unions representing state- and local-government (SLG) employees has been on their members' wages relative to the wages of otherwise comparable nonunion public employees. A detailed study using data from 1967 for noneducational municipal employees suggested that average monthly earnings of municipal employees represented by unions or employee associations exceeded those of otherwise comparable nonorganized employees by between 2 and 16 percent.[19] These estimates are no higher, and are perhaps even lower, than the union relative-wage effects observed in the private sector. Numerous studies, which use data from later periods and include analyses of educational employees' earnings, confirm this result. That is, unions in the SLG sector appear to have had more moderate effects on the relative wages of their members than unions in the private sector.[20]

As emphasized, however, wages are not identical to total compensation. In addition to those reasons presented in the previous chapter, there are other reasons to believe that the effects of public-sector unions on nonwage benefits may well exceed their effects on wages. On the one hand, public employees' wages are much more visible to the public than are their fringe benefits. The public may be more aware of the cost of a $200 increase in annual starting salaries, which is well publicized, than they are of the cost of an improvement in health-insurance benefits that will also cost $200 per employee. As such, it may be politically easier for governmental negotiators to make concessions on fringe-benefit items than on wages.

On the other hand, while the costs of increased wages must be borne in the present, the costs of improved fringe benefits are often not known at the time of settlement or are borne in the future. For example, the true cost of agreeing to pay 100 percent of employees' health-insurance costs depends upon future increases in health-insurance rates. To take another example, if public-employee pension plans are not fully funded, the costs of agreeing to more generous retirement provisions today will become evident only in the future when employees begin to take advantage of these provisions.[21] Since government officials' tenure in office is often short, and since they typically will depart from office well before the true costs of such fringe benefits become known, it is in their *short-run*

---

[19]Ronald G. Ehrenberg and Gerald S. Goldstein, "A Model of Public Sector Wage Determination," *Journal of Urban Economics* 2 (April 1975): 223–45. This study also showed that the magnitude of the union relative-wage effect for a given category of municipal employees (such as police) depended upon the extent of unionization of other categories of municipal employees (such as firefighters) in the city *and* the extent of organization of municipal employees in neighboring cities. That is, both occupational and geographic wage spillovers appear to occur.

[20]*See* Mitchell, "The Impact of Collective Bargaining . . ." and Lewis, *Union Relative Wage Effects . . .* , chapter 7 for a survey of the recent studies.

[21]That most public retirement systems are not fully funded (that is, they do not have assets sufficient to meet their accrued liabilities) is well known. For example, one study found that in 1975 state- and local-government pension funds had assets equal to only 38 percent of their accrued liabilities. *See* U.S. House of Representatives, *Pension Task Force Report on Public Employee Retirement Systems* (Washington, D.C.: U.S. Government Printing Office, 1978).

political interests to win favor with public-employee unions by agreeing to increased fringes; moreover, the short-run costs of such agreements to taxpayers may well be small.[22]

For both of these reasons then, one might expect that the effect of public-sector unions on fringe benefits would be larger than their effects on wages. Although the limited empirical evidence on this point is somewhat ambiguous, it does suggest that this has occurred.[23]

Effects on wage dispersion. One might think that the above evidence suggests that, contrary to their expressed objectives, unions increase the dispersion of labor earnings, by increasing the wages of high-paid union members and decreasing the wages of lower-paid nonunion members. In fact, however, several studies indicate that unions actually do tend, on balance, to *decrease* the dispersion of labor earnings. The major reason for this decrease is to be found in the effect of unions on the types of payment systems used in industry. In their efforts to "take the wage out of competition," unions prefer payment systems that establish a single "standard rate" for a particular job or occupation and permit upward adjustments or "progression" in the rate on the basis of seniority. Employers, on the other hand, generally favor systems that permit payment on the basis of merit reviews or some other method of making distinctions among different workers performing the same job. In the political setting within which much union decision-making occurs (see discussion in Chapter 12), it is easy to see that if the wage received by the median worker is less than the mean wage paid all workers, then a majority of union members will favor a payment system, such as the standard rate, which redistributes wages toward lower-paid workers. There is strong evidence that unions increase the proportion of workers paid by single (standard) rate plans (and reduce the percent paid by methods of individual wage determination) as compared to pay practices used in the nonunion sector.[24]

We have noted that one effect of the different wage-payment practices adopted in union and nonunion firms is to reduce the extent of wage dispersion among workers covered by union contracts. An interesting aspect of reduced wage dispersion is that the rates of return to education and job training are lower in the union than nonunion sector. These lower payoffs in the union sector are caused by the earnings there being more equal among workers with different

[22]We say short run because in the long run facts become known. The best example of this occurred in New York City where Mayor Lindsay agreed to generous fringe-benefit packages for New York City employees during the late 1960s and early 1970s. Many people subsequently blamed him for all of the financial problems that the city experienced in the mid-1970s, and when he ran for U.S. Senator in the Democratic primary in 1980 he finished well behind the winner.

[23]*See* Casey Ichniowski, "Economic Effects of the Firefighters' Union," *Industrial and Labor Relations Review* 33 (January 1980): 198–211; and David Rogers, "Municipal Government Structure, Unions, and Wage and Nonwage Compensation in the Public Sector" (unpublished Cornell University M.S. thesis, 1979).

[24]Richard B. Freeman, "Union Wage Practices and Wage Dispersion Within Establishments," *Industrial and Labor Relations Review* 36 (October 1982): 3–21.

human-capital investments than would otherwise be the case.[25] Unions also influence wage inequalities by reducing the relative-wage advantage of white-collar workers vis-a-vis blue-collar workers.

Thus, unions have conflicting impacts on the distribution of wages. On the one hand, unions tend to create wage differences among union and nonunion workers at the same occupational level in industry. On the other, unions tend to narrow the wage differences between different blue-collar occupations and between blue-collar and white-collar workers. Moreover, we have seen that unions also tend to standardize the wages paid union workers within an occupation. One study suggests that the latter effects dominate the more widely known union effects on union/nonunion worker wage differentials in the sense that, on balance, unions appear to reduce wage dispersion in the United States.[26] Finally, another study suggests that, other things equal, inequality of earnings within metropolitan areas tends to be less widespread in areas in which the extent of unionization is high.[27]

Union Effects on Productivity and Output

According to the traditional neoclassical view of unions, although they may improve the welfare of their members by improving their pecuniary and nonpecuniary conditions of employment, on balance, their effects on the economy at large are negative. Three reasons are given to support this view.

First, to the extent that unions do succeed in driving a wedge between the wage rates of comparable quality workers who are employed in the union and nonunion sectors, there is a loss of output. Recall from Chapter 3 that the demand curves for labor reflect the marginal product of labor. If the "spillover" model in Figure 17.1 holds, the union wage, W_u, exceeds the nonunion wage, W_n—and the marginal product of labor is higher in the union sector than in the nonunion sector. Consequently, output could be increased if labor were reallocated from the nonunion sector to the union sector where its marginal product is higher. Put another way, unions cause a misallocation of workers: too many workers are employed in the nonunion sector and too few in the union sector. Of course, if the union wage gain also induces some unemployment (see Figures 17.2, 17.3, and 17.4), the loss of output due to these idled resources must also be considered.

Second, union-negotiated contract provisions that establish staffing requirements or other restrictive work practices, limit firms from employing capital and

---

[25]Farrell Bloch and Mark Kuskin, "Wage Determination in the Union and Nonunion Sectors," *Industrial and Labor Relations Review* 31 (January 1978): 183–92; and Greg M. Duncan and Duane E. Leigh, "Wage Determination in the Union and Nonunion Sectors: A Sample Selectivity Approach," *Industrial and Labor Relations Review* 34 (October 1980): 24–35.

[26]Richard B. Freeman, "Unionism and the Dispersion of Wages," *Industrial and Labor Relations Review* 34 (October 1980): 3–23.

[27]Thomas Hyclak, "The Effects of Unions on Earnings Inequality in Local Labor Markets," *Industrial and Labor Relations Review* 33 (October 1979): 77–84.

labor in the most efficient ways and may cause output losses. Several examples of such provisions include minimum-crew sizes in jet aircraft, maximum apprentice/journeymen ratios in construction, provisions limiting subcontracting or mandatory assignment of overtime, and requirements that redundant employees be employed (fire stokers in diesel-operated railroad engines, typesetters in printing plants where type is set by computer). By limiting substitution possibilities or forcing firms to use redundant inputs, unions reduce output below its maximum achievable level.

Third, unions are thought to reduce output because strikes called either at the time that collective bargaining is occurring (to influence the settlement) or during the term of a contract (to protest the way the contract is being administered) result in lost work days. In this view, if strikes were eliminated, output would increase.

Actual empirical estimates of the magnitudes of these alleged losses are few and far between. In an often cited study, Albert Rees estimated that society lost no more than 0.3 percent of gross national product because of the creation of wage differentials between comparable quality union and nonunion workers.[28] Rees also estimated that the loss of output due to restrictive work practices was at least as large. Finally, Table 15.1 indicated that the estimated percentage of working time lost due to strikes over the 27-year period from 1953–79 averaged 0.2 percent. Summing these three figures yields a ballpark estimate of a loss in output of less than 0.8 percent due to these three factors. Of course, whether one considers this an acceptable or unacceptable cost depends upon the benefits that one believes society as a whole receives from unionization.

An Alternative View of Union Effects on Productivity and Output

To the extent that unions are successful in raising their relative wage, employers will have an incentive to raise the marginal product of labor by substituting capital for labor, by increasing the general quality of the work force, or by simply reducing employment. Although these employer adjustments to a higher wage will have the effect of raising observed labor productivity, the total cost of producing a given level of output will have increased. In the following section we shall consider whether union effects on productivity go beyond these induced adjustments by employers.

Recently labor economists have begun to rediscover the possibility that unions may also have positive influences on productivity.[29] The analyses of Richard Freeman and James Medoff and their associates are based heavily upon the

---

[28]Albert Rees, "The Effects of Unions on Resource Allocation," *Journal of Law and Economics* 6 (October 1963): 69–78. Rees's estimate also included consideration of output losses due to union effects on intra-industry wage differentials—for example, requiring all unionized firms in an industry to pay the same wage.

[29]For a discussion of the evidence supporting this view, *see* Freeman and Medoff, "The Two Faces of Unionism." A more detailed discussion is found in their *What Do Unions Do?* (New York: Basic Books, 1982).

assumption that unions function as institutions of *collective voice* operating within structured internal labor markets.[30] That is, because unions can communicate the preferences of workers on various issues directly to management and can help establish work rules and seniority provisions in the context of structured internal labor markets, they can contribute to increases in productivity in a number of ways.

First, by providing workers with a direct means to voice their discontent to management and by establishing job rights based upon seniority, unions may reduce worker discontent—thus reducing voluntary turnover (quit rates). As discussed in Chapter 5, reductions in job turnover increase employers' incentives to provide their employees with *firm-specific training,* which will lead to increased productivity. Considerable evidence suggests that unions do in fact reduce quit rates.[31] Moreover, seniority systems weaken the extent of rivalry between inexperienced and experienced employees and consequently increase the amount of informal on-the-job training that the latter are willing to give to the former.[32]

Second, by increasing the economic rewards to employment and providing grievance mechanisms, unions may directly enhance productivity by increasing worker morale, motivation, and effort. Third, unions provide an explicit mechanism by which labor can point out possible changes in work rules or production techniques that will benefit both labor and management.

Several studies have been undertaken in recent years that attempt to estimate the net effect of unions on productivity. These studies are summarized in Table 17.2. The methodological approach used in all but the Clark study is to estimate the extent to which value of output per worker (the *value added*) is associated with the level of unionization in an industry or establishment at a point in time, after controlling for other factors expected to influence productivity.[33] (The Clark study uses data on the physical volume of output and also looks at how productivity changes after a plant becomes unionized.)

These studies suggest that union workers are more productive than nonunion workers in manufacturing. Indeed, the size of the productivity differential appears to be large enough to offset the estimated union/nonunion wage differential; that is, the unit labor cost of unionized manufacturing workers does not appear to exceed the unit labor cost of nonunion workers. This result provides an explana-

---

[30]Albert Hirschman, *Exit, Voice and Loyalty* (Cambridge, Mass.: Harvard University Press, 1973), and Richard Freeman, "Individual Mobility and Union Voice in the Labor Market," *American Economic Review* 66 (May 1976): 361–68 provide discussions of unions' role as institutions of collective voice. Oliver Williamson, Michael Wachter, and Jeffrey Harris, "Understanding the Employment Relation: Analysis of Idiosyncratic Exchange," *Bell Journal of Economics* 6 (Spring 1975): 250–80, emphasize the interrelationship between unions and internal labor markets.

[31]*See* Richard B. Freeman, "The Exit-Voice Trade-off in the Labor Market: Unionism, Job Tenure, Quits, and Separations," *Quarterly Journal of Economics* 94 (June 1980): 644–73; and James Medoff, "Layoffs and Alternatives Under Trade Unions in United States Manufacturing," *American Economic Review* 69 (June 1979): 380–95.

[32]*See* Peter Doeringer and Michael Piore, *Internal Labor Markets and Manpower Analysis* (Lexington, Mass.: D. C. Heath, 1971).

[33]Value added is the difference in dollar terms between the sales price of a product and the value of the materials that went into making it.

Table 17.2. Estimates of the Impact of Unionism on Productivity in U.S. Industries

Industry/Year of Data	Estimated Impact of Unions on Productivity (percent)
(a) All U.S. manufacturing, 1972	20 to 25
(b) Wooden household furniture, 1972	15
(c) Cement, 1953–76	6 to 8
(d) Underground bituminous coal, 1965	25 to 30
(e) Underground bituminous coal, 1975	−20 to −25
(f) Construction, 1972	29 to 38

SOURCES OF ESTIMATES: (a) Charles Brown and James Medoff, "Trade Unions in the Production Process," *Journal of Political Economy* 86 (June 1978): 355–78. (b) John Frantz, "The Impact of Trade Unions on Productivity in the Wood Household Furniture Industry" (Honors Thesis, Harvard University, 1976). (c) Kim Clark, "The Impact of Unionization on Productivity: A Case Study," *Industrial and Labor Relations Review* 33 (July 1980): 451–69. (d)–(e) Richard Freeman, James Medoff, and Marie Connerton, "Industrial Relations and Productivity: A Case Study of the U.S. Bituminous Coal Industry" (mimeo, Harvard University, 1979). (f) Steven Allen, "Unionized Construction Workers Are More Productive" (Washington, D.C.: Center to Protect Workers Rights, November 1979).

tion of how high-wage union firms and lower-wage nonunion firms can coexist in the same competitive industry.

In the bituminous coal industry, positive union productivity differentials are found in 1965, but substantial negative ones appear in 1975. Indeed, in 1975 unionized workers were estimated to be 20 to 25 percent *less* productive than nonunion workers in the industry. This decline in relative productivity has been attributed to the well-known breakdown of the United Mine Workers' (UMW) national leadership that occurred in the late 1960s and early 1970s, which resulted in deteriorating industrial-relations practices, including increased occurrence of *wildcat* (unauthorized) strikes over local issues.[34] These results emphasize that the effects of unions on productivity are neither constant nor always positive; they vary across industries and time periods as industrial-relations practices vary.

The Allen study cited in Table 17.2 finds surprisingly large union productivity differentials in construction—surprising because in the construction industry unions were widely thought to have adverse effects on productivity owing to their restrictive work rules (limits on apprentice/journeymen ratios, limits on the jobs members of each craft can do, and so forth).[35] Because of some statistical problems associated with the Allen study, however, his results should be considered only tentative.[36]

---

[34]Richard Freeman, James Medoff, and Marie Connerton, "Industrial Relations and Productivity: A Case Study of the U.S. Bituminous Coal Industry" (Cambridge, Mass: Harvard University mimeo, 1979).

[35]Steven Allen, "Unionized Construction Workers Are More Productive" (Washington, D.C.: Center to Protect Workers' Rights, November 1979).

[36]Suppose union workers succeed in raising their wages. To cover the increased costs, employers may increase their product prices; however, this action increases value added. Thus, the association between unions and value added may reflect the effects of unions on wages and prices, not on productivity. This problem is particularly acute in construction since the market for construction products is in the main a local one and output prices are therefore set locally.

On balance, then, the studies summarized in Table 17.2 suggest that unions have *increased* productivity in certain industries. There is no consensus yet, however, as to whether these increases more than offset the losses of gross national product caused by union effects on wage structures and union strike activity. These studies suggest, however, that like most questions in economics, whether unions have had a net positive or negative effect on output is an empirical question. The answer is not as obvious as either the supporters or opponents of unions would have one believe.

Effects of Unions on Profits

The evidence that we have reviewed in this chapter gives a conflicting impression of the economic effect of unions. On the one hand, there is evidence that, *on average,* wages are about 15 percent higher for union workers than for comparable nonunion workers. The effect may be even lower, since part of the wage premium may be compensation for less attractive nonpecuniary working conditions in union jobs or for unmeasured quality advantages of union workers. On the other hand, there is also evidence that, *on average,* labor productivity in manufacturing is at least 20 percent higher in union than in nonunion establishments. Taken together, these two findings raise the possibility that profitability is greater in firms that are organized by unions. This intriguing possibility does not accord well with the rather substantial efforts of most firms to oppose demands for recognition by unions and of employer organizations to oppose proposed labor law reforms that might facilitate the process of union organization. If unions improve the competitive position of firms, why are they not welcomed by managers?

One hypothesis is related to the fact that in the process of negotiating changes in the work environment that are associated with higher employee productivity, unions place substantial constraints on the prerogatives and discretion that managers value in a nonunion employment environment. Managers may therefore oppose unionization, despite its potentially beneficial effects, in order to protect their power and discretion. That is, managers may not be maximizing profits alone; instead they may be *utility-maximizers,* where their utility is a combination of profits and job discretion. Managers therefore may be willing to sacrifice some profits to maintain their discretion. It is argued that since it is difficult for shareholders to monitor managerial performance, it may be possible for managers to take actions (such as resisting unions and their beneficial effects) that may be in their best interests but not the interests of the shareholders.

A direct approach to this issue is to examine the evidence on the effects shareholders expect unions to have on the performance of a firm, and the actual effects of unions on profitability. With respect to shareholder behavior, the literature on finance offers considerable evidence that new publicly available information on factors influencing the profitability of a corporation is quickly reflected in stock (equity) prices. Therefore, announcements of union-organizing drives and victories in representation elections could either increase the equity value of the firm (if the effect on profitability is believed to be positive) or decrease it (if the effect is believed to be negative). One study of 253 NLRB representation elections between 1962 and 1980 found that stock prices *fell* in response to both the announcement that a petition for election had been filed with the NLRB and the certification of a union as bargaining agent.[37]

A second approach is to compare the profitability of union and nonunion firms directly. Here it is important to distinguish between different product market structures. If the effect of unions is to reduce the profitability of firms in a competitive industry, those firms will earn less than normal profits and will leave the industry until the product price increases sufficiently to restore a normal rate of return. In equilibrium, therefore, the profitability of the unionized firms that survive this process and nonunion firms should be the same. In concentrated industries, however, firms may earn excess profits in equilibrium and a union may be able to capture some of these profits. One recent study indicated that unions, in fact, do reduce profits (consistent with the shareholder expectations discussed above), but, in equilibrium, the reduction of profits is observed only in concentrated industries.[38] While some of the evidence is still preliminary, it appears that the general effect of unions is to reduce profits, and that stockholders are aware of this impact.

Concluding Remarks:
Noneconomic Effects of Unions

Unions play many roles in any society and can be assessed from different perspectives. In keeping with the basic perspective of this book, we have focused our attention on the main economic effects of unions in labor markets.

The direct economic effects that have been discussed in this chapter are important and are among the most frequently studied effects of unions. In some respects, however, they provide a limited vision of the effects of unions as social institutions. Most notably, much of the analysis of the direct economic effects tends to slight the role of unions in securing workplace and political representation for workers. At the workplace, unions provide employees with an alternative to quitting in order to register dissatisfaction over working conditions.

---

[37]Interestingly, the fall in the stock price when a petition was filed (before the campaign and election) was larger in cases in which the union ultimately won the election than in cases where the union lost, a result that the authors interpret as indicating that the market is able to anticipate the outcome of the election. *See* Richard S. Ruback and Martin B. Zimmerman, "Unionization and Profitability: Evidence from the Capital Market" (Cambridge, Mass.: Sloan School of Management, MIT, October 1982).

[38]Richard B. Freeman, "Unionism, Price-Cost Margins, and the Return to Capital" (Cambridge, Mass.: National Bureau of Economic Research, January 1983).

Moreover, the alternative is likely to provide employers with more information on specific plant labor-relations problems than an increase in the quit rate. Grievances not only provide a mechanism for interpreting the labor agreement (as stressed in Chapter 16) but also provide a signal to managers about the quality of employer-employee relations. As several recent analyses of unions have stressed, the contractual rules that limit managerial discretion (for example, seniority systems and grievance procedures) may also provide a workplace environment that results in smoother production operations.

Unions also serve an important function in providing a voice for workers and for low-income individuals in a pluralistic political system in which one must be organized to be heard. Most of the important social legislation of the past two decades—for example, legislation pertaining to equal employment opportunity, occupational health and safety, and health care for the aged—has been passed with the active support of the labor movement. That economic analysis can often suggest ways in which such legislation might be structured differently to achieve greater efficiency does not alter the importance of the role of the labor movement in providing representation of the interests and rights of groups of citizens that might otherwise be ignored in the political process. Unions also seek legislation that enhances their power and supports their activities as collective-bargaining institutions. In recent years, however, labor has been able to claim more success in securing passage of legislation addressing the concerns of workers generally than in securing passage of legislation addressing the more parochial concerns of unions in their adversary relationship with employers. Ironically, the more successful are unions in securing benefits for workers generally through legislation, the more difficult it may become to convince workers that they need unions at the workplace to represent their interests.

Some observers have suggested that the function unions serve in representing the rights of workers at the workplace and in the political arena fosters a commitment of American workers to the basic economic system that is not observed in many other countries in which there is often a distinct ideological component to union activities.[39] In this sense, American unions may have a role in fostering political stability. These latter effects of unions are much more difficult to measure than the effects that we have discussed in this chapter. Perhaps because of this, they are easier to ignore. When one compares the behavior of workers and their unions in different countries, however, one cannot help but be impressed by the general political stability of workers in the United States and their acceptance of the economic system. To the extent that this is related to the direct (through collective bargaining) and indirect (through legislative efforts) effects of unions on the welfare of workers, it should be balanced against the economic effects stressed earlier in this chapter in forming a general assessment of the role of unions.

---

[39]Albert Rees, *The Economics of Trade Unions* (Chicago: University of Chicago Press, 1962), pp. 195, 202. See also Robert M. MacDonald, "An Evaluation of the Economic Effects of Unionism," *Industrial and Labor Relations Review* 19 (April 1966): 335–47.

REVIEW QUESTIONS

1. The head of a large national union is trying to decide where he should concentrate his efforts at organizing a union. He perceives three options: Firm A, Firm B, or Firm C. The three firms are identical except that: (a) Firm A faces a perfectly elastic (horizontal) supply curve of labor and a rather inelastic demand curve for its output; (b) Firm B behaves as a monopsonist (faces an upward-sloping supply curve of labor) and faces a perfectly elastic (horizontal) demand curve for its output; (c) Firm C faces a perfectly elastic supply curve of labor and a perfectly elastic demand curve for its output. This union head would like to know where a new union will pay off in large wage gains and small reductions in numbers of workers. Rank the three options from best to worst giving reasons for your ranking.
2. Is the following statement true, false, or uncertain? "The host of empirical studies that indicate that unions raise the wages of their members by 10 to 15 percent relative to the wages of comparable nonunion workers imply that unions have a negative effect on national output." Explain your answer.
3. "Craft workers generally are highly skilled, difficult to replace, and constitute a small percentage of total cost. Straightforward application of the factors governing the elasticity of derived demand for labor indicates that craft workers will benefit the most from union representation." Explain why you do or do not concur with this analysis. Is empirical evidence on union relative-wage effects consistent with the conclusion of the analysis?
4. Are unions likely to raise, lower, or leave unchanged the wages of nonunion workers?
5. In the late 1970s, Congress passed legislation that deregulated much of the air transportation industry, making it easier for new carriers to begin service on many routes and to alter their fares. Would you expect unions representing airline employees to support or oppose such legislation? Why?

SELECTED READINGS

Orley Ashenfelter, "Union Relative Wage Effects: New Evidence and a Survey of Their Implications for Wage Inflation," in *Econometric Contributions to Public Policy*, eds. Richard Stone and William Peterson (New York: St. Martin's Press, 1979).

Charles Brown and James L. Medoff, "Trade Unions in the Production Process," *Journal of Political Economy* 86 (June 1978): 355–79.

Ronald G. Ehrenberg and Gerald S. Goldstein, "A Model of Public Sector Wage Determination," *Journal of Urban Economics* 2 (April 1975): 223–45.

Richard B. Freeman and James L. Medoff, "The Two Faces of Unionism," *Public Interest* 57 (Fall 1979): 69–93.

H. G. Lewis, *Unionism and Relative Wages in the United States: An Empirical Inquiry*, (Chicago: University of Chicago Press, 1963).

Daniel J. B. Mitchell, "The Impact of Collective Bargaining on Compensation in the Public Sector," in *Public Sector Bargaining*, eds. B. Aaron, et al. (Washington, D.C.: Bureau of National Affairs, 1979).

C. J. Parsley, "Labor Unions and Wages: A Survey," *Journal of Economic Literature* 18 (March 1980): 1–31.

Chapter 18

UNEMPLOYMENT

$\mathbf{A}$s noted in Chapter 2, the population can be divided into those people in the labor force (L) and those not in the labor force (N). The labor force consists of those people who are employed (E) and those who are unemployed but would like to be employed (U). The concept of unemployment is somewhat ambiguous since in theory virtually anyone would be willing to be employed in return for some extraordinarily generous compensation package. Economists tend to resolve this dilemma by defining unemployment in terms of an individual's willingness to be employed at some prevailing market wage. Government statistics take a more pragmatic approach, defining the unemployed as those who are on temporary layoff waiting to be recalled by their previous employers or those who have actively searched for work in the previous month (of course, "actively" is not precisely defined).

Given these definitions, the unemployment rate (**u**) is further defined as the ratio of the number of the unemployed to the number in the labor force:

$$\mathbf{u} = \frac{U}{L}. \tag{18.1}$$

Much attention is focused on how the national unemployment rate varies over time, on how unemployment rates vary across geographic areas, and on how unemployment rates vary across age/race/sex groups.

It is important, however, to understand the limitations of unemployment-rate data. They *do* reflect the proportion of a group that, at a point in time, actively wants to work but is not employed. They *do not,* however, necessarily provide an accurate reflection of the economic hardship that members of a group are suffering, for a number of reasons.[1] First, individuals who are not actively searching for work, including those who searched unsuccessfully and then gave up, are not counted among the unemployed (see Chapter 6). Second, unemployment statistics tell us nothing about the earnings levels of those who are employed, including whether these levels exceed the poverty level. Third, a substantial fraction of the unemployed come from families in which other earners are present —for example, many unemployed are teenagers—and the unemployed often are not the primary source of their family's support. Fourth, a substantial fraction of the unemployed receive some income support while they are unemployed, either in the form of government unemployment-compensation payments or private supplementary unemployment benefits (SUBs). Finally, unemployment-rate data give us information on the fraction of the labor force that is not working but tell us little about the fraction of the population that is employed.

Table 18.1 contains data on the aggregate unemployment rate, the labor-force-participation rate and the *employment rate*—the latter being defined as employment divided by population—for 1948, 1958, 1968, and 1978. Although the unemployment rate rose from 3.9 percent in 1948 to 6.8 percent in 1958, because the aggregate labor-force-participation rate also rose during the period, the employment rate (the fraction of the population that is employed) fell only slightly. Focusing on the change in the employment rate suggests less of an economic downturn in 1958 than does focusing on the change in the unemployment rate. Similarly, while between 1968 and 1978 the unemployment rate once again rose (this time from 3.6 to 6.0 percent), the employment rate actually *rose*

Table 18.1. Labor-Force-Participation, Employment, and Unemployment Rates

Year	Unemployment Rate (U/L)	Labor-Force Participation Rate (L/POP)	Employment Rate (E/POP)
1948	3.9	58.9	56.6
1958	6.8	60.4	56.3
1968	3.6	60.7	58.5
1978	6.0	63.7	59.9

U = number of people unemployed.
L = number of people in the labor force.
E = number of people employed.
POP = total population.
SOURCE: Based on U.S. Department of Labor, *1979 Employment and Training Report of the President* (Washington, D.C.: U.S. Government Printing Office, 1979), Table A1.

---

[1]This discussion draws heavily on the final report of the National Commission on Employment and Unemployment Statistics, *Counting the Labor Force* (Washington, D.C.: U.S. Government Printing Office, 1979); and Glen G. Cain, "Labor-Force Concepts and Definitions in View of Their Purposes" in *Concepts and Data Needs* (Appendix Volume I to the Commission's final report).

during the decade because of the increase in the labor-force-participation rate of 3 percentage points.

Nonetheless, the unemployment rate remains a useful indicator of labor-market conditions. This chapter will be concerned with why *anyone* is unemployed; with why the unemployment rate varies over time, regions, or age/race/sex groups; and with how various government policies affect, either in an intended or unintended manner, the level of unemployment.

The next section begins with a simple conceptual model of a labor market that emphasizes the importance of considering the *flows* between labor-market states (for example, the *movement* of people from employed to unemployed status) as well as the *number* of people in each state (for example, the *number* of the unemployed). Knowledge of the determinants of these flows is crucial to any understanding of the causes of unemployment.

The chapter will then move on to discuss how unemployment arises. Economists conceptually categorize unemployment as being *frictional, structural, demand-deficient,* or *seasonal* in nature. After defining each type of unemployment and discussing its causes, we will focus on policy issues that are raised by the discussion. Among the issues that will be considered are the interrelationship between the unemployment-insurance system and unemployment, why unemployment rates vary across age/race/sex groups, why the "full-employment" unemployment rate has risen since 1960, and why firms lay off workers rather than reducing their wages in a recession. The chapter will conclude by discussing some normative issues relating to unemployment, including whether teenagers who were unemployed suffer long-run losses from such experiences.

A Stock-Flow Model of the Labor Market

Data on the number of people who are employed, unemployed, and not in the labor force are provided each month from the national *Current Population Survey (CPS).* [2] As Figure 18.1 indicates, in 1976 (when the overall unemployment rate averaged 7.7 percent) of the 156.0 million adults age 16 and over, there were 87.5 million employed, 7.3 million unemployed, and 61.2 million adults age 16 and over not in the labor force during a typical month. The impression one gets when one traces these data over short periods of time is that of relative stability; for example, it is highly unusual for the unemployment rate to change by more than a few tenths of a percentage point from one month to the next.

Focusing only on these *labor-market stocks* and their net month-to-month changes, however, masks the highly dynamic nature of labor markets. Each month a substantial fraction of the unemployed leave unemployment status, either finding a job or dropping out of the labor force. For example, in each month of 1976 approximately 1.6 million unemployed individuals found employment

---

[2]The next two paragraphs draw heavily on Ralph E. Smith, "A Simulation Model of the Demographic Composition of Employment, Unemployment, and Labor Force Participation" in *Research in Labor Economics,* vol. I, ed. Ronald Ehrenberg (Greenwich, Conn.: JAI Press, 1977).

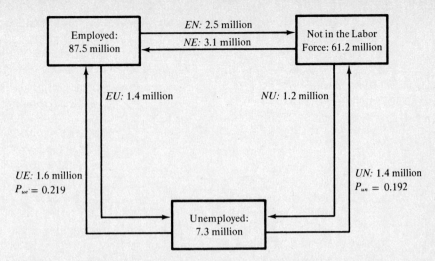

Figure 18.1 Labor-Market Stocks and Flows: 1976 Monthly Averages

SOURCE: Ralph E. Smith and Jean E. Vanski, "Gross Change Data: The Neglected Data Base" in National Commission on Employment and Unemployment Statistics, *Counting the Labor Force*, vol. II (Washington, D.C.: U.S. Government Printing Office, 1979), appendix.

(the flow denoted by *UE* in Figure 18.1), and 1.4 million of the unemployed dropped out of the labor force (the flow denoted by *UN*). These numbers represent the proportions 0.219 (P_{ue}) and 0.192 (P_{un}) of the stock of the unemployed, respectively; thus, one can conclude that approximately 40 percent of the individuals who were unemployed in a given month in 1976 left unemployment by the next month. These individuals were replaced in the pool of unemployed by roughly equivalent flows of individuals into unemployment from the stocks of employed individuals (the flow *EU*) and those not in the labor force (the flow *NU*).[3] The flow *EU* consists of individuals who voluntarily left or involuntarily lost their last job, while the flow *NU* consists of people entering the labor force. Finally, Figure 18.1 also indicates that each month there is considerable direct movement between employment and out-of-labor-force status.

When one thinks of the unemployed, the image of an individual laid off from his or her previous job often springs to mind. However, the view that such individuals comprise all, or even most, of the unemployed is incorrect, except in periods of recession. Table 18.2 provides some data that bear on this point for a period during the 1970s and early 1980s in which the unemployment rate varied between 4.9 and 9.7 percent. Only in 1975 and 1982, when the unemployment rates hit 8.5 and 9.7 percent respectively, were more than half of the unemployed job losers. In each of the years, more than one third of the unemployed came from

---

[3]Actually, in 1976 the flows of people into unemployment from both the stocks of the employed and those not in the labor force were less than the flows out of unemployment into these stocks (see Figure 18.1). As might be expected, then, the unemployment rate was declining during most of the year.

Table 18.2. Categories of Entry Into Unemployment

		Percent of Unemployed Who Are:			
Year	Unemployment Rate	Job Losers	Job Leavers	Reentrants	New Entrants
1971	5.9	46.3	11.8	29.4	12.6
1973	4.9	38.7	15.7	30.7	14.9
1975	8.5	55.4	10.4	23.8	10.4
1977	7.0	45.2	13.0	28.1	13.7
1979	5.8	42.8	14.3	29.5	13.4
1982	9.7	58.7	7.9	22.3	11.1

SOURCE: U.S. Department of Labor, *1981 Employment and Training Report of the President* (Washington, D.C.: U.S. Government Printing Office, 1981), Table A36. Data on 1982 are from U.S. President, *Economic Report of the President* (Washington, D.C.: U.S. Government Printing Office, 1983), pp. 35, 199.

out-of-labor-force status—that is, they were individuals who were either entering the labor force for the first time *(new entrants)* or individuals who had some previous employment experience and were reentering the labor force after a period of time out of the labor force *(reentrants)*. Indeed, although the vast majority of individuals who quit their jobs obtain new jobs prior to quitting and never pass through unemployment status, in each year except 1982 (a year of deep recession), at least 10 percent of the unemployed were voluntary job leavers.[4]

Similarly, when one thinks of an individual on layoff, one may envision an individual who has permanently lost his or her job and who finds employment with a new employer only after an exhaustive job search and long duration of unemployment. However, the evidence suggests that a substantial fraction (for example, 37 percent in 1974) of those individuals who *lost* their last job are on *temporary layoff* and ultimately return to their previous employer—many after only a relatively short spell (averaging 8.5 weeks in 1974) of unemployment.[5] Why some individuals "cycle" between employed and unemployed status, maintaining attachment to a single employer, will be discussed below.

Although ultimately public concern focuses on the level of unemployment, to understand the determinants of this level one must analyze the flows of individuals between the various labor-market states. A group's unemployment rate might be high because its members have difficulty finding jobs once unemployed, because they have difficulty (for voluntary or involuntary reasons) remaining employed once a job is found, or because they frequently enter and exit the labor force. The appropriate policy prescription to reduce the unemployment rate will depend upon which one of these labor-market flows is responsible for the high rate.

---

[4]For evidence that most quits do not involve a spell of unemployment, *see* J. Peter Mattila, "Job Quitting and Frictional Unemployment," *American Economic Review* 64 (March 1974): 235–39.

[5]For evidence on the magnitude of temporary layoffs, *see* Martin Feldstein, "The Importance of Temporary Layoffs: An Empirical Analysis," *Brookings Papers on Economic Activity,* 1975–3, pp. 725–44.

Somewhat more formally, one can show that if labor markets are roughly in balance, with the flows into and out of unemployment equal, the unemployment rate (**u**) for a group depends upon the various labor market flows in the following manner:

$$\mathbf{u} = F[\overset{+}{P_{eu}}, \overset{+}{P_{en}}, \overset{+}{P_{nu}}, \overset{-}{P_{ue}}, \overset{-}{P_{un}}, \overset{-}{P_{ne}}]. \tag{18.2}$$

Here F means "a function of," P_{ij} represents the fraction of the group in labor-market state i that moves to labor market state j during the period, and the subscripts n, e, and u represent the states "not in the labor force," "employed," and "unemployed," respectively. So, for example, if there were initially 100 employed individuals in a group and 15 of them became unemployed during a period, P_{eu} would equal 0.15. A plus over a variable in equation (18.2) means that an increase in that variable will increase the unemployment rate, while a minus means that an increase in the variable will decrease the unemployment rate.[6]

Equation (18.2) thus asserts that, other things equal, increases in the proportions of individuals who voluntarily or involuntarily leave their jobs and become unemployed (P_{eu}) or leave the labor force (P_{en}) will increase a group's unemployment rate, as will an increase in the proportion of the group that enters the labor force without first having a job lined up (P_{nu}). Similarly, the greater the proportion of individuals who leave unemployment status, either to become employed (P_{ue}) or to leave the labor force (P_{un}), the lower a group's unemployment rate will be. Finally, the greater the proportion of individuals who enter the labor force and immediately find jobs (P_{ne}), the lower a group's unemployment rate will be.[7]

The various theories of unemployment discussed in subsequent sections all essentially relate to the determination of one or more of the flows represented in equation (18.2). That is, they provide explanations for why the proportions of individuals who move between the various labor-market states vary over time, across geographic areas, or across age/race/sex groups. Equation (18.2) can help one understand why unemployment rates rise in recessions, how and why unemployment rates are influenced by the unemployment-insurance system, and why unemployment rates vary across age/race/sex groups.

Equation (18.2) and Figure 18.1 also make it clear that social concern over any given level of unemployment should focus on both the incidence of unemployment (on the fraction of people in a group who become unemployed) and the duration (or length of spells) of their unemployment. Society is probably more

---

[6]*See* Steven T. Marston, "Employment Instability and High Unemployment Rates," *Brookings Papers on Economic Activity,* 1976–1, pp. 169–203, for the exact functional form of equation (18.2) and its derivation.

[7]For an intuitive understanding of why each of these results holds, recall the definition of the unemployment rate in equation (18.1). A movement from one labor-market state to another may affect the numerator or the denominator, or both, and hence the unemployment rate. For example, an increase in P_{en} does not affect the number of unemployed individuals directly, but it does reduce the size of the labor force. According to equation (18.1), this reduction leads to an increase in the unemployment rate.

concerned if small groups of individuals are unemployed for long periods of time than if many individuals rapidly pass through unemployment status. Up until recently, it was widely believed that the bulk of measured unemployment could be attributed to many people experiencing short spells of unemployment. However, recent evidence suggests that, while many people do pass quickly through unemployment, most unemployment is due to prolonged spells of unemployment for a relatively small number of individuals.[8]

Types of Unemployment and Their Causes

Frictional Unemployment

Suppose a competitive labor market is in equilibrium, in the sense that at the prevailing market wage the quantity of labor demanded just equals the quantity of labor supplied. Figure 18.2 shows such a labor market, in which the demand curve is D_0, the supply curve is S_0, employment is E_0, and the wage rate is W_0. Thus far the text has treated this equilibrium situation as one of full employment and has implied that there is no unemployment associated with it. However, this implication is not completely correct. Even in a market equilibrium or full-employment situation there will still be some *frictional unemployment,* because some people will be "between jobs."

Frictional unemployment arises because labor markets are inherently dy-

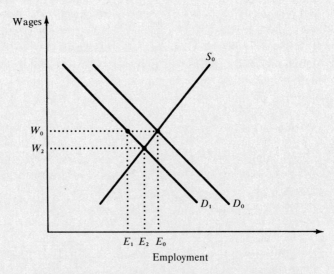

Figure 18.2   A Simple Model of the Labor Market

---

[8]Kim B. Clark and Lawrence H. Summers, "Labor-Market Dynamics and Unemployment: A Reconsideration," *Brookings Papers on Economic Activity,* 1979–1, pp. 13–60.

namic, because information flows are imperfect, and because it takes time for unemployed workers and employers with job vacancies to find each other. Even if the size of the labor force is constant, in each period there will be new entrants to the labor market searching for employment while other employed or unemployed individuals are leaving the labor force. Some people will quit their jobs to search for other employment. Moreover, random fluctuations in demand across firms will cause some firms to lay off workers at the same time that other firms will be seeking to hire new employees. Because information about the characteristics of those searching for work and the nature of the jobs opening up cannot instantly be known or evaluated, it takes time for job matches to be made between unemployed workers and potential employers. Hence, even when, in the aggregate, the demand for labor equals the supply, frictional unemployment will still exist.

The level of frictional unemployment in an economy is determined by the flows of individuals into and out of the labor market and the speed with which unemployed individuals find jobs. This speed is determined by the prevailing economic institutions, and institutional changes can influence the level of frictional unemployment. For example, instituting a computerized job-bank system, in which job applicants at the U.S. Employment Service are immediately informed of all listed jobs for which they are qualified, might reduce the time it takes them to find jobs. This system would increase the probability that an unemployed worker would become employed in any period (increase P_{ue}) and hence, as indicated by equation (18.2), would *decrease* the unemployment rate. On the other hand, one should be aware that if the time it takes unemployed workers to find jobs decreases, more employed workers may consider quitting their jobs to search for better-paying employment, thereby *increasing P_{eu}* and the unemployment rate. (This example should remind us again that social policies often have unintended adverse side effects.)

Structural Unemployment

Structural unemployment arises when changes in the pattern of labor demand cause a mismatch between the skills demanded and supplied in a given area—or cause an imbalance between the supplies and demands for workers across areas. *If* wages were completely flexible *and* if costs of occupational or geographic mobility were low, market adjustments would quickly eliminate this type of unemployment. However, in practice these conditions may fail to hold, and structural unemployment may result.

Our by-now familiar two-sector labor-market model, represented by Figure 18.3, can be used to illustrate this point. For the moment we shall assume the sectors refer to markets for skill classes of workers; later we shall assume that they are two geographically separate labor markets. Suppose that Market A is the market for semiskilled workers in the shoe industry and that Market B is the market for skilled computer programmers—and suppose that initially both markets are in equilibrium. Given the demand and supply curves in both markets $[(D_{0A}, S_{0A})$ and $(D_{0B}, S_{0B})]$, the equilibrium wage/employment combinations

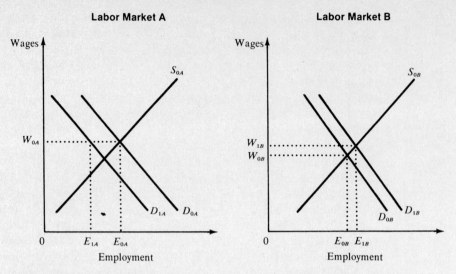

Figure 18.3   Structural Unemployment Due to Inflexible Wages and Costs of Adjustment

in the two sectors will be (W_{0A}, E_{0A}) and (W_{0B}, E_{0B}) respectively. Because of differences in training costs and nonpecuniary conditions of employment, the wages need not be equal in the two sectors.

Now suppose that the demand for semiskilled shoe workers falls to D_{1A}, due to foreign import competition, while the demand for computer programmers rises to D_{1B} as a result of the increased use of computers. If real wages are inflexible downward in Market A because of union contract provisions, social norms, or government legislation, employment of semiskilled shoe employees will fall to E_{1A}. Employment and wages of computer programmers will rise to E_{1B} and W_{1B}, respectively. Unemployment of $E_{0A} - E_{1A}$ workers would be created in the short run.

If shoe-industry employees could costlessly become computer programmers, these unemployed workers would "move" to Market B, and, since wages are assumed to be flexible there, eventually all of the unemployment would be eliminated.[9] Structural unemployment arises, however, when costs of adjustment are sufficiently high to preclude such movements. The cost to displaced individuals —many in their fifties and sixties—may prove to be prohibitively expensive, given the limited time horizons that they face. Moreover, it may be difficult for them to borrow funds to finance the necessary job training.

---

[9]Actually, this statement is not quite correct. As Chapter 17 noted when analyzing the effects of unions using a similar model, *wait unemployment* may arise. That is, as long as the wage rate in Market A exceeds the wage rate in Market B and unemployed workers in Market A expect that normal job turnover will eventually create job vacancies in A, it may be profitable for them to remain attached to Market A and wait for a job in that sector. Wait employment is another example of a type of frictional unemployment.

Geographic imbalances can be analyzed in the same framework. Suppose we now assume that Market A refers to a snowbelt city and Market B refers to a sunbelt city, both employing the same type of labor. When demand falls in the snowbelt and unemployment increases because wages are not completely flexible, these unemployed workers may continue to wait for jobs in their city for at least three reasons. First, information flows are imperfect, so that workers may be unaware of the availability of jobs thousands of miles away. Second, the direct money costs of such a move, including moving costs and the transaction costs involved in buying and selling a home, are high. Third, the psychological costs of moving long distances are substantial because friends and neighbors and community support systems must be given up. As noted in Chapter 9, such factors inhibit geographic migration, and migration tends to decline with age. These costs are sufficiently high that many workers who become unemployed, due either to plant shutdowns or to permanent layoffs, express no interest in searching for jobs outside their immediate geographic area.[10]

Structural unemployment arises, then, because of changing patterns of labor demand that occur in the face of both rigid wages and high costs of occupational or geographic mobility. In terms of Figure 18.1, structurally unemployed workers have a low probability of moving from unemployed to employed status (low P_{ue}), and any social policies that increase this probability should reduce the level of structural unemployment (other things equal). Examples of such policies include the provision of subsidized training, the provision of information about job-market conditions in other areas, and the provision of relocation allowances to help defray the costs of migration.

Each of these policies is part of the *Trade Adjustment Assistance Program,* which was initiated under the Trade Expansion Act of 1962 and expanded under the Trade Act of 1974. This program was designed to aid individuals who became unemployed because of changes in product demand brought about by foreign competition, and it also provided for an expanded form of unemployment-compensation benefits (the effects of unemployment compensation on unemployment will be discussed later in the chapter). The available evidence indicates, however, that perhaps due to restrictive eligibility rules, this program has had little effect on increasing the probability that these structurally unemployed workers will find employment.[11]

On a more general level, since the early 1960s the federal government has been heavily involved in policies to reduce structural unemployment. These policies include the provision of relocation allowances to unemployed workers resid-

[10]*See,* for example, Robert Aronson and Robert McKersie, *Economic Consequences of Plant Shutdowns in New York State* (Ithaca, N.Y.: New York State School of Industrial and Labor Relations, 1980).

[11]*See,* for example, George R. Neumann, "The Labor Market Adjustment of Trade-Displaced Workers: The Evidence from the Trade Adjustment Assistance Program" in *Research in Labor Economics,* ed. Ronald Ehrenberg, vol. 2, 1978; and Walter Corson and Walter Nicholson, "Trade Adjustment Assistance for Workers: Results of a Survey of Recipients Under the Trade Act of 1974" in *Research in Labor Economics,* ed. Ronald Ehrenberg, vol. 4, 1981.

ing in depressed areas (under the *Area Redevelopment Act of 1959*), the provision of classroom and on-the-job training to both disadvantaged and unemployed workers (under the *Manpower Development and Training Act of 1962*), and, more recently, the provision of both training and public-sector employment opportunities (under the *Comprehensive Employment and Training Act of 1973*) and of training opportunities only (under the *Job Partnership Training Act of 1982*). Indeed, in fiscal year 1978 more than 2.5 million individuals were enrolled at some time during the year in federally-funded employment and training programs.[12] Although the evidence on the effectiveness of these programs is mixed, several studies suggest that some of them have succeeded in increasing the earnings or employment probabilities of those individuals who were enrolled in the programs.[13]

Demand-Deficient Unemployment

Frictional and structural unemployment can arise even when, in the aggregate, the demand for labor equals the supply. Frictional unemployment arises because labor markets are dynamic and information flows are imperfect; structural unemployment arises because of geographic or occupational imbalances in demand and supply. *Demand-deficient unemployment* occurs when the *aggregate* demand for labor declines in the face of downward inflexibility in real wages.

Returning to our simple demand and supply model of Figure 18.2, suppose that a temporary decline in aggregate demand leads to a shift in the labor demand curve to D_1. If real wages are inflexible downward, employment will fall to E_1 and $E_0 - E_1$ additional workers will become unemployed. This employment decline occurs when firms temporarily lay off workers (increasing P_{eu}) and reduce the rate at which they replace those who quit or retire (decreasing P_{ne} and P_{ue}). That is, flows into unemployment increase while flows into employment decline.[14]

Demand-deficient (or *cyclical*) *unemployment* arises, then, when *aggregate* demand falls in the face of downward inflexibility in real wages. One appropriate government response is to pursue macroeconomic policies to increase aggregate demand; these policies include increasing the level of government spending, reducing taxes, and increasing the rate of growth of the money supply. Another policy is to use labor-market programs that focus more directly on the unemployed. Examples here include temporary employment tax credits for firms that were discussed in Chapter 4.

---

[12]*1979 Employment and Training Report of the President,* Table F2.

[13]*See,* for example, Orley Ashenfelter, "Estimating the Effects of Training Programs on Earnings," *Review of Economics and Statistics* 60 (February 1979): 47–57; Thomas Cooley *et al.,* "The Estimation of Treatment Effects for Nonrandomized Samples: The Case of Manpower Training" in *Research in Labor Economics,* ed. R. Ehrenberg, Supplement I, 1979; Nicholas Kiefer, "The Economic Benefits from Four Government Training Programs" in *Research in Labor Economics,* ed. R. Ehrenberg, Supplement I, 1979; and Bradley Schiller, "Lessons From WIN: A Manpower Evaluation," *Journal of Human Resources* 13 (Fall 1978): 502–23.

[14]*See* Steven T. Marston, "Employment Instability and High Unemployment Rates".

Of course, it still remains for us to explain *why* employers respond to a cyclical decline in demand by temporarily laying off some of their work force rather than reducing their employees' real wages. If the latter occurred, employment would move to E_2 and real wages to W_2 in Figure 18.2. Although employment would be lower than its initial level, E_0, there would be no measured demand-deficient unemployment because $E_0 - E_2$ workers would have dropped out of the labor force in response to this lower wage.

According to one explanation for rigid money wages, employers are not free to unilaterally cut money wages because of the presence of unions. However, this cannot be a complete explanation because less than one quarter of American workers are represented by unions (see Chapter 12), and unions could, in any case, agree to temporary wage cuts to save jobs instead of subjecting their members to layoffs. Why they fail to make such arrangements is instructive.[15] A temporary wage reduction would reduce the earnings of all workers, while layoffs would affect—in most cases—only those workers most recently hired. Since unions represent their entire membership, not just the newly hired, and since union leaders are not likely to be drawn from the ranks of new members, unions tend to favor a policy of layoffs rather than one that reduces wages for all members.

Although layoffs occur less frequently than in union firms, they occur in nonunion firms for two related reasons.[16] First, in the presence of investments in firm-specific human capital, which often lead to structured internal labor markets (see Chapter 5), employers have incentives both to minimize voluntary turnover and to maximize their employees' work effort and productivity. Across-the-board temporary wage reductions would increase all employees' incentives to quit and could lead to reduced work effort on their part. In contrast, layoffs affect only the least experienced workers—the workers in whom the firm has invested the smallest amount of resources. It is likely, then, that the firm will find choosing the layoff strategy a more profitable alternative.

Second, if potential job applicants and existing employees are aware that a firm is pursuing a temporary layoff rather than a temporary-wage-cut strategy, they may be willing to work for a lower *average* wage rate. Individuals are typically assumed to be *risk-averse*—that is, they are assumed to prefer a constant earnings stream to a fluctuating one.[17] In effect, a system of layoffs in which the newest employees are laid off first provides an *implicit contract* (a guarantee or form of insurance to experienced workers) that they will be immune to all but

---

[15]*See* James L. Medoff, "Layoffs and Alternatives Under Trade Unions in United States Manufacturing," *American Economic Review* 69 (June 1979): 380–95, for the following argument and evidence.

[16]*See* Medoff, "Layoffs and Alternatives Under Trade Unions," for evidence that layoff rates are higher in union than nonunion firms, *ceteris paribus* (other things equal).

[17]This line of reasoning follows that found in Costas Azariadis, "Implicit Contracts and Underemployment Equilibria," *Journal of Political Economy* 83 (December 1975): 1183–1202; and Martin Baily, "Wages and Employment Under Uncertain Demand," *Review of Economic Studies* 41 (January 1974): 37–50.

EXAMPLE 18.1

International Unemployment-Rate Differentials

Comparisons of unemployment rates across nations are difficult because the exact definition of unemployment differs across nations. For example, in the United States "discouraged workers" who leave the labor force are not counted among the unemployed, while in Italy they are. Nevertheless it is possible to adjust the unemployment data reported by various industrial countries so that the data correspond approximately to the U.S. definition of unemployment. These adjusted unemployment rates are reported in the table below for ten industrial nations and three years during the 1970s and 1980s.

Nation/Year	1974	1977	1981
United States	5.6	7.0	7.6
Canada	5.3	8.1	7.6
Australia	2.7	5.6	5.8
Japan	1.4	2.0	2.2
France	2.9	5.0	7.7
Germany	1.6	3.6	4.2
Great Britain	3.1	6.2	11.3
Italy	2.8	3.4	4.2
Sweden	2.0	1.8	2.5
Netherlands	3.8	5.1	8.9

Note: The definitions of unemployment have been adjusted to approximate the U.S. concept of unemployment.

SOURCE: Joyanna Moy, "Unemployment and Labor Force Trends in 10 Industrial Nations: An Update," *Monthly Labor Review* 105 (Nov 1982), Table 2.

This table indicates that there are large differences in the adjusted unemployment rate across these nations in each year; in 1977 the adjusted unemployment rate varied from 1.8 percent in Sweden to 8.1 percent in Canada. Part of the difference results from differences in aggregate demand across nations—labor markets were tighter in Sweden than they were in Canada in 1977. Another part of the difference, however, reflects differences in social and institutional forces that affect the underlying labor-market flows.

The adjusted unemployment rate in Japan, for example, is typically lower than that in the United States. As we first saw in Chapter 5, a large sector of the Japanese labor market is characterized by a system of long-term—often lifelong—employment relations between employers and employees. Employees in this sector rarely quit their jobs voluntarily and their employers rarely lay off workers during economic downswings. As a result, the proportions of employed workers who voluntarily leave or involuntarily lose their jobs each period and enter unemployment status (P_{eu}) are low in Japan relative to the United States—as are the proportions who leave the labor force (P_{en}). As equation (18.2) indicates, the low levels of P_{eu} and P_{en} cause the Japanese unemployment rate to be lower than the American unemployment rate, other things equal.

How are Japanese employers able to maintain almost all their employees on their payrolls during economic downswings? A recent *Monthly Labor Review* article suggests one way:

A number of Japanese enterprises with underutilized skilled labor (such as steel mills, shipbuilders, or textile producers) have adopted a novel method of maintaining employment for their regular workers. Excess workers are "loaned" for a specified period of no longer than 6 months to enterprises experiencing current labor shortages (such as automobile manufacturers). The workers maintain their affiliation with and receive their full wages from the lending company. The borrowing company usually pays temporary-worker wages, and the difference in wages plus benefits is made up by the lending employer. Thus, the borrowing company is able to temporarily increase its labor force with workers whose turnover rate is close to zero, while the lending company is able to maintain its regular work force at reduced cost.

SOURCES: Masanori Hashimoto "Bonus Payments, On-the-Job Training, and Lifetime Employment in Japan," *Journal of Political Economy* 87 (October 1979): 1086–1104 presents evidence to support the contention that P_{eu} and P_{en} are lower in Japan than in the United States; for each age group male job tenure is seen to be higher than in the United States; Joyanna Moy, "Recent Labor Market Trends in Nine Industrial Nations," *Monthly Labor Review,* 102 (May 1979); 14.

the severest declines in demand. Put another way, after an initial period when the risk of layoff is high, earnings are likely to be very stable over time.[18] To the extent that experienced employees value stable earnings streams, they should be willing to pay for this stability by accepting lower wages in such situations—thereby reducing employers' costs. Of course, during the initial period, workers will be subject to potential earnings variability and may demand higher wages then to compensate them for these risks. However, if the fraction of the work force subject to layoffs is small, on average employers' costs should be reduced.

The incentives for both employers and employees to prefer temporary layoffs over fluctuations in real wages is magnified by two characteristics of the unemployment-insurance (UI) system: the *tax treatment of UI benefits* and the system's *method of financing benefits.*[19] The unemployment-insurance system is actually

---

[18]We are ignoring here questions of real earnings growth over time.

[19]A more complete description of the characteristics of the UI system is found in Daniel S. Hamermesh, *Jobless Pay and the Economy* (Baltimore: Johns Hopkins University Press, 1977). The connection between temporary layoffs and these characteristics of the UI system was pointed out in Martin Feldstein, "Temporary Layoffs in the Theory of Unemployment," *Journal of Political Economy* 84 (October 1976): 937–58; empirical evidence on the relationship was provided in Martin Feldstein, "The Effect of Unemployment Insurance on Temporary Layoffs," *American Economic Review* 68 (December 1978): 834–40.

a system of individual state systems, and, although the details of the individual systems differ, one can easily sketch the broad outlines of how they operate.

Today virtually all private-sector employees are covered by a state UI system. When such workers become unemployed their eligibility for unemployment-insurance benefits is based upon their previous labor-market experience and reason for unemployment. With respect to their experience, each state requires unemployed individuals to demonstrate "permanent" attachment to the labor force, by meeting minimum earnings or weeks-worked tests during some base period, before they can be eligible for UI benefits. In all states covered, workers who are laid off *and* meet these labor-market-experience tests are eligible for UI benefits. In some states workers who voluntarily quit their jobs are eligible for benefits, while in only two states (New York and Rhode Island) are strikers eligible for benefits. Finally, new entrants or reentrants to the labor force and workers fired for cause are, in general, ineligible for benefits.

After a waiting period, which is one or two weeks in most states, an eligible worker can begin to collect UI benefits. The structure of benefits is described in Figure 18.4, where it can be seen that benefits are related to an individual's previous earnings level.[20] As shown in panel (a), all eligible unemployed workers are entitled to at least a minimum benefit level, B_{min}. After previous earnings rise above a critical level, W_{min}, benefits increase proportionately with earnings—up to a maximum earnings level W_{max}, past which benefits remain constant at B_{max}. Eleven states also have dependents' allowances for unemployed workers, although in some of these states the dependents' allowance cannot increase an individual's weekly UI benefits above B_{max}.

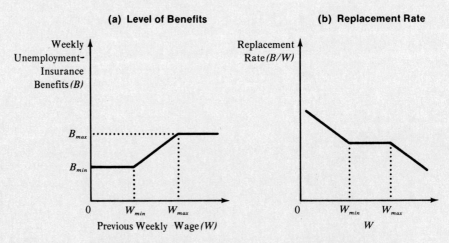

(a) Level of Benefits

(b) Replacement Rate

Figure 18.4 Weekly Unemployment-Insurance Benefits as a Function of Previous Earnings

---

[20]Benefits are calculated across states in at least three different ways: as a percentage of annual earnings, as a percentage of previous weekly earnings, and as a percent of an individual's earnings during his or her "high" earnings quarter during the past year. For our purposes, such distinctions are unimportant.

An implication of such a benefit structure is that the ratio of an individual's UI benefits to his or her previous earnings varies according to one's past earnings —see panel (b). This ratio is often called the *replacement rate,* the fraction of previous earnings that the UI benefits replace. Over the range between W_{min} and W_{max}, where the replacement rate is constant, most states aim to replace around 50 percent of an unemployed worker's previous earnings. It is important to stress that up until 1978 *UI benefits were not subject to the federal income tax;* since then, however, UI benefits received by those whose family incomes exceed a specified level are taxed. As of 1983, this level was $15,000.

Once UI benefits begin, an unemployed individual's eligibility for continued benefits depend upon his or her making continual "suitable efforts" to find employment; the definition of suitable efforts varies widely across states. In addition, there is a maximum duration of receipt of benefits that is of fixed length in some states and varies in other states with a worker's prior labor-market experience (workers with "more permanent attachment" being eligible for more weeks of benefits). Periodically, Congress also passes temporary legislation that extends the length of time unemployed workers can receive benefits in states in which unemployment is high, but the maximum total duration of eligibility for benefits did not exceed 65 weeks in the early 1980s.

The benefits paid out by the UI system are financed by a payroll tax. Unlike the social-security payroll tax, in all but three states the UI tax is paid solely by employers with no employee contribution required.[21] The UI tax payment *(T)* that an employer must make for each employee is given by

$$T = tW \text{ if } W \leq W_B \tag{18.3}$$

and

$$T = tW_B \text{ if } W > W_B,$$

where t is the employer's UI tax rate, W is an employee's earnings during the calendar year, and W_B is the *taxable wage base,* the level of earnings after which no UI tax payments are required. In 1983, the taxable wage base was $7,000 in most states; employers had to pay UI taxes on the first $7,000 of earnings for each employee.

The employer's UI tax rate is determined by general economic conditions in a state, the industry the employer is operating in, and the employer's *layoff experience.* This latter term is defined differently in different states; the underlying notion is that since the UI system is an insurance system, employers who lay off lots of workers and make heavy demands on the system's resources should be assigned a higher UI tax rate. This practice is referred to as *experience rating.*

Experience rating is typically *imperfect* in the sense that the marginal cost to an employer of laying off an additional worker (in terms of a higher UI tax

---

[21]Recall from our discussion in Chapter 3 that this fact tells us nothing about who really bears the burden of the tax.

rate) is often less than the added UI benefits that the system must pay out to that worker. Imperfect experience rating is illustrated in Figure 18.5, which plots the relationship between an employer's UI tax rate and that firm's layoff experience. (We will interpret *layoff experience* to mean the probability that employees in the firm will be on layoff. Clearly, this probability depends both on the frequency with which the firm lays off workers and the average duration of time until they are recalled to their positions.)

Each state has a minimum UI tax rate, and below this rate—t_{min} in Figure 18.5—the firm's UI tax rate cannot fall. After a firm's layoff experience reaches some critical value, l_{min}, the firm's UI tax rate rises with increased layoff experience over some range. In each state there is also a ceiling on the UI tax rate, t_{max}, and after this tax rate is reached, additional layoffs will not alter the firm's tax rate.[22] The system is *imperfectly* experience-rated because for firms below l_{min} or above l_{max}, variations in their layoff rate have no effect on their UI tax rate.[23] Further, over the range that the tax rate is increasing with layoff experience, the increase is not large enough in most states to make the employer's marginal cost of a layoff (in terms of the increased UI taxes the firm must pay) equal to the marginal UI benefits that the laid-off employees receive.

The key characteristics of the UI system that influence the desirability of temporary layoffs are the *imperfect experience rating* of the UI payroll tax and the *federal tax treatment* of UI benefits that workers receive. To understand the

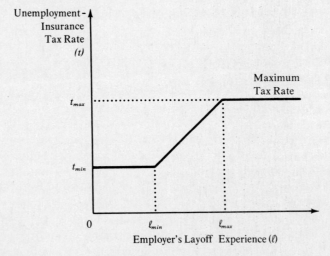

Figure 18.5 Imperfectly Experience-Rated Unemployment-Insurance Tax Rate

---

[22]In actuality the UI tax rate changes discretely (as a step function) over the range l_{min} to l_{max}, not continuously as we have drawn in Figure 18.5. For expository convenience, we ignore this complication.

[23]Such a system of UI financing leads to interindustry subsidies, in which industries (such as banking) with virtually no layoffs still must pay the minimum tax—and these industries subsidize those industries (such as construction) that have very high layoffs but pay only the maximum rate.

influence of these characteristics, suppose first that the UI system were constructed in such a way that its tax rates were perfectly experience-rated and the benefits it paid out (half of previous earnings, say) were completely taxable. A firm laying off a worker would have to pay added UI taxes equal to the full UI benefit received by the worker, so it saves just half of the worker's wages by the layoff; the *worker's* spendable income would be cut in half if he or she were laid off.

Now, suppose instead, that the UI tax rate employers must pay is totally independent of its layoff experience (no experience rating), and that UI benefits are not subject to any personal income taxes. The *firm* saves the laid-off worker's *entire* wages—not just half—because its UI taxes do not rise as a result of the layoff. The worker still gets a benefit equal to half of prior earnings, but since these benefits are not taxable, his or her spendable income drops by *less* than half. Thus, compared to a UI system with perfect experience rating and completely taxable benefits, it is easy to see that the current system—which has imperfect experience rating and does not generally tax benefits—enhances the attractiveness of layoffs to both employer and employee.[24] Put differently, these characteristics of the UI system tend to increase the level of demand-deficient unemployment over what it would be if experience rating were perfect and benefits were completely taxable.

Seasonal Unemployment

Seasonal unemployment is similar to demand-deficient unemployment in that it is induced by fluctuations in the demand for labor. Here, however, the fluctuations can be regularly anticipated and follow a systematic pattern over the course of a year. For example, the demand for agricultural employees declines after the planting season and remains low until the harvest season. Similarly, the demand for construction workers in snowbelt states falls during winter months. Finally, the demand for production workers falls in certain industries during the season of the year when plants are retooling to handle annual model changes; examples here include both the Detroit automotive industry (new car models) and the New York City apparel industry (new fashion designs).

The issue remains, why do employers respond to seasonal patterns of demand by laying off workers rather than reducing wage rates or hours of work? All of the answers cited for why cyclical unemployment and temporary layoffs for cyclical reasons exist also pertain here. Indeed, one study has shown that the expansion (in the early 1970s) of the unemployment-insurance system to cover most agricultural employees was associated with a substantial increase in seasonal unemployment in agriculture.[25]

One may question, however, why workers would accept jobs in industries in which they knew in advance that they would be unemployed for a portion of the year. For some workers, the existence of UI benefits along with the knowledge that

---

[24]This statement is not always true since unemployed workers often lose fringe benefits and the ability to take advantage of on-the-job training options.

[25]Barry Chiswick, "The Effect of Unemployment Compensation on a Seasonal Industry: Agriculture," *Journal of Political Economy* 84 (June 1976): 591–602.

they will be rehired as a matter of course at the end of the slack demand season may allow them to treat such periods as paid vacations. However, since UI benefits typically replace less than half of an unemployed worker's previous gross earnings, and even smaller fractions for high-wage workers (see Figure 18.4), most workers will not find such a situation desirable. To attract workers to such seasonal industries, firms will have to pay workers higher wages to compensate them for being periodically unemployed. In fact, casual observation suggests that the hourly wages of construction workers are substantially higher than the hourly wages of comparably skilled manufacturing workers who work more hours each year. More formally, a recent econometric study has confirmed that, other things held constant (including workers' skill levels), wages are higher in industries in which workers' expected annual durations of unemployment are higher.[26]

The existence of such wage differentials that compensate workers in high-unemployment industries for the risk of unemployment makes it difficult to evaluate whether this type of unemployment is voluntary or involuntary in nature. On the one hand, in an *ex ante* (or "before the fact") sense, workers have voluntarily agreed to be employed in industries that offer higher wages *and* higher probabilities of unemployment than offered elsewhere. On the other hand, once on the job (*ex post* or "after the fact"), the employee would prefer to remain employed rather than becoming unemployed. Such unemployment may be considered to be either voluntary or involuntary, then, depending upon the perspective one is taking.

The Demographic Structure of Unemployment Rates

Table 18.3 presents data on unemployment rates for various age/race/sex groups in 1980. The patterns indicated in Table 18.3 for 1980 are similar to the patterns for other years: high unemployment rates for teens and young adults of each race/sex group relative to older adults in these groups; nonwhite unemployment rates roughly double white unemployment rates for most age/sex groups; and female unemployment rates are higher than male rates for whites. The high unemployment rates of nonwhite teenagers, which ranged between 33.0 and 40.4 percent in 1980, have been of particular concern to policymakers and have led to numerous programs designed to reduce nonwhite teenage unemployment during the late 1970s and early 1980s.

Over recent decades, the age/race/sex composition of the labor force has changed dramatically due to the growing labor-force participation rates of females and to increases in the relative sizes of the teenage and nonwhite populations. Between 1960 and 1980, the proportion of the labor force that was female grew from 33.4 to 42.6 percent; the proportion that was nonwhite grew from 11.1 to 12.0 percent; and the proportion that was teenage grew from 7.0 to 8.8

---

[26]John Abowd and Orley Ashenfelter, "Anticipated Unemployment, Temporary Layoffs, and Compensating Wage Differentials," *Studies in Labor Markets,* ed. Sherwin Rosen (Chicago: Univ. of Chicago Press, 1981).

Table 18.3. Unemployment Rates in 1980 by Demographic Groups

Age	White Male	White Female	Nonwhite Male	Nonwhite Female	All
16–17	18.5	17.3	37.7	40.4	
18–19	14.6	13.0	33.0	34.9	
20–24	11.1	8.5	22.3	21.8	
25–34	6.0	6.3	12.5	12.3	
35–44	3.6	4.9	7.8	7.8	
45–54	3.3	4.3	6.6	6.3	
55–64	3.1	3.1	6.0	4.7	
65+	2.5	2.9	8.8	4.7	
Total	6.1	6.5	13.3	13.1	7.1

SOURCE: U.S. Department of Labor, *1981 Employment and Training Report of the President* (Washington, D.C.: U.S. Government Printing Office, 1981), Table A30.

percent.[27] The increase in the relative labor-force shares of those groups that have relatively higher unemployment rates has led to an increase in the overall unemployment rate that is associated with any given level of labor-market tightness. Indeed, one investigator has concluded that demographic shifts in the composition of the labor force alone probably are responsible for the fact that the overall unemployment rate was at least one percentage point higher in the late 1970s and early 1980s than it was in the mid-1960s, for any given level of overall labor-market tightness.[28] The demographic changes have also led to an increase in the *full-employment* (or *natural*) *rate* of unemployment—the unemployment rate that is consistent with a zero excess demand for labor. While an aggregate unemployment rate of 4 percent was considered a reasonable unemployment goal for policymakers to aim at in the mid-1960s, policymakers and academic economists rarely referred to targets below 5.5 to 6.0 percent by the late 1970s and early 1980s. (A brief discussion of why unemployment rates vary across demographic groups is found in the concluding section of this chapter.)

Search Unemployment and the Role of Unemployment-Insurance Benefits

As noted earlier in the chapter, because information about job opportunities and workers' characteristics is imperfect, it will take time for job matches to be made between unemployed workers and potential employers. Other things equal, the lower the probability that unemployed workers will become employed in a period (the lower is P_{ue}), the higher will be their expected duration of unemployment and the higher will be the unemployment rate.

Critics of the unemployment-insurance system often point out that the existence of UI benefits reduces the costs of being unemployed and may prolong

[27]U.S. Department of Labor, 1981 *Employment and Training Report of the President* (Washington, D.C.: U.S. Government Printing Office, 1981), Table A4.

[28]James Tobin, "Stabilization Policy Ten Years After," *Brookings Papers on Economic Activity*, 1980–1, pp. 19–72.

EXAMPLE 18.2

Unemployment-Insurance Benefits in Great Britain

Evidence that more generous unemployment-insurance benefits lead to higher levels of unemployment is not confined to the United States. For example, Daniel Benjamin and Levis Kochin have found three pieces of information that seem to confirm the relationship for Great Britain during the period between World Wars I and II:

1. Increases in the aggregate British unemployment rate, even after controlling for the level of aggregate demand, were associated with increases in the British UI replacement rate over the 1920–1938 period.
2. Teenagers—many of whom were either not eligible for UI benefits during this period or received very low benefits relative to their wages— had unemployment rates that were only a fraction of the adult unemployment rate. Further, the unemployment rate jumped markedly at ages 18 and 21, when UI benefits increased.
3. In 1932, the year a change in the British UI regulations reduced the possibility that unemployed married women could receive UI benefits, the unemployment rate for married women dropped sharply relative to the rate for males.

SOURCE: *See* Daniel Benjamin and Levis Kochin, "Searching for an Explanation of Unemployment in Interwar Britain," *Journal of Political Economy* 87 (June 1979): 441–78. Not all economists agree with their arguments, however, and a series of articles criticizing their evidence is found in the April 1982 issue of the same journal.

unemployed workers' job search.[29] Supporters of the UI system respond that an explicit purpose of the UI system when it was founded in the late 1930s was to provide unemployed workers with temporary resources to enable them to turn down low-wage jobs that were not commensurate with their skill levels and to keep searching for better jobs.[30] That is, many believe that while the existence of UI benefits might prolong spells of unemployment, such benefits also might lead to higher post-unemployment wages and better job matches—and better job matches might reduce subsequent job turnover, thus providing a further benefit to society.

In recent years, numerous studies have sought to estimate the effects of UI benefits on durations of unemployment and post-unemployment wages.[31] In the

---

[29]Martin Feldstein, "The Economics of the New Unemployment," *Public Interest* 33 (Fall 1973): 3–42.

[30]William Haber and Merrill Murray, *Unemployment Insurance in the American Economy* (Homewood, Ill.: Irwin, 1966), pp. 26–35.

[31]*See,* for example, Ronald G. Ehrenberg and Ronald L. Oaxaca, "Unemployment Insurance, Duration of Unemployment and Subsequent Wage Gain," *American Economic Review* 66 (December 1976): 754–66. Many of the studies are summarized in Hamermesh, *Jobless Pay and the Economy* and are critiqued in Finis Welch, "What Have We Learned From Empirical Studies of Unemployment Insurance," *Industrial and Labor Relations Review* 30 (July 1977): 451–61.

main, these studies use data on individuals and exploit the fact that the replacement rate (the fraction of previous earnings that UI benefits replace) varies (*within* states) with individuals' previous earnings levels (see Figure 18.4) and also varies *across* states. Evidence from these studies suggests quite strongly that higher UI replacement rates are associated with longer durations of unemployment; raising the replacement rate from 0.4 to 0.5 of previous weekly earnings may increase the average spell of unemployment by one half to one week. In contrast, the evidence on the effects on post-unemployment wages is much more mixed. For example, one study found that higher replacement rates were associated with higher post-unemployment wage rates for adults but not for teenagers.[32]

Normative Issues in Unemployment

Is unemployment a serious problem? Certainly some level of frictional unemployment is unavoidable in a dynamic world fraught with imperfect information. Moreover, as we have seen, the parameters of the UI system encourage both additional search unemployment and temporary layoff (cyclical and seasonal) unemployment. Nonetheless, when unemployment rises above its full-employment or natural level, resources are being wasted. More than 25 years ago Arthur Okun pointed out that every one-percentage-point decline in the aggregate unemployment rate was associated with a three-percentage-point increase in the output our society produces. That relationship appears to have held up through 1975, although since 1975 it is more in the range of a two-percentage-point increase in output. Even this latter number, however, suggests the great costs our society bears from excessively high rates of unemployment.[33] Thus, while it is unlikely that zero unemployment would be an optimal rate, policies to reduce cyclical unemployment (in a noninflationary manner) are clearly desirable. Improving the functioning of labor markets would also reduce frictional and structural unemployment; however, the benefits of reduced unemployment must be weighed against the costs generated by the policies designed to accomplish this objective in each case.

In addition to concern over the cost of unemployment, society should also be concerned about the distribution of unemployment across age/race/sex groups. As Table 18.3 indicated, the incidence of unemployment is higher among females than males, among nonwhites than whites, and among teens than non-

[32]Ehrenberg and Oaxaca, "Unemployment Insurance. . . ." The results for teens may imply that (a) unemployed teens do not search actively for work, (b) unemployed teens' job search is not productive, perhaps because of the narrow range of job opportunities they face, or (c) unemployed teens may search for jobs that offer greater training options and possible higher future wages, although not higher current wages. The available data do not permit one to determine which of these alternatives is correct.

[33]Arthur M. Okun, "Potential GNP: Its Measurement and Significance," reprinted in *The Political Economy of Prosperity,* ed. Arthur M. Okun (Washington, D.C.: Brookings Institute, 1970). Recent evidence suggests that the relationship is more in the range of 2.2 to 1. *See* Robert J. Gordon and Robert E. Hall, "Arthur M. Okun 1928–1980," *Brookings Papers on Economic Activity,* 1980–1, pp. 1–5.

teens. Evidence appears to suggest that white female adult unemployment rates are high because of proportionately large flows of women from employment to out-of-labor-force status, which implies that some of their higher labor turnover (and unemployment) may be voluntary in nature. In contrast, the major cause of high nonwhite adult male unemployment rates is the high probability of members of that group leaving or losing their jobs to become unemployed; the fact that they remain attached to the labor force suggests that their unemployment problem is serious and that the case for government intervention is strong.

What about the high teenage unemployment rates, especially those of nonwhite teens? Is the high unemployment rate for teens a serious problem that policymakers should address? Some doubt the seriousness of the problem, pointing out that unemployment rates decline rapidly as youths reach their early twenties (see Table 18.3). To these doubters, high teenage unemployment rates are symptomatic of the process of job turnover and search that occurs when new entrants to the labor force seek to acquire information about labor markets and their own productive ability. Moreover, proponents of this view could note that approximately 50 percent of the unemployed 16 to 19 year olds and 90 percent of the unemployed 16 to 17 year olds are enrolled in school.[34] Of these in-school unemployed youths, 50 percent were searching only for temporary jobs in 1976 and only 10 percent had become unemployed by losing their previous job.[35] Finally, they could cite evidence that teenage unemployment is not always associated with low family incomes. For example, data from the *1976 Survey of Income and Education,* a large national survey conducted by the Census Bureau, indicate that less than 26 percent of unemployed youths age 16 to 24 came from families whose family income fell below the poverty line.[36]

Of course, these arguments neglect a number of important points. First, a substantial body of evidence indicates that youth unemployment is highly correlated with youth criminal activity; thus there are costs to society, as well as to the youths, of youth unemployment. Second, much youth unemployment is concentrated among nonwhite youths—and the distributional implications of this fact may be unacceptable to society, especially given the higher correlation between youth unemployment and poverty that exists for nonwhites. Finally, it is possible that the effects of youth unemployment may be long-lasting and that unemployed teenagers may face reduced long-run earnings and employment prospects, as compared to teenagers who do not suffer unemployment. Although unemployment rates do decline rapidly with age for younger adults, individuals

---

[34]*See* Arvil Adams and Garth Mangum, *The Lingering Crisis of Youth Unemployment* (Kalamazoo, Mich.: W.E. Upjohn Institute, 1978), chap. 3.

[35]Adams and Mangum, *The Lingering Crisis of Youth Unemployment.*

[36]U.S. Congressional Budget Office, *Youth Unemployment: The Outlook and Some Policy Strategies* (Washington, D.C.: U.S. Government Printing Office, April 1978), Appendix Table A-5. It is worth noting, however, that this table also indicates that youth unemployment rates decline with family income and that more than 45 percent of unemployed *nonwhite* youths come from families with family incomes below the poverty line. Put another way, youth employment is much more highly correlated with poverty for nonwhites than it is for whites.

who suffer unemployment as teenagers might be "scarred" in the sense of having relatively higher probabilities of adult unemployment or commanding relatively lower adult wage rates.

Somewhat surprisingly, until recently there was no evidence on the long-run effects of teenage unemployment. Indeed, as late as 1976 Richard Freeman asserted that:

> there is no evidence that having considerable unemployment and related poor work experience at a young age "scars" a person for life. Teenage unemployment *may* have deleterious effects on work attitudes, investment in job skills, and lifetime income, and related labor market experiences, but this has *not* been documented. Teenage unemployment may be purely a transitional problem without long-term consequences.[37]

Since 1976, however, four studies using data on younger males and standard statistical methods have addressed this issue.[38] These studies do *not* all (1) use data from a common time period, (2) use the same sample restrictions (out-of-school youths or all youths), (3) focus on the same outcome variable (earnings or unemployment), or (4) use the same research methodology (simple correlation or multiple-regression analysis). Nonetheless, the evidence does appear to indicate that unemployment of *nonwhite* male teens is associated, on average, with long-run adverse labor-market effects. However, the evidence on persistence effects of white male teenage unemployment is less clear. Thus, these studies at first glance appear to support public concern, at least for nonwhites, about the long-run effects of teenage unemployment.

Unfortunately, these studies did *not* identify whether it is the experience of unemployment *per se* or some unobserved characteristics of the teenage unemployed that lead to subsequent adverse labor-market outcomes. If the experience of unemployment is responsible, then policies to reduce teenage unemployment may have long run positive effects. However, if unobservable characteristics are responsible—for example, if teens who become unemployed are less motivated or able, other things equal, than those who find employment—then it is less clear that policies to reduce teenage unemployment will have long-lasting effects. Other studies that have attempted to identify whether the experience of unemployment *per se* matters in the long run have yielded ambiguous results—such as the finding that an early employment experience has a positive effect on later employment for

[37]Richard Freeman, "Teenage Unemployment: Can Reallocating Resources Help?" in U.S. Congressional Budget Office, *The Teenage Unemployment Problem: What Are the Options?* (Washington, D.C.: U.S. Government Printing Office, 1976).

[38]*See* Wayne Stevenson, "The Relationship Between Early Work Experience and Future Employability," in Adams and Mangum, *The Lingering Crisis of Youth Unemployment;* Paul Osterman, "Race Differentials in Male Youth Unemployment" in U.S. Department of Labor, *Conference Report on Youth Unemployment: Its Measurement and Meaning* (Washington, D.C.: U.S. Government Printing Office, 1978); Joseph Antos and Wesley Mellow, *The Youth Labor Market: A Dynamic Overview* (Washington, D.C.: Government Printing Office, 1979); and Brian Becker and Stephen Hills, "Teenage Unemployment: Some Evidence on the Long-Run Effects on Wages" *Journal of Human Resources* 15 (Summer 1980): 354–72.

female teens but very little effect for male teens.[39] Thus, our knowledge about whether teenage unemployment has long-run scarring effects is still quite imprecise.

REVIEW QUESTIONS

1. Labor economists offer many reasons for unemployment. In your judgment, what are the principal explanations for today's unemployment? Justify your answer.
2. A presidential hopeful is campaigning to raise unemployment-compensation benefits and lower the full-employment target from 4 percent to 3.5 percent. Comment on the compatibility of these goals.
3. Government officials find it useful to measure the nation's "economic health." The unemployment rate is currently used as a major indicator of the relative strength of labor supply and demand. Do you think the unemployment rate is becoming more or less useful as an indicator of labor-market tightness? What other measures might serve this purpose better?
4. The unemployment rate is a stock concept (something like the amount of water in a lake at a given time). The level of unemployment goes up or down as the *flows* into unemployment exceed or are slower than the flows out of unemployment. Is it important for policy purposes to accurately measure the *flows* into and out of unemployment, or is knowing the *level* of unemployment enough for most purposes? Justify your answer.
5. Is the following question true, false, or uncertain? "Increasing the level of unemployment-insurance benefits will prolong the average length of spells of unemployment. Hence a policy of raising UI benefit levels is not socially desirable." Explain your answer.

SELECTED READINGS

Martin Baily, "Wages and Employment Under Uncertain Demand," *Review of Economic Studies* 41 (January 1974): 37–50.

Kim B. Clark and Lawrence Summers, "Labor Market Dynamics and Unemployment: A Reconsideration," *Brookings Papers on Economic Activity,* 1979–1, pp. 13–60.

Martin Feldstein, "The Economics of the New Unemployment," *Public Interest* 33 (Fall 1973): 3–42.

Martin Feldstein, "The Importance of Temporary Layoffs: An Empirical Analysis," *Brookings Papers on Economic Activity,* 1975–3, pp. 725–44.

Daniel S. Hamermesh, *Jobless Pay and the Economy* (Baltimore: Johns Hopkins University Press, 1977).

Steven Marston, "Employment Instability and High Unemployment Rates," *Brookings Papers on Economic Activity,* 1976–1, pp. 169–203.

National Commission on Employment and Unemployment Statistics, *Counting the Labor Force* (Washington, D.C.: Government Printing Office, 1979).

---

[39]David Ellwood, "Teenage Unemployment: Permanent Scars or Temporary Blemishes"; Mary Corcoran, "The Employment, Wage, and Fertility Consequences of Teenage Women's Nonemployment"; and Robert Meyer and David Wise, "High School Preparation and Early Labor Force Experience"; all in *The Youth Labor Market Problem: Its Nature, Causes, and Consequences,* eds. Richard B. Freeman and David A. Wise (Chicago: Univ. of Chicago Press, 1982).

Chapter 19

INFLATION AND UNEMPLOYMENT

Throughout most of the 1970s the United States was faced with relatively high rates of wage and price *inflation* (that is, with relatively rapid and generally pervasive increases in wages and prices). Further, these increases were taking place in the context of rather high unemployment rates, so that the country seemed to suffer the consequences of both inflation *and* unemployment at the same time. Simultaneously high rates of inflation and unemployment challenged the long-held belief that inflation would diminish if unemployment rose—a belief that seemed to have held out hope that government fiscal or monetary policies could be skillfully used to maneuver the economy to tolerable levels of both inflation and unemployment.

The causes and consequences of inflation—and the fiscal and monetary policies to remedy it—are beyond the scope of labor economics. Our intent in this chapter is to analyze the relationship between inflation and unemployment so that the connections between what happens in the labor market and what happens to prices in general are more clearly understood. Moreover, because our focus is on the labor market, we will emphasize the price of labor—the wage rate—when discussing the issue of inflation.

Measuring Wage Inflation

The overall rate of *wage inflation* in the economy is the annual percentage rate of increase in some composite measure of hourly earnings in the economy. The construction of such an index is a considerable task because *average* hourly earnings can change, even if the wage scales for every individual *job* remain constant. For example, if there is a shift in the distribution of employment towards high-wage industries (such as construction) and away from low-wage industries (such as retail trade), average hourly earnings will increase. Similarly, if there is a shift towards increased usage of highly paid skilled workers and away from lower-paid unskilled workers, average hourly earnings will increase. To take another example, if the age distribution of the work force shifts towards relatively fewer lower-paid new entrants, average hourly earnings will increase. Finally, if more overtime hours for which premium pay is received are worked relative to straight time hours, average hourly earnings will again increase, other things equal.[1]

The problem involved in all of these examples is that average hourly earnings in the economy is a weighted average of the earnings of individuals in each industry/occupation/experience group. The weight assigned to each group's earnings depends upon the fraction of all hours worked in the economy by individuals in the group and the fraction of hours worked by the group for which premium pay is received. Changes in average hourly earnings may therefore reflect changes in the weights as well as changes in the wage scales of each group. Focusing simply on the growth of average hourly earnings, then, may give one a misleading impression of what is happening to wage scales for particular jobs.

To take the above problem partially into account, government statisticians have constructed an index of adjusted average hourly earnings for nonsupervisory workers in the private nonagricultural sector. This index, which controls for changes in the industrial composition of employment and changes in overtime hours in manufacturing, is one of the most comprehensive measures of wage changes that is available.[2] As Table 19.1 indicates, over the decades of the 1960s, 1970s, and the early 1980s, this index increased at annual percentage rates of roughly 3 to 8 percent, with the annual percentage increase apparently increasing over time.

The Inflation/Unemployment Trade-Off

For many years economists believed that stable negative relationships, or *trade-off curves,* existed between the rates of wage (and price) inflation, on the one hand, and the overall unemployment rate in the economy, on the other. That is, higher

---

[1] The importance of these factors can be illustrated by referring to a rate-setting case, pertaining to a public utility on which one of us worked. As part of the regulatory case, the rate of wage inflation had to be computed for the utility's employees over the August 1973 to August 1976 period. The cumulative percentage wage increase in union wage scales called for in the company's union contracts was 32.1 percent; however, the increase in average hourly earnings was 42.1 percent. The difference in this example was primarily due to the changing skill mix and age distributions of the utility's employees. For details, *see* Ronald Ehrenberg, *The Regulatory Process and Labor Earnings* (New York: Academic Press, 1979), Chapter 2.

[2] The index only partially controls for the problem of distinguishing between changes in wage scales and changes in the composition of employment because it makes no adjustment for changes in the *occupational* or *age* distributions of the work force.

Table 19.1. Unemployment Rate and Percentage Change in Earnings and Prices in the United States

Year	Percent Change in Adjusted Hourly Earnings of Nonsupervisory Workers in the Private Nonagricultural Sector	Unemployment Rate	Percent Change in the GNP Deflator
1960	3.4	5.5	1.6
1961	3.0	6.7	0.9
1962	3.4	5.5	1.8
1963	2.8	5.7	1.5
1964	2.8	5.2	1.5
1965	3.6	4.5	2.2
1966	4.3	3.8	3.2
1967	5.0	3.8	3.0
1968	6.1	3.6	4.4
1969	6.7	3.5	5.1
1970	6.6	4.9	5.4
1971	7.2	5.9	5.0
1972	6.2	5.6	4.2
1973	6.2	4.9	5.8
1974	8.0	5.6	8.8
1975	8.4	8.5	9.3
1976	7.2	7.7	5.2
1977	7.6	7.1	5.8
1978	8.1	6.1	7.4
1979	8.0	5.8	8.6
1980	9.0	7.1	9.3
1981	9.1	7.6	9.4
1982	6.8	9.7	6.0

SOURCE: 1983 *Economic Report of the President* (Washington, D.C.: U.S. Government Printing Office, 1983), Tables B3, B29, and B38.

levels of unemployment were thought to be associated with lower rates of wage and price inflation, and vice versa. The relationship between unemployment and wage inflation was dubbed the *Phillips Curve* after the noted economist who was an early observer of its existence.[3] The Phillips Curve was thought to provide a range of feasible options for policymakers—through the appropriate use of monetary or fiscal policy they could choose any unemployment/inflation combination along the curve. For example, a paper in 1959 by two well-known economists claimed that the country could choose among the following alternatives (illustrated in Figure 19.1): 8 percent unemployment and zero wage inflation, 5–6 percent unemployment and 2–3 percent wage inflation, and 3 percent unemployment and 7 percent wage inflation.[4]

---

[3]*See* A. W. Phillips, "The Relation Between Unemployment and the Rates of Change of Money Wage Rates in the United Kingdom, 1862–1957," *Economica* 25 (November 1958): 283–99.

[4]Paul A. Samuelson and Robert M. Solow, "Our Menu of Policy Choices," in *The Battle Against Unemployment,* ed. Arthur M. Okun (New York: W. W. Norton, 1965), pp. 71–76.

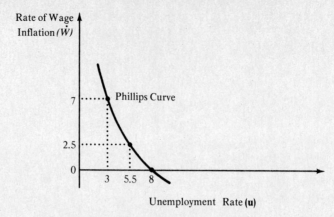

Figure 19.1   "Phillips Curve" Showing the Trade-off Between Wage Inflation and Unemployment for 1960

SOURCE: Adapted from Paul A. Samuelson and Robert M. Solow, "Our Menu of Policy Choices," *The Battle Against Inflation,* ed. Arthur M. Okun (New York: W. W. Norton, 1965), p. 74.

Unfortunately, the well-defined, stable set of choices once thought to exist appears to have vanished. Table 19.1 contains data on both the unemployment and wage inflation rate during the 1960s, 1970s, and early 1980s. These data indicate that during the 1960s a negative association did appear to exist between the unemployment rate and the rate of wage inflation. Indeed the steady tightening of labor markets and decreasing unemployment rates of the late 1960s were associated with increasing rates of wage inflation. However, during the 1970s the relationship appears, at first glance, to have broken down; one often observes a simultaneous increase in the rate of unemployment and the rate of wage inflation during that decade. The result is that while an unemployment rate of 5.5 percent was associated with a wage-inflation rate of 3.3 to 3.4 percent in the 1960s, an almost identical unemployment rate of 5.6 percent was associated with wage-inflation rates of 6.4 to 7.9 percent during the 1970s. These data tend to suggest that the belief in a stable negative trade-off between inflation and unemployment is unwarranted.

An alternative interpretation of these data, however, is that while a trade-off between the rates of inflation and unemployment exists at a *point in time,* the *position* of the trade-off curve is determined by a number of other factors that can change over time. The net effect of these other factors in recent years, it can be argued, has been to shift the trade-off curve shown in Figure 19.1 *upward and to the right.* Thus, the trade-off society faces in the early 1980s may lie everywhere above the one that prevailed during the 1970s, which in turn was itself higher than the curve that prevailed during the 1960s (see Figure 19.2). Put another way, the argument underlying Figure 19.2 is that progressively higher rates of wage inflation ($\dot{W}_0$, $\dot{W}_1$, and $\dot{W}_2$) have become associated over time with any given level of unemployment (u_0 in Figure 19.2). Conversely, progressively higher unemployment rates (u_0, u_1, u_2) have become associated with any given level of wage inflation ($\dot{W}_0$). Indeed some economists suggest that between 1960 and 1980, the

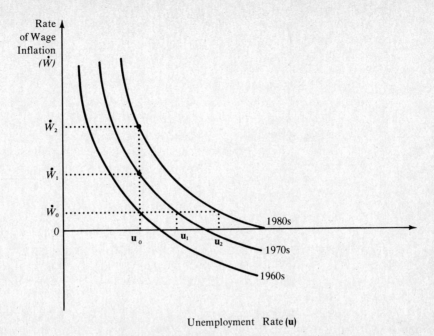

Figure 19.2   The Changing Trade-off Between the Rate of Wage Inflation and the Level of the Unemployment Rate

trade-off may have shifted to the right by as much as 3 percentage points.[5] It is also possible that the Phillips Curve has become much flatter over recent years, so that the decrease in wage inflation accompanying a one-percentage-point increase in the unemployment rate is now smaller than it once was. This growing downward rigidity of wages has caused a loss of effectiveness in the traditional macroeconomic policies to combat inflation—and has increased the importance of alternative labor-market policies.

The next section presents a simple conceptual model that explains why the trade-off between wage inflation and unemployment may exist and discusses the forces that may have caused the trade-off to shift out over time. This model provides a framework that can be used to discuss the various labor-market policies that might enable policymakers to shift the trade-off curve in a more favorable direction. It also discusses the relationship between wage and price behavior and the effect of the rate of productivity growth on this relationship.

This chapter will consider the role of unions and the collective-bargaining process also. It will explore why changing institutional arrangements—in particular the spread of *multiyear agreements* with *cost-of-living escalator clauses*—may have been partially responsible for the growing insensitivity of inflation to the unemployment rate.

---

[5]*See,* for example, James Tobin, "Stabilization Policy Ten Years After," *Brookings Papers on Economic Activity,* 1980–1, pp. 19–72.

The final section of the chapter returns to the central issue of how government policies might reduce the rate of inflation associated with any given level of unemployment. This section focuses on the various *incomes policies* that have been pursued in the United States since 1960—policies in which the government has tried directly to influence wages and prices by specifying "desired wage and price behavior," sometimes with enforcement mechanisms tied to the program (these include the wage-price guideposts of the Kennedy-Johnson years, the wage-price freeze and "Phase II" economic policies under the Nixon Administration, and the Carter voluntary anti-inflation guidelines). After discussing the available evidence on the effectiveness of these programs, we will analyze the proposals for new innovative types of *tax-based incomes policies* that were proposed during the 1970s.[6]

The Wage-Inflation/Unemployment Trade-Off

The Basic Model

Figure 19.3 represents a competitive labor market.[7] For simplicity we will *initially* take product prices as fixed so that the demand and supply curves can be drawn in terms of the money wage (W) rather than the real wage. In this labor market, the equilibrium wage is W_0, and the equilibrium employment level is E_0. We know from earlier chapters that whenever the wage is above W_0 it will fall, and that whenever it is below W_0 it will rise, to restore equilibrium.

How rapidly will the wage rate change when it is away from its equilibrium value? It seems reasonable to assume that the speed at which the wage rate changes is related to the extent to which the labor market is in disequilibrium, as measured by the excess demand for labor. Thus, although the wage rate will be increasing whenever the wage rate is below W_0 and a positive excess demand for labor exists, it is likely to be increasing more rapidly when it is at W_4 in Figure 19.3 than when it is at W_3. Similarly, while the wage rate will be falling whenever the wage rate is above W_0 and an excess supply (or negative excess demand) for labor exists, it is likely to be falling more rapidly when the wage rate is at W_2 than when it is at W_1.

The simplest possible way to formalize this idea is to assume that the percentage rate of change of wages ($\dot{W}$) is proportional to the excess demand for labor (X). Because a given *absolute* difference between demand and supply ($D - S = 1,000$, say) would indicate a greater degree of disequilibrium if 10,000

---

[6]*See,* for example, Henry Wallich and Sidney Weintraub, "A Tax-Based Incomes Policy," *Journal of Economic Issues* 5 (June 1971):1–19 and Arthur M. Okun, "The Great Stagflation Swamp," *Challenge* 20 (November/December 1977): 6–13.

[7]This section initially draws heavily on Richard Lipsey, "The Relation Between Unemployment and the Rate of Change in Money Wage Rates in the United Kingdom, 1862–1957: A Further Analysis," *Economica* 27 (February 1960): 1–31.

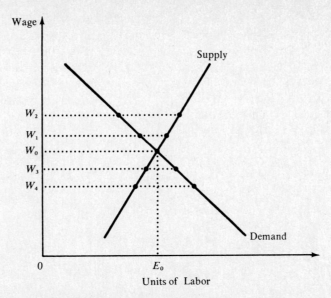

Figure 19.3   The Relationship Between Wage Changes and the Excess Demand for Labor: Prices Held Constant

people were seeking work than if 100,000 were in the market, we will measure excess demand as $(D - S)/S$, so that:

$$\dot{W} = \alpha X = \alpha[(D - S)/S]. \qquad (19.1)$$

This relationship is depicted in panel (a) of Figure 19.4; the larger α is, the faster wages adjust to disequilibrium. Note that when supply exceeds demand, X—and hence $\dot{W}$—will be negative. (One could, of course, allow the responses to be nonsymmetric to excess demands and excess supplies. For example, if wages are *sticky* in a downward direction, α would be smaller—and the curve flatter —in the region of excess supply that lies to the left of the vertical axis. However, for expository convenience we will ignore this complication here.)

Unfortunately, because the excess demand for labor is usually not observable, it is necessary to replace it with an observable variable—such as the unemployment rate—when empirically analyzing wage changes. What is the relationship between the excess demand for labor and the unemployment rate (**u**)? We know from Chapter 18 that some unemployment exists even when labor markets are in balance with the overall demand for labor just equal to the overall supply $(X = 0)$. This frictional unemployment occurs because normal job turnover and movements of people in and out of the labor market take place in circumstances where information is imperfect and job matching takes time. In panel (b) of Figure 19.4, u^* is the unemployment rate that exists when the excess demand for labor is zero; this is often referred to in the economics literature as the *natural* or *full-employment rate* of unemployment (see Chapter 18).

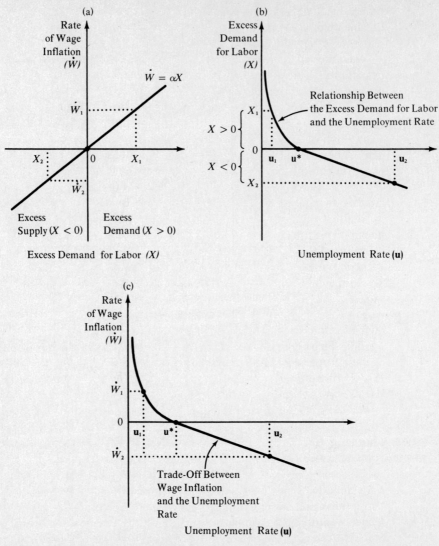

Figure 19.4   Derivation of the Trade-off Between the Rate of Wage Inflation and the Unemployment Rate

As the excess demand for labor increases and labor markets become tighter, the unemployment rate will fall. Although the time it takes to make job matches can be reduced, it will probably take some time to fill job vacancies. As a result, the unemployment rate is not likely to fall below some positive level, and as that level is approached, any increases in excess demand will call forth progressively smaller reductions in the unemployment rate. The result is a nonlinear relationship between the unemployment rate and the excess demand for labor, as drawn in the $X > 0$ region of panel (b). In contrast, in the region of excess supply (below the horizontal axis (where $X < 0$), increases in excess supply may well lead to proportional increases in the unemployment rate. Thus, the relationship between the unemployment rate and the excess demand for labor is perhaps linear in the region of excess supply, as illustrated in panel (b) of Figure 19.4.

The two relationships shown in panels (a) and (b)—the wage inflation/excess demand relationship and the unemployment rate/excess demand relationship—contain all the information that is required to derive the wage inflation/unemployment trade-off curve shown in panel (c). Refer in Figure 19.4 to the point where the excess demand for labor is zero. From panel (a), we know the rate of wage inflation is zero, and, from panel (b), we know that the unemployment rate is u^*. Thus, one point on our wage inflation/unemployment trade-off curve in panel (c) is $(0, u^*)$. When the excess demand for labor is X_1, wage inflation is $\dot{W}_1$, in (a), and the unemployment rate is u_1, in (b). When the excess supply of labor is X_2, the wage inflation rate is $\dot{W}_2$, in (a), and the unemployment rate is u_2, in (b). Thus, $(\dot{W}_1, u_1)$ and $(\dot{W}_2, u_2)$ are two additional points on the inflation/unemployment trade-off curve in panel (c). Repeating the argument for all possible values of the excess demand for labor leads one to trace out the entire trade-off curve in panel (c) of Figure 19.4.

In the context of this simple labor-market model, the trade-off between the rate of wage inflation and the unemployment rate arises from the postulated responsiveness of wages to the excess demand for labor. However, there are numerous forces that affect the *position* of the curve that traces out the aggregate relationship between the unemployment rate and the rate of wage inflation. Three of these forces are (1) the current and expected rates of price inflation, (2) the age/sex distribution of the labor force, and (3) the dispersion of unemployment rates across markets.

Forces Affecting the Wage Inflation/Unemployment Trade-Off

Price inflation. So far we have assumed the price level to be fixed. However, current and expected future rates of price inflation clearly influence the rate of *money* wage inflation associated with any given level of excess demand for labor. Since both the demand and supply curves of labor are functions of the *real* wage rate, an increase in the *price* level requires a proportional increase in the *money wage* rate simply to keep the real wage and the excess demand for labor constant. The relationship between wage changes and the excess demand for labor described in Figures 19.3 and 19.4 actually refers to changes in the real wage (prices were assumed fixed while wages changed). Hence, the effect of price inflation is to *increase* the rate of money-wage inflation associated with any given level of the excess demand for labor.

Our discussion so far has assumed that labor markets are competitive and that all real wages are renegotiated continuously as labor-market conditions change. Later in the chapter we will introduce several institutional features of the collective-bargaining process in the United States in our discussion. Here, we will consider how the introduction of one such feature—contracts that are negotiated only periodically—affects the analysis. From employees' perspectives, past price changes may influence wage demands during contract negotiations, because they signify that real wages are below the level employees expected *if* such price changes were not fully anticipated at the time of the previous contract negotiations. Expected future price changes may also matter, because they translate money-wage changes into expected real-wage changes. Similarly, from employers' perspectives, past and expected future price changes may affect their willingness to increase wages, as increases in output prices, *ceteris paribus,* reduce real wages and hence employers' costs of doing business.

Unambiguously then, higher expected price changes should lead to higher wage changes in a world where wages are adjusted only periodically. It is unclear, however, whether an extra one percent increase in expected price inflation will lead to an extra one percent increase in money wages; this depends, among other things, on the relative bargaining power of employees and employers. Let us assume that a one percent increase in the expected rate of price inflation ($\dot{P}^e$) shifts the rate of money-wage inflation associated with a given excess demand for labor up by γ percent, where γ may be less than one.[8] That is,

$$\dot{W} = \alpha X + \gamma \dot{P}^e \quad 0 \leq \gamma \leq 1. \tag{19.2}$$

Equation (19.2) is illustrated by Figure 19.5. If the upward shift in the relationship between $\dot{W}$ and X in Figure 19.5 is translated back to panel (a) of

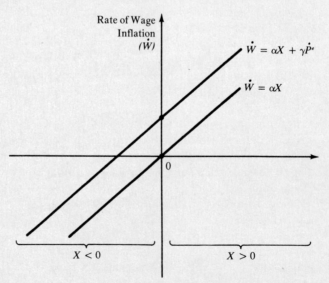

Figure 19.5   Price Inflation Shifts Up the Wage-Inflation/Excess-Demand-for-Labor Relationship

---

[8]For simplicity, we have focused only on expected price inflation and ignored past price inflation *per se* here. We also have restricted γ to be no greater than one; this need not always be the case.

Figure 19.4, and its implications for panel (c) are traced through panel (b), it should become clear that increases in the expected rate of price inflation cause the whole wage-inflation/unemployment trade-off curve in panel (c) to shift up.[9]

Age/sex composition of the labor force. Chapter 18 noted that females tend to have higher unemployment rates than males, and that teenagers tend to have higher unemployment rates than adults. The aggregate unemployment rate associated with any given degree of labor-market *tightness*—or excess demand for labor—is simply the weighted average of the unemployment rates for the various age/sex groups, with the weights being the share of the group in the overall labor force. During the 1960s and 1970s, the shares of teenagers and females in the labor force increased because of the growing share of teenagers in the population and increasing female labor-force-participation rates. Since these groups tend to have higher than average unemployment rates, the overall unemployment rate associated with any level of the excess demand for labor also increased, as illustrated in Figure 19.6.[10]

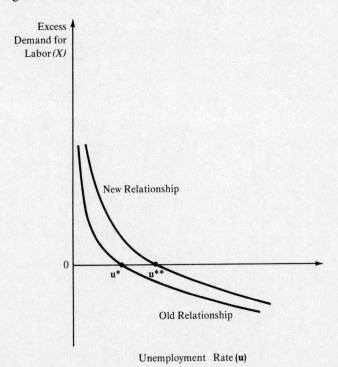

Figure 19.6   Changing Age/Sex Composition of the Labor Force Shifts Up the Excess-Demand-for-Labor/Unemployment-Rate Relationship

---

[9]Of course, since wages are a substantial fraction of production costs, increases in the rate of wage inflation should lead, other things equal, to increases in the rate of price inflation. This interdependency will be discussed later in the chapter.

[10]An early exposition of the importance of this factor is found in George L. Perry, "Changing Labor Markets and Inflation," *Brookings Papers on Economic Activity,* 1970–3, pp. 411–41.

An increase in the level of unemployment associated with each level of the excess demand for labor implies, other things equal, that a higher unemployment rate will be associated with each rate of wage inflation. Put another way, the changing age/sex composition of the labor force has also caused the wage-inflation/unemployment trade-off curve to shift up. At any level of the aggregate unemployment rate, the rate of wage inflation is higher than before. Furthermore, as indicated in Figure 19.6 (and in Chapter 18), the full-employment unemployment rate also has increased—from $\mathbf{u}_0$ to $\mathbf{u}_1$ in Figure 19.6.

The dispersion of unemployment rates. The model of the wage-inflation/unemployment trade-off that we have presented applies to a *single* labor market.[11] To obtain the wage inflation/unemployment trade-off for the *economy*, one must aggregate all of the individual labor-market relationships. If the unemployment rate differs across labor markets, the aggregate rate of wage inflation associated with any given level of aggregate unemployment may be higher than it would be if the unemployment rate were the same in all markets.

To see why this is true, suppose there were only two labor markets in the whole economy, that they were identical in size, and that the same wage-inflation/unemployment trade-off curve (represented by T_0 in Figure 19.7) existed in both.

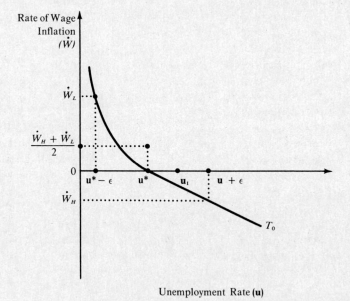

Figure 19.7   Dispersion of Unemployment Rates Increase the Rate of Wage Inflation Associated with a Given Aggregate Unemployment Rate

---

[11]The role of geographic dispersion in unemployment rates was emphasized early by Lipsey and by G. C. Archibald, "The Phillips Curve and the Distribution of Unemployment," *American Economic Review* 59 (May 1969): 124–34. The importance of dispersion of unemployment across age/sex groups was emphasized in Perry, "Changing Labor Markets and Inflation."

Given any overall level of unemployment, the aggregate rate of wage inflation is approximately equal to the average of the rates of wage inflation in the two markets.[12] If initially the unemployment rate were u^* in *each* market, the rate of wage inflation in each would be zero and the overall rate of wage inflation would also be zero.

Suppose now that the unemployment rate increases to $u^* + \epsilon$ in the first market and falls to $u^* - \epsilon$ in the second market, where ϵ is any positive number. Since the two markets are equal in size the overall unemployment rate will remain at u^*. However, wages will fall at the rate of $\dot{W}_H$ in the high-unemployment market and rise at the rate of $\dot{W}_L$ in the low-unemployment-rate market. As Figure 19.7 indicates, $\dot{W}_L$ is larger than $\dot{W}_H$ in absolute value, hence the average rate of wage inflation in the economy, $[(\dot{W}_H + \dot{W}_L)/2]$, is positive. The dispersion in unemployment rates has led to a higher overall rate of wage inflation. Indeed, increasing the dispersion in the unemployment rates (increasing ϵ) would lead to an even higher overall rate of wage inflation.

Why does this result occur? In our simple example it occurs because the relationship between the excess demand for labor and the unemployment rate is nonlinear to the left of the full-employment unemployment rate (as explained earlier in discussing Figure 19.7).[13] As a result, there is more upward pressure put on wages in the tight labor market by an ϵ-percentage-point *decline* in unemployment than there is downward pressure put on wages in the loose labor market by an ϵ-percentage-point *rise*. Thus, the average rate of wage inflation increases.

Figure 19.7 shows that an increase in the dispersion of unemployment rates will increase the aggregate rate of wage inflation (in this model) for any aggregate unemployment rate less than the full-employment rate (u^* in Figure 19.7). Since the unemployment/excess-demand-for-labor relationship was assumed to be linear to the right of u^*, small increases in the dispersion of unemployment rates around an aggregate unemployment rate like u_1 in Figure 19.7 will not necessarily lead to increases in the aggregate rate of wage inflation. However, if the dispersion is large enough that the nonlinear segment of T_0 is reached by the lower-unemployment market, then the aggregate rate of wage inflation will increase.

In sum, over a wide range of values of the unemployment rate, increases in the dispersion of unemployment rates across labor markets will increase the aggregate rate of wage inflation associated with the aggregate unemployment rate. Put another way, increases in the dispersion of unemployment rates can cause the aggregate wage-inflation/unemployment trade-off curve to shift up. (While we

---

[12]We say "approximate" because once the unemployment rate differs between the two markets a slightly higher weight should be assigned to the low unemployment market that will have relatively more *employed* workers.

[13]This nonlinearity is not necessary to derive the general result—nor is it necessary to have identical wage-inflation/unemployment trade-off curves in the two markets. (On this *see* Archibald, "The Phillips Curve and the Distribution of Unemployment.") For example, if both curves are linear, as long as the wage inflation/excess demand for labor relationship is flatter in the market that has the higher unemployment rate, the same result will occur.

have not yet defined precisely a *labor market* here, it is natural to think in terms of geographic markets. However, one could similarly analyze labor markets segmented by skill, age, sex, or race.)

Reasons for Shifts in the Trade-Off Curve Over Time

Have the three major factors discussed above been responsible for the upward shift of the short-run wage-inflation/unemployment tradeoff throughout the 1960s, 1970s, and early 1980s? First, as Table 19.1 indicates, the percentage rate of change in the gross national product (GNP) *implicit price deflator*—a broad measure of the prices of all goods produced in the economy—trended upwards over the period.[14] To the extent that past price changes affect expectations of *future* price changes, this trend should have shifted the trade-off curve out (as employees incorporated these expected price changes into their wage demands).

Second, as noted earlier in this chapter and in Chapter 18, during the 1960s and 1970s, there was an increase in the fraction of the labor force subject to higher than average unemployment rates. As Table 19.2 indicates, between 1960 and 1980 the share of teens in the labor force rose from 7.0 to 8.8 percent and the share of females rose from 33.4 to 42.6 percent. Such demographic shifts alone have increased the overall rate of unemployment associated with any given level of wage inflation, perhaps by as much as one percentage point during the 1965–80 period.[15]

Finally, there is substantial evidence that the dispersion in the demographic distribution of unemployment rates has risen over the period. In particular, the unemployment rates of teenagers and white females have risen relative to the adult white male unemployment rate, and those for nonwhite teenagers have risen

Table 19.2. Female and Teenage Shares of the Civilian Labor Force

Year	Female Share	Teenage Share
1960	33.4	7.0
1965	35.2	7.9
1970	38.1	8.8
1975	39.9	9.5
1980	42.6	8.8

SOURCE: Based on *1981 Employment and Training Report of the President* (Washington, D.C.: U.S. Government Printing Office, 1981), Table A4.

---

[14]Another widely publicized price index is the Consumer Price Index (CPI), a measure of the cost of living for urban households that is published monthly by the Bureau of Labor Statistics. This index is in fact the one that is typically used to calculate cost-of-living increases due under union contracts with cost-of-living escalator clauses. Because the GNP deflator and CPI measure different things, year-to-year percentage changes in the two indices often differ. However, over longer periods of time they yield roughly the same picture about the upward trend in the inflation rate.

[15]Tobin, "Stabilization Policy Ten Years After."

EXAMPLE 19.1

Wage Inflation and Unemployment Around the World

The existence of a short-run trade-off between the rate of wage inflation and the unemployment rate is not unique to the United States. George Perry sought to estimate the magnitude of this trade-off for nine industrialized nations during the early 1960s to mid-1970s period; some of his results are summarized in the table below. This table presents his estimates of the percentage-point reduction in the rate of wage inflation that would have occurred in each country in the first year after the country's unemployment rate was allowed to increase by 25 percent (*not* percentage points). That is, if the unemployment rate in each country were increased from its mean value during the period to a level that was 25 percent higher, the table estimates how much lower the rate of wage inflation would have been in the first year following the change.

While this table indicates that a short-run trade-off exists between the rate of wage inflation and the level of the unemployment rate in all nine countries, the marginal effects on wage inflation are strikingly different in size. In the United States, the marginal effect of unemployment on wage inflation—both in percentage-point terms and in relationship to the average level of wage inflation—is among the smallest listed. Determining why this effect in the United States is so small relative to that in other countries lies beyond the scope of this text, but these data reemphasize the fact that aggregate demand policy alone will not be sufficient to reduce the rate of wage inflation in the United States; alternative labor-market policies will also be required.

Country	Percentage Point Change in the Rate of Wage Inflation in the First Year	Average Annual Rate of Wage Inflation 1961–1974 (percent)
Belgium	−1.7	11.9
Canada	−1.5	6.6
Germany	−1.0	10.6
Italy	−6.2	13.0
Japan	−0.6	16.6
Netherlands	−0.8	13.1
Sweden	−0.3	10.3
United Kingdom	−0.5	9.3
United States	−0.3	5.0

SOURCE: George L. Perry, "Determinants of Wage Inflation Around the World," *Brookings Papers on Economic Activity* 5 (1975–2), Tables 1 and 7.

SOURCE: George L. Perry, "Determinants of Wage Inflation Around the World," *Brookings Papers on Economic Activity* 5 (1975–2), pp. 403–35.

relative to those for white teenagers.[16] However, this increase in dispersion apparently has not had a substantial impact on the aggregate wage inflation/unemployment trade-off curve.[17]

Improving the Trade-Off

The analyses above suggest ways in which government policies can reduce the rate of wage inflation associated with any given unemployment rate:

1. They can attempt to reduce the rate of wage inflation associated with any level of excess demand for labor—or shift the curve in panel (a) of Figure 19.4 or in Figure 19.5 down.
2. They can attempt to reduce the unemployment rate associated with any given level of the excess demand for labor—or shift the curve in panel (b) of Figure 19.4 down.
3. Finally, they can attempt to reduce the geographic or demographic dispersion of unemployment rates.

A number of policy tools are potentially available to achieve each goal.

Turning to the wage-inflation/excess-demand-for-labor relationship first, one obvious objective here is to reduce the expected rate of growth of prices. Over long periods of time, this goal is accomplished primarily by restrictive monetary or fiscal policy. In the short run, *incomes policies*—policies by which the government tries directly to control or influence wage and price levels by the specification of standards governing when prices or wages can be changed—may also have an effect. Examples here include wage-price guidelines, temporary wage-price freezes, and tax-based incomes policies. (The concluding section of this chapter will discuss incomes policies in some detail.)

The wage-inflation/excess-demand-for-labor relationship may also be shifted down through government policies that increase the competitiveness of labor markets and remove institutional barriers that reduce the downward flexibility of wages. Examples of such policies include eliminating or relaxing the Davis-Bacon Act (discussed in Chapter 14) and the deregulation of industries, such as airlines and trucking, that historically were regulated in ways that tended to reduce competition. While such policies could perhaps reduce the rate of wage inflation, one must of course caution that these programs have other objectives, and the cost of giving up these objectives, if any, would have to be balanced against the gains from reduced wage inflation.

With respect to reducing the rate of unemployment associated with any given level of excess demand for labor, the goal here would be to improve the efficiency

---

[16]Ronald Ehrenberg, "The Demographic Structure of Unemployment Rates and Labor Market Transition Probabilities," *Research in Labor Economics* 3 (1980): 241–93.

[17]For econometric evidence on this point, *see* Robert J. Gordon, "Can the Inflation of the 1970s Be Explained?" *Brookings Papers on Economic Activity,* 1977–1, pp. 353–74.

of labor markets.[18] Many of the policies related to this goal were discussed in Chapter 18; they include improving job-market information, improving the "job matching services" offered by the U.S. Employment Service and private employment agencies, and increasing government-sponsored training programs to help reduce skill bottlenecks. One caution here, however, is that policies designed to reduce the unemployment rate may actually serve to increase it. For example, if potential job leavers—workers with some dissatisfaction with their jobs—knew that the government was actively pursuing a policy to reduce the length of time unemployed workers spent out of work, this knowledge might increase the probability that these workers would quit their jobs. One would have to balance the benefits from shorter durations of unemployment against the costs of a higher incidence of unemployment before deciding if such policies are worthwhile to implement.

The government can seek to reduce the geographic dispersion of unemployment rates by providing information about jobs in other areas to unemployed workers, by providing relocation allowances and subsidies for job search in different areas, and by administering public employment and training-program budgets in a way that increases allocations to areas with above-average unemployment rates.[19] The government can also seek to reduce the dispersion of unemployment rates across occupational or demographic groups by targeting employment and training programs, wage subsidies, tax credits, and relocation allowances on the groups with high unemployment rates.

Finally, independent of government policies, two demographic forces will be operating during the 1980s that will tend to reduce the unemployment rate associated with any level of excess demand for labor. First, the proportion of teenagers in the labor force will be declining (compare the 1975 and 1980 teenage shares of the labor force given in Table 19.2). As a result of the decline in the birth rate during the 1960s and 1970s, less weight will be given to this relatively high unemployment rate group in computing the aggregate unemployment rate.

Second, while the proportion of females in the labor force will continue to increase, it is likely that the relative unemployment rate of females will decline. Part of the reason for the relatively high unemployment rate of females is that many of them are fairly new entrants or reentrants to the labor force whose job turnover is high while they shop for desirable positions. As these women gain labor-market experience and as the perception increases that females' attachment to the labor force is as permanent as males', females' relative unemployment rates will likely fall. These two demographic trends, then, should serve to reduce the rate of wage inflation associated with any given level of overall unemployment during the 1980s.

---

[18]A long-time advocate of such policies is Charles Holt. *See,* for example, Charles Holt et al., "Manpower Proposals for Phase III," *Brookings Papers on Economic Activity,* 1971–3, pp. 703–22. For a more critical evaluation of these policies, *see* Robert Hall, "Prospects for Shifting the Phillips Curve Through Manpower Policy," *Brookings Papers on Economic Activity,* 1971–3, pp. 659–701.

[19]*Comprehensive Employment and Training Act (CETA)* program funds were administered in this way.

Wage Inflation, Price Inflation, and Productivity Growth

To move from the relationship between *wage* inflation and unemployment to an understanding of the relationship between *price* inflation and unemployment requires a model of how producers determine their product prices. The simple model presented here highlights the role of labor productivity growth in the inflationary process and shows how increases in the growth of labor productivity can help to reduce price inflation.

Suppose that producers determine their product prices by using a *constant percentage markup* over unit labor cost rule. That is,

$$P = k \cdot ULC, \tag{19.3}$$

where P represents product price, ULC represents unit labor cost—the labor cost of producing one unit of output—and k, which is a constant that is greater than one, represents the markup. Presumably k varies across firms as the share of labor cost in total costs of production varies (with smaller labor cost shares leading to larger values of k). It is also likely that k varies with the price elasticity of demand for the firms' products.[20] Although typically the size of markups do vary over the course of a business cycle, for expositional convenience we will ignore this fact here.[21]

Now, unit labor costs are equal to the costs per labor hour divided by output per labor hour (q), or labor productivity. Suppose, for simplicity, that we ignore all labor costs other than straight-time wages. Then labor costs per labor hour are equal to the wage rate (W) and

$$ULC = W/q. \tag{19.4}$$

Substituting equation (19.4) into equation (19.3) and making use of the facts (1) that the percentage change in the *product* of two variables equals the sum of the percentage changes of the two variables and (2) that the percentage change in the *ratio* of two variables equals the percentage change in the numerator minus the percentage change in the denominator, one obtains

$$\dot{P} = \dot{k} + \dot{W} - m. \tag{19.5}$$

Here a dot over a variable represents a percentage change and m, equal to $\dot{q}$, is the rate of growth of output per labor hour (or the rate of labor productivity growth).

---

[20]Although we do not do so here, one can formally show that these statements are true for a profit-maximizing monopolist who faces a constant average-cost curve. In this case, the less elastic the price elasticity of demand for output, the greater k will be.

[21]For evidence on the cyclical variability of markups, *see* Robert J. Gordon, "The Impact of Aggregate Demand on Prices," *Brookings Papers on Economic Activity,* 1975–3, pp. 613–63.

Over time the size of markups may change; for example, the drastic increase in the relative prices of energy since 1973 surely have led to increases in k. However, since this is a text in labor economics, not macroeconomics, we shall ignore this complication and assume that k remains constant (the constancy of k implies that labor's share of output also remains constant). Under this assumption,

$$\dot{P} = \dot{W} - m. \tag{19.6}$$

Equation (19.6) asserts that the rate of price inflation equals the rate of wage inflation minus the rate of labor productivity growth. Thus, if wages increase at the rate of productivity growth *and* if markups do not change, prices will remain constant. Put another way, given any rate of wage inflation, an increase in the rate of growth of productivity will lead to a reduction in the rate of growth of prices, if markups are constant.

Moreover, if one characterizes the trade-off between wage inflation and unemployment as $\dot{W} = f(\mathbf{u}) + \gamma \dot{P}^e$, then one can substitute $f(\mathbf{u}) + \gamma \dot{P}^e$ for $\dot{W}$ in equation (19.6) to obtain

$$\dot{P} = f(\mathbf{u}) + \gamma \dot{P}^e - m. \tag{19.7}$$

That is, as Figure 19.8 indicates, as long as productivity growth is positive, the price-inflation/unemployment trade-off that exists at any time lies everywhere

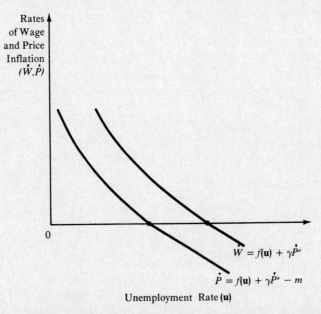

Figure 19.8   The Relationships Between the Rates of Wage and Price Inflation and (1) the Expected Rate of Price Inflation and (2) the Rate of Productivity Growth

below the wage-inflation/unemployment trade-off, with the vertical difference between the two curves being equal to the rate of labor productivity growth.

The Slowdown in Productivity Growth and Stagflation

During the late 1970s and early 1980s, one often read in the popular press that the slowdown in the rate of growth of labor productivity in the United States was at least partially responsible for high rates of price inflation that were associated with high rates of unemployment—a phenomenon commonly referred to as *stagflation*. Table 19.3 presents data on labor productivity growth in the United States that support this claim. For the entire private business sector, productivity grew at about 2.5 percent per year over the 1948–1965 period. However, during 1965 to 1973 productivity growth fell to 1.6 percent a year, and during 1973–1978 it fell further to 0.8 percent a year. Indeed, over the 1978–81 period (in which the unemployment rate rose), labor productivity growth actually turned negative. These shifts alone would cause the short-run aggregate price-inflation/unemployment trade-off curve to be some 2 percentage points higher during the late 1970s and early 1980s than it was during the 1950s and early 1960s [see equation (19.7)]. This figure should, however, be contrasted to the 5 to 10 percent annual rates of increase in the GNP deflator that occurred during the late 1970s and early 1980s. Thus, while the slowdown in productivity growth contributed to the worsening inflation/unemployment trade-off, it was not the entire cause; the other factors we have mentioned clearly were important.[22]

Unions and Inflation

Less than 25 percent of the labor force are union members (see Chapter 12). In spite of this fact, unions and the collective-bargaining process in the United States are thought to exert a considerable influence on the position and shape of the wage-inflation/unemployment trade-off curve for a number of reasons.

Table 19.3. Labor Productivity Growth in the United States (percent change per year)

Sector	1948–55	1955–65	1965–73	1973–78
Private business sector	2.5	2.4	1.6	0.8
Nonfarm	2.4	2.5	1.6	0.9
Manufacturing	3.2	2.8	2.4	1.5
Nonmanufacturing	2.1	2.2	1.2	0.5

SOURCE: *1980 Economic Report of the President* (Washington, D.C.: U.S. Government Printing Office, 1980), Table 16.

---

[22]A note of caution: one must be careful not to confuse cyclical changes in productivity growth (see Chapter 5) with changes in the underlying trend; the downward trend does tend to persist even after one controls for cyclical factors. Why this has occurred is not completely understood, although some explanations have been offered (see Chapter 4).

First, in several industries—such as steel, automobile, mining, trucking, and telephone—collective-bargaining negotiations are conducted at the national level and are well publicized in the media. The resulting settlements are often thought to set a pattern for wage settlements in other less heavily unionized industries and in the nonunion sector, either because of imitative behavior in the former or attempts to compete for labor and keep unions out in the latter.[23] Our model suggests that if the economic conditions facing firms and unions in only a few key industries heavily influence the rate of wage inflation in other sectors, the effect of the *aggregate* unemployment rate on inflation will be reduced.

Evidence to support this view is quite limited, however. For example, during the 1970s, wages in the above highly unionized industries grew substantially relative to wages in the rest of the economy, suggesting that the settlements reached in these industries do not automatically spillover to other industries.[24] Wage patterns did appear to exist among firms *within* certain industries, such as the automobile industry, during much of the postwar period, but even these patterns broke down in the concession bargaining of the early 1980s, when different firms in an industry often faced sharply different economic circumstances. For example, the United Automobile Workers granted larger concessions to the Chrysler Corporation, which was on the verge of bankruptcy, than to the General Motors Corporation or the Ford Motor Company, which were not. (When Chrysler turned a profit in 1983 and began to pay off loans ahead of schedule, however, workers at Chrysler demanded that some of the profits be used to reestablish the traditional wage equality between the major domestic automobile producers.) Generally, attempts to formally test whether or not these key wage bargains, or union wage gains in general, set a pattern for the rest of the economy have not met with success.[25]

Second, union contracts have increasingly become multiyear in nature and call for wage increases not only at the time the contract is signed, but also in subsequent years. While these increases may well be sensitive to the unemployment rate at the time the contract is signed—or, more precisely, to unions' and employers' *expectations* of the unemployment rate over the term of the contract—the contractual increases are not directly affected by the *actual* unemployment rate during the duration of the contract.

Formal econometric analyses do in fact indicate that wage increases specified in the *first* year of multiyear union contracts appear to be about as sensitive to

[23]For an early exposition of this view, *see* Otto Eckstein and Thomas Wilson, "The Determination of Money Wages in American Industry," *Quarterly Journal of Economics* 76 (August 1962): 379–414.

[24]*See* Daniel Mitchell, *Unions, Wages, and Inflation* (Washington, D.C.: Brookings Institution, 1980); and Marvin Kosters, "Wage and Price Behavior: Prospects and Policies" in *Contemporary Economic Problems, 1977,* ed. William Fellner (Washington, D.C.: American Enterprise Institute for Public Policy Research, 1977).

[25]*See* Daniel J. B. Mitchell, "Union Wage Determination: Policy Implications and Outlook," *Brookings Papers on Economic Activity,* 1978–3, pp. 537–82; and Robert Flanagan, "Wage Interdependence in Unionized Labor Markets," *Brookings Papers on Economic Activity,* 1976–3, pp. 635–73.

the unemployment rate as are wage increases in the nonunion sector. However, *deferred* wage increases specified in union contracts—those that occur in the second or third year of multiyear contracts—do not appear to be related to the actual unemployment rates during those years.[26] Hence, the increasing frequency of long-term union contracts in the economy *does* reduce the sensitivity of the overall rates of wage and price inflation to the unemployment rate, making the trade-off curves flatter.

Third, accompanying the growth of multiyear contracts has been the growth of *cost-of-living escalator clauses* in union contracts: clauses that call for wages to be automatically adjusted periodically as the price level changes. Approximately 20 percent of workers covered by major collective-bargaining agreements —that cover 1,000 or more workers—had such provisions in their contracts in 1966. However, by 1980 this proportion had grown to 62 percent.[27]

Escalator clauses typically give workers less than 100 percent protection against price inflation. Such contracts usually call for wages to increase by less than one percent in response to each one-percentage-point increase in prices, and sometimes *caps*—or maximum allowable cost-of-living increases—are also specified (see discussion in Chapter 16). Nevertheless, their existence should increase the sensitivity of wage inflation to price inflation and the evidence bears this out; union wage changes, especially those in contracts that call for cost-of-living escalators, appear to be more sensitive to price changes than do nonunion wage changes.[28] As noted earlier, larger values of γ in equation (19.2) lead to a higher short-run price-inflation/unemployment trade-off curve. Hence, the growing prevalence of cost-of-living escalator clauses in union contracts may well have contributed to the upward shift in the short-run trade-off curves.

A final reason why unions are thought to influence the position and shape of the trade-off curve is that union members are clearly concerned about maintaining their wage position relative to what they perceive are the wages of their *peer groups.* For example, at the national level, automobile workers look at the wage gains won in the steel industry and vice versa. Whichever union settles first may set a pattern for the other union to follow in its negotiations, regardless of economic conditions in the latter industry. If this occurs, the responsiveness of wage and price inflation to unemployment would again be reduced.

Wage gains in several large national industries, such as automobile, steel, and rubber clearly are highly correlated. However, it is difficult to disentangle the above *wage imitation* hypothesis from the hypothesis that wages in these industries are affected by a common set of variables. After all, steel is a major component of automobiles, as is rubber for the tires. It would, therefore, not be surprising to find that wage changes for workers in the three industries are highly

---

[26]Mitchell, "Union Wage Determination."

[27]Robert H. Ferguson, *Cost-of-Living Adjustments in Union-Management Agreements* (Ithaca, N.Y.: New York School of Industrial and Labor Relations, 1977); U.S. Bureau of Labor Statistics, *Characteristics of Major Collective Bargaining Agreements, January 1, 1980,* Bulletin 2095 (Washington, D.C.: U.S. Government Printing Office, May 1981).

[28]Mitchell, "Union Wage Determination."

correlated. Attempts to formally test whether wage imitation occurs among unions in these and other industries have not met with success.[29] Moreover, when the economic circumstances facing these industries diverge substantially as in the early 1980s, the wage settlements also diverge, as we have noted before.

Our discussion suggests, then, that the collective-bargaining process *per se* may well have contributed to the flattening and shifting up of the short-run inflation/unemployment trade-off curves during the 1970s. The increased prevalence of multiyear contracts is partially responsible for the flattening, and the increase in cost-of-living escalator clauses for the upward shift.[30] The effects of key settlements or other imitative behavior are uncertain.

Incomes Policies

The inflation/unemployment trade-offs—for both wages and prices—that we face in the early 1980s are distinctly unfavorable and appear to indicate that persistent high rates of unemployment will be required to keep inflation at relatively low levels. How then can we hope to return the economy to a situation of both low unemployment and low inflation?

Clearly, the answer is to resort to structural policies that will improve the inflation/unemployment trade-off *per se.* Many of these policies were discussed earlier in the chapter. In the remainder of the chapter we will focus in more detail on one of these—*incomes policies.* Incomes policies are policies in which the government tries to directly influence wage and price behavior by specifying *desired behavior.* Sometimes the policies are completely voluntary, and sometimes there are enforcement mechanisms built in to increase or guarantee compliance.

Incomes Policies in the United States

During the 1960–80 period, a period over which the inflation/unemployment trade-off curve steadily shifted out, the United States tried several different types of incomes policies. In the early Kennedy-Johnson years (1962–1966), the Council of Economic Advisors tried to educate the public on the relationship between the rate of wage inflation, the rate of price inflation, and the rate of productivity growth—see equation (19.6). The council observed that if money-wage growth

---

[29]*See,* for example, Flanagan, "Wage Interdependence in Unionized Labor Markets"; and Y. P. Mehra, "Spillovers in Wage Determination in U.S. Manufacturing Industries," *Review of Economics and Statistics* 58 (August 1976): 300–12.

[30]Another reason for the flattening of the trade-off curve in the nonunion sector relates to the growth of structured internal labor markets in which fluctuations in demand are met by temporary layoffs rather than money wage reductions, as discussed in Chapter 18. The "quantity adjustments" (layoffs) rather than "wage adjustments" at the individual firm level contribute to the growing insensitivity of wage changes to unemployment at the aggregate level. For an extensive discussion of this point, *see* Arthur M. Okun, "Inflation: Its Mechanics and Welfare Costs," *Brookings Papers on Economic Activity,* 1975–2, pp. 351–90; and Arthur M. Okun, *Prices and Quantities* (Washington, D.C.: Brookings Institution, 1981), pp. 351–90.

were held on average to the rate of labor productivity growth in the economy, and if markups did not change, then prices would remain stable. The council suggested in 1964 that the trend rate of growth of productivity was roughly 3.2 percent per year (but compare this to the estimates in Table 19.3) and urged that employers and unions voluntarily limit their wage settlements to this level. This limitation would cause unit labor costs to rise in firms in which productivity growth was below average, leading to increases in prices there. However, unit labor costs would fall in firms with above-average rates of productivity growth, leading to price declines there (if profit margins remained constant). On average, then, prices would remain stable, and both nominal (money) and real wages would increase 3.2 percent per year.

The guideposts worked reasonably well from 1962 to 1965 in the sense that the average rate of increase in wages was in fact below 3.2 percent during the period.[31] However, as labor markets tightened in the mid-1960s and as the price inflation rate rose above 2 percent, the guideposts broke down and by 1967 the program was abandoned.

The next experience with incomes policies occurred during the Nixon Administration in August of 1971. In response to increasing rates of price inflation (which averaged all of 5.3 percent in 1970), increasing unemployment, and a deteriorating trade balance, a comprehensive economic policy was announced. "Phase I," which lasted 90 days, called for a freeze—that is, a zero rate of increase —on virtually all wages and prices. Phase I was followed in November of 1971 by Phase II, which set standards for wage increases of 5.5 percent a year. If productivity grew at 3 to 3.5 percent a year and if profit margins were maintained, prices would then grow at 2 to 2.5 percent a year—see equation (19.6). Compliance was required by law under the program. However, a sufficient number of exemptions were granted that average hourly earnings growth was well above 5.5 percent a year (see Table 19.1). The program was terminated in January of 1973 and replaced with a voluntary program of controls with no enforcement mechanism.

Finally, in October of 1978, the Carter Administration announced a voluntary system of wage standards to help reduce inflation. Average hourly earnings and fringes per company were to increase at a rate of no more than 7 percent a year; for contracts with cost-of-living escalator clauses, compliance was evaluated at an assumed 6 percent price inflation rate over the life of the contract.[32] Several groups of workers were exempted from having to satisfy the standards, including low-wage workers.

Contract settlements under the Carter program were monitored by the Council on Wage and Price Stability. However, its enforcement power was limited to

---

[31]This does not imply that the guideposts *caused* wage increases to average less than 3.2 percent. Evidence on their effect on the wage-inflation rate will be discussed below.

[32]Actually the Carter Policy did *not* apply on a *company* basis but on an *employee-group* basis within each company. The three types of employee groups considered were supervisors, nonunion-nonsupervisory employees, and workers covered by each collective-bargaining agreement.

calling violations of the voluntary standards to public attention. Other arms of government—Congress and the President—contributed to enforcement of the standards, however, through implicit or explicit threats that firms violating the standards would lose government contracts. Threats of other government action were made to particular industries; these included relaxation of import quotas (steel), deregulation (trucking), and sale of government stockpiles (copper) if wage settlements in these industries were not in compliance. As inflation continued to accelerate in 1979, the levels of permissible wage increases were raised for 1980. After the defeat of President Carter in the 1980 election, the program was terminated.

Did U.S. Incomes Policies Work?

Numerous attempts have been made to appraise whether the Kennedy-Johnson wage/price guideposts and the Nixon Phase II economic program actually did succeed in reducing the rates of wage and price inflation below the levels that would have existed in the *absence* of the programs. It is worth emphasizing that the comparisons these studies make are *not* of actual levels of wage and price inflation during the periods that the incomes policies were in effect with levels of inflation during the *previous* periods. Since the forces that affect inflation, such as unemployment rates and expected rates of inflation, change over time, such comparisons would be meaningless. Put another way, such comparisons could not disentangle the change in inflation rates caused by the incomes policies from the change in inflation caused by changes in other variables.

Rather, the methodology used in these studies is to use historical data to estimate generalizations of the inflation/unemployment trade-off curves specified earlier in this chapter and then to ask if these estimated relationships systematically changed during the periods that the incomes policies were in effect. That is, the researchers tried to determine whether the rates of inflation that were *predicted* using the historical relationship between unemployment and inflation (after controlling for the age/sex distribution of the labor force, the dispersion of unemployment rates, and expected inflation rates) really did exceed the *actual* inflation rates that occurred. If *predicted* rates of inflation exceed *actual* rates, one could argue that the incomes policies were effective in bringing down inflation.

The answers these studies yielded are somewhat ambiguous. For example, George Perry found that the rate of wage inflation was some 0.6 to 1.2 points lower during the Kennedy-Johnson guidepost period than his model would otherwise have predicted, but Robert J. Gordon found that the guideposts had no effect on the rate of wage inflation.[33] In contrast, Gordon found that the rate of wage

---

[33]Perry's initial study was George Perry, "Wages and the Guideposts," *American Economic Review* 57 (September 1967): 897–904. Additional results are found in George Perry, "Inflation in Theory and Practice," *Brookings Papers on Economic Activity,* 1980–1, pp. 207–42. Gordon's results are in his "Comment," *Brookings Papers on Economic Activity,* 1980–1, pp. 249–57.

inflation was held down during the Nixon Phase II incomes-policy period—a result other researchers have also found.[34]

In evaluating these studies, however, one must caution that the fact that the rate of wage inflation appeared to be lower than a model predicted during the period of time that the policy was in effect does not imply that the policy *caused* the reduction in the rate of inflation. Factors not included in the model that reduced the rate of wage inflation might have occurred at the same time. For example, the period during which the Kennedy-Johnson wage/price guideposts were in effect (1962–66) was one of increased import competition for American steel manufacturers and one of rapid expansion of government-sponsored employee-training programs to remove skill bottlenecks. Both of these forces should have served to reduce the rate of wage inflation; the former by increasing the resistance of U.S. steel manufacturers to union wage demands and the latter by reducing the excess demand for labor. It is thus not an easy task to ascertain what the effects of incomes policies really are.

Incomes Policies in Western Europe

European countries have been drawn to experiment with incomes policies much more than the United States for two reasons. As we have seen in Chapters 12 and 14, there are substantial differences in the extent of unionization; unions represent about 25 percent of workers in the United States but over 50 percent of the workforce in most major countries of Western Europe. As a result, a larger proportion of the national wage bill is determined in collective bargaining in Western Europe than in the United States, and the potential impact of collective bargaining on inflation is larger. In addition, international trade accounts for a larger fraction of economic activity in Europe than in the United States. As a result, European governments are usually highly concerned about the ability of their industries to compete effectively in international markets, and are more likely to take policy actions in response to balance-of-payments deficits than is the United States.

For these reasons, Western European countries have experimented with a wide variety of policies. During the 1960s, the policies were adopted to prevent or retard the development of inflationary pressures as governments pursued full-employment growth policies. Most of the policies have included some form of guideline for the growth of wages and prices (and occasionally other incomes) accompanied by an enforcement mechanism and penalties for noncompliance. At different times and in different countries the guidelines have ranged from wage and/or price "freezes," to formulae based on aggregate productivity growth (such as the wage guide used in the U.S. wage-price guideposts, described above), to

---

[34]*See* Robert Gordon, "Wage Price Controls and the Shifting Phillips Curve," *Brookings Papers on Economic Activity,* 1972–2, pp. 385–421; and his "Comment," *Brookings Papers on Economic Activity,* 1980–1, pp. 249–57. *See also* Bradley Askin and John Kraft, *Econometric Wage and Price Models: Assessing the Impact of the Economic Stabilization Program* (Lexington, Mass.: D.C. Heath, 1974).

formulae basing wage adjustments on rates of productivity growth in particular industries.[35] Enforcement mechanisms have included exhortation by government officials, the establishment of special review committees to evaluate wage and price decisions for compliance with policy guidelines, and even the inspection of companies' books to determine whether wage payments were in compliance with the policy. Penalties for noncompliance have generally been more severe than in the United States, and in some instances included the possibility of fines or jail sentences.

At the other extreme, in Sweden, a country with very centralized collective-bargaining institutions, there has been no "official" incomes policy run by the government. Instead, the main federations of labor and employers have run what amounts to a "privately-operated incomes policy." That is, they have given weight in their negotiations to government forecasts of what would constitute "responsible" wage behavior given expected economic conditions. Both labor and management understand in this situation that if they are not able to achieve settlements roughly consistent with the government's macroeconomic objectives, the government has the option of introducing an official incomes policy that they may find less palatable than the wage restraint which they may be able to agree to among themselves. Such privately operated incomes policies appear to work best when the number of parties who must agree is small; and hence, these policies are more likely to be found in countries, such as Sweden, with highly centralized bargaining institutions.

For the most part, the European incomes policy experiments of the 1960s were not regarded as successful in their efforts to improve the trade-off between inflation and unemployment. While econometric evaluations (similar to those used to evaluate incomes policies in the United States) indicate that money wage growth was at times restrained by one to two percentage points for one to two years, these periods were often followed by outbreaks of wildcat strikes and wage "explosions" in which wages increased far more rapidly than would normally have been expected under prevailing economic conditions. The evaluations also indicated that even less price restraint was achieved, so that the net effect of the policies may have been to reduce real wages.

One interesting feature of the European experience with incomes policies during the 1960s is the breadth of the policy failure. When one reviews the experience of many countries, it is clear that at different times and in different countries, a wide variety of policy designs were imposed on a wide variety of collective-bargaining institutions. Yet the inability of incomes policies to improve the inflation-unemployment trade-off seemed independent of such factors as the centralization of the collective-bargaining institutions, the degree of political support by the trade union movement, the particular policy guidelines, and the degree of compulsion adopted by a government to enforce the policy.[36]

---

[35]For an example of the latter, *see* Jan Pen, "The Strange Adventures of Dutch Wage Policy," *British Journal of Industrial Relations* 10 (November 1963): 310–28.

[36]Lloyd Ulman and Robert J. Flanagan, *Wage Restraint: A Study of Incomes Policies in Western Europe* (Berkeley, Ca.: University of California Press, 1971) pp. 216–57.

The reasons for the difficulties encountered by incomes policies in Europe are rooted in many of the aspects of market and institutional behavior that we have discussed in earlier chapters. For example, in Example 14.4 we discussed the phenomenon of *wage drift*—the tendency of actual earnings to rise above negotiated wage rates—that is observed in countries in which collective bargaining is conducted at a relatively centralized level (for example, industrywide or nationwide negotiations). Most governments find that it is easiest to focus the enforcement of a wage guideline on the wages established in collective-bargaining negotiations, but restraint in negotiated wages may later be offset by greater wage drift, which is more difficult to observe and to control. Wage drift may develop because incomes policy guidelines imply a wage that is less than the market equilibrium wage—a situation that appeared common in Europe in the 1960s, when many governments appeared to introduce incomes policies to control inflations that resulted from excess demand and therefore would have been more appropriately addressed through restrictive fiscal and monetary policies. In this situation, wage drift (resulting from surreptitious wage increases or "paper" promotions into higher paying job categories) will tend to restore the market-equilibrium wage irrespective of the government guideline. Wage drift may also result from institutional pressures and unofficial local bargaining, as workers try to restore wage differentials that may have been disturbed by the incomes-policy rules.

The growth of wage drift also threatens the institutional security of union organizations, as workers notice that a smaller and smaller fraction of their compensation comes from wages negotiated by the union. Thus, even union leaders who are predisposed to cooperate with a government incomes policy (as can be the case, for example, if the trade union movement is affiliated with the political party that is in power) may be sharply limited in their *ability* to both support the policy and maintain the political support of the union's rank and file. The political stature of union leaders who sought to cooperate in incomes policies also was not enhanced by the fact that even with the compensating tendencies of wage drift, workers experienced a net reduction in real wages as governments were less successful in restraining price increases than in restraining wage increases.

Even in relatively decentralized collective-bargaining structures in which wage drift is less likely to arise, the ability of union leaders to comply with an incomes policy may be limited by *compliance risk.* Compliance risk arises because workers complying with a pay guideline have no assurance that other workers will exercise similar restraint. The failure of other unions to comply will result in reductions in real and relative earnings for the members of unions that comply —a result that will not increase the political security of the leaders of the latter unions. In addition, the members of noncomplying unions will benefit (in terms of increased real earnings) from whatever reduction in inflation occurs from the wage restraint of complying unions. That is, the benefit of wage restraint (lower inflation) is what we referred to in Chapter 12 as a public good; the benefit cannot be restricted to those who comply with the incomes policy.

In summary, it appeared that if incomes policies were to improve their track records, they would have to be designed in a manner that compensated union members for some of the losses that they incurred under the policies and offered some form of institutional protection for union organizations in exchange for their cooperation. This challenge became all the more difficult during the 1970s, when the combined effects of OPEC oil price-increases and reduced profitability of industry in many European countries led governments to explicitly seek real wage reductions through incomes policies. In an effort to address these issues, several governments explored the possibility of establishing a *social contract* through multilateral negotiations between labor, management, government officials, and possibly other economic interest groups. In principle, the social contract that emerged from such negotiations would include commitments regarding wages, prices, and certain government policies of interest to labor and management. The most striking difference between the social contract idea and the incomes policies of the 1960s was the presence of the government as an explicit participant in the negotiations. This difference rested on the premise that the government had policy concessions to trade that would compensate labor for wage restraint.

One bargaining tool available to governments was tax policy. In countries with very high marginal tax rates on personal income and high rates of inflation, such as Sweden and Denmark, it was increasingly difficult to achieve significant advances in the real disposable earnings of union members through bargaining over money wages. A reduction in tax rates might do as well, and this left open the possibility of a social contract involving tax reductions in exchange for wage restraint. Other policies that unions, at times, indicated might be the price of wage restraint included price controls (thereby limiting the risk of real wage losses), greater wage indexation, and legislation supporting the institutional position of unions. The basic difficulty raised by the social 1-1 contract approach under the economic conditions of the 1970s was that the policies requested by unions as compensation for wage restraint conflicted with the general objectives of incomes policies. For example, tax reductions tend to stimulate the economy, and wage drift increases with labor demand. Therefore, the negotiated wage restraint achieved through a tax reduction would tend to be canceled by increasing drift. Policies such as price controls and wage indexation tended to conflict with the need for real wages in Europe to fall during the period. While there were many experiments, by the end of the decade it was clear that, under prevailing economic conditions, the social-contract approach had been no more successful than the incomes-policy approaches of the 1960s.[37]

Why are Incomes Policies Unpopular Among Economists?

Independent of the evidence on the effectiveness of incomes policies in moderating the rates of wage and price inflation, many economists are opposed to their use because the policies create inequities and efficiency losses in the econ-

---

[37]For an extensive review and analysis of these policies *see* Robert J. Flanagan, David Soskice, and Lloyd Ulman, *Unionism, Economic Stabilization, and Incomes Policy* (Washington, D.C.: Brookings Institution, 1983).

omy.[38] The scope of this text does not permit our cataloging the case against incomes policies, but a few arguments can be mentioned.

First, rigid guidelines or standards implicitly freeze the distribution of income and create inequities. For example, individuals who recently have received large increases gain relative to those whose increases will be constrained by the policies. Unless most individuals are happy with their relative income positions at the time the policy is imposed and there is a social consensus for the need for the policy, the policy will invariably break down.

Second, such policies may create efficiency losses because rapidly expanding sectors of the economy that face personnel shortages are prevented from bidding up wages to attract labor. Once exceptions are systematically granted for the above reason, as was done in Phase II of the Nixon economic policy, the process of controlling wage increases becomes highly politicized—and the exceptions may be used to justify wage increases that exceed the standard in cases when waiving the standard is not justified by economic conditions. More generally, incomes policies tend to be unevenly applied to different groups; those with political power gain relative to those without.

Finally, the administrative costs of incomes policies that contain enforcement procedures may be enormous. Simply costing out tens of thousands of labor contracts to ascertain compliance is no trivial task, especially when numerous fringe benefits are involved—many of whose costs can only be actuarially estimated or guessed at, as is true with pensions. The resources devoted both by the government agencies monitoring the programs and by private employers to prove or assure that they are in compliance may represent a substantial cost to society.

Tax-Based Incomes Policies

In recent years proposals have been set forth to establish a new form of incomes policy that would work through the federal personal and corporate income-tax systems.[39] These *tax-based incomes policy (TIP)* proposals are based upon the notion that the tax system can be used to provide incentives for employees or employers to moderate wage and price increases.

One form of TIP uses the "carrot" of lower personal income-tax rates, or tax credits. These would be granted to employees who work for firms whose average wage settlements do not exceed a specified critical value, if the rate of price inflation exceeds another specified value.[40] Panel (a) of Figure 19.9 shows the tax

---

[38]A now classic article that presents the case against incomes policies more completely is Milton Friedman, "What Price Guideposts?" in *Guidelines, Informal Controls, and the Market Place,* eds. George Shultz and Robert Alibers (Chicago: University of Chicago Press, 1966).

[39]*See,* for example, Henry Wallich and Sidney Weintraub, "A Tax-Based Incomes Policy," *Journal of Economic Issues* 5 (June 1971): 1–19; and Arthur M. Okun, "The Great Stagflation Swamp," *Challenge* 20 (November/December 1977): 6–13.

[40]*See* Okun, "The Great Stagflation Swamp." A variant of this emerged as the Carter Administration's "Real Wage Insurance" Proposal in January of 1979. For a discussion of this proposal, *see* Robert J. Flanagan, "Real Wage Insurance as a Compliance Incentive," *Eastern Economic Journal* 5 (October 1979): 367–78.

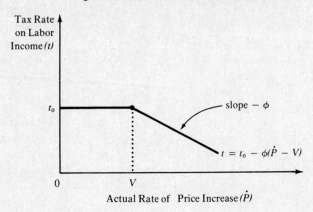

(a) Real Wage Insurance for Employees Whose Wage Increases Are Less Than the Guidelines

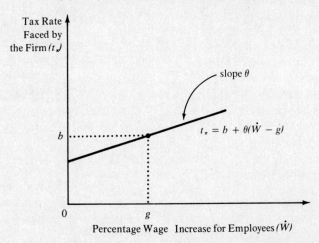

(b) Corporate Tax Rate Varies With Wage Increases

Figure 19.9 Alternative Forms of Tax-Based Incomes Policies (TIPs)

rate (t) on labor income for a representative individual whose wage settlement $(\dot{W})$ is less than the specified standard $(\dot{W}^C)$. If the actual rate of price increase $(\dot{P})$ exceeds V percent, the individual's normal tax rate (t_0) will be lowered by the fraction ϕ times the difference between the actual and critical value of the price inflation rate. That is,

$$t = t_0 - \phi(\dot{P} - V) \text{ if } \dot{W} \le \dot{W}^C; \qquad (19.8)$$
$$t = t_0 \text{ if } \dot{W} > \dot{W}^C.$$

By way of example, the Carter administration's Real Wage Insurance Proposal called for wage and price standards of 7 percent ($V = \dot{W}^C = 7$) and called

EXAMPLE 19.2

Incomes Policies During the Roman Empire

The use of incomes policies to combat inflation is not a recent innovation—and neither is the inflexibility in resource allocation caused by policies that fix prices. In the year 301 AD, after years of severe inflation, the Emperor Diocletian issued an edict fixing maximum prices and wages for the whole Roman Empire. Maximum wages were specified for more than 130 different categories of labor, and severe punishment was promised to anyone who violated the standards.

One would expect that the establishment of a rigid occupational wage structure with a maximum wage specified for each occupation would have had two effects. First, workers would have sought to leave occupations where compensation levels were fixed at relatively low levels (considering the work involved) and would have sought employment where wages happened to be fixed at relatively higher levels. These occupational flows could not be accompanied by wage changes (because wages were fixed), so one would expect that permanent surpluses and shortages would have developed. Second, some workers might have decided that the prevailing maximum-wage scales did not offer sufficiently high rewards for their labor-force participation and would have chosen not to participate. Either effect would have led to a reduction in the overall level of output.

Diocletian was apparently well aware of these potential difficulties and tried to head them off by restricting both occupational mobility and labor-force-participation decisions. Each worker was effectively tied to his job, and it was required that his children be brought up to succeed him. Not surprisingly, however, the removal of individuals' freedom of choice coupled with the wage ceilings effectively killed any incentives workers had to work hard or exhibit initiative. According to R. H. Barrow, "Production fell, and with it the standard of living; the rigid uniformity of a lifeless and static mediocrity prevailed."

SOURCES: H. Michell, "The Edict of Diocletian: A Study of Price Fixing in the Roman Empire," *Canadian Journal of Economics and Political Science* 13 (February 1947): 1–12; R. H. Barrow, *The Romans* (Baltimore, Md.: Penguin Books, 1949), p. 177.

for each one-percentage-point increase in the price inflation rate to lead to a one-percentage-point decrease in the tax rate ($\phi = 1$).[41]

The idea behind such a scheme is that if the actual rate of price inflation proves to be less than 7 percent, workers' real wages would not have declined if

---

[41]This proposal was also subject to certain "caps" or limits on the tax rebates, one of which is discussed below. *See* Flanagan, "Real Wage Insurance as a Compliance Incentive," for details.

they had confined their wage settlements to 7 percent. If, however, prices wound up increasing by more than 7 percent, workers would receive a tax credit or rebate to help protect their real earnings. However, the tax credit (and hence real earnings protection) would be granted *only* for the given year, and at the start of the next year their real after-tax earnings (assuming $\dot{W} = 7$) would have declined by $\dot{P} - 7$ percent. If $\dot{P}$ were substantially greater than 7 percent, the decline would be sizable. As such, it is not surprising that this form of TIP was opposed by organized labor and failed to win support in Congress.[42]

A TIP proposal that works through the corporate-profits tax rate and seeks to increase employers' incentives to bargain tough with their work forces seems to have more promise.[43] A representative scheme is plotted in panel (b) of Figure 19.9, where the tax rate on corporate profits faced by the firm, t_π, is assumed to vary directly with the actual average percentage wage increase ($\dot{W}$) granted by the firm. Specifically,

$$t_\pi = b + \theta(\dot{W} - g), \tag{19.9}$$

where b is the normal corporate-profits tax rate, g is the specified wage standard, and θ is the marginal effect of a one-percentage-point increase in the wage settlement on the tax rate that the firm would pay.

If the actual wage settlement is equal to the standard ($\dot{W} = g$), the corporate tax rate remains at its normal level. However, larger increases would lead to higher tax rates and smaller increases would lead to lower tax rates. This proposal thus combines both a "carrot" (lower taxes) and a "stick" (higher taxes) approach; unlike the employee tax-based proposal, it also provides an incentive for the firm to depress wage increases *below* the standard. Presumably, by tying the firm's share of after-tax profits to its wage settlement, the scheme gives employers an extra incentive to stiffen their resistance to union wage demands and to hold down wage increases. If price markups over costs remain unchanged, this policy would help reduce the rate of price inflation.

While such schemes hold out the promise of being able to shift inflation/unemployment trade-off curves down, they are not without potential drawbacks and weaknesses. First, they raise all sorts of administrative problems.[44] For example, how does one handle numerous small firms, firms with no corporate tax liabilities, private nonprofit firms, and government agencies?[45] Or how does one

---

[42]The Carter proposal also "capped" the rebate, or decrease in the tax rate, at 3 percentage points —a move that was necessary to protect against an explosion in the size of the federal deficit. Not surprisingly this limit further reduced labor support for the proposal.

[43]*See* Wallich and Weintraub, "A Tax-Based Incomes Policy." A more recent advocate of a corporate-profit-based TIP is Laurence Seidman, "Tax-Based Incomes Policies," *Brookings Papers on Economic Activity,* 1978–2, pp. 301–48.

[44]For a discussion of these problems, *see* Larry L. Dildine and Emil M. Sunley, "Administrative Problems of Tax-Based Incomes Policies," *Brookings Papers on Economic Activity,* 1978–2, pp. 363–89.

[45]One could, of course, restrict the scheme to employees of large profitable private firms; however, this creates obvious equity problems.

collect the data necessary to include nonwage forms of compensation in the calculations? In this respect, these policies suffer from the same type of problems that any incomes policy with a built-in enforcement mechanism would face.

Second, these policies focus on wages rather than prices, even though public concern is ultimately with the latter. The focus on wages is due to the difficulties involved in monitoring and measuring prices for millions of different products that are heterogeneous and whose quality can be easily varied. Employees are not likely to be receptive, though, to government intervention in labor markets if no attention is explicitly paid to product prices. Furthermore, a firm might agree to a large wage increase, resulting in an increased corporate tax rate, and then seek to negate this effect by passing the increased wage *and* tax costs on to consumers in the form of higher prices. Even supporters of such a scheme are aware of this potential problem, although they discount its importance.[46]

Finally, union leaders and members are not likely to be sympathetic to the policy.[47] On the one hand, even if the policy works and union members' real wages do not fall, the government—not union leaders—will get "credit" for the improvement. Thus, union leaders are not likely to be enthusiastic about the policy (see Chapter 12 for a discussion of the difference between the goals of union members and leaders). On the other hand, union members and leaders are both likely to resent a policy that provides direct financial incentives to management to resist union wage demands (tax cuts) but provides nothing for them. Indeed, because of this, stiffened management resistance may well lead to increases in the frequency and duration of strike activity, especially immediately after the initial adoption of the policy.

In spite of these problems, the corporate profits variant of TIP does provide certain advantages over more traditional forms of incomes policies. Unlike direct controls or standards, it does not prohibit anything. Industries in which there is an excess demand for labor can agree to relatively high wage settlements, thereby avoiding shortages, as long as they are willing to pay the price of a higher corporate-profits tax rate. Furthermore, it provides a means by which policymakers can short-circuit the inflationary process generated in the late 1960s and 1970s in which inflationary shocks, like oil price increases, fed into wage increases—which were then passed on to price increases, leading to a further wage-price spiral even after the initial shock was long past. The hope is that a decrease in the rate of wage inflation induced by a TIP would cause a decrease in the rate of price inflation leading to further moderation in future wage and price increases and a winding down of inflation.

Of course, this line of reasoning suggests that any action the government takes that causes a one-time decline in the price level—or decreases the rate of growth of prices—will lead to lower wage increases, subsequent lower price increases, and thus also help to short-circuit the wage-price spiral. As a result,

---

[46]Seidman, "Tax-Based Incomes Policies."

[47]Albert Rees, "New Policies to Fight Inflation: Sources of Skepticism," *Brookings Papers on Economic Activity,* 1978–2, pp. 453–77.

a number of such proposals have been advocated.[48] These proposals include reducing the federal payroll tax that finances social security (which enters into employers' costs and hence their product price decisions); eliminating federal excise taxes on alcohol and tobacco; and reducing minimum-wage rates and substituting a wage-subsidy program for low-income workers. Each of these proposals would directly reduce employers' costs or product prices. None would alone solve the inflation problem, but a combination of these and other proposals might cause a significant one-time reduction in the price level (compared to what it would otherwise be). To the extent that this would feed back into lower rates of wage and price inflation, such proposals would serve to improve the inflation/unemployment trade-offs that the United States faces.

REVIEW QUESTIONS

1. Why are the size of wage increases and the unemployment rate thought to be negatively related? How (and why) is this negative relationship affected by price inflation and the rising labor-force participation of women? What can the government do to reduce the wage inflation associated with any level of unemployment?
2. Great Britain recently instituted three related policies. First, it increased unemployment-compensation benefits. Second, the government agreed to pay lump-sum benefits owed to anyone permanently fired by his or her employer. (Assume that previously the *employers* paid these benefits.) Third, the government placed a tax, to be paid by employers, on wages in *service* industries (wages in manufacturing were not taxed). (a) Analyze the effects of these three policies on the labor market. (b) Judging from the effects of these programs, what is (are) the *goal*(s) implicit in these policies?
3. Suppose the government were to adopt an incomes policy that allows workers to receive wage increases each January equal to the increase in the cost of living during the previous 12 months but *no* other increases. Would such a scheme help reduce the rate of inflation?
4. Some members of Congress have supported legislation requiring the federal government to undertake massive employment programs as long as the overall unemployment rate is above 4 percent. Evaluate such a program with respect to inflation.
5. How can unanticipated inflation lower the unemployment rate?
6. If you were President, what policies would you propose to reduce inflation? Why? What are the strengths and weaknesses of your policy proposals?
7. "Incomes policies that specify that workers should receive percentage wage increases equal to their rate of productivity growth are doomed to failure because they will cause management's share of output to continually fall." Is this statement true, false, or uncertain? Explain your answer.

SELECTED READINGS

Robert Flanagan, David Soskice, and Lloyd Ulman, *Unionism, Economic Stabilization, and Incomes Policy* (Washington, D.C.: Brookings Institution, 1983).

---

[48]*See,* for example, Robert W. Crandall, "Federal Government Initiatives to Reduce the Price," *Brookings Papers on Economic Activity,* 1978–2, pp. 401–40.

Robert Flanagan, "Wage Interdependence in Unionized Labor Markets." *Brookings Papers on Economic Activity,* 1976–3, pp. 635–73.

Milton Friedman, "The Role of Monetary Policy," *American Economic Review* 58 (March 1968): 1–17.

Richard Lipsey, "The Relation Between Unemployment and the Rate of Change in Money Wage Rates in the United Kingdom, 1862–1957: A Further Analysis," *Economica* 27 (February 1960): 1–31.

Daniel J. B. Mitchell, *Unions, Wages and Inflation* (Washington, D.C.: Brookings Institution, 1980).

Arthur M. Okun, and George Perry, eds., "Innovative Policies to Slow Inflation," *Brookings Papers on Economic Activity,* 1978–2.

George L. Perry, "Changing Labor Markets and Inflation," *Brookings Papers on Economic Activity,* 1970–3, pp. 411–41.

James Tobin, "Stabilization Policy Ten Years After," *Brookings Papers on Economic Activity,* 1980–1, pp. 19–72.

Name Index

Subject Index